XXIX
(WORCESTERSHIRE)
REGIMENT.

THE BADGES, ON THE COVER OF THIS BOOK, ARE FAC-SIMILIES OF THE DEVICE ON THE OFFICERS' SHOULDER BELT PLATE, 1832-58, ALSO OF THE POUCH ORNAMENT WORN BY THE BATTALION COMPANIES.

HISTORY

OF

THOS FARRINGTON'S REGIMENT

SUBSEQUENTLY DESIGNATED

THE 29TH (WORCESTERSHIRE) FOOT

1694 TO 1891,

BY

MAJOR H. EVERARD,

3rd Battalion Worcestershire Regiment,

Late Lieut. 29th Foot.

WORCESTER:
LITTLEBURY & COMPANY, THE WORCESTER PRESS.
1891.

[*The rights of translation and re-production are reserved.*]

TO

HER MOST GRACIOUS MAJESTY

VICTORIA

QUEEN OF GREAT BRITAIN AND IRELAND

EMPRESS OF INDIA

THIS HISTORY

OF

THE 29TH (OR WORCESTERSHIRE) REGIMENT OF FOOT

IS

By Her Majesty's Gracious Permission

Most Respectfully

Dedicated.

Tho:ˢ Farington

PREFACE.

The Records in possession of the Regiment appear to have been originally collected and brought down to November, 1799, by Col. Enys, who joined the 29th in 1775. In this Officer's MS. Records, which a few years ago were kindly placed at my service by Mr. F. Enys, is the following paragraph :—" The Records were "completed at the desire of the 29th, in consequence of an order, "dated............, desiring a Book to be kept, in which all the "principal events of the Corps were to be kept in future, with as "much of its former history as they could collect. Among others, "I was applied to, and took great pains to ascertain the true "from the false part of the Reports we had heard from various "persons at various times; but when it was completed, Lieut.-Col. "(now Sir Gregory) Way, who then commanded the Regiment, "thought they were too full and particular, in consequence of which, "the copy sent to the Regiment was curtailed very much, and I "have no doubt but that they made them still shorter before they "put them into the Orderly Book."

When Col. Enys joined the 29th, Captain Roberts (who we can trace as being in the regiment in 1742) had been its adjutant thirteen years, and it is most probable that the previous history was in a great measure obtained from this officer, who, in turn, had received it from his predecessors; for although somewhat meagre, still it is substantially correct, and, with one exception, I have been able to prove all the traditions and statements. The tradition in question is—that the Regiment was either raised from the City Trained Bands, or by the Merchants of the City of London, and that such being the case, it, conjointly with the Buffs, enjoys the

PREFACE.

privilege* of marching through the City with drums beating, colours flying, and bayonets fixed.

With regard to the Trained Band theory, Sir J. B. Monckton, F.S.A., the Town Clerk, writes, that, after a careful search through the documents kept at the Guildhall, he has not been able to trace the raising of, or order to raise, any regiment in the City between 1693 and 1702.

Having carefully looked through the names of officers belonging to the Trained Bands between 1682 and 1694, I have discovered but one‡ whose name corresponds in any way with those appointed to Colonel Thos. Farrington's regiment previous to 1703. At this remote period no trace exists as to whence the non-commissioned officers or the rank and file were obtained, but "*The Declaration for the More Speedy Raising and Compleating the Foot Regiments,*" shows that the regiment was raised by order of the Government, and the following is a List of Officers§ appointed to it on the 16th February, 1694:—

Captains.	*Lieutenants.*	*Ensigns.*
Col. Thos. Farrington	Capt.-Lieut. James Howard	Barlow Wickham
Lieut.-Col.†	Richard Hargrave	Stanley Russell
Major Christopher Wray	John Danvers	John Brooks
Robert Minzeis		William Carr
John Dally (Grenadiers)	{ John Greenwood { Francis Lewis	
Anthony Hammond	John Wright	Charles Sweeting
Richard Nanfan	Robert Carr	
Charles Cracherode	Rowland St. John	James Dennis
Peter Minshull	Vere Harcourt	William Franks
John Bickley	Charles Middleton	Anthony Gawdy
Robert Thorold	William Baker	Robert Utworth
Samuel Pitman	Robert Ticke	Thomas Ashmold
Robert Cheney	David Chastelain	Peter Bonafous

Chaplain— — Hancock.   *Qr.-Master*—James Howard.
Adjutant—John Wright.   *Surgeon*—∥

---

* I am told on good authority that no regiment has a "*right*" for so doing, although from time to time this privilege has been granted.
‡ Thomas Farrington to be Lieutenant in the White Regiment, 16th April, 1690.
§ Commission Books, War Office.
† William Froude was appointed Lieut.-Col. 1st April, 1694.
∥ Abraham Silk was appointed on 28th February, 1694.

There were City Merchants at this time of the names of Lewis, Wright, St. John, Middleton, Baker, and Sweeting, and the father of Col. Farrington was also one. In the Roll of Members of the H.A.C.,* the surnames of over twenty of the officers of Farrington's regiment occur, and under that of Farrington we find a Daniel, also a Thomas, who was appointed lieutenant on July 29th, 1681.

It should here be mentioned that the photograph of our first colonel, for which I am indebted to Miss S. M. ffarington, of Worden, is taken from an oil painting by the Dutch artist, Willem Wissing, who died at Burleigh on September 10th, 1687. The fact of being painted in armour more than a year prior to being appointed to the 2nd Foot Guards‖, leads one to think that Thos. Farrington had some previous connection with the profession of arms.

Although, on returning from Holland in 1799, the privilege of marching through the City with drums beating, etc., was denied the 29th, still it appears from General Walter's letter that through the interest of Col. Hon. C. A. Wrottesley, it was in 1839 granted and exercised.

In publishing the History of the 29th Foot, which in 1797, Lord Cathcart relates, was the " Boast of the British Infantry ;" and Sir A. Wellesley, writing from Badajos in 1809 to Lord Castlereagh, was pleased to mention as "the best Regiment in this Army," I feel many apologies are due to all its ranks for the scant justice done the regiment in the following pages, and regret that the information and help which has so kindly been proffered me on all sides, should not have fallen into more able hands than mine, for I am sure the Records could by others be made much more readable.

I wish to acknowledge the great assistance received from the Earls of Cathcart and of Strafford ; from Col. R. J. Watson, Major

---

* The Ancient Vellum Book of the Honourable Artillery Company, being the Roll of Members between 1611 and 1682, by Lieut.-Col. G. A. Raikes.

‖ For many years after this, officers were gazetted to the " 2nd Regiment of Foot Guards," but occasionally, in parenthesis, is inserted "called the Coldstream Regiment ; " at other times " 2nd Foot Guards called the Coldstreamers."—*Military Entry Books, Commission Books*, and *Harleian MS.*

F. Kneebone, and Captain H. Colvill, late of the Regiment; from Mr. Chas. Dalton, F.R.S., Mr. F. Enys, and Mr. S. Milne, the latter having given me much interesting information anent the Uniform, Badges, Buttons, etc., originally worn by the 29th; from the Officials of the British Museum, and Public Record Office, especially Mr. H. Hall, of the latter Institution, who has on several occasions put me in the way of discovering most important information. I beg here to tender my sincere thanks for their kind help.

I am also greatly indebted to Major W. M. Prendergast, late 29th Regiment, for his kind assistance in illustrating these Records.

H. EVERARD,
Late LIEUT. 29TH. REGT.

NORTON BARRACKS,
WORCESTER.

LIST OF WORKS FROM WHICH INFORMATION HAS BEEN OBTAINED.

British Museum.

GREAT BRITAIN AND IRELAND (ARMY)—Army Lists and Papers, 1687-1699.
,,   ,,   ,,   Army Debentures, 1702-03.
,,   ,,   ,,   Documents relative to Army and Garrisons, 1699-1706.

BURNET—History of His own Times.
DALTON, CHAS.—History of the Wrays of Glentworth.
OLDMIXON'S History of England.
BOSE, CLAUD DE—Military History of the Wars in Flanders and Spain.
BOYER, A.—History of the Reign of Queen Anne.
BRODRICK, T.—A compleat History of the late Wars in the Netherlands.
KANE, R.—Campaigns of King William and Queen Anne, 1689-1712.
MILLNER, J.—A Compendious Journal of all the Marches, etc., in the Wars against France, in Holland, Germany, and Flanders under the Duke of Marlboro'.
MORTIER, D.—Ramillies, the Glorious Campaign of His Grace the Duke of Marlboro'.
MARLBOROUGH DISPATCHES—by Sir G. Murray.
ALLISON'S, COXE'S, AND LEDIARD'S Life of the Duke of Marlboro'.
CHURCHILL (JOHN), DUKE OF MARLBORO'—History of John, Duke of Marlboro'.
VAULT—Mémoires Militaires de le Général.
RAPIN'S History of England.
MASSUE, H. DE—An Account of the Earl of Galway's conduct in Spain and Portugal.
BEATSON, R.—Naval and Military Memoirs of Great Britain from 1727.
SMOLLETT'S History of England.
GREAT BRITAIN AND IRELAND (ARMY)—A Representation of the Cloathing of H.M. Household, 1742.
MULLER, J.—A Treatise of Artillery.

GREAT BRITAIN AND IRELAND (ARMY)—A System of Camp Discipline, etc.
,,　　　　,,　　　　,,　　The Succession of Colonels to H.M. Forces, 1745.
ARMY LISTS (NEWSPAPER ROOM)—The Quarters of the Army in Ireland, 1744-1752.
,,　　　　,,　　Official from 1754 onwards.
BOTTA, C. G. G.—History of the War of Independence in the United States of America.
STEDMAN, C.—History of the Origin of the American Revolution.
ANBUREY, T.—Travels through the Interior of America.
BURGOYNE (RIGHT HON. JOHN), GENERAL—A State of the Expedition from Canada.
,,　　　　,,　　　　,,　　Orderly Book of Lieut.-Gen. J. Burgoyne, from his Entry into the State of New York.
,,　　　　,,　　　　,,　　Remarks on Gen. Burgoyne's State of the Expedition from Canada.
HUBBARDTON—Plan of Action of 7th July, 1777.
SWORDS HOUSE—Plan of Encampment and Position of the Army under Gen. Burgoyne on 17th and 19th September, 1777.
LAMB, SERGT. R.—An Original and Authentic Journal of Occurrences during the late American War to 1783.
FONBLANQUE, E. B. DE—Political and Military Episodes of the Right Hon. J. Burgoyne.
GREAT BRITAIN AND IRELAND (ARMY)—A brief Examination of the Plan, etc., of the Northern Expedition in America, 1777.
NEILSON, C.—An original, completed, and corrected Account of Burgoyne's Campaign, and the Memorable Battle of Bemis Heights, Sept. 19th and Oct. 7th, 1777.
STONE, W. L. (THE YOUNGER)—Campaign of Lieut.-Gen. Burgoyne.
GREAT BRITAIN AND IRELAND (ARMY)—Rules and Orders for the Army, 1786.
BRITANNIC MAGAZINE—Wade's British History.
ALLEN'S Battles of the British Navy.
JAMES'S Naval History.
SCHOMBERG'S Naval Chronology.
GORDON TURNBULL—Insurrection in Grenada.
MCMAHON, F.—Narrative of the Insurrection in the Island of Grenada.
MCGREGOR—Autobiography of Sir J.
SOUTHEY'S History of the West Indies.
MUSGRAVE'S Rebellions (Ireland).
NAPIER'S Peninsular War.
WELLINGTON'S Dispatches, by Col. Gurwood.
LEITH HAY (LATE 29TH FOOT)—History of the Peninsular War.

Hamilton, Capt. (late 29th Foot)—Annals of the Peninsular Campaign.
„   „   Cyril Thornton.
Scherer, Capt. Moyle—Recollections of the Peninsula.
Landmann, Col. G.—Recollections of my Military Life.
Moore—J. Moore's Campaign in Spain.
Malleson, Col.—Decisive Battles of India.
Archer, Capt. Lawrence—Commentaries on the Punjaub Campaign.
Chiliánwálá—Sketch of the Battle of—J. Wyld.
Carter—Medals of the British Army.
Newspapers—London Gazette, Flying Post, Daily Courant, Postman, Dublin Gazette, British Journal, Daily Post, General Advertiser, Lloyd's Evening Post, Public Advertiser, Nova Scotia Gazette, St. James's Gazette, Morning Chronicle, Morning Herald, Berrow's Worcester Journal, Monmouthshire Merlin, Ross Gazette, The Standard.
Service Papers—Naval and Military, United Service, Army and Navy Gazettes, Broad Arrow.
Manuscripts—Additional, Haldimand, Harleian, Sloane, and Tyrawley.

Public Record Office, London.

War Office—Miscellanies, Original Correspondence, Military Entry Books (Henry St. John), Military Papers State Paper Office, Military Establishment Books, King's Warrants, Ordnance Warrants, Minute Books, Unnumbered Papers, Memoranda Papers, Muster Rolls, Pay Lists, Monthly Returns, Marching Orders, Abstracts of Military Accounts, Inspection Reports.
Secretary of State—Common Letter Books, Letter Books Board of General Officers, Miscellany, Succession, and Notification Books, Original Correspondence, British Army in America, on Continent, and in the Peninsula.
Home Office—Military Entry Books, Domestic State Papers, Ireland, No. 377, etc.
Colonial Office—Records, Military Returns, Correspondence, Gibraltar, Cape Breton, Quebec and Canada, America and West Indies, Grenada.
Admiralty—Secretary's Letter Books, Miscellany and Odd Volumes, Muster Books, Pay Lists, and Logs of the several Ships on which the Regiment served at various times.
Audit Office—Declared Accounts.
Pipe Office—   „   „

Record Office, Dublin.

Marching Orders, Books of Entries, Military Commissions, Military and Martial Affairs, Martial Affairs (clothing), Army States, Military Miscellanies, Abstract Military Establishments.

Royal United Service Institution.

GROSE—Military Antiquities.
PARKER, R.—Military Memoirs of.
BLAND'S Military Discipline.
LEDIARD'S Naval History.
Army List, 1740.
SYMES—Military Guide, Medley, and Military Guide for Young Officers.
REIDE—Treatise on the Duty of the Infantry Officer.
Armada, and Naval Actions.
Field of Mars.
WALSH—Expedition to Holland.
Military Chronicle, Library, Extracts, Bulletins.
Royal Military Calendar.
HAMILTON SMITH—Uniforms of the British Army, 1812.
HART'S Army Lists, 1840, onwards.
Annual Register, Gentleman's Magazine, Notes and Queries.
Regimental Histories or Records, Grenadier, Coldstream Guards, Royal Artillery, The Buffs, 25th and 34th Foot, Rifle Brigade, Royal Munster Fusiliers, and MS. Records of 29th Foot.

Junior United Service Club.

GUTHRIE, F R.S., G. F.—Clinical Lectures on the Diseases of the Peninsular Army.
Reminiscences of a Veteran.
United Service Journal.
Victoires, Conquêtes, Revers et Guerres Civiles des Français.
THACKWELL—Narrative of the Second Seikh War.
MALLESON—Indian Mutiny.

War Office.

MS. Army Lists, 1702, 1730, 1739, 1745, 1752.

Windsor.

ROUND TOWER—Picture of a Grenadier 29th Foot, 1751.

Prince Consort's Library, Aldershot.

Picture of a Grenadier 29th Foot, 1768.

Private Sources.

THE EARL OF CATHCART—Correspondence and Private Letters of William, Lord Cathcart (Colonel of 29th Foot), 1789-97.

CAPTAIN P. GROVE—Extracts from Diaries of Captain H. Grove (29th Foot), 1797-99.

MR. F. ENYS—Col. Enys' Journals and MS. Records of the Regiment, 1775-99.

Military Journal of Col. C. Leslie, K.H., late 29th and 60th Regiments, 1807-32.

*MAJOR F. KNEEBONE—Journal kept by Lieut. W. Kirby (29th Foot), during Satláj Campaign.

„ „ Journal and Letters written by Ens. W. L. D. Smith (29th Foot), during the Panjáb Campaign.

CAPTAIN H. COLVILL—Journals, 1856-1860.

---

* Present with the Regiment at Sobráon, Chiliánwálá, and Gujrát; served also from 9th November, 1858, to 28th February, 1859, with Brigadier Turner's Field Force in clearing the Palamáo, Ramgarh, and Behár Districts of Rebels.

CHAPTER I.

ON the Meeting of Parliament in November, 1693, King William III., attributing the want of success in the late campaign against Louis XIV. to the insufficiency of our forces, demanded that the army and navy should be augmented, upon which the House of Commons voted that the establishment of the former should be increased to 83,121.

On Warrants being shortly after issued for the raising of 10 Regiments of Cavalry and 15 of Infantry, the command of one of the latter was, on the 16th February, 1694, given to Colonel Thomas Farrington, of the Coldstream Guards.

Declaration for the More Speedy Raising and Compleating the Foot Regiments.

"Whereas We have directed Three Regiments of Foot to be forthwith Raised under the Command of Coll. John Gibson, Coll. Thomas Farrington, and Coll. William Northcott. We do hereby declare Our Will and Pleasure to be, That for the better and more Speedy raising and compleating thereof: the said Regiments shall be allowed as full and complete, from the Twentyeth day of this instant March, Provided the respective companys do appear in a Condition of Service, the Cloathing excepted, on or before the Twentyeth day of May next; and with all their Cloathing and accoutrements on or before the first day of June following. And if any Captain or other Officer shall be faulty herein, such Officer or Captain shall Incurr Our highest Displeasure, and shall be immediately Cashiered, as also an abatement of Pay made in proportion to the defective Numbers of men whereof the Pay Master General of Our Forces, the Commissary Generall of

1694 the Musters, and all Officers whom it may Concerne are to take due notice and to Govern themselves accordingly. Given at Our Court at Whitehall this 12th Day of March, 1693¾. In the sixth year of Our Reign.

By his Ma^{ty's} Command

WILLIAM BLATHWAYTE."

OATH TO BE TAKEN BY ALL PERSONS THAT SHALL BE HEREAFTER COMMISSIONED IN THE ARMY.

"I, A. B. Do swear That I have not made any present or Gratuity for the obtaining of the Employment of ——, neither will I, nor shall any person for me, with my knowledge at any time hereafter Directly or Indirectly make any Present or Reward for the same, to any person whatsoever. And Do further swear, that if at any time hereafter it shall come to my knowledge, That any Guift, Present or Reward has been made by any Friend either before or after my obtaining this Employment, That I will immediately discover the same to his Majesty or the Commander in Chief."

ARMS FOR COLL. LEIGH'S REGIMENT OF DRAGOONS, AND COLL. FARRINGTON'S REGIMENT OF FOOT.

WILLIAM R.

"Whereas We have Ordered a Regiment of Dragoons to be forthwith Raised for Our Service, Commanded by Our Trusty and Welbeloved Coll. Edward Leigh, consisting of eight Troops, each Troop of sixty Private Soldiers, three Corporalls, two Serjeants and two Drummers, beside Commission Officers; Likewise a Regiment of Foot, to be forthwith raised, Commanded by our Trusty and Welbeloved Coll. Thomas Farrington, consisting of twelve Companys, and one Company of Granadiers, each company of sixty private men, three Corporalls, three Serjeants and two Drums, beside Commission Officers, Our Will and Pleasure, therefore is, That out of ye Stores remayning within ye Office of Our Ordnance under y^re charge you forthwith Issue **1694** ye Necessary Arms and Appurtenances, for Arming our Said Regiments, as ye rest of Our Regiments of ye Same nature and number are, ye same to be delivered into ye charge of y^r Respective Collonells or whom they shall appoint to receive them, Taking ye usuall Indents, and for So doing this shall be y^re Sufficient Warrant. Given att Our Court att Whitehall this 26th day of March, 1694, in ye Sixth of our Reigne.

By his Maj^ty Command

SHREWSBURY."

"To our Rt Trusty & Wellbeloved cousin & Councellor
Henry Viscount Sydney Master Gen^ralle of Our
Ordnance, &c., &c."

Each Company of Infantry (the Grenadier excepted) consisted of 14 Pikemen and 46 Musketeers. "Grose" states that in 1690 Grenadiers "appear to have been armed with firelocks, and to have used cartridges, to have had slings, sword, bayonet, and pouch, with Grenades. They had also Hatchets with which, after firing and throwing their Grenades, they were, on the command 'Fall on,' to rush upon the Enemy." These still appear to have been the Arms of the Grenadier in 1694.

Each foot Soldier carried a sword, and each Pikeman a pike of 16 feet long; each Musketeer a musquet, with a collar of Bandoliers; the barrels of the musquet were about 4 feet long, and carried a ball, 14 of which weighed a pound. Until the reign of William III. hats with very wide brims and feathers were worn. The inconvenience of such brims being felt, first one, and then two sides were turned up. About the reign of Queen Anne a third side was turned up, or cocked. Captains carried pikes; Lieutenants, partizans; Ensigns, half pikes; Serjeants, halberts.

The dress of Officers at this period appears to have been as follows:—Hat, ornamented with feathers, broad brim, two sides of which

1694 were turned up; full flowing wig; square cut coat and long flapped waistcoat, with large pockets to both; breeches tied below the knee, with stocking drawn over up to the middle of the thigh; shoes; sword slung over the right shoulder; sash worn round the waist and knotted on the right side.

Leaving Norwich about the middle of June, Farrington's Regiment marched to Portsmouth, and whilst there we find that John Wright, Esq., "tooke the Oath" and received the Commission of Captain-Lieutenant.* Leaving Portsmouth in October, the Regiment took up quarters in various towns in Dorsetshire, Somersetshire, and Devonshire. In December 40 men marched from Norwich to join the Regiment, which in the meanwhile had been concentrated at Exeter.

DAILY PAY OF A REGIMENT OF FOOT, 1694.

	£	s.	D.
Colonel, as Colonel 12s., as Captain 8s.	1	0	0
Lt.-Colonel, as Lt.-Colonel 7s., as Captain 8s.		15	0
Major, as Major 5s., as Captain 8s.		13	0
Captain		8	0
Lieutenant		4	0
Ensign		3	0
Adjutant		4	0
Quarter Master		4	0
Surgeon 4s., and Mate 2s. 6d.		6	6
Chaplain		6	8
Serjeant		1	6
Corporal		1	0
Drummer		1	0
Private Soldier			8

A yearly deduction of one day's pay was made from all Ranks, and this was applied towards the purchase of Land, the Building of the Royal Hospital at Chelsea, and the better maintenance of such superannuated and disabled Officers and Soldiers as should be provided for

---

* The Senior Subaltern, who commanded the Colonel's Company.

therein: thus in a sense the place belongs rather to the Soldier than to the nation. This Hospital was founded in 1682.

1694

In January, 193 Men, 6 Serjeants, 6 Corporals, and 2 Drummers were drafted into Colonel Luke Lillingston's Regiment, then under orders for Jamaica.

1695

Early in February the Regiment left Exeter for quarters in Berkshire, Buckinghamshire, and Oxfordshire; and 558 of its Men, with their Arms and appurtenances, having been incorporated into Regiments in Flanders, orders were sent for it to recruit forthwith.

In May a change of Quarters took place, and the Companies were stationed in Kent, Herts, Suffolk, and Surrey.

Having in July been reviewed at Blackheath by the Duke of Schomberg, the Regiment marched and took up Quarters in Norfolk and Suffolk, 6 Companies being stationed at Norwich.

In September orders were received for the Regiment to march forthwith to the Hamlets of the Tower of London, where it was to remain and do such duties within the said Tower, as the Officer in chief Command there should direct.

In December, after being reviewed by the King in Hyde Park, it sailed for Flanders. Contrary winds, however, detained the Transports a short time, which was then thought a great misfortune, but afterwards proved to be the reverse, for early in January a great Jacobite plot was discovered for the invasion of England by the French, on behalf of King James, to be preceded by the assassination of King William. The assassination having failed, the threatened invasion did not take place.

Having been ordered to disembark, on the 9th January, 1696, the Regiment proceeded to take up Quarters in Clerkenwell, Islington, Holloway, and St. John Street.

1696

On 8th February orders were received to raise recruits for the Regiment, and cause them to rendezvous, 2 Companies at Leeds, 2 Richmond, 2 Halifax, 2 Manchester, 1 Ripon, 1 Barnard Castle,

1696 1 Wakefield, 1 Lancaster, and 1 at Pontefract. Although the quarters were changed from time to time, the Regiment remained in Yorkshire till October, when it marched South, and was quartered in Herts, Essex, and Middlesex. In the "Gazette" is an advertisement for two men who deserted in their Regimental Clothes, viz., "Red Coats with Brass Buttons, lined and faced with yellow, blue Breeches, and White Stockings."

At this period Regiments were called after their Colonel, as "Farrington's Regiment"; when on parade they appear to have taken precedence according to the seniority of their respective Colonels; for this year the Regiment ranked 46th, and in 1698 as the 28th Regiment of Foot. It is difficult to ascertain when it first ranked as the 29th Foot; but *vide* Royal Warrant, 14th September, 1743.

1697 On 1st July the Regiment marched to Blackheath, and there encamped for 27 days, after which it took up quarters in Essex and Suffolk.

On 20th September the Treaty of Ryswick was signed and peace concluded between England, France, Spain, and Holland.

On 12th October the Regiment marched for Cheshire, Lancashire, and Staffordshire, but two days later, it was ordered to halt till further orders. It having been decided to decrease the Establishment of the Army, the Companies were reduced from 60 to 42 private Soldiers, 2 Serjeants, 3 Corporals, and 1 Drummer in each (the Company of Grenadiers excepted.)

In December the Regiment was stationed as follows: 2 Companies Boston, 2 Horncastle, 2 Louth, 1 Spilsby, 1 Tattershall and Merton, 1 Spalding, 1 Market Deeping and Crowland, 1 Donington, 1 Wisbeach.

1698 On 17th February, 1698, it was intimated to Colonel Farrington that Brigadier Selwyn had been directed to repair to the Quarters of the Regiment, and disband it. With this object the several Companies were ordered to rendezvous at Stamford.

Extracts from Orders and Instructions sent Brigadier Selwyn. 1698
William R.

"Before such disbanding you are to take care that each Non-Commissioned Officer and Soldier be permitted to carry away with him his Cloaths, Belt, and Knapsack, and that each private Soldier, Corporall, and Drummer be payd three shillings for his Sword, which is to be delivered with the other Arms into the office of Our Ordnance. And We being pleased to allow each Non-Commissioned Officer and private Soldier fourteen days' subsistence from the time of their disbanding, to carry them home, and give them passes under your hand to the places of their former Residence, allowing them a convenient time to Repair thither, and giving them likewise strict charge that they do not presume to Travell with any Arms, nor more than three in Company together, upon pain of the severest punishment. Given at Our Court at Kensington this 16 day of February, $169\frac{7}{8}$."

Brigadier Selwyn writes to Mr. Secretary Blathwait.

"Stamford, feb. 26, $9\frac{7}{8}$

Sir,
I have this day disbanded 5 Companies of Col. Farrington's Regim^t., which are all y^t are yet arrived. I expect the rest to-morrow Munday and Tuesday, as fast as they come, will loose no time, thus far am sure I have nicely observed my instructions, and find the Officers have punctually stated their acc^t with their quarters and the men, no complaints coming against them from either, they disband pretty quietly, without mutiny or disorder, and are in a good condition most of them, so y^t I have got some extraordinary men for my Regiment. if you have any orders for me I hope to be at Grantham on wednesday, and Lincoln on thursday. next post will not faill to give you a farther acc^t, who am,

Sir, y^r most obedient Servant,
W. Selwyn."

1698 *In the W.O. Miscellany Books is the following Letter, dated 3rd September, 1698:—*

"Sir,

His Maj^ty having been pleased to order That a Comp^y be formed out of the Officers of the Reg^ts that have lately been broke, which are to march at the head of the 1st Reg^t of Foot Guards, if any of the Officers are willing to enter into this Service, you will send them to Coll. Shrimpton, Major of the said Regiment, as soon as may be convenient.

To Col. Farrington.   GEORGE CLARKE.§"

"Grose," writing about Corporal Punishments in the Army, says: "There are a great variety; but of these only one could be inflicted on "an Officer—this was boring the tongue with a hot iron for Blasphemy, "a punishment that remained in force till the Reign of Queen Anne."

NAMES OF THE OFFICERS OF FARRINGTON'S REGIMENT DRAWING H. PAY, 1698.

CAPTAINS.	LIEUTENANTS.	ENSIGNS.
Coll. Thos. Farrington	{ Capt. Lieut. John Wright { Francis Lewis	{ Dawkin Willmott { Anthony Gawdy
Lieut.-Coll. Wm. Froude	{ John Danvers { John Brooks	{ Peter Bonafous { Wm. Carr
Major Chr. Wray	{ Vere Harcourt { Charles Drake	{ Courtney Southwell { John Miller
Cha. Cracherode	Robert Uthwayte	Thos. Farrington
Thos. Phillips	Chas. Midleton	Abell Cook
John Daley (Grenadiers)	James Dennis	John Davenport
John Bickley	John Greenwood	Cha. de Castelneau
James Howard	Robert Carr	Richard Bisset
Robert Cheyne	David Castlean	
Richard Nanfan	Robert Pike	
Robert Minzies		
Saml. Pitman		
James Otway	John Hancox, CHAPLAIN.	
	James Howard, QUARTERMASTER.	

---

§ Secretary at War, in absence of Mr. Blathwayte.

In the Treasury Board Records is " an account shewing to what **1701** "time the several Officers borne upon His Late Ma^{tie's} Establishment "of Half Pay, have Received their respective Allowances, (To wch time " Paid, 24th Dec., 1701) and what Remains due to them to 8th March, " 170½."

All the above-named Officers (with the following exceptions) are included in this account :—

        Coll. Farrington ⎫ Whose Commissions were renewed
        Lieut.-Col. Froude ⎭   12 Feb., 1702.
        Captain Phillips
        Lieut. Drake
        Ensign Southwell
        Chaplain Hancox.

CHAPTER II.

1700 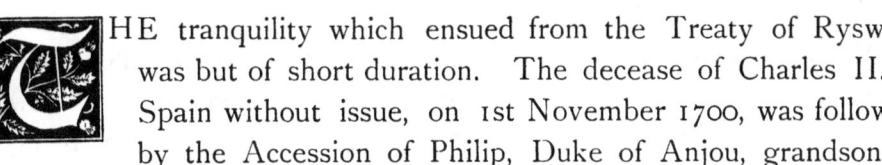HE tranquility which ensued from the Treaty of Ryswick was but of short duration. The decease of Charles II. of Spain without issue, on 1st November 1700, was followed by the Accession of Philip, Duke of Anjou, grandson of Louis XIV., in prejudice to the claims of the House of Austria. Angry feelings were further engendered by the French Monarch proclaiming the titular Prince of Wales (known as the Old Pretender), Sovereign of Great Britain, Scotland, and Ireland, on the death of King **1701** James II. at St. Germain in Sept., 1701. This combination of events induced England to enter into the War of the Spanish Succession by supporting the pretensions of Charles, Archduke of Austria, to the Crown of Spain.

The raising or reforming of Farrington's Regiment, with 8 others,† was one of the last acts of the life of William III., who had begun to place the British Army on its War footing; and on the 12th February, **1702** 1702, Col. Thos. Farrington was placed on full pay.

Upon the decease of William III. on the 8th of March, the Crown, according to the Act of Settlement, devolved on Princess Anne of Denmark (sister of the late Queen Mary), who had in 1683 married

---

† LIST OF REFORMED COLONELS OF FOOT IN ENGLAND, AND SENIORITY OF REGIMENTS :—5. Richard Coote (39F). 3. Luke Lillingston (38F). 8. John Gibson (28F). 9. Thos. Farrington (29F). 2. Henry Mordaunt (Marines). 7. Thos. Sanderson (30F). 4. Henry Holt (disbanded 1713). 6. Thos. Brudenell (Marines). 1. Edward Fox (32F).—*British Museum Documents relative to Army and Garrisons, 1699-1706.*

Prince George of Denmark. The Accession of Queen Anne did not **1702** produce any alteration in the policy of the late Sovereign, and War was proclaimed against France and Spain on the 4th of May.

In July the Duke of Marlboro' assumed command of the allied army in Flanders, whilst the combined English and Dutch fleet, under Sir G. Rook, with troops on board commanded by the Duke of Ormonde, proceeded to Spain.

Many Colonels, commanding corps broke in 1698, when their officers were placed on h.p., were in 1701-2 ordered to raise new regiments, but in several cases, instead of their former officers being re-commissioned with the new corps, an entirely new lot were brought in. Such, however, was not the case with Farrington's regiment, as the accompanying list of its officers will show. This fact, I think, establishes the connection of the regiment reduced in 1698 with the one raised in 1702, though, I know, some people fail to see it.‡

In lists of officers previous to 1756, the names of subalterns were generally entered by companies, not by seniority.

NAMES OF THE OFFICERS WHOSE COMMISSIONS WERE RENEWED, AND WHO DREW FULL PAY FROM MARCH 10TH :—

CAPTAINS.	LIEUTENANTS.	ENSIGNS.
	Capt. Lieut. Edwd. Pyles	John Miller
Lieut.-Col. Wm. Watkin	Francis Lewis	Peter Bonafous
Major Chr. Wray	John Danvers	Henry Goddard
Chas. Cracherode	Robert Carr	Alexander Mann
Robert Minzies	Ruben Caillaud	William Carr
John Dally (Grenadier)	{ John Greenwood { Richard Goddard	

---

‡ When, in 1861, the 19th and 20th Hussars were formed (chiefly from Volunteers from the H.E.I.C. Bengal European Cavalry Regiments) their connection with the late 19th and 20th Light Dragoons was so far acknowledged that they were subsequently authorized to bear on their appointments, etc., the Regimental Device, and Battle Scrolls of those Regiments which had been disbanded in 1819 and 1818.

1702

Captains.	Lieutenants.	Ensigns.
John Bickley	Vere Harcourt	Anthony Gawdy
Saml. Pitman	Robert Picke	Cha. de Boileau Castelnau
Richard Nanfan	John Brooke	Abell Cooke
Robert Cheyne	John Denise	Thos. D. Farrington
James Otway	Robert Uthwait	William Cooke
John Wright	David Chatelain	Dawkins Wilmot

Lieut. Francis Lewis, ADJUTANT.
Ensign John Miller, QUARTER MASTER.
Robert Cox, CHAPLAIN.
Abraham Silk, CHIRURGEON.

Warrant, dated 18th March, 1702, authorizing Coll. Thos. Farrington, by Beat of Drum or otherwise, to Raise Volontiers for a Regiment of Foot which is to consist of 12 Companies, of 2 Serjeants, 3 Corporalls, 2 Drummers, and 59 Private Soldiers in each Company, the Servants included, with the addition of 1 Serjeant more to the Company of Granadiers. * * * * * * ; and when the whole number of Non-Commission Officers and Soldiers shall be fully or near compleated in each Company, they are to march to Manchester, Macklesfield, Warrington, Wigan, Knotsford, Stockport, Altringham, and Leigh, appointed for the Rendezvous of the said Regiment.

The Surgeon Mate and the Non-Commission Officers drew full pay from the 1st, the private Soldiers from 20th April to 13th May, when the Regiment was placed on the Establishment of Ireland.

Colonel Farrington was paid £1316 for raising his Non-Commissioned Officers and men, being the rate of 40s. each man.

About the middle of April, orders were received for the regiment to take up quarters in the North, East, and West Ridings of Yorkshire; and, soon after, for each of the companies to be reduced to 50 private soldiers.

On 30th May orders were issued for 1 company at Bury St. Edmunds, to march to Congleton and Sandbach.

1 Company at Worcester to march to Knutsford and Altrincham. **1702**
1   ,,   Easingwold   ,,   ,, Leigh.
1   ,,   York   ,,   ,, Bury in Lancashire.
1   ,,   Knutsford   ,,   ,, Newton, and hold themselves in readiness to embark at Chester.

"Whitehall,
20 June, 1702.

Sir,
It is Her Majesty's pleasure that all the pikes, already delivered to the Regiment of Foot under your Command, be returned into the Stores of Ordnance, in lieu of a sufficient number of Muskets, which you are first to receive out of the said Stores.

I am,
Sir,
Y^{rs}, &c.,
WILL BLATHWAYTE."

"P.S.—This is not to hinder y^r carrying y^r pikes to Ireland, in case Muskets be not in time enough delivered to you.
To Col. Farrington."

Early in July, preparatory to embarkation, the Regiment again took up quarters in Lancashire and Cheshire, and sailing 1st August, arrived off Dublin the 15th, whence it proceeded to Carrickfergus, and on landing there was stationed as follows:—2 Companies at Carrickfergus; 1 Drogheda; 4 Derry, with a Detachment of 40 men at Culmore; 1 Armagh Barracks and Town; 1 Carlingford Barracks and Town; and 1 Enniskillen.

In December, Captains Cracherode and Otway, Lieut. Picke, 3 Serjeants, and 2 Drummers proceeded to England for Recruits.

1703 In 1703 the Regiment proceeded to Dublin, where it did duty from 24th April to 7th September, during which time the Non-Commissioned Officers and Private men received a penny a day in addition to their pay, as granted by King William III. to all Regiments doing duty there.

On the arrival of the Duke of Ormonde in June, to take up the duties of Lord-Lieutenant, the street from the Castle gate to the College Green was lined by Col. Sankey's and Col. Farrington's Regiments. On the Lord-Lieutenant entering the Castle, he was saluted by the discharge of 15 pieces of cannon, and soon after by three salvos of 21 guns each, and as many volleys of the small arms of the two Regiments of Foot above-mentioned who were in the Castle Yard.

ORMONDE.

"These are to pray and require your Lord^{sp} to cause to be delivered out of her Mat^s Stores of Warr under your care unto Coll. Willm Watkins, three Barrels of powder in Lieu of the like Quantity expended by Coll^o Farrington's Reg^t in firing Volleys on 23rd of Aprill, her Ma$^{tie's}$ Coronation day; upon the good news of the takeing of Bonn; and on the 29th of May, the Restoration of the royall family, as in such cases is usuall, and for so doing this, with the Receipt of the said Coll^o Watkins for the quantity of powder aforesaid, shall be your Lordsp^s sufficient Warrant.

Given at her Maties Castle of Dublin the 7th day of June, 1703.

By his Grace's Command,

EDWARD SOUTHWELL."

"To our very good Lord the Earl of Mountalex^r
    Mas^r Gen^{ll} of the Ordnance in this
        Kingdome."

The following Proceedings of Courts Martial are interesting, in **1703** that they give one an idea how Soldiers were treated, and the punishment they were awarded for various offences.

"*The Proceedings of the Court Martial held the 9th of June, 1703, are most humbly Represented.*

Present—Major Christopher Wray, *President;* and 12 Officers of the Sev^{ll} Regiments.

The Court being Sworen seet, and Serjeant Francis Parens, of Capt Wright's Company in Coll^o Farrington's Regt^t, charged James Ward, Richd Rosse, Abraham Mathews, and Alexander Vance, private Sentinells, with Mutiny.

They all pleaded Not Guilty;

And upon examination of the Wittnesses on oath against and on the Testimony of Sev^{ll} Credible Persons produced in behalf of the Prisoners, it appeared that there happened a sudden quarrell between a Townsman, who was the aggressor, and Vaunce, one of the Prisoners, which was immediately appeased, and not attended with any Circumstance to make it mutiny either in intention or consequence; the Court did therefore unanimously acquit the said James Ward, Richd Rosse, Abraham Mathews, and Alex^r Vaunce of the mutiny wherewith they stood Charged, but Abraham Mathews having during the Affray used some unfitting words, the Court did therefore adjudge that the said Abraham Mathews doe ride the Wooden horse* at the Relief of the Guard one hour, with a Musquett at each foote.

Lieut. James Dennis of Coll^o Farrington's Reg^t charg^d James Norman and John Howard, private Centinells, with mutiny, and resisting him their Commanding Officer; and Serjeant David Rust

---

* "The Wooden Horse" was formed of planks nailed together so as to form a sharp ridge or angle about 8 or 9 feet long. This ridge represented the back of the horse; it was supported by 4 posts or legs about 6 or 7 feet long, placed on a stand made moveable by trucks. To complete the resemblance, a head and tail were added. When sentenced to ride the horse, the Soldiers were placed on the back, with their hands tied behind them, and frequently, to increase the punishment, had muskets tied to their legs.

1703 charged James Commin, of the same Regiment, Drummer, with the like Crime.

The Court did adjudge that James Norman was guilty of Mutiny, but by a Majority it was carried that it was not a mutiny to that degree as to deserve death, but severe Corporall punishment, and that he doe accordingly run the Gauntlope,‡ one day six lengths of the two Regiments now in Garrisson, and that after four days' intermission the same punishm^t be repeated on him; that he remained Confined for some time afterward, and then be released, and continued in the Service. The Court being of oppinion that John Howard was in a less degree Criminall than the other, did unanimously adjudge that the said John Howard doe run but four lengths through the said Reg^{ts} on each day, and be also continued in the Service. And that James Commin was not guilty of the mutiny, but that for insolent words by him given to the Serjeant, he doe run the Gauntlope, two lengths of the said Reg^{ts} on each day, and be continued in the Service.

All wch is most humbly submitted to y^r
Grace's Consideration,
CHRISTOPHER WRAY."

"*Proceedings of the Court Martial held the 4th of August, 1703, are most humbly Represented.*
Lieut.-Coll^o Wm Watkins, *President;* Captain Robert Minzies, Captain John Dally, Captain Richd Nanfan, Captain Richd Lewis, Captain Robert Fletcher, Captain Chas. Middleton, Captain Edward Pyle, Captain Talbot Young, Captain Thom^s Candler, Lieutenant John Danvers, Lieutenant John Miller, Ensign Wm Cooke.
The Court being Sworen, satt.

---

‡ "Run the Gauntlope." The Regiment was formed 6 deep, and the ranks opened and faced inwards. Each man being furnished with a switch, the offender, naked to the waist, was led through the ranks, preceded by a Serjeant, the point of whose reversed halbert was presented to his breast, to prevent his running too fast. As he thus passed through the ranks every Soldier gave him a stroke.—Grose "*Military Antiquities.*"

Ensign Lewis . . ., charged Andrew Lawless, Corporall in Coll° ————'s Regiment, with mutinous behaviour, in pushing, resisting, and striking him, and spetting in his face. **1703**

The Prisoner denyed the Charge.

The En^s delivered in his Complaint in writeing on oath, and Nicholas ————, Adjutant, John Flood, Corporall, and Mich Tooley, Provost Martiall, was sworen, by whose Evidence it appeared to the Court that the En^s being near the Ring when orders were giving out, the Corporalls being directed to keep all clear, the Prisoner went to putt back the En^s, and as the En^s Swears, thrust him away, and tho' he asked him if he knew what he was doeing, and told him he was an Off^r, yet the Pris^r pushed him more rudely than before, upon wch the Adj^t beat the Pris^r, telling him the Gen^t was an Off^r, and that then commanding him to the Guard, the Pris^r as he was going step^t up to the En^s, spett in his face, and gave him two or three blows on the head.

The adju^t could give no acc^t of the 1st beginning of the matter but said that seeing the Pris^r pushed the En^s, he came out of the Ring, beat him, and commanded him to the Guard, and soon after, hearing a 2nd Scuffle, he came and beat the Prisoner more Severely than before, but did neither see the blows given by the Pris^r or that he did spitt at the En^s, but that the Prisoner was in drink.

" From evidence given by Corp^l Flood and the Provost Martial," it appears that as the Pris^r was being conducted to the Guard, the En^s followed and kickt the Pris^r, who turned about, struck at him with his hand, made a dent in his hand, and spett in his face.

The Prisoner confessed he was something in drink. Upon full debate and consideration of the whole course of the evidence, altho' they did not cleerly agree in all the circumstances, yett the Court was of oppinion that a Soldier strikeing and threatning an Off^r with such indignity on any acc^t whatsoever is of very ill consequence to the Discipline and Governm^t of the Army, and therefore the Court did

1703 unanimously agree to find the said Andrew Lawless Guilty of the Charge, and the question being putt whether he should suffer death for the same, it was carryd in the Negative; and thereupon the Court did adjudge That the said Andrew Lawless be tyed to a Post on the Parade in the Lower Castle Yard, and be Lasht with Six Twiggs three times by each drummer of Coll° Farrington's Reg^t, and that 4 days after he doe receive the like punishm^t from each Drum^r of Coll° Farrington's Reg^t, and that 4 days after he doe receive the like punishm^t from each Drum^r of Coll° ——— Reg^t, that he will be confined 14 days after, and be reduced to serve as a private Centinell a year following.

Captain William Higginson charged Francis Clifton, Serj^t of Coll° Farrington's Reg^t, with Mutiny.

The Prisoner pleaded not Guilty; but upon full evidence of the Cap^{tn} and another Gen^t of good Creditt upon Oath, it appeared to the Court that the Pris^r, upon pretence of an old debt of 13s. 6d. from the Captn, followed him in the Streets makeing a Loud outcry and gathering a crowd about him complained to them of the wrong done him; that the Captn demanding what he meant, the Pris^r flew into an extravagant passion and gave the Capt very ill language, and being commanded to the Guard as Pris^r, he did not goe but waited till the Cap^{tn} returned from a place he was going to, and then renewed his abuses, and made a motion as if he would have drawn upon the Cap^{tn}, but did not, and then went through sev^{ll} Streets to the Guard clamouring all the way and uttering very base and Scandallous Reflections on the Cap^{tn}, and continued so to doe after he was committed to the Mainguard.

Upon full debate of the matter, the Court did unanimously find the Pris^r Guilty of the Charge, and by a Majority it was carryed that he should not suffer death, but they did adjudge that the said Serjeant Francis Clifton be tyed to the Gallows post on the green, with a rope

1703 unanimously agree to find the said Andrew Lawless Guilty of the Charge, and the question being putt whether he should suffer death for the same, it was carryd in the Negative; and thereupon the Court did adjudge That the said Andrew Lawless be tyed to a Post on the Parade in the Lower Castle Yard, and be Lasht with Six Twiggs three times by each drummer of Coll° Farrington's Reg*, and that 4 days after he doe receive the like punishm* from each Drum* of Coll° Farrington's Reg*, and that 4 days after he doe receive the like punishm* from each Drum* of Coll° ——— Reg*, that he will be confined 14 days after, and be reduced to serve as a private Centinell a year following.

Captain William Higginson charged Francis Clifton, Serj* of Coll° Farrington's Reg*, with Mutiny.

The Prisoner pleaded not Guilty; but upon full evidence of the Cap*ⁿ and another Gen* of good Creditt upon Oath, it appeared to the Court that the Pris*, upon pretence of an old debt of 13s. 6d. from the Capt*ⁿ, followed him in the Streets makeing a Loud outcry and gathering a crowd about him complained to them of the wrong done him; that the Capt*ⁿ demanding what he meant, the Pris* flew into an extravagant passion and gave the Cap* very ill language, and being commanded to the Guard as Pris*, he did not goe but waited till the Cap*ⁿ returned from a place he was going to, and then renewed his abuses, and made a motion as if he would have drawn upon the Cap*ⁿ, but did not, and then went through sev*ˡˡ Streets to the Guard clamouring all the way and uttering very base and Scandallous Reflections on the Cap*ⁿ, and continued so to doe after he was committed to the Mainguard.

Upon full debate of the matter, the Court did unanimously find the Pris* Guilty of the Charge, and by a Majority it was carryed that he should not suffer death, but they did adjudge that the said Serjeant Francis Clifton be tyed to the Gallows post on the green, with a rope

about his neck, and be picquetted† an hour every field day of the two **1703**
Reg^{ts} now in this Garisson while they remain here; that the Adjutants
of the Reg^{ts} see it done; that he be reduced to serve as a private
Centinell and be incapable of being more dureing this warr, and be
continued on the Marshalls while the Reg^{ts} stay in the Towne.

 All which is most humbly Submitted to
   Your Grace's Consideration.
         W$_M$. W$_{ATKINS}$."

In August, Cols. Sankey's, Farrington's, Fairfax's, Gibson's, Temple's, and Tidcombe's regiments were each ordered to send a detachment of 34 men to Cork, under a captain, lieutenant, ensign, and non-commissioned officers, to complete the respective companies of Mountjoy's and Brudenell's regiments, then ordered to Portugal. No Papists, or men extracted from the native Irish, were to be amongst the detachments.

On the regiment leaving Dublin, 4 companies marched to Kilkenny, 2 Enniscorthy, 2 Arklow, 1 Bray, and 3 to Wicklow, where they remained till the following March, when it having been decided to **1704** employ the regiment in Holland, it embarked at Dublin, and on landing at Neston and Highlake, proceeded in 3 divisions to Harwich. Being placed on the establishment of the Low Countries from the 12th March, each company was augmented by 1 serjeant, and 4 private men. The regiment having embarked on the 16th May, the transports which also took recruits and horses to Holland, were detained by

---

† The Picket was another corporal punishment. The mode of inflicting it was thus: A long post being driven into the ground, the delinquent was ordered to mount a stool near it, when his right hand was fastened to a hook in the post by a noose round his wrist, drawn up as high as it could be stretched; a stump, the height of the stool, with its end cut to a round and blunt point, was then driven into the ground near the post before mentioned, and the stool being taken away, the bare heel of the sufferer was made to rest on this stump, which though it did not break the skin, put him to great torture; the only means of mitigation was by resting his weight on his wrist, the pain of which soon became intolerable.—*Grose.*

1704 contrary winds, and anchored in Hollesley Bay till near the end of the month, when starting once more, they arrived in the Maas the 10th of June.

The Duke of Marlborough having started for Bavaria on the 24th of April, left only a corps of observation in the Low Countries to restrain any attack the French troops might make during his absence; and it is most probable that Farrington's regiment formed part of that corps, no account existing of its employment elsewhere. Lieutenant Boileau, was however, more fortunate, for we find he commanded a corps of French gentlemen at Blenheim.*

1705 1705 was a memorable year in the history of this regiment, which, forming as it did part of the column that marched up the Moselle, was, for the first time since its formation, actively engaged.

As the French still occupied Flanders and the greater part of Brabant, the plan proposed for the ensuing campaign was that two columns, "the one, under the command of the Duke of Marlboro', marching up the Moselle, the other, being under Prince Louis of Baden," should penetrate into Lorraine and carry war into the enemy's country.

All preparations having been made, on the 14th of May the Duke inspected the Dutch and English troops, near Maestricht, after which the latter, under command of Gen¹ Churchill, commenced their march. Monsr. d'Auverquerque was left near Maestricht, in command of the troops intended for the protection of Holland.

---

*Charles Boileau, né le 10me Février 1673, sortit de France en 1691 pour aller dans les Mousquetaires de Brandebourg, d'où étant sorti, il passa en Angleterre, où il fut Enseigne (25 May, 1694) dans le Régiment de Farrington, qui fut cassé ou reformé en 1698. Passa en Irlande jusqu'à à 1701, quand il fut remplacé au dit Regiment, où il fut fait Lieutenant en 1703. Fut fait prisonnier à Launingen le 25 Octobre 1704, fut echangé á Valenciennes le 1re Février 1709, passa en Angleterre pour faire sa Compagnie, qu'il vendit, en 1711, et de là fut en Dublin en 1722, où il mourut le 7me Mars 1733.— *From an old MS. in possession of Surgeon-Major J. P. H. Boileau, late 29th Regt.*

1705 On the 3rd of June, having passed the Moselle, and the Saar near Consaarbruck, the army advanced by the defile of Tavernen towards Sirk, where Marshal Villars was encamped. After an arduous march of 18 miles, the troops arrived within a quarter of a league of Elft, where the enemy had an advance post.

It being too late to encamp, the troops formed up and bivouacked for the night. At daybreak it was discovered that the French detachment had fallen back on the main body, which occupied a strong position formed by the heights of Sirk.

The allies therefore made a slight advance and encamped with their right at Perle and their left at Ellendorf; in this position Marlboro' awaited the arrival of Prince Louis of Baden, whose tardy movements in a great measure frustrated his scheme for carrying on the war. Information was in the meantime received from the Low Countries that Marshal Villeroy and the Elector of Bavaria, having assumed the offensive, had captured Huy, and were advancing on Liege. It was therefore resolved to march back to the Meuse, and on the 17th of June, at midnight, the allied army decamped, without beat of drum, in the midst of heavy rain, and having without molestation repassed the defile of Tavernen, reached Consaarbruck the next morning.

It being ascertained that the enemy had not yet commenced the siege of the citadel of Liege, the march towards the Meuse was continued without delay, the Earl of Orkney being pushed forward with "all" the grenadiers of the army, and 100 men out of "each" battalion. This rapid advance caused the enemy to send back their artillery to Namur, and abandoning the siege, they retired within their lines, which reached from Marche-aux-Dames, on the Meuse, to Antwerp, and had taken 3 years to construct. Before advancing further, Huy was retaken, after which, early in the morning of 17th July, the enemy's lines were surprised and successfully forced between Neer Hespern and Elixheim, with but small loss to the

1705 confederates. The loss of the enemy, in killed and wounded, was inconsiderable, but many officers of distinction were captured, and 1200 prisoners were made the next day. Many trophies fell into the hands of the allies, amongst which were 10 pieces of cannon with 3 barrels each.

In this action, "Webb's brigade" was composed of Tatton's, Temple's, Farrington's, and Ingoldsby's regiments, and formed the right of the 2nd line of infantry.

The enemy having retreated across the Dyle, posted themselves very advantageously at Parc, near Louvain.

An unsuccessful attempt having been made there to cross the river, and Marlboro', finding he could neither induce the Dutch again to attempt the passage, nor could he baffle the vigilance of the enemy, resolved to turn it at its source. With this object the confederates, marching by Genappe, on the 17th August approached the borders of the forest of Soignies, and encamped between Hulpen and Braine l'Allieu.

In the meanwhile the enemy had taken up a fresh position, and established themselves behind the Ische.

General Churchill was now detached with 20 battalions, "including Tatton's, Sabines', Fergusson's, Lalo's, Farrington's, and Meredith's," and as many squadrons, and posted in front of the army. When the confederates advanced the next day, Churchill's troops taking the route on the left, moved towards the convent of Grœnendal, with orders to come out of the wood near Hollas, and attack the enemy in flank.

On approaching the convent it was found that the roads were broken up and trees felled across them, also that a corps of 20 French battalions was strongly posted at the opposite opening of the wood. The detachment therefore halted whilst awaiting fresh orders.

By noon the whole army was drawn up in line in sight of the enemy, and occupied the ground which in 1815 was covered by

Napoleon's army, whilst the French held the forest of Soignies and **1705** the approaches to Brussels.

The Duke of Marlboro' and Mon^{sr} d'Auverquerque, having carefully inspected the enemy's position and reconnoitred the ground, were both of opinion that the attack should be delivered at once, but General Slangenberg and the Deputies of the States absolutely refused to consent, alleging that the enemy were too strongly posted.

The Duke's project being thus defeated, General Churchill's detachment was recalled, and the confederates retired to Lane. Marching by Lower Wavre, Tirlemont was reached early in September, when detachments from each regiment were employed in dismantling it, and levelling the enemy's late lines between the river Mehaigne and Leuve. After this the troops crossed the Demer, and on the 28th marched to Herenthals, where they soon after "hutted," the weather being very cold.

The season for campaigning was now drawing to a close, and, it having been ascertained that the enemy had gone into winter quarters, towards the end of October Generals Lumley and Churchill, with the British troops, separated from the main army then encamped at Turnhout, and marched off by themselves to their winter quarters along the river Demer.

Proposal of the General Officers, relative to the clothing of the army. **1706** At a meeting in the Great Room at the Horse Guards, on the 4th of Feb., 170$\frac{5}{6}$, and at another on the 7th February, it was agreed that the quantity and quality of clothing for the Foot shall be, viz. :—

"*For the first year*—A good cloth coat well lined, which may serve for the waistcoat the second year ; a pair of good thick kersey breeches ; a pair of good strong stockings ; a pair of good strong shoes ; a good shirt and a neckcloth ; a good strong hat, well laced."

1706 "*For the second year*—A good cloth coat well lined, as for the first year; a waistcoat made of the former year's coat; a pair of strong kersey new breeches; a pair of good strong stockings; a pair of good strong shoes; a good shirt and neckcloth; a good hat, well laced. That all accoutrements, as swords, belts, patrontashes, and drum carriages be made good as they are wanted; that the recruits be supplied with a new waistcoat, and one shirt, and one neckcloth more than the old soldiers, who have some linen beforehand; and that the serjeants and drums be clothed after the same manner, but everything in its kind, better."

In a letter, dated Whitehall, 2nd April, 1706, we find by the last returns from Holland, that Farrington's regiment consisted of no more than 384 men. However, in May it again took the field, and proceeded to the general rendezvous of the army between Borchloen and Coswaren.

It being ascertained that Marshal Villeroy, "having received reinforcements, and depending on his superiority of numbers," had crossed the great Gheete and was advancing on Judoigne, the Duke of Marlboro' resolved to attack him in this position.

Early in the morning of the 23rd of May, the army of the allies was put in motion, and on approaching Mierdorp, the enemy was discovered moving towards Mont St. André, between the two Gheets and the Mehaigne, and taking up the very ground which the confederates hoped to occupy.

As the heads of the eight columns of the allies cleared the village of Mierdorp, they diverged into an open plain, and the 5th and 6th, in one of which was Meredith's brigade, were ordered to march on the steeple of Offuz.

In the approaching battle, which decided the fate of the Netherlands, Meredith's brigade was composed of Orkney's, Ingoldsby's,

Farrington's, Meredith's, and Lord North and Grey's regiments. It **1706** formed the right of the 2nd line of infantry,* and subsequently took part in the attack on Ramillies.

The enemy's left and centre, stretching from Autreglise to Ramillies, whilst protected from attack in front, by reason of marshy ground, was for the same reason unable to act on the offensive. Their right occupied the open space between Ramillies and the Mehaigne, and their position being concave in shape, afforded great advantages to the assailants.

By one o'clock, the allies were drawn up in two lines, in order of battle—the infantry in the centre, the cavalry on either flank.

Perceiving that the "Tomb of Ottomond," between Ramillies and the Mehaigne, was the key of the enemy's position, the Duke of Marlboro' ordered the British, Dutch, and German infantry composing the right, supported by the cavalry, to make a demonstration against the enemy's left. This feint had the desired effect, for Villeroy hurried up reinforcements from his centre. Marlboro' at once ordered the infantry on the right, to retire a short distance, and the 2nd line marching rapidly to its former left, formed in rear of the centre, and joined in the attack on Ramillies, which was surrounded by a ditch, and in which village twenty battalions had been posted. The enemy's right, having, after a stubborn resistance, been turned, and their troops driven out of Ramillies, the battalions, "which had made or sustained the attack on that village," supported by the British horse, were ordered to penetrate through the swamp towards Offuz.

The enemy however, gave way without waiting their approach, and were pursued by the cavalry from 4.30 to 10.0 p.m., whilst Mon^{sr} d'Auverquerque, with a detachment, followed them till 1.0 the next morning.

---

* British Museum MS. $\frac{30995}{1334}$, also Harl. MS. $3\frac{1860}{324}$.

1706 This battle cost the enemy 13,000 in killed and wounded, whilst eighty colours and standards, together with almost the whole of the French artillery, and baggage which had not been sent to the rear, were captured.

The casualties of the different corps of the allied army are not known, but their total losses were—killed 1066 (of which 82 were officers), wounded 2567 (of which 283 were officers).

The famous battle of Ramillies introduced the Ramilie cock of the hat; and a long gradually diminishing plaited tail to the wig with a great bow at the top, and a small one at the bottom, called the "Ramilie tail"; the sides of the wig consisted of a bushy heap of well-powdered hair.

The immediate result of this splendid victory was the acquisition of nearly all Austrian Flanders; Brussels, Louvain, Alost, Luise, and nearly all the great towns of Brabant opened their gates on the approach of the allies. Bruges and Ghent speedily followed their example. Daum and Oudenarde soon declared for the Austrian cause. Antwerp capitulated on the 6th of June.

Of all the towns in Flanders, Ostend, Dunkirk, and two or three smaller places alone held out for the French.

The siege of Ostend being decided upon, it was commenced the 18th of June, and carried on under the direction of Mon^{sr} d'Auverquerque.

By a plan of this siege, it appears that Farrington's, Stringer's, and Macartney's regiments were brigaded together, and formed the right of the front line of attack.

On the night of the 4th July an assault was made by fifty English grenadiers, commanded by a lieutenant, supported by a Dutch battalion. These having effected a lodgment, the next morning the enemy made a sortie and endeavoured to drive them out, but on being repulsed by the battalions which advanced from the trenches, they beat a parley.

According to the terms of capitulation, the garrison, which was **1706** commanded by Comte de la Motte, marched out with its baggage, but without military honours, and on condition the men should not bear arms against King Charles III., or his allies, for a period of six months.

This important conquest did not cost the allies above 500 men.

In the place were found 24 colours, 1 standard, and 90 pieces of cannon, besides ammunition and powder.

A design being now formed for a descent on the coast of France with an army of about 10,000 foot and 1,200 horse, the Earl of Rivers was given the command of the land forces, whilst Admiral Sir Cloudesley Shovell commanded the fleet which was to convoy them, and secure their landing near Bordeaux.

Towards the end of June, Brigadier Cadogan was directed to send to the head quarters of Farrington's and Macartney's regiments, any of their men he had, either at Dendermond or Oudenarde.

Ostend having capitulated, these two regiments were embarked, and sailed for St. Helen's, where the transports with the troops for the projected descent were assembling. Here the fleet lay in expectation of the Dutch squadron and transports, which were detained in the Downs by contrary winds till the 12th of August. This fatal delay occasioned the abandonment of the projected descent, and the destination of the forces was altered to Lisbon.

Sixty-one days' pay had been advanced to the commissioned officers to enable them to provide themselves with necessaries; the establishment of the regiment was completed to 876, and though sent to Portugal, it remained, nevertheless, upon the establishment in Flanders till the end of the year 1708.

By reason of contrary winds, the fleet was weatherbound in Torbay till the 1st October, when it weighed anchor, and after a 24 days passage, during which it encountered much bad weather, arrived at its destination.

1706　　During its stay at Lisbon, Dom Pedro, King of Portugal, died; and the attitude of the new sovereign being thought uncertain, Lord Rivers held a council of war, the result of which was that all the colonels of the forces under his command were ordered to repair to their respective posts, and hold their troops in readiness to land at once if required. This however, proved unnecessary, as the king declared he would keep true to the interests of the allies.

The Court of Spain, at Valencia, being now in disorder and danger from the superiority of the French and Gallo-Spaniards, it was resolved to proceed with the forces and join the Earl of Galway.

1707　　Leaving Lisbon the 18th January, 1707, the fleet arrived at Alicant about the 8th February, and the troops commenced at once to disembark.

Having been above six months exposed to all the inconveniences which attended long voyages in those times, the force now numbered scarcely 7,000 men, the loss by mortality being computed at about 300 men a battalion.

On the 22nd February, six regiments which had suffered most, viz., Brudenell's, Hamilton's, Mohun's, Toby Caulfield's, Allen's, and Farrington's, were "reduced," their private men being delivered over to complete the establishment of others; those of Farrington's being sent to Southwell's (6th Foot) and Breton's (afterwards disbanded).

With the exception of Lieutenants Alexr. Man, John O'Bryan, John Spark, and Ensign Lewis Griffith, who were posted to serve with the Miquelets, the officers, non-commissioned officers, and drummers of Farrington's regiment re-embarked for Lisbon the 27th February *en route* for England, to recruit.

On the 27th May orders were given for any commissioned or non-commissioned officers belonging to the six regiments lately reduced in Spain, who should arrive at Spithead, to disembark at Portsmouth, and on the 29th July, for those of Farrington's regiment, to march from London to Norwich.

1707 In September each company was ordered to be completed to 56 men, including servants, and the following month the regiment was quartered as follows:—

    6 Companies at Norwich.
    1 Company ,, Swaffham.
    1 ,, ,, Harleston.
    1 ,, ,, Attleboro'
    1 ,, ,, Buckenham, with detachments.

On the 31st of December, Captain Columbine's company was ordered from Abingdon to Thetford.

The union of England and Scotland having this year been ratified by the Scottish Parliament, St. Andrew's cross was placed on the colours of the English regiments, in addition to St. George's.

1708 Although serving in England, Farrington's regiment continued to be borne on the establishment of the Low Countries, and consisted of 1 colonel, 1 lieutenant-colonel, 1 major, 1 chaplain, 1 surgeon and his mate, and 12 companies, viz., 12 captains, 13 lieutenants, 11 ensigns, 36 serjeants, 36 corporals, 24 drummers, and 672 private centinels.

In February a change of quarters took place, when 8 companies marched to Romford and Hare Street, 2 to Mile End, 1 to Bow and Stratford, 1 to Barking; detachments being also sent to Epping and Ongar. Whilst in these quarters the regiment was reviewed by Major-General Erle, after which two companies proceeded to Ongar and supplied detachments at Kelvedon, Navistock, and Blackmore.

On the 14th of March the regiment received orders to march northwards to assist in repelling a threatened invasion of Scotland by the French in favour of the Old Pretender. The French fleet having been dispersed by Admiral Sir George Byng, near St. Andrew's, the regiment halted at Wakefield until the 3rd April, when it commenced to march *via* Nottingham, for Farnham, Guildford, Dorking, and Godalming.

1708   On the 1st May a Board of General Officers allotted the county of Surrey to the regiment to recruit from.

Early in June the regiment crossed over to the Isle of Wight, where it encamped with the troops which were to be employed in menacing the coast of France and making a diversion in favour of the allied army in Flanders. The fleet was under the command of Sir George Byng, the land forces under that of Major-General Erle.

Leaving Spithead the 6th August, the fleet made for Deal, where several of the soldiers were shifted from the men-of-war on to transports, after which the expedition sailed for the coast of Picardy, where a landing was effected. The troops subsequently returned on board the fleet, and after menacing the coast at several points, orders were received for them to return to Spithead.

The allied army, under the Duke of Marlboro' and Prince Eugene, was in the meanwhile carrying on the siege of Lille. The want of ammunition was its greatest drawback, and as all the roads to Brussels were wholly obstructed, the Duke, in order to open a new communication with Ostend, had sent for the British battalions which were being employed under General Erle.

Having, at Spithead, taken two months' provisions on board, Erle's expedition sailed for Ostend, where it arrived the 21st September.

Hearing of this, Comte de la Motte, who was advancing with a considerable force towards Brussels, returned immediately to Bruges, and cut the dykes of Leffinghen, in order to lay the country between Nieuport and Ostend under water, hoping thereby to prevent General Erle from communicating with the besieging army. In this, however, he did not succeed, for General Erle's troops drained the inundations, built a bridge over the canal at Leffinghen, and a convoy of 700 waggons with ammunition and other necessaries being dispatched, reached Lille in safety.

1708 The Duke of Vendome was so enraged at this, that he marched with a strong detachment to Oudenburg; with it, he took post along the other side of the canal between Plassendael and Nieuport, and caused the dykes to be cut in several places, which laid a large tract of land under water. General Erle therefore placed his troops, which were encamped at Raversein, in position to resist any attack the enemy might make.

Hearing of the Duke of Vendome's movements, the Duke of Marlboro' advanced against him with the greatest part of his army, on which the enemy retreated with great precipitation, and the regiments under General Erle succeeded in conveying another supply of ammunition, &c., across the inundations to places where the waggons from the army were awaiting it. These supplies proved sufficient, and the citadel of Lille surrendered on the 9th of December.

1709 On the 23rd December, the regiment was placed on the establishment of Portugal, and in February, 1709, embarked for Hull, whence on the 7th March it left for York, but in June returned to Hull to relieve Colonel Dormer's and Churchill's regiments, which were ordered abroad. A draft of 50 men having been sent to Colonel Charles Churchill's regiment, officers were sent to recruit in Edinburgh and Berwick.

In April, the regiment returned to York, and on the 25th June was placed on the establishment of land forces in Great Britain.

1710 It having been decided to employ it in an expedition under Lord Shannon, on the 25th March, 1710, Lieut.-General Farrington was ordered to provide tents and other camp necessaries for his regiment without delay.

Having embarked at Hull, the regiment landed at Portsmouth early in July, and on crossing over to the Isle of Wight, encamped with the troops which were assembling for the expedition.

1710   On the 25th August another company (the 13th) was added, which brought the total establishment up to 876. Towards the middle of October the troops embarked and proceeded to Spithead.

The Tory Ministry which came into office in November, being inclined to peace, the death of the Emperor Joseph I. of Germany, which had occurred this spring, opened the prospect of its attainment, more especially as the Archduke Charles, one of the competitors for the throne of Spain, was elected his successor. Thus the views of England with regard to the "War of the Spanish Succession" were entirely changed, and Lord Shannon's expedition was countermanded.

On the 7th November Major-General Whetham was placed in command of the troops, which still lay off Spithead, with orders to join the army in Spain.

On the 21st Lieut.-Colonel Sir Christ^r Wray, Bart., died at Portsmouth.

1711   On the 8th January, 1711, the regiment was placed on the establishment of Spain, and on arrival in that country in March, was stationed at Gibraltar.

1712   In 1712-13 thirty-two regiments were reduced or transferred to the establishment of Ireland, and orders were sent Brigadier Thos. Stanwix, the governor of Gibraltar, to cause Farrington's regiment to be reduced and incorporated with the other regiments, which were to be continued in that garrison.

On the 7th October Lieut.-General Farrington died, and was buried at Chislehurst. The command of the regiment was now given to Lord **Mark Kerr** Mark Kerr, whose own corps had recently been disbanded.

1713   Pursuant to orders, on the 22nd February, 1713, the regiment was reduced, and its non-commissioned officers and private men, with their arms, were drafted into the regiments of Pearce (5th), Barrymore (13th), and Newton (20th).

Lord Mark Kerr and his officers having paid for their own **1713** passage, were brought home on board the "St. George" galley, and on arriving at Whitehall the 12th of May, were ordered to take possession of the non-commissioned officers and private men of Colonel Chudleigh's regiment, which was quartered in Ireland, and about to be reduced.*

On the 24th November they proceeded to Ireland, and were posted to the head of Col. Chudleigh's late regiment, whose men were reported as being in possession of 320 arms, 288 whereof were not fit for any service.§

This regiment, it appears, was on the 22nd June‡ ordered to be reduced, Colonel Thos. Chudleigh and officers being placed on half-pay.

Since, by the vicissitudes of the service, this battalion eventually became the 29th Foot, which is now represented by the 1st Battalion Worcestershire Regiment, it may interest some to know when and where it was raised, and of its services; with this idea the following extracts have been made from the Records of the 34th Foot:—

This regiment was raised the 12th February, 1702, by Robert, Lord Lucas, and was composed of men from Norfolk, Essex, and the adjoining counties, one wing of the regiment having had its rendezvous at Colchester, the other at Norwich. In 1705 it embarked for Spain, and took part in storming the fortress of Montjuich and the siege of Barcelona. In 1707 being much reduced in numbers, those of its private soldiers fit for duty were transferred to other corps, and the regiment returned to England to recruit. In 1708 it served under General Erle; in 1710 under the Duke of Marlboro', being present at the passing of the French lines at Pont a Vendin, the sieges of Douay and

---

* Treasury Papers, clxv.; H. O. Ireland, No. 388; Add. MS. 22616—Record Office, London.

§ Record Office, Dublin—Books of Military Entries, 26 Oct., 1715.

‡ Record Office, London—H.O. Ireland, No. 380.

1713 Bethune, and employed in covering the sieges of Aire and St. Venant; in 1711, took part in the movements by which the enemy's formidable lines were passed at Arleux, and the siege of Bouchain; in 1712, joined the army of the Duke of Ormonde which penetrated the French territory to the frontiers of Picardy, encamping at Cateau-Cambresis; was stationed at Dunkirk until the conclusion of the peace of Utrecht, when it proceeded to Great Britain. At this time a considerable reduction took place in the army, which included Chudleigh's regiment.§

---

§ On 22nd May, 1715, a warrant was issued for Col. Thos. Chudleigh to forthwith raise a regiment (now the 34th Foot), which was to enjoy its former rank as if it had not been broke.—*Military Entry Books: and War Office Miscellany Books, 521.*

CHAPTER III.

1713 THE establishment of a regiment of foot in Ireland was fixed by Warrant dated 30th June, 1713, as follows:—

1 colonel, 1 lieut.-colonel, 1 major, 1 chaplain, 1 adjutant and quarter master, 1 surgeon, 1 mate, 10 captains, 11 lieutenants, 9 ensigns, 20 serjeants, 20 corporals, 10 drummers, and 360 private soldiers.

Queen Anne, having died on the 1st August, 1714, was succeeded **1714** by King George I., whose mother, Princess Sophia, granddaughter of King James I., had married the Elector of Hanover. The new king was proclaimed both in Dublin and Edinburgh without opposition or tumult. On the 29th instant, "the Chevalier de St. George," as the young Pretender was frequently called, who was residing in Lorraine, published a manifesto, asserting his right to the English crown.

On the 9th November, Lord Mark Kerr's regiment marched from Cork to Kinsale, where, after remaining a month, it returned to its late quarters.

On the 28th of April, 8 companies marched from Cork:— **1715**
4 to Kinsale, from which the following detachments were furnished:—

Half a company at Galbally redoubt
,, ,, Ninemile House redoubt
,, ,, Killenaule redoubt
,, ,, Longford Pass redoubt

2 companies to Youghal, 1 to Dungarvan, and 1 to Bantry.

With exception of the last-mentioned, these detachments returned to Cork about the middle of August.

1715   List of Officers of Lord Mark Kerr's Regiment of Foot 1st June, 1715:—

Captains.	Lieutenants.	Ensigns.
Lord Mark Kerr, Col.		
Chs. Cracherode, Lt.-Col.	Joseph King	Marsh Hollingworth
Benj. Columbine, Major	{ John Pittman { Ebinezer Darby	Henry Debrose
Robert Minzies	Alexr. Man, Capt. Lieut.	Howell Herd
John Greenwood	David Henderson	John Dally
Peter Bonafous	Thomas Peirson	William Shenton
Reuben Caillaud	Henry Staughton	Daniel Caillaud
John Brooke	Henry Symes	William Ash
David Paine	John Charlton	Henry Melling
Hugh Montgomery	Richard Mallen	Francis Salisbury
John Miller's "Granadiers"	{ James Steuart, 1st Lieut. { Jonathan Young, 2nd Lieut.	

Henry Bland, Chaplain.

Andrew Charlton, Adjutant.

Bartholomew Black, Surgeon.

On the 10th of August, Lord Mark Kerr was gazetted captain of that company of which Peter Bonafous was late captain.

The death of Louis XIV., which occurred on the 1st September, was a severe blow to the Pretender, who was meditating an invasion, for the views of the Duke of Orleans, who now became regent, differed from those of the late king. In the meanwhile, the Earl of Mar had prematurely and unadvisedly summoned the Highland Clans, and had at Braemar proclaimed the Pretender, king of Great Britain.

Several regiments having been sent from Ireland to assist in suppressing this rebellion, Lord Mark Kerr's was ordered to the north, there being serious apprehensions of a Jacobite rising in those parts. On the 29th, a route was issued for the regiment to march, 6 companies to Carrickfergus, 1 Newry, 2 Belfast, whilst the company which was still at Bantry was ordered to Carlingford Barracks.

In October, the several companies were directed to be made up to 50 men each, and none but Protestants were allowed to be enlisted.

1716 On the 14th of January Lord Mark Kerr was appointed commander-in-chief of the towns of Carrickfergus and Belfast, as well as of all H.M. forces quartered within the counties of Down and Antrim. Towards the middle of April, the regiment marched for Limerick, where Col. Dormer's and Col. Kane's regiments were also in garrison.

1717 Leaving these quarters in April, 1717, it marched to Navan, thence to Drogheda, and on the 19th of May arrived in Dublin, where it remained till June, 1718, when it marched to Kilkenny. **1718**

On the 26th of December war was proclaimed against Spain.

The *Serjeants' Hats* of Lord Mark Kerr's regiment, were at this period, laced with silver.

1719 In 1719 the regiment was again held in readiness to repel a threatened invasion in favour of the Pretender, this time by a Spanish force, and on the 17th of March proceeded to Kinsale, where it encamped till the 23rd of May, when the Spanish expedition having been dispersed and disabled by a storm, and the hopes of the Jacobites frustrated, the regiment proceeded to Dublin and did duty there till November, when it marched to Galway.

Lord Mark Kerr by Coll. Kennedy assigns to Mr. Jos. Kane, cloathier, in consideration of the following particulars of cloathing, the full off-reckonings* of his regiment for one year commencing the 25th of March, 1719, amounting to the net sume of £1201 9s. 2d.

For Serg^ts & Drum Major.	For Drummers.	For Corp^ls, Gran^ds, and Sentinels.
21 Coats and Breeches	9 Coats and Breeches	400 Coats and Breeches
19 Hatts and 2 Grenad^r Caps	8 Hatts and 1 Gran^d Cap	355 Hatts and 45 Gran^d Caps
21 Pairs of Shoes	9 Pairs of Shoes	400 Pair of Shoes
21 Pairs of Stockings	18 Shirts and Cravats	800 Shirts and Cravats
42 Shirts and Cravats		

* "Off Reckonings."—A specific account, so-called, which existed between the Government and the colonels, for the cloathing of their men.—*James' Military Dictionary.*

1720   By Royal Warrant, dated the 27th February, 1720, the king fixed the prices of all commissions; those in Lord Mark Kerr's regiment being—

Colonel and Captain	£6000
Lt.-Col. and Captain	£2400
Major and Captain	£1800
Captain	£1000
Captain Lieutenant	£450
Lieutenant	£300
Ensign	£200
Adjutant	£150
Qr. Master	£150

The regiment returned to Dublin the 1st April, 1720, where it **1721** remained till the 15th May, 1721.

1723   In 1723, we find that Lord Mark Kerr assigned to Jos. Kane the off-reckonings for one year, in consideration of the following arms and accoutrements :—

400 Musketts and Bayonetts
400 Pouches and Collars
400 Waist Belts
400 Slings

The strength of the regiment in October was 50 non-commissioned officers and 380 private men.

1724   Steel rammers, were this year fitted to firelocks made for wooden ones.

The wearing of swords by the N.C.O's, rank and file, appears to have been discontinued at some previous time, for in the General Officer's letter book, is a letter from the Secretary at War, dated 1st of December, 1724, saying, "His Majesty has determined that all the "non-commissioned officers and private men of his Foot forces shall "wear swords, and that the off-reckonings should be protracted a month "longer than usual, to prevent the expense falling on the officers."

1725 We also find that Colonel Mark Kerr, by articles dated 2nd of April, 1725, assigned to Joseph Kane, the off-reckonings of his regiment of Foot for one month, from the 25th of March, 1725, amounting to £102 5s. 10d., in consideration of the said Joseph Kane's furnishing the said regiment with 390 swords.

The quarters occupied by the companies this year were as follows:—

1 Company at Newmarket	1 Company at Tralee
1 ,, Dingle	1 ,, Dungarvan
2 ,, Youghal	2 ,, Limerick
1 ,, Kilmeedy & Needeen	1 ,, Colecormuck & Calleen

On the 25th of December, Colonel Henry Disney was given the **H. Disney** command of the regiment, *vice* Lord Mark Kerr transferred to the colonelcy of the present 13th Foot.

At the commencement of the next year, the Limerick garrison **1726** was composed of Col. H. Disney's, and Lanoe's regiments.‡

It being reported that the Spaniards had fresh ideas for the recovery of Gibraltar, two squadrons were equipped—one destined for the Spanish West Indies, the other, under Sir John Jennings, to cruise off the coast of Spain, and to make a descent on it, should it be thought necessary.

With a view of serving on board the latter squadron, the regiments of Anstruther, Disney, Middleton,* and Newton having embarked at Cork, arrived at Portsmouth on the 7th of June. On the 15th, the transports escorted by the "Drake," sailed for the Downs, where Disney's regiment was put on board H.M.S. "Union," "Berwick," and "Canterbury."

On board the "Union" was Sergt.-Major Patrick Quinn, a sergeant of Lieut.-Colonel Kennedy's company. This is the earliest

---
‡ Subsequently the 29th and 36th Regiments.
Re-embarked for Ireland, 15th Inst.

1726 mention I have found of a non-commissioned officer holding that rank.

Leaving the Lizard the latter end of July, the squadron arrived at Lisbon the 25th August, and after re-victualling, proceeded to Cadiz.

Having cruised off and alarmed the coast of Spain, on the 29th of September it returned to Lisbon, and sailing thence, arrived at Portsmouth the 24th of October. The detachments on board H.M.S. "Berwick," and "Canterbury," having landed early in November, were ordered to march to Chatham.

Information being again received that the Spaniards were preparing to besiege Gibraltar, measures were taken by the government to reinforce that garrison. On the 1st of December the several companies of Colonel Disney's regiment were ordered to march at once to Southampton; these, together with Col. Anstruther's, and Newton's regiments, having embarked at Portsmouth on Sir Charles Wager's **1727** fleet, landed at Gibraltar the 3rd February, 1727.

The establishment of the regiment on the 27th April, 1727, was 35 officers, 20 sergeants, 20 corporals, 10 drummers, and 340 private men.

On arriving, it was found that the Spaniards, under Conde de la Torres, were encamped within a league of the place, and had raised two batteries. At a council of war held on the 10th inst., it was decided to warn the Conde that if he did not immediately desist, suitable measures should be taken. On the enemy's continuing the work, all possible obstruction was given by the fire of cannon and small arms.

About 10 p.m. the 12th of June, a drum was heard beating in the enemy's trenches, soon after which an officer advanced, bringing a letter with advice that preliminaries of peace (treaty of Aix-la-Chapelle) were signed. A cessation of hostilities was thereupon agreed to.

The following casualties occurred in the regiment between the **1727**
11th of February and 12th of June :—†

Died—Captain Gilmour.   *Killed*—2 Rank and File.
  „   2 Rank and File.   *Wounded*—12 „
                                     Deserted—2 „

Bland, in his Treatise of Military Discipline published this year, states, that a regiment was seldom formed four deep, except when very weak or for the punishing of soldiers by making them run the gauntlet. There were four paces between each rank, and three feet allowed to each man.

The Position of a Soldier :—"His feet to be at one pace distance, the heels in a straight line, and the toes turned a little outward."

The Colours carried by a Regiment were :—1st, the colonel's; 2nd, the lieut.-colonel's; and 3rd (if one), the major's.

At a General's Inspection :—"The major, is to order the men to shoulder, as the general passes along the front; the officers are to salute him with their half pikes or partisans, and to time it in such a manner that each may just finish his salute and pull off his hat when he comes opposite to him."

When Marching Past in Grand Divisions :—"The major, is to salute on horseback at the head of the granadiers, being some paces advanced before the captain: but if he command the regiment, he is then to march on foot in the colonel's post, and salute with his half pike."

The establishment of the 10 companies was augmented from the **1728** 25th of December to 3 sergeants, 3 corporals, 2 drummers, and 50 private men each.

---

† Add. MS. 12,427 gives the list of regiments engaged in this siege and the casualties of each.

1729 On the 20th of November, 1729, the standard size of the men for the marching regiments was fixed at 5 ft. 8 in., with shoes such as were given with the clothing.

1731 February, 1731, Mr. Sutherland, son of Lord Duffus (now in the Czarina's service), to be ensign in Col. Disney's Foot.

On the death of Col. Disney, which took place the 21st of November, 1731, the colonelcy of the regiment was given to William Anne, Earl of Albemarle, "of the Coldstream Guards," who, on being promoted to the command of the 3rd troop of Horse Guards, was on the 5th of June, 1733, succeeded by Colonel George Read, 1st Foot Guards.

Albemarle

1733
G. Read

1737 Soldiers at this period appear to have worn their hair powdered and well tucked up under their hats, but none on their shoulders.

1739 Brigadier-General George Read being transferred to the colonelcy of the present 9th Foot, on the 28th of August, Colonel F. B. Fuller, 1st Foot Guards, was appointed to command the regiment.

F. B. Fuller

The strength of each company, which on the 25th of June had been augmented to 60, was in December raised to 70 private men, making a total of 815, including the officers, &c.

1742 The Spanish fleet having formed a junction with the French squadron at Toulon, orders were on the 7th of April, 1742, sent to Major-General Hargraves, "the lieutenant governor of Gibraltar," that in case Admiral Mathews should have occasion for a number of men to serve on board his ships, he should be furnished with 500 men from such regiments as were there stationed, viz., Col. Fowkes', Major-General Hargraves', Lieut.-General Columbine's, Brigadier Fuller's, and Col. Houghton's. From a State of the Garrison dated 9th of May, it appears that 313 non-commissioned officers and men of the above regiments, were then serving on board H.M.S. "Royal Oak."

Of Brigadier Fuller's regiment, Captain H. Symes, Ensign John **1742** Corrance, 2 sergeants, 2 corporals, 2 drummers, and 56 men were on board the fleet.

29TH REGIMENT OF FOOT, 1742.

During 1743, the fleet continued in Hyères Bay. The chief **1743** service it performed was blockading the French and Spanish fleet in Toulon harbour. On the 29th of November, the above detachments were turned over from the "Royal Oak" to H.M.S. "Rupert," which became engaged with the Spanish ships in the action of the 11th

February, 1744, when Admirals Mathews and Lestock engaged the Franco-Spanish squadrons off Toulon. The advantages gained in this action were lost through a misunderstanding between the English admirals.

On the 10th of May, 1744, Capt. Symes' detachment was turned over to H.M.S. "Barfleur," thence, in August, to the "Princessa," and on the 23rd of October back to the "Rupert"; shortly after this, it landed at Gibraltar.

1743 At this period, all officers (of foot) carried espontoons instead of half-pikes. The espontoon or "spontoon," had a longer and larger blade than a half-pike, and was rendered more fit for execution by a cross-stop. Officers of the flank company, always carried fusils, or "fusees" as they were sometimes called.

By Royal Warrant‡ dated 14th September, no colonel was allowed to put his arms, crest, device, or livery on any part of the appointments of his regiment.

The *First Colour* of every marching regiment was to be the great Union.

The *Second Colour* of Fuller's regiment, to be yellow, with the Union in the upper canton. In the centre of each colour was to be painted, in gold Roman figures, the number† of the rank of the regiment, within a wreath of roses and thistles on one stalk.

The *Size of the Colours* was 6 feet 6 inches flying; 6 feet deep on the pike.

The *Drummers* to be clothed with yellow, lined, faced, and lapelled with red; and laced in such a manner as the colonel should think fit for distinction's sake, the lace being of the colour of that on the soldiers' coats. From the picture of a private of the 29th Regiment dated 1742, the lace appears to be plain white tape.

---

‡ In the warrants of 1751 and '68, only alterations in the preceding warrant have been quoted.

† "Gentleman's Magazine," 1743; mentioned as the XXIX. regiment of foot.

1743 The *Front of the Grenadiers' Caps* to be yellow, with the king's cypher embroidered, and crown over it; the little flap to be red, with the white horse and motto of the regiment over it. The back part to be red; the turn up to be yellow; the number of the regiment may be in figures, on the middle part behind.

The *Bells of Arms*, or "bell tents, where the company's arms were lodged in the field," to have the king's cypher and crown and the number of the regiment under it, painted on a ground of yellow.

The *Drums* to be painted in the same manner.

The *Camp Colours* to be 18 inches square, and of yellow, with the rank of the regiment upon them.

The *Sashes of the Officers* to be of crimson silk, and worn over the right shoulder. Their sword knots to be of crimson and gold in stripes, and their gorget, silver like the lace of their uniforms.

Serjeants to wear worsted sashes, round their waists, of red striped with yellow.

1744 In April, 1744, Hargrave's, Columbine's, Fuller's, and Houghton's regiments were ordered to cause a sufficient number of commissioned and non-commissioned officers, to repair from Gibraltar without loss of time to Middlesex, London, Westminster, and Southwark, there to receive such able-bodied men as offered as volunteers, or prest men as should be delivered over to them respectively by the commissioners appointed by the Act then in force "for the speedy and effectual recruiting of His Majesty's land forces and marines."

In 1744, Col. Weideman, a German, brought light field pieces into use again.* His pieces were made of sheets of copper rolled up and soldered together; they were so very light that a 6-pdr. weighed no more than two hundredweight and a-half, and yet stood all the proofs that were required. This gave rise to our light field pieces or battalion guns.

---

* Gustavus Adolphus was the first who ordered 2 field pieces to be attached to each battalion.

1745   The mode of dressing the hair in a pigtail instead of the "Ramilie tail" is said to have been introduced in 1745.

"Grose" says that in June, 1745, battalion companies in general ceased to carry swords. (*Vide* 1784).

The regiments of Fuller and Warburton, being ordered to repair from Gibraltar to Cape Breton, embarked for Louisburg the 28th of October, but meeting with very stormy weather, the transports were obliged to stop at the Leeward Islands, and afterwards at Virginia, where the troops were mustered by the governor of that colony from the 25th **1746** of December—24th of April, 1746, when, sailing again, they reached Louisburg about the middle of May.

It having been decided to raise two regiments for the defence and preservation of the Island of Cape Breton, on arriving there, Col. Fuller found orders for him to hand over to Colonel William Shirley, 1 serjeant, qualified to be serjeant-major, 5 corporals, to be serjeants, and 5 privates, to be corporals, in order that they might be incorporated into this new regiment.

The garrison of Louisburg now consisted of Genl. Fuller's, Col. Warburton's, Col. Shirley's, Sir William Pepperell's, and 3 companies of Col. Frampton's regiment.

About the middle of September, the governor of the island, Commodore Knowles, sent the "Shirley" (Capt. Rouse), with a transport schooner as a tender, and Captain Hugh Scott, an ensign, and 40 men of Fuller's regiment, to a small island called St. John's, for stock. On their approach, the French inhabitants carried their effects, and drove their cattle into the woods. However, on the landing of French deputies (who accompanied Capt. Rouse), with proposals from Governor Knowles, the people readily consented to part with one-half of their stock of cattle, &c., which they were to be paid for, and sent a great part of it down from the woods into the town for their use. Captain Rouse therefore sent his son (a youth of 16 years of age), and a guard of soldiers, with his coopers, on shore to work, but as soon

1746 as they were landed the treacherous inhabitants sent for a party of Indians, who, taking the opportunity when the soldiers were making hay for the cattle, of surprising the tent where their arms lay, shot the sentry, seized the arms, and murdered or took prisoners the greater part of those who were ashore, except the son of Captain Rouse, who in his clothes took to the water, and swam, with his silver buckles in his mouth, to his father's ship, which was all this time firing on the Indians but with little effect, for no sooner did they see the least flash than they fell down on their faces. A grenadier of Fuller's regiment, whose wife was ashore washing, endeavoured to rescue her, but failed. The Indians then attacked him, but shooting two dead, he knocked down two others with his firelock. Seeing his ensign in danger, the grenadier took him in his arms, threw him into the sea, jumped in after him, and carried him safe on board the "Shirley." In this surprise, Captain Rouse lost all his linen which was ashore being washed, whilst 27 soldiers and 7 sailors were killed. When the Indians made their first appearance, Captain Scott was just going ashore. The governor, in a report sent home, says: "I cannot find the officer who commanded, anyways blamable."

On the 20th of October, Captain Scott, taking with him 40 French prisoners, was sent with a flag of truce to the commanding officer of the French squadron, which had recently arrived in Cherbouton (Chebuctoo) Harbour, with proposals to exchange the men captured on the island of St. John's.

This having been accomplished, he returned to Louisburg the 14th of November.

1747 Writing from Louisburg, 20th of January, 1747, to the Duke of Newcastle, Governor Knowles says:—

"As to this Place, words are wanting to represent it, the severity of the weather being now such, and the miseries and sufferings of the Troops so great, as to be beyond expression or comprehension.

1747 Many have been Froze to Death, and the Sentrys, though relieved every half hour, frequently loose their Toes and Fingers: some have lost their Limbs by mortification in a few hours. The Houses and Quarters in general are so bad they cannot be made to keep out the snow and cold, so that officers and men have but little comfort even within doors when off duty. The snow in many places laying 10, 12, and 16 feet deep, nothing is more common than for one Guard to Digg the other out of the Guard Room before they can relieve them."

In March, Lt.-Col. Peregrine Hopson, of Fuller's regiment, was appointed governor of the island of Cape Breton.

Fifes, which in 1743 had been revived by the Guards, were this year adopted by the other marching regiments, the 19th Foot being the first to set the example. They were afterwards allowed to the grenadier companies only, but most drummers were taught the use of them, as well as of the drum.

1748 On the 11th of March, 1748, a congress was opened at Aix la Chapelle, the chief parties being Great Britain, Holland, and Austria, on one side, France and Spain on the other. In October, a treaty was signed by all the belligerent powers, and it was agreed that Cape Breton should be restored to the French in exchange for Madras.

Orders were now sent to Governor Hopson, to incorporate the privates of the 3 companies of Lt.-General Frampton's regiment, "which had for some time been stationed at Louisburg," with Major-General Fuller's regiment.

In May, the colliery at the Table, near Indian river, on the east side of the island, having been attacked by a party of French and Indians, it was decided to erect a blockhouse for its future defence, and 1 lieutenant, 1 serjeant, 1 corporal, and 25 privates of the regiment were sent there, on command.

P. Hopson Major-General Fuller having died on the 9th of June, Lt.-Colonel Hopson succeeded to the command of the regiment.

On the 12th of August, Ensign FitzHugh of Hopson's, and some **1748** officers of the garrison, having obtained the governor's leave to go to Miray, after remaining there a few days, went up the river as far as the Great Lake to reconnoitre, but on endeavouring to get ashore at the house of a neutral Frenchman, were surprised by (as they afterwards computed) 160 French and Indians, who, it appears, came to the Island with the design of destroying the colliery and settlement in the N.E. harbour. Making a hideous noise, as usual, they rushed into the water, upset the boats, and dragged the officers in a barbarous manner to the shore. Some of them were then stripped, and for a considerable time pinioned with ropes. In this condition they were taken to the Frenchman's house and brought before the commanding officer Monsr. Marin, and a missionary, who, on being told that a cessation of arms had been concluded between France and England about three weeks previously, seemed much surprised.

Next morning the officers were embarked in a birch canoe and taken to the head of the lake, where they were landed and marched through the woods to Le Bras d'or. Being met here by more Indians and about 40 canoes, they were re-embarked, and after two days' paddling upon the water, and at night sleeping in the woods, they arrived at St. Peter's, and crossing over the neck of land, re-embarked for Bay Vert, which was reached after a nine days' passage.

Monsr. Marin, and the missionary having promised the officers that everything which had been taken from them should be returned on their arriving here, they applied for them, but were told if they wanted their things, they must purchase them from the Indians.

In a declaration signed at Bay Vert, the 29th of August, by the five officers thus captured, it appears that they promised to pay Monsr. Marin, commanding officer of the French and Indians, the expense he was at in ransoming them from the Indians; also that Ensign FitzHugh had been plundered of a silver spoon, 2 shirts,

1748 1 stock, 1 neckcloth, 1 pair stockings, 1 handkerchief, 5 china coffee cups, teapot and slop basin, 4 knives and forks, a powder horn, and shot bag, and had paid 10s. for his fuzee.

1749 War being now at an end, the regiments of Shirley, and Sir W. Pepperell were disbanded, and Colonel Hopson was ordered to reduce his, to Irish numbers, viz., 2 serjeants, 2 corporals, and 29 effective men per company.

It having been decided to establish a civil government in the Province of Nova Scotia, for its better peopling and settling, notice was given that grants of land would be made to such of the officers and private men lately dismissed H.M. land and sea forces as were willing to settle there. Enticed by these advantages, about 4000 persons with their families, embarked from Great Britain under command of Colonel Cornwallis, and landed in Chebuctoo harbour in June. On the arrival of the French governor and troops to garrison Louisburg, Col. Cornwallis ordered the English garrison of Cape Breton to join him, and on the 28th of July Hopson's and Warburton's regiments arrived at Chebuctoo on board French transports.

Captain John Roberts, then a private in the regiment, stated that on landing they were employed in cutting down the trees, and clearing the ground, and that he drove in pegs to mark out the new town, which took its name from the Earl of Halifax, who presided at the Board of Trade, and had the principal share in the founding of this colony.

Having remained here a short time, the regiment sailed for Ireland, **1750** and on landing was stationed at Cork. The following year it proceeded to take up quarters at Limerick.

CHAPTER IV.

QUARTERS OF THE ARMY IN IRELAND.   **1751**

Printed by Geo. Faulkner, Dublin.

XXIX Foot.	Colonel	Peregrine T. Hopson.	⎫
	C.L.	John Dale.	⎬ Castlecomer.
	2 Ens.	Will Fitzhugh.	⎭
	L. Col.	Caroline Scott.	⎫
	6 L	Robert Brome.	⎬ Phillipstown.
	6 Ens.	Will Stopford.	⎭
	Maj.	Montague Wilmot.	⎫
	2 L.	John Corrance.	⎪
	4 Ens.	George Johnston.	⎬ Kilkenny.
	1 C.	Edm. Bradshaw.	⎪
	3 L.	Francis Laye.	⎪
	9 L.	John Plukenett.	⎭
	2 C.	Will Kerr.	⎫
	1 L.	Maurice Wemys.	⎬ Castlecomer.
Agent—	8 Ens.	Edm. Bradshaw.	⎭
Capt Geo. Johnston.	3 C.	Arch. Cuningham.	⎫
	4 L.	Will Cockcroft.	⎪
	3 Ens.	John Blomer.	⎬ Kilkenny.
	4 C.	Andrew Nesbitt.	⎪
	8 L.	Kennedy Bradshaw.	⎪
	2 Ens.	James Windus.	⎭

1751

5 C.	Isaac Causabon.	⎫	
7 L.	James Barclay.	⎬	Roscrea.
7 Ens.	Richard Brown.	⎭	
6 C.	Thos. Rankin.	⎫	
10 L.	Will Massey.	⎪	
5 Ens.	Thomas Radley.	⎪	
7 C.	Barth. Blake.	⎬	Kilkenny.
5 L.	Arch. Dickson.	⎪	
9 Ens.	Saml. Barrett.	⎭	

Chapl. John Spicer.
Adjt. Will Cockroft.
Surg. Arch. Dickson.
Mate Math. Leslie.

On the 1st of July a Warrant regulating the colours and clothing of regiments of foot was issued, by which it appears that the facings of the 29th Regiment were bright yellow. The colours were now called the "King's" and the "Regimental." The motto over the White Horse, on the little flap of the Grenadier cap, was ordered to be "*Nec aspera terrent*," and the number of the regiment was directed to be worn in the middle part behind.

The uniform of the officers was to be made up in the same manner as that of the men, laced, lapelled, and turned up with the colour of the facing, and with a narrow silver embroidery to the binding and button-holes, the buttons being set on in the same manner as on the men's coats; the waistcoat and breeches to be the same colour as those of the men. Sash to be worn over the left shoulder.

The picture of the 29th grenadier of this date is taken from one in the Windsor collection. On a close inspection of the original, the regimental lace appears to be white, with two blue, and two yellow stripes, and has a blue worm on a white ground, down the centre.

On the 4th March, 1752, Capt. and Lieut.-Col. Honble. George **1752** Boscawen, 1st Foot Guards, was appointed to command the regiment, **G. Boscawen** *vice* Hopson transferred to the 40th Foot. The regiment was now

GRENADIER 29TH REGIMENT, 1752.

stationed at Cork, and on the 2nd May reviewed by the Earl of Rothes, after which it took up quarters as follows:—2 companies Kinsale, 2 Charles Fort, 4 Bandon, 4 Clonakilty.

1753
29th Foot
In 1753 it was stationed at Cork, and on the 3rd of November orders were issued for recruiting the "29th Regiment of Foot," commanded by Col. George Boscawen. This appears to be the first occasion on which the regiment's number was officially made use of in correspondence. The following year the regiment was quartered at Arklow, Wicklow, and Celbridge. It was reviewed at Kinsale by Major-Genl. O'ffarel, after which 4 companies returned to Wicklow, 1 marched to Roscrea, 3 to Castlecomer, and 2 to Nenagh.

1755
In 1755 it was stationed at Waterford, whence in July it proceeded to join a Camp formed at Thurles, where after remaining six weeks, 8 companies returned to Waterford and 2 marched to Duncannon Fort.

1756
As the quarrels which had long prevailed between French and English settlers, both in the East Indies and North America, now threatened to lead to open hostilities, the establishment of regiments at home, was raised, and each company of the 29th Regiment was augmented by 1 serjeant, 1 corporal, 1 drummer, and 17 privates.

On the 27th of April, orders were received for the raising of two additional companies, which with their officers, viz., Captains John Corrance§ and William Piers, Lieutenants John Bolton and John Warren, Ensigns Robert Graham and Charles Burton,§ were shortly after turned over to the 2nd Battalion 31st Foot, orders for raising which were dated the 25th of August. Capt. Francis Laye was also transferred to this new battalion, which two years later on was constituted the 70th Foot.

On the 5th of May war was declared against France, one of the chief subjects of complaint being its encroachments on the Ohio, and in Nova Scotia. This was the commencement of the Seven Years' War. In America, George Washington was serving with the British on General Braddock's staff.

---

§ Re-transferred to the 29th Foot.

1756 During the summer, the regiment joined a camp formed at Warrenstown, but on the 19th of October marched for Waterford. The next year it occupied the following quarters, viz., Wicklow, Arklow, **1757** Wexford, and Galway.

1758 During the summer of 1758, the regiment encamped with the 10th Foot at Kilkenny, after which it marched to Dublin. In August a draft of 150 men from the eight battalion companies was ordered to be prepared to strengthen the several regiments of foot serving in North America.

1759 In 1759, the 29th marched to Kilkenny and joined the camp formed at Bennett's Bridge, after which it took up quarters at Clonmel, Cashel, and Athy. It was while stationed here that the regiment first got its *black drummers*, which occurred in the following manner. Admiral Boscawen being at the surrender of Guadaloupe, and thinking that blacks would prove very ornamental as drummers, procured eight or ten boys, whom he brought home and gave to his brother, who then commanded the 29th Regiment. Col. Enys, in his MS. Records, states: " His Majesty's permission was obtained to retain them in that capacity, and when I joined the regiment in 1775, there were three, if not more, of the original blacks in the corps, who were remarkable good drummers." The custom of having black drummers in the regiment was continued for the better part of 84 years (the last one died on the 15th July, 1843).

Under a Warrant from the Grand Lodge of Ireland dated the 3rd of May, 1759, a Masonic Lodge was established in the regiment.

In 1760 the 29th was stationed at Limerick. **1760**

1761 On the 16th of January, 1761, George, Lord Forbes (afterwards the Earl of Granard), was appointed to command the regiment, *vice* Major-General Boscawen, transferred to the 23rd R.W.F. New colours were this year presented to the 29th.

F

1762 In 1762 the regiment left Galway for Londonderry and Belfast,
1763 and the following year was quartered at Dublin. Whilst here the 10th company was reduced, and in November orders were issued that each company should be reduced to 2 serjeants, 2 corporals, 1 drummer, and 27 privates.

This reduction was in consequence of the termination of the Seven Years' War, peace having been signed at Paris on the 10th of February.
1764 The following year, however, the companies were again made up to the numbers allowed on the Irish establishment.

1765 Leaving Dublin in May, 1765, the regiment marched to Cork, where on the 5th of June it embarked on board H.M.S. ".Thunderer," (74 guns, Captain Hood,) for conveyance to Halifax, where the head-quarters were established, detachments being sent to Annapolis and Fort Cumberland. The regiment was placed on the British establishment from 17th July, the day after its landing in Nova Scotia, and consisted of 9 companies, each of 2 serjeants, 2 corporals, 1 drummer, and 47 privates.

The year 1765 was rendered important in the annals of England by the passing of an American Stamp Act, and by the attempt to tax that colony without its consent. Dr. Franklyn, the most eminent by far of the Americans then in England, on giving evidence at the Bar, stated " that the Colonists by Charter were entitled to all the privileges and liberties of Englishmen, and that by the Great Charters and the Petition and Declaration of Rights, one of the privileges of English subjects is that they are not to be taxed but by their common consent." Petitions were also presented to Parliament from the traders of all the
1766 large towns in England, and the Act was repealed, the news of which was received in America with universal joy.

1767 From the 10th of January 1767, officers' appointments and promotions commenced to be regularly published in the " Gazette."

1767 This year, Charles Townshend, Chancellor of the Exchequer, proposed new taxes for America, namely, "Import Duties," which led to the principal gentlemen of Boston pledging themselves to encourage the consumption of their own manufactures, and not to buy anything from Great Britain beyond a few articles of indispensable necessity.

In the Army List of this year are mentioned for the first time the various regimental laces, that of the 29th being white, with 2 blue, and 1 yellow stripe.

Not only did each regiment have its own distinct pattern of lace, but the loops, *i.e.*, lace sewn round the buttonholes, were of different forms, some being square-headed, others pointed, and others frog loops. Some regiments had these loops set at equal distances, others by twos, (amongst the latter was the 29th Foot), so that at any period between 1768, and 1836, when regimental lace and the regimental mode of wearing it was abolished, a person conversant with the various patterns of lace, and the different facings, could tell to what regiment a man belonged without closely inspecting his buttons.

On the 21st of September His Majesty was pleased to direct "that the number of each regiment should be marked on the buttons, at the next clothing, as likewise on the uniforms of the officers, when they shall make new ones."

1768 In the *Nova Scotia Gazette* we find a paragraph dated Halifax, 11th February, 1768 :—

"A few days since John Dutton, a soldier of the 29th Regiment, when attempting to cross the Basin, near Fort Sackville, the ice broke in with him, and he was instantly drowned, nothwithstanding all possible means used to save him." On the 13th of June his body was found floating near the Basin, with a knapsack on his back containing 2 books and some other trifles. His corpse was brought to town and decently buried,

1768   The men's waistcoats were this year changed from red to white; and on the 27th July black bearskin caps were ordered to be worn by the grenadier company and drummers, in lieu of the yellow cloth ones.

Towards the end of June, a sloop named the "Liberty," belonging to a Boston merchant, anchored in that harbour laden with wine from Madeira, whereupon the Commissioners determined to enforce the new law, but met with resistance; their houses, and those of the other officers of Customs were attacked, their windows broken, and the collector's boat dragged through the town and burnt on the common. On account of apprehended disturbances, orders were sent to General Gage, the commander-in-chief for North America, to dispatch troops from Halifax to Boston. These reinforcements, which consisted of the 14th and 29th regiments, the grenadier and one company of 59th, and a company of Artillery, disembarked at the Long Wharf, Boston, the 5th of October, and having formed, marched, with drums beating, fifes playing, and colours flying, by King Street to the common, where the 29th, having brought their field equipage with them, encamped with the Artillery, the 14th being lodged for the night in Faneuil Hall. On the 15th, His Excellency Genl. Gage, having arrived from New York, was received by the troops under arms on the common, and reviewed the 14th and 29th regiments. On the 29th of October the regiment broke up its encampment and took up quarters in a large store by Green's Lane, belonging to Major Green, distiller, and in a house in New Boston, belonging to Mr. Forrest.

By Royal Warrant, the 19th December, 1768, we find that the *Officers' Coats* were to be lapelled to the waist with yellow, and "that these might be without embroidery or lace;" to have cross pockets, and sleeves with round cuffs and no slits. The lapels and cuffs to be the same breadth as the men's.

Officers of the grenadier company to wear an epaulette on each shoulder. Those of the *battalion*, to wear one on the right shoulder. They were to be either of embroidery or lace; those of the **1768** 29th Regiment with silver fringe. Waistcoats to be plain, without embroidery or lace.

Officers' Swords to be uniform, and sword-knots to be of crimson and gold in stripes. The hilt of the swords of the 29th to be silver, "according to the colour of the buttons of the uniform."

Hats to be laced with silver, and to be uniformly cocked.

Sashes to be of crimson silk, and worn round the waist.

The King's Arms to be engraved on the gorgets; also the number of the regiment. The *Gorgets* to be silver, like the buttons on the uniforms.

Officers of the grenadier company to wear black bearskin caps, and to have fuzils, shoulder belts, and pouches. The shoulder belts of the 29th to be white (the colour of the waistcoats).

The *Battalion Officers* to have espontoons. The whole, to have black linen gaiters, with black buttons and small stiff tops, black garters, and uniform buckles.

Serjeants' Coats to be lapelled to the waist with yellow. The buttonholes to be of white braid; those on the waistcoat to be plain.

Serjeants of grenadier company to have swords, fuzils, pouches, and caps; those of the *battalion* to have swords and halberts only.

Sashes to be of crimson worsted, with a stripe of yellow, and worn round the waist.

Corporals' Coats to have a silk epaulette on the right shoulder.

Grenadiers' Coats to have the usual round wings of red cloth on the point of the shoulder, with six loops of the regimental lace, and a border round the bottom.

Private Men's Coats to be looped with worsted lace, but no border. The ground of the lace to be white, with 2 blue, and 1 yellow stripe; to have white buttons. Four loops to be on the sleeves and four on the pockets, with 2 on each side of the slit behind. The breadth of all the lapels to be 3 inches, to reach down to the waist, and not to be wider

1768 at the top than at the bottom. The sleeves of the coats to have a small round cuff without any slit, and to be made so that they may be unbuttoned and let down. The whole to have cross pockets, but no flaps to those of the waistcoat. The cuff of the sleeve which turns up, to be three inches and a half deep. The flap on the pocket of the coat to be sewed down, and the pocket to be cut in the lining of the coat.

Regiments like the 29th, which had white waistcoats, were ordered to have white accoutrements.

Drummers' and Fifers' Coats to be yellow, faced and lapelled with red. Waistcoats, breeches, and linings to be white. To be laced as the colonel thinks fit; the lace being of the regimental pattern.

On the front of the Drummers' and Fifers' Bearskin Caps, the King's crest in silver-plated metal, on a black ground, with trophies of colours and drums; the number of the regiment on the back part.

The *Grenadiers* also wore the King's crest on their bearskin hats, but with the motto, "*Nec aspera terrent*," and a grenade on the back part, with the number of the regiment on it.

Hats of the Serjeants to be laced with silver; those of the corporals and private men with white tape. All hats to have black cockades.

Each *Pioneer* to have an axe, a saw, and an apron; a cap with a leather crown, and black bearskin front, on which is to be the King's crest in white, on a red ground; also an axe and a saw. The number of the regiment to be on the back part of the hat.

Hat Lace for the Officers, silver; waistcoat, breeches, and lining of coats, white.

1769 On the 6th of March, 1769, a Warrant was given to the Ordnance Department to issue 2 fuzils and 2 cartridge boxes for the serjeants of the 29th Grenadiers.

Early this year the regiment took up quarters at Fort William§ on Castle Island, at the entrance of the harbour.

---

§ In 1799 its name was changed to Fort Independence.

On the 3rd of November, Major Evelyn, 1st Foot Guards, was appointed Colonel of the 29th Foot, *vice* the Earl of Granard, deceased.

1769

Grenadier 29th Regiment, 1769.

In December each company was ordered to be augmented to 3 serjeants, 3 corporals, 2 drummers, and 42 privates, with 2 fifers to the Grenadier company.

1770 The following Spring, the 29th returned to Boston, where strong symptoms of discontent began to appear among the inhabitants. Unhappily, on political grounds, the troops were most obnoxious to many of the upper class, and to all the lower, and a man in a red coat could scarcely go through the streets without being insulted.

On the morning of the 2nd of March, as one of the 29th was passing the premises of John Gray, a ropemaker, he was assailed with abusive words, and afterwards beaten severely. He soon returned however, accompanied by some of his comrades; an affray ensued, in which the ropemakers got the worst of it. This affair having got to the ears of the commanding officer, orders were given the troops against quarrelling with the inhabitants. Further complaints were however made by the soldiers of their being knocked down, and otherwise ill-treated.

In the meanwhile the ropemakers and calkers,† whose occupations brought them into contact, formed a society, at the meetings of which inflammatory addresses were delivered and the most violent resolutions passed against the British Government, its agents, and instruments in America.

It was not before the 5th, that disturbances assumed a serious aspect. In the course of that day, the mob destroyed a quantity of tea (the tax on which formed their principal cause of complaint). Alarm bells were rung as in cases of fire, and on the inhabitants assembling, a considerable body collected at the gates of a barrack where two companies of the 29th were quartered. These they abused, and invited to come out to fight. Between 7 and 8 p.m. a violent tumult broke out. The multitude, armed some with clubs, others with swords, ran towards King Street,* crying, "Let us drive out these ribalds; they have no business here." They then rushed furiously towards the Custom

---

† The Tories, in derision, called these assemblies "Calker's Meetings," and the term was at length corrupted to "Caucus."—*Webster's Dictionary.*

* Now State Street.

House, and attacked the sentry on duty, with the cry of "Down with the Bloody-backs! Kill him! Kill him!" assaulting him with snowballs, pieces of ice, and every other missile they could find; with oaths and insulting epithets, they dared him to fire, and attempted to drag him into the street. He shouted to the main guard for assistance, which was immediately rendered.

The regiment happened to be on duty that day, and the main guard being commanded by Lieut. Bassett, who had not been long in the regiment, Captain Thos. Preston, the captain of the day, was induced to visit it, fearing lest so young an officer might not act with all the prudence necessary on so trying an occasion. On the way he found the tumult increasing, and as the mob seemed to be directed against the Custom House, in which was lodged a considerable sum of Government money, he made all haste to reach the guard, which was situated almost opposite to it. Finding it already under arms, Captain Preston detached a corporal and 6 men to protect the sentry and the chest of customs from the popular fury. Having posted the guard as seemed to him most advantageous, he followed the corporal's detachment.

As these approached they found the mob greatly increased, and were pelted by it worse than the sentinel had been. One of the chief leaders was a mulatto of herculean size and strength, named Crispin Attucks, who was surrounded by a party of sailors shouting, "Let us strike at the root! Let us fall upon the nest! The main guard! The main guard!" Captain Preston's party was challenged to fire, and was taunted with the assertion that they dared not fire without the magistrate's order. Meanwhile the soldiers loaded their firelocks and fixed bayonets, but the increasing mob, not at all intimidated, pressed closely upon them, and advanced up to the points of the bayonets. The soldiers stirred not a step from where they were posted, and merely used their weapons to keep off the mob. Emboldened by their apparent fear, Attucks and the sailors, giving three loud cheers,

1770 pressed closer upon the troops, and with clubs beat their bayonets and muskets, crying out to the rest, "Come on, don't be afraid of 'em; they dare not fire. Knock 'em over! Kill 'em!" Presently Attucks aimed a blow at Captain Preston, who was using every endeavour to appease the fury of the populace. The blow fell on the captain's arm, and knocked down the musket of one of the men, the bayonet of which was seized by the mulatto. At this time there was a confused cry, proceeding from some persons behind Captain Preston, "Why don't you fire! Why don't you fire!" Montgomery, the private whose bayonet was seized by Attucks, and who in the struggle was thrown down, soon rose to his feet in possession of his gun, and immediately fired. Attucks fell dead. This was followed by straggling shots from five or six others. Three persons were killed, five dangerously wounded, and a few more slightly. The populace instantly retreated, leaving the killed on the ground, but soon returned to carry off the bodies.

"On the people assembling again," said Captain Preston, in his written defence, "to take away the dead bodies, the soldiers, supposing them coming to attack them, were making ready to fire again, which I prevented by striking up their firelocks with my hand. Immediately afterwards a townsman came and told me that 4000 or 5000 people were assembled in the next street, and had sworn to take my life and every man's with me; on which I judged it unsafe to remain there longer, and therefore sent the party and sentry to the main guard where the street was narrow and short; then, telling them off into street firings, divided and planted them at each end of the street to secure the rear, expecting an attack, as there was a constant cry of the inhabitants "To arms! To arms! Turn out with your guns!" and the town drums beating to arms. I ordered my drums to beat to arms, and being soon after joined by several companies of the 29th Regiment, I formed them as a guard, into street firings. The 14th Regiment was also got under arms, but remained in their barracks.

"I immediately sent a serjeant with a party to Colonel Dalrymple **1770** (*14th Regt.*), the commanding officer, to acquaint him with every particular. Several officers, going to join the regiment, were knocked down by the mob, one very much wounded had his sword taken from him.

"The Lieut.-Governor Hutchinson, and Colonel Dalrymple, soon after met at the head of the 29th, and agreed that the regiment should retire to its barracks, and the people to their houses, but I kept the picquet to strengthen the guard. This tragic scene occurred at midnight, the ground was covered with snow, the air clear and frosty, and the moon, then in its first quarter, gave but a faint illumination, by which the features of the people were barely visible to each other."

Captain Preston and Lieut. Bassett were committed to prison about 3 o'clock next morning, and in the course of the forenoon, the eight soldiers were also arrested. When the latter were asked why they fired without orders, they replied they heard the word "Fire" from some one, and thought it came from their officer. On Captain Preston and Lieut. Bassett being examined before the magistrates, some of the witnesses swore that Captain Preston had given the word to fire, whilst others swore as positively that Mr. Bassett had done so. However, it being proved that the latter had never moved from that part of the guard which remained stationary in front of the guard house, he was discharged, whilst Captain Preston and the eight soldiers were committed for trial.

"This may be called," wrote Col. Enys, "the commencement of the American War, which in the end produced the Revolution. Certain it is, the Americans themselves looked upon this as the beginning of the contest, as they gave the 29th Regiment the name of *The Vein Openers*, from their having drawn the first blood that was spilt in that war, and by which name they were known for many years in the neighbourhood of Boston."

THE BLOODY MASSACRE PERPETRATED IN KING STREET, BOSTON, ON MARCH 5TH, 1770, BY A PARTY OF THE 29TH REGIMENT.

For many successive years the anniversary of "The Massacre,"* as **1770** it was called, was observed with much solemnity by the Bostonians, their ablest spokesmen being employed to deliver harangues by which the public resentment might be stirred and irritating reminiscences kept alive.

> Unhappy Boston, let thy sons deplore
> Thy hallowed walks besmeared with guiltless gore,
> The faithless P * * * * * n† and his savage bands
> With murderous rancour stretch their bloody hands !
> The fierce barbarians, grinning o'er their prey,
> Approve the carnage, and enjoy the day.
>
> If scalding drops, from rage, from anguish rung,
> If speechless sorrows labouring for a tongue,
> Or if a weeping world can aught appease
> The plaintive ghosts of victims such as these,
> The patriots copious tears for each are shed,
> A glorious tribute which embalms the dead.
>
> But know, fate summons to that awful goal
> Where justice strips the murderer of his soul,
> Should venal C * * * s,‡ the scandal of the land,
> Snatch the relentless villain from her hand,
> Keen execrations on this plate inscribed
> Shall reach a Judge that never can be bribed.

On the following Monday, the 12th of March, the troops were all removed to Fort William. Having remained there about a month, the 29th was ordered to the Province of New Jersey, and it appears that it marched across the country to Newport, and Providence in Rhode Island, whence it embarked, and soon after was mustered as follows :

---

* I am indebted to Mr. Chas. Pfaff, of Boston, U.S.A., for a copy of this Picture.
† Preston.   ‡ Cutts.

1770	30th May,	Captain T. Preston's Company	at Brunswick.
	,,	,, J. French's ,,	,, Brunswick.
	,,	,, P. Molesworth's ,,	,, Elizabeth Town.
1st June	,,	,, Arch. Martin's ,,	,, Perth, Amboy.
	30th May,	The Colonel's	,, Brunswick.
	,,	Captain Arch. Campbell's ,,	,, Perth, Amboy.
	,,	,, J. Corrance's ,,	,, Perth, Amboy.
	,,	Lieut.-Col. Carr's ,,	,, Perth, Amboy.
	,,	Captain Pierce Butler's ,,	,, Elizabeth Town
1st June	,,	,, Wm. Monsell's ,,	,, Perth, Amboy.

In the meanwhile Captain Preston was detained in Boston Gaol.

CAPTAIN PRESTON TO SECRETARY AT WAR.

"Boston Gaol, June 25th, 1770.

My Lord,

As I expect that Colonel Evelyn is on his way here, I know of none so conspicuously the friend of Military people in distress as your Lordship, to whom I could apply. I have therefore taken the liberty of enclosing copys of Affidavits concerning the 5th March last, should they be wanted. I sent some home before, but they are included in these, and are attested by the Justices before whom the originals were sworn, and whose hand S^r F$^{r.}$ Barnard well knows.

The madness of the people is so great that evidences are affraid to appear for us, nay, they have declared publickly that if a jury should acquit us, or we should receive his Majesty's pardon, not a man of us shall go alive out of town. Even their pulpits are echoing persecution against us, and that blood crys to heaven for Vengeance. My tryal has been put off from the setting of one Court to that of another, till finally it is defered to the beginning of September, so that I shall remain at least six months close confined in a loathsome goal, almost suffocated with charcoal, and in case of the Goals taking fire, as it did last year, must certainly be burned to Death.

My health is much impaired by my long confinement, my debts encreasi^g by my great expenses, my promotion to the Majority stopt, if not lost, my life in danger from the Mobs threatening to take me out of Goal and hang me. And lastly, the great probability of the Jury finding me guilty, in spite of all law and evidence. This, My Lord, is a melancholy situation which nothing could support me under, but a good conscience, and the hopes of his Majesty's pardon. I hope Your Lordship will excuse this trouble, and also believe me to be, with great respect,

                Your Lordships
                  Most obedient and
                    very humble Servt,
                      THOS. PRESTON, Capt
                        in the 29th Regiment.
To the Right Honble. Lord Barrington, Secretary at Warr."

"No pains," says Botta, "were spared to agitate and inflame the minds of the people from whom the jury, in the trial of Captain Preston, had to be chosen. When, however, the trial commenced on the 24th of October, it was conducted with perfect fairness. At first Captain Preston had great difficulty in obtaining counsel, many, either from popular principles or in personal terror, refused their aid, but Mr. John Adams (afterwards second President of the United States), a young lawyer then first rising into fame, who was warm and zealous on the popular side—the one on which all his hopes depended—undertook it, saying that "in a free country, counsel ought to be the very last thing an accused man should want."

At the summing-up of the trial on the 30th of October, Judge Lyndex towards the close of his speech, said: "Happy I am to find that after such a strict examination, the conduct of the prisoner appears in so fair a light; yet I feel myself at the same time deeply affected that this affair turns out so much to the disgrace of every person concerned against him, and so much to the shame of the Town in general." The

1770 jury returned a verdict of "Not Guilty," and Captain Preston was immediately discharged.

The trial of the eight soldiers did not take place so soon, but on the 5th of December the jury acquitted six, and found two guilty of manslaughter only, viz., Montgomery, who had killed Attucks, and Killroy, who was proved to have shot another man.

On the 25th of December a company of Light Infantry† consisting of 1 captain, 2 lieutenants, 3 serjeants, 3 corporals, 2 drummers, and 62 private men, was ordered to be added to the regiment, and each of the old companies of the battalion to be augmented by 20 private men. The required men were to be raised in North America, and the additional officers, brought in from reduced companies, were :

    Captain John Crozier, ... from half-pay, late 108th Foot.
    Lieutenant Thos. Robinson, ,, ,, of the 49th ,,
    Ensign John Willoughby, ,, ,, ,, ,, Regiment.

Simes mentions that the "appointments" of the Light Infantry company were :—

    (1) Jackets.
    (2) Black leather caps, with 3 chains round them, and a piece of plate upon the centre of the crown; in the front G.R., a crown, and the number of the regiment.
    (3) Small cartouch boxes, powder horns, and bags for ball.
    (4) Short pieces and hatchets.

1771 On the 5th of March, 1771, a Royal Warrant was issued, for delivering the following arms, &c., to the regiment in consequence of the addition of a Light company, viz. : 2 serjeant's fuzils, with bayonets and scabbards; 39 firelocks; 41 cartouch boxes, with straps; 39 bayonets and scabbards.

---

† *Extract from Orders dated Head Quarters, New York, 3rd March, 1771* :—The Light Company to be raised in Great Britain; the 20 additional private men, for regiments stationed in the Province of Quebec, New York, Jersey, Illinois, &c., to be recruited on the West side of the Connecticut River, and in the Province of New York, New Jersey, Pennsylvania, and Maryland to the East side of the Potomack.—*Haldimand MS.*

1771 It was proposed by a Board of General Officers that had assembled to decide on the clothing of the Light Infantry that a "Maude" would be a proper covering for these troops in the time of war, in place of a blanket, and that the waist belt should be furnished with 2 frogs, one for the bayonet the other for the hatchet occasionally, which at other times should be tied upon the knapsack.

The differences with the Court of Spain having been adjusted, recruiting in North America was stopped, and the establishment of the regiment was fixed at 20 serjeants, 10 drummers, 2 fifers, 380 rank and file. In November it embarked for St. Augustine, Florida, whence detachments were sent to Mobile, Pensacola, and one company to the Bahamas.

1772 By Royal Warrant, the 25th of May, 1772, all captain-lieutenants were authorised to rank as captains, and were henceforward called captain-lieutenant and captain.

On the 29th of July a Warrant was published regulating the prices of commissions in marching Regiments of Foot:—

1. Captain, £1500.   2. Captain-Lieutenant (having rank of Captain), £950.   3. Lieutenant, £550.   4. Ensign, £400.

In November Captain Thomas Preston was granted a pension of £200 a year upon the military establishment of Ireland, in consideration of his faithful services.

1773 In September, 1773, the regiment embarked for England, but meeting with contrary winds, was for some time detained in Charleston Harbour, and in consequence did not arrive at Dover till the end of November, when it took up quarters in the Castle, and was shortly after reviewed by Lieut.-General Irwine. The following month a detachment was sent to Archcliff Fort.

A hat of a new pattern was, in November, authorised for the Infantry.

G

1773 From the Inspection Reports, dated the 17th of December, we gather the following interesting information:—

LIST OF OFFICERS, THEIR COUNTRY, AGE, SERVICE.

		Englsh	Scotch.	Irish.	For gn.	Age.	Years of Service
Col. Evelyn		1				50	34
Lt.-Colonel Maurice Carr				1		43	28
Major Jeremiah French				1		33	13
Captains	John Corrance, *Major*	1				59	34
	Thomas Preston			1		43	18
	Pons. Molesworth			1		31	11
	Archibald Campbell		1			35	16
	William Monsell			1		35	13
	John Crozier			1		39	18
	Chas. Visct. Petersham	1				20	4
Capt. Lieut. Samuel Kathrens				1		37	18
Lieutenants	James Vibart	1				44	15
	Hugh Dickson			1		33	16
	James Bassett			1		23	11
	Paul Minchin			1		30	11
	Thomas Buckley			1		36	14
	Jeremiah Meara			1		36	13
	David St. Clair	1				27	8
	Thomas Robinson	—	—	—	—	—	—
	Alexander Mall		1			33	8
	Nicholas Aylward Vigors			1		20	4
Ensigns	Thomas Steele			1		25	4
	James Battersby			1		22	3
	John Beaumont	1				24	3
	Piers Walsh			1		25	3
	Charles Williams	1				20	2
	Sewell Monsell			1		19	2
	Thos. Hill	1				17	1
	Isaac Riches	1				19	1

1773

	COUNTRY.				YEARS OF	
	ENGLISH.	SCOTCH.	IRISH.	FOREIGN.	AGE.	SERVICE.
Chaplain John Forbes ...			1		39	6
Adjutant John Roberts ...	1				43	31
Qr. Master James Vibart	1				44	8
Surgeon Robert Scott ...		1			39	4
Mate Thos. Smith	1				27	1
N.C.O. and Men	107	22	188	17		

SIZE OF MEN.	
FROM 5FT. 6 & UNDER TO 6FT. 2 & UPWARDS.	
6ft 1 in. 1 Man	5ft. 9 in. 34 Men
6 0½ ,, 1 ,,	5 8½ ,, 21 ,,
6 0 ,, 2 Men	5 8 ,, 32 ,,
5 11½ ,, 5 ,,	5 7½ ,, 29 ,,
5 11 ,, 9 ,,	5 7 ,, 33 ,,
5 10½ ,, 18 ,,	5 6½ ,, 33 ,,
5 10 ,, 16 ,,	5 6 ,, 30 ,,
5 9½ ,, 25 ,,	Under 5ft. 6, 45 ,,

MEN'S SERVICE.	
FROM 1 YEAR & UNDER TO 35 YEARS & UPWARDS.	
35 Years	7 Years 3 Men
30 ,, 1 Man	6 ,, 2 ,,
25 ,, 2 Men	5 ,, 3 ,,
20 ,, 89 ,,	4 ,, 13 ,,
15 ,, 107 ,,	3 ,, 47 ,,
10 ,, 33 ,,	2 ,, 4 ,,
8 ,, 25 ,,	1 ,, 5 ,,

MEN'S AGE FROM 18 TO 55 YEARS AND UPWARDS.	
50 Years, 1 Man	30 Years, 57 Men
45 ,, 17 Men	25 ,, 50 ,,
40 ,, 89 ,,	20 ,, 35 ,,
35 ,, 77 ,,	18 ,, 8 ,,

Among the Remarks on the Regiment, we find that the "Officers are properly armed; salute well; uniforms according to regulation; expert at their duty."

Accoutrements, according to regulation.

Clothing, good; made according to regulation, and well fitted.

Hats are ill-cocked and not of the size or pattern ordered by the King.

1774 The following spring new firelocks and bayonets were issued to the regiment, which was inspected at Dover on the 25th of April by Major-General Sir W. Howe, who in his report made the following remarks :—

Drummers and Fifers.—Beat and play well. Ten drummers are negroes.

Men.—A serviceable corps for present duty. Many old men in the regiment.

Manual Exercise.—Well performed, and in good time.

Firings.—Loads quickly, presents low and well. The ramrod is drawn with the backhand, which is supposed to contribute to the quickness of loading. The platoons, shouldered by signal from their respective flank men.

Gayters.—Good ; those of the battalion according to regulation. Those of the Grenadiers have white metal buttons.

General Observations.—Steady, attentive, and silent under arms. In some of the firings, when formed three deep, the front rank stood up ; in others, as well as for the oblique firing, the front rank kneeled. An able-bodied Light Infantry, and well trained, was drawn up three deep on the right of the Grenadiers, and was posted upon the left of the battalion for the manual exercises and firings. The Grenadiers remained on the right in one platoon.

The officers have a sutler, eat together, and live in friendship.

In July, the Light company under command of Captain, Chas. Viscount Petersham, was ordered to march to Salisbury, where, on arrival, it joined a brigade, formed of the Light companies of the Buffs, the 11th, 21st, 32nd, 36th, and 70th regiments, to practice a set of manœuvres invented by General Sir W. Howe, who was appointed to instruct them. This officer had under him, as second in command, Major Jeremiah French, 29th Regiment.

On the 4th of October this brigade was reviewed by H.M. King **1774** George III., in Richmond Park, after which Lord Petersham was quartered with his company at Dartford, whilst the regiment, being relieved by the 36th Foot, marched to Chatham, there to be stationed.

Towards the end of February, the several companies were **1775** augmented by 1 serjeant, 1 corporal, 1 drummer, and 18 privates each.

Disturbances in America assuming now a warlike aspect, several regiments were ordered to prepare for active service. Orders were issued to enlist men for the term of three years, or during the war, and as no one thought it could last so long, a great many men were procured.

Major General Evelyn and the officers used their utmost endeavours to get the regiment completed to its new establishment, and being the first corps reported as such, His Majesty was pleased to express his approbation in a very generous manner, saying "he would employ the 29th Regiment directly, in a situation where he trusted it might distinguish itself."

CHAPTER V.

1776 N the 4th of January, 1776, orders were received for the regiment, "strength, 1 lieut.-colonel, 1 major, 8 captains, 11 lieutenants, 8 ensigns, 1 chaplain, 1 adjutant, 1 quartermaster, 1 surgeon, 1 mate, 642 non-commissioned officers and private men, under command of Lieut.-Col. Patrick Gordon," to be held in readiness to embark for Quebec, which the Americans, under command of General Montgomery (formerly an officer in H.M. 17th Foot), were besieging.

As it was to be augmented to the same numbers as the other regiments of foot serving in North America, two additional companies (to remain at home on recruiting service), each consisting of 1 captain, 1 lieutenant, 1 ensign, 3 serjeants, 3 corporals, 2 drummers, and 56 private men, were raised. The sum of five guineas was allowed to the recruiting officer for each approved recruit, of which the latter received three guineas, agreeable to regulation.

On the 22nd Major-General Evelyn was desired to give the necessary directions for the immediate providing of tents for the officers, and camp necessaries complete, for the men of his regiment.

List of Camp Necessaries ordered:—12 bell tents, 12 silk camp colours, 20 drum cases, 140 tin kettles with canvas bags, 140 hand hatchets, 642 water flasks with strings, 642 havresacks, 642 knapsacks, 10 powder bags.

Extra Necessaries:—Hand hatchets. 140; sunks,* 22; water decks,† 22; forage cords, 30; scythes, with stones, 20.

---

* A canvas pack saddle stuffed with straw.—*Grose.*
† A covering of painted leather, for the saddle, bridle, &c.—*Stocqueler.*

On the 15th of February, Captain Bassett's company embarked **1776** at Sheerness, on board the "Dorothy" transport for conveyance to Plymouth, where, on arrival, it was to be transhipped to the "Surprise" frigate and "Martin" sloop. This company was followed a few days later by the Grenadiers, under command of Lord Petersham, and embarked at Chatham on board the "Isis" of 50 guns. Of the remaining companies some embarked at Dover, others at the Nore, or Sheerness, on board the "Lord Howe," the "Bute," the "Agnes," the "Swift," and the "Aldborough." On their way down Channel these ships experienced very bad weather, and when off Portland, on the night of the 17th of March, the "Swift" took fire and was completely burnt. Several of the soldiers and seamen were, however, got off by the boats of the other ships, but Lieut. Thos. Bernard, Ensign John Bennett, and five privates were drowned. After a very stormy passage, and having encountered much difficulty and danger from drift ice, the "Isis," "Martin," and "Surprise" met on the 2nd of May at the Isle aux Coudres, where they were again detained by contrary winds.

On the evening of the 4th, orders were received for the "Surprise" to proceed as soon as possible to Quebec, and a light breeze having sprung up, the frigate arrived the following evening within six miles of that town, but being uncertain whether the garrison still held out, it was considered advisable to anchor for the night. On the morning of the 6th, both wind and tide being favourable, the "Surprise" came in sight of Quebec, and the signal previously agreed upon having been answered, she immediately approached the town. The detachments of the 29th, and marines then disembarked, and climbed over the barricades which had been erected upon the wharf. The "Isis" and "Martin" coming up almost immediately after, also landed the troops they had on board, which brought the reinforcements up to about 300 men, and determined General Carleton to make a sortie. The two principal gates having been cleared and opened, about noon 100 of the regiment,

1776 80 marines, and 720 of the garrison marched out upon the heights of Abraham, upon which the Americans retired towards the Sorel River, leaving all their guns in their batteries and one loaded 6-pr. brass field piece on the field. This they had attempted to spike, but had done it so badly that one of the 29th Grenadiers, partly with his fingers and partly with his teeth, soon removed the nail which had been driven into the vent. In the evening the troops returned to Quebec. Four days after this the remainder of the regiment landed, and Ensign John Enys was detached with 20 men to Cape Rouge. Shortly after this, the 47th Regiment, which had arrived from Halifax, together with the flank companies of the 29th, were ordered to march along the river to Point à Tromble. The remaining companies having embarked at Quebec, on the 22nd of May, on small transports, proceeded, under command of Lieut.-Col. Nesbit, 47th Regiment, up the St. Lawrence towards Three Rivers, and came to an anchor about two miles from that place, where the headquarters of the army under General Carleton were established.

Nothing, however, of importance occurred till the 8th of June, when, at daybreak, the Americans, wholly ignorant of the force assembled there, made an attack. Meeting with a warm reception from the flank companies of the 9th, 21st, 24th, 29th, 31st, 47th, 53rd, and 62nd regiments, they retired into the woods. In the meanwhile the troops were landed from the ships, and, having taken post at the bridge over the River Machiche, cut off the enemy's retreat. Early next morning many of the rebels surrendered, amongst others General Thompson, and Colonel Irwin the second in command. After this the troops returned to Three Rivers, and their vessels respectively, but being detained by bad weather, it was not till the 13th that they were able to proceed towards Sorel, a strong post, where it was thought the enemy would make a stand; but when, the following afternoon, this place was reached, it was found that the enemy had evacuated it, and retired to Forts Chambly and St. Johns.

The Grenadiers and Light Infantry of the army were therefore **1776** immediately landed, and ordered to pursue them up either side of the river, the main body taking the same route as fast as the troops came up. The 29th however, and some other troops remained on board their ships, and proceeded towards Montreal. When within 30 miles of that town, information was received of its evacuation. On account of the unfavourable state of the weather, it was deemed best to land the troops and march thither.

They had not been long in the town when a very strange noise was heard. This was found to proceed from a party of Loyalists and Indians, who, with Sir John Johnson, had arrived from his estate on the Mohawk River. On their way they had defeated a party of the enemy at the Cedars, and captured a brass 6-pr., which they brought with them. Everyone was much surprised and amused at the arrival, and dress of this new kind of force. The Indians consisted of about 100 very fine young men, all highly painted. The dress of the Loyalists was nothing more than their ordinary clothes, but that of Sir John Johnson was somewhat remarkable, it being made of dressed deerskins, and fitted him as tight as his skin. In his hand he carried a tomahawk, and on his breast hung a scalping knife, whilst the skin of a rattlesnake was twisted round his hat, with the rattle in front.

After burning both Chambly, and St. Johns, the Americans embarked for Lake Champlain. The want of boats rendering further pursuit for the present impossible, the army encamped near St. John's, the advance corps at Isle aux Noix, and the 29th at Montreal. On the 3rd of July 4 companies marched to La Chine, whence all stores for Upper Canada were embarked.

On the 25th of July Brigadier Patrick Gordon, "having been to see Lord Petersham, who, with the 29th Grenadiers, was stationed at St. Johns," was passing through a small wood on his way back to his quarters at La Prairie, when he was shot at and severely wounded by Lieut. Whitcombe, of the Connecticut Rangers, who had offered his

1776 services to venture through the wood and bring in prisoner, an English officer. For this purpose he had stationed himself among the thickest copses situated between La Prairie and St. Johns. The first officer who chanced to pass was the brigadier. He was mounted on a high-spirited horse, and Whitcombe, thinking there was little probability of seizing him, fired at and wounded him, two balls entering the shoulder. Colonel Gordon, however, did not lose his seat, and the horse setting off at a gallop, brought him to the first settlement, where he was discovered, nearly insensible, by an officer's servant, who, taking him off his saddle, conveyed him in a cart to the quarters of Lieut. Hepburne, 21st Regiment, where every attention was paid him. After suffering extreme agony, Colonel Gordon died on the 1st of August. When Whitcombe returned to Ticonderoga and informed General St. Clair, who commanded there, how he had acted, the latter expressed his disapprobation in the highest terms, and was so displeased at the transaction that Whitcombe again offered his services, professing he would forfeit his life if he did not return with a prisoner.

On the 29th of August, Bt.-Major Thos. Carleton, of the 20th Foot, was appointed Lieut.-Colonel of the 29th, *vice* Gordon, whose brigade was ordered to be broken up. The 29th, for the remainder of the campaign, was attached to the headquarters of the army. Early in September the regiment left Montreal, and joined the camp at St. Johns.

It was about this time that Whitcombe, accompanied by two other men, proceeded down Lake Champlain in a canoe to a small creek, where, having secreted the boat, they repaired to the same spot where Brigadier Gordon had been shot. The two men then concealed themselves a little way in the wood, whilst Whitcombe skulked about.

Quartermaster Alex. Saunders, having occasion to get some stores from Montreal, was going from the camp to procure them. On account of the late outrage, he was advised not to take the road, but to go by way of Chambly. Being a man of great personal courage, he resolved **1776** not to go so many miles out of his way, for any Whitcombe whatever. He jocosely added that he would "be very glad to meet him, as he was sure he should get the reward which had been offered for that individual's apprehension!"

Previous to setting out he took every precaution, having not only loaded his fusee, but charged a brace of pistols. On approaching the woods he was very cautious, but in an instant Whitcombe and the two men, springing from behind a thick bush, seized him before he could make the least resistance, deprived him of his weapons, tied his arms behind him, blindfolded him, and marched him off.

Four days after this they arrived at Ticonderoga, when Saunders was brought before the General, who, failing either by threat or entreaties to gain any information relative to the British troops, ordered him as prisoner of war on his parole to some of the interior towns.

On the 6th of September, a detachment, under command of Ensign J. Enys, consisting of 2 ensigns, 2 serjeants, 82 rank and file, which had been trained to big gun drill, embarked on board the "Thunderer," as additional gunners, and as such they served during the campaign.

About the same time, three companies, with Captains Campbell and Dickson, Lieut. Alexr. Mall, Ensigns F. W. Farquhar and J. Williamson, embarked on board the "Inflexible," whilst the remainder of the regiment was put on board the "Carleton" schooner, and the gunboats, of which there were 21. This flotilla, which assembled at Point au Fer on the 10th of October, was destined to operate against the enemy on Lake Champlain.

It being ascertained that the enemy's fleet was anchored higher up the lake, at daybreak of the 11th, the flotilla advanced, and about noon arrived at Valcore Island, where the Americans were found. The early part of the action which ensued was confined to the "Carleton"

1776 schooner, and the gunboats which were a good deal knocked about; but on the arrival of the "Inflexible" and the "Maria," the result was no longer doubtful.

In the course of this day the following casualties occurred in the regiment: On board the "Carleton," 1 drummer and 6 privates killed; 2 privates wounded. A private, also, was wounded on board one of the gunboats. During the night, the enemy, aided by their accurate knowledge of the lake, and the great darkness that prevailed, passed undiscovered between the fleet and some high land on the main, and effected their escape. It was not till the 13th, that the British fleet again sighted them and renewed the action, when Arnold* ran his vessels aground, and setting fire to them, escaped with his men to the woods. General Waterbury, the second in command, on the contrary, continued for some time to oppose his vessel, the "Washington," which carried very heavy metal, to the "Maria," but on receiving a broadside from the "Inflexible," struck his colours; whereupon Capt. Campbell was sent on board to receive the brigadier's sword, and conduct him to Sir Guy Carleton. A sloop was also captured, but the remainder, having lightened themselves by throwing their guns overboard, escaped, but were captured the following year near Ticonderoga.

In this day's action a few of the regiment were wounded, but none killed.

On the 14th, the fleet anchored off Crown Point, when Captain Campbell was ordered to land his detachment, and take possession of the old works of Fort Frederick. The British colours were then hoisted on a temporary flagstaff, and the men, expecting at any moment to be attacked by General Gage, lay on their arms for three nights.

---

* Benedict Arnold, who, as a private soldier, had in early life twice deserted from the British Army, received the rank of colonel in the insurgent forces early in the revolutionary struggle. This officer's subsequent treachery, and desertion from the colours under which he was serving, led to the ignominious death of Major André, 7th Fusiliers, as a spy.—*E. B. de Fonblanque. Political and Military Episodes of General Burgoyne.*

1776 The advanced brigade, consisting of Royal Artillery, the 24th Foot, and the remainder of the 29th, arrived soon after, and encamped, as did the 1st brigade, at Chimney Point. The 29th, however, was detailed to cover the head quarter staff, and furnish the commander-in-chief's guard at Crown Point.

Winter now set in with great severity, and there being no accommodation for the army, Sir Guy Carleton decided to defer the attack on the enemy's lines at Ticonderoga, where they were strongly posted, till the ensuing spring. Accordingly, on the 2nd of November, the troops re-embarked and sailed for Canada; but the "Inflexible" remained at Crown Point, a few days, to prevent the enemy harassing the troops on their passage down the lake. On reaching Fort St. John, Captain Campbell's detachment landed and marched to Montreal, to rejoin the regiment, which, with the head quarters of the army, was stationed there.

The Grenadier company, under Lord Petersham, took up quarters at Verchere.

On the 12th of August, Lieut. Gawen Vaughan having embarked at Gravesend on board the "Maria" transport, with a detachment of the 15th, 24th, 29th, 33rd, 53rd, and 62nd regiments, proceeded to Cork, where, with the above details, he was tranferred to the "Nottingham," armed ship, and reached Halifax, Nova Scotia, early in December. Instead of proceeding to join his regiment at Montreal, he was, on the 20th, ordered to re-embark on board the "Lark" for New York, which had been captured in September. On arrival there, he was by General Sir W. Howe's orders, attached to the 7th Fusiliers, till the 7th of April following, when he embarked on board the "Integrity," and shortly after arrived at Halifax, where, by order of Brigadier McLean, he was again transferred to the "Nottingham." It was not till the 2nd of June, 1777, that he landed and proceeded to join the head quarters of the 29th.

1776   All the clothing of the regiment which was shipped on board the "Mellish" transport, in August, 1776, was taken by the rebels.

By the Monthly Returns it appears that Mr. George Turner, the regimental chaplain, proceeded on King's leave the 21st of June, 1776, and that he remained so absent till the 24th of June, 1794. Lord Cathcart, writing in 1790, says: "Our chaplain is head of a college at Oxford, with 5s. a day; 2s. 6d. is deducted from him when any man is appointed to do his duty; which I think very essential."

1777   On the 13th of March, 1777, General Sir G. Carleton reviewed the regiment on the ice at Montreal.

After the troops had repassed Lake Champlain, a considerable number of insurgents, finding their presence no longer necessary near Ticonderoga, joined the American forces in the Provinces of New York, and Jersey, and broke in, with some degree of success, upon the winter quarters of Sir W. Howe's troops. Upon this account, and with a view of quelling the rebellion as soon as possible, it was decided to send two expeditions from Canada the following spring, one, under Lieut.-General Burgoyne, to force its way to Albany, the other, under Lieut.-Colonel St. Leger, to make a diversion on the Mohawk River.

Orders,† fully as imperative as those sent to General Burgoyne, were to have been sent to Sir W. Howe (who was to have advanced and co-operated with the expedition from Canada), but owing to the carelessness of Lord George Germain, who preferred going to a good dinner in Kent to waiting for a few moments to attach his signature, they were pigeon-holed in London, where they were found, after the Convention of Saratoga, carefully docketed, and only wanting the minister's signature.

In the approaching operations under General Burgoyne, the Grenadier and Light Infantry companies of the 29th Foot, formed part

---

† Fonblanque—"Life of Burgoyne." Lord E. Fitz-Maurice—"Life of Lord Shelburne."

of the advance corps under Brigadier-General Fraser, of the 24th Regiment.

1777

The battalion companies, leaving Montreal on the 19th of June, encamped near Ste. Thérèse, and detaching two companies to Chambly, were employed during the campaign in assisting to forward stores of all kinds for the expeditionary force.

Expedition from Canada.

On the 17th of May, General Burgoyne assumed the command of the army.

The officers of the 29th employed with this force were:—

Captain	Archibald Campbell	Commissary of Musters.
,,	Chas. Visct. Petersham	Grenadier Company.
,,	Nich. Aylward Vigors	Light Infantry Company.
Lieut.	Thomas Steele	Grenadier Company.
,,	James Battersby	Light Infantry Company.
,,	Charles Williams	
,,	Sewell Maunsell	
,,	James Douglas	Light Infantry Company.
Ensign	Fra. Wm. Farquhar	
,,	William Johnson	
,,	York	
,,	James Dowling, appointed from 47th Foot on death of Lieut. Douglas.	

The troops having encamped at Crown Point, remained there a few days in order to establish magazines, hospitals, &c. On the 30th of June, the advance corps, under General Fraser, moved from its camp at Putman Creek, and advanced up the west side of Lake Champlain, to Four Mile Point, whilst the German reserve advanced along the east.

The Grenadier battalion was commanded by Major Ackland, of the 20th; the Light Infantry, by the Earl of Balcarras, 53rd Foot.

The following day the whole army made a forward movement, the naval force keeping in the centre. By the 3rd of July, Mount Hope, which lay to the north of the old French lines at Ticonderoga, was

1777 occupied in force by General Fraser's brigade, and within a few days, three-fourths of the enemy's works at Ticonderoga,† and Fort Independence were surrounded. On Sugar Loaf Hill (Mount Defiance), which had been taken possession of by the light infantry, and which completely commanded the enemy's position, and cut off their communications with Lake George, a battery was commenced. About daybreak, the 6th of July, intelligence was brought that the enemy, having previously set fire to their block houses, saw mills, and other works, were retiring. General Fraser therefore ordered the picquet to advance at once, and the brigades as soon as they were accoutred, marched down to the enemy's works. Orders were then given for the grenadiers and light infantry to pursue the enemy, who had retired in the direction of Hubberton. Having marched from 4 a.m. till 1 o'clock, in a very hot and sultry day, the troops halted to refresh themselves, after which they again moved forward to an advantageous position, where they lay on their arms for the night.

At 3 o'clock the following morning, the march was continued, and two hours later, the advance guard under Major Grant, 24th Regiment, having come up with the enemy, succeeded in forcing their picquets to retire on to the main body. The light infantry, and the 24th regiment then came into action, and the former suffered very much from the enemy's fire, particularly the companies of the 29th and 34th regiments. The grenadiers were now moved to the front, to prevent the enemy getting to the road that led to Castletown. In this they succeeded, upon which the enemy attempted to retreat by a very steep mountain to Pittford, but the grenadiers having slung their firelocks, climbed, with the aid of the branches of trees, and projecting rocks, up the side of a very steep ascent, and gained the summit before the enemy, who, notwithstanding their great losses, were still far superior in numbers to the British. Fraser's left, having met with a stubborn resistance, the issue of the contest appeared doubtful, but the arrival

---

The garrison was commanded by General St. Clair.

on that flank of General Reidesel with a large body of Germans, **1777** decided the fortune of the day, and the Americans retired, leaving their commander, many officers, and above 200 men dead upon the field. About 5 p.m., the grenadiers were ordered down to join the light infantry and the 24th. During this day's action the light company of the 29th had half its effective strength either killed or wounded.

Lieut. Douglas, whilst being carried off the field wounded, received a ball directly through his heart. Lieut. Steele was also wounded.

The sick and wounded, having to be escorted back to Ticonderoga, were left in charge of a subaltern's guard, and Fraser's brigade, marching by Castletown, rejoined the main body of the army at Skenesborough (Whitehall), on the 9th. On the 12th of July, Captain Lord Petersham was appointed Supernumerary A.D.C. to General Burgoyne, and as many officers in Fraser's brigade had been killed or wounded, Captain Campbell was given a command in the battalion of grenadiers, with which he did duty, and was present in all the subsequent actions of this campaign.

To follow up the advantages already gained, proved a difficult undertaking, for the Americans, now under command of General Schuyler, neglected no means of adding by art, to the difficulties which nature seemed to offer to the passage of Burgoyne's army. Large trees were cut down on either side of the road, so as to fall across, and lengthways with their branches interwoven. The troops had not only layers of these to remove, but also to construct more than 40 bridges, one of which was of log-work across a morass two miles in extent. By great exertions, these difficulties were overcome, and on the 30th of July, the army reached the banks of the Hudson. As the retreating enemy destroyed, or removed all stores and cattle, it was found necessary to make another halt, in order to allow of a further supply of provisions and stores being transported from Lake George to the

1777 Hudson. In the meanwhile, intelligence having been received that the enemy had established a store of provisions at Bennington, a place about 20 miles distant, a detachment, under Lieut.-Colonel Baum, was sent thither with a view of surprising it. Captain Fraser's Rangers, a company composed of 50 picked men from different regiments, amongst whom were some of the 29th, accompanied this expedition, which however did not prove successful.

A short time previous to the departure of Colonel Baum, General Fraser's brigade had passed the Hudson by a bridge of rafts, and some boats (which a few days after were washed away), and taken post on the Heights of Saratoga, but after the failure of the attack on Bennington it was recalled. On the 4th of August, the Indians, who formed part of the expedition, finding they were not allowed to plunder at their will, began to desert, whilst those nearest their homes begged permission to return to their harvest, which was granted.

On the 19th, General Gates, an Englishman by birth, and one who had served with distinction against the French in Canada, was appointed to the command of the enemy's forces. This officer, with Colonel Arnold as his second, having superseded General Schuyler, raised the whole country. By this time, provisions for about 30 days having been brought forward, and a bridge of boats completed, Burgoyne's army passed the Hudson on the 13th and 14th of September, and on the 17th encamped about 4 miles from the enemy, who were strongly fortified in the neighbourhood of Stillwater.

The passage of a great ravine, and other roads leading to their position having been reconnoitred, on the 19th, the troops advanced in 3 columns—Fraser's brigade, in order to cover the right of the line, and to pass the ravine without quitting the heights, had to go some distance round, before arriving at its allotted position.

The left column, under Major Generals Phillips and Reidesel, kept to the great road, and meadows near the river, whilst the centre, led by General Burgoyne in person, passed the ravine in a direct line, and formed up in order of battle as it gained the summit. All **1777** preparations being completed, a general advance took place. The enemy in the meantime, unacquainted with the combined advance of the three columns, had moved out of their intrenchments in great force, with a view of turning Burgoyne's right. In this however, owing to the position of Fraser's brigade, they failed; whereupon they directed their attack against the British left, and being continually reinforced with fresh troops, the action became general, and was continued with great obstinacy till after sunset, when the enemy retired.

During this engagement, which is known as that of Stillwater, or Sword's House, Fraser's brigade, which remained on the heights on the right, was not so actively engaged as were the other troops, but the grenadiers and 24th were at times brought into action, as were part of the light infantry.

Darkness having rendered pursuit impracticable, the troops lay on their arms that night, and the following day took up a position nearly within cannon-shot of the enemy.

From this time till the action of the 7th of October, the outposts of General Fraser's brigade were within half a mile of those of the enemy, whilst the remainder of his troops were employed in securing their own post, and clearing the country in their front. The left of the army was now extended so as to cover the meadow through which the river flowed, and where the boats and the hospital were placed.

It was soon found that no advantages were gained by the preceding victory. The enemy's right, being unassailable, they worked with redoubled energy to strengthen their left.

It was now found necessary to diminish the men's rations, and the Canadian Indians deserted in a body. Although thus weakened, the army continued to confront the enemy, whose numbers increased daily.

No intelligence having been received of the expected co-operation from Sir W. Howe, on the 7th of October, it was judged advisable to make a movement against the enemy's left, not only to discover

1777 whether there were any possible means of forcing a passage at that point, should it be necessary to advance, but also to cover a forage of the army, which, on account of scarcity of provisions, was then in great distress. This led to the action of Bemis Heights, or Saratoga, as it is also called. Night put an end to the fighting, but the enemy had gained an opening on Burgoyne's right, and rear.

In this day's action, the following casualties occurred amongst the officers of the 29th Foot :—

Wounded { Lieutenant Battersby.
                ,,   Dowling, doing duty with 20th Foot.
                ,,   Williams.

Prisoners { Ensign Johnson.
                   ,,   York.

After this action, the army fell back in good order, but on account of heavy rains, and the difficulty of guarding the boats which contained all the provisions, Saratoga was not reached till the night of the 9th. The enemy, who were hourly being reinforced, now pushed on, and intrenched themselves opposite all the fords. Their position, which nearly surrounded Burgoyne's army, was, from the nature of the ground, unassailable.

Under these circumstances the army took up, and fortified the best available ground, and remained there until the 13th, in anxious hope of succour, or an attack from the enemy. During this time the men, who lay continually on their arms, were cannonaded in every part, even rifle and grape shot fell into all parts of the line. At this period an exact account of the provisions was taken, and it was found that only 3 days' rations, upon short allowance, remained. Disappointed in the last hope of any timely co-operation, reduced by losses to 3,500 fighting men, not 2,000 of whom were British, a council of war, extending to all field officers, and captains commanding corps, was summoned, and the Convention of Saratoga ensued. Soon after this, Lord Petersham was sent home with dispatches, by General Burgoyne.

The sketch of Lord Petersham is taken from an oil painting, **1777** "Burial of General Fraser," at Saratoga, 8th of October, 1777, by J. Graham.

CHA. VISCT. PETERSHAM.
Captain 29th Grenadiers.

It will be observed that the officers of the 29th did not wear any lace round the button-holes of their coats. The epaulettes, shoulder belt plate, and buttons were of silver. The original picture, which is in the possession of Captain Fraser, of Balnain, was exhibited at the Royal Academy of 1791.

The British troops, which according to the Convention, were to have embarked at Boston, were detained by the Congress, under the most frivolous pretences, at Cambridge.

We find that in the summer of 1778, the Artillery and the 9th Foot, together with the flank companies of 29th, 31st, 34th, and 53rd regiments were quartered in barracks, at Rutland. The officers were allowed to go amongst their men for the purposes of roll call, and other matters of regularity. In September, 1779, they were at Charlottesville.

In the autumn of 1780, an exchange of Officers of Convention,* on parole in New York, or in Europe, was proposed by General Washington. This was followed soon after, by the exchange of the flank companies of the 29th, when all their men, fit for service, were drafted into the regiments at New York.

1777 After the Convention of Saratoga, the battalion companies of the 29th Foot (which in September, 1777, had marched to St. John's to relieve the 34th, ordered to Ticonderoga), being no longer required on the line of communications, returned to Montreal, where they remained during the winter. About this time, Ensign Williamson began, and made much progress with that humorous little book which he afterwards published, under the title of "*Advice to the Officers of the British Army.*"

"During this winter," wrote Col. Enys, "a serjeant, and 14 rank and file of the Germans, in passing from Sorel to Three Rivers, were overtaken by a snowstorm on Lake St. Peter, and subsequently found frozen to death in an upright position, with their arms in their hands."

1778 Early the next year, the detachments left in Canada by the 6 British regiments which formed part of General Burgoyne's army, were drafted into the 8th, 29th, 34th, 53rd, and the 3 companies of the 47th regiment which had remained near Quebec.

On the 11th of September, the regiment moved to Isle-aux-Noix, the advance post on that side to New York, and relieved the Royal Highland Emigrants, who had suffered much from sickness.

---

* New York, 24th of January, 1781. List of British Officers of the Troops of Convention. Exchanged. 29th Foot, Captain Vigors; Lieuts. Battersby, Williams, and Monsell.—"*Dispatches Quebec and Canada.*"

On the 24th of October, an expedition under command of Major **1778** Christopher Carleton, 29th Regiment, composed of detachments of 29th, 31st, 53rd, and the Royal Regiment of New York, was ordered out to destroy the forage and stores which had been collected by the enemy on the frontier.

The detachment of the regiment was composed as follows:—

29th Regiment—1 major, 2 captains, 5 lieutenants, 1 surgeon, 6 serjeants, 6 corporals, 2 drummers, and 100 privates.

29th Rangers—1 lieutenant, 1 ensign, 1 serjeant, 1 corporal, and 20 privates.

Colonel Enys, who at this time was an ensign, serving with the 29th rangers, or scouts, wrote:—

"Many of the officers at one time had so little to do, that, for want of better amusement, they played tetotum on the drumhead, from which it got the name of the "Tetotum expedition."

"It is surprising with what indifference the inhabitants saw their farms destroyed, but I cannot help taking notice of one old woman, who said not a word whilst her house and barns were burning, but soon after broke out into a most violent lamentation, for which I confess I thought she had good reason; but what was my surprize when I found the only part of her effects which caused her distress, was the loss of her tobacco pipe, and when Capt. Ross, 31st Regiment, procured her another in its place, she again appeared perfectly happy."

"During this expedition, Major Carleton used to send the men into the woods a little way, to practice 'treeing' as they called it, that is to say, the manner of hiding ourselves behind the trees, stumps, &c."

"On the 30th of October, a very unlucky accident happened by one of the 29th cutting down a tree carelessly, which fell on a wigwam where there were several men sitting, by which three were hurt, and one died of his wounds the same morning."

1778   On the following day, the expedition returned to Isle-aux-Noix, except one boat, which had on board presents from the Indians, with a serjeant and 14 privates of the 29th, a serjeant and a private of the 53rd, and which, on account of the bad weather, was thought to be lost.

On the 25th of December, the regiment was ordered to consist of 12 companies, of 3 serjeants, 4 corporals, 2 drummers, and 70 private men each.

It being found necessary that the garrisons of Isle-aux-Noix and St. John's should keep out constant scouting parties, each regiment was ordered to appoint 1 subaltern, 2 serjeants, 2 corporals, and 20 privates for that duty. These detachments received the title of "Rangers," **1779** and in January, the 29th rangers were increased to 2 subalterns, and 40 privates. With a view of sending parties across Cumberland Bay, Lieut. Walsh was sent to report on the state of the ice; whilst Ensign R. Battersby succeeded in bringing in 6 prisoners taken at Missiqui Bay.

In November, the latter officer with 20 rangers accompanied an expedition of about 180 Indians, with an equal number of royalists and rangers, which started for Fort Edward.

About the same time, 4 companies of the regiment proceeded to St. John's, to relieve the 31st Foot, ordered to Quebec, and 3 others followed later on, leaving only one company at Isle-aux-Noix.

1780   In May, 1780, Major Carleton received orders to endeavour to intercept scouts sent by the Americans into the Province of Quebec, and for this purpose small parties of the regiment, clothed and armed like the rebels, were dispatched in search of them.

It having been ascertained that the Americans were again collecting and storing forage on the frontier, an expedition under command of Major Carleton was ordered out to destroy it. The force, "which consisted of 968 of all ranks, was composed of detachments of 29th (1 major, 2 captains, 3 lieutenants, 2 ensigns, 5 serjeants, 5 corporals, 1 drummer, and 182 privates), 34th, 53rd, and 84th

Regiments, of Chasseurs, Royalists, Royal Yorkers, Rangers, and some Mohawk Indians," left St. John's, the 28th of September. On entering Lake Champlain, the advance posts were entrusted to Bt. Major Campbell, of the 29th. On landing at the head of South Bay, the troops proceeded towards Fort Anne. Failing to surprise it, Major Carleton, at 3 a.m. the following day, ordered Lieut. Farquhar, of the 29th, with 30 British, and as many Loyalists, to cut the enemy's communication on the Fort Edward road, whilst Lieuts. Kirkman of the 29th, and Johnson of the 47th, were sent to demand its surrender. This being agreed to, the fort was set on fire, and the stock destroyed. Burning parties having been sent out on either flank, Major Carleton's force marched the following day towards Fort George, and halted that evening within 9 miles of it. The advance was continued the next morning, and when within a mile and a half of the place, a small party of Indians saw two men, who ran off and alarmed the fort. A halt was thereupon called, and a party sent forward to reconnoitre. On its being discovered that the enemy were advancing, the company of the 34th Foot, with about 25 Loyalists, was sent to support the Indians who were now engaged with the Americans. As the remainder of the expedition moved forward to take possession of Gage's Heights, several shots were fired from the fort. Advantage was now taken of a small hollow, near at hand, in which the troops formed under cover, and from whence Major Carleton sent Lieuts. Kirkman and Johnson, with a flag of truce, to summon the fort, which agreed to surrender. "During the time," wrote Col. Enys, "that the flag was there, we saw some men leading a wounded person, who we at first supposed to be an Indian, from his head looking so red and shining, but on his nearer approach found him to be one of the rebels who had been scalped. This man had not been long brought in, when some of our men recognised him as being a deserter from my party when serving with the artillery in 1776; this he at first denied, but, being questioned by a man who had formerly been his comrade, acknowledged it. Surely never poor fellow suffered more than this one did; he had one of his

1780 arms broken by a shot, a violent contusion, and three very deep tomahawk wounds at the back of his head. Notwithstanding these injuries, he lived some days, but died on board one of the ships on Lake Champlain."

Having destroyed the fort and adjacent buildings, the expedition returned by the west side of the lake, and landed at Crown Point the 15th of October.

On the 20th of November, the regiment went into winter quarters on the River Sorel, 2 companies being stationed in each of the following parishes, viz., Belloeil, St. Charles, St. Denis, and St. Antoine.

1781 A warrant, dated 27th of July, 1781, was issued for reducing the strength of each company from 70, to 56 privates.

In September, orders were received for the formation of new flank companies; those which had served with General Burgoyne having been drafted into other regiments. The raising of these companies had scarcely been completed, when, about the middle of October, an expedition under command of Lieut.-Colonel St. Leger, 34th Foot, was ordered out on the frontier. The force was composed of the Light company of the 29th, 31st, 34th, and 44th regiments, detachments of the 29th and 34th Battalion companies, together with Royalists and Indians. Having proceeded to Ticonderoga, the Light company of the 29th, with some Royalists, was sent to Diamond Island, on Lake George, but not meeting with any of the enemy, they were ordered to rejoin the main body, which returned to St. John's on the 15th of November.

The regiment which had only awaited the return of its Light company, now crossed the St. Lawrence, and took up the following quarters:—The Grenadier, and the Colonel's company, with music, at La Chenage; the Light infantry, and 2 battalion companies, St. Henri de la Mascouche; 4 companies Terrebonne; and 1 at Mascouche le Page.

On the 22nd of February, 1782, a Warrant was issued to the **1782** Master General of Ordnance to supply the regiment with 57 stands of arms and 22 drums,* with pairs of sticks, to replace those lost at Saratoga (7th Oct., 1777).

On the 6th of July, the *serjeants of infantry regiments*, were ordered to wear their swords over their coats, in the same manner as the private men carried their bayonets.

During this year, in order to facilitate the procuring of recruits, regiments were given *County Titles*, with reference to which the following order was received :—

"London, 31 August, 1782.

Sir,

His Majesty having been pleased to order that the 29th Regiment, which you command, should take the county name of "The Worcestershire Regiment," and be looked upon as attached to that county, I am to acquaint you it is His Majesty's further pleasure that you should in all things conform to that idea, and endeavour, by all means in your power, to cultivate and improve that connexion, so as to create a mutual attachment between the county and the regiment ; which may at all times be useful towards recruiting the regiment. But as the compleating the several regiments now generally so deficient, is in the present crisis, of the most important national concern, you will, on this occasion, use the utmost possible execution for that purpose, by prescribing the greatest diligence to your officers and recruiting parties, and by every suitable application to the gentlemen and considerable inhabitants ; and as nothing can so much tend to conciliate their affection as an orderly and polite behaviour towards them, and an observance of the strictest discipline in all your quarters, you will give the most

---

* This I think should be 2, for the complement of Drummers and Fifers for the 10 Service companies was but 20, and only the 2 Flank companies were employed under Burgoyne. The strength of the Flank companies of the 29th, 31st, 34th, and 53rd regiments, was on the 1st September, 1779, 5 Captns., 13 Subs., 1 Adjt., 1 Qr. Master, 1 Surgeon, 16 Sergts., 14 Drummers, 185 Rank and File. "Wanting to complete," 5 Sergts., 9 Drummers, 263 Rank and File.

1782 positive orders on that head; and you will immediately make such a disposition of your recruiting parties as may best answer these ends.

I have the honour to be,

&c., &c.,

(Signed)   H. S. Conway."

" Lieut.-Gen. Evelyn,
or the Officer Commanding
the 29th Regiment."

Captain Chas. Williams and Ensign Wm. C. Strachan are by the Muster Rolls, shown as being at Worcester from the 5th of June to the 24th December, 1782.

Had this plan been firmly and constantly adhered to, there is but little doubt that it would have answered the purpose intended. For, in the first instance, the 29th Regiment procured many very good men, who, on their joining, appeared to be very pleased with their county regiment; and it will be shown hereafter how this advantage was lost, with no fault on the part of the corps.

In August, the Regiment marched to Montreal, and thence to winter quarters at St. Johns, and Isle-aux-Noix.

In December, orders were issued to reduce the two additional companies raised seven years previously, and to augment the regiment with a recruiting company. This company, to be raised in the county of Worcester, was to consist of 6 serjeants, 8 corporals, 4 drummers, and 30 privates.

In the course of the winter a report prevailed that the Americans, under Le Marquis de Lafayette, intended to cross Lake Champlain before the ice broke up, and make an attack on Canada. In consequence of this, the Light companies of the 29th, 31st, and 53rd regiments, with a detachment of the 29th battalion companies, some

Royalists, and Indians—the whole under command of Major Campbell, **1782** of the 29th—advanced across the boundary line of the Province, and hutted themselves in the woods not far from Point-au-Fer. On preliminaries for a general Peace being entered upon, these companies were withdrawn, and rejoined their respective regiments.

In anticipation of peace, a reduction in the establishment of **1783** regiments took place, and all men who in 1775 had enlisted for three years, or during the war, became entitled to their discharge. Some of these received grants of land at Cataraqui, and the Bay of Chaleurs. A great number, however, re-enlisted, and thus the regiment was completed to its reduced establishment, viz., 1 colonel, 1 lieut.-colonel, 1 major, 1 chaplain, 1 adjutant, 1 quartermaster, 1 surgeon, 1 mate.

Companies.	Captains.	Lieutenants.	Ensigns.	Serjeants.	Corporals.	Drummers.	Fifers.	Privates.
6 Companies each of	1	1	1	2	3	2		48
1 Company of Grenadiers ...	1	2		2	3	2	2	48
1 Company of Light Infantry	1	2		2	3	2		48

The 9th and 10th Companies being reduced, their commissioned officers remained *en seconde*.

In August, on the death of Lieut.-General Wm. Evelyn, Lieut.-General Wm. Tryon, colonel of the 70th Foot, was transferred to the colonelcy of the 29th Regiment.

On the 3rd of September, definite treaties with America, France, and Spain were signed, the former at Paris, the two others at Versailles. In the Treaty with America, the 13 United States were acknowledged to be free, sovereign, and independent. France gave up her West

1783 Indian conquests, except Tobago; Spain retained Minorca and West Florida; East Florida being ceded in exchange for the Bahamas.

CAPTAIN JOHN ENYS.   1783.

A picture of Captain J. Enys, done this year, shows that the officers wore their hair clubbed (*vide* 11th April, 1786).

1784 By Warrant, dated the 21st of July, 1784, it was ordered that "the whole quantity of ammunition carried by each soldier was to be 56 rounds, 32 of which were to be carried in a pouch on his right side, and 24 in a cartridge box, by way of a magazine, upon a new principle, to be worn occasionally on his left side. The *flap of pouch* to be **1784** plain, without any ornament,* and the bottom part of it to be rounded at the corners. The *cartridge box by way of magazine*, to be fixed to the bayonet belt in such a manner as to be easily taken off or put on, it not being intended to be worn except on a march or on actual service. The *cross belt* for the pouch, and magazine to be made of buff leather, two inches broad. The *gayters* to be made of black woollen cloth (instead of linen), with white metal buttons, and without stiff tops. The *Grenadier swords*, matches, and match cases‡ to be laid aside.

The Light Company to have a small priming horn, to hold about two ounces of powder (instead of the horn, and bullet bag now in use, which are both to be laid aside). The horn, and hatchet not to be fixed to the accoutrements, but to be carried either with the knapsack, or in such other manner as the commanding officer shall think convenient. *Light Company Cap* to be of black leather.

In a Return of Accoutrements, dated the 20th of August, 1784, the serjeants, rank and file, both of flank, and battalion companies, were shown as being in possession of swords.

In 1785 the crime of desertion prevailed throughout the army to **1785** such a degree that orders were issued "that any man who (being regularly convicted thereof) shall by a General Court Martial be adjudged to suffer death, must expect a certain, and speedy execution of the sentence."

On the 24th of May, the regiment under command of Major Campbell (having been selected to relieve the 8th "King's"), marched

---

* The issue of new accoutrements took place in 1789-90, a few months previous to the 29th being stationed at Windsor.

Captain K. V. Bacon, late of the Regiment, "whose grandfather, Captain Charles Williams, retired from the 29th Foot in 1790," states that he was told that the Regiment was permitted to retain its *star* pouch ornament through the influence of Queen Charlotte.

‡ See remarks of Inspecting Officer, 26th Aug., 1828; and Lord Strafford's letter of 2nd April, 1838.

1785 from Montreal to La Chene, where it embarked for the upper posts, in the Province of Quebec; and, on landing, was stationed at the Fort of Niagara, Cataraqui, Carleton Island, and Oswego.

Brigadier-General Barry St. Leger, as a particular mark of his opinion of Major Campbell's conduct, gave that officer a Letter of Service, appointing him commandant of all the posts situated on the five great lakes, with more power and privileges than had ever been conferred on anyone prior to this.

1786 In April, 1786, orders were issued for *battalion officers* to use swords, in lieu of espontoons. Both officers, and men in general, when under arms or on duty (the Fusilier Corps, Grenadier, and Light Infantry companies, when they wear their caps, excepted) were for the future to wear their hair "clubbed." The non-commissioned officers and men to have a small piece of black polished leather, by way of ornament, upon the club. The whole to wear black leather stocks.

Officers to wear black cloth gaiters, uniform with those of the men, on all duties except upon a march, when they might be permitted to wear boots.

The following is Col. Enys's description of

Dark Sunday.

"Whilst I was at Montreal, procuring provisions and stores for the regiment, on the 16th September, 1786, a phenomenon took place which is worthy of mention, and was called the " Dark Sunday," from its happening on that day. The weather had for some time been extremely hot, and for two or three days very dark and close, but on that day more so than usual; so that about 9 or 10 o'clock in the forenoon all the cattle sought shelter under their sheds, and the poultry and birds of all kinds went to their roost as they do in the evening. About noon it was so dark that people could not do their common business. Before two, they were obliged to light candles in all the houses, when they began to be considerably alarmed, and crowded into the churches, where mass was performed. Various were the conjectures **1786** on the occasion : some expected an earthquake, whilst others conceived the end of the world was approaching, and 3 o'clock was expected to be the time at which it was to take place—which was confirmed by the darkness continuing to increase until that hour, when it was at its worst, and so dark was it that I and many others ran against each other in the street. After this time it became gradually lighter, which was again succeeded by a second darkness, but not quite so dark as the first, which after some time again cleared off; and again a third time became dark, which was again less than the former one, after which it became by degrees lighter, until the darkness was wholly dissipated, by which time the evening was closing in fast. Shortly after, the moon shone out with unusual splendour, and the streets were filled with people walking about for several hours, apparently very happy to find themselves still in existence. During this time I remember only one clap of thunder, and that not very loud ; but there was a good deal of lightning playing round the mountains, and some very hard rain, which some of the priests said was full of ashes, but I cannot think there was anything remarkable in it, as I was out in some part of it, and being dressed in uniform, had there been any such thing, it must have been seen thereon."

The 65th Foot, having arrived at Niagara to relieve the 29th, the **1787** several detachments assembled at Carleton Island, and sailed thence, early in July, under command of Major Campbell, for Quebec, where, on arrival, orders were found for the regiment to be held in readiness to return to England. Before embarking, however, Admiral Sawyer's fleet arrived, and as one of the ships, H.M. " Pegasus," was commanded by Prince William Henry, afterwards King William IV., this visit was made the occasion of much gaiety in the way of balls and dinners ; the Prince being entertained by each regiment in turn.

Landing in the character of a Prince of the Blood Royal, he was received by the Governor, and Council, all the principal clergy, and

1787 four officers who had been appointed to attend him during his stay ashore. One of the latter was Captain Hugh Dickson, 29th Foot, the flank companies of which formed the Prince's personal guard. On the 29th of August, a grand review of the troops in garrison and cantonments took place near Quebec. This was followed by a sham fight, in which the right wing of the army was commanded by Lieut.-Colonel Cotton, 31st Regiment; the left by Major Campbell, of the 29th; whilst 10 Grenadier and Light Infantry companies, under Lieut.-Col. Hastings, 34th Foot, represented the enemy.

On the 5th of October, the regiment embarked on board the "General Elliott" and "Jane" transports. After a very boisterous passage, it landed at Portsmouth early the next month, and marched to Petersfield. Having remained here about three weeks, it proceeded to Alresford, Alton, and thence to Worcester, where it was quartered in the Tything of Whistones, and parishes of St. Clement, St. John, St. Michael, and St. Peter. Ever since the 29th received its county title, the recruiting company stationed at Worcester, had been very successful; but, strange as it may seem, at the time when the regiment was almost daily expected to land in England, the recruits were all ordered to join the 43rd Foot. This so offended the Worcestershire men, that the recruiting interest in the county, for the regiment, was lost from that time for many years.

CHAPTER VI.

N the death of Lieut.-General Tryon in January, 1788, **1788** Charles, Earl of Harrington, was on the 28th instant, transferred from the colonelcy of the 65th Foot to that of the 29th.

Previous to the County Militia assembling at Worcester for its annual training in April, the 29th was ordered to march to Pershore, and whilst there was, on the 31st of May, reviewed by Lieut.-General J. Douglas, who, in his report, made the following remarks :—

"*Officers.*—Only 3 captains and 4 subalterns present with the regiment, all the rest being employed on the recruiting service.

Men.—Only 28 file under arms ; several old men.

Recruits since last Review.—101 ; some rather under size.

Number of Men to be Discharged.—26, for reasons approved.

Arms.—Bad and deficient.

Clothing.—Good, what was seen.

Gaiters.—According to order."

As swords for the non-commissioned officers, rank and file, are not mentioned in the Return of Arms and Accoutrements, it appears they were discontinued on the regiment's return to England.

Leaving Pershore in July, the 29th marched to Tewkesbury, whence a detachment was sent to Cheltenham to do duty over Their Majesties. On the 26th, the King and Queen, accompanied by the Princesses, passed and repassed through Tewkesbury, on their way to, and from, the seat of the Earl of Coventry, upon which occasion the

1788 inhabitants gave every proof of their loyalty and attachment to their Sovereign. A grand triumphal arch, adorned and decorated with flowers and garlands, was erected across the street at the post-office. On the top of the arch were placed Their Majesties' arms, with the following inscription: "King George I., before his Accession to the Throne, was Baron Tewkesbury. May the illustrious House of Hanover flourish to its latest posterity." A band of music was placed on an eminence close by, which, as Their Majesties passed, played "God save the King." The 29th Regiment was drawn up by the Earl of Harrington, and every other method was used to testify the pleasure the inhabitants received from the visit of the Royal Family.

Towards the end of August, the King having left Cheltenham, the detachment rejoined head quarters, and the regiment marched, by Worcester, for Scarborough, where, on arrival, it was ordered to aid and assist in preventing owling† and smuggling, by seizing uncustomed goods, and by apprehending and securing the offenders, but not to repel force by force, unless in case of absolute necessity.

On the 13th of October, new looping was approved of for the 29th Foot.

1789 On the 11th of May, 1789, Major-General G. Scott reviewed the regiment, and made the following remarks:—

"*Officers.*—Dressed according to regulation, except that they have adopted the use of feathers, which is not sanctioned by H.M. Regulations, either for officers or men.

Accoutrements.—A new supply ordered; as also the Grenadier caps.

Colours.—Bad, want replacing; very nearly worn out.

Towards the end of the month, the regiment was ordered to Tynemouth, and such a detachment as the magistrates and principal

---

† Owling—the offence of transporting wool, or sheep, out of the kingdom, was usually carried on at night. "Owler" is said to be a corruption of Wooller.

inhabitants of Sunderland might think expedient was to proceed there, **1789** and to Newcastle, to aid in preserving peace, and quelling any riots or disturbances that might happen.

On the 6th of July, all officers of infantry regiments were ordered, when on duty, and appearing with their sash on, in future to wear their swords slung upon their right shoulder, over their uniform. When off duty, and having their uniform on without the sash, to wear the sword slung over their waistcoats.

The regiment received new colours on the 17th of August.

On the 6th of October, William, Lord Cathcart, exchanged from the Coldstream Guards to the lieutenant-colonelcy of the 29th Foot; and on the 14th instant the regiment left Tynemouth *en route* for Dover.

LETTER FROM LORD HARRINGTON TO LIEUT.-COL. LORD CATHCART.

"Harewood House, Oct. 18th, 1789.

"My dear Lord,

I beg you a thousand pardons for not having before answered a Letter which I received from you previous to my departure from Tynemouth, which place I left with the Regiment on Wednesday. I marched with them to Durham, from whence L^{dy} Harrington and I went on a visit for a day to Ld Darlington, and passed them again to-day at North Allerton. I must beg you, my dear Lord, to intirely consult your own convenience in regard to residence with the twenty-ninth, we shall be flattered with your company when you have no calls elsewhere, but as there is a Field Officer constantly resident, and ready to supply both your place and mine, you will be perfectly at liberty on that head. I propose being myself in London about the time the Regiment will pass through it, and shall be happy to introduce you to it. You will find us excessively week & equaly undisciplined, there not being more than a hundred men fitt for duty, & many of them totaly worn out—the rest are all Recruits. There is an Officer at Chatham with 30 or 40 Recruits who are to join us on our march

1789 through it, together with about the same number of men on Furlough, who are ordered to rendezvous there on account of the distance of our former Quarter.—I inclose a march-route which will shew you the detail of our progress. We have given, as you will see, a Halt of 3 days, that the Soldiers may get their shoes repaired on the road.—There has been such a continuance of rain that the Roads are in a terrible state, & a great deal of the Country under water, the Corn is still in the fields in many places, & the Beans almost everywhere. Should you have any Commands for me, I beg you to direct to me at Elvaston, near Derby, where I shall probably remain till I sett off for London. I beg you to be assured of the truth & regard with which,

  I am,

   My dear Lord,

    Your most faithful

     and obedient Servand,

      HARRINGTON."

To LORD CATHCART.

"Elvaston, Novr 7th, 1789.

My dear Lord,

  As I am about to sett off from hence for London, & propose overtaking the first Division of the Regiment at Barnet on the tenth, I shall be excessively happy to present the Officers who are with it to you, either there or on their Way through London the following day——You will find us extremely weak having very little more than a hundred men in each Division owing to the number of our recruiting Parties & to so many men having been left in the north on furlough; most however of the latter will join the Regiment on its Way through Chatham together with about 40 Recruits who are now in those Barracks.——Lady Harrington joins me in congratulations on the addition to your family, & in hopes that Lady Cathcart will Speedily **1789** recover from Her present Confinement.

Believe me, with great regard,
   My dear Lord
     Your most faithful
      & obedient Servant,
        Harrington."

Lord Cathcart having kindly supplied me with several copies of a correspondence between his grandfather (the lieut.-colonel, and afterwards full colonel of the 29th) and his grandmother, extracts have been made, and the letters numbered consecutively 1 to 28.

[Letter 1].

"Dartford, 15th Nov^r, 1789.

"Having on Friday (13th) ridden to Barnet to take command of troops, I invited the officers to supper at 9 o'clock. I marched from Barnet a little before 5 o'clock a.m., and reached Dartford about 4, without leaving a man behind us. It is full 30 miles; and as I found the officers with this division much mortified at being smuggled through the City, lest people should say the best men were picked to be seen in the first division, I marched boldly down St. James Street and through the Horse Guards, where Lord Henry FitzGerald's guard was getting ready for him. But it was too early, as we passed under the Horse Guards as the clock struck 9. I am quite pleased with the 29th Regiment; they are mere boys, almost children; but so willing, so good humoured, and so well-behaved. Not a prisoner on the whole march; not a man confined or punished.

I halted an hour and a-half on Blackheath, and gave them a breakfast to the same amount as I had given the others. I then put their

1789 knapsacks in a cart, and I am sure they would have gone on to Rochester. I have the adjutant, one lieutenant, and 2 ensigns with me, and in excellent quarters. They gave us a good dinner, and we had a rubber of shilling whist, and were all in bed before 10. Most of them lay above 14 hours, for, as they make a point of marching on foot every step with the men, they were not a little fatigued.

I have given up all that idea, as I know a field officer is of much more use mounted. However I walked several miles in the course of the day. I am now in expectation of Ld Harrington, with whom I shall go on to Rochester; and indeed, if he does not, I shall go by myself, as I should like to pass the entire day of to-morrow there. The whole regiment will be there to-morrow."

[LETTER 2].

"Chatham Barracks,

Monday, Nov. 16, 1789.

"Who should arrive at Dartford at 3 o'clock but Major Campbell and Major St. Clair, and who should they be followed by but L^d and Lady Harrington and their charming 5-year-old boy Leicester. They dined with us and went on to Rochester, and they go to Dover with us.

I marched before 7 this morn^g, and got to Rochester at half-past 11 o'clock, when I marched in with the band, &c., in great style.

We march again to-morrow all together to Sittingbourne, when I shall go with five companies to Faversham, and, if I can do it well, shall go and dine at Eastwell, and get back to march to meet the other five companies at Aspringe, when we shall all proceed to Canterbury on Wednesday, and either halt there on Thursday or march on to Dover.

The day has been spent in barracks, where the parade has been filled with a succession of corps. Colonel Crosby has shown us his regiment, and all our officers dine with that corps; the 22nd are in very fine order, and Crosby, a wonderful prince, at their head. I marched most of the way from Dartford, and I am very hungry. But I shall go early and drink tea with Lady Harrington, where several of our officers are to be. I have not seen such a military world a great while. Lord H. is delighted, and is strutting about the parade with Crosby, viewing a parcel of raggamuffins of different corps who are being tormented in different corners by a variety of drill serjeants. The Botnay Bay Corps are too fit for that service to be what we hoped to find them. Our recruits are in general good, and we shall march to-morrow near 300; which, considering all, is very strong. Adieu! here comes Crosby. I send his compliments at a venture."

[LETTER 3].

"Sittingborne, Nov. 17, 1789.

"Pleasant march. Dinner of yesterday agreeable; the band and much laughing, without much drinking, and no pressing. The band good; they introduce the fifes in lively tunes with good effect. We have left one of the band to learn this. I do not choose to go to Eastwell because it is so against my own principles that officers should absent themselves on the march. Lady Harrington dines with us, and we drink tea with her. There was a supper in her appartment last night, but, being sleepy, I took my milk and went to bed. I am up at 5 every morning, and generally call up the house. I am wonderfully pleased with everything but your absence. Had we remained at Chatham B[ks] I would certainly have brought you. You would like these officers much better than any you have seen me with. No noise and swaggering, but the fashion is to be as well bred and gentlemanlike as possible. We march early to-morrow for Canterbury."

1789

[LETTER 4].

"Canterbury, Nov. 18, 1789.

"Pleasant dinner; drank tea with Lady H.; and all asleep by 10 o'clock. Marched at 6 this mor^{ng}, arrived soon after one. I walked almost all the way, and fell asleep whilst dressing, to be aroused by Governor Graham [of Georgia], who came to offer the regiment all sorts of hospitality, and was vastly civil. My morning is gone, dinner is coming, and by mistake the Lt Dragoons dine with us. We met Lord Eardley a mile from here on a prancing troop horse, w^h took fright at the reg^t and carried his lordship off, but not till he had splashed Lord Harrington from head to foot. We sent after him to invite him and his friend to dinner, and this friend understood the invitation was for all the corps.

The regiment marched in by divisions, and really made a good appearance."

[LETTER 5].

"Dover Castle, Nov. 20, 1789.

"We arrived about half-past 1. Pleasant march. The women were there, having, with the stores, come by sea. Dinner for the men was served the instant the parade was dismissed. The officers found bare walls. We chose our rooms, and then went down to the "City of London" where we all dined and slept. To-day we begin a mess in barracks. I have chose my rooms next to Lord Harrington's, so that when one is away the other may have his rooms. Lord H. has a slight fit of the gout, brought on by walking on the Canterbury march. People are assembling for breakfast, and I am writing on their table."

[LETTER 6].

"Dover Castle, Nov. 22, 1789.

"Poor Lord H. is unable to walk; no pain, but weakness and swelling, and is forced to hop about his room with the help of the walls. Molineux,† in following me to the inn, was made prisoner by a watchman, as a suspicious person, and detained from 9 to 12, when the watchman got tired of standing sentry, and let my man go. Lord & Lady H. had furniture w^h came by sea, and they are quite comfortable. I have got a small bed, 3 chairs, and a dirty table, with no other furniture for two large rooms; but I never slept better. I am now going to breakfast with Lord Harrington. No milk can be had for money; we must order that better, otherwise I will hire an ass or buy a goat. I continue much pleased with everything and everybody. Our mess will be extremely comfortable and well-regulated under 1s. 6d. a day. Nor is there any tendency to drinking; there are a sufficient number of elderly people to keep up all matters in very steady order. Lady H. dined with us yesterday."

(LETTER 7].

"Dover Castle, Dec. 13, 1789.

"I missed the post, because I had the band in my outer room to play over new music that I might select, & I kept them longer than I intended. Lord H. has his leg on a stool and has had three relapses, and has suffered much pain; they will return to town as soon as he is able. We had a card party in their room last night, and this evening a little supper. I have now my baggage unpacked. I am to have 2lbs. of the finest tea at 6s. 6d., and other things as cheap in proportion. They have got the mess in very good order. Candlesticks & knives from Birmingham; a good cook and good wine; so that I

---
† Lord C's civil servant.

1789 never saw a mess better served. Major Campbell breakfasted with me, and we have had our parade within the keep. Our men would have been very healthy but for the itch, which they contracted on the march, and w^h it has been very troublesome to eradicate, and for a nest of the most abandoned women who have concealed themselves under the old gateways of this place, but who are now banished."

[LETTER 8].

"Dover Castle, December 15, 1789.

"We have a frenchman in the ranks, Guibert, who is a very good draftsman. Great interest is made for his discharge. Lady H. has been learning perspective of him, and has made great progress. If I find I can allot an hour to such a purpose, I think I will take some lessons in return for those he receives on parade."

[LETTER 9].

"Dover Castle, Dec. 17, 1789.

"Thanks for the haunch of venison, w^h will be a treat to the mess, and it will arrive the very day the command devolves on me. Stormy weather continues. The rooms of the keep are so spacious that 2 of them hold the whole reg^t, and in bad weather we parade there, and even march off our guards with drums and music. I like being here very much. Poor Lord H. is again laid up as bad as ever; his ankle and foot much swelled, so lame, he cannot put it to the ground."

Lord Cathcart sends for his violoncello and music books.

[LETTER 10]. **1789**

"Dover Castle, Dec. 20, 1789.

"Lord and Lady H. dined with us, and as she and my lord happen to like venison, I was glad it was there. They are to leave us, and their things are packed; so I invited Lady H. to tea in my room, and I also asked the whole reg^t and Mrs. Monsell. I had two card tables, and some cold meat, &c., in the mess room; all which succeeded extremely well. Lord and Lady H. left us at eleven this morning. You will like her because she really wishes to be agreeable and civil; I do not recollect to have heard her abuse anybody, or say anything illnatured or satirical. I am to dine on Xmas day at Major Monsell's. The great rooms of the keep were King Arthur's rooms of State. There are 2, each of which is capable of holding a wing of the reg^t, and there we parade in bad weather. The effect of the band in these rooms is very fine when we "beat the troop," and march off the guard. I began the command by desiring the major not to take the trouble of taking post on the ordinary parades, but to walk about with me; and that really worthy man seemed pleased with that trifling attention. I shall really be proud in Town to introduce almost all who are here to you; and when I except any, it is only they are not so much formed as the rest. It is a prodigious advantage when the Com. Off. is not called upon to interfere in keeping order in the mess room, and in the domestic behaviour of young officers, as is the case here.

The captains and senior lieutenants are in themselves perfectly well bred, and never suffer the slightest indecorum to pass unnoticed. The allowance of wine is half-a-pint a man; when that is out, the President calls for more, which is a signal for those who choose it to take their hats and withdraw. The cost to them is 1s. 6d. for dinner, 4½d.—5d. for wine. Surely in these times no gentleman can live cheaper. My bill for 6 days' dinners, and every expense, with, on one day, two guests besides—Saturday to Friday—was £1 1s. 0½d. The bills are paid every Friday. The men buy coarse beef at 3d. per lb."

1789

[LETTER 11].

"Dover Castle, Dec. 24, 1789.

"From ten to four, officers call on me; then I have the parade; now and then attend drill; reg^{tl} letters and papers, and the number of soldiers' letters to be 'franked,' time goes fast. A visitor, a young gentleman from Dublin, but last from France, caused a drinking bout at mess. Even my friend the major sat late, and made a night of it. I retired early; the seniors are all in bed; the youngsters none the worse. But this is the first time since I have been down that the mess has sat after 8 o'clock. I am not sorry this Irish gentleman's visit is over, as I do not wish for more of his countrymen at this juncture. We have but two, and they do extremely well by themselves.

I worked my parade about in the long room, making the best of bad weather. They were like horses in a 'manage,' marching round in single file, in slow time, without music and without arms, saluting the serj^t major with the opposite hand; this gives the men wonderful grace and air. The men have Christmas dinners given by the officers, and ½ a guinea per company given by Lord Harrington. Lady H. has given a brown flannel great coat, neatly made up like her own children's, to every soldier's child in this reg^t; you cannot imagine how comfortable and creditable it makes the little things look. I have also been tempted to deal in flannel. The men are miserably in debt to their captains; we are here in rags and tatters, that we may get out of debt and be able to keep ourselves out of rags when we go to Windsor. Our waistcoats & breeches are all darned and patched, and scarce hold together, and many men have nothing to turn the wind under their jackets but their shirts. I have bought a quantity of flannel, and have given each man in the reg^t a flannel shirt to wear next his skin. I have 20 or 30 hands at work 6 hours by candlelight, and make 50 in an evening. They will not cost 15d. each when made up. Flannel at 11d., the whole will cost £23, and for that extravagance, w^h I can recoup from public places and club dinners, I am sure I shall save many useful lives and constitutions."

[LETTER 12].

1789

"Dover Castle, Dec. 29, 1789.

"One of my lieut^s of Light Infantry, who was major of brigade and confidential friend to poor Col. Hope, in Canada, and who stands very high in my estimation, is going to town to meet his sister. His name is Farquhar. If he calls when you are at home, and it is not inconvenient, pray see him. I have been all morning fitting on new clothing and penning orders for certain interior arrangements of cleanliness. We have a dinner in the town, ladies and men; also a private ball. I shall go, because the people are inclined to be extremely civil to the regiment & because it is not inconsistent with my system to encourage balls, and the service of the ladies, for my young officers. We have Strephons amongst us, and whose toasts are repeated as regularly as the port is set before them. I have a party of about 7 or 8 every evening, half-past 7 till 10. I ask all the elder officers and boys in turn; this is well, and makes the day go off pleasantly enough.

You would laugh could you see me to-morrow evening superintending the washing of the feet of half the regiment, an operation which I have ordered to be repeated by half the regiment at a fixed hour every Thursday and Saturday, and seen by an officer; the water to be milk warm. I have got 260 of my flannel shirts made up & given out. They are to be washed once a fortnight, half at a time, every Saturday; They are to be worn night and day. I shall be much mortified if I do not reduce the sick list considerably, before I leave the Castle, by these regulations, and some other attentions."

[LETTER 13].

1790

"Dover Castle, 6 Jan^{ry}, 1790.

"My men are all cased in flannel, and I hear less coughing in the ranks. We have 5 low-fever cases, which have lasted several weeks; the dangerous symptoms have gone off, but they do not recover,

1790 nor do I expect they will till the frost sets in, and I have the mortification to see the wind veering back to the old rainy quarter. I have had a letter from Lord H. to say he has been to inquire for the Grenadier caps he bespoke a year ago, and has been told they were sent many months ago. I have searched the stores and found the package all in good order, and I have a Grenadier dressing in my ante-chamber, that I may report his appearance. All our boys are so much pleased with this novelty that I fear it will distract their devotion. The caps have a plain brass front, the rim of which goes all round with the 'Plait en bandeau,' like the Coldstream, and a small neat leather shade for the eyes, like my Light Infantry cap. The last part I do not like; yet, on the whole, they are the handsomest and most martial-looking caps I ever saw. The Grenadier cap^{tn} was lamenting to me yesterday that the caps were not bespoke—he does not yet know they have been found; but I am going to send for him and surprise him."

[LETTER 14].

"Dover Castle, April 4th, 1790.

"I find all going on well here, the men growing in height, and really grown fat and healthy-looking; which is all I can yet judge of. We have been at church, where I find the institution I have planned answers in every respect. The band are very much improved, and had prepared an hymn for the day to surprise me. It was extremely well performed, and set with a great deal of taste and variety, and would have surprised any audience. The accompanyment was rather too powerful, as the men were shy of singing loud, but it had a fine effect. They also sung a psalm very well. I have got the offer of a house at Windsor."

[LETTER 15].

"Dover, April 7th.

"I am out from 8 o'clock until dinner enjoying myself and fancying myself busy. We dine at $4\frac{1}{2}$ o'clock. This day the ladies

LORD CATHCART.   LADY CATHCART.

PHOTOGRAPHED FROM MINIATURES BY COSWAY.

Woodbury print, Waterlow & Sons, Limited.

of the reg^t dine with us, and it is now dinner time. But this early hour is very tiresome.

I am provoked the major's horse is lame; the whole regiment have been playing with it, like children with a toy, ever since it arrived. The serjeant-major has been 'lounging' it, and riding it with the soldiers; and now it has two evils, a sprain and a farrier."

[LETTER 16].

"Dover Castle, April 9, 1790.

"It rains and blows; yet I have been out with the regiment in a valley near, where I made experiments and marched the reg^t about for an hour or two. I mean to leave to-morrow, and, having sent on a fresh horse, to sleep at Sittingbourne. A pleasant incident happened this morning. Just as I was preparing to march off the parade with the regiment, I saw Mrs. Tinling, the lady lately married to an officer of the regiment, arrive breathless, and almost blown away by the wind. I went up to her and recommended her to take a more sheltered situation. She said she was not come from curiosity, but that she had just received accounts that a brother of her husband's, whom they had supposed to have been killed in a duel abroad, and for whom they had been some time in mourning, was alive and safe. Her husband and their servant being under arms, she could not resist running up the hill herself with the news. I immediately sent the lieutenant to her, and it produced an interesting scene of emotion."

On the 31st of May, Major-General Scott reviewed the regiment at Dover, and reported that the officers were dressed conformable to regulations, with exception of feathers in their hats.

The Spaniards having this year sent an armed force to dispossess the British traders and settlers of their possessions on the N.W. coast

1790 of North America, demands were sent to the Court of Spain for the restitution of these places, and a powerful fleet, under the command of Lord Howe, was ordered to be equipped, and to rendezvous at Spithead, in case the demands should be refused. With the view of doing duty as marines on board this fleet, in June the regiment marched from Dover, for Portsmouth, where, on arrival, detachments were embarked on board the following ships:—

23rd July—on H.M.S. "Egmont," 74 guns; 4 serjeants, 2 drummers, 94 rank and file, from the Colonel's, Lieut.-Colonel's, and Grenadier company. The officers were Captain Hugh Dickson, Lieut. Alexander Saunders, Ensign Daniel White. On the 21st of September, Lieut. Saunders was ordered to rejoin the head quarters of the regiment, and Lieut. Sir John Wrottesley, Bt. (afterwards 1st Baron Wrottesley) to relieve him. On the 15th of November the detachment was transferred to the "Royal William," from which it was soon afterwards discharged.

24th July—H.M.S. "Courageux," 74 guns; Captain John Mallory, Lieut. Stuart Douglas, Ensign James Allen; 3 serjeants, 2 drummers, 84 rank and file. These, on the 16th November, were turned over to the "Alfred," and landed, by order, at Chatham on the 24th inst.

29th July—H.M.S. "Gibraltar," 80 guns; Major Wm. Monsell, Lieut. John Riky, Ensign Patrick Ewing; 4 serjeants, 2 drummers, 92 rank and file. These were discharged to the "London" on the 16th of October; thence, on the 16th of November, to the "Bellerophon," and shortly afterwards landed.

July—H.M.S. "Charlotte," 100 guns (Lord Howe's ship); by the Monthly Returns dated the 1st of November, a detachment of 1 serjeant, 9 rank & file, were still serving on board the admiral's ship. Colonel Enys wrote that "the band which served on Lord Howe's ship received 10 guineas from the admiral when they went ashore."

23rd October—H.M.S. "Duke," 98 guns; Ensign Joseph Clavey;

1 serjeant, 43 rank & file.   These were discharged at Chatham on the **1790** 16th of November.

October—H.M.S. "Captain," 74 guns; Monthly Returns, dated the 1st of November, show Ensign Wm. Hosea as being on board this ship.

In consequence of a Convention signed at the Escurial on the 28th of October, the armaments were discontinued; several ships of war ordered to be paid off; and the detachments of the regiment rejoined their head quarters, which had returned to Dover Castle. In December, Lord Cathcart presented the drum-major with a large silver-headed bâton.

It having been intimated that the regiment was to take the Windsor duty on the 15th of February, 1791, every effort was made that time allowed to improve both its discipline and appointments after its service on board the fleet.

[LETTER 17]. **1791**

Writing from Dover Castle on the 18th of January, 1791, to Lady Cathcart, Lord Cathcart says:—

"At 6 this mor^{ng} it was a stark calm, but at 7 there came a sudden squall, with hail, and it has blown hard ever since. Our parade (Queen's Birthday) was much disturbed by it, and the wind perversely attacked the very place I had yesterday pitched upon. However, I marched to it in great pomp, and was very much pleased with the appearance of the men and their numbers. We took up a line according to the exact Prussian principle, w^h line required no correction; and as soon as the Castle had fired all the great guns they could fire, we fired three volleys; the first, and last, as good as I ever heard, the other not much amiss. But the wind blew so hard, I have roared myself as hoarse as a bullfrog! We marched back and formed a line better than the first, and the whole was over in less than an hour."

1791   On arrival at Windsor, the regiment relieved a party of the Guards on the King's duty. It was no doubt a great honour to be so employed; but as 4 companies were detached to Salthill, Datchet, Slough, and Clewer-cum-Chalvey, 1 company to Maidenhead and Maidenhead Bridge, the remaining 5 companies at Windsor, 'being on guard every third day,' found the duty very hard.

On the 27th of May, Major-General Hyde reviewed the regiment at Windsor, and in his report made the following remarks:—

Officers.—Dressed with great uniformity, extremely attentive, and expert at their duty.

Drummers and Fifers.—The drummers, black, beat and play well.

Men.—A fine corps of young men, in general tall, upright, and well dressed.

Clothing.—The Grenadier and Light Infantry caps have useful flaps to shade the eyes, and are at the same time ornamental. These, as well as the hats, are of a better size to fit the head than some regiments at present; but as they are still so small as to make it necessary to tie them on, they are, in my opinion, smaller than the covering for a soldier's head should be, for use and convenience.

The regiment wear worsted tufts, in imitation of feathers, but they were given by the colonel.

	COUNTRY.			
	English.	Scotch.	Irish.	Foreign.
Officers	18	4	6	
Staff, do.	5			
Men	318	50	35	23

Size from 5 ft. 6 and under to 6 ft. 2 and upwards.			
	Men.		Men.
6 feet 2 inches	4	5 feet 9½ inches	27
6 ,, 1½ ,,	3	5 ,, 9 ,,	39
6 ,, 1 ,,	3	5 ,, 8½ ,,	47
6 ,, 0½ ,,	2	5 ,, 8 ,,	45
6 feet	4	5 ,, 7½ ,,	57
5 ,, 11½ ,,	11	5 ,, 7 ,,	51
5 ,, 11 ,,	14	5 ,, 6½ ,,	43
5 ,, 10½ ,,	12	5 ,, 6 ,,	34
5 ,, 10 ,,	30	Under 5ft. 6 ,,	20

Age from 18 Years & under to 55 Years & upwards. **1791**

	Men.
55 years	
50 ,,	1
45 ,,	7
40 ,,	12
35 ,,	22
30 ,,	44
25 ,,	124
20 ,,	169
18 and under	47

At this period it was the custom to employ the troops on Windsor duty in making roads or some other work about the park, with the intention of benefitting the soldiers, whose pay was certainly very small; and we find that towards the end of June, 200 strong spades, 50 large stout pickaxes, 50 stout mattocks, 50 large strong shovels, 50 strong iron wire sieves, and 100 wheelbarrows were issued to the regiment, which was to be employed during the summer on the rides in Windsor Forest. Early in July, the regiment encamped just outside the Great Park, on Egham Wick Common, and was employed in an attempt to turn the turnpike road near the tower at Virginia Water; but for some reason this plan was given up, and the road remained in an unfinished state for many years.

[Letter 18].

"Camp at Egham Wick, July 7, 1791.

" I was out before 5 yesterday morning, and did not return to dress till past 10, having breakfasted near the work. My toilet was interrupted by reg^{tl} business, and I was in my shirt when a serjeant

1791 came running into my tent to tell me the King was approaching the camp on horseback. I immediately put on my coat and sword and went to receive him about an hundred yards from my lines.

His Majesty began by rallying me about my fall, and then was pleased to dismount and minutely to visit every part of the camp—beginning with the men's kitchens, and doing me the honour to go into my tent, which the servants had the attention to have cleared out and put into order. After viewing the rear of the camp, mess tent, &c., His Majesty came upon the parade, where he was received by the major, the officers of the day, and 2 ensigns, who touched the colours which were displayed. The King then examined the new tents, and after walking some time with Colonel Campbell and me, got on horseback, when I conducted him to see the work, which already makes considerable figure, and afterwards, when I took my leave, I was commanded to ride with the King to see the ridings about Virginia Water, which are beautiful and well kept, and in short I was carried to a place near Windsor, where I was most graciously dismissed. In the evening I presented myself on the Terrace, and returned to camp extremely ready for my bed."

Having been employed on duty in the forest till the 16th of October, the camp was broken up, and five companies returned to King's duty at Windsor, whilst the remainder re-occupied their former detachments.

During the winter Princess Augusta presented the regiment with the music of a March* of her own composing, which received the name

---

* Note from Lord Cathcart, June 8, 1885: "This fact is quite familiar to me—the March, and the Princess Augusta, and I am pretty sure I have, or have seen, a note from the Princess to Lord C. on the subject. I have often heard the March mentioned in conversation; my impression is that Lord C., who was a musician himself, and well instructed, got the air somewhere abroad, and that the Princess arranged the music; or the Princess may, at his suggestion, have altered and improved the original. Curious Captain Everard should have heard a Russian origin attributed. Lord C., his brothers, and sisters, were all brought up at St. Petersburg in the time of the Empress Catherine."

of "The Royal Windsor March." In 1881 it became by authority the *Quick Step* of the four battalions of the Worcestershire Regiment.

1791

On the 10th of December, an order was issued that the effective field officers of all regiments should in future be distinguished by wearing an epaulette on each shoulder. The officers of the flank companies, who already wore two epaulettes, were to have the addition of a grenade, or bugle-horn, embroidered on each.

The men were this year supplied, by their colonels, with black stocks, instead of rollers or neckcloths; also with cockades, as being equally with their hats, a part of the soldiers' clothing.

On the 24th of March, 1792, 1 serjeant and 12 privates were ordered to Kensington, and on the 29th inst. were brought before the King, Their Royal Highnesses the Prince of Wales, the Dukes of York, and Gloucester, and Sir Wm. Fawcett, at the Queen's Riding House, Pimlico, where they went through the new manual exercise which had been brought forward by their two commanding officers, the Earl of Harrington and Lord Cathcart. The King, Prince, and all the officers present seemed highly pleased with this plan of shortening the drill.

1792

On the 4th of April, serjeants of infantry regiments were ordered to be supplied with, and make use of, pikes, instead of halberds, which were to be laid aside.

On the 8th of May, officers of Grenadier, Light Infantry companies, and Fusilier regiments were ordered to make use of their swords, instead of fusils, and the serjeants of Grenadiers, and Fusiliers to carry pikes, but the Light Infantry serjeants were to keep their fusils.

Major-General D. Dundas had in 1788 compiled a set of movements and manœuvres, principally from the writings of Prussian tacticians, but it was not until the 1st of June, 1792, that His Majesty, thinking it highly expedient and necessary that a uniform system of field exercise, &c., be adopted, was pleased to direct that the Rules and

1792 Regulations for the Formations, Field Exercise, and Movements of H.M. Forces approved of by him, and published that day, be implicitly complied with. Previous to this there had never been any general system of discipline; on the contrary, a few review regulations excepted, every commander-in-chief, or officer commanding a corps, adopted or invented such manœuvres as were thought proper.

Early in June, the Maidenhead detachment was withdrawn, and on the 11th, Major-General Ainslie reviewed the regiment at Windsor.

On the 2nd of July, 1 serjeant, 1 corporal, and 11 privates were detached to Oakingham.

H.M. Queen Charlotte to Lady Cathcart.

"My dear Lady Cathcart,

I know you can do much with Ld Cathcart, pray use all the influence you have to obtain a Holiday for your two Etonians to-morrow, that I may have the pleasure compleat in seeing the 29th. I hope for a fine day, and still more to hear that you are better w^h will give every pleasure to

Your affectionate friend,

Charlotte."

"The 16 July, 1792."

On the 23rd July, the regiment joined the Camp of Exercise, formed about eight miles from Windsor, at a place called Cæsar's Camp, or Wickham Bushes. There were assembled here 2 battalions of Royal Artillery, the 10th and 11th Light Dragoons, the 2nd, 3rd, 4th, and 29th Regiments of Foot, the whole under command of the Duke of Richmond, with Sir Wm. Howe as second in command.

After practicing the new system of drill, arrangements were made for a sham fight and an attack on a wooden redoubt constructed for the occasion. After a continued series of field days and reviews, the grand review before His Majesty took place on the 6th of August. The day was remarkably fine, the concourse of people prodigious, and, as usual on such occasions, the troops did less than on any other day; **1792** they were, however, under arms, and the band played the greater part of the day for the amusement of the spectators.

The sutlers had a plentiful harvest, for "Wade" relates that for a single mutton chop, a cucumber, and a pint of bad wine they charged 18s.; and 5s. for tea or coffee, with two thin slices of bread and butter.

On the 8th, the camp broke up, and the troops returned to their respective quarters, with the exception of the 29th Foot, which encamped close to the park, at Bishop's gate, and was again employed on the rides, till the 22nd of October.

On the 5th of December, Lieut.-Colonel Lord Cathcart was appointed colonel of the regiment, *vice* Lord Harrington, transferred to the command of the First Regiment of Life Guards, and Lieut.-Col. Archibald Campbell, who a short time previously had been promoted into the 21st Foot, was transferred to the lieut.-colonelcy of his old regiment.

STANDING ORDERS OF THE 29TH REGIMENT OF FOOT, CONCERNING THE DRESS AND APPEARANCE OF THE OFFICERS, &C.
WEYMOUTH, 24 OCTOBER, 1797.†

A Copy of the Standing Orders of the Regiment is to be made out for every Officer.

Hair.—The hair to be dressed with one curl on each side; the toupee turned up, and not too long; the club to be tyed high, and to be more spread at the top than at the bottom.

The rosette to be of ribband, and not more than three inches in diameter; the ribband and rosette to be perfectly black, and put on after powdering.

---

† These MS. Regulations appear to have been in force previous to this date, as the attention of officers is, in several places, called to alterations made in 1793—96, &c. These Standing Orders, together with those published in 1812 and 1863, besides several chacos, and badges of the regiment, I have since presented to the Royal U.S. Institution, Whitehall.—H. EVERARD.

1792   The Grenadier and Light Infantry officers to have their hair dressed the same as the men, excepting their side locks, which may come down so as to cover the open part of the ear, but never lower, and must be frizzed so as not to blow about.

Hats.—The hats, and caps of all sorts, to be worn very high behind, and the exact centre of the front close upon the nose before, the left-hand corner of the hats a good deal raised, and the right-hand low; the Battalion officers at all times to wear their laced regimental hats, which are expected to be cocked exactly according to the regimental pattern.

The Grenadiers to wear plain hats, with a small grenade button and black loop, a silver cord round the bottom of the crown, and roses at the corners the same as the officers of the battalion; the button and loop to be worn forward, and no part of the loop to be concealed by the cockade; the button to be at equal distance from the lace, and the bottom of the hat.

The feathers to be white, and exactly nine inches above the brim of the hats; they are to be very small, and equal in circumference at the top and bottom, and must be fixed so as to be perfectly upright and steady.

Stocks.—The stocks to be made of black silk, plaited and stiff, without any appearance of the shirt above them.

Coats.—The officers to have standing collars, the same as the men; one button on the collar and nine on each lappel; the buttons to be put on very distinctly two and two, beginning from the top, including the one on the collar; the lappels to reach as low as the top of the hip bone, to have one hook and eye at the second button-hole from the top, and another in the middle of the space between the fourth and fifth button; the first of these to be hooked through the frill; the breadth of the lappels and cuffs, must be exactly according to the King's regulations; the yellow cloth must be of a pale lemon colour originally, and must be kept bright and clean, by using English pink; the pocket **1792** must be in the inside of the coat, the flaps on the outside to be sewn down, and to have an edging of white cloth round them and round the skirts; the skirts to be fastened back at the corners, and to have one button, with two hearts,* which are to be laced with a braid the same as that which confines the epaulette; the skirts are never to be let down. The length of the coat to be such that if an officer was to kneel down, the skirts of his coat should be exactly three inches from the ground.

N.B.—This order is not meant to countermand the exceptions made for the flank companies.

Epaulettes.—The epaulettes are to pass under a silver band, which is to be put upon yellow cloth and sewed to the coat, and buttoned to a button which is to be put on close to the collar, and very near, but rather behind, the seam on the shoulder; the braid is to be sewed on so tight as to confine the epaulette and keep it perfectly steady; the pad of the epaulette must come up close to the braid, and it must often be new stuffed to prevent it from getting lower. When the epaulette is fixed, the centre of that part to which the bullions are fastened must be half an inch to the rear of the highest part of the shoulder.

The length of the strap of the epaulette down the middle, where it is longest, five inches; width in the broadest part above the fringe, two inches; breadth at the lower part of the button hole, one inch and three-quarters. The epaulette to be sewed on yellow cloth and very stiff.

Waist Coats.—To have a flap to the pockets and four buttons under.

Breeches.—To be white cloth or casimir, and not to come lower than the upper part of the calf of the leg; they must buckle at the knee.

---

* With these "skirt ornaments" the hearts were generally made of red cloth, the button being sewn on where the narrow points of the hearts met.

1792 White leather breeches, with regimental buttons, may be worn with boots, but not till they have been made perfectly white.

Gaiters.—Gaiters must be constantly worn with the sash and gorget, except by the mounted officers; they are to come up before, fully to the point of the knee, and close into the hollow of the joint behind; allowances must be made for their shrinking, and they are to be fixed by a button behind, the same as the men's; the shoe buckles, if any, must not be seen.

Boots.—Boots, and steel spurs, to be constantly worn by the field officers and adjutant; boots may also be worn by the other officers at common parades and when not on duty; they must be uniform, and come up fully to the cap of the knee.

Gorgets.—To be worn as high as possible; the loops and roses to be of crimson ribband, and to be renewed whenever they lose their colour.

Sashes.—To be of sufficient length to go twice round the body and tye before; they are to have taggs at each end; the knott is to be over the left pocket of the waist coat, and the ends to be drawn through, under the sash, so that the taggs may hang over the knott and cover it, so as to hang down nine inches from the top to the end of the taggs.

Great Coat.—Great coat to be blue, with a single row of regimental buttons in front; white lining and edges; square pockets, with four buttons, under the sleeve; not to be made too long, and to have buttons and braids for the epaulettes.

Shoes.—In the evening, and when there is no parade of any kind, officers who are engaged to balls, or parties with ladies, may wear shoes with silver buckles, but never with shoe strings. Officers are never to be seen on the parade of their own, or any other corps, in regimentals, without boots or gaiters.

Swords.—Regimental swords, only, to be worn with regimentals; they are always to be carried in the belt, and never in the scabbard.

1792 Officers are particularly requested to accustom themselves always to wear their swords when in regimentals,† except in their own rooms ; and the sword must never be worn without a sword knott, the oldest rag of a sword knott being better than none.

Regimentals to be always worn at Quarters.—No officer must appear at head quarters, or any quarters of the regiment where there is an officer's command, even though he may be on leave of absence, or belonging to a different quarter, or upon the recruiting, or any other detached service, otherwise than in regimentals.

Exceptions.—The only exceptions which can be made to this Order are as follows :—

The day officers arrive at quarters ; the day officers are going from quarters ; when officers are going to ride, or walk above a mile from quarters, or when going out of quarters for the purpose of any sport or amusement ; but on all these occasions they are to observe that they are to shew themselves as little as possible in quarters.

Absent Officers.—Officers are never to wear their regimental coat, either with the regiment or when absent from it, without being regimentally dressed in every respect ; and officers will oblige the colonel if they will pay as much attention to the uniformity of their dress in regimentals when absent from the regiment, even when in foreign countries, as they do at head quarters. The staff officers, except the chaplain, will conform to these regulations as far as their particular uniform will allow.

Horses.—His Majesty having been pleased, by a late regulation, to order the field officers and adjutant of regiments, to do their duty in the field, and on some other occasions, mounted, those officers will in future have their horses brought to the parade, regimentally appointed, every time the regiment is under arms.

---

† The sobriquet, "Eversworded," probably originated from this order.—*Vide Extracts from Diary kept by Lieut. H. Grove, 1797.*

1792   *Leave of Absence.*—A book will be kept in the orderly room in which the dates of officers' leave of absence are to be entered.

No officer is to absent himself a night from quarters till he has made a memorandum of his leave of absence; and when officers obtain permission to exchange duties, or to take duty for each other, a memorandum must be made or affixed to this book, signed by both officers, before any notice can be taken of it by the adjutant. No memorandum of leave or exchange of duty to be made without the knowledge of the commanding officer.

Words of Command.—Words of command to be given *strong* and *smart*, but more particularly *sharp* in the latter part; and to whatever number of men addressed, should be given loud, to the full extent of the voice. Words of command given in a careless manner, will always produce motions equally so.

Mess Regulations were also drawn up this year [*v.* 1835].

1793   Early in January, 1793, orders were received for the regiment to go to Ireland, and on the 17th inst. it marched in 2 divisions, viz., 5 companies to Petersfield, and 5 to Alton, Chewton, and Farringdon, where, on arrival, instructions were received for the detachments to halt.

STANDING REGIMENTAL ORDERS.

"Petersfield, Jan^{ry} 22nd, 1793.

"To prevent misconceptions of the King's order, or of regimental orders concerning mounted officers, it is thought necessary to define what is expected as to the appearance of those officers when on duty. Unless when these orders are expressly dispensed with, mounted officers, viz., the field officers and adjutant, are expected to be provided with horses fit for the duty required of them; they are by no means expected to purchase high-priced, or tall and showy horses; hardy, stout little horses, under 15 hands, and not less than 14 hands high, are, on the contrary, quite sufficient. But, although figure and action, are not insisted upon, it is presumed that field officers will not, for their own sakes, or the credit of the corps they belong to, think of appearing under arms, on horses that bear evident marks of being draft horses, or are otherwise deform'd so as to be unfit to be rode by gentlemen. The horse appointments consist of, a pair of pistols, a regimental bridle with nose band, a black bredoon, and a white bredoon, a saddle, regimental stirrup irons, crupper, half cover with holsters, and black bearskin flounce; a regimental saddle cloth. The saddle cloth is only to be worn when the colours are carried, and the white bredoon at reviews, or field days in review order: on other occasions the bridle, holster, and crupper are to be worn. The bridle is always to have a noseband, which is not to be buckled over the headstall of the bredoon; the front is to be covered with yellow ribband, and to have a yellow rosette at each end of the same size as the hair rosettes (not more than three inches in diameter). The end of the ribband is not to be seen.

On a march, or without white bredoons, the front may be covered with facing cloth, and kept clean with English pink.

The furniture, with black bredoons, to be worn when on duty or grand parades.

[LETTER 19].

"Petersfield, Jan 23, 1793.

"I am interrupted by General Dundas, who has drank tea with me on his way to take the command at Guernsey and Jersey.

I am very unlucky in getting recruits, and two of my recruiting officers have independent companies of their own; and I am so weak in officers that I cannot at present replace them. I have not lost a man since Windsor, nor had reason to find fault with a man; nor has there been a fault in the other division. I have been out with five companies here, and Campbell with the others, to fire ball, in which we succeeded tolerably considering the badness of the flint. I fired divisions,

1793 and volleys three deep with ball, which they did full as well and regularly as with bran and powder cartridges. I go to-morrow to Alton to see the 5 companies there. The miserable difference of the English and Irish Establishment ensures the 29th going Cork."

The destination of the regiment was, however, altered, orders being received for it to march to Hilsea Barracks, and subsequently to act as Marines, on board the fleet then fitting out at Portsmouth. In consequence of these latter orders, detachments were embarked, but as the services afloat of some of these extended over four years, they will be dealt with separately.

On the 4th of February, each company of the regiment was directed to be augmented by 1 serjeant, 1 drummer, and 17 private men.

[LETTER 20].

"Hilsea Barracks, Feb^{ry} 6, 1793.

"Our serjeants teach those of the Militia in the morning and evening, and there are now above 20 squads of Militia learning to march, under my window, exactly in our time and upon our principle, with 'my pendulum' swinging in the middle of the parade. The Lieut.-Governor and the officers of the Suffolk Militia dine at our mess to-day. I have put the militia captains on duty with ours; they are exceedingly correct, and anxious to be so. I have a strong party in the Isle of Wight, all Grenadiers in caps, with drum and fife, w^h has taken the lead of all the partys, and are very popular. We have got one very fine recruit there, and sent him back dressed out, and covered with ribbands."

[LETTER 21].

"Hilsea Barracks, Tuesday, Feb 12, 1793.

"I have been disappointed of seeing Capt. Kirkman, which is essential. He commands on the other side of the harbour where he has much to do in guarding the roads by which those seamen who would attempt to escape the 'Press' must fly. To-morrow Cap^{tn} Marton is to embark with Clavey and Egerton, the Light Comp^y, Enys', and Farquhar's (late St. Clair's), in all 70 men. I shall see them embark, and try to be with you by noon.

Do not think me idle. Since last Friday night I have equipped my regiment in trousers, check shirts, and blue jackets lined with flannel, and with yellow capes* and shoulder straps, by which they will look like soldiers even when mixed with tar and oakum; and when they are called upon to take up their arms, they will have their regimentals fit to appear as becomes H.M. infantry. The eagerness to punish the French is the first consideration, and nothing can equal the sobriety and good behaviour of the men."

REGIMENTAL ORDERS.
"7 July, 1793.

"During the present campaign, and until further orders, the side curls required by the Standing Order concerning officers' dress, are dispensed with. The officers of the regiment, them belonging to the flank companies included, are to wear their hair short, both upon the toupee and at the sides, so that the hair, when undressed, should not come lower than to cover half the ear, and no hair to be on the cheek lower than the point of the ear.

"The Colonel takes this opportunity of repeating the directions formerly given to officers absent from head quarters, or commanding detachments, that they will on all occasions maintain that uniformity of appearance by which the 29th Regiment has been so much distinguished."

The King having been pleased to appoint Lord Cathcart, Brigadier-General with local rank, to serve with the Earl of Moira, Lord Cathcart on the 23rd of November, applied for Capt. Jas. Kirkman to act as his

---

* Collars which were made to turn down.

1793 Major of Brigade with the army serving in Germany, and the following day handed over the command of the regiment to Lieut.-Colonel Campbell.

In November, another plan for recruiting the army was made by offering to such regiments, as could raise a certain number of men in a given time, an additional lieut.-colonel, and major; the promotion to go in the regiment; each officer benefitted thereby to pay a certain sum towards the recruiting service. This proposal was cheerfully embraced by the regiment, and the band was sent to Birmingham, Manchester, and Nottingham with such success that the required numbers were obtained, and Major Hugh Dickson promoted to the junior lieut.-colonelcy, whilst Captain John Enys obtained the majority, on the 1st of March following.

On the 1st of December, 17 serjeants, 10 drummers, and 576 rank and file, in addition to officers, were serving on board the fleet.

1794 Early the following year, Lieut.-Colonel Campbell, who had remained in command of the part of the regiment ashore, moved out of Hilsea Barracks to make room for the Irish volunteers, and his men were billeted in the neighbouring villages. On the 12th of June, the staff of the regiment, with all the recruits, having assembled at Hilsea Barracks, embarked for Plymouth, where, on the 4th of August, they moved into the Dock Barracks.

Extracts from Letters* of Lieut.-Colonel Campbell to Lord Cathcart.

"Plymouth Dock, 20 Sept., 1794.

"My Lord,

* * * Would it be practicable to exchange an equal number of our Draughts, for the Detachments of our Our Old, and best men, serving on board the "Alfred" and "Minotaur," the first is now in Torbay, and the latter in the Sound of this Harbour. I heartily

---

* The original letters are in possession of Lord Cathcart.

wish your Lordship would exert your Interest with the *Mighty Lords of the Main* to bring a measure to bear, which must tend so much to the good of the King's Service and the credit of the Regiment.

Shall we carry with us the Grenadier caps, and shall they be the Brass front or those of Order? The Brass Drums I think had best be left in Store."

"Plymouth Dock, 28 Sept., 1794.

"My Lord,

By yesterday's post I had the Honor of receiving your Lordship's letter of 24th, by which I find the destination of this part of the Regiment is still a secret; we have received no Orders here since my last, except that the Draughts are to have a Guinea and a half allowed to each man, for the purpose of putting them on necessaries. Your Lordship may assure yourself, that there is nothing I shall at all times have more at heart, than the appearance, and Discipline of the 29th Regiment, and that what I mentioned in my last, respecting the *Band* was in consequence of the information given here, that every part of the pageantry of Parade was discountenanced by the Duke, and in consequence of which the Band of the 25th Regiment were disposed of the manner formerly mentioned (put on board the Marlboro'), much to the Dissatisfaction of Lord George Lennox, but more particularly to Lady Louisa, whose chief amusement they were. I shall beg leave to assure your Lordship that no change of plan shall make a change in any part of the present Dress of the Regiment, which I think must suffer by any alteration."

"Plymouth Dock, 23 October, 1794.

"Here we still remain in the same state of uncertainty as when I last wrote to your Lordship, except that the last letter from the Adjutant-General expressly says, we are intended for the Continent. We received two days ago a hundred and thirty-three Draughts, from the 91st Regiment now at Plymouth, which will still leave a deficiency

1794 of 45 men to compleat this part of the Regiment to the numbers ordered of 600 Rank and File. I have not heard a syllable upon the subject of the Exchange of Officers and men your Lordship flattered me with a prospect of in your last, and cannot help looking toward the "Glory," "Robust," and "Minotaur," now here; the two former, together with five more Sail of the Line, are a Detached Squadron from the Grand Fleet, under the orders of Sir Thos. Rich, sent to take in a large supply of Stores, Provisions, &c., at this place, and to sail to-morrow, 'tis Conjectured, for the West Indies. We have a Captain Fitzherbert, from the Independents, attached to the 29th. There has been nothing as yet said respecting the person from the Life Guards of whom your Lordship formerly spoke.

Your Lordship's
Most obi^{dt}
Most Humble Ser^{vt}
A. CAMPBELL."

On the 28th of December, Lieut.-Colonel Campbell embarked with all the effectives, their destination, however, being kept a secret. Major Enys was left ashore in charge of the sick, viz., 2 serjeants and 75 rank and file, with orders to collect the detachments then serving on the fleet, whenever they might be landed.

On the 31st, Mr. Joseph Skinner, surgeon 29th Foot, died at Plymouth; he had been a faithful American Loyalist, and, contrary to the sentiments of his mother and relatives, had joined the King's army at Bunker's Hill in 1775, and afterwards Lord Cornwallis, by which he forfeited for ever the affection of his family.

CHAPTER VII.

ET us now trace the detachments of the regiment, which, on **1793** reaching Hilsea Barracks towards the end of January, 1793, embarked on board the following ships :—

H.M. Frigate "Regulus," 44 guns; 11th of February. Captain Alexr. Saunders, Lieut. Wm. Jaques; 2 serjeants, 1 drummer, 42 rank and file. These, on the 14th, were turned over to

H.M.S. "Leopard," 50 guns; and, on the 8th of March, to

H.M.S. "Brunswick," 74 guns. On the 22nd, twenty-two privates were lent to H.M.S. "Boyne," 98 guns, which sailed with Rear-Admiral Gell from Spithead on the 2nd of April. When off Corvo (Azores), on the 10th of May, it is stated in this ship's log that Private Thos. Robson,* 29th Regiment, was punished with one dozen. This detachment rejoined the "Brunswick" on the 7th of June following.

---

* Mr. Chas. Dalton, writing on the 3rd of February 1883, said " I send you a notice of a 29th man who possessed both a naval, and military medal. These two medals were bought by me in 1866, in Durham, for a few shillings, and sold in 1878, for over 10 guineas to Mackenzie of Seaforth, who valued them exceedingly, and obtained from the War Office a description of Thos. Robson, 29th Foot. I believe the two medals are now in the collection of Captain Eaton, late Grenadier Guards, who bought Seaforth's collection. The medal for the Peninsular War, was issued in 1849 to the survivors of certain general actions.—Medal with 4 clasps "Albuhera," "Talavera," "Vimiera," "Roleia," (Thos. Robson, 29th Foot).

Naval War Medal, issued 1849, to the survivors of certain general actions between 1793 and 1841, medal with one clasp " 1st June, 1794 " Thos. Robson, &c., &c.

On the 17th, Ensign Harcourt Vernon, 1 serjeant, 35 rank and file, were taken on the muster rolls of the "Brunswick," which sailed, under Lord Howe on the 14th of July, to cruise at the mouth of the Channel, and was with him when, on the 18th of November, he fell in with a French squadron.

On the 15th of December, Lieut. Jaques was transferred to H.M.S. "Glory."

In March, 1794, the "Brunswick" was cruising, under Rear-Admiral Bowyer, in the Channel, and Soundings. On the 2nd of May, she sailed from St. Helens under Lord Howe, and formed part of the centre squadron on the glorious 1st of June.

Extracts from Log of H.M.S. "Brunswick."

1st June. "At 10 past 10, fired into and raked our intended opponent; at 15 past 10, fell on board another ship of the French line, and engaged her side by side about four hours. At ½ past 11, Captain Hervey received a wound; continued the engagement, though much disabled in our hull, guns, and rigging: shipping great quantities of water into our lower deck ports, 10 of them being knocked off, and all our anchors on the starboard side. Enemy alongside."

13th June. Moored at Spithead.

6th July. Returned sails and guns to gunwharf, and rigging to dockyard.

14th July. Carrying ship's company to the "Robust."

H.M.S. "ROBUST," 74 guns. On the 20th of August, Lieut. James Monsell was transferred to this ship from the "Ramillies." On the 3rd of September, the "Robust" sailed from St. Helens, and continued to cruise during the winter under Lord Howe; the detachment on board her consisting of 2 subalterns, 2 serjeants, 1 drummer, 83 rank and file.

In February, 1795, she formed part of the fleet which sailed to escort the East and West India convoys, to clear the Channel, and which afterwards cruised off Brest and in the Bay. In May she returned to Spithead, and on the 12th, landed the detachment of the Regiment at Portsmouth.

H.M.S. "EDGAR," 74 guns. 13th February, 1793. Captain Geo. Richd. Marton, Lieut. Joseph Clavey, Ensign Chas. Bulkeley Egerton; 2 serjeants, 1 drummer, 76 rank and file. This ship sailed from Spithead with Rear-Admiral Gell in April, and on the 15th, the "Edgar" and the "Phaëton" fell in with and captured the French privateer "Dumourier," and the "St. Jago," a Spanish register ship from Lima (the latter had recently been captured by the French privateer after an engagement of five hours). The following day, the "Edgar" was ordered to sail with the "St. Jago" in tow, and the "Dumourier" in company, for Spithead, where they arrived on the 28th.

In *Lloyd's Evening Post* is a correct account of the cargo of the re-captured Spanish register ship. It mentions that "This cargo has been two years in collecting from different parts of the coast, and is without exception the richest that was trusted on board any single ship. It is impossible to form a just estimate of its value, but it is certainly not over-rated when it is stated at £1,300,000."

Colonel Enys wrote: "Captain Marton received as his share of this prize £2,000; Lieut. Clavey and Ensign Egerton £1,200 each; the serjeants £300, and privates £60 each."

On the 14th of July, the "Edgar" joined Lord Howe, and continued to cruise during the winter, as did the "Brunswick" (q.v). In February, 1794, she moored at Chatham, when 1 lieut., and 30 seamen, with 1 serjeant, and 13 privates of the 29th, were sent to the "Thunderer" to assist in fitting her for sea; and, on the 25th, the "Edgar" paid off, and turned over her crew to

H.M.S. "THUNDERER," 74 guns. On the 9th of March, Captain Marton was discharged. This ship formed part of the fleet that sailed on the 2nd of May, from St. Helens under Lord Howe, and was present on the 1st June, but in the rear squadron.

On the 19th of June, Captain Clavey (from head quarters, Portsmouth), was entered on the muster rolls of this ship.

On the 23rd of June, received from La Juste, a prize belonging to H.M.S. "Alfred," Lieut. John Tucker, 1 sergt., 25 rank and file of 29th Foot; these were discharged on the 30th to the "Latona," who returned them on the 4th of July to the "Alfred."

On the 3rd of September, the "Thunderer" sailed from St. Helens, and continued to cruise under Lord Howe during the winter. In March, 1795, she was cruising in the North Sea, under Rear-Admiral Henry Harvey; and, on the 20th of May, Captain Clavey, Lieut. Egerton, &c., were discharged, with orders to forthwith join their regiment.

H.M.S. "DUKE," 98 guns. 18th February, 1793. Captain James Kirkman, Lieut. D. White, Ensign W. S. Bertrand; 4 serjeants, 2 drummers, 94 rank and file.

Deputies from the Islands of Martinico and Guadaloupe, having arrived in London to solicit the protection of the British Government against the French, the "Duke" formed part of a fleet which sailed from Spithead on the 24th of March, under Rear-Admiral Gardner, for the West Indies. On the 10th of May she anchored in Carlisle Bay, Barbadoes, and on the 24th was standing off, and occasionally close to, the shore of Martinico, between Case Navire and Case Pilote.

Admiral Gardner, and Major-General Bruce "commander-in-chief of H.M. forces in the West Indies," being encouraged by the disputes which existed between the Royalists and Republicans in that island, and invited by the former to join in an attack on the town of St. Pierre, on the 14th of June the 21st Regiment was ordered to land at Case Navire, and there take post, so as to enable the officer who commanded the Royalists to collect his forces in that neighbourhood. On the 16th, additional forces were disembarked ; these joined the 21st and the Royalists at a very strong position within about five miles of St. Pierre.

Extracts from the "Duke's" Log.

17th June. "At 2 p.m., landed at Fond Capot 3 officers and 77 men belonging to the 29th Regiment serving as marines on board : at the same time the rest of the fleet are landing troops. At 4 p.m., in company with the "Hector," "Ephigenia," and "Ulysses," made sail to the northwards. Several shots and shell were fired at us from several batteries in the town of St. Pierre, and from one northward of it, but received no damage. At 5.40 was fired at by the battery on the Point a la Mer, which was soon silenced. Steered down towards the village of La Precheur, and received several shots from two batteries at that village, and at 7.20, having silenced them, left off firing. Weather cloudy and calm, with much lightning. At half-past ten a ball of lightning, with a tremendous clap of thunder, struck our main-top gallant masthead, and shivered the topgallant mast and topmast to small pieces, but luckily no person was hurt."

When, on the 18th instant, the troops were put in motion to attack St. Pierre, some alarm unfortunately took place amongst the Royalists, who by mistake fired on one another, and severely wounded their commander; nor would they submit to the control of any other officer, but returned to their former position. The British not being strong enough to deliver an attack by themselves, with any prospect of success, and not having become engaged, commenced the following day to re-embark.

The "Duke," having now rejoined the Admiral's fleet, took on board the detachment of the 29th; on the 21st she parted company with the fleet and anchored in Prince Rupert's Bay, Dominica. Sailing thence by Antigua and St. Kitts, she anchored at Spithead on the 2nd of October, and on the 7th of November the detachment was turned over to

H.M.S. "Glory," 98 guns. On the 18th instant, Captain Kirkman and Lieut. White were discharged by order, and the following day Ensign Patrick Henderson came on board from Plymouth. Lieut. Jaques, having been discharged from H.M.S. "Brunswick," was entered on the muster rolls of the "Glory" on the 17th of December. On the 1st of January, 1794, the detachment on board this ship consisted of 3 subalterns, 3 serjeants, 1 drummer, 90 rank and file. On the 5th of February, Lieut. Jaques was discharged, on obtaining his promotion.

In March the "Glory" was cruising under Rear-Admiral Bowyer in the Channel and Soundings. On the 21st of April, Lieut. Bertrand was discharged at Haslar. On the 2nd of May this ship sailed under Lord Howe from St. Helens, and formed part of the rear squadron on the 1st of June. Sailed again in September, under Lord Howe, and continued to cruise during the winter.

On the 12th of May, 1795, the detachment was discharged.

H.M.S. "ALFRED," 74 guns. 28th February, 1793; Ensign Barker Edmeston, 2 serjeants, 1 drummer, 32 rank and file.

In a decree of the French Convention of November, 1792, the Republic declared their intention of extending their assistance to the disaffected and revolted subjects of all monarchial governments. The British Ministry demanded a disavowal of this assertion, but it not being complied with, war was the result. Alliances were formed with Austria, Russia, Spain, Portugal, Holland, and Prussia, all of whom agreed to shut their ports against French vessels. The French army then invaded Holland, where it met with several repulses from the allies. Orders were now sent to Admiral Macbride to sail from the Downs with all the frigates and armed vessels that he could muster, to blockade the port of Ostend, and not to allow any of the French vessels there to escape. On the 19th of March Ensign Edmeston's detachment was transferred to

H.M. FRIGATE "FLORA," 36 guns; and on 1st April to

H.M. FRIGATE "REGULUS," 44 guns, which, on the 6th, was sent to Ostend.

LETTER FROM LORD CATHCART.*

"Albemarle Street, April 23, 1793.

"The promotion of Cap^{ts} Sir John Wrottesley and Dundas makes two vacancies. Lord Cathcart recommends the two eldest ensigns, Bertrand and Edmestone, for promotion. It is true they are both young, but they are both on actual service, and Ensign Edmestone had the singular good fortune and honour to relieve the Austrian garrison at Ostend, and to remain there for some time with a considerable detachment of the 14th and 29th Regiments under his command, and the detachment having been landed without subsistence, he subsisted them himself for several days."

---

* Memoranda Papers. Record Office, London.

On the 27th of April the detachment was transferred at Ostend to

H.M.S. "CUMBERLAND," 74 guns, which sailed, under Lord Howe, on the 14th July, and was with him when, in November, he fell in with a French squadron. On the 28th of June the detachment was augmented by Captain J. Mallory, Lieut. Augustus Colman, 43 rank and file; these two officers were discharged in December, but on the 1st of March, 1794, Lieutenant Edmeston, 1 serjeant, 1 drummer, 68 rank and file were transferred to

H.M.S. "MINOTAUR, 74 guns. Lieut. Edmeston having received his promotion, was discharged on the 21st of May, and the following day Ensign Wm. Seymour was taken on this ship's muster rolls. On the arrival of the intelligence of Lord Howe's victory, the "Minotaur," which was cruising between the Lizard and Portland, was ordered to reinforce Rear-Admiral Montagu's squadron, after which she cruised in the Bay under Rear-Admiral Cornwallis.

In February, 1795, she formed part of the fleet which sailed under Lord Howe to escort the East and West India and other convoys, after which she cruised off Brest and in the Bay.

In May, formed part of Rear-Admiral Waldegrave's squadron cruising to the westward.

In July, cruising in the Soundings, under Vice-Admiral Colpoys. On the 15th of August the detachment was discharged.

H.M.S. "STATELY," 64 guns. 31st May, 1793. Captain Edwd. E. Coleman, Ensigns Montagu Burrows, Wm. Edgell Wyatt, 2 serjeants, 1 drummer, 52 rank and file. This ship formed part of the squadron stationed at Newfoundland under command of Vice-Admiral Sir Richard King. On the 26th of December, Ensign R. Duddingstone joined the detachment.

On the 4th of January, 1794, Capt. Coleman was sent ashore with orders to join the head quarters of the regiment, Ensign Burrows being likewise discharged the following day. On the 8th of April the detachment was turned over to

H.M.S. "COLOSSUS," 74 guns, which during this year was employed in a similar way to the "Minotaur." (q.v.)

On the 12th of May, 1795, Lieut. Wyatt, Ensign Duddingstone, 2 serjeants, 1 drummer, 73 rank and file, were discharged at Portsmouth.

H.M.S. "RAMILLIES," 74 guns. On the 30th of June, 1793, Captain Lawrence Dundas (discharged by order 25th December), Lieut. James Monsell, Ensign Patrick Henderson (discharged 17th November, 1793, to the "Glory"), 2 serjeants, 2 drummers, 73 rank and file, embarked on board this ship. The stations for this ship were the same as those of the "Brunswick." (q.v.)

On the 28th of January, 1794, Ensign G. Dalmer was entered on the ship's muster rolls. The "Ramillies" was present with Lord Howe's fleet on the glorious 1st of June. On the 19th of August Lieut. Monsell was transferred to the "Robust." Ensign Dalmer's detachment, consisting of 2 serjeants, 68 rank and file, was, on the 30th September, turned over to

H.M.S. "ORION," 74 guns, which cruised during the winter, and in February, 1795, sailed to escort the East and West India convoys. On the 19th of March the detachment was turned over to

H.M.S. "LEVIATHAN," 74 guns, and on the 15th of April was disembarked at Portsmouth.

H.M. FRIGATE "PEGASUS," 28 guns. On the 1st of July, 1793, Lieut. James Allen (discharged 14th December), 2 serjeants, 1 drummer, 22 rank and file came on board. Was cruising with Lord Howe on the 14th, at the mouth of the Channel; was also with him when, on the 18th of November, he fell in with a French squadron. Sailed from St. Helens with the fleet on the 2nd of May, 1794, and on the 1st of June was attached to the centre squadron to repeat signals.

Sailed under Lord Howe in February, 1795, as did the "Minotaur." The detachment was discharged at Sheerness on the 26th of June.

H.M.S. "VANGUARD," 74 guns. 27th of July, 1793. Lieut. R. Harrison, Ensigns John Tucker and L. Augustus Northey, 2 serjeants, 1 drummer, 73 rank and file. In July was cruising under Lord Howe, also on November 18th, when he fell in with a French squadron. On the 9th of February, 1794, the detachment was turned over to

H.M.S. "ALFRED," 74 guns, which cruised under Rear-Admiral Bowyer in the Channel and Soundings. Was present in the Rear Squadron of Lord Howe's fleet on the 1st of June.

Extracts from Log of H.M.S. "Alfred."

1st June. Had two ensigns shot away with the staff, six men wounded. The "Rattler" brought orders for us to take possession of a dismasted French ship. Sent an officer on board, and found her to be the "Vengeur," of 74 guns. Hoisted out all our boats to save her people. She began sinking in about an hour. Got out 213 men, when she went down with the rest at 7.

Took "La Juste," of 80 guns, in tow after action.

9th June. Cut off "La Juste," and delivered her to the "Valiant."

(*Vide* "*Thunderer,*" *23rd. of June. Lieut. Tucker, 1 sergeant, and 25 rank and file*).

13th Novr. On 13th Novr the ship's company, including the detachment of 29th, was turned over to

H.M.S. "Blenheim," 98 guns. Although borne on the muster rolls of this ship till the 15th of August, 1795, it appears that Captain Robert Harrison had been left behind at Plymouth, without leave.

The "Blenheim" sailed from St. Helens on the 3rd of September, and cruised under Lord Howe during the winter.

In February, 1795, escorted convoys, &c., as did H.M.S. "Minotaur," but on the 20th parted company with the fleet, and joined Admiral Hotham in Myrtello Bay, Corsica, on the 27th of March.

Formed part of Admiral Hotham's squadron, which on the 13th of July discovered the enemy's fleet off the Hyères Islands, and, together with the "Gibraltar" and "Captain," was closing on the rear ships of the enemy when the recall was made.

Extract from Log of H.M.S. "Blenheim."

13th July. Off Cape de la Coòps. 12.12, "Victory" and "Culloden" began to engage the enemy.

1.15, Opened our fire.

3.10, Answered signal to discontinue action; ceased firing; had one man killed and two wounded.

After this, the "Blenheim" cruised about Corsica, Leghorn Roads, and on the 12th of January, 1797, when moored in the Tagus, the last detachment of the regiment serving on board the fleet (consisting of Lieuts. Northey, Tucker, 5 serjeants, 1 drummer, 59 rank and file) was turned over, by order of Sir John Jervis, to

H.M.S. "GIBRALTAR," 80 guns, which moored at Spithead on the 30th of January. On the 10th of March, 1797, the detachment landed, and marched to join the head-quarters of the regiment, then stationed at Weymouth.

MOVEMENTS OF THE CHANNEL FLEET IN CONNECTION WITH THE GLORIOUS 1ST OF JUNE, 1794.

1793 The Channel Fleet passed most of the winter of 1793 between the ports of Torbay, Plymouth, and Portsmouth; but the following spring Lord Howe collected the East India ships and his own fleet at St. Helens, having the following objects in view, viz. :—

    1st—To convoy the East India fleet of nearly 40 sail to a sufficiently south latitude.

    2nd—To force the French fleet to action, should it put to sea.

    3rd—To intercept the French convoy returning from the ports of America richly laden with the produce of the West Indian Islands, and with provisions and stores for the Republic.

1794 By noon on the 2nd of May, a fair wind having sprung up, the ships were all clear of their anchorage. On reaching the Lizard, Rear-Admiral Montagu's squadron was detached to escort the East India ships to a certain latitude, whilst Lord Howe steered for Ushant, and early on the morning of the 5th, with his fleet reduced to 26 sail of the line, arrived off that island. Finding that the enemy's fleet was still at Brest, he steered for the latitude in which he imagined the French convoy would run in its passage from America. From the 5th to the 19th of May the English fleet swept the bay in various directions, but without success. On returning to Brest it was ascertained that the French had sailed thence some days previously. Lord Howe therefore steered eastward for the Bay, but it was not till about 7 o'clock on the morning of the 28th, the weather being hazy and cold, with a stiff breeze, that two or three sail were discovered directly to windward; **1794** these the advanced frigates signalled as the enemy's men-of-war. The British fleet therefore cleared for action, and a general chase to eastward was commenced. A partial action then ensued, and the firing on both sides, for nearly two hours, was very brisk; but when darkness came on the enemy's fire began to slacken. In the evening the wind increased, the sea ran high, and, the firing having ceased, both fleets stood under easy sail, parallel to each other. They resembled a long street lighted up on both sides. Every British ship carried a light, those of the admirals' two each. Of the enemy's fleet, the admirals' ships only were lighted. Next morning the sea moderated, but the wind was still strong. During the partial action which ensued several ships on both sides suffered severely in their rigging and sails.

Very hazy weather prevailed on the 30th and 31st, and though only a few miles apart, the fleets got but occasional glimpses of each other; the men, however, were kept constantly at their guns. On Sunday morning, the 1st of June, the haze having cleared away, the enemy was discovered in order of battle, but so far to leeward that their lower deck ports were not visible. The wind being moderate from S. by W., the British admiral made the signal, "Are you ready to renew the action?" to which every ship answered in the affirmative.

As the fleets had each lost a ship, the British were now 25 to the enemy's 26.

At 7.16 a.m., Lord Howe made signal that he intended to attack the enemy's centre, and engage to leeward. The fleets at this time were about four miles apart, and the crews of the British ships after the fatigue of sitting up three nights, needing some refreshment, Lord Howe hove to, and gave the men time to breakfast.

At this time the following detachments of the 29th Foot were serving on board Lord Howe's fleet:—

1794 MONTHLY RETURNS—1ST JUNE, 1794.

SHIPS.	CAPTAINS.	SUBALTERNS.	SERJEANTS.	DRUMMERS.	RANK & FILE.	NAMES OF OFFICERS.
"Brunswick"	1	1	2	1	76	Captain A. Saunders, Ensign Harcourt Vernon.
"Ramillies"		2	2	1	73	Lieut. Jas. Monsell, Ensign George Dalmer.
"Alfred"		3	2	1	75	Lieuts. R. Harrison and John Tucker, Ensign L. A. Northey.
"Glory"	1	2	2	1	98	Captain Wm. Jaques, Lieut. W. T. Bertrand, Ensign Patk. Henderson.
"Thunderer"		2	2	1	73	Lieut. (Josh. Clavey‡)? and C. Bulkeley Egerton.

At 8.12, the British fleet filled and bore up, and signal was made for each ship to steer for, and engage her proper opponent. At 9 o'clock the enemy's van opened fire upon the "Defence," and half an hour later the "Queen Charlotte" (Lord Howe's ship) steered for "La Montagne," 120 guns, on board of which were Admiral Villaret de Joyeuse, and Jean Bon St. Andre, member of the National Convention.

The French ships astern of "La Montagne" were "Le Jacobin," 74; "Le Pelletier," 80; "Le Patriote," 74; and, fourthly, "Le Vengeur," 74 guns. The "Queen Charlotte," whilst steering for the French admiral's ship, was fired at by "Le Vengeur," but Lord Howe did not permit a shot to be returned until he got the broadside of his ship under the stern of his intended opponent.

The "Brunswick" (Captain John Harvey) suffered much from the fire directed at the "Queen Charlotte," and her cockpit was filled with wounded before she fired a shot. It was Captain Harvey's intention to

---

‡ *Vide* preceding account of H.M.S. "Thunderer."

have cut the enemy's line between "Le Jacobin" and "Le Pelletier," but finding them in very close order, he bore up for an opening which he saw between "Le Patriote" and "Le Vengeur." The latter ship, on seeing this, pushed forward to close the interval. Captain Harvey then kept his helm aport, which brought his ship alongside "Le Vengeur," the "Brunswick's" anchor hooking the French ship's port fore shrouds and channels. On being asked by the master, Mr. George Stuart, if they should endeavour to cut her clear, Captain Harvey exclaimed, "No, we have got her, and will keep her." The ships then swung broadside to broadside, and so close were they to one another that eight of the "Brunswick's" starboard ports could not be opened ; but this difficulty her crew soon overcame by firing their guns through them. Thus fiercely engaged, they dropped out of the line. On the "Brunswick's" quarter deck, forecastle, and poop "Le Vengeur's" musketry proved very destructive, but on the lower deck the seamen, profitting by the rolling of the French ship, frequently drove home the coins, and depressed the muzzles of their guns, each of which was double shotted ; then again withdrawing the coins, and pointing the muzzles upwards, alternately fired into their opponent's bottom and ripped up her deck. So furious was the fire and dense the smoke, that at 11 o'clock "L'Achille" having her rigging and gangways crowded with men, as if intending to board, managed to approach unperceived upon the port quarter of the "Brunswick," but the discharge of a well-directed broadside, added to the cannonading she had previously received, brought down all three of her masts, the wreck of which, falling over her starboard side, rendered her incapable of further resistance, and she struck her colours, which were, however, subsequently re-hoisted.

1794

The "Brunswick" and "Vengeur" continued their destructive operations, during the early part of which Captain Harvey was hit in the right hand; but he bound the wound up in a handkerchief and still kept on deck. The "Ramillies," commanded by Captain Harvey's brother, now emerged from the smoke of the action, and stood towards

1794 the still tightly-locked ships. The crew of the "Brunswick" then raised a cheer for the two captains, and their captain, who had by this time partially recovered from the effects of a severe concussion, was in the act of waving his disabled hand, when the crown of a double-headed shot, which had split, struck this gallant officer, and shattered his arm near the elbow.

This brave man waited a short time while the "Ramillies" took up a position, then, faint from loss of blood, was obliged to go below. A seaman offered to help him, but Captain Harvey said, "No man shall leave his quarters on my account. My legs still remain to bear me down to the cockpit;" and turning back as he descended, he cried, "Persevere, my brave lads, in your duty! Continue the action with spirit for the honour of our King and country! And remember my last words: The colours of the 'Brunswick' shall never be struck."

The difficulty of striking one ship and not the other, obliged the "Ramillies," after attempting a few broadsides, to haul off.

About 1 p.m. "Le Vengeur" ceased firing, and showed a union jack over her quarter; this she afterwards displayed at her cross-jack-yard-arm, but the "Brunswick" had not a boat to send to take possession of her. Every man on her forecastle had been killed except the boatswain; such also (with the exception of two men) was the fate of Captain Saunders, 29th Regiment, and his party, who were stationed on her poop. Glorious as was the behaviour of Captain John Harvey during the action, still more conspicuous was it after it was over, for the "Brunswick," having lost her mizen mast, her other masts being so badly wounded that she was unable to haul up for the fleet, having been on fire three times from the "Vengeur's" wads, and 23 of her guns disabled, her starboard quarter gallery knocked away, and the best bower anchor with the starboard cathead towing under her bottom, she drifted to leeward, and 13 sail of the French fleet separated her from the British.

Such was the state of affairs when the 1st lieutenant sent to apprise **1794** Captain Harvey of his danger, and ask for orders. His answer was to " sustain and return the fire as long as possible, even from every one of those 13 ships, and to let the " Brunswick " sink, rather than strike after such a glorious day."

In this action the casualties on board H.M.S. " Brunswick " were 45 killed; 113 wounded. Of these, some were of the 29th Foot, viz. :—

Killed.

Captain—Alexr. Saunders.
Corporals—Adsley, Wm.   Blood, Wm.
Privates—Brown, Thos.   Grace, Thos.   Lawless, Thos.
  „   Potts, David.   Todd, Robert.
  „   Wingfield (Wagfield) Henry.   Wright, Abraham.
  „   Wright, Samuel.

Wounded.

Ensign—Harcourt Vernon; 20 Rank and File.

Shortly after the parting of the " Brunswick " and " Le Vengeur," the latter's fore and main masts fell, and, with her mizen mast only standing, she lay rolling, her lower deck ports, many of which had been torn off or shot away by the " Brunswick " being under water. In this state she soon filled, and, although fast sinking, her colours, which had been re-hoisted, were kept flying. Fortunately for her, at 6.15 p.m., H.M.S. " Alfred," " Colloden," and " Rattler " (cutter) approached, and, observing her state, humanely sent their boats alongside, and by great exertions saved about 400 of her crew.

The " blowing up " of " Le Vengeur " is a favorite subject with French artists, notwithstanding it has been proved to the satisfaction of French investigators that the ship sank in the ordinary way.

The casualties on board H.M.S. " Alfred " (Captain John Bazeley) were 8 wounded, two of them being 29th men.

1794   H.M.S. "Glory" (Captain John Elphinstone) was a very slow-sailing ship. On getting into action, she passed under the stern of "Le Scipion," hauled up, and closely engaged her to leeward. In a little time she had knocked away that ship's three masts, she herself losing her foretopmast, main and mizen top gallant masts; then shooting ahead she engaged the "Sans Pareil," whose fore and mizen masts had just before been shot away by the "Royal George." Although the "Sans Pareil" surrendered, neither of the British ships were in a condition to take possession of her. The "Glory" and the "Royal George" then together raked "Le Républicain," and compelled her to retreat with her masts in such a tottering state that shortly after her main and mizen masts fell over the side.

There were 13 killed and 39 wounded on board the "Glory." Among the latter were Ensign Patrick Henderson and eight privates of the 29th Foot.

The action had for some time been continued with great fury, when "La Montagne" crowded off, and was followed by most of the French ships which were in a condition to bear sail. The "Ramillies" then made sail for "L'Achille," of which ship she made a prize.

Although on retiring the enemy had left 10 or 12 of their ships behind crippled and dismantled, owing to the disabled condition of the greater part of the British fleet, only six of these were captured.

The casualties on board H.M.S. "Ramillies" were—2 seamen, &c., killed on the 28th and 29th of May; 7 seamen, &c., wounded on the 1st of June. Amongst the latter was Drummer Thos. Dormer, 29th Foot, who died of wounds on the 8th of June.

On board H.M.S. "Alfred," two privates of the 29th Foot were wounded on the 1st of June. No casualties whatever occurred on board H.M.S. "Thunderer."

Sunday afternoon, and the whole of the 2nd of June, were **1794** occupied in adjusting the rigging, shifting sails, removing prisoners from the captured ships, and manning the latter with British sailors and marines. On the 3rd, the fleet with the captured ships in tow, bore away with a fair wind for Portsmouth and Plymouth, where on arrival, they were heartily welcomed by all classes of His Majesty's subjects. In honour of Lord Howe's victory the metropolis was illuminated for three successive nights.

On the arrival in England of the news of Lord Howe's victory, Rear-Admiral Montagu's squadron, which had returned to Plymouth on the 31st of May, was at once reinforced by H.M.S. "Colossus" and "Minotaur" (on board of which were detachments of the 29th Regiment), and ordered to sea in hopes of being able to pick up some of the enemy's stragglers. In this, however, they were not successful.

I have endeavoured in previous pages to record the care taken of the health of the regiment, and the interest shown by its commanding officers, Lord Harrington and Lord Cathcart, in all ranks of it; even the welfare of little children, in these busy times, was not overlooked. An extract from the Will of Captain Saunders, who was killed on the " glorious 1st of June," will, I think, show how Lord Cathcart was looked up to by his subordinates :—

"On board the " Brunswick," 29th July, 1793.†

" Be it known to all concern'd that I, Alex^r Saunders, Captn in His Majesty's 29th Reg^t, do will all that I Die possess'd of to be equally divided between * * * * * * , And I do constitute and appoint (in Hopes that his Lordship will serve me in this Request) the Right Honb^{le} Lord Cathcart, Col^n of the 29th Regm^t my Executor, and do hope and trust that his Lordship, as Father of the Regim^t, will provide

---

† A true copy of this will is in the possession of Lord Cathcart.

1794 for my Sons in any way that his Lordship may think best, either in the 29th Regim^t or otherwise.

A. SAUNDERS, Capt.
29th Regim^t."

"Lord Cathcart, Col.
29th Regiment."

1795
2nd Battn.

2ND BATTALION 29TH REGIMENT.

On the 12th of March, 1795, an order appeared in the *London Gazette* for the formation of second battalions to the 2nd, 25th, 29th, and 69th Regiments.

The detachments of those corps then serving on board the fleet were directed to be disembarked, those of the 29th, when landed, to assemble on the Island of Jersey.

The following letters from Major Enys to Lord Cathcart are copies of those made by Captain R. Watson in 1872, when the regiment was in Barbadoes. The originals have since then disappeared from the orderly room, and are supposed to have been destroyed:—

FROM MAJOR ENYS TO LORD CATHCART.‡

"Plymouth Dock, March 15, 1795.

"My Lord,

I have no doubt that your Lordship has heard of the long reported Second Battalion for the 29th Regiment, which report was so strong just before the Regiment Sailed from hence, owing to the paper No. 4, which I herewith transmit to you, that Lt.-Colonel Dickson applied to Lord George Lennox to know whether he was to embark with the Regiment, or remain for the prospect of the New Battalion, on which subject His Lordship wrote to the War Office, and for answer received a negative. Dickson of course embarked with the Regiment, who on going from hence took every man they could,

---

‡ Copied by Captain R. J. Watson from the original, which has since been lost.

leaving me only the sick. The 25th have acted quite contrary, having left several Officers, about 25 Non-Commissioned Officers, with their music, &c. In this state things stood until a few days ago, when an order came down to the 25th to say they were to form a Second Battalion without delay, in consequence of which they immediately began to enlist for it, and have procured a few men since that time. But yesterday proved a day of intelligence, as the *Gazette* not only announced a Second Battalion to the 25th, but also to the 2nd, 29th, and 69th Rg^{ts}, at the same time it brought orders for disembarkation of the men of the 25th who are on board the men-of-war at this port, in consequence of which I have received orders to quit the Barracks we now occupy, and remove to country quarters anywhere in the Western District, but have represented the very great danger and inconvenience such a removal will occasion, and am in hopes of getting some of the detached Barracks near this place for our people until I hear something further on the Subject, either from your Lordship or the War Office, for at present I have no Order or any intimation about the New Battalion, not seeing Dickson's name and my own in the *Gazette* as appointed to it. I therefore presume the Official Orders are gone to your Lordship, that you may make your arrangements, and send me orders accordingly, in which case you may wish to know the exact state we are in, here, at present. I therefore lose no time in sending you such papers as I conceive may be useful to you in so doing. No. 1† is a copy of the Weekly State sent to the Adj^t General last Friday, with which I sent a letter saying I had received no kind of Orders respecting the Second Battalion I that day heard was in the *Gazette*, and requesting, if I was expected to do anything in it before I received your Orders, that he would be so good as to point out to me what was to be done, at the same time requesting to know whether our detachments now on board were to be disembarked or remain on their present duty, as it required that very different necessaries should be provided according to circumstances.

---
† This paper is missing.

1795
2nd Battn.

No. 2† is a particular state of my Detachment, mentioning under the different heads how many men were left on board, and how many on shore with me on the 28th Dec' when the Regiment first went on board, to which I have added all the Casuals which have happened since that period, by which return you will see in what a very destitute state I am left, and how very little it is in my power to do, having in fact only myself and two sickly Serjeants, Doyle and Spalding, to do anything. It was with difficulty I procured one Corporal to be left, in order to assist me in my accounts, and am in hopes I shall get some others from the Hospital, who may in time be useful, but still we shall be in a total want of Drills, and another useful kind of creature called Tailors. As to the stations of the different ships, I am told that the "Blenheim" is gone to the Mediterranean, and the "Thunderer" and "Orion" to the North Sea, the "Pegasus" is in the Downs, all the rest with the Grand Fleet at Spithead.

No. 3† contains a list of all the Non-commissioned Officers left me, as well on board as on shore, with the dates of their appointments, together with a list of such Privates as Colonel Campbell and Johnstone seem to think would answer best for Corporals.

I fear your Lordship's absence at this time will put us to very great difficulties in procuring proper persons for the Staff, if you are not already prepared in case of such an event, as the person you expected from the Life Guards‡ came down in time to sail with the regiment, and Perry, our late Serg' Major, is now Ensign and Adjutant of the 91st Reg', so you will have to look out for an entire new list.

No. 4 is a copy of the first paper we received relative to the 2nd Battalion which was never sent officially, nor had it any date to it. On its being shown who had gone on board, they all to a man rejected the proposal. I have now a copy of the order for the 25th Regiment

---

† This paper is missing.
‡ Ensign Joseph Bailey from Corporal-Major 1st Life Guards.

1795
2nd Battn.

before me, and for fear you may not have gotten the order for Ours, I mention that the Establishment is the same, bearing date from 24th of last month, but the terms of reduction entirely different, a copy of which part I have put upon the back of the former paper, which will no doubt alter the whole of their late determinations, particularly as I am told they are to get their New Commissions gratis: but how their determination is now to be known I cannot tell, unless by application to the Regiment abroad, whose destination we are yet ignorant of, and the Return of Officers is required to be given in to the Duke of York as soon as possible. Thus I have endeavoured to place the whole before your Lordship in as small a compass as possible, and hope I shall either see or hear from you soon on the subject: in the meanwhile if I get any further orders from either the War Office or Adjutant-General, I will acquaint you with them. But most sincerely wish you may be on the spot to assemble the New Corps yourself, as I feel myself unequal to the task, having been for more than three months confined by the Gout, and yet hardly able to walk. The Regiment embarked in health and spirits, but were sickly after they were on board, particularly the "Maria," on board of which was Col. Campbell and most of our men. I received 5 men from them the day they sailed, 4 of whom are since dead.

It is rather remarkable we have not had a man desert from the Reg^t since the time of embarkation inclusive, and only three men from naval parties, two of whom were taken, and are confined. The "Lively," frigate, Captain Burlton, has taken and brought unto this port, two French frigates, and two other prizes, within these two days, which seems the principal news at this place. Whilst I remain

Your Lordships most obedient,

Humble Servant,

J^n Enys."

1795
2nd Battn.
P.S.—I have opened this again, to say it will be necessary for Your Lordship to say whether you mean to have Black Drummers for the 2nd Battalion; you remember we have now two whites on our strength.

The following is a copy of No. 4 paper; a like, with the exception of the last paragraph, was sent to the 25th and 29th Regiments :—

"War Office.

"The King having thought fit to direct that the 2nd or Queen's Reg^t of Foot, under your command, shall be formed into two battalions, I have the honour to acquaint you herewith, and to send you the annexed state of the regiment, as it is to stand from the 25th inst. It is intended that the Lieut.-Col. and 2nd Major of the regiment shall be transferred to the new battalion, that your companies and second lieutenancies in the new battalion shall be offered to the officers of the regiment, and that the other companies, and lieutenancies in the battalion shall be bestowed on the independent officers now serving therewith. You will in course be allowed the nomination of the staff officers, the surgeon and mate excepted, who are to be recommended by the Army Medical Board. His Majesty, conceiving it very material that the situation of the officers in the event of a reduction of the 2nd Battalion should be clearly understood, is graciously pleased to declare his Royal intention, that notwithstanding from precedent, the commissions in the two battalions shall be made out distinctly for each, and that reduction of the 2nd Battalion shall only effect the officers actually commissioned thereto at the time of reducing the same. The detachments now employed on marine duty are to be relieved and landed without delay, which may enable you (if there should be time) to make any further arrangements in regard to the commissioned and non-commissioned officers that you shall judge necessary, both in regard to that part of the corps which is embarked, and that which will continue in Great Britain; taking care, however, that nothing shall interfere to prevent the former from going on service complete both as officers and men (600 rank and file)."

On the back of this paper Major Enys had written:—In case of **1795** reduction, the present order runs thus: His Majesty, conceiving it **2nd Battn.** very material that the situation of the officers, in the event of a reduction of the 2nd Battalion, should be clearly understood, is graciously pleased to declare his Royal intention that on a reduction of the 2nd Battalion, the youngest officers of each rank throughout the regiment should be placed on half-pay without respect to the particular battalion in which they may happen to serve, the same rule of reduction having been uniformly observed in all former occasions.

PROPOSED ESTABLISHMENT OF THE 2ND, 25TH, AND 29TH REGIMENTS.

1ST BATTALION.	2ND BATTALION.
1 Colonel, with a Company	1 Lieut.-Colonel, with a Company
1 Lieut.-Col. ,, ,,	1 Major ,, ,,
1 Major ,, ,,	8 Captains
7 Captains	12 Lieutenants (no Capt. Lieut.)
1 Captain and Lieutenant	8 Ensigns
11 Lieutenants	1 Chaplain
8 Ensigns	1 Adjutant
1 Chaplain	1 Qr. Master
1 Qr. Master	1 Surgeon
1 Adjutant	1 Mate
1 Surgeon	32 Serjeants
1 Surgeon's Mate	40 Corporals
32 Serjeants	22 Drummers and Fifers
40 Corporals	760 Privates
22 Drummers and Fifers	
760 Privates	

TO LORD CATHCART.†

"Plymouth Dock, Apl 22nd, 1795.

" My Lord,

In anxious expectation of your arrival, I send this to wait for you in London, to beg you will send me your Orders respecting

---

† Captain R. J. Watson's MS.

1795
2nd Battn. the New Battalion of the 29th as soon as possible, as I have no authority to make the least alterations until you do, not having received an order of any kind about it, and am told they were all sent to your Lordship to Germany in the beginning of last month, about which time I also sent you a Packet, in which I mentioned everything respecting the Reg^t I could think of, and although I have been constantly in expectation of your answer, no such thing has yet reached me. I have a few days ago received an Order from the War Office to say that the 1st Battalion of the 29th were to go to Jersey as soon as the parties could be relieved from on board the Men of War, which was ordered to be done without delay. I am sure I need not mention to your Lordship that Jersey is one of the worst places in the world to form a Regiment, provisions being extremely dear, and liquor of all kinds very plentiful and cheap, which, with the large sums of money our men have coming to them, will be enough to ruin the whole Regiment. The 25th have got off from going there, and I believe the 69th also. With Regard to the formation of the New Corps, I told you in my last letter that I could give you no information as to the choice of the Officers, for although they certainly all rejected the first proposal, which was known before they sailed from here, yet I think the present terms so much better, that I hardly think they would reject these also.

There are also one or two things respecting the Men which occurs to me; provided the New Establishment is to take place from the 24th of last February, are all the men who were then on our strength to be drafted and transferred to the New Battalion from that day, or are we only to transfer such men as may be on our strength at the time the new arrangements actually took place, as it will make a very material difference, not only from men that have died, but also from a number who have been returned unfit for any service, and are to be discharged by a Board of Officers and Surgeons lately assembled here for that purpose. There is also a report here that the Regiment is gone to

Corsica; if this is true, are the men of the Battalion now in the **1795** Mediterranean to be esteemed a part of the old or new Battalion, those **2nd Battn.** numbers are, 2 Officers, 2 Serjeants, 1 Drummer, and about 64 or 65 Rank & file. I do not know what arrangements your Lordship may have made with regard to your staff, but Colonel Dickson seems to wish very much for our late Serj^t Major Perry, as Adjutant, who is now Adjutant & Ensign in the 91st, at this place, but being very near eldest Ensign, it will not be worth his while to come to us unless he gets a Lieutenancy, for which I believe he will pay the regulation if you think him an object worth gaining at such a price. There are many things more which may be mentioned but I will leave them until I am sure of your being in England; but if it is necessary that I should come to meet you, some Officer must be sent here, as Lord George Lennox does not wish I should go until some other comes in my place, while I am

    Your Lordships most obedient Servant,

          J^n ENYS."

In June, Major Enys received orders to proceed from Plymouth with the men under his command, and there join the detachments which had disembarked from the fleet, and assembled at Jersey under the command of Captain Jaques. Accurate returns were now made out, and it was discovered that owing to deaths, and men receiving their discharge, the strength of the battalion was but 567 rank and file. As these were all old soldiers, the regiment was formed of as fine a body of men as any in the army, and fit for any service.

During their stay in Jersey the men received very large sums of prize money, which became due to them whilst serving on board the fleet. " I was rather surprised," wrote Major Enys, " one day to hear that a soldier of my company, named William Davis, one of those who had received prize money, had invited the whole company to sup with him on roast duck and green peas. On enquiry I found it was not

1795
2nd Battn. only true, but that the same man, on a former payment of prize money, not being able to go ashore at the moment he wished to spend it, had eaten a £20 note!!"

In the Muster Rolls kept at the Record Office, Chancery Lane, is the following list of officers:—

2ND BATTALION 29TH FOOT. 25TH DEC., 1794—24TH JUNE, 1795.

LIST OF 2ND BATTALION OFFICERS.

Colonel	William, Lord Cathcart			Serving on the Continent.
Lieut.-Colonel	Hugh Dickson	25 Feb., 1795		Serving with 1st Batt. in Grenada.
Major	John Enys	25 ,, ,,		From 1st Batt. 29th Foot.
Captains	Francis Wm. Farquhar	16 April ,,		,, ,, ,,
	William Jacques*	17 ,, ,,		,, ,, ,,
	James Allen	18 ,, ,,		,, ,, ,,
	Robert Harrison	19 ,, ,,		,, ,, ,,
	James Monsell	21 ,, ,,		,, ,, ,,
	W. S. Bertrand	23 ,, ,,		,, ,, ,,
	John M. Doherty	26 ,, ,,		,, 75th Foot
	Chas. Thos. Grant	27 ,, ,,		,, 77th ,,
Lieutenants	William Seymour	21 ,, ,,		On board H.M.S. "Minotaur."
	Geo. Saville Burdett	23 ,, ,,		From 1st Batt. 29th Foot.
	Edmund Rolleston	6 May ,,		,, 24th Foot.
	Henry B. Lynch	6 ,, ,,		,, 20th ,,
Ensigns	George Tod	16 April ,,		,, The Northern Fencibles.
	Nathaniel Forster†	20 Aug. ,,		
Adjutant	Thomas Comber	16 April ,,		Serving with 1st Batt. in Grenada.
Quarter Master	Richard Nosworthy	3 June ,,		
Surgeon	Saml. Irving	6 May ,,		
Mate	Alexander Hodge			

* Signs himself Jaques.   † From Acting Surgeon 2nd Batt. 29th Foot.

[LETTER 22].

LADY CATHCART TO LORD CATHCART.

"Windsor, July 6, 1795.

"The King asked me several questions about the 29th, and amongst others, where Majors Mallory and Enys were; the official accounts of Major Mallory's death had not arrived. When I told the King, I took the opportunity of saying that the eldest captain of the regiment was your A.D.C., and that he had served all the time with you, and every one who knew him, knew what a remarkable good officer he is; in short, I said as much as I thought I might venture without doing mischief. The Princesses . . . . and . . . have also entered warmly into the business. I have no doubt of success, it needs only to state the pretensions: however such strange things do happen! I thought in your absence I had better do what I could, knowing that if the vacancy is otherwise filled it will be a mortification and disappointment to you. I shall regret very much if Captn Kirkman is obliged to leave you; he has been with you so long, I do not know how you can supply his place."

TO LORD CATHCART.*

"Grouville B^{ks} Jersey.
11th August 1795.

"My Lord,

It is now three months since I did myself the honor of writing to you from Plymouth Dock, and am sorry to say have not yet received any answer. I however hope my letter reached you safe as I find it impossible to enter again, at length, into the various subjects I then wrote upon; indeed the hurry with which everything now seems to be pressed forward with, seems to preclude me from making a point of dressing the Regiment with that attention I could otherwise wish to

---

* Captain R. J. Watson's MS.

1795
2nd Battn. do. Our people were not put ashore from the fleet until the 18th of May, long after the other Regiments had been embarked, and some of them are not even yet landed, as you will see by the enclosed card. But that is not all; when they had landed about 350, they sent them to this place, keeping me still at Plymouth with only a few sick men, until the 24th June, by which means I did not join the Regiment until the 1st July, when I immediately set to work arranging the companies, getting their confused accounts settled as well as I could to their satisfaction, and getting our Regimental Books & Returns put as forward as I possibly could. I had not been ten days employed at this work before I received an order for the Battalion to be in readiness to embark on the shortest notice, under which order we still remain without the least idea of our future destination. On our arrival at this place, the arms we had on board ship were found to have been so spoiled on that duty, that most of them were returned into stores of this place before my arrival, in place of which we are now using the 400 stands, sent in Decr last, for the augmentation. I was also fearful for some time that we should have embarked without our clothing, but finding some Breeches cloth in the Stores, I made it all up and procured as many Waistcoats and breeches as I could from St. Heliers, by which we have partly covered our nakedness. Aid, a few days ago, arrived, consisting of about 600 Coats and 850 sets of Half-mounting,* but no Waistcoats or Breeches with them; indeed I do not know the reason, but they do not seem to pay the least attention, either to the orders or returns I sent them, nor will they even deign to answer either my letters or those of Mr. Nosworthy, who joined us a short time since, and seems to be attentive to his business, whilst the arrangement of the Corps, and our being under orders, has prevented me from going to London to see things done myself, or to learn how others in the same situation are doing. As to any of the ornamental parts of the Regiment, they are mostly unordered, except when I found we were

---

* A Half-mounting consisted of—a pair of shoes, a shirt, 2 pairs socks, and a stock.

likely to embark, that I desired the agent to order Colours for us to be ready whenever we sent for them, but my whole view has been to get the arms, clothing, and accounts in as good a state as I can, at which I am constantly employed, so that if from the want of the ornamental parts, we may not be said to be a parade Regiment, I think no one can deny we are as noble a Detachment as ever were seen. I take the opportunity of sending you a Morning State of the Regiment, and a list of the Non-Commissioned Officers as they now stand, and a third, of the Officers now with me at this place; you will see by the State, that we have 62 on the Sick Report, but they are the same set of fellows you always remembered to have been there, with sore legs, sore backs, and Venerial, or I do not think we have what can be called a sick man in the whole place. The large balances due to our men when they landed, with the extreme cheapness of liquor in this Island, has been the cause of some irregularities, which have not yet ceased, but from what I can find no Regiment has been so well liked by the inhabitants for many years, except the 63rd, and I hope, as their cash is now nearly expended, they will improve upon us. Captain Clavey has been so good as to superintend our Drills whilst I am at other things, and the men improve daily from his attention to them; so much for the 2nd Battalion.

**1795
2nd Battn.**

Would to God I could send you so good an account of the first, but their melancholy horrors meet us at every line of their letters, but as you may not have heard from them yourself, I think it my duty to inform you of some of the particulars I have learned, although it will give you I am sure as much pain as it has done all here.

The *first letter* is of the 20th April, from Dickson, in which he says very little more than a detail of the passage, landing at Barbadoes 30th of March, and sailing next day for Grenada, and of their landing, and some of their attacks afterwards; he then says that Mallory was hurt in a struggle with two negroes, who attempted to take him prisoner, and that he and Vernon were gone sick to St. George's; he then says

1795 that Serg^t Clarke and Corporal Hindmarsh were killed in the first
2nd Battn. attack; in the second Ensign Bayley was killed, Mr. Comber wounded in the arm, and Dr. Wm. Archer in the head.

The *second letter* was from Campbell, in which he says Mallory was dead, and refers me to Dickson's letter for the rest.

A *third letter*, from Dickson, dated 15th May, after some particular details, says death is now making great havoc among them; he then mentions the death of Mrs. Dalgetty, the Serg^t Major (that is I presume Comber),‡ and Serjeant William McLean, and that many others of all ranks were very ill, and that of the 600 who embarked, only about 380 remained fit for duty.

A *fourth letter*, from Dickson, is worse than all; he says but little of their movements or actions, but that, within the last six weeks, they had lost by Yellow Fever, 5 Officers, 6 Serjeants, and about 80 Rank and file, and adds, that about 120 more were in the Hospitals, very few of which he ever expected to see come out of them.

The names of the officers lost are—Captains Allen and Williams, Lieutenants Vernon, French, & Love; of Serjeants, he mentions the Serjeant Major, Mr. McLean (Master of the Band), with two of the Band, Serg^t Swopp, the Drum Major, and his wife, with most of the Women, and children who went with them.

To this account I may add from other accounts, the death of Serj^{ts} Dalgetty, Clay, Cotton, and Walker who I hear died on the passage, not mentioned by Dickson. But let me finish this dreadful account which it rends my heart to write, as I am sure it will yours to read, and to proceed to another part of my duty, which is, that by Comber's death, we have lost our Adjutant. I beg leave to mention the person who has done duty as Serjeant-Major, Serjeant Owenson, and has been of infinite use to us, all through the formation of the Battalion, as a proper person to succeed to this office. I have every

---

‡ Had been appointed Adjutant 2nd Battalion 29th Foot, 16th April, 1795.

reason to think Captain Clavey means to write to you on the same subject by this day's post, and means to mention Serj^t . . . .§ as a person worthy of attention, which I must also say I think, his having received great assistance from him also. There is also a gentleman here, named Nathaniel Foster,‖ who has been acting as Surgeon to us for some time, and who is extremely beloved by every officer present, who wishes to change his line, and if possible get an Ensigncy without purchase, and it is by desire of the Corps in General, that I beg leave to recommend him to you for one of the many vacant Ensigncies in this Battalion. Mr. Nosworthy also requests I would remind your Lordship of your naming him to an Ensigncy. In a letter to Colonel Brownrigg of this, I have told him that I had this day recommended the above gentlemen to your Lordship, and hope they may not be forgotten if they were obliged to fill up the vacancies before an answer came from you on the subject, of which I hope you will approve, as it may be long before we hear from you, and I know not how soon we may embark. Be so good as to make my best compliments to Major Kirkman, to whom I would write if I had time, which I really have not, whilst I am,

1795
2nd Battn.

Your Lordship's most obed^t Humble Servant,

JOHN ENYS."

You will I presume have heard before this reaches you that Mr. Irving who was appointed Surgeon to the Battalion, has exchanged with Mr. Lenon, who joined us this day, so I can say but very little about him, more than that first appearances are well enough. We have also a person here named Mr. Hodge, who Mr. Irving sent down here as Mate, some time ago, whose assistance I have accepted of, Although I have not heard that your Lordship has given him any

---

§ Name nearly obliterated, but looks as if it might be "Doyle."
‖ Ensign 2nd Battalion 29th Foot, 20th August, 1795.

1795 Warrant. But as those kind of people are not often to be found, if
2nd Battn. forced on Service before his Warrant arrives I shall be obliged to answer for you.

Yours, &c., J. E."

From a Morning State* of the 2nd Battalion 29th Regiment, dated Grouville, 11th August, 1795, the total strength was 31 serjeants, 39 corporals, 10 drummers, and 513 privates; of these 7 serjeants, 9 corporals, 2 drummers, and 116 privates were "on command."

LIST OF OFFICERS OF THE 29TH REGIMENT NOW SERVING WITH THE 2ND BATTALION.—GROUVILLE, 11TH AUGUST, 1795.

Major	John Enys	2nd Battalion 29th Regiment.
Captains	William Jacques	,, ,, ,,
	Robert Harrison	,, ,, ,,
	James Monsell	,, ,, ,,
	John Doherty	,, ,, ,,
Lieutenants	Geo. Saville Burdett	,, ,, ,,
	Blois Lynch	,, ,, ,,
	Edmund Rolleston	,, ,, ,,
Quarter Master	R. Nosworthy	,, ,, ,,
Surgeon	Mr. Turner§	,, ,, ,,
Mate	Mr. Hodge	,, ,, ,,

OF THE 1ST BATTALION.

Captains	Joseph Clavey
	Chas. Bulkeley Egerton
	Will Edgell Wyatt
Lieutenants	Robert Duddingstone
	George Dalmer
	Pat Henderson
Lieutenants	Northey and Tucker, 1st Battalion, on board H.M.S. "Blenheim" in Mediterranean, with 4 Serjeants, 1 Drummer, 62 rank and file.

---

* Captain R. J. Watson's MS. § Was not gazetted to the Regiment.

Lieutenant   Seymour, on board H.M.S. "Minotaur," with 2 Serjeants, 1 Drummer, **1795**
61 rank and file.   **2nd Battn.**

Not yet Joined.
⎰ Captain Chas. Thomas Grant   2nd Battalion.
⎱ Ensign George Tod   ,,
⎱ Lieut. Samuel Gauntlett   1st Battalion.

Not yet Appointed. 8 Lieutenants, 7 Ensigns, 1 Chaplain.

In August, Lord Cathcart received notice from the War Office, dated 17th inst.,* "that, from the utmost impossibility of procuring recruits to complete the old regiments, as well as from the extreme difficulty of finding officers for this very extensive establishment, it had been judged absolutely necessary to reduce a considerable number of young battalions, transferring the rank and file to the old regiments, but continuing their officers in pay until opportunities were found to provide for them in the corps remaining on the Establishment. In pursuance of this above arrangement, His Majesty was pleased to order that the 2nd Battalion of the 29th Regiment should forthwith embark for Portsmouth, where all rank and file fit for service were to be transferred to some of the regiments in the Southern District, and that the battalion should be discontinued on the Establishment from the 24th of November inclusive."

The following paragraph appeared in the *Morning Chronicle* :—

"Jersey, 27 August, 1795.

Eight transports, under convoy of the "Rattler" ship of war, are just arrived to take away the 29th Regiment, commanded by Major Enys. The politeness and urbanity of that gentleman, and of the other officers, and the regularity of the privates, has endeared them to the islanders in general. The good order, and discipline kept among them, were the more remarkable, as every man brought with him £50 prize money, acquired while the regiment served on board the fleet as marines. The farmers, and public-houses about

---

* Captain R. J. Watson's MS.

1795
2nd Battn.

the barracks, will long feel the good effects of the soldierlike propensity of the men, to part with their money. One of the soldiers had yesterday still remaining a bank note of £25, but finding that his comrades had spent all their cash, he determined to swallow the note between two pieces of bread and butter, and by this ingenious expedient avoided the implication of being singular."

Having marched to St. Aubins, the regiment embarked thence on the 28th, and landing at Southampton on the 2nd of September, marched to, and encamped on, Nursling or Nutshalling Common, with the troops there assembling under Major-General Sir Ralph Abercrombie, destined to complete the deliverance of the French West India Islands from the power of the Republican Government, and to reduce to obedience the islands of St. Vincent, and Grenada.

Whilst in this camp, and in conformity with War Office letter of the 17th of August, orders were received for the battalion to be drafted into the 42nd (Royal Highlanders). This, however, does not appear to have been approved by Lord Cathcart, who brought his influence to bear, and before the order could be carried out the Duke of York arrived and countermanded it.

[LETTER 23].*

"Brinkum, n^r Bremen,

August 30th, 1795.

"I have received a notification of His Majesty's commands for drafting the 2nd Battalion. If I cannot obtain that the 2nd should be drafted into the 1st, the regiment will be utterly ruined for many years to come, as I shall not have a single old serjeant or man left. I have wrote to the War Office, to guard them against the fatal mistake of reducing the troops which were embarked as marines, as the 2nd Battⁿ, whereas they are from every reason the "first," and the West

---

* Lord Cathcart to Lady Cathcart.

India Battⁿ the 2nd ; but if they must go to the West Indies, why not send them to the other battalion, which is already nearly worn out, and make one regiment out of the two battalions ?"

The following reply was received with reference to Lord Cathcart's representation to the War Office anent the proposed reduction :—

"Adjutant-General's Office,*
16 September, 1795.

"My dear Lord,

I take the first opportunity to acknowledge the receipt of your Lordship's favor of 28th of last month, and to acquaint you in reply, that the 2nd Battalion of the 29th Regiment, under your Lordship's command, is in conformity to your wishes, to be incorporated into the 1st. Your Lordship's reasoning on the subject is evidently just, and has accordingly been productive of the desired effect. I have the honor to be, with great regard and truth,

My dear Lord,
Your Lordship's most faithful, humble Servant,
WM. FAWCETT,
A.G."

"Right Honble
Lord Cathcart,
&c., &c., &c."

Although incorporated with the 1st Battalion then serving in Grenada, and under orders to proceed to the West Indies with Sir Ralph Abercrombie, it was intimated that most likely on its arrival there, it might not be sent to join the regiment, but have to act as a separate corps.

---

* Captain R. J. Watson's MS.

1795

2nd Battn.

[LETTER 24].

LADY CATHCART TO LORD CATHCART.

"Sept. 28, 1795.

"I am so happy I don't know how to write. The Duke of York arrived last night. He was at the rooms where we were at tea, drew his chair very kindly by me, and after saying handsome things of you, whispered in my ear a secret! I was almost wild with joy; I ought not to doubt I shall soon see you, after what was so kindly and humanely imparted. God grant me strength to support myself under such happiness . . . . [In the middle of a closely-written quarto sheet the Princess Augusta interpolates]: 'I cannot resist having the pleasure of writing a few lines to you, with Kate's permission. I have had a very good account of my dear 29th, my Brother says it really is a very excellent battalion, and I am most happy to hear it. Pray pardon the liberty, and believe me your most sincere well-wisher, A. S.' [Lady C. goes on to say]: "Princess Augusta has been playing 'reels' in my room, and insisted on adding a few lines, which will give you pleasure. It is very true what she has prettily told you. The Duke of York told the King he was surprised and delighted with the 29th, which he had just seen: the men fine and the regiment in good order, notwithstanding they had been so long on board ship. He said they were the original 29th, all the old men, and it would have been a shame to have drafted them into other regiments. I joined in the conversation, and we three talked over both battalions, officers, and men, the losses in the West Indies, and all the losses and hardships, &c. The Duke talked of Major Kirkman in the highest terms, and explained to me how he came not to be major in poor Major Mallory's place, and apologised for it, telling the King what a valuable officer Major Kirkman was, and useful in every situation."

On the 18th of October, the regiment was ordered to embark at Southampton on board the "Sebastiana," "Somerset," and "Sally" transports. As scarcely three hours' notice had been given, this sudden move created a certain amount of surprise amongst the officers, and men; still greater was their astonishment when the following General Order was issued :—

GENERAL ORDERS.†

"Southampton, October 15, 1795.

"Major-General Sir R. Abercromby thinks it his duty to make in this pointed manner, his disapprobation of the shameful Desertion which has taken place from the 29th Regiment, which will also render it necessary to bring the Deserters now in confinement to a General Court Martial."

The effect of this order upon the regiment, which had been but shortly before pronounced as in a satisfactory and well-disciplined condition, was, to say the least, somewhat startling. This unpleasant impression, however, was partially relieved the next day, by the issue of another General Order, and Lord Cathcart's letter which follows, explains fully the circumstances of the misunderstanding :—

GENERAL ORDER.

"19th October, 1795.

"Major-General Sir R. Abercromby was induced to mark his disapprobation of the conduct and discipline of the 29th Regiment in the Orders of yesterday, from the inaccuracy, and inattention of the Commanding Officer of that Regiment in camp, on the 17th inst., who returned 42 men deserted in place of four."

[LETTER 25].

"Hastedt, Nov. 12, 1795.

"I have had letters from the 29th. General Abercrombie has been in a passion, and treated them very harshly.

---
† Captain R. J. Watson's MS.

1795
2nd Battn.
"Major Enys happened to be at Southampton, looking after the packages of the regiment, and the Weekly State was signed by the officer commanding in camp. There were 42 sick and 4 deserters: by mistake they put down 4 sick and 42 deserters. Without asking a question, or thinking of the extraordinary recovery of near 50 men in one week, the Adjutant-General, the General, and all the family, became outrageous against the regiment for desertion, and the most cutting and violent order was given out, attended by orders for the regiment to be instantly embarked as a punishment, and no man to be allowed to land, but under strong checks. The regiment did embark, on three hours' notice, unconscious of having given any offence, with a regularity and marks of loyalty that did them high honour in the eyes of the army. In the evening a new order came out, which explained the blunder, and threw the blame on the officer who signed the return, but without taking off or softening the asperity with which the regiment had been treated. Some people honour, and keep up the pride of a soldier; others perhaps doubt, or forget, that such things exist, but such is the history of the anticipated embarkation of my poor regiment."

The regiments destined for the West Indies having all embarked, the transports, with Major Enys' battalion on board, sailed with the rest of the fleet on the 15th of November. On the 17th, it blew so hard that early in the afternoon signal was made to anchor, but on account of the increased violence of the gale, only a few ships succeeded in so doing. The greater number bore up for St. Helens, where, on arrival, it was discovered that several of the men-of-war had suffered so much that it was necessary either to replace, or repair them. This detained the expedition until the 9th of December, when it again sailed, accompanied by a division of the Royal Navy under Admiral Christian. Again the weather proved unfavourable, for on the 12th, a S.W. wind freshened to a gale, and orders were signalled to bear up for Torbay.

The storm which ensued compelled each ship to look to its own safety. **1795** Some wrecks occurred, but the majority of the transports returned to **2nd Battn.** St. Helens, where (with the exception of the "Sally") those having the 29th on board anchored on the 28th of January. It was a long **1796** time before it was ascertained that the "Sally" had made good her passage to the West Indies.

On the 8th of February, Major Enys' battalion was ordered to disembark, and place itself under command of its colonel, Lord Cathcart, who then commanded the troops at Southampton. On account of various delays, Southampton was not reached till the 15th. In March, the battalion marched to Hamble.

MAJOR ENYS TO LORD CATHCART.‡

"Hamble, April 3rd, 1796.

"My Lord,

Agreeable to my promise I went to Southampton yesterday in hopes of meeting the 12th and 33rd Regiments, which I expected would be there, in place of which I found only a part of the 90th, from whom nothing was to be gathered.

Mumbler,* however, purchased two Octave Flutes which he said were wanting, and not part of what were expected from Germany, and he has found one old Oboe, and a Clarionet, the whole purchase of which, I am told, is not much more than 2 guineas . . . . But if I was unfortunate on the subject of the Music I did not wholly lose my labour, having met Champané, and attacked him for the Black they have so long promised us, who, he says, shall be sent as soon as ever we send a White man in his place.

Would your Lordship wish me to send, this years new suit of Cloathes, out with the Recruiting parties.

---

‡ Lord Cathcart's MS.   * Master of the band.

1796
2nd Battn. There are also other things which should be thought of, if we are likely to remain in England, particularly our Camp Equipage as what we now have is only a Collection of what we could collect from the Regiments that were drafted, about the time of our arrival in Nutshelling Camp. We of course want many things such as Quarter Guard Tent, Camp Colours, &c., &c. . . . . I must also observe that all our Serjeants have not got Pikes, for no more were sent than to compleat the Augmentation of one Serjeant per Company; of course many Serjeants who were such in the Second Battalion, and who now remain as such, have never had any such thing, But have been furnished with the Lance part of the old haldberts as far as they would go towards compleating them. I have also in compliance with your desire, made all the inquiry I can for a proper person to succeed to the honourable office of Crimp for the 29th Regiment, in the place of Mr. Hoffard, deceased: in consequence of which I have received the enclosed letter from one of that honourable profession, But having no acquaintance with the 133rd Rgt, or Lt. Col. Simon Fraser, I transmit it to your Lordship who may possibly get Kirkman, or some other person to make the necessary inquiry into his Character whilst I wait your further orders on the subject. . . . .

I have the honour to be your Lordships

Most obedient Servant

JNO ENYS."

A disturbance having taken place (on the 28th of April) among the men at work on the canal near Southampton, on the application of the Mayor, a detachment, of 100 men, under command of Captain C. B. Egerton, was sent to assist in preserving order; these, after an absence of three or four days, rejoined their regiment. The thanks of the Mayor and Corporation, together with a sum of money to be divided amongst the men who had been employed on this duty, was afterwards received by the regiment.

The following is a copy of the vote of thanks:— **1796**

"SOUTHAMPTON, 11 MAY, 1796. **2nd Battn.**

At a Common Council held at the Audit House of the Town, and County of Southampton, it was unanimously resolved:

That the thanks of the Mayor and Corporation of this Town, and County, be presented to Major John Enys, commanding the 29th Regiment of Foot, at Hamble, for the readiness with which he complied with the request of the Magistrates, by ordering a detachment of that regiment into the town for the purpose of assisting the civil power, in case it had been necessary at the time of the late disturbance, also to Captain Egerton, the other officers, non-commissioned officers, and privates of the detachment, for the strict discipline they observed, and their very regular behaviour whilst in the town.

Ordered—

That their resolutions be signed by the Town Clerk, and by him transmitted to Major Enys, requesting that he will be pleased to have them communicated to the detachment.

By order of the Common Council,

(Signed) THOMAS RIDDING,

Town Clerk."

"Adjutant-General's Office,

4 May, 1796.

"His Majesty has thought fit to signify His Royal Pleasure, that all Officers without distinction, belonging to the Infantry of the Line, shall in future have the undermentioned articles of their Regimental Dress here specified, made exactly according to the following Regulations, viz.:

A crimson and gold cord round the Hat, with crimson and gold rosettes, or tufts, brought to the edge of the brim.

1796
2nd Battn.
The Sword to have a brass guard, pommel, and shell, gilt with gold; with the gripe or handle of silver twisted wire.

The blade to be straight, and made to cut, and thrust; to be one inch at least broad at the shoulder, and 32 inches in length, conformable to former orders given in April, 1786.

The Sword Knot to be crimson and gold, in stripes, as required by His Majesty's present regulations.

The Gorget to be gilt with gold, with the King's cypher, and crown over it, engraved in the middle, and to be worn with a riband, and tuft or rosette at each end, of the colour of the facing of the regimental clothing respectively.

WM. FAWCETT,
Adj^t General."

[LETTER 26].

" Salisbury, June 27, 1796.

" The Worcester Militia* have been marching through this place ever since I have been here, in small divisions, and as they march at 2 in the morning, they keep up an incessant drumming in the middle of the night for two hours, so a stranger would suppose the French had landed. I have recommended to them to practice turning out in silence, as a very useful military operation, but I do not like to forbid the noise because they seem to enjoy it. They are a very fine regiment, and have been at pains to imitate the Worcestershire Regiment of Foot, in dress, and many other things."

About the middle of July, the regiment relieved the 28th Foot at Gosport, but on the 9th of August, marched for Weymouth Camp, where a force was assembled under General Sir William Pitt, K.B., and one of the brigades of cavalry was commanded by Major-General Lord Cathcart.

---

* Became in 1881, the 3rd Battalion of the Worcestershire (late 29th) Regiment.

1796
2nd Battn.

[LETTER 27].

"Weymouth, Sept. 16th, 1796.

"At 8 o'clock a.m., received the King. The 2 cavalry brigades exercised much to His Majesty's satisfaction. By 12, the King went to Lord Uxbridge's lines, where there was a most magnificent breakfast in many tents. After breakfast, country dances, &c., after which the line of infantry was reviewed, and made a very good figure. I put myself at the head of the 29th when the King passed them, and also marched past, at their head, but left the exercise to Col. Sneyd. This review also gave great satisfaction, and lasted till half-past 3."

During Their Majesties' stay at Weymouth, the 29th was encamped on a hill (Sutton Camp) overlooking the bay, but on their departure the regiment took up quarters in the town, where, on the 7th of October, it was joined by the remains of the battalion which embarked for Grenada in 1794.

About this time the sword exercise was introduced into the army, and was practiced before His Majesty.

On the 15th of September, it was ordered that "the brigade of Foot Guards, and the Infantry of the Line, in general, are to wear plain hats with white feathers in them, white tufts at the corners, for the brigade of Foot Guards; and white mixed with the colour of the facing of the regiment, for the Line; with a white loop round the button, and the edges bound round with black worsted tape.

1796 The cross-belt plate worn by the officers of the 29th Foot, at this
2nd Battn. period was an oblong, octangular silver plate, 3 inches long, 2¼ broad.

SHOULDER-BELT PLATE OF CAPT. EDGELL WYATT.*

A wreath of laurels was engraved round this plate, on the centre of which was a raised device, consisting of a Lion *crowned* statant guardant, encircled by a Garter bearing the motto "Honi Soit," &c., surmounted by a crown. This is the earliest trace I have been able to discover of the *Lion Device*.

---

* Now mounted as the lid of a snuff-box, and in possession of Colonel A. Wyatt Edgell, of Cowley House, Exeter.

CHAPTER VIII.

T will be remembered that on the 28th of December, 1794, **1794**
Lieut.-Colonel Campbell and the effectives embarked at
Plymouth, their destination being, however, kept a secret.

At this time, 3 captains, 9 subalterns, 20 serjeants, 6 drummers, 603 rank and file were doing duty as Marines on board the fleet. In order to bring the head-quarters up to a service strength, a considerable number of recruits had to be obtained, and large drafts were received. The majority of these, it appears, were too young to stand the fatigue of the campaign upon which they shortly afterwards embarked, but more especially the trying, and, at that time pestilential, climate of the Island of Grenada.

For the correspondence between Lieut.-Col. Campbell and Lord Cathcart, I am again indebted to Col. R. J. Watson, who, whilst serving with the regiment in Barbadoes, fortunately copied the originals, which are supposed to have been destroyed, as they have not been seen in the Orderly Room since 1872.

Owing to the very few sources of information about this expedition to Grenada, I have thought it advisable to publish these letters intact.

"To Lord Cathcart. **1795**

"Maria" Transport, 10 Jan^ry, 1795.

" My dear Lord,

The 29th have been embarked for about a week, but for what purpose, I am yet a stranger to. The 25th, 32nd, 48th, & 67th

1795 are in the same situation; I could not, consistent with my duty, leave this shore without making your Lordship acquainted with the distribution of the regiment, which I flatter myself the Returns therein enclosed will in a great measure explain. It will be, however, necessary to remark that the " Wanting to Complete," mentioned in the Return of the Battalion embarked for foreign service, was to complete it to 1000, and Drafts for that purpose are immediately expected at Plymouth, though probably too late to join us, as we expect to move to Cossand Bay to-morrow, where probably our stay will be short, indeed the situation cannot permit of its being long. Your Lordship will observe on the General Return that the greatest part of our officers in the battalion are attached ones from Independent companies, who, however, by the order, are not to expect to succeed in case of vacancies that may take place in the regiment, except by particular appointment. The Drafts we have got to augment this battalion to a Service establishment of 600, have been in general of a description by no means adequate to the purpose, exclusive of their being quite recruits, without either a knowledge of the use of arms, nor any part of a soldier's duty, they are on two extremes in point of years, very inadequate to bear the fatigues which probably must be imposed upon them. I am sorry to add that the whole of the regiments have been sickly since embarkation. We have landed several with fevers, of which a great part have died since, in the General Hospital. Major Enys is left at Portsmouth in charge of the convalescents, as well as to superintend the business of the part of the regt. embarked in the Fleet. Exclusive of the Returns before mentioned, I have likewise sent enclosed a proposal for forming the 2nd, 25th, and 29th Reg^{ts} of two battalions each, and it appears from the letter to Lord George Lennox on the subject, that it was intended to have landed the above regiments upon the 4th December, when the arrangement was immediately to take place, but circumstances having occurred that rendered their remaining on board necessary, until after cruise now intended by the Grand Fleet; the letter to Lord George, was to know whether under such circumstances His Lordship thought such an arrangement could take place consistent with the good of the Service, and this he has answered in the affirmative. For my own part I doubt the situation of the battalion will receive much benefit. I applied to Lord George for permission to exchange both men, and officers with some ships now here, viz., the "Minotaur," "Blenheim," "Colossus," and "Orion," and was promised that application would be made accordingly, but it is probable we shall be off before anything can be effected. I begged that Lord George would have it explained to us what purchase money would be expected from the Lieut^s, &c., on their promotion, and whether the Independent companies were to take rank of them in the proposed battalion, circumstances I conceived necessary to be made acquainted with, suspecting it would hardly be worth while of the oldest Lieut^s to pay much more for young companies in a battalion which was certain to be reduced. I am sorry to say that particularly under the present circumstances, we shall lose Perry, he has been some time since promoted by Col. Hunter to the Adjutancy of the 91st Reg^t, and expects the commission by every post; he has besides, the promotion of an Ensigncy. I have repeatedly written to Mr. Greenwood, as likewise to Lord Harrington, on the subject of the person you wished from the Life Guards, but have not heard from either on the subject, though I understand your Lordship wishes to have the matter carried into effect.

May your Lordship enjoy the blessings of good health and everything which may contribute to happiness, is the very Sincere wish of

Your most Obedient and much obliged Humble Servt.,

A. CAMPBELL."

"My best wishes attend Kirkman."

1795 Copy of Return enclosed.

State of a Battalion formed from His Majesty's Twenty-ninth Rgt., and now embarked for Foreign Service.

"Maria" Transport, 6 Jan^ry, 1795.

Officers Present.										Present.			Wanting to Complete.		
Commissioned.						Staff.									
Colonel.	Lieut.-Colonels.	Major.	Captains.	Lieutenants.	Ensigns.	Chaplain.	Adjutant.	Qr.-Master.	Surgeon.	Mate.	Serjeants.	Drummers.	Rank and File.	Serjeants.	Drummers.	Rank and File.
	2	1	7	5	3		1	1		1	27	18	595	15	4	405

A. CAMPBELL, Lieut.-Col.,

29th Regiment.

Owing to continued contrary winds, the transports with the 2nd, 25th, 29th, 34th, 81st, and 96th regiments, were detained in Plymouth Sound, till the middle of February. It appears that about this time, a very bad fever, prevailed among the inhabitants, and troops at Plymouth, which also communicated itself to those who were embarked. With such fury did this fever rage, that in one day over 70 men were buried, and we read of a regiment, quartered at Stoke, losing 400 out of 600 men, the remaining 200 being left unfit for any duty. The 29th was not so much affected by this fever as were many regiments; still it continued to send its sick ashore, up to the day of its sailing.

On the 15th of February, Admiral Parker, and the convoy, started from Plymouth with sealed orders, and on leaving the Sound, were joined by the Channel Fleet, under Lord Howe, which, after escorting them a certain distance, proceeded to cruise off Brest, and in the Bay.

Not until the transports were off Cape Finisterre, was the destination of the Expedition known. On its proving to be the West Indies, each part of the convoy made the best of its way to its respective destination. After a fair passage, during which the sick recovered in a most surprising manner, the 29th arrived in Carlisle Bay, Barbadoes, on the 30th of March, and on the 1st of April, together with the 25th Foot, and a detachment of Royal Artillery, the whole under command of Lieut.-Col. Campbell, of the 29th, was despatched to quell an insurrection which had broken out early that month in Grenada.

1795

As it may interest some to know the origin of the outbreak in that island, whose climate proved more destructive than the enemy, a sketch of the events which took place previous to the arrival of these reinforcements is here given.

Early this year, the French made great efforts to recover their possessions in the West Indies. Emissaries were sent among the negroes, and correspondence with discontented French inhabitants was set on foot with a view of raising simultaneous insurrections. These attempts in Grenada, Dominica, and St. Vincent, although attended with a temporary success, were finally defeated.

The commencement of the insurrection in Grenada was probably due to the success which had attended the Republican arms in Guadaloupe. The meeting place of the conspirators was the plantation called Belvidere, situated in the very centre of the island ; it belonged to their chosen leader, a mulatto named Julien Fedon.

Two of their band, who had been despatched to Guadaloupe to concert measures with Hugues, and other Republican Commissioners, in that island, returned a few days before the insurrection broke out, and landed at Charlotte Town, or "Gouyave," with arms, ammunition, Liberty caps with national cockades, and a flag on which the words "Liberté," "Egalité, ou la Mort," were inscribed. They were furnished with commissions signed by Hugues, Goyrand, and Le Bas.

1795 About midnight on the 2nd of March, the small towns of Grenville, or "La Baye," and Charlotte Town, were taken possession of, and 11 out of the 15 English inhabitants of the former, were butchered. At Charlotte Town, the governor of the island, Lieut.-General Home, and 46 others, after being surprised in bed, were conducted on foot, under a strong guard, to the insurgents' camp at Belvidere.

The only troops in the island consisted of 190 men, and the militia of St. George's. The former, which were in garrison at Richmond Hill, near St. George, were commanded by Captain Sandeman, 9th Foot. On the 5th of March, 150 men, forty of whom were regulars, embarked under Captain Gurdon, 58th Foot, to retake Charlotte Town. With the exception of St. George, or "Ville et Fort Royal," the fortifications, and a few estates near the town, the whole of the island was now in the possession of the insurgents. The rising of the slaves became general, and the work of plunder, and devastation by fire, were of a daily occurrence.

On the 6th of March, Fedon sent a flag of truce, demanding the surrender of all the fortifications, giving also notice "that the instant an attack was made on the post where the prisoners were confined, every one of them should be put to death."

On the 12th, Brigadier-General Lindsay arrived from Martinico, with 150 men, and on the 17th proceeded to attack the enemy, but without success. Captain Sandeman and 16 privates were wounded, 9 were killed. At the commencement of this engagement, Fedon ordered the governor and other prisoners to be put to death; they were, however, spared for a time, and conducted from the insurgents' lower camp at Belvidere, to the higher one, where their chief had his head-quarters. Here they were placed under a strong guard.

It had been General Lindsay's determination to renew the attack the following morning, but the heavy rains which commenced, and continued up to the time of his death (22nd inst.), rendered any movement impracticable.

The command of the troops now devolved on Lieut.-Colonel **1795** Schaw, 68th Regiment, who, together with the other officers, was of opinion that the force then in the island, was insufficient to assume any offensive operations with a prospect of success.

Such was the state of affairs when the reinforcements, under Colonel Campbell,* disembarked at Charlotte Town.

A detachment of 250 men, under Major Wright, 25th Regiment, was at once ordered to march through the woods, and support Captain Gurdon who was stationed about five miles distant, at the Observatory; whilst Captain Ewen, of the same regiment, was ordered to take post at Madame Chadeaux's, about half-a-mile in front of Belvidere Camp; and Major Mallory, of the 29th, with 300 men, re-embarked for St. George's, it being intended that he should take up a position on a hill, a few miles from the Grand Étang, which commanded the principal line of communication between Grenville Bay and the enemy's camp, hoping thereby to intercept their supplies, and cut off their retreat.

Major Mallory's detachment marched from St. George's on the 4th of April, and took post near one of the enemy's camps in the vicinity of Madame Aché's house (Fôret Noir), which was attacked, and captured the next morning, with the following losses:—

Killed { Sergeant: Clarke, James. Corporal: Hindmarsh, Wm. Privates: Dyke, Richard; Freeman, Thos.; Hillory, John; Hopewell, George; Hughes, Francis; Phillips, Henry; Shelton, George; Williams, Richard.

Wounded—15 Rank and File.

Shortly after this, Major Mallory, who went out by himself to reconnoitre a position at a distance from his men, was assailed by three negroes, armed with muskets and bayonets. Though he had only his sword and a brace of pistols, he refused to surrender, and defended himself with such determination that he killed two of his assailants,

---

* Appointed Brigadier-General, 3rd April, 1795.

1795 and obliged the third to save himself by flight. In this conflict unfortunately, Major Mallory received some wounds, none of which were at the time thought dangerous. The night of the 5th passed pretty quietly, a few harmless shots only being fired at the sentinels. Fearing that, if the detachment made a further advance without first securing this post, his communications with St. George's might be cut off, and having but three days' provisions, Major Mallory determined to remain where he was, but fever having set in, he died on the 22nd. Lieut.-Colonel Este, 68th Regiment, who had in the meanwhile started from Charlotte Town, arrived on the 6th, and assumed command, and thinking the force unequal to the difficulties which were to be encountered, no further advance was for a time made. Major Wright also reported that he had found a large body of the enemy strongly intrenched, and having ascertained that they had lately received a further supply of arms and ammunition, he judged it unadvisable to attack their position until he was reinforced. The failure of these two enterprises put an end to the idea of a general co-operation of the different detachments against the enemy's camp, whilst the vast quantities of rain which fell during the next few days precluded the possibility of carrying on any further operations. In the absence of the Governor, and death of Brigadier Lindsay, the command devolved on the President of the Council, who, considering that any further delay would prove advantageous to the enemy, judged it best to make an assault on their camp, from the post before Belvidere, which was still held by a detachment. In so doing he did not take into consideration the state of the weather.

On the 7th, the President arrived at Mount St. John, where the troops were now principally collected, and ordered an attack to be delivered without loss of time. Accordingly, Brigadier-General Campbell, having the following morning collected all available forces, an advance by two columns was made on the enemy's principal position at Morne Quaco. The column under command of Lieut.-Colonel

Hope, 25th Foot, was composed of detachments of the 91st and 68th regiments, under Major McLean, 68th Regiment, the Light company, and the remainder of the 25th, not already employed; whilst Lieut.-Colonel Dickson, 29th Foot, had charge of the second column, which consisted of some seamen of H.M.S. "Resource," the Light company, and remainder of the 29th not otherwise detached. The Grenadiers of the 25th and 29th regiments formed the reserve.

1795

On the approach of the troops, the enemy retired to their upper post, situated on a ridge of the mountain, which, on account of the inaccessible nature of the ground, was in itself a strong position, but had been rendered more so by the felling of trees. In addition to this, they had two guns, one of which was served by French soldiers.

Notwithstanding these obstructions, the ardour and resolution of the seamen and troops induced them to press forward, and endeavour to gain possession of one of the guns which had been advanced from the summit of the position. On account of the heavy rains which had lately fallen, it was scarcely possible for the men, whilst climbing the hill, and making their way through the dense brushwood and fallen trees, to keep their feet, much less to use their musquets with effect.

The troops having for some time been exposed to a very heavy and galling fire, with scarcely an opportunity of returning it, Brigadier-General Campbell decided to withdraw his men under cover of the two companies of grenadiers (that of the 29th was commanded by Captain Augustus Colman, who himself shot one of the insurgent chiefs), and, having first collected the wounded, returned to his former positions at Mount St. John and Madame Chadeaux's.

In the return of killed and wounded on the 8th of April, 1795, signed by A. Campbell, Lieut.-Colonel, Commanding the Troops and Seamen, the casualties in the 29th Foot are :—

1795

Killed†—1 Subaltern, 9 Rank and File.
Wounded—1 Serjeant, 1 Drummer, 8 Rank and File.

During the above attack, Fedon put the governor of the island to death in the presence of his wife and daughter, and then the remaining prisoners, with the exception of three, were shot in detail at his word of command.

To Lord Cathcart.

"Grenada, 19 April, 1795.

" My good Lord,

Enclosed herewith I have the honour of enclosing a State of the Regiment as near as our detached situation will permit, but am afraid they will contain many errors, which, however I shall endeavour to correct in our next. I write this in a negro hut, on the top of the highest mountain in this rugged island.

I need not mention how blackguard a service we are employed upon. The insurgents (mulattoes and negroes, with a few of the old French inhabitants) are posted at about three miles distant; they occupy the summit of a very extensive mountain, the access on every side seems so steep that I fear it is hardly possible to face them, at least with the force now assembled upon the island. We have felt for them upon two or three different points, and am sorry to say came off with loss without gaining anything; the last was an attempt to force their chief post on the hill before-mentioned, but were taught to our cost that the strength of the ground was beyond our strength, and was

---

† The Muster Rolls give the following names: Ensign Joseph Bailey, acting adjutant; Privates—Adams, Edward; Bailey, John; Briggs, Wm.; Jaques, James; Manwairing, Thos.; Murphy, Thos.; Oldwright, Jas.; Partington, Wm.; Riley, James.

defended by cannon, and numbers which our best information flattered us it was impossible to expect; so that everything considered, we came off well, though at the expense of a good deal of blood. Poor Bailey, who I had appointed a few days before to act as adjutant, fell on this occasion. We seem entirely left to poke out our own way in the dark wilds, and fastnesses, not yet having found a guide who knows a yard beyond the beaten tracks, which are here improperly called roads, neither can you get for love or money a person who will venture a hundred yards to gain intelligence, consequently we either fall into ambuscade, or are led to error, through false information. Immediately on my arrival in this country, I recommended Dalgetty to the Commander-in-Chief to succeed to the vacant ensigncy, in room of a Mr. Bird, who was either promoted or exchanged some time before we left Europe, and this morning received the appointment, together with a Mr. Campbell in room of Bailey. I have on this occasion only to hope that the vacancy of Mr. Bird has not been previously filled up at home, and to request your Lordship's good offices to prevent it; Dalgetty's commission here is dated the 1st instant. There is a heavy cannonade from an outpost at this instant, therefore conclude with telling you that this goes by Capt. Brown of the Navy, who took a very spirited part in our late attack on the enemy.

Believe me, my dear Lord, with every sentiment of

Respect and Esteem,

Your most obedient humble Servant

A. CAMPBELL."

"The cannonade proves of little importance."

1795 COPY OF ENCLOSED STATE.

State of His Majesty's Twenty-ninth Regiment of Foot, Commanded by Major-General Lord Cathcart, between 15th Feb^ry & 26th April, 1795, inclusive.

COMPANIES.	OFFICERS. COMMISSIONED.						OFFICERS. STAFF.						*		RANK AND FILE.						WANTING TO COMPLETE.			ALTERATIONS SINCE LEAVING ENGLAND.				
	General.	Lieut.-Colonels.	Majors.	Captains.	Lieutenants.	Ensigns.	Chaplain.	Adjutant.	Quarter Master.	Surgeon.	Mate.	Serjeants.	Drummers.	Fit for Duty.	Sick at St. George's.	Sick at Barbadoes.	On Command.	On Furlough.	Recruiting.	TOTAL.	Serjeants.	Drummers.	Rank and File.	Joined.	Died.	Discharge Recommended.	Discharge not Recommended.	Deserted.
General Lord Cathcart's...	1							1	1			2	1	18	4	2	28			52			8	2				1
Lt.-Col. Arch. Campbell's		1												19	3	6	28			56	1		4	4				
Major Mallory's													1	27	4	1	26			58			2	2				
Capt. James Kirkman's ...				1	1							1	1	39		9				48	2		10	1				
Capt. F. W. Farquhar's...												1	1	14	6	9	26			55	1		5	2				
Capt. Geo. Johnstone's ...				1										28	6	2	26			62								
Capt. Daniel White's ...												2		24	6	2	28			60								
Capt. Jas. Allen's				1	1							3	1	53	3	4				60								
Capt. Richd. Pigot's ...					1							3	1	16	3	2	35			56			4	2				
Capt. T. B. Deverall's ...					1							1		17	4	2	35			58			2	4				
TOTAL....	2		3	4				1	1			13	6	255	39	39	232			565	4		35	17				1

* 2 Serjeants dead, included in that Column.
4 Serjeants and 8 Drummers sick at St. George's.
1 Serjeant and 2 Drummers sick at Barbadoes.

Absent Officers. Rank and Name.	Since What Time.	For What Time.	Officers on Duty, and What Duty.	Vacancies, by What Means.
Ensign T. Campbell	Not joined since		Major Mallory	1 Ensign, by promotion of Ensign Vernon.
Chaplain Geo Turner	Appointment.		Capt. White	
			Capt. Pigott	1 Ensign, by promotion of Ensign Northey.
			Lieut. Williams } On Command.	
			Ensign Love	1 Mate, by promotion of Gregg.
			Ensign Walton	
			Capt. Deverall, at the Observatory.	Number of Serjeants on Command, 7.
			Ens. & Qr.-Mr. Dalgetty, on duty at St. George's.	Number of Drummers, ditto, 2.
			Capt. Bruce	
			Lieut. Vernon } Sick at St. George's.	
			Ens.	

1795

A. CAMPBELL, Lieut.-Col.,

29th Regt.

On the 16th of April, Brigadier-General Nicholls arrived from Martinico and took over the command. Having examined the positions occupied by the troops, he determined to change the scene of operations, and to attack a large force of the enemy assembled on the east side of the island, at Pilot Hill, near Grenville Bay. With this object, Major McLean, with about 200 men, was stationed in Charlotte Town. On the 26th, the posts on the heights above that town, and at Madame Aché's, were evacuated, and on the following day Brigadier-General Campbell, with about 900 men, embarked for Grenville Bay. The second night after their landing there, the enemy abandoned their position, and retreated to some inland heights.

During the wet and sickly season which now set in, it was judged best to station the troops at different positions along the coast, and to postpone for a time all further operations.

1795   Major Wright (25th) was therefore left in command at Pilot Hill; the garrisons of Charlotte Town and St. George's were reinforced, and new posts were taken up in the north of the island at St. Patrick, or "Sauteurs," and in the south-east at St. David's, or "Maigrin," the latter being under command of Captain D. White, 29th Foot, who had with him 60 men of his own regiment, and 26 of the St. David's regiment of Militia.

Fever now began to tell on the regiment. Lieut. P. T. Campbell had died on the 22nd of April; on the 14th of May, Adjutant Thomas Comber and two privates succumbed, on the 18th, Captain James Allen, on the 19th, Lieut. Robt. French, 1 serjeant, 1 drummer, and 4 privates, on the 21st, Lieut. Harcourt Vernon, and 1 private. Casualties amongst the men were almost of daily occurrence.

On the arrival of Captain White at St. David's, the parish church, being a stone building, and considered a strong and safe position, was at once occupied by the detachment. All went on quietly till the 25th of May, when about 2 a.m. some of the enemy, by creeping through the brushwood, succeeded in surprising two sentinels. The first intimation the garrison had of the enemy's approach was a volley of musketry fired in at the door, and windows. Captain White being at the time down with a bad attack of fever, Lieut. Hugh Rowland Williams (29th), who was also suffering from its effects, immediately called the men to arms. The cries, and shrieks of the sentinels who had been surprised, were more appalling than the fire of the enemy, who, it appeared, were torturing their victims, instead of dispatching them at once. Lieut. Williams, ill and unable to move, was wounded where he lay; from the effects of this, combined with the malignant fever which ensued, he died on the 11th of June. This officer had, on the 24th of April, been gazetted to a company in the 1st Battalion 29th Foot, but the notice of his promotion had not been received at the time of his decease.

Although the garrison of the church was surprised, still the men **1795** were undaunted, and determined to sell their lives as dearly as possible. The church door was hastily barricaded, and Sergt. Sully (29th Regiment) placed ten of his best men with fixed bayonets at the entrance. In a few minutes all was ready, and the men, cool and obedient, were directed not to fire at random, but to watch, and be guided by the enemy's fire. There being a light in the church, the enemy for some time had the advantage, but a stray bullet soon extinguished it.

During this attack, the little garrison was much annoyed by the fire of one of the enemy, who had posted himself in a large tree close at hand; this man, Mr. May, the rector of the parish, was determined to dislodge. He therefore climbed up into the belfry, and watching his opportunity, discharged his musket with such good effect, that all further annoyance from that quarter ceased. At daybreak the enemy retired, having lost, according to the best information, 100 killed and wounded. Of the garrison, 36 killed or wounded lay in the church.

In the gallant defence of this post, which was of considerable importance, the losses of the 29th Foot were :—

Killed*—5 Rank and File.
Wounded—Lieut. H. R. Williams (captain), 1 Serjeant, 33 Rank and File.

Serjeant Sully died of his wounds on the 20th of June. On the day previous Lieutenant John Marco Love succumbed to fever; this was the eighth officer who had died in a little over eight weeks. On the 6th of July, Ensign Smith Palmer, and on the 21st, Surgeon Thos. Gregg, died.

---

* Muster Rolls 29th Foot. Died 25th of May, 1795; Privates—Castler, Geo.; Creswell, William; Evans, Robert; Lush, John; Summers, John.

Other accounts state 15 rank and file; these most likely include 10 privates returned in Muster Rolls as having died the following day.

P

1795   The casualties which occurred in the regiment between the 15th of February and the 20th of June, 1795, will be found annexed to the following letter.

To Lord Cathcart.

"Richmond Hill, St. George,

Grenada, 20 June, 1795.

"My dear Lord,

Herewith I have the honour of enclosing a Return of part of the 29th Regt. at present under my command, to which there is joined a list of Casuals, the magnitude of which your Lordship will join with me in regretting, but more particularly when by the very recent date of many, it is manifest that the cause is by no means abated. I was in great hope that on the regiment coming to this garrison, the general health might be restored, the situation having the most promising appearance; it is almost a mile and a half from the town, and fort of St. George's, by a road that winds up to the summit of a steep ridge, on which the Garrison is built, and in direct distance, sufficiently near to cover both the fort and town with its cannon, we have the advantage of enjoying the finest and best air that the island or climate can afford, and have taken every precaution possible to guard against infection from other quarters, though I am sorry to say without the effect desired. A fever now rages in the town, with very destructive violence; it appears to be a species of plague, never being known to attack a person twice, indeed very few have survived the first; our loss by the enemy has not been many in comparison, though they merit much regret, as having died by the hands of so unworthy a Banditti, over which I cannot say we have as yet had any very decided superiority, as they maintain much the same situation as when I first came into the island. We have had several reconnoitres, and premeditated attacks, all which, though they prove the inferiority of their spirit or discipline even with our recruits, yet they always ended with a certain loss of men on our part, which with the contingent loss occasioned by sickness, has reduced the 29th Regt. to what your Lordship now finds it. Brigadier-General Nicholls has lately rescued us from the command of a President of the Council, who, on the death of the lieutenant-governor (murdered by the insurgents) assumed the military command, and issued orders for attack, &c., with all the confidence of a Veteran ; in one of these we lost poor Bailey, and other valuable lives, as by the Returns, but the whole loss, including seamen (of whom we had a detachment), part of the 25th Regt., and other detachments, was about 100 men ; the service was in storming the strongholds of the insurgents, which ended in proving what must have been the opinion of every military person before it commenced, a matter without any probability of success. This post is on the summit of the highest mountain in the island, defended with artillery, and a fire of musketry much superior to what we could bring against it, the ascent is so difficult, that of about 200 Seamen who began to climb up at the head of the attacking columns, there were not 30 up when it was found necessary to return to the low ground, and the whole so very much spent, and fatigued, that a spirited enemy might have made us pay very dear for the temerity of our attempt, but luckily, we had not such to deal with, for though they made a show of following to the plain, yet were kept sufficiently in check by the grenadiers of the two battalions, and the whole were allowed to march to their camp without insult. Under Major Mallory, an attack was made on the enemy at this side of the Island, while a detachment was sent to windward to attack the enemy at La Baye ; these being planned by the same military genius, had a similar effect with that already mentioned under your Humble Servant. I have perhaps taken up too much of your Lordship's time in setting forth the follies of a person not otherwise worthy of attention, but to show how dangerous it is to trust power of any sort, but military in particular, into the hands of ignorance and presumption.

1795

1795   My not knowing where to address Lady Bulkeley obliges me to request that your Lordship will take the very disagreeable trouble of communicating to her Ladyship the death of Lieut. Williams; his death was caused by wounds, and bruises received in the defence of a post where Captain White commanded with 60 men of the 29th; it was an old church at a place called Maigrin; they were attacked in the night by almost 400 of the insurg^{ts}; these appeared after, to have been a chosen band, determined on the total destruction of our small party. However, after many violent and fruitless efforts to force them, they were obliged to retire in the morning, leaving 30 corpses on the ground, and from information since received, the loss of the enemy, killed and wounded, could not be less than 90.

When I left England, the uncertainty of our destination prevented my making many arrangements, and among them I left the Black Horse, in charge of Major Enys, but without mentioning at that time anything further relative to the matter. I however, on my arrival at Barbadoes, wrote a few lines directing that the horse should be sent to the person to whom he certainly belongs, and flatter myself your Lordship has had some pleasant days hunting with him, over the happy plains near Windsor. Pray present my best respects to Lady Cathcart, and believe me with every sentiment of respect and esteem.

Your Lordship's
Most obedient & most Humble Servant,
A. CAMPBELL."

Abstract of the enclosed State of the Regiment, with Casualties since leaving Plymouth, 15 Feb^y, 1795.

Present.—2 Lieut.-Col^s, 4 Capt^s, 2 Lieut^s, 3 Ensigns, 1 Adju^t, 1 Q^r M^r, 1 Surgeon, 21 Serj^{ts}, 11 Drummers.

Rank and File.—244 Fit for Duty; 125 Sick in B^{ks}, Hospital, or at Barbadoes; 87 On Command.

Wanting to Complete.—3 Serjeants, 3 Drummers, 141 Rank and File.

Alterations.—Died 115; Deserted 3.

This Return was made up for the 11th of June, but could not be sent.

Casuals up to 20th June.—*Since Dead:* 3 Serjeants, 13 Rank and File.

"Richmond Hill, St. Georges,   **1795**

Grenada 6 July 1795

"My dear Lord,

    Herewith I have the honour of transmitting a Return* of the part of the 29th Regiment, in which I am sorry to say your Lordship will find the loss considerably increased since the last up to the 20th June, and which I hoped reached you before this. I flatter myself the Majority, vacant by the death of Mallory has fallen to Enys, and that Kirkman has succeeded to his. The other vacancies, though I recommended them for the regiment at large, will without doubt be filled up by the Commander-in-Chief. That cursed destructive fever, continues still to rage with unabating violence, two or three men of a day, fall a sacrifice to it. Richmond Hill, the present head-quarters of the regiment, appears to have every advantage which can be procured in this climate, for preserving good health. A high commanding situation, with a constant refreshing wind that preserves the temperature of the air in a state not (to my feeling) better than what is common in our English summers, and has neither swamp nor bog to occasion a nauseous vapour of any sort. The insurgents continue at present quiet in their fastnesses, where they are reduced to much misery, even for provisions, and indeed every article of the necessaries of life, this has occasioned great desertions among them, and many have risked the sentence of the law, to avoid present distress—upon the whole, should our cruisers prevent them receiving their necessary supplies from Guadaloupe, there will not remain with General Fedon, except such whose crimes preclude them from any mercy. We have had some report of a Second Battalion, and a newspaper gives the promotions, but a total silence in way of letters leaves the matter still doubtful, pray have the goodness to let me into the secret as soon as

---

* This document is missing.

1795 possible.——Not having the address of the friends of any of the poor fellows we have lost in this country, I have to request you will direct the Agent, or other perhaps more eligible person, to communicate the unfortunate tidings.

The amount of which their effects sold for shall be transmitted to the Agents by next Packet. In my last, I requested your Lordship to communicate the melancholy tidings of poor Williams' death to Lady Bulkeley. The great want of medical assistance, as well as the great merit of the man, induced me to appoint Pipes, to act as Surgeon's Mate, until your pleasure was known on the subject, and if not otherwise engaged, I should thank your Lordship to send him a warrant. His professional knowledge is perfectly satisfactory to the Surgeon, his modesty, and application is very much so to myself. Finding that your Lordship was serving on the Continent, I flatter myself good health, and satisfaction have accompanied your return, and that you found Lady Cathcart, and family in every respect as I wish them. Pray offer my best respects to Her Ladyship, with my love to all the young folk, and believe me to be with unalterable respect, and esteem,

Your Lordships

Humble Servant,

A. CAMPBELL."

"Richmond Hill,

Grenada 22 July 1795.

"My good Lord,

I cannot allow Colonel Dickson to depart for England without enclosing a State § of the Regiment, though I sent one by the last Packet, this will show the progress of our misfortunes by comparing it with the last, and on that melancholy subject am sorry to add that

---

§ Missing.

there seems to be no abatement in our misfortune. Poor Dr. Gregg, the Surgeon, died yesterday. In my last, I concluded you were long before, in possession of the Black Horse, but by a letter from Enys, I find he is still in his possession at Plymouth, and the same letter gives me to understand that your Lordship was still on the Continent, in command of the Light Cavalry, on that service, therefore you could have no great want of the horse, which however I have directed should be sent you on your return to England. I am happy to hear of the Second Battalion in the arrangement of which your Lordship has most certainly had particular attention to the interest of the Old Corps, not much to the satisfaction of Independent officers serving with us in this country. The state of the blackguard war in this Island is not materially altered since my last, though I think, if matters on the part of the insurgents continues much longer in their present state, they have no other alternative but to starve or submit to mercy, which last, has I think been wisely proffered to such as cannot be accused of murders, or other crimes particularly specified. This, with the inattention, or (what I hope is more probable) inability of their friends, at Guadaloupe, in offering them succour, has visibly damped their ardour, and several under the description of mercy, have claimed, and found it ; so that at this time we have only the enemy "climate" to contend with, which indeed seems to baffle every effort of medicine, and constitution, so much so, that according to the present mortality, a few weeks, will put a period to the existence of this deserted battalion.

For my own part, I never enjoyed better health, than since my arrival in the West Indies, nor have I the smallest apprehension of the contrary, it is not however without reason, that I should bless the power in which I received orders to your side of the Atlantic. The species of war in this Island is such that a man may easily lose credit by the least *misfortune*, but cannot gain any degree of honour in beating what may be termed a despicable enemy, which nothing could prevent from annihilation, except the strength of their fastnesses, which

1795 they have to retire to; but enough of so bad a subject. Pray present my best respects to Lady Cathcart, with the sincerest good wishes for all the young folk. I hope Kirkman does not forget his old Friends, either with, or without the, s,

>Believe me my dear Lord
>
>With much esteem and respect
>
>A. CAMPBELL."

In August, the insurgents assembled in great force, and on the 15th of October, captured Charlotte Town, where Colonel Schaw commanded. After this, 300 men landed from Martinico to help the troops to hold their own until further reinforcements arrived from England, for the climate proved more destructive than the enemy, and the 29th was, by the 3rd of September, reduced to 13 serjeants, 228 rank and file.

On the 24th of October, a reinforcement of 270 of the 17th Light Dragoons, and the 40th Foot, arrived.

According to the Regimental Muster Rolls, between the 15th of February and 16th of December, 26 serjeants, 17 corporals, and 359 privates had died or been killed since leaving England—in addition to these, Major & B^t.-Lieut.-Colonel R. Ramsay and Ensign Jas. Forbes had died during the autumn; and Captain A. Colman on the 16th of December.

1796 On the 4th of February, 1796, the "Sally" transport, with Captains J. Clavey and Edgell Wyatt, Lieut. R. Duddingstone, Ensign Samuel Galindo, 4 serjeants, 3 drummers, 129 rank and file, arrived at Grenada.

Further reinforcements being expected, Brigadier-General Nicholls decided, on their arrival, to attack the enemy's post at Port Royal, situated on the windward side of the Island. The position occupied by the insurgents was situated on a hill with very steep ascent, particularly towards the summit, on which a fort had been constructed, **1796** armed with four 6-pounders, and some swivel guns.

On the 22nd of March, General Nicholls, with two troops of 17th Light Dragoons, 200 men of the 9th, 10th, 25th, and 29th regiments, together with 500 of the Island Black Corps, marched to join the reinforcements, which were daily expected, and ordered to disembark near Port Royal.

On the 24th, detachments of the 8th and 63rd regiments, with part of the "Buffs," disembarked; two 6-pounders and a 5½-inch howitzer were also got ashore, and placed on a ridge about 1000 yards south of Port Royal.

During the night, a battery was constructed, and the following morning at daybreak, fire was opened on the enemy's redoubt. This disconcerted them very much, but General Nicholls' object being to close with the enemy as soon as possible, he determined to get on the same ridge with them, or, if he saw an opening, to attempt to carry the work by assault. For this purpose it was necessary to try and dislodge some strong parties which were posted on some heights to the left, as if intending to turn or threaten that flank. A strong black corps, and 50 of the 88th Foot, the whole under Major Houston, of the latter regiment, were therefore detailed for this service, but meeting with a reverse, the 8th (King's) was ordered to support them, which it did effectually.

At this moment an alarming fire broke out in rear of the troops, near a place where on landing all the stores had been deposited. By the exertions of the men these were all saved.

In the midst of these untoward circumstances, firing was heard from the ships-of-war, which lay at anchor, and it was ascertained that two French schooners, with reinforcements for the enemy, had arrived, and were making for "Marquis." As these were well within range of the 6-pounders, General Nicholls immediately ordered one to be turned

1796 against them. The situation of affairs was now so critical, that not an instant was to be lost, and Brigadier-General A. Campbell was ordered to proceed to the assault without delay. He therefore advanced with only the Buffs and 63rd Regiment. The 8th (King's) having, as before mentioned, been detached on another service, General Nicholls ordered up half of the 29th to replace them, also half of the 9th, to assist if necessary. The 29th having to march from Grand Bacolet, although it pushed forward as quickly as possible, did not arrive till after the Buffs had met with a check, in consequence of the advantage the enemy had of the ground, and of a very galling fire to which they were exposed. Brigadier-General Campbell then offered to carry the position with his regiment.

The 29th, accordingly, with orders not to fire, advanced to the assault, led by their colonel waving his hat and cheering them on.

The enemy, elated by their recent success, delivered a sharp fire, and advanced to meet them. The brushwood fence, where the Buffs had been checked, was passed steadily, and in perfect order ; then, with a rush, the position was forced, and, scrambling in at the embrasures, the fort was carried at the point of the bayonet, Captain Clavey being the first to enter. On this, the enemy fled in all directions ; some threw themselves down precipices, others tried to escape down the hill under cover of the bush ; but so heavy was the fire kept upon them, that they were forced to try and escape along a valley, where the detachment of the 17th Light Dragoons, under Captain Black, and the St. George's troop of light cavalry, rode them down, and though themselves exposed to a heavy fire of grape from the French schooners, cut down every man they saw ; but few who had been in the fort escaped. It was afterwards ascertained that the garrison had chiefly been composed of the Sansculottes companies from Guadaloupe.

The following day the insurgents evacuated, and burnt their fort on Pilot Hill, and retired to Morne Quaco, where they succeeded in maintaining their ground for some time.

Return of Killed and Wounded of the 29th Regiment at the Attack of Port Royal, Grenada, March 25, 1796.

Killed.—Serjeant—Combs, John ; Privates—Normanton, Jas. ; Pope, Isaac ; Woodcock, Geo.

Wounded.—Lieutenant—A. Brunton Tandy ; Ensign—Thos. Arbuthnot ; 12 Rank and File.

To Lord Cathcart.*

"Port Royal 4 June 1796

" My dear Lord,

Give me leave to assure your Lordship that I shall find a particular mortification if it should so happen that I shall be obliged to send this without the regular Return of the part of the 29th in this Country, to attend it ; but flatter myself should that be the case, that the present hurry of my situation will be accepted as an apology.

I am just informed that the Reinforcement of Troops after the Reduction of St. Lucia (which took place on the 26th of last month) are now on their way for this Island, and being likewise told that I shall have the Honor of commanding the Division of the Troops on this side of the island with which I shall probably march in the course of a very few days towards the Enemys stronghold at Morne Quaquo, taking such Position as is most likely to keep them in Check, and at the same time co-operate with two other considerable Columns, to move upon that point best from different situations on the other side of the Island ; I much doubt the possibility of having time to collect the necessary information from St. Georges, before my Departure from hence ; however shall keep this open to the last moment.———

---

* Original in possession of Lord Cathcart.

1796 The Commander-in-Chief is now at one of the neighbouring Islands, Carriacu, where B^r Gen. Nicolls is gone to meet him with every necessary information respecting the situation of matters in this Island.——But whether His Excellency will Honor this, or St. Vincent, with his presence first is yet uncertain. Both are the object of his present attention——the Business here, I have no doubt will very soon be settled; When I flatter myself I shall have it in my power to perform my Duty to your Lordship in a much more regular manner than hitherto, from the divided state of the Regiment.——

8th June. An opportunity offers immediately for St. Georges, and the Packet being hourly expected at that place, I think it best to send this to wait her arrival; therefore with my best Respects to Lady Cathcart, and every wish for the Health and Happiness of Her Ladyship, your Lordship, and Family, Believe me with the greatest respect and Esteem

   Your Lordships

    Most obed^t Hum^{le} Servt

     A. CAMPBELL."

On the 10th of June, the French in the island, under their commander, Jossy, surrendered all their posts, and by the 19th, the British were in full possession of all the enemy's positions. Fedon, with a few followers, escaped to the woods, but is supposed to have met with a watery grave whilst attempting to leave the island in a canoe.

By this time the 29th was so reduced in numbers that it was thought necessary to send it home, the effectives being first drafted into other corps. From the Regimental Muster Rolls, it appears that on the 24th of June, 6 corporals were drafted to the 4th West India Regiment, and 196 privates to the " Buffs."

On the 11th of July, what remained of the regiment embarked for England, and on the 15th, sailed for Tortola to join the homeward-bound convoy. During the passage Captain Clavey, Lieut. Duddingstone, and 13 privates died. Gosport was reached on the 29th of September. On disembarking, the detachment—a mere skeleton of the regiment, for it consisted of but 2 captains, 3 subalterns, 10 serjeants, 14 corporals, 10 drummers, and 53 privates—marched to Weymouth, where its late 2nd Battalion was stationed, under command of Major Enys.

The following officers were left sick in the West Indies: Lieut. Samuel Gauntlett, Ensigns Dudley Simper and John Quayle (the latter had recently been promoted from serjeant).

Brigadier-General Campbell, who remained behind on the staff, was soon afterwards appointed lieut.-governor of the island, but he never lived to hear of his promotion, for whilst making an inspection of the defences of Grenada, he was attacked by yellow fever, and died on the 15th of August, to the very great regret of all those who knew him, more especially of the 29th, with which regiment he had served over 38 years.

By a warrant issued on the 23rd of September, 1796, His Majesty was pleased to order that all "*Regimental Chaplains*" who did not join their respective corps before the 20th of December ensuing, should retire on the reduced subsistence of 5s. per diem, to commence from that day, and to continue during their natural lives. No chaplains hereafter were to be allowed to appoint a deputy.

The Rev. Geo. Turner, regimental chaplain, who had been absent on King's leave ever since the 21st of June, 1776, is in the Muster Rolls shown as "present with the regiment" between the 25th of June and the 24th December, 1796. This is the last mention of a regimental chaplain.

CHAPTER IX.

1796 Y the return of the detachment from Grenada, the regiment, after having been for over three years dispersed in different hemispheres, was, with the exception of those still serving as marines on board H.MS. "Blenheim," once more assembled together. The re-forming of the several companies, and posting of non-commissioned officers to them, was therefore shortly after commenced.

[LETTER 28].

"Weymouth, October 10, 1796. Sunday.

"I went to church with the regiment, and much as I had heard of the singing, it was beyond what I had conceived. The sermon by a young Scotchman, who left his text, and amused himself with every address he could think of most calculated to affect the feelings of those who had lately lost their relations; of that number were many of the poor 29th, and many persons who were very strongly affected. I afterwards passed some time with the regiment on parade * * * * Everything in this county is excellently contrived by Lord Milton, in case of any alarm, so as to prevent confusion, and to afford the greatest assistance to troops.

Yesterday I passed with my regiment, in and out of doors. I selected a Light company, then posted officers, non-commissioned officers, and drums to 10 companies. These went into an house, and drew lots for eight Battalion companies, the men's names being classed in three sizes, and numbers opposite to each name, with corresponding numbers in a tin box. Eight officers were placed in line, and the box **1796** handed round successively till all the numbers were drawn. These officers represented the eight companies, so that each had an impartial lot of each size. I then inspected the invalids, and men unfit for service."

On the 21st of November, orders were sent for a detachment of commissioned and non-commissioned officers to proceed to Worcester, and receive an allotment of recruits, agreeable to the late Act of Parliament.*

As this seemed a good opportunity of endeavouring to regain the county interest, which, as already mentioned, had been lost by no fault of the regiment, Col. Enys had particular orders to explain the cause of the former difficulty, and to essay, by every means in his power, to re-instate the 29th in the favour it had formerly enjoyed in Worcestershire. Great pains were taken to effect this, and his efforts were at first attended with considerable success; but after having attended many public meetings, and, on the faith of orders received, assured all the men so raised, that there could be no doubt that in this instance, they should join their county regiment, judge the surprise of all parties, when orders were received from the War Office to return to Weymouth, and to transfer the "*quota men*" raised in Worcestershire! to the 46th Foot.

Thus, for very many years the 29th (Worcestershire) Regiment lost every hope of deriving any benefit from bearing the name of that county.

---

* Act (passed 11th November, 1796) for raising a certain number of men in the several Counties in England, for Service in His Majesty's Army and Navy. The number of men to be levied for the said respective Services by virtue of this Act shall be as follows:—For the County of Worcester, with the City and County of the City of Worcester, 156 for the Army.

1796

"Worcester. Dec. 8, 1796.*

"My Lord,

I have the pleasure to inform you the party under my command arrived here this morning and I have every reason to be satisfied with their appearance. But I think it will surprise you to hear that I found orders from the Adjutant-General on my arrival that the men I receive are not to join the 29th Regiment, but to be attested for the 46th I am nevertheless ordered to remain here and take charge of the whole until the arrival of an officer of that Regiment. I am very sorry to find this is the case as we should probably have gotten many very good men as I am told several very respectable Magistrates have exerted themselves very much under the Idea they were serving their County Regiment who now as well as myself feel themselves hurt at being duped in such a manner. I find there is a Surgeon sent by the Medical Board to inspect the men so that Mr. Carter may if he pleases return to the Regiment whilst I have the honor to be

Your most obedient
Humble Servant,

"Lord Cathcart." Jno. Enys."

"W.O. 10 Dec. 1796.†

"Sir,

I am desir^d by the S at W to ac^{qt} you, that in conseq^{ce} of a new Regulation it being found expedient for the Recruits furnished by the County of Worcester to be rec^d by the 46th Reg^t of Foot, you will cause the Party under your com^d on being relieved by a Party of the said 46th Reg^t to return to their former Quarters at Weymouth.

I am Sir

"Officer Com^g M. Lewis."
   the Party of the 29th Foot
   at Worcester."

---

* From the original in possession of Lord Cathcart.
† From Secretary of State's Common Letter Book, 1796, vol. 14.

By the Monthly Returns, dated Weymouth, 1st January, 1797, it **1797** appears that the following were "on command" at Worcester: Lieut.-Col. Enys, Captain W. E. Wyatt, Lieutenants Blois Lynch, R. Ross Rowan, Francis Rawdon, Surgeon Carter, 6 serjeants, 11 rank and file. These rejoined head-quarters during the month.

Information having been received that the French intended to attempt a landing on the coast of Dorsetshire, similar to those which had but recently taken place at Bantry, and in Pembrokeshire, it became necessary to be more than ordinarily watchful, and prepared, especially as, with a view of invading England, and helping the disaffected Irish, Spain and Holland now threw in their lot with France, and large fleets were being got ready at Texel, Brest, and Cadiz. On the 14th of February, Admiral Sir John Jervis defeated the Spanish fleet off St. Vincent. Towards the end of that month, the regiment marched to Bridport *en route* to Bideford. Just previous to this it had been joined by its last detachment, till then serving on board the fleet.

The following is a Return of a Detachment of Royal Artillery, attached with battalion guns ‡ to the 29th Regiment of Foot.

Weymouth, 27 February, 1797.

	Bombadier.	Gunners.	Conductor.	Drivers.	Horses.	Light 6-Pdrs.	Ammunition Waggon.
The Conductor, Drivers, and Horses of Thomas Wellen, Esqr., Contract................ Joined the 29th Regt. the 10th day of November, 1796							
Total	1	4	1	2	9	2	1

‡ Colonel Duncan, in his "History of the Royal Artillery," says :—" Battⁿ guns were drawn by 6 drag-rope men; the guns, although attached to different battalions, in pairs, were occasionally brigaded. The Detach^{ts} of R.A. present with such guns in Ireland ('98) were six in number, each consisting of 1 N.C.O and 9 men, the whole under command of Captain Geary assisted by 3 Subalterns. After the Rebellion, the men of the R.A. returned to England. The regiments to which they were attached were 3 Batt^{ns} of the Guards, the 'Queen's,' 29th, and 100th. Infantry regiments took guns with them to Holland in 1799, but they seem to have fallen into disuse a few years before the Peninsular War."

1797 *Return§ of Stores and Ammunition with the Two Light Six-Pounders attached to the 29th Regiment of Foot.*

Laboratory Stores.

Fixed to Wood Bottoms, and Flannel Cartridges. Shot filled with Powder	Round, 1½ lb. each	120
	Case, 1¼ oz. each	80
	Total...	200
Flannel Cartridges Filled with Powder	With 1½ lb. each	63
	1¼ oz. each	33
.... 10 oz. Cartridges		35
	Total...	131

And^R McBeath, Bom^{dr}
Royal Artillery.

On the 8th of March, the regiment arrived at Bideford, and on the 26th, Lieut.-Colonel H. Dickson received information that the 2nd (or Queen's Royal), 29th, and 58th regiments were to be formed into a brigade, to do duty in the Western District under command of Major-General Wm. Grinfield. In order that they might be in readiness to pass over to Ireland, should re-inforcements there be required, this brigade remained in North Devon for some months.

On the 31st of May, notice was sent to Major-General Lord Cathcart that His Majesty had been pleased to direct that a reduction of 12 lieutenants (being one per company) should be made in the establishment of the regiment.

The officers who, in consequence of this measure, became supernumerary, were to continue to do duty with the regiment, and fall into

---

§ Lord Cathcart's MS.

vacant lieutenancies on the establishment as they occurred, without purchase, but were not to be replaced by other officers. **1797**

In consequence of many attempts made to seduce soldiers from their allegiance, the non-commissioned officers, drummers, and privates of the regiment addressed the following letter* to their commanding officer :—

"Bideford, June 4th, 1797.

"Sir,

We the Noncommissioned Officers, Drum^{rs}, and Privates of His Majesty's 29th (or Worcestershire) Regiment of Foot do request Lieut.-Col. Dickson to make known to Major-Genl, William, Lord Cathcart, Colonel of the said Regiment; and also to General, Lord George Lennox, Commander in Chief of the Western District, ——Our firm, and unshaken Attachment to our King, and Country; and to assure them that no art of designing Men, shall ever seduce us from our former Allegiance to our Sovereign and his Government; that we shall ever hold in just abhorrence any attempt at the Subversion of that good order which has ever characterised the 29th Reg^t.—And we trust ever inviolably to preserve the Character of a corps, whose Loyalty, love of Discipline, and Subordination, have never yet been questioned.——We also gratefully serve the present opportunity of expressing the sense we entertain of His Majesty's favour, and more particularly of the late signal Instance of his goodness to us, and our fellow soldiers in the augmentation of our Pay.——We have therefore with duty, and respect unanimously commissioned Serjeant Major Thomas Stott to sign the above for the whole of the Non Commissioned Officers, Drummers, and Privates of the 29th Regiment.

THOS. STOTT,

"To Lieut Col Dickson "Serg^t Maj 29th Reg^t."
 Command^g 29th Reg^t of Foot
 at Bideford."

---

* Original in possession of Lord Cathcart.

1797   Two days after this regimental declaration, an Act of Parliament was passed, for the better prevention, and punishment of attempts to seduce persons serving in His Majesty's Forces, by sea or land, from their duty and allegiance to His Majesty, which decreed, that from and after the passing of this Act, any person, on being legally convicted of such offence, be adjudged guilty of felony, and shall suffer death, as in cases of felony, without the benefit of clergy.

Colonel Enys, writing from Bideford, on the 19th of July, to Lord Cathcart, says . . . . "Mr. Dalgety also wishes me to inform you, that Mr. Dukie has been very tardy, and inattentive with regard to the Clothing, That the Clothing written for from Weymouth is not yet come, and that some of the last he did send, is far from being agreeable to the Regimental Pattern, having ten Buttons on the Lappells, exclusive of the one on the Collar, Nor is there any Lace on the inside of the Lappells, as ordered."

On the 8th of August, Major-General Lord Cathcart was transferred to the Colonelcy of the 2nd Life Guards, and Major-General Gordon Forbes, Colonel of the 81st Foot, was appointed to that of the 29th.

In consequence of a report that a large number of French troops had embarked at Brest, with the intention of making a descent on the Cornish coast, the "Queen's" and the 29th were ordered to Truro.

On the 17th, the former regiment, with the artillery, left Truro, and marched by way of Torrington; whilst the 29th, in order to try the route through Camelford, which had never been passed by troops since the civil war, was directed to proceed by Stratton. The only part of the road out of repair, lay between these two places, it having a few days previously been very much damaged by the bursting of a waterspout. Truro being reached on the 23rd, the regiment halted for about six days, and then proceeded to Falmouth, where, on account of the crowded state of that town, it encamped between the end of the town and the sea, on what was then known as Bath's Farm. There **1797** were at this period stationed in Falmouth Harbour two squadrons of frigates, the one commanded by Sir John Warren, the other by Sir Edward Pellew; these took it in turn to visit the French coast, and ascertain the movements of the force expected thence.

MUSTER ROLLS.—FALMOUTH CAMP, 16TH SEPTEMBER, 1797.

LIST OF OFFICERS OF 29TH REGIMENT.

Colonel William Lord Cathcart

Lieut.-Colonels { Hugh Dickson / John Enys

Majors { James Kirkman / Francis W. Farquhar

Captains {
George Johnstone
Wm. Jacques
Daniel White
Robert Harrison
Chas. B. Egerton
W. Bertrand
W. Edgell Wyatt
Chas. T. Grant
Thos. B. Egerton
Wm. Shairp
}

Capt.-Lieut. Thos. Fitzgerald

Lieutenants {
John Tucker
L. Augustus Northey
George Dalmer
Patk. Henderson
Wm. P. Seymour
Geo. S. Burdett
Saml. Gauntlett
Edmund Rolleston
Hen. B. Lynch
Alexd. Dalgety
George Tod
A. Brunton Tandy
Arth. Wilkinson
Emd. Hutchinson
Ralph R. Rowan
Francis Rawdon
Nathl. Forster
John Drury
John Rose
Eugene Nestor
Saml. Holden
Stewart Barclay
Edmd. Ormsby
}

Ensigns {
James Linklater
J. Blake Lynch
Dudley Simper
David Delancy
John Quayle
John Johnston
.... Webb
Thos. O'Neil
John Balderson
}

Adjutant Thos. O'Neil

Qr. Masters { Alexd. Dalgety / R. Nosworthy

Surgeon Hen. Lennon

Asst. Surgeons { Alexd. Hodge / John Wilson / Edwd. Walsh

When, on the 8th of October, orders were received to return to Truro, everyone was well pleased, for their present camp occupied an exposed position, and the weather had been very bad. Detachments having been sent to Penryn, Pendennis Castle, and Redruth, the head-quarters of the regiment shortly after left Falmouth.

1797 The French—notwithstanding the defeat inflicted in February on their Spanish allies—had by no means abandoned their projected invasion, and during the summer, a fleet under the command of Admiral de Winter, was prepared at Texel to convey 15,000 men to Ireland. When, in October, it sailed for Brest, Admiral Duncan, who had been watching the enemy for some time, gave them battle off Camperdown, and, after a desperate engagement, came off victorious. This victory being followed up the next year by the blockade of Havre, and the battle of the Nile, all projects of invasion were, for a time, effectually checked.

LIEUT.-COLONEL JOHN ENYS.

By a Return dated Truro, the 9th of November, it appears that both the King's, and Regimental Colours were in a bad condition. Such being the case, Major-General Gordon Forbes, the colonel of the regiment would present it with a new set, which in all probability were those carried by the 29th in the expedition to Holland, and throughout the Peninsular War.

On the 22nd of December, the regiment marched for Plymouth, **1797** where, on arrival, it took up quarters in the Mill Prison Barracks, and was brigaded with the "Queen's," and 25th Regiment, under command of Lord Dalhousie.

Extracts|| *from a diary kept by Lieut. Henry Grove, who purchased a lieutenancy in the 29th, and subsequently a company in the 57th Foot* :—

"In the summer of 1797 I joined the 29th at Falmouth, where they were then encamped with the 2nd (Queen's), and a brigade of the Royal Artillery.

"The 29th was always one of the most exact Corps in the Service, even to trifles, and to this day every officer sits down to dinner with his sword on,† but one of our very best men, weighing 20 stone, found it so inconvenient, that he was allowed to dine without his sword, provided it hung up immediately behind him.

"The youngest member at the mess table, was obliged to wear a green leathern apron, to prevent any wine being spilled over his white kerseymere 'shorts,' as he had to draw all the wine which was drunk. If he left the room, he had to hand over the apron to the next youngest member.

"I never saw a mess waiter of the 29th draw a bottle of wine.

"Colonel Enys undertook the Mess accounts, and every Friday afternoon, each officer was called upon to pay his week's bill.

"We wore powder in those days, and the hair was formed in a club behind, with a black rosette; shoes, and black cloth gaiters to the cap of the knee, with Regimental buttons. The Coat was cut off at

---

|| Supplied by Colonel R. J. Watson.

† This old custom, which is mentioned in the Standing Orders of the regiment in 1792, was altered during the tour of service in the East Indies, 1842-59, when only the Captain, and Subaltern of the Day, were required to dine with their sword on. Such is still the case. Tradition relates that the custom of being "*eversworded*" dates back to September, 1746.

1797 the sides, and turned over like those of the Greenwich Pensioners: in front, a hook was passed through an eyelet in the frill of the shirt which was displayed to advantage. The other parts of our dress were, a white kerseymere waistcoat, cut off in front, with flaps to the pockets, with 4 buttons to each: the Breeches of white kerseymere, with Reg^{tl} buttons at the knee; a cocked hat worn square to the front, the least more over the right eye than the left.

"We had a corps of Black Drummers: the one beating the Big Drum in the centre was a handsome man, 6 feet 4 inches."

1798 On the 27th of March, 1798, the regiment received orders to march in two divisions to Barnstaple and Pilton. Early the next month nine companies proceeded to Bideford, and one to Appledore; the latter rejoined head-quarters in May. About this time the Irish Rebellion broke out, and it having been decided to send the "Queen's" and the 29th Foot to that country, agents of transports were sent down. On the 14th of June, the regiment sailed from Appledore, and Passage was reached on the 17th, but it was the 19th before orders were received from Major-General Fawcett, who commanded at Duncannon Fort, for the 29th to disembark at Ballyhack, and proceed two or three miles along the road towards Ross, where he would meet it. These orders were carried out, and after having waited almost the whole day at the appointed place, without either seeing or hearing from the general, as evening was closing in, it was decided to return to Ballyhack. The "Queen's" being the leading regiment on the return march, filled the village so full that Colonel Enys ordered his men to return on board the transports for the night. Here we will leave them for a time, in order to obtain a glimpse of the state of affairs previous to their arrival in Ireland.

From the time of the failure of the French expedition to Bantry (December, 1796), the disaffected Irish kept up the spirits of their party by circulating reports that another descent would soon be attempted. In order to supply themselves with arms, nocturnal domiciliary visits in

search of weapons took place, and scarcely a night passed without some **1798**
dreadful enormity being perpetrated. To compel people to join them,
houses were demolished or burnt, cattle destroyed, and people being
dragged from their beds, had their ears cropped off and were otherwise
maimed or murdered. Thousands, in order to save their lives, were
obliged to compromise with the rebels, to give up their arms, and take
the oath of secrecy. In March, some of the most influential amongst
the rebel leaders were arrested, but those who succeeded them, devoted
themselves with the utmost energy to hurrying on the arming of the
people, and in endeavouring to seduce soldiers from their allegiance to
the King.

Many rebels enlisted in the King's forces, for the purpose of
obtaining a knowledge of discipline, and then deserted with their arms
and ammunition. The 23rd of May was fixed on as the day for a
general rising, and the first intelligence of the rebellion having broken
out at Rathfarnham, about three miles from Dublin, was received in
that city the following morning. The nature of the surrounding
country enabled troops to move with rapidity, and within a fortnight
the rebels were dispersed, but only to join similar parties in Counties
Wicklow and Wexford, where mountains and wooded defiles were of
great advantage to them.

A general massacre of Protestants now commenced. Some were
shot, some stabbed to death with pikes, whilst others, stripped almost
naked, had pitch caps put on their heads, and were compelled to march
several miles, previous to their execution. Houses were set fire to,
and when the inmates, driven upstairs by the flames, endeavoured to
escape by leaping from the windows, the rebels received them on the
points of their pikes. In one unfortunate affair with the insurgents, a
drummer boy, aged 12, of the Antrim Militia, fell into their hands.
The rebels, having intentions of making him serve them as a drummer,
desired him to beat his drum, but the brave and loyal little fellow
exclaimed that, "the King's drum, should never be beaten for rebels,"

1798 and instantly broke through both its heads. His body was immediately perforated by pikes.

The county of Wexford now became the centre of attraction, for the rebels had gathered in two large encampments—one on Vinegar Hill, above Enniscorthy; the other on Carrickbyrne Hill, a few miles from Ross. On the 16th of June, Lieut.-General Lake, commanding the forces in Ireland, issued orders preparatory to the attack on these two positions, and the occupation of Wexford. Sir John Moore was directed to land on the 18th at Ballyhack-ferry, to move at 3 a.m. the 19th to Foulkes's Mill, unite with General Sir Henry Johnson (who was advancing from Ross) in driving the rebels from Carrickbyrne Hill, and afterwards to take up a position near Foulkes's Mill for the night, and intercept the escape of rebels between that place and Clonmines. The general forward movement, and investment of Wexford was to take place on the 21st. This is how matters stood when on the 19th of June the regiment landed.

DISEMBARKATION RETURN OF THE 29TH FOOT AT BALLYHACK, 19TH JUNE, 1798.

2 Lieutenant-Colonels, 1 Major, 6 Captains, 18 Lieutenants, 7 Ensigns, 1 Paymaster, 1 Adjutant, 1 Quarter Master, 1 Surgeon, 1 Assistant Surgeon.

Present fit for duty	37 Sergeants	20 Drummers and Fifers	532 Rank and File
Sick in England			7 ,,
On command			4 ,,
Recruiting			47 ,,
Wanting to complete	8 ,,	1 ,,	10 ,,

Absent Officers
- Captain Thos. Egerton, by leave of Genl. Lord George Lennox, for recovering his health.
- ,, Wm. E. Wyatt, left sick at Bideford.
- Ensign John Johnston, absent without leave.

Absent on Duty
- Major Farquhar, at Chatham.
- Captain Robert Harrison, recruiting.
- Lieutenant Patrick Henderson ,,
- ,, A. Brunton Tandy ,,
- ,, Edward Ormsby ,,

Vacant
- 1 Captain-Lieutenant, by Capt.-Lieut. Fitzgerald app^{td}. Paymaster.
- 1 Lieutenant, by promotion of Lieut. Armstrong to 83rd Foot.

During the night orders were received for the "Queen's" and **1798** 29th, who had returned to Ballyhack, to proceed to Foulkes's Mill, and place themselves under the command of Sir John Moore. It being daylight before the boats could be got ready, the "Queen's," who had passed the night ashore, had more than an hour's start of the 29th, and were taken by General Fawcett to dislodge a party of rebels supposed to be in the vicinity of Duncannon Fort, but failing to discover any trace of an enemy, the two regiments proceeded together towards their destination. In the evening, from the top of a hill about two miles off Foulkes's Mill, firing was heard, and it was discovered that Sir John Moore was engaged with a considerable body of the rebels under command of their General Roche, who, instead of waiting to be attacked at Carrickbyrne, had taken the initiative.

Every effort was now made to reach the contending parties as quickly as possible, but at the approach of the two regiments the rebels dispersed, and fled towards Enniscorthy and Wexford. After this "pretty sharp action," as Sir John termed it, he returned to his position at the cross roads near Foulkes's Mill, where the reinforcements joined him. The 29th lay on their arms that night, and took the opportunity of cooking two days' provisions.

On the morning of the 21st, Sir John's force was joined by a battalion of light infantry from the Irish Militia, some of Hompesch's mounted riflemen, and two curricle* guns, with a party of the Irish Artillery; with these he marched to Taghmon, *en route* for Wexford. During the day, the firing of cannon in the distance, was heard; this afterwards proved to be the engagement at Vinegar Hill. When the rebels saw a numerous, and well-appointed army, march into the county of Wexford, and commence to surround them, they resolved to indulge their fanatical hatred against Protestants, by murdering such as were their prisoners. Numbers were killed by the mob in Wexford on the 20th. The general manner of putting them to death was this :—Two

---

* Small pieces drawn by two horses.

1798 rebels pushed their pikes into the breast of the victim, while two were pushed into his back, and thus, writhing with torture, he was held aloft till dead, and then the body was thrown over the bridge into the water. Ninety-seven alone, thus ended their days on the bridge. The mob, consisting of more women than men, expressed their joy on the immolation of each of their victims, by loud cheers. Whilst thus amusing themselves, information was received that Vinegar Hill was beset, and reinforcements wanted, on which several immediately set out for that camp. The news of the victory at Foulkes's Mill was received at Wexford the same evening on which it was gained, and after the bloody massacres which had been perpetrated, a number of the rebel leaders who had been present at them, assembled at Governor Keugh's house, and, in hopes of procuring an amnesty, concerted measures of conciliation. These proposals they despatched the following morning to Generals Lake and Moore, by some officers, their prisoners. Sir John, hearing of the state of affairs in Wexford, and the atrocities which were being committed, thinking he might be the means of saving the town itself from fire, as well as the lives of many loyal subjects, pushed forward as fast as possible. On the way, Major Kirkman, 29th Regiment, who commanded the advance guard, saw a large body of rebels near the "Three Rocks." This was afterwards ascertained to have been part of their force retiring from Vinegar Hill, which had passed through Wexford, and which, on getting into the Barony of Forth, dispersed itself so effectually that nothing more was heard of it. On nearing Wexford, the 29th were just in time to save several Protestants, who were shut up in a barn, from being burnt to death, for on the sudden arrival of the King's troops, the rebels beat a hurried retreat. When Sir John got within two miles of the town, the "Queen's" was ordered into Wexford, whilst the remainder of his troops halted. The 29th lay on their arms for the night on some ground near the house of Mr. Jacobs, mayor of that town. The next day General Lake's force approached Wexford, and in the evening the regiment advanced nearer the town, and formed on some ground just outside the suburbs, with the object of intercepting any rebel stragglers **1798** who, having remained concealed in Wexford, might now attempt to escape; and in this they were successful. The regiment again bivouacked for the night, and about noon on the 23rd marched into Wexford, and was placed under command of Major-General Peter Hunter, in what was called the "English brigade." This brigade consisted of the "Queen's," 29th, and 100th regiments, with two six-pounders from the British artillery, and, although serving in Ireland, remained on the English establishment, and made all reports to the War Office. In the meanwhile Lord Cornwallis arrived in Dublin to assume supreme power, both civil and military.

On the 26th of June, General Lake's force left the vicinity of Wexford, and only the "Queen's" and 29th, under General Hunter, remained in the town.

During their stay here, a great many people were tried and executed for being concerned in the rebellion. Among these was Mr. Keugh, formerly a captain-lieutenant in the 65th Foot, but who had been dismissed the service two years previously. Mr. Bagenal Harvey, who had commanded at Ross, Cornelius Grogan the rebels' quarter-master-general, Mr. Colclough (all three men of position and fortune), and Father Roche, their priest and commander-in-chief, who pretended he was invulnerable, and could catch musket balls in his hands, were also launched into eternity.

The regimental baggage, and camp equipage having arrived on the 7th of July, the regiment marched out of the town, and encamped where it had passed the night, previous to entering Wexford, in June. Here it remained till the 24th of August, when information being received that two days previously, three French frigates had cast anchor in Killalla Bay, and troops, under the command of Général Humbert, were being landed, General Hunter's brigade was directed to march to Kilkenny, and there await further orders which were to be issued from day to day.

1798 The marches the regiment now commenced were as follows :—

26th August	Wexford to Ross	19 Miles.	
27th „	to Killkenny	21 „	
28th „	to Castle Durrow	12 „	
29th „	to Barrow in Ossory	12 „	Marched across country.
30th „	to Birr	15 „	
31st „	to Ballinasloe	24 „	Marched across country.
1st September	to Glentaine	13 „	There being only one house, the regiment encamped.
2nd „	to Tuam	11 „	Joined the army under Lord Cornwallis, and encamped two miles from the town.
3rd „	Halted whilst General Lake, with the Reay Fencibles, the Armagh Militia with their Battalion guns, and a detachment of Roxborough's Fencible Cavalry, started off in a more northerly direction to join a brigade under Major-General Taylor, at Ballyhadirreen.		
4th „	Tuam to Hollymount	12 „	Encamped.
5th „	to Ballyhaunis	16 „	„
6th „	to French Park	15 „	„
7th „	to Carrick-on-Shannon / to St. Johnstown	20 „ / 30 „	} 50 Miles.

On passing the bridge at Carrick-on-Shannon, the regiment was ordered to keep back all women, and baggage, and take post on some high ground commanding a road along which it was expected the enemy might advance. On a report being issued that the French had changed their line of march, and were making for Manor Hamilton, it was with a certain amount of pleasure that the troops, after a long day's march, received orders to encamp, and cook two days' provisions. Before this order could be carried into effect, intelligence was received that the French, and rebels, after being attacked at Coloony by the Limerick Militia, were being closely pursued by General Lake, and had but four hours previously crossed the Shannon, at Ballintra Bridge, about seven miles above Carrick.

The men, tired not only by their late march, but also by collecting turf to cook with, and grass to sleep on, were therefore ordered to resume their march. During the night the regiment passed through a small village which paid it the compliment of illuminating the houses, and a piper was stationed at one of the windows playing national tunes as it marched through. As day was breaking, Mohill was reached, where some prisoners were found, and information was received that the enemy, with General Lake close on their rear, was marching on a nearly parallel road about two or three miles distant. By 8 a.m. on the 8th of September, the Flank companies of the "Queen's" and 29th Regiment, the Bucks and Warwickshire Militia, came in view of the enemy, who had halted for the night at Cloone. Lord Cornwallis, not deeming it prudent to attack with these troops only, waited for the remainder of his column. The enemy in the meantime had moved off, but were soon overtaken by General Lake. About 11 a.m., the sight of the engagement, and the blowing up of a tumbril, cheered the men considerably, and they pushed on with all speed until the Bridge of St. Johnstown, a distance of 50 miles from French Park, was reached and occupied. It now became evident that the object of this forced march was to cut off the retreat of the French to Granard, where it was said Général Humbert expected to be joined by many friends.

Whilst in this situation, intelligence was received that the French had surrendered to General Lake, and shortly afterwards, their generals, Humbert and Sarrasin, with the principal officers of their staffs, were brought before Lord Cornwallis, who was on a small height near the front of the 29th. After this, the troops encamped for the night, on the ground they occupied.

On the 8th of September, many prisoners were brought in, and disposed of as follows. The French generals with their staffs, were sent to Dublin; the remaining officers, and men being despatched to Longford.

1798   On the 10th, a Military Court was assembled for the trial of rebel prisoners, who may be said to have been divided into three classes :—

> The 1st consisted of 13 deserters from the Kilkenny and Longford Militia; these were sentenced to death, and executed the next day.
>
> The whole of the 2nd class were sentenced to death, but it is believed that in most cases the sentences were commuted.
>
> The 3rd class were dismissed to their homes, being told that should they ever again be found in such circumstances, they might not be let off so easily.

On the 12th, the regiment marched from the camp at St. Johnstown to Longford, and the following morning took charge of and proceeded with French prisoners to Mullingar, and thence, on the 14th, to Philipstown, where they handed them over to a party of militia, sent from Dublin with boats, to convey them by means of the canal to that city.

In consequence of a report that a part of another French expedition had been seen off Bantry Bay, General Hunter's brigade left Philipstown on the 26th, for Cashel, where it arrived on the 28th, and encamped till the 3rd of October, when it again returned to Philipstown. When within a short distance of that place, an orderly arrived, bringing information of the capture of the French fleet, which had caused the alarm, by Admiral Sir J. Borlase Warren. Thus ended the long-projected French invasion.

On the 23rd instant, the regiment marched for Maryborough; on the 24th it proceeded to Castle Durrow, and the following day arrived at Kilkenny where it took up quarters for the winter.

On the 18th of November, a number of prisoners, under sentence of transportation, arrived at Kilkenny. After a day's halt, they continued their route to Waterford, under escort of 150 of the 29th Foot,

and 30 of the 9th Light Dragoons, the whole under command of Col. **1798**
Enys, who wrote the following account :—

"We halted the first night at Thomastown, when the weather proved the most inclement I ever saw in Europe, and I am sorry to say that, notwithstanding every care possible was taken, one man of the 29th, and two prisoners, were so much affected by the cold, that they died in course of the night, and many did not recover for many days after, which obliged me when I returned on the 23rd to leave an Officer behind to bring them up when able to march. I also found on enquiry, that the Dragoons were as much affected as the Infantry, for they acknowledged that had they been called on to act, they were all so benumbed that they could not have drawn their Swords.——Most happy was I to give up my charge to Lord Rolle, who was quartered at Waterford with the Devon Militia. Having halted a day at Waterford, the weather became more moderate, and the escort returned without difficulty."

On the 25th of December, the "Queen's," and 29th, were placed on the Irish establishment, and from that time ceased to report to the War Office in London.

The following detachments were for a time furnished by the 29th, but rejoined head-quarters 1st February, 1799 :—

    1 Company at Graigue
    1   ,,   Borris
    1   ,,   Gore's Bridge.

The remainder of the winter passed off very quietly, and early in the spring, on Major-General Hunter being appointed Lieut.-Governor **1799** of Upper Canada, Major-General Gardiner took over the command of the brigade.

On the 7th of May, in consequence of reports that the French were again meditating a descent, and had been seen off the coast, the brigade left Kilkenny; the "Queen's," with General Gardiner, marching

1799 to Tullamore, the 29th to Philipstown. On the 11th of June, both regiments returned to Kilkenny, soon after which the former received orders to embark for England.

Previous to the 29th leaving Philipstown, Captain Wm. Shairp, who "had been out," received a ball in his groin, which completely disabled and prevented him taking part in the approaching campaign in Holland.

Late in the evening of the 13th of July, orders were received by express, for the regiment to march with all possible speed to Cork, and there embark for England. On the arrival of frigates, no time was lost, and having embarked on board the "Melpomene," "Naiad," "Proselyte," and "Pomone" (on which were the head-quarters), the ships sailed from Cove on the 24th. After a favourable passage, the regiment landed at Deal early in the morning of the 30th, and marched to Barnham Downs, where it was brigaded with the "Queen's," 27th, 55th, and 85th regiments, under command of Major-General Sir Eyre Coote, and encamped with the army there assembling for the expedition to the Helder, under command of Sir Ralph Abercromby.

Previous to this the British Ministry had decided to send an army to Holland, with the desire of bringing that country once more under the dominion of the House of Orange, believing that numbers of the Dutch would combine with them, as soon as they could with safety act according to their sentiments. Negotiations were also entered upon with Emperor Paul I. of Russia, with the view of obtaining the assistance of an auxiliary corps of Russian troops, and on the 22nd of June, a treaty to that effect had been concluded.

On the 8th of August the camp broke up, and on the 11th, the 29th marched to the village of Birchington, on the coast of the Isle of Thanet. Here it encamped till the 13th, when it marched for Margate, and embarked on board the "Royal Admiral," an old East Indiaman, which accommodated the whole of the regiment, together with all its **1799** light baggage. The heavy baggage, and sick were sent to Deal, under command of Major George Johnstone.

Sailing on the 14th inst., the "Royal Admiral" was joined by various transports which had embarked troops at Dover, Deal, and Ramsgate.

On account of the very stormy weather, the Helder was not reached till the 21st, and the following morning the "Royal Admiral" got near enough to anchor, but in a few hours the wind blew so hard that it was found necessary to weigh anchor, and put to sea. It was not till the morning of the 26th that the whole expedition again approached the shore, and anchored. That evening instructions were received for Major-General Coote's brigade, and a detachment of light artillery, the whole under the command of Lieut.-General Sir James Pulteney, to effect a landing the next morning, in front of the right of the line of transports.

That the 29th was always a very exact corps one may gather from a Regimental Order issued that evening preparatory to its disembarking, viz.: "Officers are to be clubbed,* and powdered, but may wear blue overalls provided they have regimental buttons."

At 3 a.m. on the 27th instant, two flat-bottomed boats from the "Melpomene," together with the ship's boats, were filled with the Flank companies of the regiment, under the command of Captain D. White. The men had each been supplied with 60 rounds of ball ammunition, two days' provisions, and had their canteens filled with spirits and water. Major Ramsay, of the "Queen's," commanded the Flank companies of the brigade. When everything was ready, a gun fired from the admiral's ship, gave the signal for the simultaneous

---

* Circular Memo., 2nd May, 1799.—Officers and Men to wear their hair queued; tied a little below the upper part of the collar, and to be ten inches in length, including one inch of hair to appear below the binding.

1799 advance of the landing parties, whose approach covered by a heavy and incessant fire from all the men-of-war, and gunboats, met with but small opposition.

On landing, the troops found themselves on a ridge of sandhills stretching along the coast, north and south. Scarcely, however, had the 1st Division formed up than it was met with volleys of musketry, and a continued fire of light artillery.

The right flank being unavoidably exposed to the whole force, and fire of the enemy, many casualties occurred. The first object of contention, was a signal station situated on a slight eminence, which, after a sharp contest, was carried by the Flank companies of the "Queen's," 27th, 29th, and 85th regiments. This position afterwards proved of great service in directing the fire from the fleet, and gunboats.

The following anecdote is related by Mr. Edward Walsh, assistant surgeon to the regiment :—

" The gallantry, and spirit of the 29th Grenadiers deserves to be mentioned.

" Finding themselves encumbered with their knapsacks, &c., while charging the enemy through the heavy sand, they threw away both them, and their provisions. After the battle they petitioned to have these necessaries replaced, which in truth they very much wanted, but from a strict adherence to the rules of military discipline the request could not be granted."

Lieut. H. Grove, in his diary, writes :—

"I was Lieutenant of the Grenadiers, commanded by William Edgell Wyatt. We had 3 subalterns, Henderson, † Tod, and myself, Tod being the only one who was not wounded. Wyatt was shot through

---

† *Extract from the " Military Chronicle."*—Lieut.-Colonel Henderson of the Royal York Rangers, b. near Aberdeen 16 Sept. 1775, accompanied the 29th Foot on board H.M.S. " Glory," was present at the Action of 28th and 29th May, and 1st June, 1794,

the thigh, Henderson was saved by having a thick map in his pocket, six folds of which were shot through. I was shot in the chin, and for this wound, twenty years after, received a year's pay. I was taken with others on board the "Romney," 50 guns, and the regimental surgeon ordered me off, saying my wound was not likely to spoil my beauty or destroy my constitution; had I been a little older I should not have left the field; in short I was more frightened than hurt. Admiral Mitchell who commanded the fleet, now turned his thoughts to the Dutch fleet, all chained together in the Zuyder Zee. A Russian 64 took the lead, but as she got aground, the "Romney" took her place. Captain Lamford advised me to go below when the Action commenced, to keep out of danger, to this I demurred, so he gave me the command of a gun on the main deck. At last a flag of truce, announced the surrender of the Dutch fleet. When the Duke of York arrived with reinforcements, the army advanced to Schagen, and I re-joined the 29th."

In the meanwhile the remainder of the regiment was anxiously awaiting the arrival of the boats to take it ashore, for those of the "Royal William" had been detained near the beach. At length a lugger came alongside, and by means of it, the men were landed in detachments, which advanced until met by General Coote, who ordered them to halt, and await his further orders. About 1 o'clock the head-quarters of the regiment were joined by Captain White and the Flank

---

when he was wounded. Served with the regiment in Holland, and commanded the Grenadier company (his captain being wounded at the landing.) Was honoured by particular thanks of the Commanding Officer Sir Eyre Coote, and Colonel (afterwards General) McDonald, the latter in particular, who having afterwards occasion to speak of him officially, stated "that he first fell in with Lieut. Henderson in command of the Grenadier comp^y of the 29th, in a trying situation, pressed by the enemy on the sand hills in Holland, where he conducted himself, as he remembered to have expressed at the time, 'with the gallantry of a soldier, and judgement of an officer.' In 1806 Captain Patrick Henderson was appointed Major of the Royal African Corps. He died 1809."

1799 companies which had been engaged nearly the whole morning, and had suffered the following casualties :—

Killed ‡—3 Rank and File.
Wounded—Captain Edgell Wyatt, Lieut. H. Grove, 3 Serjeants, 1 Drummer, 30 Rank and File.

The wounded were sent on board the fleet as quickly as they were brought down to the beach.

It was late in the afternoon, when orders were received for the regiment to advance as fast as possible; no time was lost in so doing, yet before it reached the front, the action was over and the enemy in retreat. That part of the army which had been most engaged now fell back, thus leaving Coote's brigade in front, and the 29th Regiment in the advanced part, which post it retained as long as the army kept its position on the sand-hills, which, from the north point at the Helder, extended about seven miles to the village of Kallends Oog.

The troops now suffered severely from the inclemency of the weather, for the nights were unusually cold, and there were frequent showers. On the evening of the 1st of September, the army took up a fresh position, but the regiment did not move until the following morning, when it took up cantonments about a mile in rear of the village of Oud-Sluys. On the 4th instant, it occupied part of that place, and after two or three days, marched to Schagen.

Having established his right at Petten on the German Ocean, his left at Oud-Sluys on the Zuyder Zee, and with his front protected by the Zyp, Sir Ralph Abercromby awaited the arrival of the Russian allies. At daybreak on the 10th, the enemy made a sharp attack on the British right, and centre, from Petten to St. Martins, the neighbouring village to Schagen, but were repulsed by the troops there stationed. Coote's brigade was not called upon to take any active part, though the 85th Foot had one rank and file killed, and three

---

‡ Pay Lists 29th Foot.—Privates—Ferguson, Dundas; Slack, Stephen; Smithurst, Jno.

wounded. After this both armies resumed their original positions, and **1799** the British head-quarters were established at Schagen, those of the enemy at St. Pancras, a village north of Alkmaar.

From the Weekly State of Coote's brigade, it appears that on the 12th inst. the strength of the 29th Foot was as follows :—

Present and fit for duty.............. { 2 Lieut-Colonels, 1 Major, 4 Captains, 17 Lieutenants, 4 Ensigns, 5 Staff. 37 Sergeants | 16 Drummers | 502 Rank and File
Sick .... | | | 43 ,,
On command ...... | | | 35 ,,
Recruiting .... | | | 15 ,,
Wanting to complete | 5 ,, | 2 ,, | 5 ,,

On the 13th of September, H.R.H. the Duke of York assumed the chief command, and having been reinforced by 7,000 Russians under General d'Herman, considered his force strong enough to take the offensive. All being in readiness, the advance of four columns was commenced in the following order :—

The left column, under Lieut.-General Sir R. Abercromby, being destined to turn the enemy's right, marched at 6 p.m., the 18th inst., and the next morning the remainder of the troops were put in motion.

The other three columns commencing from the right were : 1st, that commanded by Lieut.-General d'Herman, which was ordered to advance against the enemy's left, which rested on the sea. The 2nd, under Lieut.-General Dundas, to attack Schorldam, and the enemy's centre. The 3rd, under Sir James Pulteney, "consisting of two squadrons of 11th Light Dragoons, Major-Generals Don's and Coote's brigades," was to take possession of Oud-Karspel, a fortified village at the head of the Lange dyke, or canal, leading to Alkmaar.

The country over which the two last columns had to pass was a plain, intersected every three or four hundred yards by broad, deep, wet ditches, and canals. The bridges across the roads which led to Oud-Karspel had been destroyed.

1799   Coote's brigade, "consisting of the 'Queen's,' 27th, 29th, 69th, and 85th regiments" (with a troop of 11th Light Dragoons, two 6-pounders, and one howitzer), was directed to attack the village in front, whilst the remainder of the column stormed its flanks.

Leaving Schagen at 2 a.m., the brigade marched to Nieu-Diep-Verlaat, where it arrived at five o'clock, and finding the bridge broken, its advance was for some time delayed. The 85th Regt. was then left in reserve, part at Nieu-Diep, the remainder in Oos-Nieu-Diep; a patrol of cavalry was sent to Rustenburg, and the "Queen's," 29th, and one 6-pounder, and the howitzer were directed to proceed along the dyke leading to Oud-Karspel, in order to turn the battery that commanded the road from Nieu-Diep-Verlaat. The Light companies of the brigade, under Major Knight of the "Queen's," were at the same time directed to clear the wood upon the left of the road leading to the battery, whilst, to protect the left, the cavalry patrolled the road, and the 27th Regt. with one 6-pounder, occupied the cross at the turn to the middle way. These dispositions having been made, the "Queen's" and the 29th Regiment continued to advance until stopped by a broad canal, which protected the front of the enemy's work. The bridge across this obstruction having also been broken, and there being no means provided for crossing the dyke, which was very deep, full of water, and about 40ft. wide, a constant cannonade was kept up on the village, and battery; and the two regiments had the extreme mortification of being mere spectators of all that was occurring, so that it was not until the Guards and the 40th Regiment had taken the place, and furnished materials from a neighbouring house, that the "Queen's" and 29th were able to cross the canal, and join in the pursuit

The Dutch troops which had occupied the village were so completely defeated, that eighteen of their guns, with ammunition waggons, and horses complete, were captured.

The 29th being comparatively fresh, now found themselves well in front, but having advanced to within three-quarters of a mile of the enemy's camp were halted. A great number of people could now **1799** be seen near the gate of Alkmaar, and it being observed that many of them were dressed in green uniforms, it was supposed that they were Russians, and that the 1st column had been as successful as that of General Pulteney. At this time Coote's brigade occupied a bridge at the end of Oud-Karspel, this as evening approached the 29th was endeavouring to strengthen, when orders were received to retire as soon as possible. So peremptory was the order, that time was not even given to destroy the bridge. The Dutch cannon, and ammunition waggons, however, were hastily disabled, and turned over into the ditches on either side of the road. No communication having been kept up between the advancing columns, the defeat of the Russians was not heard of until this moment, when it was ascertained that those seen in the neighbourhood of Alkmaar were prisoners.

Some few of the inhabitants having remained in their houses, Colonel Enys took two into custody, to act as guides. This proved a very useful precaution, as the night was very dark, and rain fell in torrents. To the left could be seen the route of the retreating Russians, for they burnt all the villages, and houses they passed.

About daybreak of the 20th, the brigade returned to its old quarters near Schagen. The retreat of Pulteney's column, which was conducted without any confusion, need not have been so hurried, for the enemy never pursued.

For some days after this, the state of the weather prevented any further operations, but on the morning of the 2nd of October a vigorous attack was made on the enemy's left at Bergen. This large village was surrounded by woods, through which passed the great road leading to Haarlem, and between it and the sea, lay an extensive range of sandhills, impassable for artillery, and, on account of their broken surface, unfavourable for cavalry. The enemy's right was protected by dykes, and canals, easily to be defended; their centre rested on the town of Alkmaar.

1799   The 1st, or right column, under command of Sir Ralph Abercromby, with a view of turning the enemy's left, was directed to march against Egmond-op-Zee, by way of the beach.

The 2nd column, composed of Russians under Major-General D'Essen, advancing through the villages of Groet, and Schorl, was to co-operate with Major-General Burrard's brigade in the attack on Schorldam, and then march on Bergen.

The 3rd column, under Lieut.-General Dundas, consisted of Major-Generals the Earl of Chatham's, Coote's, and Burrard's brigades, together with a squadron of the 11th Light Dragoons.

The 4th, commanded by Sir James Pulteney, was destined to turn the enemy's right, and covered the whole of the left, to the Zuyder Zee.

The state of the tide determined the march of the right column, which proceeded from Petten at 6.30 a.m. This was followed at seven o'clock by Major-General Coote's brigade, which on reaching Kamp turned to the left, and advancing as far as the extremity of the Slaper Dyke, and the village of Groet, cleared the road for the Russian column.

The brigade had not proceeded far when Colonel Enys was ordered to form the 29th on the edge of the sand-hills, and to continue to advance, keeping always slightly ahead of the Russian line, which was moving upon Schorl. In this formation the regiment continued the greater part of the day, clearing the sand-hills above Schorl, until the Russians halted not far from the scene of their former defeat. After some delay the enemy was driven from Schorl and Schorldam. In pursuing them, the regiments of Coote's brigade, whose left was now above Schorl, became separated by very great intervals, and extended a long way into the sand-hills. On the right, the 85th Foot were considerably in advance, and warmly engaged. As the enemy showed a disposition to attack this part of the line, Lord Chatham's brigade was ordered from the plain to support it, and the enemy, being now outflanked, and having their rear threatened, retired to another range of hills above Bergen.

1799

Colonel Enys was about this time ordered to proceed towards the front, and place the 29th under the command of Lord Chatham, but before this could be effected, fresh orders were received from Sir David Dundas, for it to dislodge a party of the enemy posted on a hill near Bergen. The regiment was now joined by the Light companies of the "Queen's," and 27th, which, taking part in the charge, drove the enemy into a thick wood at the bottom of the hill. The advance of the 29th was the signal for all the troops on its right to move forward, and the enemy retired into the village, whilst the victorious troops occupied the surrounding hills, and made as many and as large fires as they could find fuel for.

Although the action might be said to have been decided at sunset, yet the firing of the Flank companies of Coote's brigade, and of the enemy, posted in a small angular wood, did not cease before 11 p.m.

In this day's action the 29th Foot suffered the following casualties:—

Killed—Serjeant—Cook, John. * Privates—Butler, Simon; Gilbert, John; Holt, Jas.; Robinson, Jas.; Swindall, Richd.
Wounded—1 Captain, 3 Lieutenants, 1 Serjeant, 30 Rank and File.
Missing—1 Serjeant, 10 Rank and File.
Officers Wounded—Captain D. White, Lieutenants A. Brunton Tandy, R. Ross Rowan, and Thos. Bradgate Bamford.

At daybreak of the 3rd of October, it was discovered that the enemy had evacuated Bergen, and their line of retreat in the direction of Alkmaar was plainly visible. The allied troops therefore quitted their positions, and occupied those from which the enemy had retired. On passing through the wood to its front, the regiment marched into

---

* These names are taken from the Regimental Pay Lists. The official return of Killed in the 29th Foot in the Battle of Bergen is 1 Serjeant, 7 Rank and File.

1799 the plain, and took up cantonments in the neighbouring farm-houses to the right of the village. These, being very large, and having barns, stables, cow-houses, and all such conveniences under the same roof, and being attached to the dwelling, furnished most excellent quarters for both men and officers. In the course of the day intelligence was received that Alkmaar had been occupied, and that the enemy, in expectation of reinforcements, were taking up a strong position between Beverwyck and Wyck-op-Zee.

The Duke of York therefore determined, if possible, to force them thence before the reinforcements could arrive. The regiment remained in cantonments until the 6th of October, when it moved into Bergen, and had been there but a little while when orders were received for it to advance without loss of time. When, after passing round Alkmaar, it got on the great road leading to Beverwyck, it was ascertained that part of the troops in front were in action, and on approaching the village of Haloo, the enemy were seen retiring along the sand-hills to the right. After a short halt near Haloo Bridge, the regiment advanced about a mile and a half, when the village of Castricum, through which the enemy's rear-guard had just passed, came in view.

Firing, on the sand-hills, having altogether ceased, and as evening was approaching, it was not judged expedient to continue the pursuit, so the regiment returned to Haloo Bridge, and took up a position on the banks of the river. Early the following morning it advanced to Egmond-op-den Zee.

The position on which the Duke of York wished to direct his forces was Haarlem, but hearing that the enemy had been reinforced by 6000 men, that Vandamme had strengthened the position of Beverwyck, and stationed a large force at Purmerend, a position now rendered by inundations almost inaccessible, and one which it was necessary to take, or mask, before a further advance; failing also to find the expected support from the Dutch, or to obtain the necessary supplies, together with the impossibility of covering the troops in the narrow district of country in possession of the allies, a Council of War was **1799** summoned, and it was decided to withdraw the army to England. No time was lost in embarking the sick, wounded, and stores, and on the evening of the 7th, the troops received orders to return to their old lines. Taking the road by the sea-shore, the regiment reached Petten before daybreak, and continuing its march, proceeded to its former quarters at Schagen.

Thus may be said to have ended the expedition to North Holland, for although there were some slight affairs between the rear-guard of the allied army, and the enemy's advanced troops, they were of but little consequence.

On the 17th, a suspension of hostilities was agreed to, when it was decided that all prisoners on both sides should be given up, and that the allies, on liberating 8000 Dutch and French seamen, then prisoners in England, should be allowed to re-embark without molestation. After this, the Russian troops were landed, and quartered for some time in the Channel Isles.

On the 28th of October, the 29th and 85th regiments embarked on board H.M.S. "Trusty," 50 guns, and when, on the 5th of November, the regiment landed at North Yarmouth † "the men were all dressed in white breeches with black gaiters to the cap of the knee, and all wore cocked hats (with one unfortunate exception who was paraded in rear in a forage cap.) Upon this occasion the 29th was hissed by the crowd, who supposed that on account of the uniformity, and smartness of the corps, it had not seen any service, whilst other regiments were cheered from a supposition that they had done everything, because they landed in round hats tied up with pack-thread, and fastened with pieces of tobacco pipes, and in trousers of all sorts, and fashions.

"The 29th, at a subsequent embarkation for service, was reported by a General officer to be perfect in every respect, except in the want

---

† *Morning Herald*, 17th March, 1840.

1799 of a commanding officer ; this remark might almost have been omitted. On another occasion, this gallant regiment was deprived by sickness, of the service of its only Field officer who happened to be present, and the general in command entreated the officer to leave the parade, saying that " the youngest officer could command the regiment."

From Yarmouth, the regiment marched to Dover Castle, where it arrived on the 29th of November, and remained during the winter.

On its route, the regiment had to pass through London, and with regard to this march, the following note in Colonel Enys' handwriting, still exists :—

" Upon this occasion I made application at the Guildhall for permission to allow the 29th to march through the City of London with their Drums beating, &c., the regiment having always been pre-possessed with the idea that they, in common with the Buffs, had that privilege—but they would not allow of it, indeed the person to whom I spoke would not allow that the Buffs had any such privilege, but said they once had done so by the authority of the then Sheriff, who put himself at the head of the regiment, and marched through with them ; at any rate the 29th were not allowed to Beat their Drums, which being the case, they cased their colours, and marched through in silence like all other regiments."

CHAPTER X.

THE following Circular was addressed to the Officer Commanding the 29th (or the Worcestershire) Regiment :— **1800**

" Horse Guards,
January 17, 1800.

" Sir,
I have the honor to inform you that it is His Royal Highness, the Commander in Chief's intention to form a Corps of detachments from the different Regiments of the Line, for the purpose of its being instructed in the use of the Rifle, and in the system of exercise adopted by Soldiers so armed. It is His Royal Highness' Pleasure that you shall select from the Regiment under your Command 2 Serjeants, 2 Corporals, and 30 private men for this duty, all of them being such men as appear most capable of receiving the above instructions, and most competent to the performance of the duty of Riflemen. These N.C. Officers and Privates are not to be considered as being drafted from their regiments but merely as detached for the purpose above recited; they will continue to be borne on the Strength of their Regiment, and will be clothed by their respective Colonels. His Royal Highness desires you will recommend 1 Captain, 1 Lieutenant, and 1 Ensign of the Regiment under your Command who Volunteer to serve in this Corps of Riflemen,* in order that His Royal Highness may select from the Officers recommended from the regiments which furnish their quota on this occasion, a sufficient number of Officers for the Rifle Corps. These Officers are to be considered as detached on duty from their respective Regiments, and will share in all promotion that occurs in them during their Absence.

Eight drummers will be required to act as Bugle Horns, and I request you will acquaint me, for the information of His Royal Highness, whether you have any in the 29th Regiment qualified as such, or of a Capacity to be instructed.

I have, &c., &c.,
HARRY CALVERT,
A.G."

---

* Now the Rifle Brigade (The Prince Consort's Own), then known as Colonel Coote Manningham's Corps of Riflemen.

1800 On the 20th, orders were issued for the detachment, intended for the Rifle Corps, to march to Horsham Barracks, and there remain.

GENERAL ORDER.—24TH FEBRUARY, 1800.

It is His Majesty's Pleasure, that in future, the use of Hats is to be entirely abolished throughout the whole of the Infantry of the Army, and that instead thereof, Caps are to be worn. [These Caps made of lacquered felt, were seven inches deep, had a leather peak two inches broad; and the cockade and tuft were worn in front.]

His Majesty is pleased to permit the Colonels to engrave the number of their respective Regiments on each side of the Lion, on the lower part of the brass fronting [an oblong plate about six inches high and four broad]; and likewise to the Regiments which are entitled to that distinction, His Majesty grants permission to bear their Badges in the centre of the Garter.

The Grenadiers who are allowed to wear these Caps occasionally, when they do not use their proper Grenadier Caps, may, if their Colonels choose it, bear the Grenade, in the same manner as regiments entitled to them, wear their Badges.

It is His Majesty's Pleasure that the Tufts used by the Grenadiers shall be White; those of the Light Infantry (who are likewise included in this order) dark Green. All soldiers shall bear the buttons of their respective regiments in the centre of the Cockade, except the Grenadiers, who shall use the Grenade.

The Caps are to be made of sufficient size to come completely on the soldiers' heads: they are to be worn straight and even, and brought forward well over the eyes.

The Field and Staff Officers, as also the Officers of the Battalion Companies, are to continue to wear Hats as usual.

The Grenadier Officers are permitted to wear Hats when their men do not parade in dress Caps.

The Officers of the Light Company are to wear Caps, similar to those ordered for the Light Infantry.

REGIMENTAL ORDERS.

"Dover, 20 March, 1800.

"His Majesty having been pleased to appoint Major John Byng from the 60th Foot to be Lieut.-Colonel in the 29th Regiment, Lieut.

Colonel Enys cannot take leave of a Regiment, in which he has passed **1800** almost the whole of his life, and from which he now retires only because he finds himself unequal to the fatigues of so active a profession, without returning his most sincere thanks to all and every part of the Corps, from whose Officers he has at all times (since he had the honour to command it) found the utmost, cordial and zealous support whenever necessity required, and whose Non-Commissioned Officers have at all times been so attentive to the support of their respective commands, nor does he feel himself less obliged to every individual Soldier in the Corps for that tranquillity and regularity in quarters and on the march, that patience when on the most fatiguing duties, and that steady and uniform obedience which they have ever paid to the discipline of the Regiment, by which its character has been raised to such an height of military fame, as to render it the pride and envy of the British army. To leave such a Corps, after having served in it nearly twenty-five years, must naturally be a very painful task, but it is a great satisfaction to know that he leaves the command in the hands of a nobleman, who has for nearly three years witnessed the courage and conduct of the Regiment, and who is well-acquainted therewith; one whose conduct has deservedly acquired the esteem of every officer in the Corps; and he flatters himself that the officer whom His Majesty has been pleased to appoint as his successor will by following the steps of his Lordship equally become himself an acquisition to the Regiment, and he most ardently entreats every part of the Corps to pursue the same line of conduct in future as the only means by which they can preserve that character they have so deservedly gained, and he begs leave to assure them that although he has no longer the honour to belong to the Regiment, that their conduct and behaviour will ever remain deeply impressed in his mind, and that it will be at all times one of the greatest pleasures of his retirement whenever any opportunity is offered him, of showing his gratitude (not by words only) but by using every means of serving those, who have served with him."

1800   Writing from Enys, Penryn, Cornwall, 12th August, 1885, Mr. F. G. Enys says:—

"I send you the inscription on the sword, made by Rundell and Bridge, London.

On the hilt opposite his coat of arms—"*A Present from the Officers of the 29th Reg^t. to L^t.-Col. Enys.*"

On the blade in embossed letters are the following words—"*As a Tribute of Sincere Regard and as a Testimony of their Perfect Approbation of his Conduct during Twenty Five Years' Service, This Sword is Presented to John Enys, late Lieut.-Colonel of the 29th Reg^t., by his Brother Officers.*"

Monthly returns, dated the 1st of June, show the following as being *on command* :—

Lieut. T. Langton,	2 Sergts., 1 Drumr., 32 Rank and File,	at Shorncliffe.
„ H. Birmingham,	2 „ 1 „ 20 „	at Bagshot.
„ *Blois Lynch Ens^n. *Chas. Douglas	2 „ 1 „ 32 „	Detached to Rifle Corps.

With a view of establishing a uniform system of manœuvring, it was now decided to form a camp of about 14,000 at Swinley, under command of Lieut.-General D. Dundas. On the 6th of June, the regiment marched from Dover, and on arriving at the camp on the 14th, was brigaded with the three battalions of the 9th Foot under Major-General Robert Manners, but afterwards with the 2nd battalion of the 1st (Royals), and the 1st and 2nd battalions of the 27th Foot, under Major-General W. Morshead.

The King frequently came from Windsor to attend the drills, and on the 17th of July, a grand review of about 32,000 troops took place on Winkfield Plain.

---

*Lieut. Lynch, Ensign Douglas, 1 Sergt., and 2 Privates were on the 24th October following discharged to the Rifle Corps.

The following account of this review is taken from the daily **1800** *papers :—*

"The 7th Regiment of Light Dragoons was first on the ground, the Stafford Militia appeared next, preceded by their field guns. The 27th Foot, with their band, drums, and fifes playing, marched in companies abreast, as did the whole of the infantry. The 29th and 2nd battalion of the "Royals" then followed in the same manner.

"His Majesty, attended by the Prince of Wales, Duke of Cumberland, his A.D.C's and a number of officers, arrived on the plain at 10.30, followed by the Queen, the Princesses Augusta, Elizabeth, and Mary, the Princess of Orange, and the Countess of Harrington, in two sociables, and His Serene Highness the Stadtholder in another open carriage. On His Majesty's arrival, a royal salute of 21 guns was fired. The troops were drawn up in two lines, the cavalry being at each extremity with their artillery.

"Having passed and re-passed the front of the lines of troops, His Majesty took up his station in the middle of the plain; the whole line of cavalry and infantry immediately fired in quick succession: beginning with the cavalry on the right in front, and ending with the cavalry on the right in rear, the "*battalion guns*" of each regiment, firing as signals, and the music playing after each salute. This part of the review, which was repeated three times, had a most striking effect.

"A signal gun was soon afterwards fired for the cavalry and infantry to form into single companies, in order to march off the ground, past the king; each regiment with its artillery at its head.

"The Duke of York, who acted as Commander-in-Chief, marched on to the ground at the head of the Guards; he wore in his hat a large bough of laurels. The review was over at 1.30 p.m. The Light infantry wore their new caps, similar to those worn by the Austrians."

1800 On the 1st of August, the Light company marched for Weymouth, and on the camp of exercise being shortly after broken up, the remaining companies of the regiment set out in three divisions (the first marching on 1st September) for Canterbury, and proceeding thence to Deal, embarked on board the "Dido" and "Resource" transports for Guernsey. On arriving there, the regiment occupied the New Ground Barracks for the night, and the following morning moved into Fort George. Whilst in these quarters two companies were detached to Sark, and two to Rocquaine. The Weymouth detachment did not join head-quarters till about the first week in November.

The Union of Great Britain with Ireland having been effected on the 2nd of July, on the 15th of December a H.G. Circular was issued, ordering all *Colours* to be sent to the Ordnance Office, Tower of London, for alteration to the new pattern. This was the conjoining of the crosses of St. George and St. Andrew with that of St. Patrick, the addition of the Shamrock to the wreath of Roses and Thistles, and the placing *on the regimental colour* of a small Union in a "canton."

It was directed that every regiment and corps in the service should display the new *Colours* on the 1st of January, 1801.

1801 On the 30th of January, the regiment embarked on board the "Sea Nymph," "Polly," "Isabella," and "Ceres" transports for Spithead, where on arrival it disembarked and marched to Winchester. During the assizes, it moved to the neighbouring towns of Bishops Waltham, Warnford, Exton, Meonstoke, Hambledon, East and West Meon, and returned to Winchester on the 9th of March. About this time an order was received for the formation of two additional companies (the 11th and 12th), each to consist of 1 captain, 2 lieutenants, 5 sergeants, 5 corporals, 2 drummers, and 95 privates; these were to be borne on the establishment from the 25th inst.

On account of disturbances in the West of England, on the 4th of April the regiment commenced to march in three divisions for Exeter.

Having halted at Taunton on the 13th inst., two companies were **1801** detached to Shepton Mallet, and one to Chard. On the 16th these companies, under command of Major Johnstone, proceeded to Exeter, where on the 6th of May they were joined by the remainder of the regiment. On the 8th, head quarters with five companies, under command of Lt.-Col. Lord Fredk. Montagu, marched for Berry Head, whilst Lt.-Colonel Byng and two companies proceeded to Taunton, Major Johnstone with three companies to Totnes, one company to Dartmouth, and one to Chard. Detachments were subsequently sent to Exeter, Newton Bushel, and Paignton.

On the 23rd of April, a Warrant was published for providing each man with a great coat. Previous to this there had only been a few watch coats allowed per regiment.

Early in June, the head quarters and eight companies marched to Plymouth Dock, and occupied the barracks in George and Cumberland Squares. Three companies remained on detachment at Berry Head, and one at Exeter. In July, head quarters and 11 companies were assembled at Plymouth. One company, under command of Captain A. Creagh, with Lieuts. Burdett, Tandy, and Rowan, was on duty at Woodbury Camp from July to October, when it rejoined head-quarters. About this period the idea of regimental schools appears to have been started, as in the *Military Extracts*, at the Royal United Service Institution, is the following paragraph, which has been cut out of a newspaper :—

"We find that the plan of Regimental Schools is not limited to the Devonshire Regiment of Militia alone. There are in the Plymouth Garrison two Schools for the children of the Privates and N.C.O.'s; the 29th Regt. of Foot, under the patronage of Lieut.-Colonel Lord Frederick Montagu and the Officers of that Regiment, and the Plymouth Division of Marines under the patronage of Major-General Bowater and the Officers of that invaluable Corps. The happy idea

1801 of infusing a portion of useful knowledge into the children of our brave defenders, formerly too much neglected, has already been productive of the most salutary effects."

1802 On the 25th of February, 1802, a notice of payment of prize money due to the army engaged in the expedition against Holland, in 1799, appeared in the *Gazette*. The sum amounted to a little over £21,830.

The 23rd, 25th, 27th, and 29th regiments were to be allotted their share on the 4th of March; the state of distribution being as follows:—

Each Field Officer	£62	8	3
„ Captain	£10	8	3
„ Lieutenant, and Ensign	£4	14	3
„ Serjeant	£2	0	7
„ Corporal, Drummer, and Private		6	8

On the 24th of June, the regiment embarked at Stonehouse, on board the "Matthew and Thomas," the "Queen," "Hilberts," and "Camilla" transports, for Halifax, Nova Scotia.

Previous to the sailing of the transports, Major-General England caused the following order to be published:—

"Plymouth Dock, 24 June, 1802.

"Major-General England begs to express his thanks to the 29th Regiment for the regular, sober, and soldierlike manner in which they embarked this morning for Foreign Service; such meritorious conduct must ensure to them the approbation of Lieut.-Colonel Byng, under whose immediate command the Regiment is now ordered; and the Major-General will not fail to inform him of the high state of discipline of the Corps, and the very great satisfaction he felt, during the time they were under his direction in this Garrison."

By a General Order dated the 14th of July, 1802, the wearing of Epaulettes and Shoulder Knots by the Non-Commissioned Officers of the Foot Guards, and Regiments of Infantry was directed to be discontinued; Chevrons of Regimental lace worn on the right arm being substituted: 4 Bars for a Sergt.-Major, or Quarter-Master Serjeant. All other Serjeants, 3 Bars; Corporals, 2.

On landing at Halifax in September, the regiment was quartered **1802** in the North Barracks, and whilst here several eligible volunteers were received from the 66th Foot and the Loyal Surrey Rangers.

The following story is related by Judge Haliburton in " Sam Slick's Wise Saws " :—

" The Sable Island Ghost."

" 'Now,' said Cutler, 'sit down here, Mr. Slick, and I'll tell you one of the strangest stories you ever heard. In the year 1802, the ship 'Princess Amelia' was wracked off Sable Island, having the furniture of the Queen's father, Prince Edward, on board, and a number of recruits, sodger officers and their wives, and women servants. There were 200 souls of them altogether, and they all perished. About that period, some piratical vagabonds used to frequent there, for there was no regular establishment kept on the island then; and it's generally supposed some of the poor people of that misfortinate ship reached the shore in safety, and were murdered by the wrackers for their property. Well the Prince sends down Captain Torrens *— of the 29th Regiment, I think it was—from Halifax to inquire after the missin' ship; and, as luck would have it, he was wracked too, and pretty nearly lost his life in trying to drag others through the surf, for he was a man that didn't know what danger or fear either was, except by name. There was but few that could be rescued before the vessel went to pieces. Well, he stationed them that survived at one eend of the island, and off he goes to the other so as to extend his look-out for aid as far as he could, but first they had to bury the dead that floated about the troopship, and gather up such parts of the Prince's effects as came ashore, and were worth saving. It was an awful task and took them a long time, for the Grave was as large as a cellar a'most. There they are, just where that long bent grass grows. Having done this, and findin' fire-arms in the Government shelter-hut, off he goes alone

---

* H. Torrens, Ensign 29th Foot, 28 July, 1801.

1802 to the other eend of the island. One day, having made the circuit of the lower half here, he returned about dusk to where we now are.

" 'Where you see that little hillock, there was a small hut in those days, that had fireworks in it, and some food and chairs and tables, that had been saved out of wracks, which were placed there for distressed people; and there were printed instruction in French and English, telling them what to do to keep themselves alive till they could be taken off. Well, he made a fire, hauld down some hay out of the loft, and made up a bed in one corner, and went to take a walk along by the side of the lake, afore he turned in. As he returned, he was surprised to see his dog standin' at the door, lookin' awfully skeered, growlin', barkin' and yelpin' like mad. The first thing he saw inside was a lady sittin' on one side of the fire, with long drippin' hair, hangin' over her shoulders, her face as pale as death, and havin' nothin' on but a loose soiled white dress, that was as wet as if she had just come out of the Sea, and had sand stickin' to it, as if she had been rolled over and over on the breakers.

" 'Good Heavens, Madam,' said he, 'who are you, and where did you come from?' But she didn't speak to him, and only held up her hand before her, and he saw one of the fore-fingers was cut off, and was still bleedin'. Well, he turned round, and opened a case that he had picked up in the mornin' from the drift-ship, in which was materials for bandagin' the wound, and was goin' to offer her some assistance, when she rose up sudden, slipped past him, and went out of the door and walked off. Well, he followed and called to her, and begged her to stop; but on she went, and thinkin' she was out of her mind, he ran after her, and the faster he went, the swifter she raced, till she came to the lake, and dived right into it headforemost.

" 'Well, he stood some time there considerin' and ponderin' over what had happened, and at last he strolled back, and sat down by the fire a good deal puzzled. Arter studyin' it out for some time, sais he, ——'There can't be no mistake here. That is not a ghost, nor a demented person, but a murdered woman. If I catch a wracker here while I am on the island, I'll ask no questions but I'll shoot him as I would a wolf.

"'Poor thing, she wants me to tell her friends I have seen her, and that she is actilly dead; but who is she, and who are her folks? But the finger,' said he, 'that is very odd. I suppose in putting up her hand to save her life, it was cut off. Confound the villain, I wish I could once get my eyes on him,' and he look'd at the primin' of his gun and went out and kneeled down, and takin' off his hat, held his head close to the ground, to see if anybody was a movin' between him and the horizon; and findin' there warn't, and feelin' tired, for he had been on his feet all day, he returned to the hut again, and who should be there but the selfsame lady in the selfsame place.

"'Now,' said he to himself, 'don't go too near her, it's evidently onpleasant to her; but she has some communication to make.' Well, what do you think, it's a positive fact, she held up the mutilated hand again. He paused some time afore he spoke, and took a good look at her, to be sure there was no mistake, and to be able to identify her afterwards, if necessary. 'Why,' sais he, after scrutenizin' of her (for he was a man, was the brave Captain Torrens, that the devil himself couldn't daunt), 'why," says he, 'it ain't possible! Why, Mrs. Copeland is that you?' for he knew her as well as I know you. She was the wife of Dr. Copeland† of the 7th Regiment, and was well known at Halifax, and beloved by all who knowed her. She just bowed her head, and then held up her hand, and showed the bloody stump of her finger.

"'I have it,' sais he, 'murdered for the sake of your ring.'——She bowed her head. 'Well,' sais he, 'I'll track the villain out, till he is shot or hanged.' Well, she looked sad, and made no sign. 'Well,'

---

† Surgeon John Copeland was appointed to the 7th Foot (or Royal Fuziliers) on the 14th of May, 1795.

1802 sais he, 'I'll leave no stone unturned to recover that ring, and restore it to your family.'

"Well, she smiled, bowed her head, and rose up and waved her hand to him to stand out of the way, and he did, and she slipped by him, and then turned and held up both hands, as if she was pushin' some one back, and retreated that way, makin' the same motion; and he took the hint, shut to the door, and sot down to digest this curious scene.

"'Now, that story is a positive fact,' sais the Superintendent. 'Them is the real names. My father heard Torrens tell it word for word, as I tell it to you; and there is people now living at Halifax who knew him well, for he was a great favourite with everybody. Just after that, there was an awful storm, and another wrack, and he was mainly the means of saving the people at the risk of his own life. His name is on the Chart as the 'brave Captain Torrens,' the House of Assembly voted him a large sum of money, and the Prince thought everything of him. I dare say the Duchess of Kent has often heard the story, and if she hain't——'

"'But about the ring?' sais I.

"'Oh, yes!' said he, 'that is the curiosest part of it.' Captain Torrens got hold of the names of three of the most noted wrackers, and set out to track 'em to their hidin' places. One of them lived to Salmon River, just about as solitary and lonely a place as he could have found to escape observation. When the Captain got there, the feller had gone to Labrador. Well, Torrens soon knocked up an acquaintance with the family by stayin' at the house, and makin' it his head quarters while he was fowlin' and fishin' in the neighbourhood. One evenin' he put on a splendid ring, which he brought down for the purpose, so as to draw the talk to the subject he wanted. The eldest girl admired it greatly; and he took it off, and it was handed round, and commented on. At last one of the darters said she didn't think it was half so pretty as the one daddy got off the lady's finger at Sable **1802** Island.

"'No, my dear,' said the mother, who got behind his chair to telegraph, 'he got it from a Frenchman, who picked it up at the sand there.'

"'Oh! I believe it was,' said the girl, colourin' up, and lookin' a little confused.

"'Well, at last the ring was handed back, and he put it on his finger again; and when he was kinder pretendin' to admire it, sais he carelessly,—' Show me your ring; if it is as handsome as this I'll buy it of you, for I am a great ring fancier; but I don't suppose it would go on my great coarse finger—would it? Where is it?'

"'It's at Halifax, sir,' said she. 'The last time daddy was there, he left it with a watchmaker to sell. He gave him twenty shillings on it, and told him if it fetched more he should have it.'

"'Oh,' said he, quite unconsarned, 'it's no matter.'

"'Oh, yes! it is, sir,' said she, 'for it's a most beautiful one; you had better buy it'; and she described it most minutely.

"'He was quite satisfied; and arter breakfast the next mornin' he started for Halifax as fast as he could. Well the town warn't then what it is now. Two watchmakers was all that was in it, so a search couldn't last very long any how; but in the window of the fust shop he went to was the identical ring. Says he to the shopman—

"'Friend,' sais he, 'give me the history of that ring, as far as you know about it.'

"'Well, the account was just what he had heard himself, omittin' of course all mention of the finger. Says he 'Give it to me; here are the twenty shillings advanced, and if the owner wants more, tell him to bring the finger that was cut off to get at it, and then come to me.'

1802 "'Well it was identified at once by the ladies of the regiment, and some of the Doctor's brother officers ; and the moment the Prince saw it, he knew it, for it was a curious old family ring, and the Captain sent it to England to Mrs. Copeland's friends.'

"'Torrens was ordered home soon after that, and there the matter dropt.'

"'That's a strange story,' said the Skipper ; 'what do you think of it, Mr. Slick?"

"'Why,' sais I, 'It seems to come very straight, and looks as if it was true ; and nothin' ought to be considered impossible because it is uncommon.'

"'Well, says Eldad, that story is as true as Gospel, for I've heard it from Mr. Collingwood's father, who was with the Prince at the time, and saw the ring himself; and more than that, I could tell you the name of the wracker, but I won't, for some of his descendants are still living, and are decent people. I have seen the old coon several times and the devil himself with all his arts and insinevations never could coax him out of the house arter dark.'" *

Although on the 27th of March, 1802, the Treaty of Amiens had been concluded, yet both England and France were ready to renew the **1803** conflict, and early in 1803, on account of the extensive warlike preparations being carried on in the ports of France and Holland, an explanation was requested from the French Government.

On the 12th of May, the ultimatum of the British Government was presented, which being rejected, war was declared on the 18th instant, but it was not till 1808 that the 29th Foot was called upon to take a share in the active operations.

In June, 1803, the Field Officers' companies were taken from them, and the rank of captain-lieutenant and captain abolished ; the latter officers were promoted captains of the colonel's late company, and the two senior lieutenants succeeded to the command of the lieut.-colonel's, and major's companies.

---

* *Note by Judge Haliburton.*—This story is given with the real names, and is well known to an Officer of the 7th, still living who was intimately acquainted with the parties.

In "*James' Regimental Companion*," published this year, it is **1803** stated "The *Sash* is now usually worn outside the coat and crossbelt. There is not however any specific regulation on this head, as in many regiments, the officers have their sashes made so as to tie with ribbands, under the coat. The tuft or tassels, on duty, hang on the right side for cavalry officers, on the left for infantry. As the original purpose for which sashes were ordained (being for the immediate conveyance of a wounded officer off the field of battle), is now wholly defeated by its diminutive size, there appear to be only two points of view in which this article can properly be considered; these are, designation of duty, and convenience to the wearer. The sash was originally made full enough to hold the human form, and was worn across the shoulder."

The following were the rates of pay at this period :—

	Infantry of the Line, per Diem. £ s. d.	H.P. Infantry of Great Britain. s. d.	Infantry of Ireland. s. d.
Colonel	1 2 6	12 0	12 6
Lieut.-Colonel	15 11	8 6	8 6
Major	14 1	7 6	7 6
Captain	9 5	5 0	5 0
Lieut., with additional allowance	5 8	2 4	2 4
Ensign	4 8	1 10	1 10
Paymaster	15 0		7 6
Adjutant	8 0	2 0	2 0
Qr.-Master, with additional allowance	5 8	2 4	2 4
Surgeon	9 5	5 0	2 0
Assistant Surgeon	5 0	2 6	2 6
Surgeon's Mate	4 6		
Serjeant-Major	2 0¾		
Qr.-Master-Serjeant	2 0¾		
Paymaster-Serjeant	1 6¾		
Serjeant	1 6¾		
Corporal	1 2¼		
Drummer, and Grenadier Fifer	1 1¾		
Private	1 0		

1804 On the 19th of August Lieut-General Bowyer inspected the regiment at Halifax. The *Colours* were reported as being good:—

"Queues" were this year shortened to 9 inches. As it may interest some to know the mode of dressing such appendages, the following account is taken from "*Notes and Queries*":—"A lock of hair at the back of the head was allowed to grow a little longer than the rest, and upon this was placed a piece of whalebone of regulation length and of the size of a small quill; a narrow black ribbon was then wound round the lock of hair and the whalebone, and continued along the latter until near the end of it, when another lock of hair, kept for the purpose, was placed on the whalebone, projecting about two inches beyond it, and the ribbon wound to the end of the whalebone, where it was fastened off. The whole thus resembled a continuous tail of hair terminating with a curl."

REGIMENTAL ORDERS.

Halifax, 18th Oct., 1804.

Lieut.-Colonel Byng, having been appointed to the 3rd regiment of Guards, wishing, in taking leave of the officers of the 29th regiment, to express his high approbation of their conduct and to acknowledge the very great assistance he received from them in maintaining the discipline of the regiment whilst he had the honour to command it; for the very great happiness he experienced in their society he returns them his most grateful thanks, and his sincere wishes for their future welfare, will ever attend them. To the non-commissioned officers and privates, he has only to say that he considers them in every point of duty, surpassed by none, and equalled but by few regiments in His Majesty's service, and he hopes that every one of them will always consider themselves entitled to call upon him whenever they think he can in anyway serve them—and he hopes that these few lines will be considered by every individual of the regiment, not as a commonplace compliment, but as the sincere effusions of gratitude, and good wishes towards them.

1805 During 1805, the regiment supplied the following detachment at Melville Island, viz.:—1 captain, 1 lieutenant, 1 ensign, 3 serjeants, and 74 privates. Subalterns were sent in command of parties detached to Forts Charlotte, Clarence, and Sackville; Point Pleasant, York **1805** Redoubt, Dartmouth, and Cape Breton, whilst at Camperdown, and the Light House respectively, 3 privates were on command.

Black canvas knapsacks‡ were this year adopted by most infantry regiments, but as late as 1810, the 29th Regiment were still in possession of calf-skin ones, with the hair on the outside. Much trouble was taken in matching the skins as to markings. As the regiment did not return from the Peninsula till December, 1811, it is most probable that it continued to wear the calfskin pack till the following year.

In 1806, the above-mentioned detachments were still on command. **1806**

By General Order dated the 20th of October, black felt Caps were substituted for those of lacquered felt; the brass plate in front was of a smaller and a more oval shape than that of 1800. It was surmounted by a crown, and bore the G.R. in a cypher, with the number of the corps immediately below it, on the centre. The worsted tuft and cockade were fixed on the side of the cap. Suspended across the front of the officers' cap was a crimson and gold twisted cord, with tassels; the same cord in white worsted was worn by the non-commissioned officers and privates of the battalion; and in green, by the Light infantry company.

From later accounts, it appears that the officers of the 29th continued to wear their cocked hats for some years after this.

An account of the dress of the officers of the regiment at this period says :—"They wore large cocked hats, white leather breeches, and long boots reaching above the knee. Their evening dress consisted of grey cloth tights, Hessian boots with tassels. Before setting down to dinner, the facings of the coats were buttoned back, and the hair dressed in a queue powdered. When on duty, the men wore black cloth leggings with 25 white metal buttons."

On the 15th of January, Lieut. Henry Birmingham was granted **1807** six months leave of absence, and soon after sailed for England. Unfortunately, the ship in which he was coming home was captured by a French privateer, and he was detained, a prisoner, in France till May, 1814.

---

‡ *United Service Journal*, 1830, and *Broad Arrow*, 2nd of October, 1886.

1807   On the 2nd of April, Major-General Martin Hunter inspected the regiment at Halifax.

The *Colours* were reported as good.

The following returns are taken from the inspection report:—

COUNTRY.	ENGLISH.	SCOTCH.	IRISH.	FOREIGN.	HEIGHT.	PRIVATES.	SERGTS.	CORPLS.	DRUMRS.
Officers	18	4	12	*1	6ft. 2in. and upwards	5	—	—	—
Staff	5	—	—	—	6ft. 0in.	26	3	2	—
Serjeants	32	10	2	—	5ft. 11in.	34	3	3	1
Corporals	26	6	8	—	5ft. 10in.	35	8	5	—
Drummers	—	—	2	20	5ft. 9in.	87	9	5	4
Privates	410	83	133	12	5ft. 8in.	107	8	12	1
					5ft. 7in.	117	11	9	2
					5ft. 6in.	119	2	3	2
					5ft. 5in.	68	—	1	6
					Under 5ft. 5in.	40	—	—	6
					TOTAL	638	44	40	22

Having received orders to return to England, on the 19th of June, the regiment embarked on board the "Dominica," "Crisis," "Zephyr," "Amphitrite," and "Sceptre" transports.

One company, under command of Captain Thomas Egerton, consisting of Lieut. W. Birmingham, 3 serjeants, 1 drummer, 65 rank and file, did duty as marines on board H.M.S. "Mermaid" during the voyage. Previous to leaving Halifax, N.S., the following district order was issued :—

"Halifax, 18th June, 1807.

"Major-General Hunter cannot allow the 29th regiment to embark for England, without assuring them, that there is not a regiment in His Majesty's service, he would prefer having under his command, either in garrison or in the field; he will report the regiment to His Royal Highness the Commander-in-Chief, in the highest state of

---

* Lieut.-Col. White, aged 35, $19\frac{9}{12}$ years service.

discipline, and fit for any service His Majesty may be pleased to order them upon; and that the conduct of officers and men has been most exemplary since he has had the honour to command the garrison."

The inhabitants of Halifax having presented the officers' mess with a very handsome silver cup, sent the following letter to General Gordon Forbes, Colonel of the 29th Foot:—

"Halifax, Nova Scotia,

"13 July, 1807.

"The inhabitants of the town of Halifax, although strangers to you, are encouraged with the hope that as Colonel of the 29th Regiment you will oblige them by communicating to the Officers, Non-Commissioned Officers, and Soldiers, of that highly distinguished Corps, the Esteem in which they are held by all descriptions of His Majesty's Subjects in this Town and Province, and that you will express to them, our sincere regret at the departure of a body of men whose Exemplary Conduct, during their residence in this Garrison, has excited our highest respect and admiration. We are all aware Sir, that the Praises of a remote Colony like Nova Scotia can but add little to the Reputation of a Regiment long accustomed to receive the tribute of respect and admiration, which it has on all occasions so justly merited.

"But when we recollect the pleasure which many of us for several years enjoyed in the Society of the Officers, the correct and gentlemanly manners which marked their intercourse with all classes among us, the orderly and becoming behaviour of the Non-Commissioned Officers and Private men, and reflect on the Confidence and Security with which the presence of such a corps would have inspired us had danger approached Our Shores, we feel it a duty highly incumbent on us, to express the interest we shall ever take in the welfare and happiness of every Individual of the 29th Regiment, and the pleasure and satisfaction it will at all times afford us to hear of any event which can tend to its Fame and Glory.

T

1807   "In the hope, Sir, that a Corps which resided Five Years in this Garrison, will not think us unworthy of its remembrance, we take the liberty of offering a Silver Cup with our sentiments inscribed on it; and we beg through you to have it presented to the Regimental Mess, and to request the Officers will be pleased to allow the small tribute of our Sincere Regard to have a place on their table.

"We hope, Sir, you will deem the occasion to be a sufficient apology for the liberty we have taken in troubling you; and allow us to express to you the sentiments of high respect with which we have the honour to be,

                          Sir,

        Your very obedient & humble Servants,

             Signed *(by the principal inhabitants, and addressed to)*

Lieut.-General Gordon Forbes,
     Colonel of His Majesty's 29th (or Worcestershire) Regiment of Infantry."

It will be remembered that in 1749, Colonel Hopson's Regiment, afterwards known as the 29th Foot, was employed in clearing and marking out the site for the future town of Halifax.

In "*Cyril Thornton*" (by Capt. Thos. Hamilton, late 29th Foot) is a most interesting account of the regiment whilst quartered in Nova Scotia, and its subsequent services in the Peninsular campaign.

After a favourable passage, the regiment under command of Bt. Lieut.-Colonel D. White, arriving at Deal towards the end of July, was in full expectation of being employed with the expedition then assembling in the Downs and destined to proceed to Copenhagen. To the great disappointment of the officers and men, instructions were however received to disembark, and occupy the barracks at Deal. The reason for this order was afterwards ascertained, viz., that the authorities at the Horse Guards thought that the regiment, owing to **1807** its lengthened absence from England, could not be in a fit state for immediate active service. Never was there a greater mistake, for all the general officers who witnessed its landing, declared it to be one of the finest corps they had ever seen.

The following description of the regiment is taken from the "Adventures of Captain J. Patterson":—

"In August 1807, I joined the 2nd Battalion of H.M. 50th (or West Kent) Regiment at Deal Barracks.

"In the adjoining barrack lay the 29th (or Worcestershire) Regiment, commanded by Lieut.-Colonel Daniel White. It had lately returned from Halifax, where it had been stationed many years. Being in preparation for active employment, it was now passing through the usual ordeal of drill, and ball practice; and consequently the interminable sounds of drums and bugles, the monotonous din of the drill serjeants 'as you were,' accompanied by the clamour from the adjutant's stentorian lungs, were continually ringing in our ears.

"The 29th was a fine regiment, although it had been trained up after the manner of the old school. Their Lieut.-Colonel, a gallant veteran, showing the example, made his officers dress with cocked hats, square to the front, long queues, and wide-skirted coats, fastened or looped back with hook and eye. We were enlivened by their excellent band; and their corps of black drummers cut a fierce and remarkable appearance while hammering away on their brass drums."

It appears that about this time the College of Arms became more particular as to the Colours, and also the devices borne on them, for the following correspondence still exists there, for a copy of which I am indebted to Sir Albert Woods, C.B., Garter King of Arms:—

"Sir, "Deal, August 12, 1807.

"In answer to your letter of the 2nd May, I have the honour of enclosing you, Sketches of the Colours borne by the 29th

By Regulation, the Colours should have been "*The King's.*" The great Union, only.

"*The Regimental*," in the centre $\frac{\text{XXIX}}{\text{REG}^{\text{T.}}}$, encircled by a wreath of roses, thistles, &c.; in a canton, a small Union.

"*The Camp Colour*," which was of yellow, without any device, should have had "XXIX REG$^{\text{T.}}$" straight across it.

Regiment, in which you will find a slight deviation, but cannot state by what authority the alteration took place.

1807

I have the honour to be

Sir

Your obedient Servant

D. WHITE, Lt. Col.

George Nayler, Esqre   Major 29th Regt."
&c. &c. &c."

As these Colours were carried by the regiment throughout the Peninsular War, an exact copy of the sketches mentioned is inserted.

One evening in September, the officers whilst at mess, were startled by the sound of musketry, and on going into the square, several shots passed over their heads. On repairing to the barrack gate, which opened almost on to the beach, it was discovered that a large smuggling boat had passed through the fleet, which was lying at anchor, and had been run ashore. The smugglers, having been observed by some of the boats of the men-of-war, fire had been opened on them. As soon as their boat touched ground, the smugglers landed, drew up, and returned the fire, whilst their accomplices emptied the boat of its cargo. The regiment having neither authority nor orders to interfere, could but remain spectators of what was going on. It was not till after this affair was over, that the Custom House authorities applied for assistance. The Light company was immediately turned out, and on searching the houses on the outskirts of the town, some fifty kegs of brandy were secured, but the greater part of the cargo had been successfully carried off into the country.

On the 7th of November, orders were received to march to Brabourne Lees, situated on a low-lying common between Hythe and Ashford, where some temporary wooden barracks had been erected.

1807 On the 28th, the regiment set out for Portsmouth, and passing through Tenterden, Cranbrooke, Tunbridge Wells, East Grinstead, Cuckfield, Horsham, and Petworth, reached Petersfield on the 6th of December. Here it was met and inspected by its colonel, General Gordon Forbes, who entertained the officers at a dinner, and informed them that they were to embark the following day, and be employed on a secret expedition, but that they were not to divulge this to the men. The march was continued early the next morning, and on reaching Cosham, Lieut.-Colonel the Honble. G. A. F. Lake, who in 1804 had retired on half-pay of the regiment, now re-joined and took command of it. Having ordered it to halt, he invited all the officers to breakfast, and gave the men a substantial meal, after which they continued their route to Portsmouth, marching directly to the point, where flat-bottomed boats were found ready to convey them to the transports. This was the first intimation the men had of their embarkation for foreign service. Their spirits rose immediately, and they got into the boats with as great coolness and regularity as if they had only been going to cross a ferry. They embarked * to the sound of martial music and to the cheers of an immense crowd, to which they heartily responded. It was, however, very distressing to hear the wailings of many poor women and children who were thus suddenly separated from their husbands, and fathers, and left destitute on the beach. A certain number belonging to each company were, however, afterwards permitted to embark.

It was now ascertained that a force (consisting of the 29th, 32nd, 50th, and 82nd regiments, the 3rd, 4th, 6th, and 8th battalions of the King's German Legion, a brigade of British, and one of German artillery, the whole under command of Major-General Sir Brent Spencer, with Brigadiers-General Sir Miles Nightingale and Sir

---

* Lieut. James Nestor, Ensign Samuel Hardy, 3 Serjeants, 3 Corporals, 1 Drummer, and 16 Privates were left at home for Recruiting purposes. On the 23rd of May, 1808, the Recruiting company was directed to be augmented to 1 Captain, 2 Lieutenants.

Robert McFarlane, commanding brigades, the 29th and 50th being in **1807** that of the latter) was to be employed on a secret service, and that the transports had been provisioned for six months.

The 29th were put on board the following ships :—the "Dominica" (head-quarters of the regiment), "London," "Scipio," "John," "Neriod," and "John Taylor."

LIEUT.-COLONEL LAKE.

The Peace of Tilsit (7th July, 1807) having restored Buonaparte, victorious, to his capital, he now took advantage of the dissensions in the Spanish Court, to get its Royal Family into his power, when he

1807 at once sent a *corps d'armée* into Spain, and made his brother Joseph, king. At the same time the Prince Regent of Portugal having refused to carry out Buonaparte's decrees with regard to British shipping, French troops were marched into Portugal, on which the Royal family fled to Brazil. But though thus abandoned, neither the Spanish nor Portuguese were inclined to submit to the universal enemy, but determined to apply to England for help.

The destination of General Spencer's force being kept a profound secret, the ships were directed to sail with sealed orders, with the first fair wind after the 10th of December. It was not until the 20th inst., when the wind having changed to the eastward, that the convoy got under weigh, and passing through the Needles, was on the 22nd, fairly in the Bay. The next day the wind failed, it became a dead calm; so smooth was the sea that boats were lowered, and visits exchanged with the other transports. During the night a S.W. wind began to rise, which increased to a gale, so bad was it on Christmas day, that all sail was shortened, and the men were only able to get a small quantity of meat cooked, which they eat, seated like Turks, on sails on the cabin floor. As the storm continued with unabated fury, signal was made to bear up, and sealed order No. 1 being opened, it was found that the fleet was directed to rendezvous off Lisbon. On account of the hurricane which still raged, it was found impossible to make this rendezvous, so the transports bore up for Falmouth, where, those with the 29th on board, with the exception of the "Neriod," were re-
1808 assembled by the 23rd of January, 1808. The "Neriod" (on board which was Captain E. Nestor's company with Lieut. R. Stannus, Ensigns Wm. Duguid and Benj. Wild), having become separated from the convoy, made for Gibraltar, where on arrival she was despatched to strengthen the British force assembled in Sicily, under Lieut.-General Sir James Stewart, Bart., to support and protect King Ferdinand IV., who had been driven by Buonaparte from the throne of Naples.

On the 23rd of February, the fleet having re-assembled, it once **1808** more sailed from Falmouth with a fair wind and sealed orders. On arriving off the Tagus, it being ascertained that the French under Marshal Junot, had occupied Lisbon and the surrounding forts, the expedition proceeded to Gibraltar and anchored at the New Mole on the 12th of March.

Dr. Geo. Guthrie, surgeon of the regiment, gives the following anecdote:—

"One of the transports having a detachment of the 29th on board, anchored on the bank in the Bay, and being in harbour, all turned in, except the watch and mate. Being a bad sleeper on board ship, and knowing the carelessness of the sailors, I went on deck in the middle of the night, and to my astonishment, found the ship was drifting. The mate, on being awakened from his nap, would not believe it, until I showed him the cable, nearly right up and down. Well, we turned up all hands, got sail on the ship, and the moment we tacked, the battery at Algeçiras opened fire upon us (the Spaniards were not yet our allies), and after some trials, they sent one shot through the accommodation box on the poop. We got half-a-dozen more shots from Cabrito Point, on passing, and then beat our way back, to the astonishment of the fleet and the garrison, who could not understand what we had been after."

On the 14th, the English regiments disembarked (leaving, however, detachments and all their baggage on board), and occupied the South Pavilion. This division was guided by orders distinct from those of the garrison, and its destination was still kept a mystery.

About the 8th of May, the troops were surprised to hear the batteries of Algeçiras firing a salute, and it was shortly afterwards ascertained that on the 2nd inst. the Spaniards at Madrid, had risen against the French.

On the 14th, orders were issued for the immediate embarkation of General Spencer's division. An east wind having sprung up, the whole of the convoy got under weigh early on the 17th, and the

1808 following day arrived off Cadiz, where it joined the blockading fleet under Lord Collingwood and Rear-Admiral Purvis.

The favourable disposition of the people now induced the British Admiral to endeavour to open a private communication with the Spanish officers, but the Governor, the Marquis of Solano-y-Socoro, not feeling himself either strong, or bold enough, to oppose the views of the French, declined all overtures.

On the 28th, this officer, having been considered as gained over to the French cause, fell a victim to popular vengeance. The people now turned their fury against the French troops, who retired on board their vessels. The new Governor, General Morla, immediately entered into negotiations with the British, and the Spaniards separating their fleet from that of the French, prepared to attack their ships then in Cadiz Harbour, at the mouth of which Admiral Purvis and the transports remained anchored, ready to give assistance if necessary. The French admiral, hemmed in on all sides, determined not to yield without a fight, which took place in full view of the British. As soon as the French ships were captured, the port was opened to the English, who were received with acclamations of joy from all ranks.

Abstract of the Description of Service of the Non-Commissioned Officers and Rank and File of the 29th Regiment of Foot. Cadiz Bay, 1st June, 1808.

	SERJEANTS.	DRUMMERS.	RANK AND FILE.
Men Serving for Life.....................	40	18	677
Men Serving for a Limited Period ...			126
Boys Serving for Life			
Boys Serving for a Limited Period ...			7
Total	40	18	810

1808

On the 7th, Captain Nestor's company re-joined from Sicily.

The Spaniards, thinking themselves now capable of defending Cadiz, General Spencer's expedition cruised between that port and Lisbon, touching occasionally at Ayamonte, as it was reported that the French army, then collecting at the mouth of the Guadiana, intended to enter Spain by that route, but on the approach of General Spencer, the French retired towards Lisbon.

On the 1st of July, the transports, with the regiment on board, were once more in Cadiz Harbour, and, on the 3rd, the whole of the troops disembarked and occupied barracks at Puerto Santa Maria, on the opposite side of the town of Cadiz. These were the first British troops to land in the Peninsula, § and were received with shouts of " Viva. Viva los Ingleses! Rompez los Franceses!"

The patriots, having assumed a red cockade, with the cypher $\frac{F}{VII}$ worked upon it, the Spanish ladies took a pride in embroidering and presenting the English officers with this national emblem, which they had been ordered to place above their black one. General Spencer's force was kept in constant readiness to take the field, and the 29th were actually under orders to march to the aid of Generals Reding and Castaños, when information was received that General Dupont's army had been surrounded at Baylen and compelled to capitulate. After these successes, General Spencer communicated to the Junta his intention of joining, on the coast of Portugal, the expedition which had sailed from England under Sir Arthur Wellesley. With this object

---

§ Extract from Military Journal of Colonel Chas. Leslie, K.H., who was gazetted to the 29th Foot, 18th Dec., 1806; was present at Roliça, Vimiero, Oporto, Talavera, Albuhera, Siege of Badajos, besides various other affairs and skirmishes:—

"We had the honour of being the first British troops who landed in the Peninsula."

Captain Leslie, who was severely wounded at Talavera, retained the musket ball in his right leg for the remainder of his life. He received the Peninsular medal with four clasps, and was in 1813 transferred to the 60th Rifles.

Colonel Leslie was 26th Baron of Balquhain, and died January, 1870.

1808 the whole of the troops re-embarked on the 19th of July, and, sailing the following day, arrived in Mondego Bay on the evening of the 6th of August, where orders were received for them to disembark the next morning. Owing to the swell and surf, several boats were upset whilst endeavouring to get ashore, and one containing a party of the 29th Grenadiers, lost arms and everything, the men narrowly escaping with their lives.

General Spencer's division being the last to land, it was found that every animal in the neighbourhood had been purchased, so that it was impossible to get horses or mules to carry the tents and baggage. The officers were therefore obliged to carry in their haversacks a few shirts, stockings, shaving articles, &c.; their cloaks were slung over their shoulders on one side, and a canteen of rum on the other.

It was late in the evening, before the regiment reached Sir Arthur Wellesley's army, then encamped above the small town of Lavos, on joining which the 29th and 82nd, under command of Brigadier-General Sir M. Nightingale, formed the 3rd brigade.

The army which landed in Mondego Bay, expected to meet the enemy forthwith, but no arrangements had been made for sick or wounded. Dr. Guthrie was therefore ordered by Colonel Lake to purchase a mule, or an ass, to carry the instruments and medicines.

Dr. Guthrie said:—" I had two one-handed men, attached to me, whose hands I had cut off, after maiming themselves in America, and who had hitherto been necessary cleaners. These fellows could saddle a horse or mule nearly as quickly and as well as if their hands had not been amputated. They took care of the jackass that carried the physic and surgical stores in a biscuit bag, which I begged from the master of the transport, there being nothing else to be had; and thus the regiment set off to fight two or three battles and take Lisbon."

When Nightingale's brigade arrived in camp, it was so dark that the regiments had some difficulty in finding their tents, and in regard to food, nothing whatever could be obtained, so the men had to content themselves with a morsel of ship's biscuit from their haversacks, and a glass of rum. They then wrapped themselves up in their coats, and lay down in hopes of getting some rest.

At 2 a.m. on the 8th of August, without a bugle sound or beat of drum, the whole army was under arms, and remained so till an hour after sunrise, lest the enemy should attempt a surprise.

Extract from " Recollections of My Military Life," by Colonel G. Landmann, R.E.

" On the next day, Monday, the 8th of August, 1808, we discovered a large fleet ahead, already at anchor in Mondego Bay. Having arranged my luggage, I gave it in charge of . . . It now occurred to me that my long 'queue' might be inconvenient on service, so after very serious consideration, I resolved on cutting it off, for it was my own natural hair. From this day, the dropping of *'Queues'* * throughout the army may be dated, excepting the 29th Regiment, of whom I shall hereafter have occasion to say a few words on the subject."
—(*Vide this Officer's account of meeting the 29th, with Colonel Lake at its head, on the 17th of August, page 278*).

---

* The 29th was the last regiment of the Peninsular Army to retain the "Queue."— " *Notes and Queries,*" 2nd Series, *Vol. II.*

"*Queues*" were doomed by Horse Guard General Order, 20th of July, 1808, but officers continued to wear the Flash, made of black ribbon, attached to the collar of the coat behind, to distinguish them as flankers. This custom has been for years preserved in the 23rd Royal Welsh Fusiliers.—*Records of 44th Foot.*

"*Broad Arrow," 30th October, 1886.—" The Flash, and the Royal Welsh Fusiliers."*— After the Queue was done away with, Colonel Pearson retained the Flash on the officers' coats until the regiment came home in 1834. The dress regulations had been revised and materially altered a short time before the 23rd landed, and the General commanding at Portsmouth questioned the right of the officers to wear the "flash." Colonel Harrison, then commanding, referred the question to the Horse Guards, and through the interest of Sir Willoughby Gordon, permission was obtained from King William IV., for its retention.—(*Records of the Royal Welsh Fusiliers.*)

1808 On the afternoon of the 10th, the army commenced its first march in the Peninsula, and the 29th bivouacked for the night near a wood.

The next morning it marched for Leira, and on the 13th bivouacked at Caviero, near Batalha, from which the enemy's advanced posts had but a few hours previously retired. The following day the march was continued towards Alcobaço, and the regiment, when halted at a short distance beyond that town, could trace the retreat of the enemy by the clouds of dust which they raised for a considerable distance. Having passed through Caldas on the 15th, the regiment bivouacked in a vineyard. About 6 p.m., the alarm being given that the outposts were engaged, Nightingale's brigade instantly turned out, and marched off to their support. Having advanced about two miles, it was ascertained that the enemy had been repulsed, and driven from Obidos. The brigade therefore retraced its steps, but remained accoutered the whole night. During the 16th, the army remained perfectly tranquil, but two of the 29th being caught in the town against orders, were tried by drumhead court-martial. One of these was Private Needham, a grenadier of the finest order of men, a man of the kindest heart, an excellent soldier; but he could not resist rum. In America, in summer or in winter, for heat or cold were nothing to him, he would swim across the harbour of Halifax, on a stormy night, and return to his post with as many bladders of rum tied round his neck as he could get money to buy. Of course everybody got drunk, and poor Needham was detected and flogged; he never disputed the justice of his sentence, but readily admitted that he could not possibly refrain from doing the same thing again. "This man eventually died in the element he had so often braved with impunity, for he was carried off the forecastle of a transport, by a heavy sea in the Bay of Biscay, and was long seen buffeting the waves in vain, and without hope or prospect of relief."

That evening, there was every reason to believe the 29th would be among the first troops to be engaged with the enemy the following morning, and when Colonel Lake formed up the regiment for the punishment of the two culprits, he knew full well that every man was satisfied they deserved it, but he did not say so. He spoke to the hearts of his soldiers, he told them he flogged these men not only because they deserved it, but that he might deprive them of the honour of going into action with their comrades in the morning, and that he might not prevent the guard, who was stationed over them, from participating in it. The regiment was in much too high a state of discipline to admit of a word being said, but the colonel's remarks were repeated all the evening from mouth to mouth, and the poor fellows who were flogged, declared to Dr. Guthrie, that they would willingly have begged on their knees, at Col. Lake's feet, if they dared, as the greatest favour he could bestow on them, to be allowed to run the risk of being shot first, with the certainty of being flogged afterwards if they escaped.

1808

The outlying picquet this evening, which consisted of fifty men under Major Thos. Egerton, Lieutenants Robert Stannus and Chas. Leslie, was posted in an open wood, with a chain of sentinels along its outer edge.

Soon after daybreak on the 17th, these were called in, and joined the regiment which had commenced its march towards Obidos.

On reaching the plain in front of that town, the whole army was formed in mass, each brigade in contiguous columns of battalions at half distance. After a short halt, an order was received for all the women and baggage to go to the rear, and for the troops to stand to their arms. The enemy's position having in the meantime been reconnoitred, and the final dispositions for an attack been made, the army was again put in motion. Soon after passing through Obidos, the various columns of attack struck off into different routes, and Nightingale's brigade, with the 29th Foot leading, proceeding along the main road marched direct for the enemy. Drawn up in line, on an elevated plain

1808 beyond the village of Mamed, with Columbeira in rear of their left, were discovered two battalions of the French 70th Regiment of the Line.

A momentary halt was now made, and the 29th and 82nd having deployed into line, the men were ordered to prime and load. Then, with shouldered arms, and in perfect order, these regiments advanced until the red tufts, and even the enemy's faces, were easily distinguished.

On Dr. Guthrie asking what was his place on such an occasion, he was told it was seven paces in rear of the colours. Colonel Lake, who was about the same distance in front of them, now turned round, and called out, "Gentlemen, display the colours," the colours flew, and shortly afterwards he again turned round and addressed the line thus, "Soldiers, I shall remain in front of you, and remember that the bayonet is the only weapon for a British soldier!" On arriving at the position where the French were first seen, it was found that their right was filing to the rear, and that their left had retired through Columbeira, to their principal position on the heights of Roliça,* which commanded that village. To attack these heights, five columns had been formed, and to each was assigned the carrying of a pass. The forcing of the 3rd or centre one was entrusted to Nightingale's brigade. The 82nd Regiment was ordered to another point of attack, and on the right of the 29th, again meeting the road, it advanced in column of sections through Columbeira.—— Colonel Landmann states :—"On reaching the main road, the 29th regiment was at this moment coming up with Lieut.-Colonel the Honble. G. Lake, at their head, the band playing a country dance. Lake was mounted on a complete charger, nearly 17 hands high, with a famous long tail, and was dressed in an entire new suit, even his leathers, boots, hat, feather, epaulettes, sash, etc., being all new, and his hair powdered and queued, his cocked hat placed on his head square to the front, and, in fact, accoutered in the strictest accordance with the King's Regulations."

---

* By an error of a copying clerk in Lord Bathurst's office miswritten "Roleia," and which spelling has since been continued.

"I was so struck with the marked distinction between the 29th Regiment and all others, then with the army, that I could not refrain from observing to Lake, 'Well, colonel, you are dressed as if you were going to be received by the king.'——Lake smiled and replied with a dignified air, 'Egad, sir, if I am killed to-day, I mean to die like a gentleman.'"

In passing through Columbeira the 29th became much exposed to the fire of the enemy's sharpshooters on the heights, and to a cannonade of round shot from the left; this being the case, the left wing was ordered to march round the village to the left, and thus it did not reach the entrance of the pass until a considerable time after the right wing.

On the Light company being detached (with those of the 5th and 82nd, the whole under command of Major Andrew Creagh of the 29th) with the object of making a demonstration against a pass further to the right, some of the old grenadiers called out, "We can do it as well as them, colonel!" but Col. Lake replied, "Never mind, my lads. Let the 'light bobs' lather them first, we will shave them afterwards."

Having passed through the village, the right wing of the regiment turned to the left through some vineyards, and advanced along the foot of the heights in order to gain the pass, and during this movement it became necessarily exposed to a flank fire, from which it suffered considerably.

On approaching the pass, it was found to be extremely steep and narrow, and being overhung with rock and groves, it afforded excellent cover to the enemy's light troops, whilst in some places, only two or three men could ascend at a time. About half-way up, there was a small olive grove in which the men were halted to form, and ordered to take off their haversacks, great coats, etc., which was done under a hot fire. It was about this time that Colonel Lake, who was leading the attack at the head of his grenadiers, had his horse shot under him,

1808 upon which Major Gregory Way dismounted and gave him the charger he was riding, "*Black Jack,*" which had been lent him by the colonel.

After clearing the narrow defile, the right wing reached some open but thinly wooded ground, and in order to make room for the left wing to form up when it should arrive, the leading companies, already much reduced in numbers, were obliged, under a heavy fire, to take ground to the right. The officers then lost no time in forming their men in line, and the remains of the three or four companies having advanced, gained the heights.

Some of the enemy who had been lining a broken fence, then suddenly rose up and opened fire, upon which Colonel Lake called out, " Don't fire, men ; don't fire ; wait a little, we shall soon charge !" These were nearly his last words, for, as he was moving towards the left to superintend the prolongation of the line, he was shot by one of the French skirmishers, and "*Black Jack,*" who galloped into the French lines, was taken prisoner, and became the property of General Delaborde.

The right, not receiving any orders to advance, now opened fire, and some of the enemy in front of the extreme right, either as a ruse, or in earnest, called out that they were poor Swiss, and did not want to fight the English ; some were actually shaking hands, and a parley ensued, during which the French troops (1st battalion, 70th) which had been posted on the side of the ravine, finding that it had been forced, and that they were likely to be cut off, began to retire, and coming in rear of the right of the 29th, dashed through, carrying away with them Major Way (who was dismounted, and whose sword had been broken by a ball), five other officers, 1 serjeant, 1 drummer, 32 rank and file. Owing to this accident, and the tremendous fire now poured in from all sides, there were but three officers remaining with the right wing, one of whom was Lieut. Charles Leslie. The senior officer, Major Thos. Egerton, seeing the impossibility of making an effectual resistance with the few men remaining, ordered them to fall back, and under cover of the wood, await the arrival of the left wing, which was fast **1808** advancing. The enemy, on observing this, set up a shout, and then, but not till then, advanced, as if with the intention of charging. Some individuals on both sides got mixed, and had personal encounters with the bayonet; but the French did not venture to press, or follow.

On being joined by its left wing, and supported by the 9th Foot, which had been sent to reinforce it as soon as it was found to be so seriously engaged, the regiment pushed forward, regained the dangerous footing above, and succeeded in maintaining the position against all attacks. The 29th was then halted, and on mustering the regiment, it was found that those who had been taken prisoners all belonged to the 3rd and 4th right companies.

It may here be added, that one of the men who had been punished the previous day, scorning to remain in the rear while his regiment was engaged, gallantly broke away from the hospital serjeant, joined his company, and fought most daringly against the enemy.

The army having taken up a good position, and re-formed in order of battle, strong picquets were posted in front and rear. Orders were then received for the regiment to remain accoutered, and ready to fall in at a moment's notice.

Among the men who escorted the prisoners to Lisbon, were two brothers named Bellegarde, one a " sous-officier," the other a private. Both laid claim to having shot poor Colonel Lake. The " sous-officier" insisted that it was he who did it, and that he was lying behind a bush when he fired seven shots at the colonel, who was in front of his men superintending their forming in line. Once he observed that he seemed to stagger as if hit, but it was only at the seventh shot that he fell.

It is probable that this was correct, for the colonel was slightly wounded in the back of his neck, but the ball that killed him passed quite through from side to side beneath the arms. Major Campbell, A.D.C. to Sir Arthur Wellesley, being near when the colonel fell,

1808 immediately went up and expressed a hope that he was not seriously wounded. Colonel Lake lifted his eyes, took Major Campbell's hand, which he pressed with all his remaining strength, and soon expired. The body was then covered with a cloak, and after the action removed for interment.

As Major Campbell was passing, many of the wounded called out to him, "Never mind us, sir ; for God's sake take care of the colonel."

The spot where this gallant officer was buried † is marked by a plain square stone monument, surmounted by a cross of the same material, bearing on one of its sides the following appropriate inscription :—

> Sacred
> to the Memory of Lieut.-Col. Lake
> of the 29th Reg^t
> who fell at the head of his Corps
> in driving the Enemy from the heights
> of Columbeira,
> on the 17th August, 1808.
> This Monument is Erected by his Brother Officers
> as a Testimony of their Regard and Esteem.

The expenses of the above memorial, as well as of a handsome tablet erected in the north-west tower of Westminster Abbey, were defrayed by a subscription of so many days' pay from the officers, non-commissioned officers, drummers, and privates of the regiment.

The end of a more humble, though as brave, a soldier should also be mentioned, viz., that of Serjeant-Major Richards, who, seeing his colonel fall, stood over defending him, until he himself fell wounded in thirteen places by shot and bayonet. Dr. Guthrie, who gave him some water in his dying moments, said his last words were, "I should have died happy, if our gallant colonel had been spared"—a sentiment shared by almost every wounded man of the regiment.

---

† *United Service Journal*, 1844.—"Stray Gleanings from British Battle Fields."

Killed, Wounded, and Missing of the 29th Foot in the Battle of Roliça, 17th of August, 1808.

1808

Killed*—1 Lieut.-Colonel, 2 Serjeants, 31 Rank and File.
Wounded*—1 Major, 3 Captains, 4 Lieutenants, 6 Serjeants, 105 Rank and File.
Missing—1 Major, 2 Captains, 5 Lieutenants, 1 Serjeant, 1 Drummer, 32 Rank and File.

In the *Broad Arrow* of the 2nd of October, 1886, is the following paragraph :—" On this occasion the brunt of the fight was borne by the 29th Regiment, which was considered one of the finest corps in the army. It is recorded that the men of the regiment fought in queues, and powdered hair, and carrying hairy packs of a pattern long forgotten ; and the officers in cocked hats, worn athwartships, in the fashion of the preceding decade."

The men stood to their arms at about 2 a.m. on the morning of the 18th, and as the enemy had entirely disappeared, the troops advanced to Lourinha, where they bivouacked that evening.

The next day, with the view of covering the disembarkation of reinforcements, the army took up a position at Vimiero, a village situated in a valley through which the Maceira, flanked at right angles on either side by a range of steep hills, flowed into the sea.

About 11 o'clock on the night of the 20th, the alarm was given that the enemy was advancing. All the inlying picquets were immediately ordered under arms, and a brigade was sent to occupy some heights on the left of Vimiero. As nothing further occurred, the rest of the troops again laid down by their arms. The morning of the 21st dawned in all its brilliancy, and the troops, who as usual were under arms an hour before daylight, were dismissed at about 6 a.m., on the arrival in camp of the reinforcements. Two hours later, the bugles sounded the alarm, and the drums beat to arms, for distant clouds of

---

* The names of the officers will be found in the Monthly Returns inserted on page 286 ; those of non-commissioned officers, rank and file, killed in the Peninsular War, will be found on pages 332 and 333.

1808 dust announced the approach of the enemy. A breakfast of biscuit and water, with a bunch of grapes, had to be hastily swallowed, and the men were directed to leave their knapsacks in the camp under charge of the quarter guard. In order to support the force which was posted on the heights to the left of the village, towards which the enemy appeared to be marching, the 29th and 82nd were moved across the valley in which Vimiero stands. On reaching the foot of the heights, the road was found to be so steep and heavy, that two companies of the 29th were ordered to assist in dragging up the guns. After gaining the ascent, the 29th, being the leading regiment, moved along the edge of the heights which sloped abruptly to the valley below, and after advancing some distance, it deployed into line. Observing that the enemy were endeavouring to force his centre, Sir Arthur Wellesley immediately ordered the Grenadier, and another company of the 29th whose right was resting on the slope of the height commanding this route, to retire a short distance, and some artillery being brought forward, a well-directed fire was opened on the French column, which retired.

It was about this period of the battle that Lieut.-General Sir Harry Burrard, Bart., arrived on the field, and took over the command of the army.

Scarcely had the enemy been repulsed by the right wing, than they attempted to turn the left of the British position. The 29th had at first but little to do, but its Light company, with that of the 82nd, both under command of Major Andrew Creagh, became warmly engaged in its front, during which time the regiment was ordered to lie flat down. The men being under fire, were impatient to advance, and at last orders were received for them to move against a column of the enemy; they, however, were not allowed to fire, but marched steadily on, ready to charge. Before they could close with the French, the latter retreated, and abandoned all their guns. The brigade was then halted, and as the enemy appeared to have gone completely off, the men were allowed to stand at ease. Whilst resting in this manner, another **1808** column of the enemy was observed to dash suddenly down some opposite heights, as if meaning to attack the brigade, and a body of cavalry appeared on the right flank, which it threatened to turn.

The 29th was therefore ordered to form four-deep, which formation afforded the advantage of showing a front to meet the enemy in line, and at the same time was of sufficient strength to resist cavalry. On the enemy's infantry arriving on the low ground, it was received by a destructive fire from the 71st, and the Light companies of the 29th and 82nd, which had been lying concealed by willow beds and bushes, from both friend and foe. After returning an irregular fire, the infantry retired, and the cavalry, observing their discomfiture, followed their example. This was the last effort the French made that day. The 29th, which was still halted, was much disappointed at its forced inactivity; the men were never in better humour for a brush, or in better fighting trim, for their knapsacks had been left in camp, and having only marched a short distance, they were comparatively fresh; but enough had been overheard of a conversation between Sir A. Wellesley and Sir Harry Burrard, to judge that no advance would take place that evening. Fatigue parties having been left to bury the dead, the regiment, after a short rest, marched back to its bivouac with band playing and colours flying. The general feeling amongst the troops was, that had Sir Arthur been allowed to carry out his plans, the advantage gained by this victory would have been far greater.

In the battle of Vimiero, fought 21st August, 1808, the regiment suffered the following casualties:—

Killed—2 Rank and File.
Wounded—Brigadier-Major Andrew Creagh, 1 Serjeant, 10 Rank and File.

Early on the morning of the 22nd, Lieut.-General Sir Hew Dalrymple disembarked to assume the chief command, so that within twenty-four hours the army had had three different commanders.

1808 List of Officers of the 29th (Worcestershire) Regiment, taken from the Monthly Returns.

All the officers were present with the head-quarters of the regiment on the 1st of August and 1st of September, except where otherwise specified.

	1st August.	1st September.
	On board "Dominica" Transport at Sea.	Sobral de Monte Grape.
Colonel	Gordon Forbes, LG. Absent with leave,	His Majesty's permission.
Lieut.-Colonels	Fred Maitland, MG. Absent with leave,	His Majesty's permission.
	Honble. G. A. F. Lake. Killed, Rolica, 17th August.	
Majors	Daniel White, lc.	
	Gregory Way.—Wounded, 17th Inst.	Prisoner of War.
Captains	Thos. Egerton, m.—Severely Wounded, 17th Inst.	Sick in Portugal.
	Andrew Creagh, m. — Wounded at Vimiero, 21st Inst.	Sick in Portugal.
	John Tucker. Absent. Brigade Major, Nova Scotia.	
	L. Augustus Northey. Absent. A D Q M G., England.	
	Peter Hodge. Wounded, 17th Inst. (Arm broken.)	Sick in Portugal.
	Saml. Gauntlett.	
	George Tod.	Prisoner of War.
	Eugene Nestor.	
	Chas. W. Davy.	
	Andrew Patison. Wounded, 17th Inst.	Prisoner of War.
Lieutenants	H. Birmingham. Absent. Prisoner in France.	
	Walter Birmingham.	Prisoner of War.
	Robt. Birmingham. Severely wounded, 17th Inst.	Died of Wounds, 10th September.
	Ambrose Newbold.	Prisoner of War.
	John Humfrey.	
	Wm. Wade, Adjt.	
	Charles Smyth.	
	Thomas Gell.	
	Thos. Langton. Wounded, 17th Inst.	Prisoner of War.
	St. John W. Lucas. Wounded, 17th Inst.	Prisoner of War.
	Elmes S. L. Nicholson.	
	James Nestor. Recruiting at Killashandra, Ireland.	
	Robert Stannus. Wounded, 17th Inst.	Prisoner of War.
	James Brooks.	
	Wm. Duguid.	
	Adam Gregory.	
	Charles Leslie.	
	Thos. Popham.	
	Wm. Penrose.	Absent. Not yet joined.
	Charles Stanhope.	
	Wm. Champain.	Absent without leave.
	Wm. Elliot.	Absent. Not yet joined.
	Andrew Leith Hay.	Absent. Not yet joined.
Ensigns	Thos. Lewis Coker.	
	Henry Pennington.	
	Samuel Hardy.	Recruiting at Manchester.
	Alexr. Young.	
	Benjn. Wild.	
	John Marshall.	Absent. Not yet joined.
	Henry Reid.	Absent. Not yet joined.
Pay Master	Thos. Stott	
Adjutant	Wm. Wade.	
Qr. Master	Wm. Gillespie.	
Surgeon	Geo. Guthrie.	
Assistant Surgeons	Edwd. Curby.	
	Lewis Evans.	Attending the Sick on board the Transports.

Whilst Sir Hew Dalrymple was examining the state of affairs, a party **1808** of French cavalry approached the British advance guard. They were escorting General Kellerman, who, with a flag of truce, had been sent by Marshal Junot, to demand a cessation of arms, and propose the groundwork of a Convention, by which Junot offered to evacuate Portugal without further resistance. As several delays occurred in the negotiations, it was thought that the enemy wished to gain time, so on the 23rd the British army pushed forward towards Lisbon.

On the 2nd of September, the 29th approached Bucellas, but on learning that the French rear-guard had not yet evacuated that place, it halted on the heights above the town, and as soon as it was ascertained that the enemy had marched off, the route was continued to Antonio-de-Tozal, near which the regiment bivouacked and remained for a few days. During its stay here, the 29th was brigaded with the 40th and 50th regiments, and attached to the reserve under General Spencer. The Convention of Cintra was also concluded, and the officers who had been taken prisoners at Roliça, rejoined their regiments. These now informed their comrades of some of their adventures during their captivity. Major Way, who at the time of being made prisoner had but the hilt of his sword, with a few inches of the blade in his hand, was saved from the bayonet of a French grenadier by General Brenier. On being brought before General Delaborde, he requested permission to retain the hilt, which was very politely granted, and the General said, "Gentlemen, now that you are prisoners, we are no longer enemies." Another soldier made a thrust at Lieutenant Langton, but the bayonet fortunately struck his buff cross-belt; the thrust was about to be repeated when a French officer knocked up the bayonet with his sword, and saved Langton's life. The prisoners were hurried off to Lisbon, and put on board the "Vasca de Gama," then lying in the Tagus.

Marshal Junot, on returning to Lisbon, after his defeat at Vimiero, and before the Convention was concluded, was very civil to the British officers, and invited them to dinner every day.

1808   An officer of the 29th, writing to his brother in Edinburgh, said:—
"The dinner service was all silver plate, and the dessert was served completely on gold; in short, it was the most splendid thing of the kind I ever sat down to. There were about 20 French officers, high in rank, of the party, who were all very attentive; General Junot himself was equally so."

On the morning of the 12th of September, the 29th and 50th regiments marched into Lisbon, and took post in the Campo St. Anna, a large Square in the upper part, whilst the French occupied all the lower part of the town, and had pointed loaded cannon up each street leading to it.

The officers of the regiment were much amused on observing a proclamation of Marshal Junot's posted on the walls, announcing that he had defeated the English, and that the 9th and 29th regiments had been cut to pieces.

On the 14th, the British troops marched out of Lisbon, and joined the main part of the army then encamped on some heights commanding the town. It having been decided by the Convention that the French flag was to be hauled down, and the Portuguese hoisted on the towers of Lisbon on the 15th inst., on that day, a grand guard was formed (consisting of the Grenadiers of the 29th, 40th, 50th, and 79th regiments, with a party of the 95th and some pieces of artillery, the whole under command of General Cameron), and marched off at 6 a.m. to take possession of the citadel. At the same time the 29th Regiment, with colours flying and band playing, proceeded to Plaço de Rocio, the grand Square of Lisbon, which it occupied, relieving all the French posts in that quarter. About mid-day the French flag was struck. Three companies of the 29th, under command of Major Way, were then ordered to cover the embarkation of the French army, and marching from the Rocio to the small Square in front of the Naval Arsenal, were there drawn up in line opposite the principal entrance, through which **1808** the French troops had to pass to get to the boats waiting at the wharf to convey them to the transports. Several of the French officers felt so grateful for the protection which had been afforded them, that they made presents of their horses to officers of the covering party. The 29th were most anxious to recover "*Black Jack*," * their late colonel's charger. On a communication being made to General Delaborde that any sum he chose to name would be paid him, if he would part with the horse, the general, in the most handsome manner possible, sent the charger back as a present to the regiment, saying " that he was happy to have in his power the means of gratifying a corps which had displayed such determined gallantry against him."

The three companies of the regiment which were on duty covering the embarkation of the French, remained in the Square in front of the Arsenal all night, and on being relieved the following morning by the 50th Regiment, returned to their camp. On the 17th, the regiment marched into Lisbon, and relieved the 79th in the Black Horse Square.

Towards the end of the month, further reinforcements having been received, the army took up another position some miles from Lisbon, the 29th encamping near Monte Santa.

Previous to Sir Arthur Wellesley's return to England, the commanding, and field officers of corps, who had had the honour of serving

---

* " Black Jack " afterwards became the property of Major Gregory Way, who rode him at the Passage of the Douro, Battles of Busaco, Talavera, and Albuhera. On the latter occasion, when Major Way fell from his charger badly wounded, " Black Jack " again fell into the hands of the enemy, but was returned the following day, with a note from the French general, saying " he had been so struck with the gallant behaviour of the 29th, on the day previous, that he begged to return the charger to its owner, with his compliments."

1808 under his command, presented him with an address, and a piece of plate.

Sir Hew Dalrymple was next recalled, and the command devolved on Sir Harry Burrard, who, from bad health and other causes, requested leave to resign the appointment.

On the 27th of September, the Emperors Napoleon and Alexander met at Erfurt, and offered peace to England. This being rejected, on the 6th of October, Lieut.-General Sir John Moore, K.B., was given chief command of the British forces, and appointed to lead an army into Spain.

Owing to the losses the regiment had sustained, and the many wounded and sick still remaining in hospital, it was not destined to form part of Sir John's force, but on leaving Monte Santa, early in October, moved into Lisbon, and took up quarters in the St. Domingo convent, from which it subsequently marched into the citadel.

GENERAL ORDER.

"Head Quarters, Lisbon, 15th October, 1808.

"Before entering Spain, in compliment to the Spanish nation, the army will wear the Red cockade, in addition to their own."

On the 27th, Sir John Moore left Lisbon. Sir John Cradock, K.B., having been charged with the conduct of military proceedings in Portugal, resolved, early in December, to make the reinforcing of Sir John Moore's army his first care, and therefore sent the 29th, who had lately received a draft of recruits from England, and whose sick and wounded had mostly recovered, to join it.

Communications with Sir John Moore being suddenly interrupted, and Napoleon having entered Madrid, the line of the River Tagus acquired greater importance; therefore, on reaching Castello Branco, the regiment was ordered to halt, whilst two companies, under Captains **1808** Tod and Davy, were detached to Villa Velha, to protect the flying bridge. The Portuguese force failing to support him, and hearing that 30,000 French were on the road to Badajos, Sir J. Cradock determined to concentrate his troops near Lisbon, and having destroyed the Villa Velha bridge, Captains Tod and Davy's detachment rejoined the regiment, which, returning by Abrantes and Santarem, on the 20th of January, 1809, arrived at Lisbon and was quartered in the convents.   **1809**

This brigade (General Richard Stewart's) had been marching incessantly for over a month, often in the rain; the men's uniforms were worn out, their accoutrements nearly destroyed, and, in common with the rest of the army, they were suffering from the want of shoes.

As the account of the Battle of Roliça, and the subsequent movements of the 29th, are partly taken from the military journal of Colonel Charles Leslie, it may be as well to quote the following letter from that officer to the editor of the *United Service Journal* :—

THE 29TH REGIMENT AT ROLIÇA.

"Mr. Editor—In justice to a gallant old corps, I have to request that you will give the following statement a place in your most impartial and excellent journal. I observe, with much regret, in Colonel Napier's work on the Peninsular War, several inaccuracies in the account which he gives of the operations of the 29th Regiment, in the action of Roliça. To a regiment jealous of its reputation, it is at all times a matter of great interest that its deeds in arms should be fairly recorded, but infinitely more so that no misstatements, even by mistake, should be made tending to its prejudice and disadvantage. I feel confident Colonel Napier would not willingly hurt the feelings, much less tarnish the fame and blight the laurels, of a corps which, during several arduous campaigns, distinguished itself in every action that was fought, as testified by his Grace the Duke of Wellington's General Orders, when the regiment was sent a skeleton from the field, in consequence of the severe losses it had sustained in the numerous actions in which it had been engaged.

I have long wished that somebody more capable than myself, would have undertaken the task of correcting these mistakes. However, as no abler advocate has yet appeared, and as the Colonel has since, in a reply to General Brenier, called upon the officers of the 29th to confirm or deny the General's statement, wherein he affirms that, he with only two companies broke the 29th Regiment, I shall by simply stating matters of fact, as they occurred, endeavour to show that both are mistaken.

I may add that, however inadequate to the task, I am entitled to do this without much presumption, having had the honour and good fortune to serve in that gallant corps during the whole period of their service in the Peninsula.

I have the honour to remain,

Sir,

Your Obedient Servant,

An Officer late of the 29th Regiment."

"Cork, 21st August, 1830."

Colonel Napier states, "that the 29th and 9th Regiments forced the two strongest passes;"

"That the 29th Regiment arrived first in disorder at the top;"

"That ere they could form, a French battalion broke through the midst of them, slaying the Colonel and many others, and making one major and 50 or 60 men prisoners."

I flatter myself that I shall satisfactorily prove, by the following extract from a journal kept at the time, that the Colonel has been misinformed when he makes the above assertion.

In Colonel Leslie's journal are the following paragraphs relating the Battle of Roliça:—

"To show that the regiment was not in disorder when we arrived at the top, I may state that after clearing the wood where we had reformed, and were advancing in column of sections, a ball knocked off the steel of a serjeant's halbert, who was leading the section in front of me, which came flying backwards and struck Major Way, who being dismounted, was walking alongside. Soon afterwards, when we were forming line, I saw his sword broken by a ball, whilst in the act of waving it and cheering the men. When he was taken prisoner, as before related, General Laborde gave him permission to retain the hilt of his sword, in which a part of the blade was still remaining; however, the escort (who behaved very brutally to him) afterwards made him throw it away.

We afterwards understood that it was not intended the 29th should have so soon attacked the strong pass, nor penetrate so far as we did, but were merely in the first instance to have occupied the village of Columbeira, and make a demonstration on the enemy's centre, whilst General Ferguson on the left, and General Hill on the right, should attack and turn his flanks. By some mistake, however, the order was misunderstood, and our gallant Colonel pushed on."

This account of the battle of Roliça, the correctness of which can be established by the testimony of several officers, I deem sufficient to prove—

I. That the 9th Regiment did not force a separate pass;
II. That the 29th Regiment did not arrive in disorder at the top; and
III. That the French did not break through the midst of the regiment, slaying the Colonel and making sixty prisoners, as was asserted by Colonel Napier in his " History of the Peninsular War."

With regard to General Brenier's assertion, that he, with only two companies, broke the 29th Regiment, I have to observe that it may no doubt be true that he sent two companies from his own left, but it ought at the same time to have been stated that those companies could only have come in support of troops already defending the debouch of the pass, and that neither they, nor others broke through the centre of the regiment; because at the time stated it is sufficiently proved that there were not formed more than the remains of three or four weak companies, reduced by the dreadful fire they had been exposed to, so that he would have had no great achievement to boast of, even if correct. While we were engaged in this desperate conflict, the enemy's balls which passed through our ranks or over our heads, fell amongst the 9th Regiment, which was moving up in our rear to support us. They, not being aware that we were so immediately in their front, because the wood concealed us from their view, some of their leading companies opened their fire upon us, nor could this be stopped until they had occasioned serious casualties in our ranks. They, however, soon afterwards rushed up, and formed upon our left. We all dashed boldly on. The enemy gave way at all points. They again attempted to make a stand at Zambugeira. We continued to pursue them, but as our cavalry was not up to follow the pursuit, we were at last ordered to halt, and the enemy continued their retreat on the road to Torres Vedras. We took up a good position."

1809 In consequence of the failure of Sir John Moore's expedition, it was now suggested to secure Cadiz, as a future base of operations.

The 29th Regiment, having received drafts from England, and most of its wounded having returned to duty, on the 27th of January, 1809, it was reviewed by the commander-in-chief, Lieut.-General Sir John Cradock, in the Rocio Square, when he gave it his most unqualified praise, and two days later, it received orders to be in readiness to embark at a moment's notice. The force destined for this service, consisted of the 2nd battalion 9th, the 27th and 29th regiments, and a brigade of artillery, the whole under General Mackenzie. It embarked at 8 a.m. on the 31st instant, and arrived off Cadiz on the 5th of February, but not being permitted to land, the troops remained on board the transports in the harbour till the 6th of March, when the convoy sailed for the Tagus, where after a stormy passage, it anchored on the 12th. The following day the 29th landed, and the men were quartered in a convent, the officers in billets.

The sudden recall of General Mackenzie's expedition was now ascertained to be due to Marshal Soult having entered Portugal and taken possession of Oporto.

Further reinforcements having arrived from England, and Marshal Beresford having collected the bulk of the Portuguese regular troops between the Tagus and the Mondego, Cradock resolved to advance against Soult.

On the 18th, the army took up cantonments in the villages of Loires and Lumear; the 29th being at the former on the 1st of April. On the 8th, the advance was commenced, and the regiment marched to Bucellas. Leaving there on the 11th, it arrived at Leira, where the different corps of the army concentrated on the 22nd, the same day on which Sir Arthur Wellesley landed at Lisbon to take over the supreme command. On the 29th instant, the regiment marched to Pombal, on the 30th to Condeixa, and on the 1st May to Coimbra.

On the occasion of the commander-in-chief's arrival there on the 3rd, **1809** the 29th Grenadiers had the honour of being selected to form the guard of honour to receive him. It being ascertained that the enemy's advance guard had been pushed forward, and was two or three days' march from Oporto, the outposts and inlying picquets of the allies were strengthened.

On the 4th, the regiment was placed in Brigadier-General R. Stewart's brigade, in which were the 16th Portuguese and the 1st provisional battalion of detachments. When, two days later, Sir Arthur reviewed the allied army in the Campo de Mondego, it is stated that, with the exception of the Guards, the 29th Foot, and the Germans, most of the soldiers were very young.

It was now decided to advance towards Oporto, in two columns, one marching by Adiga on the Vouga, the other by the Bay of Aveiro, to Ovar. The advance guard of the first-mentioned column (consisting of the King's German Legion, Brigadier-General R. Stewart's brigade, with a battery of 6-pounders, and one of 3-pounders) under Lieut.-General Paget, marched from Coimbra to Mangaforaz on the 7th, and the following day to Mureska, a small village on the left bank of the Vouga. Having remained inactive the whole of the 9th, the troops were roused about midnight and ordered to get under arms with as little noise as possible, and to march immediately with the view of surprising the enemy's advance guard, which was at Oliveira. On account of the intense darkness, the artillery missed the way, and it was found necessary to halt the column. It was near daybreak of the 10th before the march was resumed, and on reaching Albergaria Nova, it was discovered that the enemy had retired but an hour before. The light troops were at once pushed forward, some skirmishing ensued, in which the 29th Foot had

1 Rank and File wounded,

and the French were driven through Oliveira. That evening the outposts were placed close up to the enemy, the sentries being within half

1809 musket shot of each other. When at daybreak of the 11th, it was ascertained that the enemy had retired, a pursuit was immediately commenced, and their advance guard, consisting of 4000 infantry and some squadrons of cavalry, with its front covered by woods and broken ground, was discovered strongly posted on the heights above Grijo. Two companies of the 29th were then thrown into a wood on the right side of the road, to clear it, and at the same time to act as a flanking party to the advanced troops. These companies, on being relieved by the riflemen of the K.G.L., rejoined their regiment, which had halted on a height immediately opposite the enemy. Line was then formed, the cavalry and artillery on the right, the 29th in the centre, and the 16th Portuguese on the left. The riflemen of the 95th and the Flank companies of the 29th, 43rd, and 52nd regiments, under command of Major Way of the 29th, then advanced against the enemy's centre, and soon became warmly engaged. Whilst this was taking place, the remainder of the brigade was ordered to lie down. Sir Arthur Wellesley and his staff were immediately in rear of the colours of the 29th, and as the skirmishing in front continued with great obstinacy, Sir Arthur was heard to say, "If they don't move soon, I must let the old 29th loose upon them!". On the enemy's left flank being turned by a well-executed movement of Major-General Murray's with the K.G.L., and their right threatened by the 16th Portuguese regiment, they gave way. After moving through the village, the 29th Foot halted in the French bivouac, and became indebted to their foes for shelter and food, for slaughtered cattle had been left lying about.

In the action fought on the 11th of May, 1809, on the heights of Grijo and Calvahos, the casualties in the regiment were :—

Killed—2 Rank and File.
Wounded—6 ,,

Sir Arthur Wellesley, in his despatch to Viscount Castlereagh anent the fight at Grijo, wrote : "I have also to request your Lordship's attention to the conduct of the riflemen, and flank companies of the 29th, 43rd, and 52nd Regiments under command of Major Way, 29th."

The following morning, the regiment pushed on with great expedi-**1809** tion to Villa Nova, a suburb of Oporto, situated on the left bank of the Douro. Here it halted in the steep narrow streets, in column of sections well closed up. Word having been passed from the rear, to open out right and left, to let the Guards pass, it is related that the 29th, wishing to remain at the head of the column, passed back word that it was impossible to do so.

In the meantime, three companies of the "Buffs" had crossed the river higher up, and occupied the convent of St. Augustino da Serra, and on General Murray showing himself on the enemy's left, Soult commenced to retire from Oporto. The French having collected all the boats to their side of the river, apparently considered them so secure as to make it unnecessary to place a sufficient guard over, or to destroy, them. This being observed, it was immediately taken advantage of. Signs were made to the inhabitants, who, availing themselves of the confusion in the enemy's army, instantly brought over several boats, into which the 29th jumped, and pushing across, succeeded in gaining the opposite shore with but slight opposition. Having landed and formed, the regiment at once moved up the main street, and the Grenadiers opened fire on the retreating enemy. The "Buffs" now dashed into the town, and cut off a battery of light artillery, which becoming wedged in between that regiment and the 29th, received the fire of both, and was captured. The 29th then drove the enemy from a rocky height and continued pursuing them very closely, but when on the point of charging them, a staff officer rode up to the head of the regiment, and placing his horse across the road, said to the commanding officer, "Sir, I order you to halt, to let the cavalry pass to the front!" This, as may be conceived, was very disappointing to the men. The cavalry having cleared the front, the 29th continued to advance, until ordered by Sir Arthur in person, to form line along a wall on the edge of a wood to the left of the road, and not to move without his own positive orders. Having remained in this position till about 7 p.m.,

1809 the regiment marched back to Oporto, where a street was given up to it, and the officers were allowed to choose the best houses they could find.

EXTRACT FROM THE GENERAL ORDER PUBLISHED WITH REGARD TO THIS ACTION.

"Oporto, 12 May, 1809.

"The timely passage of the Douro, and subsequent movement on the enemy's flank by Lieut.-General Sherbrook with the brigade of Guards and 29th Regiment; and the bravery of the two squadrons of the 14th Light Dragoons, under command of Major Hervey and led by Brig^{dr} General the Honble C. Stewart, obtained the victory which has contributed so much to the honour of the troops on this day."

I have not been able to trace any regimental list of the killed and wounded in this action, but the 29th Regimental Pay Lists and Muster Rolls do not return any of the men as killed.

The following anecdote was related by Dr. Guthrie:—

"The Portuguese boatmen having procured more boats, ferried me over, with my horse. The alarm was perfect, for the enemy, who appear not to have suspected such a surprise, fled in all directions, leaving horses, mules, and baggage all in the greatest confusion; every one took to his horse or his heels, and no one thought he could leave Oporto fast enough.

"The inhabitants seemed afraid to touch anything themselves, but called out to us to seize every horse and baggage mule we saw as being French. Being the only mounted officer, I could ride about and take my choice of lots of loaded horses and mules. It was not yet considered officer-like to deal in baggage, and so I occupied my time looking for some riding-horses, until I lost the British, and was overtaken by Sir J. Milley Doyle at the head of the 16th Portuguese, also looking for them. I offered to show him the way, as they were only a

little before us, and placed myself by his side at the head of his regiment. **1809**
On turning a corner I showed him the 29th Grenadiers drawn up in line on the rising ground at the end of the road. They soon perceived us, and after a minute or two I saw Sir J. Sherbrooke himself face the Grenadier company towards us, and to my astonishment they very quietly 'made ready' as if on parade.

"Sir John and the Portuguese called out it was all over with them, and I thought so myself, for, knowing the old Grenadiers very well, I took it for granted we were as good as dead. We were too far off to be heard in time, yet close enough to be shot, and it was quite plain they took us for French. I bethought me I had a red round jacket on, under my blue undress coat, and as little time was to be lost, I stood up in my stirrups and opened the blue coat as wide as possible, so that none of the red one should be lost. The Grenadiers at this moment came to the 'present;' I thought we were gone: when in an instant I saw them irregularly changing to the 'recover:' they knew me, and called out 'the doctor and the Portuguese.' I never was so delighted in my life, and galloped up to them forthwith.

"Sir J. Sherbrooke saluted me with, 'By God, Sir, if you had not shown that red jacket, I would have sent you all in a second more to the devil!' I knew Sir John very well, and said I hoped at all events he would have sent us elsewhere, but he would not hear of it. 'No, sir,' said he, 'I would have sent you all to the devil: you should have gone there and nowhere else!' and as it was well known that Sir John would always do what he said as far as depended on him, there was nothing to be done but submit. From that day the Portuguese never went into action, that I saw, without a white band round the left arm.

"Shortly after this I accompanied the light troops to the front, and had a little skirmish with the French runaways, who were making their escape from the end of every street. Some of them brought up a gun, but on seeing us, and also that the road was occupied, as it turned in front of us, dismounted and left the gun with the four mules that drew

1809 it. These I seized, but what to do with a gun and four mules I did not know, more particularly after my failure in horse-stealing; so I settled the matter by taking possession of the best mule, which I carried off, and it served me very faithfully through the Talavera campaign."

Owing to the rapid advance made by the army during the last few days, and the difficulty of getting the necessary supplies across the river, Stewart's brigade remained at Oporto till the 15th, when it followed the direction taken by the French in their retreat, and marched to Villa Nova de Famelicao. Braga was reached the following day. On the 17th, it was ascertained that Soult, having destroyed his artillery and stores, had escaped across the frontier, breaking down all bridges with a view of retarding the pursuit. Sir A. Wellesley therefore came to the conclusion that to pursue any further with his whole force, would be harassing the men for very little purpose. Stewart's brigade was therefore immediately countermarched, and moved into cantonments at Povo de Lanhoso. On hearing that Marshal Victor had taken Alcantara, and was threatening to enter Portugal by way of Castello Branco, the regiment left its cantonment, and on the 22nd, returned to Oporto, where the army had re-assembled. It will not be necessary to record the daily marches now made by the troops, but sufficient to state that, on the 24th, Stewart's brigade re-passed the Douro, and subsequently marched to Ovar, where it embarked on board some boats, and proceeding down the Vouga, reached Aveiro early on the morning of the 28th. On the 1st of June the 29th was at Coimbra, and on the 8th at Abrantes. Whilst here, it was ascertained that Marshal Victor, on hearing of Soult's defeat, had retired to Talavera de la Reyna, and that a Spanish army, under General Cuesta, was on the Tagus watching the French. Sir A. Wellesley, having determined to march into Spain and attack the enemy, now commenced to concentrate his troops, and on the 12th Stewart's brigade crossed to the left bank and took up a position about a league from it. On the 18th, the brigades of Major-General

Hill and Brigadier-General Stewart were ordered to form the 2nd **1809** division. On the 9th of July, this division reached Plasencia. By a Return, dated Plasencia the 15th of June, Stewart's brigade was composed of the 1st battalion of detachments, 1st battalion 48th, and the 29th regiments, the strength of the latter being 1 lieut.-colonel, 1 major, 6 captains, 14 lieutenants, 5 ensigns, 6 staff: 36 serjeants, 15 drummers, 600 rank and file, present and fit for duty. A hospital depôt having been established here, under the command of Captain Patison,* of the 29th, the regiment marched on the 16th for Talavera, where on arriving on the 21st, it bivouacked in the olive groves to the left of that town. On the 22nd, the enemy's advanced corps were driven in on to their main body, which occupied a position about two leagues distant, on the other side of the Alberche. When, early on the morning of the 24th, the troops advanced to attack the enemy, it was discovered that Marshal Victor had fallen back to meet Joseph Buonaparte, who, with reinforcements, was hastening to his support. Sir A. Wellesley therefore halted his troops, but Cuesta, becoming full of fight, dashed forward in pursuit. Nothing was heard of the Spanish army till the morning of the 26th, when the report of artillery announced its return, and it was found that Cuesta had sustained a severe check.

That night and the following morning, the Spaniards continued to pass to the rear in full retreat; first from 4000 to 5000 runaways, then the baggage, cattle, sick, wounded, &c., all in terrible confusion.† A heavy cannonade, and fire of musketry, announced the rapid advance of the French, and all this confused mass had to be got out of the way, and line formed in a very short space of time. The position now taken up

---

* Was made prisoner on the 31st July, 1809, when Marshal Mortier, with the 5th Corps, entered the town.

† I am indebted to Colonel Alexander S. Leith Hay, C.B., for the use of a letter written from La Puebla de la Calçade, September 19th, 1809, by Lieut. Leith Hay, of the 29th Foot, to his uncle, General Sir Jas. Leith, G.C.B., describing the part taken by the 29th at Talavera.

1809 by the allies, was about half-a-mile in front of Talavera. Their right rested on the Tagus, at a short distance from, and parallel to which, ran the main road to Madrid. To command this road, and the space between it and the river, some field works had been thrown up, and a battery of Spanish artillery placed in position; from this, and for a mile towards the left, the country was level, but on account of the olive groves, and vineyards, and of its being intersected by thick earthen walls, it was easy to defend. Here the Spaniards were posted. The British right flank rested on a knoll just clear of these enclosures, and the ground which now became perfectly open, rose gradually until it reached the summit of a hill on the left, which formed the key of the position. Beyond this hill was a valley, on the other side of which, the country being broken, rocky, and mountainous, was therefore impracticable for troops. The bed of a dried-up stream ran along the whole front of the position.

The Spanish army having taken up its position on the ground until then occupied by General Hill's division, between 4 and 5 p.m. Stewart's brigade received orders to move to its left, and when passing between the lines of the allies was greeted by the valiant cries of "Rompez los Franceses!" On getting clear of the enclosures, and gaining the lower slope of the hill on the left, the brigade (which had been marching left in front, the 48th Regiment leading) was halted and drawn up in rear of the front line. Whilst in this position, the regiment becoming exposed to a continued fire of shot and shell directed against portions of the advance guard which was now falling back, the men were ordered to lie down. As evening approached, the firing ceased, and all seemed quiet. Marshal Victor, perceiving that the eminence on the left was the key of the position of the allies, and that Donkin's brigade, which occupied it, was too weak to defend every part, conceived the idea of seizing the hill by a sudden assault, and, without communicating his design to King Joseph, directed General Ruffin's division, which consisted of the 9th Léger, the 24th, and 96th Regiments of the Line, to attack it. About 9 p.m., a sudden and tremendous fire was opened **1809** on the hill, and it soon became evident that the enemy were in possession of the top. General Hill was then ordered to reinforce Donkin. Stewart's brigade was approaching the base of the hill when a sharp fire issued from the leading regiment, which although assailed in its progress, continued to advance. It was about this time that General Hill, galloping down the descent, met the 29th advancing in column of companies, and, without a moment's hesitation, led it up at the double. So dark was it, that the blaze of musketry alone displayed the forms of the assailants. The leading company, when close to the enemy's bayonets, poured in a volley, and with a glorious cheer charged the French, who after a short but desperate struggle, were driven off the summit. The regiment having then wheeled into line, advanced in an oblique direction, and the right companies being some way down the slope of the hill, opened fire on the French reserves, which were fast advancing. All the battalions of the 9th Léger having re-formed, it again advanced with re-doubled vigour. The fighting became vehement, for the combatants were scarcely 20 yards apart, but soon the shout of the British soldiers made itself heard above the din of arms, and the enemy's broken troops were once more driven into the ravine below. Line having been re-formed, the 29th took possession of the top of the hill; picquets were immediately thrown out, and a chain of sentries having been posted, the men lay down on their arms in the the midst of fallen enemies, the furred shako of a dead French soldier forming in many cases a pillow for the night.

Sir A. Wellesley having arrived on the scene of action, immediately ordered up artillery, and the early part of the night was employed in placing the guns in position, after which a stillness prevailed for some time; this was at length broken by the rumbling of gun carriages to the front, which betokened preparations for renewed hostilities on the morrow.

1809   At dawn on the 28th, all eyes were anxiously turned towards the enemy, the whole of whose dispositions became clearly visible from the hill as the sun rose. Immediately in front, and on the brink of the ravine at the foot of the hill, appeared a very strong column with reserves in its rear, and field batteries on either flank, whilst light troops were thrown out as skirmishers to cover the front, and prepare the way for an assault. The first move on the part of the French, was made by their artillery directing the muzzles of their guns up the hill.

Soon after this, the picquets of Stewart's brigade were withdrawn, the Light companies being ordered out to cover its front. Sir A. Wellesley now rode up in rear of the 29th. A breathless silence prevailed on both sides, till a signal gun, which was to put the enemy's attacking column in motion, was fired; at the same time a heavy cannonade was opened against the hill, from the afore-mentioned batteries, which never ceased until the French had so nearly reached the summit, that they were unable to make their shot tell without endangering their own troops.

In capturing the hill the previous evening, the formation of Stewart's brigade had become somewhat altered, and the 29th now found itself on the extreme left of the British line of infantry, whilst the battalion of detachments, and the 48th Regiment, were formed on the slope extending towards the right.

Being exposed to a heavy fire, the 29th had been ordered to lie down a short distance behind the brow of the hill, but ready to start up at a moment's notice, and by this judicious arrangement the regiment suffered but little. An old Scotch serjeant, who was crouching close to Lieut. Leith Hay, permitted his head to attain a very slight elevation, and with a groan said, " Good God, sir, this is dreadfu!" Without discussing the merits of the situation, he was advised to keep down his head, a hint instantly adopted without any apparent reluctance. No other part of the army was at this time engaged.

General Hill, on seeing the overwhelming force advancing against his position, gave orders for the light troops to fall back. **1809**

General Ruffin's columns, notwithstanding the well-served fire of the British artillery directed against them, had nearly surmounted all the difficulties of the ground, when they received a check, as the summit, which had up to the present appeared deserted, suddenly supported a regular line of infantry, for General Stewart had called out, "Now 29th! Now is your time!"

The men instantly sprang to their feet and poured in a heavy fire. The French, however, continued the battle with small arms, when Sir Arthur, who was standing near the colours of the 29th, ordered a charge. With a tremendous shout, the right wing of the regiment, together with the 48th, rushed down like a torrent, bayonetting and sweeping back the enemy, even across the ravine, to where their reserves were formed. It was in this charge, that the 29th had the honour of securing two silk standards.* On the top of each pole was a plate with screw-holes, which unquestionably indicated that "Eagles" had surmounted them.† At this moment a column of French infantry appeared close upon the right flank. By great exertions, the pursuers were collected, and forming a front, they charged their new assailants. So completely had all attacks been repelled, that the British infantry were quietly collected in the ravine, and marched back to the height without being seriously assailed. Line was then again reformed a short distance in rear of the crest of the hill, so as to shelter the men as much as possible from the effect of the cannonade, which was for some time kept up along the whole line. After these repulses, great indecision appeared to prevail in the enemy's army, and their columns remained

---

* The official account states that, one Standard was captured, and another destroyed, by the 29th Foot.

The attacks on the 27th and 28th July appear to have been led by the 9me Léger.

† It was the custom of the French to unscrew the "*Eagle*" when in danger, and for the "Eagle-bearer" to conceal it about his person.

1809 immoveable for some hours. When about 10 o'clock, the firing having ceased and everything being quiet, Sir Arthur descended the hill, repaired to the Spanish position, and held a conference with General Cuesta.

Detachments from both armies were now sent to collect the wounded, and friend and foe intermixed in the most friendly way without fear or suspicion. Suffering from excessive thirst, occasioned by the heat of the weather and their recent exertions, they descended in parties to the stream in their front.

Lieut. Langton took this opportunity of giving a French officer two Crosses of the Legion of Honour which had been taken off the bodies of officers killed far up the hill.

For a time all symptoms of strife seemed to have ceased, but early in the afternoon, appearances again indicating renewed action on the part of the enemy, Sir Arthur immediately returned to his former position on the hill. The whole of the enemy's line now stood to arms, heavy masses were seen to be forming against the centre of the allies' position, and soon after, clouds of dust marked the advance of troops against the British right. The scene from the hill was now of a grand description. The columns advancing against the centre were serious in aspect, and caused some anxiety, which, however, was soon relieved by the bayonet, and those on the hill had the pleasure of seeing the enemy give way at every point.

During this great struggle Stewart's brigade had remained comparatively disengaged, for the fire of the enemy's artillery and light troops produced but slight effect. The favourable termination of the battle in the centre, had created great excitement. The cheer which had been re-echoed from the height had scarcely died away when a movement of another character attracted Sir Arthur's attention, for Marshal Victor, having failed to force the centre, now tried to turn the left of the allies' position. The movements of the divisions of Ruffin and Villatte, had, during the contest just described, been vacillating and uncertain. Formed to all appearances with a determination again to attack the hill, they had even advanced some distance towards its base, and their light troops skirmished closely and seriously, but nothing like the attack of the morning was again attempted. A similar repulse would in all probability have attended the effort, for 6000 cavalry were now in the immediate vicinity, and could have instantly fallen on the broken ranks. A turning movement having been checked by the 23rd Light Dragoons and the K.G.L., no further attempt was made to gain possession of the hill. Towards the evening, the enemy, repulsed and defeated at all points, drew off their infantry under cover of their cavalry.

After the French attack on the centre, the wadding of the guns lying smouldering on the ground, set fire to the long grass in the valley, which burnt and extended with such rapidity that the face of the hill on which Stewart's brigade was posted, soon became a scorched mass, studded with bodies of dead and wounded. Sir Arthur Wellesley, who had been on the hill during the whole action, was in the evening hit by a spent ball.

The casualties which occurred to the 29th (Worcestershire) Regiment in the actions with the French, commanded by Joseph Buonaparte in person, were as follows:—

27TH JULY, 1809.

Killed—10 Rank and File.
Wounded *—1 Lieutenant, 42 Rank and File.
Missing—1 Rank and File.

28TH JULY.

Killed—1 Serjeant, 25 Rank and File.
Wounded *—1 Captain, 5 Lieutenants, 98 Rank and File.
Missing—2 Rank and File.

---

* For the names of the officers *vide* Monthly Returns page 311.

1809   Exhausted from want of food, oppressed by heat, tired by the duration of a struggle which seemed interminable, the approach of night was not unwelcome. The fire of cannon had not yet altogether ceased, and it was not till the close of twilight that the dull rumbling sound of artillery heard at intervals, and at a distance, seemed to indicate the close of this sanguinary but most interesting battle. A cold damp night succeeded the excessively warm and fatiguing day, and the regiment, without food or covering of any description, bivouacked on the same spot as on the preceding day. A morsel of bread, with some pure water, would have been considered luxurious fare.

At daybreak, on the 29th of July, it becoming evident that the main body of the enemy had retreated from view, and that there was no necessity for the troops to retain their positions, at 9 a.m. the regiment marched down from that height, which, from the commencement to the end of the action, it had had the honour of defending against repeated and desperate attacks, and which it now left behind strewn with dead bodies, broken arms, shattered tumbrils, and fragments of shell. It encamped in the olive groves at its base.

The gallantry and discipline evinced by the 29th and the 1st battalion 48th Regiment, on the night of the 27th inst, was specially noticed by the commander-in-chief, in General Orders, dated Talavera de la Reyna, the 29th of July, 1809 :—

" Talavera," said Sir Arthur, " was the hardest fought battle of modern times, and each party engaged lost a quarter of its numbers."

On the morning after these battles, every exertion was made to inter the dead ; each regiment furnishing its quota of men on fatigue duty for this purpose, and this last sad duty was performed as far as possible to both friend and foe.

The town of Talavera now became crowded with wounded, those of the 29th, through the activity and energy of Dr. Guthrie, were however soon lodged.

Captain Gauntlett, who in the second day's action had been struck **1809** on the side of the head by a ball, which carried away a portion of his skull and brain, lingered until the 31st inst., when he was interred, in presence of the regiment, on the heights where he had fallen.

THE ADJUTANT-GENERAL TO LIEUT.-COL. WHITE, 29TH REG^T.

" 30 July, 1809.

" I have presented the French Standard taken by the 29th on the 28th instant to the Commander of the Forces, and I am directed by his Excellency to return it to you, that it may remain in possession of the 29th Regiment as a testimony of their gallant conduct."

In the "*Memoir of George Weale, formerly of the 29th Regt. of Foot*," one reads : " The regiment succeeded in taking one and destroying another of the French eagles. The one captured, was sent by Lieutenant Elliot (afterwards Major) to be presented to Lord Wellington, who directed it to be retained with the regiment as a trophy of their valour."

It is much to be regretted that all trace of this standard has been lost; the only information attainable being that of General Sir R. P. Douglas, Bart., who joined the regiment in 1820, and wrote as follows in 1885 :—

" Heatherton Park,
Wellington,
Somerset.

" 7th March.

"My dear Captain Everard,

If I possessed any old 29th records, I would willingly contribute them towards your future publication.—My memory is still fresh as to many persons and things, which I could narrate by word, but which I do not think worthy of committing to paper.

With regard to the French Standard captured by the 29th at Talavera, I think it was either given into the care of the Dean and Chapter of Worcester, or was left in the possession of the late Lord Strafford,§ who, as Sir John Byng, was Colonel of the Regt.

---

§ There is not any trace of it at Worcester, nor is the Earl of Strafford in possession of it.

1809   Do you know the present Lord S.? If not I could with pleasure write to him on the subject. We were brother Sub[s] in the 29th.

Have you a drawing of the 29th Grenadiers in old days? Long black gaiters to the kneecap, and white breeches.—The Grenadier Co. carrying the port fire and slow match on their belts—and the bayonet carried in a *sliding* frog on the cross belt, this was quite an exception to all other corps. Hoping you will find ample materials for your interesting publication,

I remain,

Yours faithfully,

R. P. DOUGLAS."

During the 30th and 31st of July, the French were not seen. On the 1st and 2nd of August, intelligence was received, that Soult, with intention of cutting off the British communications with Portugal, was advancing against Plasencia. Prompt measures were therefore necessary, and Sir Arthur Wellesley proposed to march with the entire British army against Soult, provided that Cuesta would remain at Talavera in charge of the wounded, and to secure the rear.

As the regiment was to accompany Sir Arthur, its sick and wounded were left behind in charge of Assistant-Surgeon Curby.

On the morning of the 3rd, the army marched to Oropeza.

Scarcely were the British out of sight, when the Spanish general began to doubt the security of his quarters, and giving orders for the immediate evacuation of Talavera, made ready to follow Sir Arthur. In doing this he sacrificed the whole of the wounded who had been entrusted to his charge, and that, too, when no enemy was even in sight. Three days after this hasty and uncalled-for retreat, Marshal Victor's advance guard entered Talavera without opposition, and Lieut. Stanhope, Assistant-Surgeon Curby, and 27 privates of the regiment, who were too ill to be moved, were among those who fell into the enemy's hands. The wounded privates having died, their two officers were sent prisoners to France, *via* Madrid. Dr. Curby was, however, released the following year, and rejoined his regiment in October, but Lieut. Stanhope remained a prisoner till 1814.

The following Monthly Returns for May and August give the names of the Officers serving with the **1809** *Regiment on the 1st of May and 25th of August. All the Officers were present with the Head-Quarters of the Regiment, except where otherwise specified:—*

HEAD QUARTERS, 29TH REGIMENT.

1st May, Coimbra. *25th August, Medillen.*

Colonel	G. Forbes, L G.	Absent with leave,	His Majesty's permission.
Lieut.-Colonels	{ F. Maitland, M G.	Absent with leave,	His Majesty's permission.
	{ D. White.		
Majors	{ G. Way.		
	{ Thos. Egerton. Left Sick at Loires since 2nd April, 1809.		Absent with Lieut.-Genl. Sir A. Wellesley's leave, 3 months from 9th June, 1809.
Captains	A. Creagh, *m.* Absent without leave from 27th Dec., 1808.		Promoted in the 95th Foot.
	J. Tucker. Brigade Major, Nova Scotia.		Joined the Head Quarters of Regt. 24th July.
	P. Hodge. Absent without leave since 2nd Feb., 1809.		In charge of a Detachment at Lisbon.
	S. Gauntlett.		Severely Wounded 28th, died 31st July.
	G. Tod		
	E. Nestor.		
	C. Davy. Left Sick at Lisbon on 18th March, 1809.		Left Sick at Lisbon.
	A. Patison.		In Charge of Sick at Plasencia. Made Prisoner 31st July.
	W. Birmingham.		
	T. Gell.		
Lieutenants	H. Birmingham.	Prisoner in France since 13th January, 1807.	
	A. Newbold.		Slightly Wounded 28th July.
	J. Humfrey.		
	Wm. Wade, *Adjt.*		
	T. Langton.		
	St. J. W. Lucas.		
	E. S. L. Nicholson.		Slightly Wounded 28th July.
	J. Nestor.	Recruiting at Killashandra, Ireland.	
	R. Stannus. Left Sick at Caldas, 21 April, 1809.		Severely Wounded 28th July. Left Sick at Elvas.
	J. Brooks. Left Sick at Loires, 9th April, 1809.		Absent with Lt. Genl. Sir A. Wellesley's leave, 3 months from 14 June, 1809.
	W. Duguid.		
	A. Gregory.		
	C. Leslie.		Severely Wounded 28th July. Left Sick at Elvas.
	T. Popham.		Severely Wounded 27th July. Left Sick at Elvas.
	W. Penrose.		
	C. Stanhope.		Severely Wounded 28th July. Left Sick at Talavera. Prisoner 7th August.
	W. Elliot		In charge of Sick at Elvas.
	A. Leith Hay. Absent without leave since 1st August, 1808.		"*Present with Regiment on 27th and 28th July*."
	T. L. Coker.		
	A. Young		In charge of a Detachment at Lisbon.
	H. Pennington.		
	S. Hardy.	Recruiting at Manchester.	
	Chas. Western. Appointed 25th May.		Absent with leave. Not yet joined.
Ensigns	B. Wild.		Left Sick at Plasencia.
	H. Reid.	Recruiting at Aberdeen.	
	Edwd. Swinbourne.		In charge of Sick at Coimbra.
	John Evans.		
	Thos. Biggs. Left Sick at Oporto 24th May, 1809.		Left Sick at Oporto.
	Wm. Stirling. Left Sick at Oporto 24th May, 1809.		Left Sick at Oporto.
	Mills Sandys.		
	George Hillier. Appointed 23rd March, 1809. Not yet joined.		
	John Vesie. Appointed 13th April, 1809.		Not yet joined.
	George E. Ironside. Appointed 8th June, 1809.		Not yet joined.
Pay Master	T. Stott.		
Adjutant	W. Wade.		
Qr. Master	W. Gillespie.		
Surgeon	G. Guthrie.		
Assistant Surgeons	{ E. Curby.		In charge of Sick at Talavera. Prisoner 7th August.
	{ L. Evans.		In charge of Sick at Elvas.

1809   In order to secure his retreat to Portugal, and extricate himself from the position in which he had been placed by Cuesta's untimely move, Sir Arthur decided to at once cross the Tagus by Puente del Arzobispo, and so place the river between himself and Soult. Marching by Deleytosa and Jaraicijo, on the 24th Hill's division reached Medillen, where having remained a couple of days, it continued its march to Merida.

On the 30th of August, Sir Arthur Wellesley established his headquarters at Badajos, and distributed his army along the frontier of Spain and Portugal, in a position where it could subsist with ease, and also give protection to both countries. On the 3rd of September, Major-General Hill's division was ordered to be cantoned in Montijo, and Puebla de la Calçada, the 29th being at the latter place. All the sick were now directed to be sent to Elvas.

In his "*Recollections of the Peninsular War*," Captain Moyle Scherer, of the 34th Foot, gives the following description of the 29th Regiment:—

"On the 7th September, 1809, we marched into cantonments in Spanish Estramadura. We reached Torre Major, the village allotted to our brigade, in two days. Some regiments of Hill's division, to which our brigade was attached, lay at Montijo: amongst others, the 29th. It was the first corps distinguished for its service, which I had ever seen under arms. Nothing could possibly be worse than their clothing; it had become necessary to patch it; and as red cloth could not be procured, grey, white, and even brown, had been used; yet under this striking disadvantage, they could not be viewed by a soldier without admiration. The perfect order and cleanliness of their arms and appointments, their steadiness on parade, their erect carriage, and their firm and free marching, exceeded anything of the kind I had ever seen. No corps of any army or nation which I have since had an opportunity of seeing, has come nearer to my idea of what a regiment of infantry should be, than the old Twenty-ninth."

The following is an extract from the Wellington Dispatches:— **1809**

"TO VISCOUNT CASTLEREAGH.

"Badajos, 12 Sept., 1809.

"My dear Lord,

∗ ∗ ∗ ∗ ∗ ∗ ∗ I wish very much that some measures could be adopted to get some recruits for the 29th Regiment. It is the best Regiment in this Army, has an admirable internal system, and excellent Non-Commissioned Officers; but for the want of a Second Battalion, and somebody to attend to its recruiting, it is much reduced in numbers by the losses in the Actions of Roliça and Vimiero, in the Expedition to the North of Portugal and at Talavera. ∗ ∗ ∗ ∗ ∗

Believe me, &c.,

ARTHUR WELLESLEY."

"Viscount Castlereagh."

On the 4th of October, Lord Wellington reviewed General Hill's division on the plain of Montijo.

Fever and ague now caused many casualties amongst the troops cantoned on the plain bordering either side of the Guadiana, and Captain Ambrose Newbold succumbed after a few days' illness.

Extract from " The Weekly State of the Forces in Spain and Portugal under command of Lieut.-General Lord Vis^{ct} Wellington, K.B.

"Head Quarters, Badajos, 1 Nov., 1809.

2nd Brigade (Major-Genl. R. Stewart's), 2nd Division: 29th, 1/48 and 1/57th Regts.
29th Foot, Puebla de la Calçada.

Officers Present, 1 Lt. Colonel, 1 Major, 9 Captains, 11 Lieuts., 7 Ensigns, 5 Staff.

Serjeants	,,	22	4 Present, Sick		7 Absent, Sick		4 On Command.	
Drummers	,,	14	1	,, ,,	2	,, ,,		
Rank & File	,,	439	111	,, ,,	179	,, ,,	7	,, ,,

Alterations—7 Rank and File dead.

1809   While the greater part of the forces under Lord Wellington marched northwards, General Hill's division was left to watch the Tagus, and the province of Alentejo. On the 14th of December, this division was quartered at Portalegre, and on the 25th, General Hill established his head-quarters at Abrantes, the 29th Foot being also stationed there. Captain Gell, Lieuts. Elliot and Penrose, together with Assistant-Surgeon Evans, were left at Elvas in charge of the sick.

On the 28th of March, 1809, a General Order was issued that Officers of Grenadier and Light companies should wear wings, in addition to epaulettes.

The French, in consequence of their various victories over the Spaniards, were now nearly masters of the whole of south Spain. Soult was advancing on Cadiz, whilst General Regnier threatened Spanish Estramadura. It being necessary that General Hill should watch the latter, and act decisively in opposition to him, on the 5th of **1810** January the 2nd division marched to Punhete, a small town situated at the junction of the Zezere with the Tagus, but on information being received that Badajos was threatened, General Hill was ordered to return to Portalegre, which was reached on the 18th of February.

On the 31st of March Lieut. Gregory, and on the 4th of April Capt. W. Birmingham, were ordered to place themselves under the orders of Marshal Beresford, with a view of being attached to the Portuguese army. On the 20th, Lieut. A. Leith Hay was appointed A.D.C. to Major-General Leith.

On the 23rd, when the regiment was about to celebrate St. George's Day, information was received that the French had attacked and driven out the Spanish garrison of a frontier town a few leagues distant. All further thoughts of celebrating the anniversary of the patron saint were therefore dismissed, and the 29th marched that afternoon to Allegrete, where it halted and bivouacked. On its being ascertained the following day that the enemy had retreated, the division returned to its former quarters. On the 15th of May, the division was again ordered out, **1810** this time to Arronches, but, two days later, returned to Portalegre. In July, it being reported that the French were again threatening Badajos, the division marched to Arronches, where on arrival, it was found that this was but a feint on the part of the enemy, their main body being actually on the march northwards with the design of crossing the Tagus, and seizing Castello Branco. General Hill therefore immediately retraced his steps, crossed the Tagus at Villa Velha, and on the 21st, the division reached Castello Branco. After halting here a day, the troops advanced to Atalaya, near which place the regiment bivouacked. It was now discovered that the enemy had got command of the road leading thence to the north of Spain. Communications by that route, between General Hill and Lord Wellington, being thereby cut off, the former retired further back into Portugal, and marched by another, but less practicable, road across the mountains. On the 2nd of August, Hill's division took up a position at Sarzedas, which commanded the roads to Villa Velha and Thomar. On the 7th, Major-General the Hon. W. Stewart was appointed to command the 2nd division, under General Hill, and shortly after, on the illness of Major-General R. Stewart, Col. Inglis, of the 57th Regiment, took over the command of the brigade.

In consequence of Massena's advance against Lisbon, in September, Lord Wellington decided to take up a position on the left bank of the Tagus, near Pena Cova. Three days later, Stewart's division crossed the Mondego, and, on joining the main body of the army, Hill's corps was placed in force on the extreme right of the position, across the road leading over the Serra to Pena Cova.

The next day, the 27th of September, was fought the battle of Busaco, in which it was not the fortune of the 2nd division to be actively engaged.

1810 *By the Monthly Return dated the 25th of September, Camp on the Mondego, the following Officers were present with the Head-quarters :—*

Major—Way.
Captains—Hodge, Tod, Nestor, Gell, Humfrey, Wade.
Lieutenants—Nicholson, Stannus, Brooks, Duguid, Popham, Penrose, Elliot, Coker, Young, Pennington, Hardy, Evans, Sandys, Hillier.
Ensigns—Vesie, Ironside, Lovelock, King, Furnace, Lucas.
Adjutant—B. Wild.
Quarter-Master—Gillespie.
Surgeon—Jos. A. Stanford.

The French having been repulsed in the battle of the 27th, Massena, finding Wellington's position impregnable, now endeavoured to turn his left. Lord Wellington therefore retired his forces to the first series of the celebrated lines of Torres Vedras, which extended from the Tagus to the mouth of the Zizandre, a distance of 29 miles. Having recrossed the Mondego and retired by Espinal, Thomar, and Santarem, the 2nd division reached Alhandra, the extreme right of the new position, on the 9th of October.

From Alhandra to the valley of Cadandrix, a distance of five miles, there ran a continuous lofty ridge, defended by thirteen redoubts, and for two miles its brow was rendered inaccessible by the erection of a scarp from 15 to 20 feet high. This portion of the lines was to be held by the British and Portuguese divisions, under General Hill. A strong flotilla of gunboats, manned by British seamen, was stationed in the Tagus, to flank the right of the lines.

On the morning of the 10th of October, the 2nd brigade took post at the village of Sobral Piqueño, about two miles to the west of Alhandra. It was here that Major-General Houghton succeeded to its command *(vice* General R. Stewart, deceased), and that the brigade became the 3rd.

Soon after this, the regiment marched to Bucellas, and on the 25th of October was encamped at St. Jago, where, after a short stay, it was ordered to occupy the Quinta de Cunha, a large solitary chateau in the **1810** hills. The walls of this building being loop-holed, armed with a few pieces of light artillery, and protected by the surrounding batteries, formed a place of some strength. During the time the regiment was here stationed, nothing of importance occurred.

Massena, finding it impossible to force the lines without strong reinforcements, broke up his cantonments, and retired on the night of the 14th of November. The following morning being very foggy, the retreat of the French marshal was not discovered for some hours after daybreak. The enemy's intention not being clearly developed, Lord Wellington kept the principal part of his army in position, but directed General Hill's and the light division to follow the French.

On the 16th, Houghton's brigade marched from the lines; the route lay through deserted, desolate villages, and the rain fell heavily without intermission. It was not till long after dark that the 29th reached Villa Nova, where it halted for the night. On it becoming known that Massena had established his army on the heights about Santarem, which had been fortified with numerous batteries and redoubts, Hill's division was ordered to cross the Tagus opposite to Magem. Finding the enemy had no intention of falling back any further, the 2nd division went into winter quarters in a series of small towns and villages bordering the river, the 29th being stationed at Chamusca. The inhabitants proved kind and hospitable; sutlers brought copious supplies of comforts and luxuries, so the regiment had an easy and pleasant time. The river being here of no very great breadth, it was a favourite morning amusement of the officers to ride down to its banks and hold conversation across the water with the French, who came for a similar purpose to the opposite side. In these dialogues offence had been taken, possibly at some national reflections, for the meetings eventually assumed a more hostile form. Captain Thos. Hamilton relates that the daily routine became as follows:—" A Frenchman would advance close

1810 to the river, when an English officer, taking the musket of a neighbouring sentry, would deliberately take aim at the Frenchman and fire. The Englishman, after waiting to receive the fire of his antagonist, would yield his place to some other competitor. General Hill, on hearing of these contests, very judiciously put a stop to them."

In December, General Hill being compelled by sickness to return to England, and it being ascertained that Soult was collecting a strong force, Lord Wellington ordered the troops on the left bank of the Tagus to be reinforced; Marshal Beresford being at the same time appointed to their command.

The following General Order was published on the 9th of February, 1810:—

"Field Officers to wear an epaulette on each shoulder. A Colonel to wear a crown and star; Lieut.-Col., a crown; Major, a star, on the strap.

Captains, Subalterns, and the Quarter Master, one epaulette only, on the right shoulder.

Officers of the Flank Companies to wear a wing on each shoulder, with a Grenade or Bugle thereon, according to their respective Company.

The Paymaster, and Surgeons to wear a Regimental Coat, but without epaulette or sash."

[At this period, every regiment had its own pattern of epaulette. The Adjutant wore one on his right shoulder, and an epaulette strap, on his left. The Paymaster and Surgeon carried their sword suspended from a black leather belt, worn under the coat.]

"Horse Guards,
9th Sept., 1810.

"His Majesty is pleased to command that, in commemoration of the brilliant victories obtained at Roleia, Vimiera, Corunna, and Talavera, the under-mentioned Officers present on those occasions shall enjoy the privilege of wearing a medal, to be worn by Commanding Officers of Corps (not being under rank inferior to Lieut.-Colonel) attached by a ribbon of the colour of the Sash, with a blue edge, to the button hole of their uniform. H.M. has also been pleased to command, that the Medal which would have been conferred upon the Officers who have fallen at, or died since, the above-named actions, shall, as a token of respect for their memories, be deposited with their respective families.

29th Foot. Lieut.-Colonels—Honble. G. A. F. Lake, and Daniel White."

In January, 1811, the regiment proceeded to Carraguera where **1811** it remained till the enemy retired from the neighbourhood of Santarem on the night of the 5th of March. The following morning, the 3rd brigade crossed the Tagus and joined the pursuing army. The enemy's track was found literally strewn with carcases of mules and horses, which had succumbed to famine or fatigue.

On reaching Thomar, Houghton's division,* which formed the rear of the pursuing force, halted for a day; and when, on the 12th, the leading division of Lord Wellington's army attacked the enemy at Redinha, Houghton was ordered to bring up his troops with all possible speed, but on nearing the scene of action, the 29th were halted in rear of an eminence, and held in readiness should their services be required. Such, however, was not the case, as the French continued their retreat to Condeixa. This was the last night that the 29th served with the pursuing army, for intelligence being received of the surrender of Badajos, General Houghton was ordered to retrace his steps and place his troops under command of Marshal Beresford, who had received orders to retake the fortress. Having crossed the Zezere at Punhete, and the Tagus by a bridge of boats near Tancros, General Houghton's troops advanced by Oralo, and Portalegre, to Arronches, in the neighbourhood of which they halted for two days. On the 25th, the enemy having been surprised at Campo Major, abandoned that place, and retired to Badajos. The next day Beresford advanced to Elvas, where the troops halted for a few days. On the 4th of April, the division marched to Borba, where it remained whilst the engineers were engaged in constructing a bridge across the Guadiana, near Jurumenha. It was late on the night of the 6th before all the troops had crossed the river, and taken up a position on the heights of Villa Real. On the 9th, the division encamped near Olivenza, where General Sir Lowry Cole was left to conduct its siege, whilst the main body under Beresford

---

* A temporary command, consisting of the 3rd brigade, and one of Portuguese infantry.

1811 proceeded to cover all the roads by which Soult could advance to the relief of Badajos.

On the 25th, the head-quarters of the regiment were at Almendralejo. The French having retired from Estremadura, on the 6th of May the division moved towards Badajos, to take part in the first siege of that fortress.

On the evening of the 13th, it being the turn of the 29th to go on duty in the trenches, about sunset the regiment marched from its encampment, and when night approached covering parties were sent to the front. The remainder of the regiment having piled arms, took off their packs, and having been served out with entrenching tools, advanced with great caution to within three hundred yards of the walls. In an hour or two, when the trenches were so far advanced as to afford some cover, orders were received for the working parties to retire, and the siege to be raised; also for the 2nd, and the Portuguese divisions, to join Marshal Beresford, for Soult had quitted Seville and was advancing to the relief of Badajos.

On the afternoon of the 15th, the British army took up its position on a ridge about four miles long, which ran nearly parallel to the rivulet of Albuera and about six hundred yards distant from it. On the right, these heights were steep and more detached; somewhat in advance of the centre of the position was a bridge and the village of Albuera. On the opposite side of the stream, the main body of the French army was hidden from view by a gentle slope covered with trees.

On arriving at this position, the 2nd division under General W. Stewart, was drawn up in line, its right resting on a commanding hill over which the Valverde road passes, its left on the road from Badajos. The Portuguese troops prolonged the line to the left. As the Spanish army, which was to occupy the right of Beresford's position, had not yet arrived, Houghton's brigade, viz., "the 29th, 57th, and 1/48 regts.," was moved to that flank, and formed into line, with its right thrown back.

The Spaniards having come up during the night, early on the **1811** morning of the 16th of May, Houghton's brigade resumed its place in the line. Scarcely had the men time to get a little tea and a morsel of biscuit, when the alarm was given that the enemy were advancing towards the bridge and village of Albuera, in two strong columns, supported by cavalry and artillery. This attack proved to be a feint, for in the meantime the main body of the French attacked the Spaniards, and a sharp firing was heard in that direction. Such being the case, the 2nd division broke into column and moved rapidly along the heights to its right. Nearly at the commencement of the battle, a heavy storm of rain came on, which with the smoke, rendered it impossible to discern anything distinctly. The enemy having already established themselves on some heights, opened a tremendous cannonade on the advancing troops, and Captain Humfrey, who was struck on the hip by a cannon ball, which carried away the limbs of two men behind him, died, encouraging the advance of his company, "for the honour of old Ireland," of which country he and many of his men were natives.

The Spaniards being attacked with an impetuosity they were unable to resist, were also put into some confusion when in the act of throwing back their right, to meet an unexpected flank attack.

Colonel Colborne's brigade (consisting of the "Buffs," 2/48th, 66th, and 31st Regiments), the first, of Stewart's division, to come into action, behaved in the most gallant manner, and notwithstanding a loss of two-thirds of its numbers, kept its ground until the arrival of Houghton's brigade, the conduct of which, said Marshal Beresford, "was conspicuously gallant." As the latter brigade came up, the 29th leading, the regiment closed to quarter column, under cover of the heights, and deployed. Before the other two corps could complete this formation, a body of Spaniards in front of the left of the 29th gave way, and came rushing back on the regiment. On the assurance that if they would only keep their ground for a few moments they should be relieved, and by the exertions of some of the officers, together with

1811 those of Lieut. Wild, the adjutant of the 29th, who rode amongst them, they rallied, moved up the hill again, but very shortly returned in the utmost confusion, closely followed by the enemy's lancers, who were cutting and thrusting without mercy. Many of the Spaniards attempted to get through the ranks of the 29th, which was now in line on the slope of the hill, but this could not be permitted, since an opening, if made to allow the former to pass, would also have admitted the enemy. There being no alternative, the regiment stood firm, and had in self-defence to fire on both. This shortly decided the business, and whilst the lancers made the best of their way back to their own lines, the surviving Spaniards were permitted to pass to the rear. Houghton's brigade being now deployed, General Stewart rode up, and after a few stirring words, said, "Now is the time, let us give three cheers!" This was responded to with heart and soul, and the brigade immediately advanced, under a sharp fire from the enemy's light troops, without returning a shot. General Stewart was twice hit; the gallant Houghton, after receiving many wounds without shrinking, fell pierced by three musket balls whilst in the act of cheering on his men. Colonel Daniel White, of the 29th, was mortally wounded. On arriving at the crest of the hill, the French were seen a little in rear, apparently formed in masses, or columns of grand divisions, with light troops and artillery between the intervals, whilst some artillery, posted on a bank in rear, fired over their heads.

Notwithstanding this formidable array, the 29th, 57th, and 48th continued to advance, without even a piece of artillery to support them, whilst Soult afterwards stated he had forty pieces of cannon bearing on the advancing troops. The 29th was at this time on the extreme right of the line, for the 4th division, which was advancing to the new front, was still at a considerable distance below, in the plain to the right. It was at this period that the desperate fighting began, when a most overwhelming fire of artillery and small arms was opened on the brigade, which was vigorously returned. There the men unflinchingly stood, and there they fell, their ranks at times being swept away by sections. Nothwithstanding this, the struggle was continued with unabated fury.

"The regiments of this brigade," said Lord Londonderry, "vied with one another in deeds of heroism, the 57th and 29th in particular, the former under Col. Inglis, the latter under Major Way, performed prodigies of valour."

Major Way had his bridle arm broken by a shot, and fell from his charger, *Black Jack*, badly wounded. Ensign Edward Furnace, ‡ only 17 years of age, who had, whilst carrying the colours, received a severe wound, but declined to leave the field, soon after received another, which proving fatal, terminated his short but honourable career.

The regiment at length became so reduced in numbers, that what had formerly been a line, now resembled detached groups of skirmishers ; in fact not one-third of the brigade remained standing. From its constantly diminishing numbers, and the necessity of closing in towards the colours, the right of the 29th became further exposed. The supply of ammunition was now falling short, when Sir Lowry Cole brought up his Fusilier brigade, from the plain, on the right of the 29th. The two battalions of the 7th, and the 23rd then bringing their right shoulders forward, took the enemy obliquely in flank. Nothing could withstand the undaunted bravery of these soldiers who continued to advance notwithstanding the fearful discharges of grape poured upon them. At the same moment, Abercromby's brigade passed the left of Houghton's, and the enemy's masses, after a desperate struggle for victory, being forced to give way at all points, were driven in disorder beyond the Albuera.

Sir William Napier writes :—" In vain the French reserves joining with the struggling multitude, endeavoured to sustain the fight; their efforts only increased the irremediable confusion, and the mighty mass giving way like a loosened cliff, went headlong down the ascent.

---

‡ Youngest son of Thos. Furnace, Esq., of Baldoyle, co. Dublin.

1811 The rain flowed after in streams discoloured with blood, and fifteen hundred unwounded men, the remainder of six thousand unconquerable British soldiers, stood triumphant on the fatal hill."

The battle, which had commenced at 9 a.m., had been continued without interruption until two in the afternoon; during the remainder of the day there was but cannonading and skirmishing.

In the battle of Albuera, fought on the 16th of May, 1811, the 29th Foot suffered the following casualties:—

Killed—1 Captain, 1 Lieutenant, 3 Ensigns, 1 Serjeant, 76 Rank and File.
Wounded—1 Lieut.-Colonel, 1 Major, 3 Captains, 4 Lieutenants, 3 Ensigns, 1 Staff; 12 Serjeants, 220 Rank and File.
Missing—11 Rank and File.

After the action the field presented a sad spectacle, the English dead lying generally in rows, the French in large heaps, from their having fought principally in masses. The 29th was brought out of action by Captain Thos. Gell, who ensigncy in the regiment dated from the 5th of October, 1804. For having succeeded to the command of the regiment during action, this officer afterwards received the gold medal. On calling the roll, it was found that only 96 men, two captains, and a few subalterns of the regiment remained unwounded. Every field officer of Houghton's brigade, being either killed or wounded, at the close of the action it remained in command of Captain Cémétiere, of the 48th.

Some affecting incidents which occurred on this memorable day may not prove uninteresting:—

Early in the morning, General Houghton, hearing of the enemy's advance, had in the hurry turned out in a green frock coat. Whilst on horseback, in front of his brigade, his servant rode up with his red uniform, and, without dismounting, a change was immediately made. This public display of the national colour, and British coolness, took place under fire of French artillery.

Ensign Richard Vance,* who was amongst the killed, had scarcely **1811** been gazetted seven months to the 29th: his heroism during the action had been most conspicuous. Seeing the terrible loss his regiment was suffering, and fearing lest the regimental colour, of which he had charge, might fall into the hands of the enemy, he tore it from the pole. Shortly after so doing, he was killed, and when the action was over the colour was found concealed in the breast of his coat, the standard lying near his body.

Lieut.-Colonel White, who had been severely wounded whilst leading his regiment into action, died at Eylas on the 3rd of June, and his remains were interred near those of his late brigadier.

During the following day, both armies retained their respective positions, and Marshal Beresford, having received reinforcements, the 2nd division was enabled to re-occupy its former ground between the Valverde and Badajos roads.

On the 18th, Soult, "the Duke of Dalmatia," commenced to retire. On the same day the Duke of Wellington reached Albuera, for on hearing of the French marshal's advance, he had used all possible exertions to come up and command in person.

After examining the state of affairs, the Duke desired Beresford to follow the French cautiously, whilst he returned to Elvas, and the siege of Badajos was re-commenced. A call was now made for volunteers from line regiments to assist the Engineers, and it appears that some of the 29th offered their services, for by the Returns of the killed and wounded in the trenches between the 6th and 11th of June, one rank and file of the regiment was reported as wounded.

In the meanwhile General Hill, who had returned to Portugal, was given the command of the covering army, which consisted of the 2nd and 4th divisions and some Spaniards.

---

* This officer also appears to have been of Irish extraction. The notice of his death states him to have been a "nephew of the late Alderman Vance, of Dublin." Previous to appointment in the 29th Foot, he held a lieutenancy in the Dublin County Militia.

1811 By Monthly Returns dated the 25th of May, the head-quarters of the 29th were at Almendralejo.

		25th April. Almendralejo.	25th May. Almendralejo.
Colonel		Gordon Forbes, L G.	Absent with His Majesty's leave.
Lieut.Colonel		D. White.	Absent. Severely Wounded 16th May. Died 3rd June.
Majors	{	G. Way.	
		Thos. Egerton.	Absent without leave, since 18th April.
Captains	{	J. Tucker.	Commandant at Belem.
		P. Hodge.	Absent. Slightly Wounded 16th May
		G. Tod.	Absent. Slightly Wounded 16th May.
		E. Nestor.	Absent. Slightly Wounded 16th May.
		C. Davy.	With Depôt of Regiment at Droitwich.
		A. Patison.	Prisoner of War.
		W. Birmingham.	Attached to the Portuguese Army.
		T. Gell.	Commanding the Regiment.
		J. Humfrey.	Killed 16th May.
		W. Wade. On duty at Elvas.	
		T. Langton.	Absent. Marshal Sir W. Beresford's leave, 1 month from 21st inst.
Lieutenants	{	H. Birmingham.	Prisoner of War.
		St. J. Lucas.	Recruiting at Mullingar.
		E. Nicholson.	
		J. Nestor.	Absent without leave since 31st March.
		R. Stannus.	Absent. Severely Wounded 16th May.
		J. Brooks.	Absent. Slightly Wounded 16th May.
		W. Duguid. Absent without leave since 7th April.	Killed 16th May.
		A. Gregory.	Attached to the Portuguese Army.
		C. Leslie.	
		T. Popham.	Absent. Severely Wounded 16th May.
		W. Penrose.	
		C. Stanhope.	Prisoner of War.
		W. Elliot.	
		A. Leith Hay.	A.D.C. to Major-General Leith.
		T. Coker.	
		A. Young.	On duty at Elvas.
		H. Pennington.	
		S. Hardy.	Recruiting in England.
		Chas. Western.	
		B. Wild, *Adjt.*	Absent. Severely Wounded 16th May.
		H. Reid.	Recruiting at Aberdeen.
		J. Evans.	
		T. Biggs.	Absent. Severely Wounded 16th May.
		M. Sandys.	
		G. Hillier.	
Ensigns	{	J. Vesie.	On duty at Lisbon.
		Cornelius Sullivan. Recruiting at Manchester.	With Depôt at Droitwich.
		J. B. Lovelock.	Absent. Slightly Wounded 16th May.
		Francis King.	Killed 16th May.
		Edward Furnace.	Killed 16th May.
		Richard Lucas.	Absent without leave since 20th April.
		Thos. Hamilton.	Absent. Severely Wounded 16th May.
		Henry Brodrick. On duty at Belem.	
		Edwd. Kearney. On duty at Belem.	Absent. Severely Wounded 16th May.
		Richard Vance.	Killed 16th May.
Pay-Master		T. Stott. Absent with leave since 25th June, 1810, till appointment of a successor.	
Adjutant		B. Wild.	Absent. Severely Wounded 16th May.
Qr.-Master		W. Gillespie.	On duty at Lisbon.
Surgeon		Josh. A. Stanford.	On duty at Elvas.
Assistant Surgeons	{	E. Curby.	Attached to the 4th Division.
		L. Evans. On duty at Elvas.	

Fit for Duty at Head Quarters:—

1 Lieut.-Colonel, 1 Major, 6 Captains, 14 Lieutenants, 5 Ensigns, 1 Adjutant, 1 Surgeon, 1 Assistant-Surgeon, 25 Serjeants, 10 Drummers, 460 Rank and File.

2 Captains, 9 Lieutenants, 1 Ensign, 13 Serjeants, 10 Drummers, 144 Rank and File.

All these Officers were present with the head-quarters of the Regiment on the 25th of April, and 25th of May, except where otherwise specified.

It is related that when Lord Wellington was inspecting the **1811** hospitals at Elvas, on seeing some of the 29th, he said, "Oh, old 29th, I am sorry to see so many of you here!" The men instantly replied, "Oh, my lord, if you had only been with us, there would not have been so many of us here!" So implicit was the confidence, of even the humblest individual, in this great man.

EXTRACTS FROM GENERAL ORDERS PUBLISHED ON THE 6TH OF JUNE.

"Quinta, in front of Elvas.

Para. 8. The 3rd Regiment or Buffs, 29th, 2/31st, 57th, and 2/66th, are for the present to be formed into a provisional battalion under Lieut.-Colonel Colborne.

,, 9. The N.C.O.'s and Soldiers, are to remain in their companies in their several regiments at present, but for the purpose of the formation, those present and fit for duty of each of these regiments are to be divided into two companies.

,, 10. The Colours of these regiments to be sent to Elvas, under the charge of the senior officer of each, who will be there.

,, 11. The provisional battalion is to be in Major-Genl Lumley's brigade, in the 2nd division of infantry.

WELLINGTON."

Information having been received that the forces under Marshals Marmont, and Soult, had formed a junction, and were again advancing to relieve Badajos, the covering army was ordered to concentrate at Albuera. The blockade having been raised on the 17th, the troops re-passed the Guadiana, and the 2nd division joined the main army under Lord Wellington, at Elvas. Soon after this, the 2nd and 4th divisions were cantoned near Evora. On the 25th of June, the headquarters of the regiment were in bivouac near Torre de Mora, and on the 25th of July the regiment was quartered at Villa Viçosa.

z

1811   Extracts from General Orders, 7th August, 1811.

1. The provisional battalion, consisting of the Buffs, 29th, 31st, 57th, and 66th, to be broken up, and the Buffs and 57th each to resume their separate formation in the usual manner.

2. The officers and men present fit for duty, in the 29th, 31st, and 66th are to form a provisional battalion under command of the senior officer of the three who shall be present fit for duty; and the officers, non-commissioned officers, and privates fit for duty of the 29th and 66th are to be formed into three companies of each regiment, and those of the 31st into four, for the purpose of this battalion.

5. The Buffs, 57th, and the provisional battalion are to form a separate brigade in the 2nd division.

On the 27th of August, the 29th were at Portalegre. From the beginning of September, this brigade under command of Lieut.-Colonel W. Stewart, of the Buffs, was occupied in movements along the valley of the Tagus; between Niza and Peña Macor, and in communicating with the main body of the army near Fuente Guinaldo, during the combat of El Boden.

On the 25th, the regiment was stationed at Aldea D'Bispo, and when, on the 28th, the French army fell back towards Salamanca, the British troops resumed their cantonments, whilst Lieut.-Colonel Stewart's brigade retired gradually to Portalegre.

The three regiments which had suffered most severely in the recent campaign being ordered home to recruit, on the 3rd of October the following orders were published :—

Provisional Battalion Order.   3rd October, 1811.

"The 29th Regiment being ordered for England, Lieut.-Colonel L'Estrange cannot take leave of them without testifying his satisfaction at the manner they have conducted themselves whilst under his command; if his approbation can be considered as a gratification by a Corps which has distinguished itself on every occasion, he is happy in taking the opportunity of expressing it, as well as his regret, at its removal from his provisional battalion."

GENERAL ORDER, FRENEDA, 3RD OCTOBER, 1811.

"The Commander of the Forces has received the orders of the Commander-in-Chief, to send to England the 29th Regiment, the 85th, and 97th.

These regiments have all been distinguished since they have belonged to this army, particularly the 29th and 97th, which have been with the army so long. The 29th landed with the army three years ago, and they have been distinguished in every action that has been fought in that period: and the Commander of the Forces is happy to add, that the conduct of all these troops has been equally regular in their cantonments and camp, as it has been gallant in the field.

WELLINGTON."

GENERAL ORDER BY LIEUT.-GENERAL HILL.

"Portalegre, 7th October, 1811.

"Considering the length of time the 29th Regiment has been under his orders, and the distinguished manner in which it has always conducted itself, as testified in the General Order of the Commander of the Forces, Lieut.-General Hill cannot allow it to quit the 2nd division of infantry without expressing to it his warmest approbation and thanks for its good conduct, and his regret at being deprived of their services."

On the 25th of October, the head-quarters were at Lisbon, and Lieut. Gregory was ordered to rejoin. On the 2nd of November, the regiment, under command of Major Tucker, embarked on H.M.S. "Agincourt," 64 guns, which left the Tagus two days later, and after a rather boisterous passage, arrived at Portsmouth on the 1st of December. Having disembarked on the following day, the regiment

1811 marched to Havant, and thence to Steyning Barracks, where it was joined by its depôt, under command of Captain St. John Lucas, with Lieut. James Brooks and Ensign Ensor. These had left Worcester on the 9th of September, for Horsham Barracks, where they were stationed awaiting the arrival of the head-quarters from Portugal.

On the 10th of December, the regiment was reviewed at Steyning Barracks by Major-General Houston, when the following officers and men were reported as being absent :—

Prisoners of War.—Captain Patison, Lieuts. H. Birmingham, C. Stanhope, and 33 Privates.

Attached to the Portuguese Army.—Captain W. Birmingham, Lieuts. C. Western and George Hillier.

In Charge of Sick in Portugal.—Ensign Geo. Ford.

The nationality of the officers, &c., and height of non-commissioned officers and privates, were as follows :—

	English.	Scotch.	Irish.	Foreign.
Officers	25	9	20	
Staff	4		1	
Serjeants	27	10	6	
Corporals	21	11	7	
Drummers	1		2	9
Privates	337	64	236	4

Height.	Serjeants.	Corporals.	Drummers.	Privates.
6 ft. 2 & upwds.				2
6 ,,	4	2		5
5 ,, 11	2	2		14
5 ,, 10	7	4		27
5 ,, 9	3	4	1	63
5 ,, 8	11	11		102
5 ,, 7	8	9	3	109
5 ,, 6	7	5	1	123
5 ,, 5	1	2	4	113
Under 5 ft. 5			3	77
Boys				6

On the following day the regiment was inspected by its colonel, **1811** Lieut.-General Gordon Forbes, who caused the following Regimental Order to be published :—

"Steyning, 13th Dec., 1811.

"Lieut.-General Forbes has charged the commanding officer to express to the regiment his perfect satisfaction with their appearance on parade yesterday. He offers all his best congratulations on their arrival in England, and feels every confidence that their conduct in this country will ensure them the continuance of that high and distinguished character which accompanied them during all their services in the Peninsular War."

List of Officers of the 29th Foot on whom gold medals, clasps, and crosses had been conferred in reward of military services from 1806—1815, with their rank at the time ‖ :—

Name.		Rank.	Service.	Action.
Creagh, Andrew	M*	Bt. Major, 29th Foot.	Light Companies of a Brigade.	At Roliça and Vimiero.
Gell, Thomas	M	Captain ,,	Succeeded to Command of Regiment.	At Albuera.
Honble. G. A. F. Lake	M	Colonel ,,	Commanded Regiment.	At Roliça.
Way, Gregory, H. B.	M	Major ,,	Succeeded to Command of Regiment.	At Albuera.
White, Daniel	X †	Lt.-Colonel ,,	Succeeded to Command of Regiment.	At Roliça, Vimiero, Talavera, Albuera.
Western, Chas. M. T.	M	Major 8th Caçadores.	Major 8th Caçadores.	Salamanca.

* M—Medal.   † X—Cross.

Medals for the Peninsular campaign were not issued till 1849.

‖ *United Service Gazette*, July, 1841.

1811 NAMES, FROM MUSTER ROLLS AND CASUALTY RETURNS, OF OFFICERS, NON-COMMISSIONED OFFICERS, RANK AND FILE OF 29TH, KILLED IN THE PENINSULAR WAR.

Roliça, 17th August, 1808.

Lieut.-Colonel—Honble. G. A. F. Lake.
Serjeant-Major—Richard Richards.   Serjeant—Henry Rostern.   Corporal—Mark Brown.
Privates—

Barker, Josh.	Featherston Fras.	Parkins, Josh.	Stevenson, Archd.
Barnsley, John.	Giles, Alexr.	Pass, Chas.	Stubbs, Benjm.
Bell, Wm.	Grogan, Sylvester.	Perry, Geo.	Thompson, Wm.
Brown, Mark.	Henderson, John.	Peterson, Nichs.	Townsend, Jas.
Clarke, Geo.	Husband, Richd.	Pinnager, Thos.	Want, Edward.
Cluff, Jas.	Knox, Jas.	Reardon, Denis.	Warnell, Jno.
Cockayne, Geo.	Lewis, Thos.	Richardson, Jas.	Watts, Thos.
Connor, John.	Massey, Thos.	Rigby, Jas.	Weimar, Joseph.
Curtis, H.	Millbank, Henry.	Sharp, Fred.	Whelan, John.

Vimiero, 21st August, 1808.

Corporal—Richard Franklyn.   Private—Gunn, Thos.

Heights of Grijo and Calvahos, 11th May, 1809.

Drummer—Forbes, Robert.   Private—Clough, James.

Talavera de la Reyna, 27th and 28th July, 1809.

Serjeant—Joseph Martin.   Corporals—Geo. Duckworth, Jno. Palmer.
Privates—

Alleson, Robt.	Gladson, Thos.	Kenagh, Jas.	Schofield, Jno.
Armstrong, Jno.	Garside, Robt.	Lord, John.	Shelmardine, Thos.
Aspinall, Richd.	Griffith, Jno.	Newlands, Wm.	Slater, Jno.
Barnes, Wm.	Hayes, Wm.	Newton, Wm.	Smith 2nd Thos.
Bayles, Josh.	Hefferman, Jas.	Pearson, Wm.	Teston, Thos.
Collingwood, Josh.	Hird, Thos.	Quinn, Pat.	Tyler 1st Jas.
Evans 1st Jno.	Johnston, Jno.	Ragg, Edmd.	Tyler 2nd Jas.
Findley, Robt.	Jones, John.	Rhodes, Josh.	Watts, Jas.

Williams, Wm.

Albuera, 16th May, 1811.

Captain—John Humfrey.   Lieut.—Wm. Duguid.
Ensigns—Francis King, Edward Furnace, Richard Vance.
Serjeant—Jas. Farmer.   Corporal—Jas. M'Intyre.   Drummer—Joseph Creeber.

Privates—

Adams, Jno.	Craig, Patrick.	Hall, Joseph.	Pierce, Hugh.
Allen, Francis.	Dalton, Garret.	Hawkins, Wm.	Poole, Chas.
*Bailies, Joseph.	Davellan, Joseph.	Henly, Thos.	Ridley, Robert.
Barclay, Absalom.	Dean, Robert.	Holding, Wm.	Ryder, Thos.
Barker, Jno.	Devine, Patrick.	Holmes, Wm.	Shepherd, Robt.
Birch, Wm.	Dickie, Alexr.	Hughes, Barnaby.	Shore, Rodger.
Bolton, Jno.	Dingwell, Jno.	King, Lawrence.	Siddle, Jno.
Bonsanger, Jacob.	Doherty, Jno.	*Lane, Jno.	Smith, Alexr.
Boston, Joseph.	Donaldson, Jas.	McConville, Pat.	Stewart, Jas.
Boyle, Thos.	Douglas, Thos.	McDowall, Peter.	Stewart, Robert.
Brooks, Thos.	Eddie, Wm.	McKeon, Benjm.	Sweeney, Wm.
Caple, Thos.	Everleigh, Jno.	McNamara, Patk.	Taylor, George.
Carig, Thos.	Faghey, Thos.	Mackay, Thos.	Thays, Saml.
Cassidy, Jas.	Gardiner, Robert.	Neil, Luke.	Tierney, Thos.
Chadwick, Jno.	Good, Wm.	Ogden, Thos.	Weazer, Jas.
Charlesworth, Jonathan.	*Gould, Wm.	O'Hara, Danl.	Whitcraft, Wm.
Clegg, Jas.	Graham, Wm.	Olliver, Jno.	Youle Wm.
Coogan, Jno.	Grimes, David.	Pendergrass, Richd.	
Couts, Finley.	Grimshaw, David.	Perry, Wm.	

Died of Wounds—Sergt.-Major John Robinson, 3 Serjeants, 2 Corporals, and 47 Privates.

Colonel Leslie relates that "during the march from Portsmouth to Havant some fine pigs happened to pass the regiment, and a soldier remarked to his comrade, 'My eyes, Jack, them's fine pigs!' This remark being overheard by a patriotic bystander, he exclaimed, 'Pigs! would you like pigs?' and there and then bought them for the men, and the regiment continued its march, driving not prisoners, but—pigs before (or after) it."

---

* The only three Worcester men in the regiment amongst the killed.

1811 General Order. Horse Guards, 24th Dec., 1811.

"Officers of the Infantry are to wear—a Cap of a pattern similar to that established for the Line: a Regimental Coat similar to the Private men's, but with lapells to button over the breast and body: a grey cloth Great Coat, corresponding in colour with that established for the Line, with a stand-up collar, a cape to protect the shoulders, and regimental buttons.

In case of regiments employed on foreign service, the Officers are to wear grey Pantaloons, or Overalls, with short boots, or with Shoes and Gaiters such as Private men's.

The Field and Staff Officers of Regiments are to conform to the foregoing Regulations, the same as the Officers of companies.

When at Court the Officers of Infantry are to appear in long Coats, with cocked hats, as at present.

The Epaulettes and Wings of all Regimental Officers, are in future to be of the same description without any other distinction than what is prescribed by the General Order of 9th February, 1810.

Captains of Flank Companies who have the Brevet rank of Field Officers are to wear 'Wings' in addition to their Epaulettes, Officers of the Grenadier Company to have a 'Grenade,' those of the Light Company a bugle horn below the previously mentioned badge of rank on Epaulette strap."

About this period officers of the Light Company carried a curved scimitar-shaped sword, suspended by slings from the shoulder-belt.

CHAPTER XI.

ON the 3rd of March, 1812, H.R.H. the Prince Regent, in the **1812** name and on the behalf of the King, was pleased to approve of the word "ROLEIA" being borne on the colours and appointments of the 29th (or Worcestershire) Regiment in recognition of its distinguished conduct in that battle.

The regiment was selected for Windsor duty, and marched from Steyning in two divisions on the 20th and 21st of April; on arriving at Windsor it relieved the Staffordshire Militia, which had been quartered there nearly fifteen years.

On the 18th of June the Congress of the United States of America declared war against England.

EXTRACT FROM "*Knight's Passages of Working Life.*"

"Sunday evening, 16th August, the Band which was playing in the Long Walk, was suddenly ordered back to Barracks, the reason for which was the arrival of the Extraordinary Gazette, containing Lord Wellington's dispatches relating to the Victory of Salamanca, whereupon the regiment marched to the inspiring tune of 'Ça ira,' into a field adjoining Frogmore Gardens, and fired a feu-de-joie.' . . . . A practical joke, with a somewhat ludicrous termination, was here played on a sentry of the 29th, a man who had more than once crossed bayonets with the French, and had been twice wounded at Talavera. Being one night posted beneath a private appartement under Queen Elizabeth's Gallery, the sentry saw a figure in black approaching; he

1812 challenged it, but not receiving any answer, brought his musket to the charge, and advanced towards it, on which the figure disappeared, but on its re-appearance the sentry, crying out 'I'm lost! I'm lost!' fell prostrate. Even when a mischievous artist was shortly after compelled

PRIVATES OF LIGHT, AND OF GRENADIER COMPANY, 1812.

to leave his pleasant appartment, carrying with him his phantasmagorian devices, it was difficult for many, in the somewhat benighted town, to comprehend that optical delusions were not difficult to manage."

The regiment was inspected by Major-General Disney on the **1812** 25th of May and on the 12th of October. On the former occasion its strength was 43 serjeants, 40 corporals, 16 drummers, 634 rank and file. The colours were represented as being "bad," but according to regulation.

Extracts from Standing Orders of H.M. 29th (or Worcestershire) Regiment of Foot, printed in London, 24th June, 1812 :—

Uniformity of Dress.

"Upon home service, Field and Mounted officers, to appear in white leather breeches, high military boots of the same pattern, and regulation spurs. At morning parades, all other officers will dress in white pantaloons and half boots; but at all reviews, inspections by general officers, public and regimental duties, in black cloth leggings and white breeches; the former to come close up to the knee, with two buttons of the breeches knee, only to appear above the top of the gaiter.

No other than black stocks clasped behind, agreeable to the regimental pattern, to be worn.

Gorgets—Upon all reviews, field days, marches, public and regimental duties, fastened close up the stock with ribbands and rosettes corresponding in colour to the facings.

Three button holes, of the jacket lappel to turn back, and frills worn outside; the same number of buttons and white edging to the jackets as were worn on the coats.

Sashes, to be tied uniformly over the left side.

Caps, being the established uniform for the army, they are to be worn perfectly straight over the forehead, and in paying compliments never to be taken off, but the right hand brought over the peak to the salute.

1812   Upon service, marches, and duties of fatigue, grey pantaloon overalls will be worn, six buttons opening at the bottom; and great coats, of the same colour, agreeable to the late established pattern for the army.

Officers' Epaulettes must be all of the same pattern, and uniformly put on; they are to pass under a silver braid, fastened so as to keep the epaulette perfectly steady, and the pad must come up close to it. The epaulette to be sewed on cloth of the same colour as the facing, which should be, when new, of a pale lemon colour, and kept clean with English pink.

Regimental Swords only to be worn, and always in the belt.

Officers will wear their swords at all times when in uniform (excepting in their own rooms), and always a regimental sword knot, and white leather gloves at all parades and duties.

The Colours.

The Colours are to be at all times treated with the highest respect; they are to be carried by the two senior ensigns present. In times of danger, the officers carrying the Colours will consider themselves as responsible for the honour of the regiment, and to defend them at every personal risk. The minds of soldiers must be impressed with the duty incumbent upon all, to defend their Colours to the last extremity; and of the infamy and disgrace that attends the base deserter of this important pledge entrusted to their fidelity and valour. Officers passing the Colours of their own, or other corps, to mark their respect by taking off their hats, or saluting in caps. Non-Commissioned officers and soldiers to observe the same.

Men's Necessaries.

The complement of necessaries must always be kept up to the following Establishment:—

    3 Good shirts, 2 pairs hose or socks, 2 pairs of good shoes, 1 pair indifferent.

1812 1 Pair good black leggings, 1 pair indifferent, 1 good forage cap. 1 Regimental stock and clasp. Brushes and black ball. Worm, screw, brush and picker. Buff stick, hair comb, and razors. Any changes or additions according to climate, will be ordered accordingly.

Music, Drums, and Fifes.

The Master of the Band, and the Drum-Major are always to be serjeants in the regiment, and obeyed as such. Cymbals, Big Drum, and Tambourines, when employed are considered as belonging to the Band."

In the Miscellany Books at the War Office, is a Warrant authorizing the Commissioners for the Affairs of Barracks to appropriate and fit up barrack rooms for regimental schools, and to issue coals and candles for the same, dated 24th July, 1812.

In the Army Lists published about this time, the facings of the 29th are given as being yellow, and the lace silver. It may be as well to mention that the latter referred only to the epaulettes, and hat lace.

Officers of the 29th did not wear lace on their jackets, or coatees, till 1830.

The regimental braid (half-an-inch broad) worn by privates was white, with two dark blue, and two yellow stripes, the latter being on the outside.

Serjeants' sashes were crimson, with one yellow stripe.

It appears that about this time the officers' shoulder-belt plate and skirt ornaments were altered; for those at present in use were—

Breast Plate. †—Plain silver, with gilt, raised ornaments; *i.e.*, in centre, on a wreath, was the Lion crowned, *statant guardant*, encircled by a garter (with the motto, "*Honi soit*," &c.), surmounted by a crown; from the bottom of the garter and extending either way was a branch of laurels, below which was a scroll with "ROLEIA."

The Skirt Ornament,† about two inches in diameter, was a wreath of laurels surmounted by a crown; in the centre of the wreath was "29," with "ROLEIA" above it. The whole was embroidered in silver, on scarlet cloth.

---

† I am indebted to Mr. S. M. Milne, of Calverley, near Leeds, for information about these badges.

† *Jacket Epaulette*, on yellow cloth, 2½ in. silver braid strap, with binder, a twisted bullion silver crescent, with a gilt metal scroll with "ROLEIA" between palm and laurel branches.

1812 It is quite possible that the silver button, "with '29' encircled by a laurel wreath,"‡ which was worn by the officers, up to 1833, was in use at this period.

General Order dated 6th July, 1812, instituted the rank of Colour Serjeant, whose distinguishing badge was a "Regimental Colour," supported by crossed swords, and was worn above the chevrons.

So high was the character borne by the regiment, that its numbers were soon completed, and it once more received orders to proceed on foreign service.

1813 Leaving Windsor on the 4th, 5th, and 6th of February, in three divisions, the regiment, under command of Lieut.-Colonel Gregory Way, marched for Portsmouth, and there embarked on board the "Malabar" transport, for conveyance to Cadiz, where on landing on the 23rd of March, it went into quarters at Isla de Leon, and Major Hodge proceeded on command to Tarifa.

Shortly after the inspection of the regiment, in December, by Colonel the Honble. Edward Capel, Lieut.-Colonel Way, who was still suffering from his wounds, was obliged to return to England on leave. H.M. King George III., having previously granted this officer permission to wear the Order of the Tower and Sword, presented by the King of Portugal, now made him a K.C.B.

Depôt, 1813.

When the regiment left Windsor, its Depôt marched to Chichester, where it was inspected in May by Major-General Houston, and in October, by Major-General Richard Bingham. On both of these occasions two colours "good" were returned as being in its charge. As the Depôt was not in charge of any colours when inspected on the 9th of May, 1814, it is quite possible they had been

---

‡ It is said that this "*wreath*" was adopted to commemorate the services of the regiment on board the fleet.

sent out to replace those carried by the regiment through the Peninsular **1813** War. In the mess-room at Norton Barracks, Worcester, is one side of

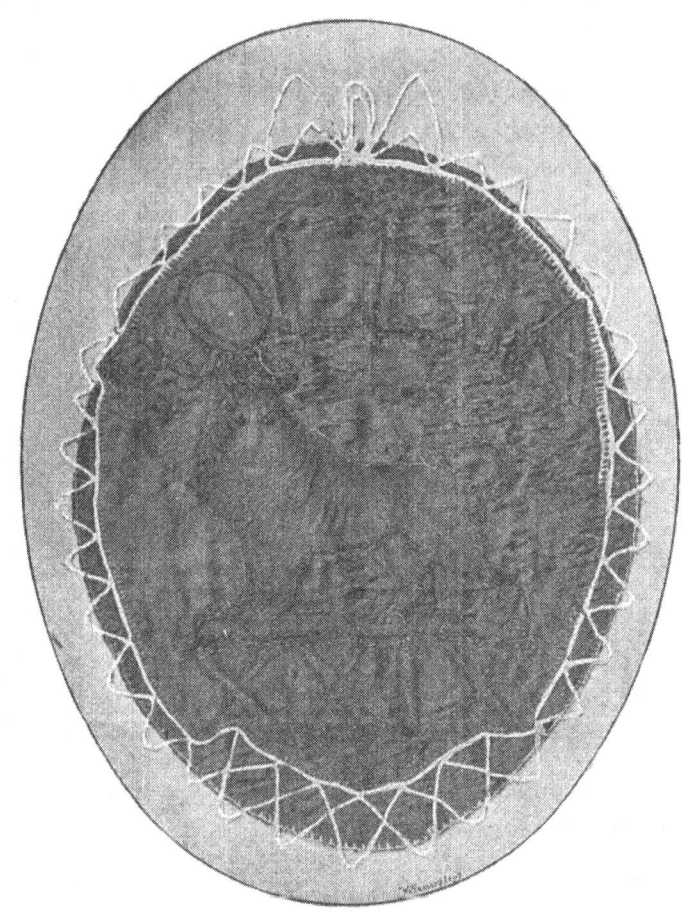

FRAGMENT OF REGIMENTAL COLOUR CARRIED IN THE PENINSULA.

the centre of a *Regimental Colour*, which was presented by Colonel A. A. Dick to the regiment when stationed at Aldershot in 1877. It was afterwards mounted and framed, and on the 29th being ordered to

1813 India in 1879, it was left in charge of the Depôt. It will be observed by the accompanying illustration that "ROLEIA," which was granted in in March, 1812, is the only battle borne on the colour. From the present appearance of the gold wire with which that word, the lion, and regimental number, are worked, it would seem that they were all embroidered at the same time, and therefore it is quite probably a piece of the colours which the Depôt had charge of in 1813, for those presented in 1824 are now in possession of Lord Strafford.

1814 Early in January, 1814, the regiment took up quarters at San Fernando, and in February, embarked at Cadiz, on board the "Leyden," a Dutch 64, for conveyance to Gibraltar, where, on landing it occupied quarters in the King's Bastion, Town Range, and Blue Barracks.

The following paragraph, concerning the Calpe Hunt and the 29th Regiment, is taken from the "Histories of Gibraltar," by Colonel Gildea and Lieut.-Colonel Gilbard :—

"The origin of the Calpe Hunt is rather doubtful. It certainly appears from the only documents connected with the Cadiz Club, still extant, that on the breaking up of the Cadiz garrison, the hounds were presented to the 29th Regiment, in joint ownership with the other regiments quartered on the Rock. The entry, in the Account and Record Book of the Isla de Leon Hunt, is as follows :—'April 29, 1814. It was this day resolved by the remaining members of the Real Isla de Leon Hunting Club, that the hounds shall be offered to the officers of the 29th Regiment, who originally subscribed to them, and to the officers composing the Hunting Club now established at Gibraltar.'

"The Isla de Leon Hunt Club established by the British garrison at Cadiz, claims, therefore, the honour of having supplied the nucleus round which the Calpe Hunt was formed."

On the 30th of April, the regiment, under command of Major Hodge, was inspected by Major-General Widdrington, who reported the colours as "good, and according to regulation," but in his "*Confidential Report*" the following remark appears : "The colours have seen so much honourable service in the field that little of them is left on the poles."‖ The inspecting officer also caused the following Order to be published:— **1814**

BRIGADE ORDERS. 30TH APRIL, 1814.

"In expressing the very great satisfaction Major-General Widdrington has derived from his inspection of the 29th Regiment this day, he feels it a duty incumbent upon him, and an act of justice to Major Hodge, and the officers, and non-commissioned officers of the corps, for the manner in which they have fulfilled with so much honour to themselves, and the public service, the important duties attached to their particular stations, both in training, and securing health and comfort to the soldiers; and by an example, conspicuous, in directing their minds to patriotism and enterprise.

"The distinguished honour, this corps has received for Intrepidity, during the greatest and most awful events the eye of a soldier ever gazed on, leaves the Major-General little more to say. The military prowess of the 29th Regiment will add an illustrious page to the records of British valour and heroism. Nothing but the greatest attention on the part of the officers, and a zealous application on the part of the men, could have brought the battalion to such a forward state of discipline, so highly creditable in all respects. The Major-General will most sincerely state in his Report, as strongly as is in his power, his entire approbation and how much he has been gratified by the soldierlike appearance, the correct movements, and good conduct of the corps. If the Major-General might be permitted to obey the impulse of his own heart, he cannot conclude without wishing Major Hodge, the officers, and men, after so honourable a return from the fatigues, hardships, and dangers to which they have been so much exposed, a comfortable and uninterrupted enjoyment of the remaining years of their life."

‖ This must refer to the colours carried by the regiment through the recent campaign.

1814 Nothing of moment, except the death of the lieutenant-governor, Lieut.-General Colin Campbell, and his interment in the presence of the whole garrison, occurred during the stay of the regiment on the Rock.

The Treaty of Paris having been signed on the 11th of April, troops were now withdrawn from Spain and Portugal, and sent to America to carry on with greater vigour, the war which the Congress had declared two years previously.

The regiment having been minutely inspected on the 8th of June, was placed under the command of Major-General Gosselin, and shortly afterwards embarked for America. Having arrived at Teneriffe, it remained in the harbour of Vera Cruz till the 24th instant, when it left for Bermuda, where transports having been changed, it sailed again for Halifax, Nova Scotia, and on arriving there on the 20th of August, it encamped near the Freshwater Run.

Six days later, a combined naval and military expedition (of which the 29th formed part), under command of Rear-Admiral Griffith and Lieut.-General Sir J. C. Sherbrooke, G.C.B., sailed for the Penobscot River.

The Fort of Castine, situated on a peninsula on the eastern side of the river, was summoned on the 1st of September, but on the American officer in command refusing to surrender, arrangements were made for disembarking the troops; before however this could be effected, the enemy, having blown up their magazine, evacuated the place.

The fort having been occupied, it was determined to obtain possession of the U.S. frigate "Adams," which had run up the river to Hamden, where her guns had been landed, and by way of defence, mounted on the shore.

It being judged advisable to establish a post on the western bank, so as to be able to afford support, if necessary, to the force going up the river, Major-General Gosselin was directed to occupy Belfast, with **1814** the battalion companies of the 29th. The Flank companies, under Captains Gell and Coker, were attached to the force, commanded by Lieut.-Colonel John, 60th Regiment, which was ordered to proceed by river to Hamden. On reaching Ball's Head Cove, on the afternoon of the 2nd, the troops immediately commenced to land, and the enemy's picquets having been dislodged, the force bivouacked for the night, during which it rained incessantly.

Having got under arms about 5 o'clock the following morning, the troops advanced; the ships and gunboats on their right, moving up the river at the same time. The fog was so thick that it was impossible to form a correct idea of the features of the country, or to reconnoitre the enemy, who were reported to be 1400 strong, and under command of Brigadier-General Blake.

Between seven and eight o'clock, the Rifle company of the 7/60th, which formed the advance guard, being sharply engaged, half of the Light company of the 29th, under Captain Coker, was sent to its support.

The column had not advanced much further, when the enemy, drawn up in line, were discovered occupying a very strong and advantageous position in front of the town of Hamden. Their left rested on a high hill, on which were mounted several heavy pieces of cannon commanding the road and river.

In order to rake the road and narrow bridge, by which their assailants were obliged to advance, the enemy had placed some light field pieces in advance of their centre; their right rested on a strong point d'appui, where an 18-pounder had been placed in position.

A heavy, but somewhat ill-directed, fire of grape and musquetry was opened on the attacking column, and Captain Gell, who was leading the advance, fell severely wounded.

1814   The bridge having been crossed, the troops immediately deployed, and charged up the hill to get possession of the guns. Some of the advanced ones, having been captured by the riflemen of the 60th, the enemy's fire commenced to slacken. When Captain Coker, with the Light company of the 29th, gained possession of the heights on the enemy's left, it was discovered that the " Adams " frigate was on fire, and that the battery which defended her, was deserted. The enemy being now driven in at all points, and their position captured, the expedition pushed on to Bangor, which was reached without any opposition, and here Brigadier-General Blake, with several others, surrendered themselves.

Twenty-two pieces of cannon, and three stands of colours, this day fell into the hands of the expeditionary force.

In the affair at Hamden, 3rd of September, 1814, the Flank companies of the 29th suffered the following casualties :—

Killed—Private Peter Bracewell, Light company.
Wounded—Captain Thos. Gell (severely), 2 rank and file.

One of the latter, Private Isaac Holt, of the Grenadier company, died shortly afterwards from effect of his wounds.

Lieut.-Colonel John's force returned to Castine on the 9th, where Major-General Gosselin, with the battalion companies of the 29th, was also directed to rejoin General Sherbrooke.

The Fort at Machias being now the only remaining post in the enemy's possession between the Penobscot and Passamaquady Bay, Lieut.-Colonel Pilkington was ordered to proceed and occupy it with a detachment of Royal Artillery, and the 29th Regiment. On the evening of the 10th, a landing was effected at some distance from the fort, which after a very difficult night march, was taken possession of early the next morning. A capitulation was signed, by which the enemy engaged not to bear arms against his Britannic Majesty during the remainder of the year. On this occasion 24 pieces of cannon were taken possession of. Having destroyed the fort, Colonel Pilkington's force returned to **1814** Castine, which was now strongly fortified. In December the Treaty of Ghent was signed, Peace was concluded with America, and the evacuation of Castine agreed upon.

DEPÔT, 1814.

The following officers, who had for some time been prisoners in France, rejoined their Depôt this year, viz.:—Captains H. Birmingham, A. Patison, and Lieut. Charles Stanhope.

On the 29th of September, Lieut.-Colonel Sir Gregory Way, K.C.B., exchanged to the 22nd Foot,* with Lieut.-Col. John Tucker, who had a short time previously been promoted into that corps from the 29th.

On the 31st of December, a circular was received from the Adjutant-General, directing a Bugle Horn, with the number of the regiment below it, to be worn on the Caps of the Light Infantry company.

It may interest some to know that William Vincent Wallace, the composer of the charming operas of Maritana, Lurline, Amber Witch, &c., &c., was the son of the bandmaster of the 29th Regiment; he was born at Waterford 1st of June, 1814, and buried in October, 1865, in Kensal Green cemetery, by the side of Balfe.

---

* On leaving the 29th Regiment, Sir G. Way was presented by the officers with a piece of Plate with the following inscription surmounted by the "Tower and Sword":—

Presented
By the Officers of His Majesty's
29th Regiment of Foot, to
Lieut.-Colonel Sir Gregory Way, K^{nt}. C. B. and K^t. T^t. and S^d.,
Deputy Adjutant-General for N.B.,
And late in Command of that Corps,
In Acknowledgment of their Gratitude for
the Warm Interest he invariably displayed
wherever their welfare and happiness
was concerned.
Dec. 1st, 1814.

1815 On the 18th of April, 1815, H.R.H. the Prince Regent, in the name and on behalf of His Majesty, was pleased to approve of the word "Peninsula" being borne on the Colours and Appointments of the 29th Regiment, in commemoration of its services during the late war in Portugal and Spain, under Field-Marshal the Duke of Wellington.

On account of Buonaparte's escape from Elba, and his subsequent operations, the regiment, under command of Major G. Tod, sailed from Castine in May, and having arrived at Spithead on the 4th of June, landed, and marched to the Portsea Barracks, where it proceeded with the least possible delay to complete its equipment for service in the Netherlands. Colonel Tucker having now taken over the command of the 29th, issued the following order :—

Regimental Orders, 8th June, 1815.

"Lieut.-Colonel Tucker was particularly desired on taking over the command of the 29th Regiment, to express the pain and regret felt by Lieut.-Colonel Sir Gregory Way, when another appointment obliged him to relinquish the proud situation which he held at the head of the corps.

His high feeling of their conduct on every occasion involving the credit and honour of the regiment, renders all commendation weak and unnecessary ; it is only in his warm interest for the character of the 29th Regiment that Lieut.-Colonel Tucker presumes to rival him ; having now succeeded to a command which has long been the object of his proudest wishes, he only entreats the assistance of his brother officers, and soldiers will surely never forget the corps to which they belong.

In a few days more we shall be called into the field, by the express desire of His Grace the Duke of Wellington, and I trust our conduct there, will not weaken the gracious kindness and regard by which he has never failed to distinguish the 29th Regiment."

Having re-embarked on the 10th, on board the "Leyden," the regiment landed at Ostend on the 13th, and proceeded in boats up the Bruges canal to Ghent, which was reached on the 15th. Pushing on from thence in all haste, it arrived near enough to distinctly hear the firing, but, to the great disappointment of all ranks, too late to take part in the battle of Waterloo.

1815

After this, it was employed in escorting prisoners for embarkation at Ostend. Returning to Ghent, the regiment did duty over H.M. Louis XVIII. till the 24th, when it marched, with part of the 7th Fusiliers, under command of Colonel Sir E. Blakeney, for Paris. The King of France, escorted by about 200 of his Guards, left Ghent at the same time, but it is a question whether his troops would have proved an acquisition in the event of an attack, as they were conveyed in waggons, and had only the appearance of soldiers.

A Return, dated Grammont, 25th June, gives the names of the following officers as being present with the regiment:—

Lieut.-Colonel	Tucker.
Majors	Hodge, and Tod.
Captains	Patison, Birmingham, H., Gell, Elliot, Mahon, Coker, Stannus, Gregory, Stanhope.
Lieutenants	Popham, Pennington, Reid, Evans, Biggs, Vesie, Sullivan, Lovelock, Lucas, Brodrick, Ford, Richardson, Arth.; FitzGerald, Chas.; Doyne, Richd.; Gibbons, Stephn.; Hilton, Wm. L.; Bovill, Edwd.
Ensigns	Johnstone, Wm.; Dixon, Henry; Parker, Wm.; Akers, J. L.; Fitzgerald, John; Wright, Chas.; Wild, Henry; Sitwell, Robt.
Paymaster	Humfrey, Chrisr.
Adjutant	Wild, Benjn.
Quarter Master	Gillespie.
Surgeon	Stanford.
Assist. Surgeons	Parker, Wm., and Lawder, Jas.

On the 6th of July, the regiment arrived at St. Germain, where it joined the army under the Duke of Wellington in camp near Paris. It was placed in Major-General Sir Morley Power's brigade (which formed part of the 6th division) and the following day moved to Neuilly.

1815   During the occupation of Paris by the allied army, Frenchmen took every opportunity of insulting its officers, and it has been alleged that a club of French officers existed, the members of which had sworn to devote their lives to the killing of them one by one. Most people have read "Harry Lorrequer," in which Lever tells us of a French captain, a member of such a club, who boasted of already having killed a dozen English officers, and promised to go on with this work, and how that one evening, having swaggered into his usual café, and finding his accustomed seat in possession of one of them who was quietly reading a newspaper, proceeded to insult him, first by taking away the lights, and then snatching the paper out of his hands; failing to obtain the explanation he sought for, he brought his heel down on the officer's foot, who still took no notice of the insults. The Frenchman then called for a glass of brandy, and putting his face close to the Englishman's, said in a loud voice "à votre courage Anglais," and tossed off the liquor. Scarcely had he time to swallow it, when the Englishman rose slowly from his chair, and with one stride was beside the Frenchman; seizing his nose with one hand, while with the other he grasped his lower jaw, with the strength of a man standing 6 feet 6, and broad and strong in proportion, he wrenched open the bully's mouth, and spat down his throat. The Frenchman rushed from the room, holding his lower jaw with both hands (for it was fractured), and was never again seen at that café.

"We may add," says Mr. Douglas in his book on '*Duelling Days in the British Army*,' "that the English officer in question was the late General Sir James Simpson,[†] who for a time commanded the army in the Crimea."

The following reason is given by officers who served for many years in the 29th with Sir James Simpson, for his conduct on this occasion. Whilst Simpson was recovering from wounds received at Quatre Bras, a great friend of his had unfortunately fallen by the

---

[†] Captain Simpson exchanged from the 1st Foot Guards to the 29th Foot in 1826.

hand of this Frenchman, whose name and habits Simpson having ascertained, as soon as he was convalescent, he repaired to the café, the bully's place of resort, and purposely placed himself in his way.   **1815**

On the 24th of July, the allied troops were reviewed by H.I.M. the Emperor of Russia.

On the 10th of September, a squadron of Life Guards and the 29th Regiment were ordered to St. Cloud, and placed at the disposal of Sir George Scovell.

On the 23rd of October, Sir Manly Power inspected the regiment (strength 61 serjeants, 56 corporals, 22 drummers, and 858 privates) at Neuilly camp. The only officers reported absent were—General Gordon Forbes, Captains H. Birmingham (Commander-in-Chief's leave), W. Elliot (Brigadier-Major 16th Brigade); Lieut. Thos. Hamilton, and Assistant-Surgeon W. Parker (sick leave).

It having been decided to keep a British contingent in France of 30,000 men, of which 10,000 were Hanoverians, on the 30th of November the regiment, together with the 1/16th and 1/71st, was placed in Major-General Sir T. Bradford's brigade. The 29th was at first quartered at Andrésy on the Seine, but on the 10th of December marched to Versailles, where it joined the 6th brigade. On the 28th it continued its march to St. Just, and thence to Chaumontel.

Depôt, 1815.

On the 24th of February, 1815, the Depôt, under command of Captain W. Wade, marched from Chichester to Hilsea Barracks, and later on embarked for the Isle of Wight, where on arrival, it took up quarters in the Albany Barracks.

On the 2nd of August, a General Order was received relative to the arms of the Infantry being "browned," and on the 22nd another Order that the cap then in use by the Infantry of the army should be discontinued, and one of an approved pattern adopted.

1815 † The new head dress was the broad-topped chaco, then common to all continental armies. It was 11 inches in diameter at the top, and 7½ deep. The officers' chin scales were silver, and could be tied up in front to a black cockade, and upright white feather which was 12 inches high; their chaco plate was an oblong silver star (3¾ inches by 3⅛) marked with concentric circles; in the centre, on a blue enamel ground, was a gilt lion, encircled by a solid garter of the same metal (with the motto, "*Honi soit*," etc., in raised burnished letters) surmounted by a gilt crown. In 1828 this star device, with the exception of the crown, was fixed on the universal large gilt star-plate then introduced, an illustration of which will be found on page 369.

The Light Company cap badge was a white metal bugle horn.

The officers' chaco had silver lace, 2½ inches broad round the top, flower and ring pattern, and half-inch vellum lace round the bottom.

The feather worn by the Light company was green. The Grenadier company retained their bearskin caps with a white feather; silver tassels for the officers, white for the other ranks.

When this first chaco was introduced, the officers had a feather plume, the non-commissioned officers, rank and file, a worsted one.

1816 Early in February, 1816, the regiment took up quarters at Chocques, Pas de Calais, where its head-quarters were stationed the greater part of the two succeeding years.

On the 10th of April it was cantoned as follows:—

Head Quarters at Chocques ...	7 Officers	136 Men
Gonnelrem	8 ,,	235 ,,
Hinge	5 ,,	154 ,,
Mont Berninchen	4 ,,	141 ,,
La Bœuvières	4 ,,	110 ,,
La Pugny	3 ,,	85 ,,

On the 6th of August, the 29th marched to Blandecques, where it encamped till the 15th of October, when it marched and encamped near Mastaing. On the 22nd it was reviewed near Valenciennes, with the remainder of the British contingent, by the Duke of Wellington, after which it proceeded to Guenain, and on the 30th, was inspected at Chocques by Sir Thomas Bradford.

---

† For these details I am indebted to Mr. S. M. Milne.

On the 25th of December, the establishment of the regiment was **1816** fixed at 1 colonel, 1 lieut.-colonel, 2 majors, 10 captains, 12 lieutenants, 8 ensigns, 6 staff; 45 serjeants, 22 drummers, 800 rank and file. In consequence of this the recruiting company was done away with, 1 captain and 12 lieutenants were placed upon half-pay, and all supernumerary serjeants and corporals discharged.

Depôt, 1816.

In March the Depôt was stationed at Yarmouth, Isle of Wight, where it embarked early in April for Dover, and on landing, marched to Deal Barracks.

The following General Orders with regard to dress were published this year:—

16th June, 1816. Officers, when at Court, or on other occasions in their Regimental Uniform, to appear in a Cap, in lieu of a cocked Hat.

20th December. All Mounted Officers of Infantry to wear the white buff leather Shoulder Belt with Slings, and not waistbelt. Officers of all Infantry Regiments are required to button the lapels of their jackets close across their breast, without showing any part whatever of their facings.

In March 1817, several volunteers were received from the 1st, **1817** 5th, 52nd, and 88th regiments. On the 4th of July, the regiment marched to Helfaut, where it encamped till the 1st of September, when it moved to Valenciennes, and together with the remainder of the British infantry, was there reviewed by the King of Prussia. On the 12th, it marched to Denain, where the British contingent was, on the 15th, reviewed by the Duke of Wellington. After this, it returned to Chocques.

On the 2nd of June, 1818, the regiment again encamped near **1818** Helfaut where it remained till the 16th of August, when it marched, by Lens and Auberchicourt, to Valenciennes, and there encamped on the glacis.

1819   On the 21st instant, permission was granted the 29th Regiment to bear on its colours and appointments the words "Vimiera," "Talavera," "Albuhera," in recognition of its distinguished services in those battles.

In September, H.R.H. the Duke of Kent reviewed the troops encamped near Valenciennes, after which the 29th marched to and encamped near Neuville.

On the 23rd of October, H.I.M. the Emperor of Russia, and the King of Prussia, reviewed the British, Danish, Russian, and Saxon contingents, after which the regiment returned to Auberchicourt.

Orders having about this time been received for the withdrawal of the British contingent, the regiment embarked at Calais on the 31st, and landing the next day at Dover and Ramsgate, marched to Deal.

The peace establishment being now fixed at 1 colonel, 1 lieut.-colonel, 2 majors, 10 captains, 12 lieutenants, 8 ensigns, 5 staff, 35 serjeants, 22 drummers, 650 rank and file; 1 assistant-surgeon was placed on half-pay, 10 serjeants, 10 corporals, and all men above the establishment, were discharged.

On the 12th of November, the regiment embarked on board the "Brilliant" and "Lady Hamilton" transports, for conveyance to Cork, and having landed at Cove on the 24th, it marched in two divisions for Armagh, where, on the 10th of December, it relieved the 82nd Foot, and detached 1 company to Lifford, 1 to Strabane, 1 to Monaghan, and 2 to Omagh. Smaller parties were also sent to Dungannon, Cookstown, Pomeroy, and Aughnacloy.

1820   On the 15th and 17th of July, 1820, the head-quarters marched from Armagh in two divisions for Dublin; the company at Monaghan joining the second division at Drogheda. The detachment from Omagh, under command of Captain Wade, and that from Strabane, under Lieut.-Colonel Hodge, arrived in Dublin on the 25th and 26th instant respectively. On the 22nd of November, the regiment embarked **1820** at Pigeon House, and sailing for Liverpool, arrived there on the 24th. On landing, it marched to relieve the 12th Foot at Macclesfield, and two companies were sent to Northwich, two to Middlewich, and one to Knutsford.

<small>All ranks were this year ordered to discontinue the wearing of short coats.</small>

In February, 1821, these detachments under Lieut.-Colonel Tod, **1821** relieved the 12th Foot at Manchester. In May, three of these companies, under Major Gell, proceeded to Liverpool, the head-quarters and remaining companies marching to Chester.

Previous to this change of quarters, the regiment was inspected at Macclesfield, on the 1st of May, by Major-General Sir James Lyon, K.C.B., who in his report made the following remarks:—

"*Accoutrements*—2 Colours, good and according to regulation.

"*Band*—There are 4 men of colour in it, who were enlisted by authority from H.R.H. the Commander-in-Chief.

"*Clothing* of Officers, Non-Commissioned Officers, and Men is in strict conformity to H.M. Regulations."

The following paragraph is taken from "*Military Extracts*" in the R.U.S. Institution:—

<small>"MACCLESFIELD.—'*A Singular Occurrence.*'—On the 21st April last a serjeant of the 29th Regiment of Foot stationed here, escorting a party of men of the 12th Regiment thence to Portsmouth, was quartered at the King's Arms Inn, Bishops Waltham; the next day being (Sunday) a halting day, and on which day he left the house and never returned, search was made, but without effect until the 28th, when he was found in a ditch, having formed a determination to starve himself to death, and had actually been there the seven days without food. He had got a curious bed made in the ditch, with sticks laid across, and a large quantity of moss. He was taken to Mr. Clarke's house, who gave him some food, which he ate very little of, and he was allowed to depart, and he was not heard of again until Saturday, 12th May, being three weeks, and during which time he had also been without food, having been in the wood about a mile from Bishops Waltham, the last fourteen days without any sustenance whatever, except a little muddy water, which was near the place where he made his bed. He rose up on the morning</small>

1821 named, with a determination of beginning a new life, that being his birthday (the 32nd year of his age), and came wandering like a skeleton, to the King's Arms again. He told Mr. Clarke that it was his intention to place himself under his protection; he said he had got the better of his weakness, as he found he could not put an end to his existence which he had tried to effect by making incisions in his arm to bleed himself to death, as he did not die of hunger, which he thought he should in 10 days: the means he had used to prevent his feeling the pains of hunger, was—by tearing the sleeves off his shirt, and binding them round his body, and drawing them closer as his body decreased in size, by which means he thinks he could have lived fourteen days longer. The reason for his committing this act was, as he states—On his march from Macclesfield with the party of men under his command, he took two £1 Bank of England notes, which he considered to be bad, by their being refused, which notes he had in his possession, and finding that he had not money enough to pay the men, it hurt his feelings so much that he could not bear it, having been in the regiment 10 years, without the least stain on his character; which appears to be correct by the Commanding Officer's letter which has been since received, stating him to be one of the most trustworthy men in the regiment, and was particularly selected for the purpose.

"He is recovering as fast as nature will allow."

In August, a further reduction took place; the establishment of the regiment being ordered to consist of 1 colonel, 1 lieut.-colonel, 2 majors, 8 captains, 10 lieutenants, 6 ensigns, 5 staff, 29 serjeants, 24 corporals, 12 drummers, and 552 privates; 2 captains, 2 lieutenants, and 2 ensigns were therefore placed on half-pay, 6 serjeants, 6 corporals, and all men above the new establishment, being discharged.

In September, detachments under command of subalterns, were sent to Macclesfield, Stockport, and Liverpool.

Towards the end of the following month, the regiment and its detachments marched to Liverpool, and (with exception of 1 company stationed in the Isle of Man) embarked thence on the 6th of December for Dublin, where, on arriving, it took up quarters in the Royal and Palatine Squares.

When, on the 21st, the Marquis of Wellington entered Dublin to take up the Lord-Lieutenancy, the 29th Foot lined Dame Street and College Green.

On the 22nd of January, 1822, the company from the Isle of Man **1822** joined head-quarters. Leaving Dublin in two divisions on the 9th and 10th of July, the regiment marched for Mullingar, 2 companies being sent to Longford, 1 to Tullamore, 1 to Maryborough, and 1 to Philipstown.

The *Officers' Dress Trouser Lace* was 1⅝ inch silver, crooked bias and vellum pattern, with scolloped edge.

By General Order, Horse Guards, 18th of June, 1823, " His Majesty was pleased to **1823** approve of the discontinuance of breeches, leggings, and shoes, as part of the clothing of the infantry soldier ; and of blue grey cloth trousers and half boots being substituted." White linen trousers were also introduced for the rank and file in lieu of a second pair of cloth ones.

The regiment was inspected at Mullingar, on the 21st of June, by Major-General W. G. Harris, who reported that " 4 men of colour had been enlisted since the last Inspection.

"*Colours*—2, good, are as far as can be made out from their very tattered condition in conformity to H.M. regulations."

On the 28th of August head-quarters and the detached companies marched for Limerick, 1 company, under command of Captain Denis Mahon, for Bruff, and 16 other detachments to different parts of the country ; ten of these parties were commanded by subalterns, the other six by non-commissioned officers.

On the 30th of September, another change of quarters took place, the regiment marching for Tralee, where it arrived on the 3rd of October, and 1 company proceeded to Listowel, 1 to Castle Island, 1 to Millstreet, 1 to Killarney, and a detachment under the command of a subaltern to Tarbert.

On the 4th of November, Major-General Sir John Lambert inspected the 29th at Tralee, when he made the following remarks on the colours :—

"*Colours*—2, bad, worn out, and new ones ordered in conformity to H.M. regulations."

Soon after this, a company proceeded on detachment to Abbeyfeale.

1824 On the 26th of May, 1824, the regiment was again inspected at Tralee by Sir J. Lambert, who this time reported the *Colours* as "good, and in exact conformity to regulation."*

"*Band*—11 vacancies are reserved for black boys, who are on their way from Africa for the purpose."

Early in October, Nos. 1, 3, 6, and 8 companies, under command of Major Stannus, marched for Kinsale. On their route they were joined by the Millstreet detachment, and No. 6 was left at Macroom, from which company detachments were sent to Inchigeelah and Ballyvourney.

On the 7th, the head-quarters, under command of Major Elliot, left for Kinsale, where, on arrival, the Grenadier company, under Captain Brodrick, was sent to Charles Fort, and a detachment of No. 1 company to Camden Fort. The Light company was left at Bandon, when the head-quarters passed through that place.

1825 In April, 1825, the establishment of the regiment was raised to 1 colonel, 1 lieut.-colonel, 2 majors, 10 captains, 12 lieutenants, 8 ensigns, 5 staff, 42 serjeants, 36 corporals, 14 drummers, and 704 privates.

Orders having been received for the regiment to leave its present quarters, the following Address was presented to Lieut.-Colonel Sir John Buchan:—

"We the Sovereign and Inhabitants of the town of Kinsale, impressed with feelings of the highest esteem, beg leave to express our regret at the departure of the 29th Regiment from our town.

"During your residence here, no circumstance has occurred to interrupt that intercourse which, commencing in civility, has grown into friendship, and we feel as if about to part with friends whose value has been appreciated by an acquaintance of years.

---

* On new colours being presented to the regiment in 1841, these were given to Lord Strafford.

"Such are the sentiments with which the inhabitants of Kinsale **1825** and its vicinity will witness the departure of the 29th Regiment.

Independent of those private feelings we deem it incumbent upon us to acknowledge our sense of the truly admirable good conduct of the non-commissioned officers and soldiers of the regiment, as not even a solitary instance of complaint of any irregularity has occurred since its arrival in these quarters. Allow us to conclude this imperfect, but sincere, expression of our sentiments, by assuring you, and the officers, that the regiment will long retain a large share of our esteem, and that the hearty good wishes of the inhabitants of Kinsale and its vicinity for their welfare, happiness, and success will always accompany you and them.

Kinsale, 3rd October, 1825.

(S^{d.}) WILLIAM NEWMAN,

Sovereign."

Signed	Kinsale	Signed	John C. Cramer
,,	H. Taylor, Capt. R.N.	,,	J. T. Heard
,,	R. B. Warren	,,	Thomas Buller
,,	Robert Warren, M.D.	,,	Henry Honack
,,	J. T. Newman	,,	Edward Heard
,,	J. M. Daniel	,,	R. G. Foley
,,	Dennis Daly	,,	James Sandys
,,	Martin Sayer	,,	William Lawder
,,	Archd. Taylor	,,	H. Massey
,,	R. H. Lewis	,,	T. Crosbie Hamitt
,,	C. G. Fryer	,,	H. Nairn, Lt. R.N.
,,	Saml. Heard	,,	G. E. Bevan, Lt. R.N.
,,	Edward Standish	,,	John Walton
,,	H. Burgoyne, Capt. R.N.	,,	George Newman
,,	Roger E. Green	,,	Edward Supple
,,	Michael O'Connor	,,	J. D. Walton
,,	J. Hurley, J.P.	,,	G. W. Dunn
,,	W. J. Browne	,,	Richard Webb
,,	W. Markham	,,	G. Nason
,,	Edward Bishop, M.D.		

1825   Sir John Buchan's Answer :—

"*To William Newman, Esq. Sovereign, and Inhabitants of Kinsale.*

"Gentlemen,

"I have received with true feelings of gratification, the expression of your friendly sentiments towards the officers of the 29th Regiment, and I beg to assure you how cordially we all reciprocate those which have primarily arisen from your hospitality and kindness.

"The testimony which you are pleased to bear to the good conduct of the non-commissioned officers and men of the 29th Regiment, have excited in my mind feelings of a high order, but without derogating from the willing good conduct of that body of men, whom it is my pride and happiness to command, I must attribute a large share of that total absence of complaint which has so favourably marked their residence in Kinsale, to a spirit of kindness and goodwill which they have uniformly experienced from the inhabitants.

"With the sincerest wishes of the officers of the 29th Regiment for your individual welfare, and for the prosperity of your interesting town,

I have the honour to be,

Gentlemen,

Your obedient and obliged humble Servant,

(S[d.])   John Buchan, Lt.-Colonel

Com[dg], 29th Regiment."

"Kinsale,

October 6th, 1825."

On the 7th, the head-quarters left Kinsale for Waterford. The Light company, together with Nos. 4 and 5, under Major Stannus, proceeded to Wexford. Companies were also detached to Ballynamult, Cappoquin, Dungarvan, Duncannon Fort, and Kilmacthomas.

When, on the 26th, Major-General G. R. Bingham inspected the **1825** regiment at Waterford, he was pleased, in his general remarks, to report that "The officers of this corps are of the highest description, and that the *esprit-de-corps*, for which the 29th Regiment has been for so many years remarkable, exists in its full force and vigour, and contributes to keep the battalion in as high a state of discipline and in as effective a state as any in the country."

At this period* the officers' *shoulder belt plate* was of plain silver, with gilt raised ornaments; below the garter was a scroll inscribed "PENINSULA," on either side above the latter, were two other scrolls, those on the left facing one, bore the words, "ROLEIA," "VIMIERA," those on the right, "TALAVERA," "ALBUERA."

The *skirt ornament* for the officers of the battalion companies was a garter bearing the words "ROLEIA," "PENINSULA," surmounted by a crown, embroidered in silver on red cloth. In the centre of this device was "29" embroidered in silver on yellow cloth; that of the Grenadier company, had a grenade in the centre of the garter; the Light company wore an embroidered bugle only.

On the *epaulette strap* was a gilt scroll, bearing the word "ROLEIA;" the grenadier wings, which were of silver-plated chain, had a long gilt grenade above the "ROLEIA" scroll.

The *buttons* bore "29" encircled with a wreath of laurels.

In an old MS. copy of the "Regimental Records" is a picture of a private of the Grenadier company, a drummer and a bandsman of this period. The bearskin cap of the grenadier is represented as being very tall and the same size the whole way up, but in front, the top projects slightly; it has a large brass plate in front, and a white plume on the left side.

The drummer, appears to have worn the same pattern of regimental braid as was in use in 1866, viz., chevroned with yellow, dark blue, and and white, alternately.

---

* For the details of these badges and ornaments I am indebted to Mr. S. M. Milne.

1825 The bandsman's dress is a busby, with a scarlet plume, and yellow cap lines like those of a hussar. Yellow shell jacket with six rows of black braid, in pairs, across the breast, and a silver button at end of each row. Below the waist belt, which is of buff leather with an oblong brass plate, the jacket is edged with black fur, with which the collar and cuffs are also trimmed. Crimson overalls, with an Austrian knot of black braid down the outside seams.

1826 About the middle of May, the regiment marched to Cork, preparatory to embarkation for the Mauritius. On the 7th of June, two companies, under command of Major Elliot, embarked at Cove on board the "Diadem" transport; the officers who sailed with these companies were—Captains T. B. Hickin and Jonathan Davidson, Lieutenants A. G. Faden and Sackville Thatcher, Ensigns Christopher Humfrey and Andrew Hawthorn, Assistant-Surgeon John Hawkey, M.D.

One company, together with the Grenadier company (under command of Captain Brodrick), Lieutenants R. P. Douglas, Henry Blunt, and R. F. Walond, Pay Master Nathaniel Farewell, and 30 men of Captain Champain's company, sailed the same day on board the "Vallyfield" free-trader.

The head-quarter division, under command of Lieut.-Colonel James Simpson,‡ consisting of the staff, the Light company (Captain Evans'), Captain Popham's, and the remainder of Captain Champain's company, with Lieutenants Henry Bell, Christopher Eaton, Ensigns Henry Phillpotts, P. S. Fitzgerald, W. W. Drake, W. G. Alves, Adjutant M. Morgan, Quarter-Master Thos. Kneebone, and Surgeon Chas. Ingham, M.D., having sailed from Cove on the 19th, on board the "Prince Regent" East Indiaman, disembarked and occupied the barracks at Port Louis, Mauritius, on the 21st of September.

Detachments were shortly after this sent to Tonneliers, Flacq, Grand River S.E., and Poudre d'or.

---

‡ Lieut.-Colonel James Simpson (appointed from half-pay *vice* Col. Sir J. Buchan, who exchanged) assumed command of the regiment on the 13th of June, 1826.

On the 5th of February, 1827, the following letter was received **1827** by Lieut.-Colonel Simpson :—

"Horse Guards,

26 June, 1826.

"Sir,

Your letter of the 22nd inst. has been submitted to the Commander-in-Chief, who has received your report of the conduct of the 29th regiment on their embarkation, with great satisfaction, and considers it highly creditable to the character and discipline of that distinguished corps, and to the zeal and attention of its late commanding officer.

I have the honour to be,

Sir,

Your ob^{dt} Servant,

"To Sir Jno. Buchan, (Signed) H. TAYLOR."
H.P."

After the arrival of the regiment in the Mauritius, dysentry for a short time prevailed amongst all ranks, but fortunately caused no considerable loss of life.

On the 12th of June, His Excellency Lieut.-General the Honble. Sir G. Lowry Cole, G.C.B., inspected the 29th at Mahébourg. Shortly after this, a change of quarters took place, and on the 25th, the Light company, under Captain Evans and Lieut. Blunt, proceeded to Dardanne; head-quarters, together with four battalion companies, marching the following day for Port Louis, where on arrival they occupied the barracks, conjointly with the 82nd Regiment. The Grenadier company, under command of Capt. Brodrick, having marched to Black River, detached thence a subaltern's party, under Lieut. Faden, to Poste Jacoté; and another to Camp Dardanne.

In July, Capt. Evans, with 1 subaltern, 3 serjeants, and 50 rank and file of the Light company marched to Curepipe, the remainder of

1827 the company being detached to camp Dardanne, where also was Capt. Douglas' company.

In August, Lieut. Fitzgerald proceeded on detachment to Tonneliers. Whilst occupying these posts the men were employed in working parties. Towards the end of December all the detachments marched into Port Louis.

CAPTAIN GEORGE CONGREVE.

It appears that about this period, officers of the Light company wore a chaco with a silver bugle in front, and black cap lines; a crimson rifle sash with cords and tassels; and a buff shoulder belt with whistle attached. A plain single-breasted blue frock coat with 8 regimental buttons down the front, 2 smaller ones on the cuffs, and a plain

1827 Prussian collar, was this year authorized as undress for the officers. With this, the sash was worn round the waist, the sword was suspended from a black patent leather waist-belt, with a sliding frog (slings for mounted officers) and snake clasp; whilst as an undress cap, the chaco (without plume) was worn covered with an oilskin.

1828 General Gordon Forbes, dying on the 17th of January, 1828, Lieut.-General Rt. Honble. Sir John Byng, K.C.B., G.C.H., was appointed colonel of the 29th Regiment.

On the 29th of May a working party, under command of Capt. Hickin, left head-quarters for Camp Berthault, for the purpose of making a road to the Post of Souillac. Having been employed on this duty till the 29th of December, the detachment was broken up, and parties marched to the following stations :—Grand River, S.E., Powder Mills, and Cannonier Point.

On H.E. Lieut.-General the Honble. Sir Chas. Colville, G.C.B., G.C.H., inspecting the regiment at Port Louis on the 26th of August, he made the following remarks in his report :—

"With the exception of the Badge on the Pouch, the Match and Fuzee Pipe, and Brass loop on the Bayonet Belt, so long worn peculiar to this regiment, the clothing, accoutrements, and appointments of the officers, non-commissioned officers, drummers, and privates of this regiment, are strictly in accordance to the King's Regulations."

During this year the silver lace and black rosette cockade were stripped off the officers' chaco, and its height reduced to 6 inches. An universal pattern gilt star plate surmounted by a crown, the whole about 6½ inches in diameter, was adopted by the officers [*vide 1830*]. On the gilt plate was a smaller silver star, in the centre of which was a gilt lion on a ground of blue enamel, encircled by a solid gilt garter, with the motto "*Honi Soit, &c., &c.,*" in burnished letters.

Gold cap lines were also introduced, to be worn by officers on parade occasions only; these were wound round the cap across the front in a heavy braided festoon, and then hung down, terminating in two tassels, which were looped to one of the coat buttons. The cap lines for the Light company were of green worsted, those of the remaining companies being of white [*vide 1830*].

1828   On the 15th of November, 1 captain, 2 subalterns, 1 serjeant, 1 corporal, and 53 privates arrived from Chatham.

FIELD OFFICER IN UNDRESS, AND SERJEANT OF LIGHT COMPANY.

1829   By warrant dated 10th February, 1829, the coatee with yellow lappels, was ordered to be discontinued, and one of a new pattern was introduced [*v. 4 June, 1830*], which remained, with but little alteration, the dress of the infantry officer until 1855. An universal pattern epaulette, with stripes of the regimental facing, on the strap was also ordered to be adopted. All ranks of officers to wear two epaulettes, the badges of rank remaining on the straps as formerly.

A plain scarlet shell jacket was ordered to be worn by officers in certain climates. **1829**
Those of the 29th were fastened down the front with hooks and eyes, had two small regimental buttons on each cuff, shoulder straps of two twisted crimson silk basket cords with a small regimental button, and collar and cuffs of the regimental facing. This jacket was worn by the officers of the regiment, till the introduction of a very similar one in 1855.

By circular letter, dated the 21st March, a forage cap (with a large flat stiffened top) was authorized for the first time for officers.

Whilst at Port Louis the regiment supplied detachments for the following stations:—Grand River, S.E., Black River, Powder Mills, Cannonier Point, Jacoté, Réduit, Fort Blanc, Curepipe, and Souillac.

On the 26th of May the regiment marched to Mahébourg, to relieve the 82nd Foot. Parties were detached to Réduit, 22 Mile Post, and Isle de la Passe, also Capt. Sharrock, Lieut. Faden, Asst.-Surgeon P. Robertson, 3 serjeants, 4 corporals, 51 privates to Camp Berthault to be employed in making a road to the Post of Souillac. This detachment rejoined head-quarters on the 5th of January, 1830.

On the 28th of October Sir Chas. Colville inspected the regiment at Mahébourg, and reported as follows:—

> "*Musicians.*—Three blacks, the remnant of a corps of black drummers, authorized in the regiment. Two have been 27 years in the corps.
>
> "*Clothing, Accoutrements, and Appointments.*—Those of the officers are strictly according to the King's Regulations; those of the rank and file are not, dispensation having been regularly granted for the departure from regulation with regard to those now in wear."

Attached to the inspection report of 1830 is the following letter:—

"London, 9th May, 1829.

"Sir,
We have the honor to transmit herewith the Copy of a letter from the Adjutant-General, dated 2nd Inst., authorizing the accoutrements

1830 now in possession of the 29th Regiment being continued in use until worn out, although not in strict conformity with H.M. Regulations.

We have, &c.,
(Signed)   GREENWOOD, COX & Co."

"P.S.—The Pouch and Side Belt sent as a pattern to our office shall be immediately returned."

"Officer Commanding   A true copy
Depôt 29th Reg^t. of Foot,   W^M. ELLIOT,
Plymouth."   Major 29th Reg^t.
     Com^{dg}."

On the 2nd of November, 2 subalterns, 1 drummer, 20 rank and file, arrived from England in the "Amity" transport.

On the 7th of December, Major Evans, Capt. G. Congreve, Lieut. Humfrey, Ensign P. G. Beers, 2 serjeants, and 50 rank and file, marched from head-quarters for Flacq, to relieve Lieut.-Col. Grant and a detachment of the 82nd Regiment.

Gold and crimson shoulder cords were this year ordered to be added to the plain blue frock coat; the sword to be worn suspended in a white shoulder belt with a regimental breastplate, in lieu of the black waist belt. Sash to be worn round the waist.

On the 4th of June, 1830, in conformity with directions contained in the Circular Memo, dated Horse Guards, the 22nd of December, 1828, the new regulation dress cap, and feather, was taken into wear by the officers, who also appeared for the first time in the new pattern coatee, with silver lace and two epaulettes for all ranks, as pointed out in Circular Memo dated the 10th of February, 1829.

The new forage cap described in the Circular Letter of the 21st of March, 1829, was also adopted, as well as trousers of Oxford mixture, in lieu of those of blue grey.

On the 8th of June, the head-quarters, with the companies of Captains Champain, Sharrock, and Congreve, marched to relieve the 99th Foot at Port Louis, the Grenadier company, under command of Captain Douglas, was detached to Réduit, the Light company, under Captain Davidson, to Flacq, No. 1, Captain Hickin's, to Grand River,

N.W. Later on in the year, detachments were sent to Grand River, **1830**
S.E., Black River, S.E., Tonneliers, Cannonier Point, and Poudre d'or.

On the 7th of August, 1 serjeant, with 22 rank and file, arrived from England, on board the "Sir Joseph Banks" transport.

OFFICERS' CHACO PLATE, 1830—1846.

The following alterations in the uniform of the officers and men were this year ordered to be made :—

The uniform of the officers of the regular forces to be laced gold [*v. 4 Dec. 1832*].

Cap lines and tassels on caps of officers and men to be abolished, and their cap feathers to be shortened to eight inches.

1830   Officers and men of the Light company to wear a green tuft instead of a feather.

The gorget to be abolished.

Band of infantry regiments § to be clothed in white, with regimental facings.

Serjeants of infantry to be armed in future with fusils instead of pikes." [*v. 1 Aug. 1834*].

Staff serjeants retained the silver lace on their coatees till 1855.

1831   Circular Memo, Horse Guards, 5th March, 1831 :—" The coats of the drummers of regiments of infantry shall be red. With regard to the lace which is at present worn, no alteration is intended."

On the 13th of June, Lieut. Humfrey, 1 sergeant, 29 rank and file, embarked on board H.M. sloop "Jaseur" for conveyance to the Seychelle Islands, with a view of aiding the local Government in the prevention of the slave trade. On arriving at the Mahé, the most important island of the group, the detachment landed and relieved a similar party of the 99th Foot. Whilst here stationed, the detachment sent a party to Desroches Island, for the purpose of suppressing an outbreak amongst a number of slaves. Happily, on landing, its immediate services were found unnecessary; still the party remained there till May, 1832, when it returned to Mahé, and thence, in September, 1833, to the Mauritius.

Detachments were this year also sent to the following stations :— Flacq, Black River, Tonneliers, Cannonier Point, Poudre d'or, Grand River, N.W., Réduit, Fort Blanc, Powder Mills.

The several detachments having returned to Port Louis on the 27th of August, on the 14th of October the regiment was inspected by Sir C. Colville.

From Returns furnished at this inspection, it appears that the drummers no longer carried "hangers" but were in possession of swords.

---

§ Circular Memo, Horse Guards, 4th January, 1837.—The undress jacket, for bands, shall also be white.

By Circular Memo, dated Horse Guards, 30th April, 1832, field officers of infantry **1832** were ordered to discontinue wearing the shoulder belt with slings, a buffalo leather waist belt, with a gilt plate 2¼ × 1⅝ inches, bearing in raised silver " 29," surmounted by the Royal cypher and crown, being substituted; they were also directed to wear in future, a brass instead of a leather scabbard. Adjutants to wear a steel scabbard, and retain the old method of carrying the sword.

On the 5th of September, Captain Lloyd, Civil Engineer, Lieut. Taylor, R.A., Honble. T. R. Keppel, R.N., and Captain H. Phillpotts, 29th Regiment, started from Port Louis, for the foot of the Peter Botte, a mountain about ten miles distant.

Extract from a letter written by Captain Phillpotts soon after their ascent:—

"Early next morning (6th Sept.), after a hasty breakfast, we commenced our ascent from the S.E. side. We were in number about 16, two Englishmen belonging to our Engineer Department, one an overseer, the other a master carpenter, together with nine or ten black Sepoy convicts. The head of this singular mountain (2600 ft.) is in shape an inverted cone, about 40 feet high, and at the foot 30 feet in circumference; it overhangs its own base on every side. There is a ledge of rock about 3 feet broad which forms a sort of socket for the head to rest on. This ledge extends all round except on one side, where it appears to have fallen away.

" Lloyd ascended the cone first, I second, Taylor third, and Keppel fourth. On our arrival at the top, we hoisted the Union Jack which we had with us, on the end of a boat hook, and joining hands gave three hearty cheers. By the time we had reached the top it was well known in the town of Port Louis, and to the squadron, that we intended to attempt to scale the Peter Botte. All our friends were on the look out, and on the flag appearing on the top of the mountain, the " Undaunted " frigate, and the batteries in the town, fired a royal salute.

" I forgot to mention that there is a legend in the Isle of France, that a Dutchman, named Peter Botte, succeeded in reaching the summit of the mountain called after him, but broke his neck in coming down.

1832 It is also said that a Frenchman accomplished the feat, and having planted a flag, returned in safety. I much doubt the truth of these stories, more especially as the French account gives a list of the number of yards of rope, &c., &c., which he is said to have carried on his back, and which would weigh as much as, or more than, any man, in these degenerate days, could lift. It also states he sunk his flagstaff into a hole which he made in the rock. We looked very closely for this hole, or for any trace of man having been there before, but in vain.

"Before making the descent, Lloyd and the two others set about making a hole in the top of the rock, to admit our flagstaff. We then made the blacks tie a rope to a ladder which had been left on the shoulder by Lloyd and Dawkins (Mil. Sec.) on their former unsuccessful excursion; this we intended to be the lower portion of our flagstaff. The hole having been made in the rock, we fixed it in firm, having previously tied the boat hook to the top of it. Having done this, we descended, cutting away, or bringing with us anything which might be of use in a future ascent."

On the 12th of September, the regiment marched to relieve the 87th Royal Irish Fusiliers, then stationed at Mahébourg, and detachments were sent to Souillac, Réduit, Curepipe, 22 Mile Post, Point Colville, and Isle de la Passe.

On the 15th of November, 1 lieutenant, 1 ensign, 1 serjeant, 1 drummer, with 58 rank and file, arrived on board the "Arab" transport from Cork.

On the 4th of December, the officers of the regiment appeared in coatees laced with gold, epaulettes, &c., to correspond, in conformity with General Order, Horse Guards, 2nd of August, 1830. The alteration from silver lace to gold, entailed a change of buttons, breastplate, and coatee skirt ornaments.

The buttons were simply changed from silver to gilt.

A gilt breastplate, with gilt ornaments, was now adopted. This plate was oblong. In the centre, on crimson velvet, was the "Lion" encircled by a garter pierced with the motto ("*Honi soit*," &c.), over blue enamel; the garter was surmounted by a crown. This breastplate was worn till the introduction of the tunic.

Officers' Skirt Ornaments.—Embroidered in gold on red cloth. Grenadier company, **1832** a grenade 3¾ inches long. Light company, a bugle. Battalion companies, a Star of the Order of the Garter (same length as the grenade). The garter, and centre of ornament in which "29" was worked, were of dark blue velvet. The skirt ornaments of the non-commissioned officers, rank and file, were of metal. Those of the Battalion companies, the flat pewter regimental button, with a small "29" in centre, and a narrow circle round the numerals.

The Flank companies wore metal grenades, or bugles, as the case might be. These several skirt ornaments were worn till the introduction of the tunic.

Circular Memo, Horse Guards, 16th January, 1833.—The grey cloth trousers of **1833** officers, non-commissioned officers, and privates of regiments of infantry, to have a red stripe down the outward seam. The above alteration to take place from the 1st of the ensuing year. [*Vide 1 April, 1835.*]

On the 16th of May, H.E. Major-General Sir William Nicolay inspected the regiment at Mahébourg, and made the following remarks in his report:—

"The silver-laced coatees are still in wear until the whole of the officers shall have the new coatee completed.

"The officers' clothing and appointments are all supplied by the regimental tradesmen, viz., Mr. Hibbert and Mr. Prosser.

"Men's accoutrements, good, but not according to regulation. It appears, however, by authority from the adjutant-general, dated 2nd May, 1829, they are permitted to be worn until the regiment receives a fresh supply.

"There are 2 blacks, the last of the corps of black drummers."

On the 6th of September, 1 lieutenant, 1 ensign, with 32 rank and file, arrived from Cork on board the "Voyager" freight ship. On the 27th inst. the regiment relieved the 9th Foot at Port Louis, and was joined the following day by the Souillac and Seychelle detachments. Whilst stationed here detachments were sent to Grand River, N.W., and Réduit.

1834 By Circular Memo., Horse Guards, 31st May, 1834, an approved pattern of forage cap for officers "of blue cloth for the grenadier and battalion companies, of dark green for the Light company," was ordered to be adopted [*v. 11th January, 1836*]; that of the battalion companies had a small "29" encircled by a wreath of laurels, embroidered in gold in the centre of the black silk oak-leaf band which was round the cap; the Grenadier company an embroidered grenade, with "29" in silver on the centre of the ball; Light company, a bugle, with the number of the regiment in the centre.

The gold and crimson shoulder cords hitherto worn with the undress frock coat, were by General Order, Horse Guards, 4th June, directed to be abolished, shoulder straps of blue cloth, laced round with regimental lace, with metal crescents, being substituted.

The rank of a field officer continued to be denoted on the shoulder strap, by the addition of the crown, or star badge. Officers of the Flank companies wore a silver grenade, or bugle (according to the company to which they belonged) within the crescent. In undress, the sword was once more worn suspended from a black patent leather waist-belt, with snake clasp. The coatee of this period was ordered to be scarlet, with two rows of uniform buttons, ten in each row, which by the 29th were worn in pairs: the distance between the rows at the top was 3 inches, at bottom 2½ inches, Prussian collar, with two loops and small uniform buttons at each end. Scarlet slashed flap on the sleeve, with four loops and large buttons; two large buttons and four short twist loops at the waist; white kerseymere turn-backs and skirt linings.

Collar and cuffs of the regimental facings.

The bullion on the epaulettes varied in length and size, according to the officers' rank.

Officers of the Flank companies wore "wings," with a silver grenade, or bugle, on the centre plate.

Chaco of black beaver, 6 inches deep, lacquered sunk top, 11 inches in diameter, and with gilt scales on the sides.

Feather, white upright hackle, 8 inches long, with a gilt socket.

Trousers.—15th October to 30th April, Oxford mixture, with red stripe down outward seam.

,, 1st May to 14th October, white linen.

On the 1st of August the serjeants of the 29th appeared on parade for the first time with "fusils," in accordance with General Order, Horse Guards, 31st July, 1830.

On the 25th of October, 1 captain, 3 subalterns, 1 serjeant, and 4 privates arrived from England on board the "Arab" freight ship.

The Circular Memo. relative to the adoption of laced shoulder straps with the blue **1834** frock coat was received on the 6th of December.

The following description of the dress of the 29th was given by Major Murchison :—

"4 Almorah Road,

"Jersey, 4th March, 1877.

"Dear Everard,

"In reply to your request, I have much pleasure in giving you, as far as my memory will serve, a description of the gorgeous dress of our black drummers. When I joined the 29th* there were three black drummers time beaters in the band, viz., Geo. Carvell, Big drummer; Peter Askins, Kettle drummer; and Geo. Wise, Tambourine beater; each on Sundays and state days, such as General's inspection, &c., was dressed as follows—A muslin turban with a silver crescent in front, surmounted with a scarlet hackle feather 12 inches long, with silver cord and tassels, entwined round the turban. A silver-plated stock for the neck which opened with clasps and fastened behind. Yellow cloth jacket, hussar fashion, trimmed with black fur on collar and cuffs, the breast was embroidered with black silk cord, and three rows of silver buttons in front. This jacket was worn open.—The waistcoat was of white cloth embroidered with crimson silk cord, and had a row of silver buttons down the front.—A yellow and crimson silk sash round the waist.

"They also wore Turkish scimitars, brass scabbards with sling waist belts. The pantaloons were scarlet with a broad silver stripe on the outside seams, and fitted tight at the knee. Yellow Hessian boots with large black silk tassels in front.

"The dress on other occasions was a bearskin busby (somewhat similar to what the R.H.A. now wear), with a yellow bag, worsted tassels and line, with a scarlet feather.

---

* Joined head-quarters of the regiment, 25th of October, 1834. Cr. Serjt. and Actg. Serjt-Major of Depôt companies from the 1st of March, 1831.

1834   "Jacket and waistcoat as above. Silver grey coloured trousers with yellow stripes down the outside seams. On all full dress parades the serjeants wore the cane (which was malacca and silver-mounted) secured under the left arm and fastened with a knot of light buff leather to the left breast of the coat by a plain silver-gilt button with "29" on it. On ordinary parades, they carried the cane in the hand. It was done away with in 1833.

"The Grenadiers wore the bearskin cap, 21 inches high, a large brass plate in front, brass scales worn under the chin, white hackle feather on the side white line and tassels.

"The officers' and serjeants' were of silver cord, and the rank and file of cotton.

"The Grenadiers wore white worsted wings, and immediately over the breast-plate was a brass grenade fusee case, about 3 or 4 inches long, and attached to it and extending under the right arm to the back of the pouch belt was a coil of buff leather cord. The slow match was made of twisted cotton cord, and was fastened to the belt with small brass grenades at top and bottom of the match. The brass match box, perforated with holes to allow the match to burn slowly, was made to grip the side belt with brass claws. On the pouch was a cypher surmounted by a crown† inside of which was a grenade and "29," and motto, with garter, '*Honi soit qui mal y pense.*'

"The Light company had a similar 'cypher' on the pouch, somewhat smaller, with a bugle, and motto as grenadiers; they also wore a waist-belt, fastened in front with a plain brass plate. They had green wings, and a green feather.

"The whole of the Battalion companies wore the 'Star' on the pouch.

---

† I have not been able to get any corroborative evidence with regard to this "Cypher" device of the Flank companies. Other old officers of the regiment say that the Flank companies wore a similar star as the battalion companies, with the exception of a grenade, or a bugle in the centre, instead of "29."

1834 " The Light company officers and serjeants wore a silver whistle, in front under the breast plate, fastened by a rosette and long green ribbon about half an inch in width.

" I may mention that the belts of the 29th were different to those of other regiments. The frog of the bayonet belt was not a fixture, it was a kind of circular swivel of buff leather, however odd, it was very awkward, but woe to the man of any other corps who should say a word against it. It was done away with in 1838.

" The breeches and leggings were abolished in 1823.

" A fly, like a frill, was worn by all, down the outside seams of the white trousers, 1½ inches wide; it was discontinued in 1834. God forgive me, many a time I cursed them as they interfered when shouldering from the order, the men's thumbs would often catch and prevent them shouldering all together.

" We were the last regiment to give up wearing the frills to the shirts; they were discarded in 1832. They were worn by all, in front of the stocks. The officers wore the frill in front of the coatee, with two or three buttons undone to allow the frill to come through the opening.

" At times the officers wore a gold gorget, which fell in front of the breast of the coatee, close up to the stock and fastened to the collar with yellow silk ribbon; when this was the case the frill was not worn. On all state occasions the *golden lions** were attached to the colour poles, at other times a spear head was substituted.

---

* Sir R. P. Douglas, who was an ensign, in the regiment from the 16th of March, 1820, to February, 1824, writes:—"To the best of my recollection the colour pole I carried very often was capped with a lion."—Major Richard Erwin *(vide* List of Quarter Masters), writes: "The colour poles had lions on the tops, similar to those worn at that period on officers' shako and breast plates; there was a screw at the top of the pole, which went through the brass plate on which the lion stood. I cannot remember what became of them. They were very heavy and tiresome to carry on the line of march."

Major F. Kneebone also corroborates the above statements.

From other accounts, it appears that these lions were occasionally used after the regiment landed in India in 1842.

1834   "The last time I saw the lions was, I think, in 1834; they were in the Qr. Master's stores, in a box with the Masonic jewels, &c., of the regiment.

"I think I have given you all the information you require, and hope it may be of some use to you.

"Believe me,

"Yours very truly,

"K. Murchison."

1835   Lieut.-Colonel Simpson, having caused the Mess Regulations which were drawn up when the regiment was stationed at Windsor, in 1792, to be revised by a committee consisting of Major J. V. Evans, Captains J. Davidson and R. Lucas, Lieutenants A. Hemphill and S. Palairet, convened a full meeting of the officers, at Port Louis Barracks, on the 21st of March, 1835, for taking them into consideration, and it was unanimously agreed that the new regulations then submitted should be considered the Standing Mess Rules of the 29th Regiment.

The following are extracts from the new Mess Rules:—

Public Officers.

3. The President, or Vice-President, if absent from mess, without having appointed a substitute, is to be fined one bottle of wine—and at the discretion of the Mess, on a repetition of the offence.

6. The authority of these officers is not to be called in question during the Mess.

The President.

1. It is the particular duty of the President to keep order and regularity at all times in the Mess Room.

3. In order to enable the President to keep up his authority, he **1835** is hereby empowered to inflict fines, not exceeding six bottles of wine, on any member or members, who may so offend or infringe any known rule, or custom of the Mess, although not particularly mentioned in the written rules.

4. Should any member prove refractory on being so fined, the President is to caution him against the consequences; but if that fails, he may repeat the fine as often as necessary, still repeating the caution before every addition made to the original fine.

Vice-President.

1. It is the duty of the Vice-President to sit at the foot of the table, where he is to pass the bottle, and assist the President in calling for Toasts,† and in keeping order and regularity.

The Mess.

4. Any officer, asking a private friend to the celebration of an anniversary, or other public dinner—unless by the sanction of the Mess Committee—shall forfeit six dozen ‡ of wine for each friend invited by him.

6. No conversation relative to bets, and fines, shall be carried on before strangers.

---

† The first Toast, the King or Queen, as the case might be, was proposed by the President, and on guest nights, when the wine was passed round the second time, the Vice gave, "The Custom of the Mess." The origin of this Toast is not even known to officers who joined the regiment over 50 years ago, and whose relations served in it many years before that. This Toast, it is said, was discontinued by order of the officer who was in temporary command of the 29th when stationed at Dánápur. He had but recently exchanged to the regiment, and set his face against this old regimental custom.

‡ Altered by a mess meeting held at Kasauli to six bottles.

1835

7. Any officer appearing at Mess, in any way unregimentally dressed, shall forfeit one bottle of wine for every deviation, and the President overlooking any such deviation shall himself suffer the penalty as well as the defaulter.

12. If the dog of any member, or that of his servant, comes into the room during Mess, that member shall forfeit one bottle of wine, whether the dog follows him or not. If proved that another member purposely enticed the dog into the room, the owner shall be acquitted, and the offender shall forfeit two bottles of wine.

20. No smoking allowed, at any time, in the Mess Room, nor in the Ante-room, until after the Mess is broken up. Any person infringing this rule will be fined one bottle of wine.—*(Added by Mess Meeting):* "This obnoxious practice is, however, so lamentably increased in India, it is permitted to smoke in the Billiard and Ante-rooms, except during the hour of meals. This rule does not apply to hookahs."

Bets.

1. All bets made in the Mess Room, shall be considered for the general good, and the loser, shall pay the Mess.

2. The better of odds is always to be considered the loser.

3. Any member arranging a bet in the Mess Room, and, endeavouring to evade the consequences by saying, "I will bet so and so, out of the Mess Room," etc., etc., shall be considered to have made the bet as much as if such words had never been used.

4. Bets not originally made in wine, shall be converted thereto, as soon as determined, and be recorded amongst the fines; provided that no bet be considered as incurring a loss of more than six dozen of wine.

5. The sum to be charged for all bets and fines shall be at the rate of five shillings a bottle.

6. The amount of all bets and fines to be placed to the credit of the Mess Room.

Fines.

1. In order to prevent all disputes about the period at which fines may be inflicted, the Mess is understood to be assembled, as soon as any three members meet in the Mess Room after the second drum or bugle has sounded, and continue until the President leaves the room.

2. Any member proposing another to be fined, shall, if it be decided against him, pay the same fine he himself proposed.

On the 1st of April, the new pattern grey cloth trousers, with red stripe down the outward seam, as prescribed by Circular Memo on the 16th of January, 1833, were issued to the regiment.

On the 1st of May, Sir Wm. Nicolay inspected the regiment at Port Louis, and by the Return of Accoutrements the serjeants are shown as being in possession of swords, sword and bayonet belts, pouches and pouch belts.

On the 11th, the regiment marched to Flacq, to relieve the 87th Royal Irish Fusiliers, and detachments were sent to the Powder Mills, Villa Bagne, Black River, Cannonier Point, Poudre d'or, Grand River, S.E., and Réduit.

Circular Memo, Horse Guards, 27th of August, abolished the feather plume worn by the officers, and the worsted one worn by the men, a worsted ball tuft being substituted, that of the Light company being green. [*Vide 1 April, 1836.*]

On the 9th of October, in consequence of the removal of the 9th Foot to Bengal, the head-quarters of the 29th returned to Port Louis, and the strength of the various detachments was reduced. " The close

1835 friendship," writes General Sir A. Borton, "which existed in 1833-34 between the 29th and my old regiment the 9th, when we were quartered together in the Mauritius, owed its origin to the traditions of Roleia; when, if I remember rightly, the gallant impetuosity of the 29th led them into trouble until timely supported by the 9th, when the two regiments were enabled to hold their own against long odds until victory crowned the efforts of our army, each corps losing its commanding officer during the fight. In the days of which I speak, such events remained in the memory of corps, long after they ceased to retain in their ranks any of those who had taken part in them."

Having some years ago been told by an old officer of the 29th, that in his time it was understood that the 9th and 29th were permanent honorary members of each other's mess, I took the liberty of writing to the P.M.C. 1/9th to inquire if there were any foundation for the report, and in answer received the following communications:—

" Wellington, Madras,

" 17th May, 1889.

" Dear Sir,

I have not been able to ascertain from the Officers now serving in the Batt. whether the 29th Regt. are permanent honorary members of our Mess; one of the Majors in the Regiment believes that one Regt. is, but he does not know which. Colonel Massey, late commanding the 1st Batt., has been written to, and if he does not know if it is the case, has been asked to make inquiries on the subject, and will write to you.

Yrs truly,

S. D. SHORTT,

Capt. P.M.C."

"Wessex Cottage,

"Winchester,

"June 11th, 1889.

"Dear Sir,

I have just been forwarded a letter from the 9th 'Norfolk' Regiment, in which I have been asked to endeavour to find out, if not able to reply myself, with reference to the fact 'whether any foundation for the report that on account of the 9th and 29th having been in the same brigade at Roleia, as well as in the Sutlej Campaign —the 9th Regt. conferred the privilege on the Officers of the 29th of being perpetual hon. members of the Mess of the 9th Regt.', as I only joined in 1846, just after the Sutlej Campaign. I have heard that such was the case—I knew that there was a very brotherly feeling between the two corps, but I have just written to Genl. Elmhirst, who was serving at the time in the Regt., who may throw some light on the matter, when I will communicate with you on receiving his reply.

Yrs truly,

W. P. TERRY,

Major, late 9th Foot."

"24th June, /89.

"Dear Sir,

I enclose a letter from Major-General Hawes, bearing on the subject of our correspondence, and I am writing to Captain Wallack to trace the matter, but General Hawes, I feel sure, comes nearer to the clearing up the question than either Generals Elmhirst or Borton. Please return the letter, and I will write on hearing from Captain Wallack.

Yrs truly,

W. P. TERRY."

[*Copy of General Hawes' Letter*].

"Holly Lodge,
"Lexden Road,
"Colchester,
"23—6—89.

"My dear Terry,

I have a vague recollection that the old 29th were permanent honorary members of our Mess, but whether dating from the Peninsula or at the time of the Sutlej Campaign, I cannot well remember.

The circumstances under which the close friendship between the Regts. in my time were as follows :—They relieved us at the hill station of Kussowlie* just before the war, when the comradeship existing between the Regts. at Mauritius (before my time) was renewed.

The 29th joined us the day after Moodkee by forced marches, and were almost destitute of baggage animals and tents.

We were comfortably well supplied as we advanced from the base of supplies at Umballa, and we shared our tents and animals to a great extent with them, and this of course tended to intensify the feeling of good fellowship already existing, and they were already, or were made at this time, permanent honorary members of our Mess. That there is no record of the fact in our books is easily explained, as all were left behind at Umballa with the Depôt, and we had no Mess equipage with us till some days after the battle of Ferozeshuhr, all baggage being packed at Moodkee on our advance to relieve Ferozepore, and which resulted in the battle of Ferozeshuhr.

I have little doubt that the permanent Mess books remained at Umballa until the end of the war, when all went to Meerut—but of this I am not sure.

---

* The head-quarters of the 29th reached Kasauli, 20th November, 1845.

"I think Capt. Wallack, now one of the Corps of Gentlemen at Arms, was a member of the Mess Committee about this time; he might remember more of the circumstances than I do. . . . . . "

Yrs truly,

G. H. Hawes."

"July 8, /89.

"Dear Sir,

I enclose some extracts from the letters I have received with reference to y^r letter. As Captain Wallack was not able to clear up the matter, I puzzled over my mind which way to turn, and I then remembered if Col. Hook was alive I might get some more tidings, so I wrote to the Army Agent for his address, if living, and enclose his reply. I know of no one else that can assist, and if all my efforts have in any way assisted you in your researches, I am very glad to have been able to be of use. One thing is very marked, that a most cordial feeling of comradeship existed between the 9th and 29th wherever they have met, and tho' the two regiments have not been stationed together for many years, yet I feel that the same feeling will never cease to exist. The extracts I have sent you will be forwarded to the head qrs. of the 1st Batt. 9th, the Norfolk Regiment, so that possibly the subject may be ratified.

Yrs truly,

W. P. Terry."

[*Copy of Extracts from Letters mentioned by Major Terry*].

Extract from a letter from Captain Wallack, late, 9th Regiment :—

"I am quite aware of the cordial feeling that existed between the two Regts. since the days of the Peninsula, but I am astonished that Sir A. Borton and Elmhirst, who were in the Rgt., should not remember anything about it."

Extract from a letter from Colonel Hook (Adjutant of the 9th Foot, in 1845):—

"With regard to your question about the 29th, they relieved the 9th at Kussowlie just before the Sutlej war. On the arrival of the 29th at Kalka, at the foot of the hills, there was such a scarcity of carriage that they could only send up one company at a time, and the 9th sent down one comp^y with the return coolies, so that it took some days before the relief was effected. During the time, they were honorary members of each other's Messes. The 9th Regiment kept up their Mess at Kussowlie till the last company and Hd Qrs left, and the 29th at Kalka, and a very jolly time we had of it. The 9th marched for Meerut taking over the 29th camp equipage, but were halted at Umballa, where a few days after we got the order to advance on the Sutlej: the 29th got the same order, but had to march without tents, &c., as we had taken them over, and which we saw little of during our advance. After the battle of Moodkee, the 29th caught us up, and of course we shared what we could with them, but they were in the 2nd div^n, and we in the 3rd.

"The very best feeling existed between the Regts., and I have heard the old officers often talk of the good fellowship at the Mauritius, and Roleia is a matter of history. I am unable to say I recollect if the 29th were made permanent honorary members of the Mess, but I can fully believe they might have been."

1836   On the 5th of January, 1836, 1 lieutenant with 14 rank and file, arrived from England, by the "Atlas" freight ship.

On the 11th, the officers appeared in the new regulation forage cap, as prescribed by Circular Memo, Horse Guards, 31st of May, 1834.

On the 23rd of January, the new regulation forage cap, as prescribed by Horse Guards Circular, 4th of January, 1834, was adopted by the regiment, and on the 1st of April the worsted ball tuft, as described by the Memo dated Horse Guards, 27th of August, 1835.

On the 2nd of May, the regiment withdrew its detachments and **1836** marched to Mahébourg, to relieve the 87th Fusiliers. Subalterns' parties were sent thence to Grand River, S.E., Souillac, Isle de la Passe, and three privates to Réduit.

By Circular Memo, Horse Guards, 10th of June, the following alterations were sanctioned in the make of the coat for the infantry :—Skirts were cut across, instead of being made in one piece with the body; bottom of each skirt five inches in breadth; the tops so cut that the coat rested on the hips, and the turn-backs were not seen when looking at a man in his front at the distance of two yards. Skirts to be rounded over the hips. Breadth of cuff 2¾ inches, its upper edge being even with the centre point of the slashed flap on the sleeve.—(*Vide 1st April, 1837*).

On the 20th of June, Captain John Weir, 1 serjeant, with 12 rank and file, all invalids, embarked for London, on board the "Doncaster." It is supposed that the ill-fated ship was wrecked about the 18th of July on the Agulhas Bank, about 70 miles N.E. of the Cape of Good Hope, and that all hands were lost, for nothing more was ever heard of the ship, and the bodies of many of the men picked up on the shore, were identified by their regimental buttons.

By General Order 525, Horse Guards, 20th of September, 1836, the white tape hitherto worn on the coatees of the non-commissioned officers, and the regimental lace § on those of the rank and file, were abolished; in the latter case plain white tape was substituted (*Vide 1st April, 1838*). The 29th retained its custom of wearing the "loops" in pairs, and with pointed ends.

Serjeants of infantry were directed to wear double-breasted coats, without lace, but with white epaulettes; those of the Flank companies to wear wings.—(*Vide 1st April, 1838*).

On the 4th of November, 2 captains, 3 ensigns, 1 serjeant, and 50 privates arrived at Port Louis, from England, in the "Stirling" freight ship.

On the 1st of April, 1837, the regiment took into wear coats made according to **1837** directions contained in Circular Letter of the 10th of June, 1836.

---

§ Drummers continued to wear regimental lace up to 1866.

1837 On the 20th of April, Sir William Nicolay inspected the regiment at Mahébourg, and reported on the *Colours* as being "rather the worse for wear. The men are encouraged to play cricket, fives, &c., &c."

Having been relieved by the 35th Foot, on the 19th of June the regiment marched to Port Louis, whence detachments were sent to Isle Bénitiers (a quarantine station), Black River, Flacq, Réduit, Cannonier Point, Fort George, and Fort William.

On the death of H.M. William IV., the following orders, dated the 20th of June, were issued from the Horse Guards :—

"Officers to wear black crape over the ornamented part of the cap or hat, the sword knot, and on the left arm. Officers on duty to wear black gloves, the sash to be covered with black crape; and a black crape scarf over the right shoulder. The drums to be covered with black crape, and black crape to be hung from the pike of the colour staff of infantry regiments."

The size of Colours was this year ordered to be 6 feet 6 inches flying, and 6 feet deep on the pike. The cords and tassels of the whole to be crimson and gold mixed. No regiment was henceforth to display a third stand of Colours. Any regiment having a third Colour as a mark of distinction, was ordered to abandon such claim.

Orders having been received for the regiment to return to England, it assembled at Port Louis on the 1st of December, and on the 5th was inspected by Lieut.-General Sir Wm. Nicolay, C.B., K.C.H., who caused the following General Order to be published :—

"Head Quarters, Réduit,

"Thursday, 7th December, 1837.

"*General Orders.*

"The troopship "Athol" having been reported ready to receive the head quarters of the 29th Regiment, the baggage will be embarked to-morrow at 6 a.m., and the troops at 4 p.m.

"The Commander-in-Chief, while he congratulates the 29th Regiment on its approaching return to Europe after so long a period of service in a tropical climate, cannot refrain from expressing the regret which he personally feels at its departure.

"His Excellency has considered it his duty to report to the **1837** General Commanding in Chief, in the highest terms, his opinion on the general state of the 29th Regiment, and has only to add the assurance of his most fervent wishes for the future welfare of all ranks of that distinguished regiment.

      (Signed) WM. STANLEY,

        "D^y Q.M. General."

Being relieved by the 12th Foot, the 1st division, with headquarters, consisting of the Flank companies and No. 1, under command of Lt.-Colonel Simpson, with the following officers, viz., Captains T. B. Hickin (*m*), and R. Lucas (Light company); Lieutenants Honble. W. F. Byng, J. O. Lucas, Wm. Hemphill, and G. L. Way; Ensign A. St. G. Stepney; Paymaster N. Farewell; Adjutant A. T. Hemphill; Surgeon C. T. Ingham, M.D., embarked for England on the 8th of December, on board H.M.S. "Athol."

Having touched at Cork on the 1st of March, 1838, this division **1838** landed at Plymouth and marched into the citadel on the 9th, where it was joined the same day by the Depôt companies, under command of Major J. Walter.

The 2nd division (consisting of Nos. 2, 3, and 4 companies, with Captains Alex. Sharrock, C. E. Eaton, and H. Blunt; Lieutenants S. H. Palairet, G. Brown, Tho. A. Gerard, and Assistant-Surgeon P. Robertson, which, under command of Major Evans, embarked on board the "Parmelia" transport, on the 14th of February, arrived at Spithead on the 31st of May. Disembarking on the 4th of June it marched to Cumberland Fort, but a few days later re-embarked on board H.M. steamer "Messenger," for conveyance to Plymouth, where it joined the head-quarter division on the 9th.

Reserve, or Depôt, Companies, 1826 to 1838.

1826
Depôt
On the 27th of April, 1826, previous to the regiment leaving Kinsale, Major Robert Stannus, Captains A. Richardson, J. Weir, G. Gosselin, and R. Lucas, Lieutenants Thos. Biggs, J. Lacon Akers, Geo. Foskey, Geo. Congreve, and Wm. H. Shippard; Ensign A. T. Hemphill, actg. adjt.; Assistant-Surgeon Geo. Dunlop, 12 serjeants, 4 drummers, with 205 rank and file, were selected to form the regimental depôt on the embarkation of the 29th for foreign service.

The above details left the head-quarters then stationed at Cork, for Bantry on the 1st of June, whence on arrival, detachments were sent to Clonakilty, Macroom, Skibereen, Bere Island, and Whiddy Island.

On the 28th of September, the 1st division of the Reserve companies commenced its march from Bantry for Killarney and Listowel. The 2nd division, with head-quarters, left on the 2nd of October for Tralee.

1827
In January, 1827, there were detachments at Blennerville, Tarbert, Carrig Island, and Listowel. On the 28th of May, these detachments having been withdrawn, the Reserve companies marched for Buttevant, whence, on the 4th and 5th of September, they proceeded in two divisions to Boyle, and detached parties thence to Carrick-on-Shannon and Keadew.

Major R. Stannus having retired from the service towards the end of November, Major Wm. Elliot succeeded to the command of the Reserve companies.

By special desire of Lieut.-General the Right Honble. Sir John Byng, K.C.B., G.C.H., the Reserve companies were directed to march to Cork, for conveyance to England. Leaving Boyle, in two divisions on the 8th and 9th of February, that under the command of Capt. Richardson, proceeded by Fermoy and Ballinacorra, to the Cove of Cork, where, having embarked on board the "Amphitrite" transport, it sailed for Plymouth, where it arrived on the 2nd of March. The 2nd division, with head-quarters, under command of Major William Elliot, on reaching Cork on the 27th of February, went into barracks and did garrison duty until the return of the transport. **1827 Depôt**

The Reserve companies were now quartered together in the Granby Square Barracks, Devonport, but early in October they moved to the Longroom Barracks, Stonehouse.

In July, Captain A. Sharrock, Lieut. G. Congreve, Ensign Uriah Boyd, Assistant-Surgeon P. Robertson, 1 serjeant, and 55 rank and file, sailed to join the service companies in the Mauritius.

This draft, under command of Captain J. Weir, had left Ireland for Chatham, early in February.

On the 26th of May, 1829, Lieut. R. Beaufoy, Ensign P. Groove Beers, 1 drummer, 20 rank and file, embarked at Plymouth on the " Amity " transport for passage to the Mauritius. **1829**

On the 1st of April, 1830, a draft of 1 serjeant, 22 rank and file, sailed on board the " Sir Joseph Banks " to join the service companies. **1830**

Being ordered to Ireland, the Reserve companies embarked on the 19th of November, on board the " Sir William Fawcett " steamer for Dublin, and on disembarking six days later, took up quarters at Pigeon House Fort, and formed part of the Dublin garrison, then commanded by Major-General Sir Edward Blakeney, K.C.B.

Orders being received to complete the establishment of the regiment to 740 rank and file, about the middle of December, recruiting parties were sent to Armagh, Castle Dawson, Coleraine, and Omagh, in addition to similar parties already at Worcester and Sheffield.

On the 19th of May, 1831, being relieved by the Depôt of the 1st battalion 60th, the Reserve companies marched to the Beggars' Bush Barracks. **1831**

DD

1831
Depôt
In August, a detachment, under command of Captain Hickin, with Ensigns C. Adams and Wm. Hemphill, proceeded to Pigeon House Fort.

On the 30th of September, No. 1 company, with Captain Shippard and Ensign J. O. Lucas, marched from Dublin for Cavan, and No. 2 for Armagh, where it was joined a few days later by the head-quarters, with Nos. 3 and 4 companies.

When on the 12th of October, the head-quarters moved to Newry, No. 4, under command of Captain R. Lucas, with Ensigns C. R. Storey and E. H. Moore Kelly, was detached to King's Court. Captain Shippard's company, which rejoined head-quarters on the 1st of November, proceeded the next month on detachment to Armagh.

1832
On the 20th of February, 1832, the King's Court detachment rejoined head-quarters. These left Newry in May, and arrived at Belfast on the 12th inst. Two companies were now sent to Downpatrick.

On the 5th of June, Lieut. Edward Bayly, Ensign Lucas, with a draft of 1 serjeant, 1 drummer, 60 rank and file, embarked at Cork on board the "Arab" transport for passage to the Mauritius.

On the 13th of July, Major Elliot being promoted on the half-pay unattached, Major John Walter was appointed to the command of the Reserve companies, but did not join them till the 12th of September.

On the 16th of July head-quarters and 2 companies left Belfast *en route* for Cork; the following day the Downpatrick detachment marched for Newry, where, having joined the head-quarters, the Reserve companies, under command of Captain Hickin, continued their march *viâ* Cahir to Spike Island, Cork Harbour, which was reached on the 4th of August. Here but a short stay was made, for on the 27th, they moved into Cork Barracks.

On the 7th of November, Captain Shippard, Ensigns Storey and G. L. Way, &c., &c., proceeded on detachment to Mill Street, whence in January, 1833, they marched to take up quarters at Milltown and

Kilorglin, Co. Kerry, and on the 28th of April following rejoined head-quarters at Cork. **1832 Depôt**

On the 14th of December, Captain Hickin, Ensign Kelly, &c., &c., proceeded on detachment to Ballincollig, but rejoined head-quarters on the 3rd of January, 1833.

On the 9th of May, Lieut. A. T. Hemphill, Ensign Wm. Hemphill, with 32 rank and file, embarked at the Cove of Cork on board the "Voyager" freightship to join the service companies. **1833**

After the passing of the Irish Reform Act on the 7th of August, 1832, disturbances took place in many parts of the country, which rendered it necessary, in 1833, to proclaim martial law in many districts.

On the 2nd of June, a detachment of the 7th Dragoon Guards, 1 captain, 2 subalterns, 3 serjeants, and 65 rank and file of the 29th Foot (under command of Captain Lucas), together with a force of police, proceeded to Midleton, co. Cork, in aid of the civil power in serving tithe processes.

As of late years some rather exaggerated accounts, appeared in Irish papers, of this affair, the following paragraphs are taken from *The Cork Mercantile Chronicle*, Wednesday, 5th June, 1833 :—

"The following account of this transaction appears in an evening contemporary, and is, of the conflicting statements we have seen, the one most entitled to attention.—It appears that the Rev. Dr. Austen sent for the military on Sunday evening, and Monday morning Captain Hoare, M. Cummins, junr., Esqre., and Captain Nangle, proceeded with about 150 of the 29th Regiment, 30 of the 7th Dragoon Guards, and 5 policemen, to the house of a man named Power, on whom a subpœna was served without the slightest resistance. They next went to the house of a person named Butler, and having found the people much excited, and likely to offer resistance, some of the soldiers of the 29th Regiment were ordered to go up to the hill which was situated above the house, and the remainder of the regiment was desired to

1833
Depôt remain before the house, where the people were collected. Captain Hoare having in vain remonstrated with the people, and entreated them to disperse, the Riot Act was twice read, after which the soldiers and police fired, when one of the men on the hill belonging to the 29th regt. fell. It is not ascertained whether or not an order was given by the Magistrates to fire, but it is believed, from the firmness and clemency which the soldiers observed towards the people during the day, that they discharged their guns over their heads for the purpose, if possible, of intimidating them, and inducing them to retire to their houses. The fact however is as I have stated, namely, that the soldier fell accidentally by the shot either of the police or his companions. I can give no fuller account at present, but you may rest assured that the circumstances which I have stated are the most accurate that can now be collected, and gathered from the most impartial and unbiassed individuals who were present at the transaction."

Friday, June 7th, 1833.

THE CARRIGTOHILL AFFRAY—CORONER'S INQUEST.

" The first witness, George Witkins, private 29th Regiment, who, being duly sworn, and examined, said : I know the lands of Rossmore ; I was on duty there last Monday with part of my regiment ; we were all under the command of Captain Lucas ; and in consequence of seeing the people disposed to resist, near the house of a person living at Immogeesha, he ordered our party to divide, directing some of us to proceed to the hill above the house, while he commanded others to remain in the plain before it. The people immediately commenced throwing stones, and I think there were about 100 thrown before the firing commenced. There were five or six shots fired, when I turned to the rear and desired the men to stoop, and on turning round, I heard a ball whizz by me, and saw the deceased, who was directly in my front, fall dead. These shots must, I expect, have been fired by the party placed before the house. I think we were about a hundred yards from the party on the strand. I cannot say by whom the shot was fired which caused the death of the deceased. There were drawn up on the strand four or five policemen, ten dragoons, and twelve of the infantry, all of whom fired together. . . . . . . Joseph Barry, Esq., M.D. : I examined the body of the deceased, Michael Maguire, and found his death to have been caused by a gunshot, which entered his right side between the fifth and sixth rib, penetrating the heart and wounding the lungs on either side, and passing through near the left breast. Captain Nangle, commander of the police, and Mr. W. Byng, of the 29th, having given evidence, the Jury retired for a short time, and on returning gave the following verdict—" That the deceased, Michael Maguire, came by his death on the 3rd instant, in consequence of a gunshot which entered his right side, and passed through his body —which shot was fired, either by the police or soldiery, in protecting a tithe process-server, and the Jurors further say that the homicide was caused by misfortune."

On the 15th of August the head-quarters of the Reserve companies proceeded from Cork Barracks to Spike Island, two companies, with Captain Hickin, Lieut. A. G. Alves, and Ensign Way, to Camden, and one company, with Captain Lucas and Lieut. G. Foskey, to Carlisle Fort. On the 2nd of September, the whole moved to Charles Fort, Kinsale, whence on the 19th of December, Captain Shippard, Ensign Kelly, 2 serjeants, with 51 rank and file, were sent to occupy the barracks at Clonakilty; these rejoined head-quarters on the 27th of March, 1834.

On the 12th of July, 1834, Captain Lucas, Lieut. the Honble. W. F. Byng, Ensigns Storey and Kelly, Serjt.-Major K. Murchison, and four privates, embarked at London on board the " Arab " freight ship for passage to the Mauritius.

On the 10th of November, Captain Eaton, Ensign G. Brown, 2 serjeants, 2 corporals, and 46 privates, were detached to Mitchelstown.

1834 In the Depôt Inspection Returns for this year is the first mention
Depôt of the men being in possession of Bibles, Testaments, and Books of Common Prayer, viz., 310 in possession, 5 in store, 59 required.

On the 18th of December, 100 men, with a proportion of officers, under command of Major Walter, were ordered to proceed to the parish of Gurthroe, county Cork, for the purpose of aiding the civil power in the collection of tithes; a small party of the 4th Dragoon Guards accompanied this detachment. On their arrival at the farm where the tithes were to be collected, it was found to be strongly defended, and several hundred of the peasantry, armed with sticks, lining the ditches in all directions.

The Riot Act being read, orders were given to the military to force an entrance, which was opposed in a most violent manner, several of the soldiers were knocked down, and their arms broken. At length it was found necessary to give the order to "fire," when several of the peasantry were killed and wounded.

The following detailed accounts of this sad collision are taken from the Irish papers :—

"*Dublin Evening Post*," Tuesday, 23rd December, 1834 (from "*The Constitution*" of this morning).

"On the morning of Thursday, the 18th December, the Revd. Archdeacon Ryder proceeded to distrain for tithes due to him from the parish of Gortroe (adjoining the town of Rathcormac). He was accompanied by two Magistrates, Captains Collis and Bagley, and by a small detachment of the 4th Dragoon Guards, under Lieut. Tait. They were subsequently reinforced by 100 men of the 29th Depôt, under Major Walter, and also by a very small party of police. For two or three nights previous to Thursday horns had been sounded on the hills throughout the country, and on the night immediately previous, large bodies of peasantry marched through various towns, distant eight, ten, and twelve miles from the threatened parish. A formidable plan of resistance had been evidently organised. On the approach of Mr. Ryder and his party to a place called Bartlemy's Cross, they were assailed by the countrymen on the hills, with hootings, and several stones were thrown.

"The military advanced without making any return to these hostile demonstrations. The country people then drew down from the hills, and in a dense body, surrounded the farm-yard, or haggard, of a widow Ryan, which had been previously blocked up with logs, stones, and carts with their axles so disposed that they could not be easily withdrawn. Here the entrance of the military and distraining party was resisted with every species of violence. The country people fought eagerly with spades, sticks, and stones. All was borne patiently by the soldiers for a considerable time, and frequently the widow Ryan was called on to pay the demand and put an end to the strife. The Riot Act was read three times, blank vollies were fired, all in vain. The country people gained courage from the passiveness of the military, and it was not till after every art had been tried to stop their savage fury, and that Major Walter and Captain Ailes,† with many of the soldiers, had been desperately wounded, and several of their muskets been broken, and 45 minutes from the first reading of the Riot Act, that the fatal order to "fire with ball" was given. On the bugle sounding a stop to the fire, and the smoke clearing away, 20 bodies were seen prostrate on the ground.

"The country people, who had, it is supposed, been persuaded by the agitators that the military would not dare to fire on them, frightened by this dreadful and unexpected slaughter, dispersed in every direction. A deathlike silence ensued. . . . The widow Ryan, who had been called on so often in vain, now came out and paid the demand, and all resistance immediately ceased throughout the parish."

---

† Lieut. W. G. Alves.

1835
Depôt

The following evidence was given at the inquest :—

"*The Cork Evening Herald*," Saturday, 3rd January, 1835.

CONTINUATION OF THE INQUEST AT GURTHROE.—ELEVENTH DAY.

"At 11 o'clock the Court assembled.

"Major John Walter, of the 30th* Regiment, being sworn, was examined by Mr. Wood : recollects Thursday, 18th December; was in command of the party which went out that day to assist in preserving peace according to order—the substance of which order was 'that he should proceed with 200* men of the 29th Depôt, and a proportion of officers and non-commissioned officers, to Rathcormac on 18th December, leaving their barracks at half-past eight o'clock, to enable them to reach that place by half-past ten o'clock on that day, when they would be met by the Rev. Mr. Ryder and Captain Collis, Magistrates, and under whose directions they were to act, for the preservation of peace, during the removal of some corn seized and distrained for tithe due in the parish of Gortroe and Dysert; Lieut. Tait, of the 4th Dragoon Guards, to accompany Major Walter ; the troops to breakfast before they started, as there was little prospect of their being detained more than two or three hours, provisions would not be required to be taken with them. —Signed, George Edward Jones, Lieut.-Colonel, commanding the garrison of Fermoy.' Witness took out that force and proceeded to the Tallow road. When the small body of Dragoons was detached from the main body, he saw a large concourse of people on the Tallow road ; Mr. Tait's party joined his in a minute or two after ; the people had sticks in their hands, and were speaking in a violent manner ; heard expressions used by them to the purport of which was that ' they'd pay no tithes'; the Riot Act was read ; heard Captain Bagley's name used when applauding him after he addressed the people ; he (Captain Bagley) addressed them in a long speech, to the effect that if they (the

---

* Errors in this newspaper; they are correctly stated in the other Irish papers.

people) continued in a body, they were breaking the law, and that he did not come among them but as a friend; he addressed them in a friendly manner; they did not disperse on Captain Bagley's addressing them; Captain Bagley then took a card out of his pocket, and told them he was going to read the Riot Act for their own good; Captain Bagley read the Riot Act; Captain Bagley addressed them again after the Act was read, telling them that now the Act was read, if they continued together, they would break the law; the people did not disperse after the second address. When he was going to read the Act, he desired the Witness to have the men fix bayonets, and after the Act was read he desired him to order the men to load; the troops then moved up a narrow lane to the widow Ryan's, on which the crowd moved across the fields, flanking his detachment in such a manner, that he had to send out flanking parties to protect his flanks from being broken; finding a number of them moving upon his left, he threw out detachments right and left to protect the troops, fearing an attack upon them; some of the people went through the fields flanking the troops, and others towards the haggart; when Captain Bagley was speaking, the mob shouted as if to drown his voice; when the troops moved the people cried out, ' Now to the haggart, now to the haggart, boys!!' Saw no women amongst the crowd; witness sent the cavalry in front down the boreen, and headed the infantry, and proceeded thence to the haggart; the cavalry in the first instance went towards the haggart, and the infantry halted at the widow M'Auliffe's, as he heard Mr. Ryder was going into the haggart; sent the cavalry on in front as an advance guard, as he thought it necessary; part of the infantry then passed the cavalry; at this time, witness, seeing a number of people lining the wall of the haggart, and fearing they might close on his party, he threw out skirmishers on the opposite potato field to keep his retreat clear; he did so for the protection of his men; he will not say at that time he did so from the demeanour of the people, but from their great numbers and from their previous demeanour he thought it expedient to keep a place open for retreat; when in the act of throwing

1835 Depôt out the flanking parties, he heard Captain Bagley call out, 'Send up men to the front;' he then ordered a detachment to move forward; and when he came to the entrance of the haggart, he saw a cart across the entrance; saw a dense crowd in the yard; all with large sticks in their hands; the sticks were not as large as the handle of a spade, but they were very large; when Captain Shippard moved up with the detachment, Captain Bagley was in the act of addressing the people; there were certainly in the yard at the cart, about 150 people as closely chucked together as possible; Captain Bagley at this time begged of them to disperse, and allow the military to go through without opposition; and the people did not disperse on Captain Bagley addressing them; they said they would not disperse, 'there should be blood before a soldier should enter,' and that 'they would pay no tithes;' Captain Shippard's party was then at the boreen side of the cart; the people, at the time they were making use of the expression 'that there should be blood before the soldiers should enter,' were striking the cart with their sticks; Captain Bagley then said, 'Major Walter, you must force an entrance.' Witness then ordered the men to charge and disperse the crowd; he said, 'Charge and disperse the crowd.' Captain Shippard, who headed the party, got on the cart, and was immediately thrown back, and two or three of the men in the same manner; five men might charge abreast at the spot; the opposition at this time was most violent, the bayonets were struck and many of them bent, so much so that he was obliged to call up more men to the spot; every exertion was used at this time to force an entrance; then Captain Bagley said, 'Major Walter, you must force an entrance, you must fire;' previous to that he saw but two or three stones thrown; every possible exertion had been made with the bayonet, the stones were thrown from the yard by the people at the military; every exertion that could be made by soldiers to force an entrance with the bayonet had been resisted; after the fresh party was brought up, witness was struck by a stone; after he had received the order to fire, from Captain Bagley, he directed his men to fall back, determined to do everything in his power to avoid that last alternative, and effect his object without it; he (Major Walter) spoke to the people for two or three minutes, 'begging of them for God's sake, to disperse, and allow the soldiers to pass quietly; that they had heard the Magistrate give the order to fire, and he assured them on his honour he had balls in the muskets, and fire he must;' at this they flourished their sticks and swore 'the troops should never enter without loss of life on either side;' this was spoken in English, but there was a good deal of Irish spoken, which he did not understand; in speaking he held a small switch in his hand, to show he was a peace maker, not wishing to hold his sword for fear they might think he was menacing them, but they struck the switch, and broke it; finding his efforts had no effect, he again desired the military to charge and force an entrance, but in the same manner they were repelled, several of the bayonets being again bent; it was then suggested to him to take the wheel off the cart, by one of the soldiers, when he desired them to 'do it, my men;' they attempted it, but the blows were so violent at their heads that they had to desist; the term was, 'take the linchpin out of the wheel;' he stated these circumstances to show that everything was done to effect an entrance; after trying to remove the wheel, he (Major Walter) again addressed them, when he received a blow from a stone on the shoulder, which cut his coat and bilged his brass epaulette; at this time several of his men were in such an irritable state, from blows they had received, that he determined to take some other step; they were so irritated that two or three of them were cocking their pieces, on which he called out 'For God's sake, men, do not fire,' and they immediately resumed their position at the charge; from the time Captain Bagley desired him to 'fire' to this period was about twenty minutes; cannot say whether it was his own suggestion, or suggested to him that he might force an entrance into the haggart, and force their flank; believes he took the idea from seeing Captain Bagley endeavour to enter there; he desired Lieut. Alves to go round with his party to another part, so that the people might move from the cart to oppose Lieut. Alves, and then give him an opportunity of entering at the cart;

1835

Depôt

1835 Depôt his order to Lieut. Alves was, to force them with the bayonet; he did not attempt it, and after some time Lieut. Alves got upon the ditch; at this time part of the people were facing the haggart ditch, and another party of them inside the wall facing M'Auliffe's house; calls both of them walls from being built with stone; saw the soldiers attempt to get into the haggart; on the instant the troops succeeded in getting the officer (Lieut. Alves) on the ditch; every one of the soldiers made a simultaneous attempt to fight on it, but they were repelled and thrown back; as fast as the soldiers got on the ditch they were knocked off; in fact, he should not say they got on the ditch, for as soon as their hands were on the ditch, they were forced back; at this instant he saw Lieut. Alves with his sword in the defensive position; at first they let him get on the ditch, but when the people saw the soldiers endeavour to get up, there was a dreadful rush of the people against them, which forced them back; the entire crowd in the haggart rushed towards Lieut. Alves' party; at this moment the noise and excitement were immense; saw Lieut. Alves opposed to 40 or 50 with his sword, and his men not able to back him, he was standing on a height on loose straw; witness then felt, if he was knocked down, that the consequence might be fatal to Lieut. Alves; he then turned round to Captain Bagley, who was standing by his side, and said, 'Captain Bagley, you see I can't force an entrance without firing;' he replied, 'Then you must fire,' upon which he gave the word 'Fire!' He did not give the word, 'ready, present,' feeling that if he did so every man would feel it his duty to come down to a level and take aim, but left it discretionary with them, thinking that, if two or three of the people were wounded or killed, it would have the desired effect; at that moment he directed his attention towards the car, to see what effect the fire would have, and saw the opposition at the car as violent as ever; it is impossible to say how many soldiers fired; the first fire was into the haggart, the opposition at the car continuing as violent as ever; Captain Shippard then addressed the witness and said, 'Major, must I fire?' when witness said, 'You must;' the soldiers at the car fired, and he immediately ran up to see the effect, in hopes that they had gained their object; on coming up he saw the crowd coming in as thick as ever; the crowd opened first after the fire, but closed in immediately as thick as ever; at this instant, a second fire was given; he saw then eight or ten men flourishing sticks at the cart; he then cried out, 'Advance!' and called out as loud as he could, 'Cease fire;' that was in the boreen; he was then at the rear of his men; some stray shots were going on at the time he was crying out 'Cease fire,' but the bugler came up to him, and he ordered him to sound 'Cease firing;' he sounded, and only one stray shot, he thinks, was fired just as the bugle ceased to sound; he then ordered the cart to be removed, and directed the cavalry to move up; he then got into the yard, and found three bodies lying at the cart; the cavalry moved into the orchard field; the bodies were dead; heard no firing in the yard; finding the people had gone from the farm, he desired his men to form entirely round and keep possession of it; when giving this order a policeman came up and said they (the people) had formed at the back of the orchard field, at the north end, and were taking up stones; looked towards it, and saw heads; at this time a Magistrate [thinks it was Captain Collis] came up and said, 'Major Walter, form your men up in the field;' he said 'No! I'll surround the farm, and keep what I have got, for if I leave it, they'll take it again, and I'll have the same work to go over,' fearing the people would come up from another, where they were, and take possession of the yard; heard no shots fired in the orchard field; is sure there were not any; had not compelled his detachment to surround the farm when Mr. Ryder came up and said, 'Major Walter, you may draw off your men—the tithe is paid, or settled,' cannot say which; he then retired; from what the policeman said, he thought it was a necessary precaution for the protection of his men to throw out flanking parties; was standing within five or six yards of the stable when he gave the word 'Fire!' There was an interval of half an hour from the time Captain Bagley gave the first order to fire, until the second, which was obeyed; was standing close to the cart when the first order was given.

1835 —By Captain Bagley: Should not have withdrawn his men from the
Depôt widow Ryan's, by the direction of Mr. Ryder, had he not known him
to be a Magistrate.

"Cross-examined by Mr. F. M'Carthy: There were five officers and 100 of the infantry, an officer and nine dragoons, three foot police, chief of police, and his mounted orderly. * * * * As the soldiers attempted to get over the wall of the haggart, which was five feet high, the people struck at them; as the soldiers attempted to get in they were struck, but cannot say whether on their persons; he certainly saw them struck in the caps; several of the men told him they were struck; cannot say the soldiers' bodies were not injured, for he knows they were, but did not see them at the time they received the injuries—there were three companies out that day, divided into three divisions; Captain Hickin's company was broken up in making flank and rear guards."

The examination of this witness closed at five o'clock, when the Court adjourned till Monday.

Captain Wm. H. Shippard and Lieut. G. Alves, of the 29th Regiment, were then examined, the latter by Mr. Wood :—

"Remembers the 18th of last month * * The company he commanded was on the left; two companies preceded him, Captain Hickman's* in the front, and Captain Shippard's immediately preceding his (Lieut. Alves'); Captain Shippard's company was ordered up by two sub-divisions towards the haggart at different times; Captain Hickman* passed the word for 'More men,' when witness sent up his left sub-division and about four men of his right sub-division; when he halted his men he was at the extreme left of the southern gable end of the stable, fronting the stable; the wall of the haggart was thickly lined with people, and a great mob behind them; as near as he could judge the entire of them had clubs in their hands; thinks the wall was five feet high; it was not an easy matter to climb over the wall opposed

---

* Hickin's.

to such a mob; the straw inside the wall was nearly level with it; as soon as he came up he received orders from Major Walter to charge the mob with the bayonets and disperse them. * * * When he ordered his men to charge he desired those behind him to help him up on the wall; the mob that were immediately in front of him were kept back by the soldiers extending their bayonets whilst he was gaining the top of the wall; on getting up he immediately called to his men, 'Follow me—Charge!' One man, more desperate than the rest, lifted his stick as if to strike him, when he put out his sword to check the blow, and the man said, 'Do not run me through;' he replied, 'I will not, but I am ordered to charge, and you must keep back;' upon this they seemed more desperate. * * * None of the soldiers got on the wall; they said, 'we cannot get up,' on which he said, 'Major Walter, we cannot force this with the bayonets'; the demeanour of the crowd in the haggart, at this time, was particularly furious; the collision continued at the wall for about five minutes. Major Walter was immediately behind him at the time; the mob was particularly furious until the word 'Fire!' was given, so much so that not a single soldier was able to get on the wall. * * *"

After the Coroners' inquest, which lasted 14 days, at 6.30 on Wednesday, February 7th, the Coroners entered the Court, and having called for the counsel on both sides, informed them that there was no likelihood of the Jury agreeing as to their verdict. The Jury were then brought in, and their names called over. Thirteen were for returning a verdict of Wilful Murder, two of Manslaughter, and eight of Justifiable Homicide."

The following letter was afterwards received with reference to the duty at Gurthroe on which the detachment had been employed :—

"Horse Guards,

"Sir, "8th January, 1835.

"In reference to your several letters and the papers

1835 which they contain relative to the late melancholy collision at Gurthroe
Depôt and Rathcormac, I have received the General Commanding in Chief's directions, to request that you will convey to the officers and men employed on the occasion referred to, the satisfaction with which he has learned that their conduct, under circumstances the most trying, was such as to call for the most unqualified approbation on the part of the Magistrates.

" I have, &c.,

(Signed) Fitzroy Somerset."

" Lieut.-General
   The Right Honble
   Sir P. R. H. Vivian, Bart."

On the 29th of June and the 1st of July, the Reserve companies marched in two divisions from Fermoy for Tralee, where the Mitchelstown detachment joined them on the 2nd.

On the 5th of September, Lieut. H. Cosby, 1 serjeant, and 14 privates, embarked at Chatham on board the " Atlas " freight-ship for passage to the Mauritius.

1836 On the 25th of April, 1836, head-quarters and two companies of the Depôt marched from Tralee for Cork, where they arrived on the 28th; the remainder started on the 27th, and leaving a company under command of Captain Phillpotts with Ensign Jerningham, on detachment at Macroom, reached their destination on the 30th.

On the 3rd of May, the whole embarked at the Cove, on board the " Stakesley " transport for conveyance to Devonport, where on landing they occupied the Ligonier Barracks, and formed part of the Plymouth garrison under command of Major-General Sir Willoughby Cotton, K.C.H.

In June, a detachment of 1 lieutenant, 1 serjeant, 36 rank and file, was sent to Pendennis Castle; these returned to Devonport in October.

On the 26th of July, Captains Hickin and Eaton, Ensigns Way, Brown, A. St. G. H. Stepney; 1 serjeant, and 50 rank and file, embarked at Plymouth on board the "Stirling" freight-ship to join the service companies. **1836 Depôt**

Early the following year a subaltern's party, under command of Ensign E. Durbin, was detached to St. Nicholas Island. **1837**

During this summer, strong symptoms of opposition to the arrangements which had been made for carrying the provisions of the Poor Law Administration Act into effect, having made their appearance amongst large masses of the miners in Cornwall, it was found necessary to have detachments of military ready on the spot, and with this purpose, on the 31st of August, Major Walter, Captain Drake, Ensigns Durbin, and Donaldson, 3 serjeants, 2 corporals, and 49 privates, embarked on board the "Vulcan" steamer for Falmouth, but their services being found unnecessary, they shortly afterwards returned to Devonport.

On the 1st of March, 1838, the following officers were serving with the Reserve companies:— **1838**

Major—John Walter; *Captains*—Geo. Congreve, H. Phillpotts, W. W. Drake, and W. G. Alves; *Lieutenant*—Hen. M. Cuninghame; *Ensigns*—Fred W. Jerningham (acting Pay Master since 1st October, 1837), J. McNeill Walter (acting Adjutant since 1st September, 1837), Edm. Durbin, Alex. S. O. Donaldson, Geo. Molle, John Power, Honble. J. W. Fortescue, Lewis Coker; *Quarter Master*—T. Kneebone; and *Assistant-Surgeon*—J. Hawkey, M.D.

The head-quarters of the regiment having landed at Plymouth on the 9th, and marched into the citadel, its Reserve companies joined them there the same day.

CHAPTER XII.

1838 HORTLY after the arrival of the 29th in England, several of the most distinguished officers in the army came to Plymouth and were entertained by the regiment. Amongst those who were, or had formerly been, connected with it, were Lieut.-General John, Lord Strafford, G.C.B., G.C.H. (its Colonel), Major-General Sir John Buchan, K.C.B., and its late surgeon, Dr. G. Guthrie, who presented the regiment with a copy of his work on "Gunshot Wounds."

On the 1st of April, the clothing for the present year was taken into wear. The serjeants' coats were double-breasted, without braid, and with white epaulettes or with wings. The lace on the coats of the privates, white.

On the 5th of May, authority dated Horse Guards 1st May, 1838, was received from the General Commanding-in-Chief for the regiment to continue to wear the "*Star*" on their pouches. This star was similar to that worn at that time by the Coldstream Guards,§ with exception of the grenade, bugle, or "29" in the centre, according to the company which wore it. The correspondence relating to this

---

§ In the Zeughaus at Berlin, are the regimentals and accoutrements of some of the Coldstream Guards (*temp. 1788*), and on the oval, brass, cross-belt plate, of the Grenadier company, is engraved a Star, with St. George's Cross in the centre encircled by a garter inscribed "Coldstream Guards;" above this device is engraved, a grenade; on the flap of the pouch is a similar device, but with a detachable grenade.

An eight-pointed Star, with garter, is the distinguishing badge of Prussian, Russian, and Saxon Regiments of the Guard. The 29th (Worcestershire) is now the only British Regiment of the Line, permitted to wear a pouch ornament.

**1838
Depôt**

distinction, and authority of the General Commanding-in-Chief, is to be found in the Adjutant-General's Office.

" No. 6, Portman Square,
                    2 April, 1838.

" My dear Sir John,

" The 29th Regiment on its return to this country require new accoutrements, which will be ordered strictly in accordance with the Regulation pattern, but from time immemorial they have been allowed a " Star" on the pouch, an ornament, which the officers and men are very proud of; and are desirous for permission to continue. I hope such distinction may not be considered at variance with the Rules of the service, and that you will kindly apply to the General Commanding-in-Chief, for his permission, as I am very anxious to comply with the general wish of the regiment.

              Believe me, &c.,
                    (Signed)   STRAFFORD."

" The
    Adjutant-General
        of the Forces,
            Horse Guards."

" Horse Guards, 1st May, 1838.

" My Lord,

" I have had the honor to lay before the General Commanding-in-Chief, your Lordship's letter of the 2nd ultimo, and am directed to acquaint you, that under the circumstance therein stated, and in compliance with your Lordship's recommendation, Lord Hill is pleased to approve of the continuance of the ' Star ' on the pouches of the 29th Regiment; to which effect the necessary notification has been

1838 made to the Consolidated Board of General Officers, and to the officers appointed to inspect the clothing and appointments of the Army.

I have, &c.,

(Signed) JOHN MACDONALD,
A.G."

" Lt.-General

Lord Strafford, G.C.B.,

Colonel of the 29th Regiment."

Several years after this, whilst the regiment was at Moulmein, some correspondence took place between Captain Hugh G. Colvill[*] (commanding the Light company) and Lord Strafford, anent the origin of the *Pouch Star*. His Lordship's reply was as follows:—

" London,

26 August, 1854.

" Dear Sir,

I have great pleasure in answering to the best of my power your letter of the 18th June, but regret that I can give you but little information on the subject you wrote upon. When I joined the old 29th in 1800, Major Johnstone[†] who had served in it for many years, was the person we used to look to for records, but to the best of my recollection he could not inform us how we obtained the privilege of wearing the Star upon our pouches.

I think it was before the regiment went to the Mauritius, at half yearly inspection in Ireland, the General of the District reported them to the Horse Guards for having a Star on the Pouch, as contrary to the regulations, and they were ordered by the Commander-in-Chief to take

---

[*] Adjutant of the regiment from the 22nd of October, 1850, to July 29th, 1853, when promoted.

[†] George Johnstone, Ensign 29th Foot, 1st November, 1780.

it off, at which both officers and men were very much distressed, and the commanding officer wrote to me (it was either Sir John Buchan or General Simpson) telling me how much it was felt, and praying of me to intercede for retaining it, adding that the men offered to pay for it themselves, which the Captains of companies would not hear of. I hope you will believe that I was equally ready; I would not have allowed anyone but myself to be at the expense. I made a very strong application to Lord Hill, who kindly granted my request, the Adjutant General kindly helping, by telling him how much we valued the distinction, and his Lordship for his great regard both for the regiment and myself, made us all happy in retaining the ornament.

I am sorry to say this is all I can tell you.

Believe me to be,

Faithfully yours,

STRAFFORD."

On the 8th of May, a party consisting of 1 serjeant and 30 rank and file, under command of Lieut. H. M. Cuninghame, was detached to do duty at Pendennis Castle.

The Coronation of Her Majesty Queen Victoria having been fixed for Thursday, the 28th of May, all troops were ordered to be assembled on that day at their respective stations for the purpose of firing a "feu de joie."

Having read in the *United Service Gazette*, of the 26th of May, 1838, the following paragraph referring to the 29th Regiment, " It is understood that in a short time this distinguished regiment is to be made Fusiliers," I wrote to some of the surviving officers, who had, at that time, been serving with it, asking if there were any grounds for the above statement.

1838   Their replies were as follows :—

The first answer received was from Major Gregory L. Way, who served with the 29th from 1832-50.

"Wick Hall, Brighton,
March 30—86.

"Dear Captain Everard,

When quartered at Plymouth shortly after our return from the Mauritius in 1838, the offer of becoming Fusiliers was made, but declined by Colonel Simpson.

If a meeting of officers was held on the question, it must have been when I was on leave, for it was on my return that I first heard of the offer, and of the unanimous wish against any alteration or addition to the well known and well loved—29th.

Yrs truly,

GREGORY WAY."

The second reply came from Lieut.-General John McNeill Walter,* C.B. :—

"27 Holland Park, W.,
6 April, 1886.

"My dear Sir,

"I am in receipt of your letter of the 29th March—it will give me much pleasure to give you any information relative to the old 29th that I can recollect or may have noted. My father served with the Regt. for a long period. I was with him as a boy, and served in the Regt. from 1835 to '39. I have ever entertained the greatest regard for the Regt., which I consider one of the most distinguished in the Service—none in my opinion have a higher record.

---

* Lieut. Walter exchanged to the 90th Foot on the 8th of May, 1840.

What you read in the *United Service Gazette* is perfectly true. **1838** The Service companies of the Regiment landed at Plymouth on the 9th of March, 1838, from the Mauritius—the Depôt companies had been quartered at Mount Wise Barracks for two years previous. My father was in command of the Depôt comp^s and I was the Adjutant.

Colonel Simpson, who had been Adjt. of the Guards at Waterloo, received an invitation to dine with the Duke of Wellington at the Waterloo Banquet—and on his return it was notified to the Regt. that they could be made into a Regt. of *Grenadiers* or *Fusiliers* if they wished it—all of us juniors were anxious for it—but the senior officers were opposed to it, and it was declined. The reason I heard given was—that to be made a *new* Fusilier or Grenadier Regt. would distract from the great distinction that the 29th had earned. We Subs. were disgusted, as we would have been made 2nd Lieuts., and ranked over all Ensigns.

Amongst the officers opposed to the change were the following:—

Majors { John V. Evans.
{ John Walter.

Captains { Thos. B. Hickin (M).
{ Richard Lucas, Comd^r Light Company.

Lieut.   J. G. Weir.

There were many strange and grand old customs kept up in the old corps—At Mess we always dined with cross belt on and dared not take off our swords. Before all parades were formed,—guards paraded, picquets marched—a drum and fife beat off 'Hearts of Oak.'

After dinner—after the Health of the Queen was given, the Vice-President gave 'The Custom of the Mess'—this led to many questions when there were ladies at dinner.

1838   Do you recollect a very large and old snuff box* that the regiment had; have they it now? It used to afford great fun when any young fellow joined, as it was supposed for the time being to belong or to be held by the ugliest man in the regiment. For years it was held by Major . . . . . . Shortly after the arrival of the regiment from the Mauritius, it was decided to have a new service of plate, and that of the Service and Depôt companies joined. Each officer of the regiment, serving, received some small memento of the old silver. I got the enclosed [*a saltspoon, date 1802*] and have kept it in my desk ever since, and I now ask your acceptance of it.

    Sincerely yrs,

    J. McN. WALTER."

"Hd. Qrs.,

York, 20 June, '84.

"My dear Everard,

"About the year 1826 (I think) my father was to have got the command of the 29th, but he was given the 93rd instead. He often told me (he died a few years ago) that the Regt. was offered the distinction of being made Fusiliers or Light Infantry about that time. That is all I know. The Regt. had also black drummers. I wish I could give you more information.

    Yrs sincerely,

    H. G. McGREGOR." §

    Colonel the Honble. H. Manners Monckton, who in 1850 exchanged as captain to the 3rd Light Dragoons, says:—"After

---

* When the regiment was stationed in Jersey in 1875-76, Major Murchison used often to mention this snuff box. It is said to have disappeared about the time the regiment went to India, viz, 1842.

§ Now Col. H. G. McGregor, C.B., A.D.C.; half-pay the Worcestershire Regiment; exchanged to the 29th from the 17th Foot in 1869, as Captain.

watch setting 'Rule Britannia' was often played instead of 'God Save **1838** the Queen,' in memory of the 29th having served on board the fleet as marines;" and Major Lyle writes :—" For years after I joined *(1843)*, the drums alternate nights at tattoo, played off with 'Hearts of Oak,' which tradition said, was instituted to commemorate for ever, the action of the glorious 1st of June, 1794, in which our regiment had serious losses."

While mentioning these old regimental customs and toasts, it may not be amiss here to give two sobriquets* by which Col. Monckton, Surgeon-General Trousdell, and many other old officers of the regiment say, the 29th was known in years gone by: these were " The Old and Bold," and " The Guards of the Line."

On the 29th of May, Major-General Robert Ellice inspected the head-quarters of the regiment at Plymouth citadel, and reported :— " There is one black drummer, the last of a corps of black drummers. The arms are old and unserviceable; application for new arms will be made when the whole corps is assembled. The accoutrements of the regiment have always varied from other regiments. New accoutrements are now ordered for the whole regiment according to regulations, with the exception of the Star on the pouch, which is sanctioned by authority."

On the 1st of September, the new accoutrements were taken into wear by the regiment. In this supply the old regimental bayonet belt was discontinued, the new belt being of the regulation pattern.

Being relieved on the 17th and 18th of October, by the 46th and 85th Depôts, the regiment marched in two divisions from Plymouth citadel to Devonport, where it occupied the Mount Wise, George's Square, Picquet, and Granby Barracks.

---

* The "Vein Openers," "The Eversworded" "Two and a Hook," are also old regimental nicknames.

1838   On the 9th of November, Lieut. Brown, with 1 serjeant, 29 rank and file, embarked on board the "Devon" tender, for Pendennis castle to relieve Lieut. Cuninghame's detachment, which returned to Devonport the next day.

On the 29th, the funeral of Captain and Paymaster Farewell took place at St. George's Chapel, Stonehouse.

Early in December, orders were received to recruit to the full establishment of 739 rank and file.

1839   On the 5th of February, a detachment, under Ensign Walter, embarked on board H.M. steamer "Meteor" to relieve Lieut. Brown's party stationed at Pendennis castle. It rejoined head-quarters on the 12th of May.

On the 18th of February, five companies, under command of Major the Honble. C. A. Wrottesley, marched to Tavistock; the remaining five, under Major Hickin, proceeded to Plympton and Ridgeway, where they were billeted during the re-election of Sir George Grey at Devonport.

By Warrant, dated the 22nd of February, 1839, the universal pattern big star plate, worn on the chaco of non-commissioned officers, rank and file, was abolished, a round brass plate three inches in diameter, ribbed horizontally and edged with a raised wreath of laurel leaves, the whole surmounted by a crown, being substituted.

The Battalion companies had the regimental number in raised burnished numerals in the centre; the Light company, a small bugle above the figures. On the discontinuance of bearskin caps by the Grenadiers of the regiment, and adoption of the chaco, a similar plate to that worn by the Light company, but with a grenade in its centre in lieu of a bugle, was introduced. These chaco plates were worn up to 1855. A patent leather chin-strap, and a fall behind, was also, by the above Warrant, directed to be added to the hat. [*Vide 3rd of May, 1840*].

On the 23rd, the regiment returned to its former quarters, and on the 9th of April a detachment consisting of 1 serjeant, with 21 rank and file, under Ensign Molle, was sent to Nicholas Island; it returned to head-quarters on the 11th of May.

On the 30th of April, four companies which were in the Mutton **1839** Cove Barracks moved into Cumberland Square.

The unfavourable harvest of the two preceding years having occasioned much distress among the lower classes, the opportunity was seized by people of a revolutionary character, to excite the masses to riot and disorder. "Chartists," was the name assumed by a considerable body of the lower orders, who shortly after the passing of the Reform Bill in 1832, demanded a new Charter, or thorough re-organization of the Lower House of Parliament. In the autumn of '38, these people, armed with guns, pikes, and other weapons, held many large meetings in the North of England, and in '39 the country was so much disturbed by such assemblages, and the many excesses committed by the Chartists, more especially in the large manufacturing districts in the north, that the strong arm of law was found necessary to curb them. In the meanwhile these disturbances were extending further south, and on the 23rd of April, in consequence of intelligence received of a serious riot having taken place at Taunton, a detachment, under command of Major Wrottesley, consisting of three companies, viz., the Grenadiers with Captain Drake, Lieuts. Way and Cuninghame; the Light company, under command of Lieut. Byng; and that of Captain Congreve, with Lieut. Gerard; Assistant-Surgeon Hawkey, M.D., 6 serjeants, 2 drummers, with 104 rank and file, marched to that town, but its services being no longer found necessary, it was ordered to South Wales, where disturbances were threatened by the audacious conduct of the Chartists. Marching therefore to Bristol, it crossed thence by Packet to Newport, Monmouthshire, where it was received with welcome by the inhabitants, and billeted in the licensed houses of that town. Later on, one of the companies marched to the workhouse, there to be quartered. From an early hour on the 10th of May, the town was in a state of great excitement in expectation of the arrival of the Chartist leader, Vincent, who two days previously had been arrested at his house in London. The Mayor and Magistrates of the

1839 borough, attended by all those within a circuit of 20 miles, together with the Lord-Lieutenant of the County, were at their posts at 7 a.m., and proceeded to swear in special constables to the number of 500. The detachment of the 29th Regiment was under arms at daybreak. These preliminary arrangements having been made, the police arrested one Townsend, junr., and on the arrival of the Packet, Edwards, another notorious Chartist, was taken into custody. A slight and ineffectual attempt at a rescue was made. During the whole day the banks and shops were closed, business was at a standstill, and the utmost consternation prevailed throughout the town, as reports were rife that a large band of colliers would make an onslaught towards the evening.

Although public meetings were for a time abandoned, it was ascertained that secret organizations continued to exist. It was therefore thought advisable, in case of further disturbances in Wales, or the manufacturing districts of Wiltshire and Somersetshire, to have a force concentrated at Bristol to form a *point d'appui*. With this idea a detachment of artillery was ordered there from Woolwich, a troop of the 10th Hussars from Dorchester, and the 29th Foot from Devonport.

On the 8th of May, two companies under command of Major Hickin, marched for Bristol, where they arrived on the 16th; these were followed on the 13th by two other companies, under Captain Eaton, and on the 14th by the head-quarters and three companies, under command of Lieut.-Colonel Simpson.

Previous to this, Major-General Ellice addressed the regiment on parade in George Square, and expressed in the highest terms, his approbation of the general conduct of the corps during the period it had been under his command. On the head-quarter division reaching Ivybridge, Colonel Simpson proceeded on leave of absence, pending his exchange to half-pay, and Major Evans, who joined the head-quarters from leave of absence, took over the command. As the division was marching **1839** from the Cheddar Cliffs into Bristol, Ensign Walter, who was carrying one of the colours, being taken unwell, requested to be relieved; the Adjutant, Lieut. A. T. Hemphill, asked Major Evans' permission, on which the latter rode back, halted the battalion, and dismounting, took the colour, and carried it for some time, making known to the regiment that the last time he carried colours was as a volunteer at Roliça or Vimiera. That night Major Evans was taken seriously ill, and being shortly after sent to his sister's house, died there on the 2nd of July.

On arriving at Bristol, part of this division went into billets, and part occupied the Armoury in Stapleton Road.

After the arrest of Vincent, the Chartists in the neighbourhood of Newport being more quiet, the Light company, under command of Lieut. Byng, was ordered to rejoin head-quarters, and reached Bristol on the 4th of June. On the 19th, Ensign Power, 1 serjeant, with 25 rank and file, marched to Trowbridge; and on the 1st of July Ensign Croker, with 1 corporal and 30 privates, proceeded to Newport to relieve the Grenadier company. Captain Congreve's company, with Ensign Croker's party, remained at Newport till the 9th of October, when they both marched to join the regiment at Woolwich, where they arrived on the 17th instant.

The 29th was now ordered to Northamptonshire, but previous to its departure from Bristol, Col. Farmer, C.B., issued a Garrison Order, dated the 10th of July, expressing his approbation of the conduct of the regiment whilst stationed there.

The following day, Captain Alves, Lieut. Stepney, 1 serjeant, with 29 rank and file, marched for Trowbridge, where they were stationed till the 6th of October, when they marched for Woolwich.

On the 11th of July, three companies, under Captain Sharrock, and the next day, head-quarters and two companies under Major Wrottesley, marched for Weedon, where they arrived on the 18th and 19th.

1839   Major Hickin, with three companies and the following officers, viz., Captains Eaton and Phillpotts, Lieuts. W. Hemphill, Brown, Durbin, and Molle, remained at Bristol in the temporary barracks at the Armoury, till the 5th of October, when they marched for Woolwich, where they arrived on the 12th.

On the 22nd of August, orders were received for the establishment of the regiment to be augmented from the 12th inst. so as to consist as follows: 10 companies, 1 colonel, 1 lieut.-colonel, 2 majors, 10 captains, 12 lieutenants, 8 ensigns, 1 pay-master, 1 adjutant, 1 quarter-master, 1 surgeon, 1 assistant-surgeon, 1 serjeant-major, 1 quarter-master serjeant, 1 paymaster serjeant, 1 armorer serjeant, 1 schoolmaster serjeant, 1 hospital serjeant, 1 orderly room clerk, 10 colour serjeants, 30 serjeants, 40 corporals, 1 drum major, 13 drummers and fifers, 760 privates.

On the 6th of September, the head-quarters and the Flank companies marched into the Northampton Barracks. A detachment under command of Major Lucas, consisting of 2 captains, 4 subalterns, 1 staff, 12 serjeants, 1 drummer, and 242 rank and file, was left at Weedon.

On the 9th of October, Captains Weir's and Palairet's companies from Weedon, and the Grenadiers from Northampton, proceeded under command of Major Sharrock, by rail to Deptford and Woolwich. The next day, head-quarters from Northampton, under command of Lieut.-Col. Wrottesley, being joined at Roade by a detachment from Weedon, under command of Lieut. Walter, consisting of 2 subalterns, 1 staff, 5 serjeants, with 135 rank and file, proceeded by rail to London and Woolwich.

Writing on the 26th of April, 1886, Lieut.-General Walter said:— " I met the head-quarters at Roade, and marched with them through the City of London, and arrived at Woolwich barracks the same day. The officers with us were Col. Wrottesley, Lieutenant J. O. Lucas, Ensigns Fred Coventry, Geo. H. Jones, and Surgeon C. T. Ingham. We marched through Temple Bar, passed the Horse Guards, over Westminster Bridge, to Woolwich. I commanded, and marched with the leading com^y, but I could not say *for certain* whether our bayonets were fixed, but I feel sure the band played †—I at the time was under the impression that the same privilege had been granted to the Regt.

1839

Officer of—
"Battalion" Company.   "Grenadier" Company.

as to the Buffs, and for the last 45 years have mentioned this circumstance when speaking of the regiment, and it was never contradicted.

---

† In a previous letter this officer wrote—"and marched through the City of London, with drums beating and colours, *thus establishing our right to do so*—the same as the Buffs."

1839 I understood that it was Colonel Wrottesley's interest that settled the matter, his relations being connected with the city."

On the 1st of November, the regiment was inspected at Woolwich by Lieut.-General Lord Bloomfield, who the next day caused the following General Order to be published:—"The Commandant has great satisfaction in conveying to Lieut.-Colonel Wrottesley, the officers, non-commissioned officers, and privates of the 29th Regiment, his entire approbation, not only of their appearance in the field, but of the steadiness and precision with which the several manœuvres were directed and executed."

On the 30th, two companies, under Lieutenants Cuninghame and Walter, marched from Woolwich Barracks to join Major Sharrock's detachment at Deptford, and assist in performing the duties at the Docks and Victualling Yard.

On the 1st of December, the Grenadiers and No. 3 company proceeded to Deptford to relieve No. 2 and the Light company.

1840 On Serjeant Tyler being appointed bandmaster of the 69th Foot, Lieut.-Colonel Wrottesley and the officers presented him with a silver snuff box, on the lid of which was a representation of "Mazeppa on the wild horse," and the following inscription:—"Presented to Serjeant, and late Bandmaster, William Tyler, by the Officers of the 29th Regiment, on his leaving after a service of 21 years.—2 April, 1840."

On the 3rd of May, the new chacos, with a patent leather chin strap, instead of scales, were taken into wear.

Nos. 2, 5, and 8 proceeded on the 30th to Deptford to relieve Nos. 4, 6, and 7 companies.

Orders having been received for the regiment to proceed to Edinburgh, on the 4th of July, the head-quarters and seven companies, under command of Lieut.-Colonel Wrottesley, embarked on board H.M.S. "Apollo," 46 guns, for passage to Leith. Major Hickin's detachment, stationed at Deptford, being relieved by the 60th Rifles, embarked at Deptford Dockyard on board the Government steamer **1840** "Vesuvius." Having disembarked on the 10th, the regiment marched from Leith to Edinburgh castle, where it relieved the 78th Highlanders. Small parties under command of serjeants were now detached to Greenlaw and Leith.

On the 15th of August the regimental band attended the ceremony of laying the foundation stone of a monument to Sir Walter Scott, the Lord Provost of Edinburgh and the Grand Master Mason of Scotland commencing the ceremony, with the usual masonic rites.

It having been decided to present new colours to the regiment, **1841** General the Earl of Cathcart, who in 1797 was promoted from the colonelcy of the 29th to that of the Life Guards, was invited by Lord Strafford to perform the ceremony, but being unable to attend, sent the following reply :—

"Cathcart,
May 16, 1841.

"My dear Colonel Wrottesley,

"I lose not a moment in sending to you my best thanks for your letter of the 14th inst., and for the most obliging recollection and sentiments which you have so kindly expressed on the subject of my having belonged to the 29th Regiment.

There is no event in my life, that I look back upon with more pleasure, than the years I had the happiness to pass in that regiment which I never expected to leave, had it not been His Majesty King George the Third's gracious pleasure to move me to the Cavalry and to his Life Guards. I heard with great delight that the 29th were to be stationed at Glasgow, and was rejoiced to think that, that circumstance would place me within the reach of seeing them again; but my health will I fear not allow me to profit as much as I was in hopes. I still indulge myself in the expectation of doing so during the time you are stationed here. I fear I dare not undertake any active exertion, which however desirous I should be to place myself in relation with the

1841 regiment to which I shall never cease to feel the most affectionate regard, but which I fear I cannot hope to be able to perform, and I must beg of you my dear Colonel to accept the will for the deed, and to be assured of my most sincere regard and unceasing affection for the 29th, which I should be most happy to prove by any exertion of mine.

I will take as early an opportunity as I am able to express to Lord Strafford how much I am flattered and obliged by his proposal that I should have the honor of presenting to the regiment the new colors, which are to replace, in due time, those which I have often sworn fealty and been so proud to follow, as long as I had any right to that honor. Meanwhile accept the assurance of my sincere affection and regard.

(Signed) CATHCART,

General."

On the 17th of May, the regiment was inspected on the Bruntsfield Links by Major-General Lord Greenock, K.C.B., commanding the forces in Scotland.

On the 1st of June, the left wing, under Major Sharrock, marched from Edinburgh castle for Glasgow. Halting at Linlithgow that night, the following day two of the companies proceeded to Cumbernauld, and three to Kilsyth, and thence on the 3rd to Glasgow, where they relieved the 58th Regiment. The next day, Lieut. Brown went by steamer with 1 serjeant, 18 rank and file, to Dumbarton castle, where the detachment remained till the 29th of July.

The right wing and head-quarters, under Lieut.-Colonel Wrottesley, left Edinburgh *en route* for Glasgow on the 3rd of June.

On the 16th, Major-General Lord Greenock, in presence of a numerous and fashionable assemblage, presented new colours to the 29th, in the Queen's Park; his lordship's father, Lord Cathcart, though most anxious to be present, was unequal to the fatigue and excitement of so interesting a ceremony.

1841 After the new colours had been consecrated by the Revd. M. Aitcheson, Lord Greenock came forward, and in a forcible speech, in which he dwelt feelingly on the peculiarly strong tie which had bound him to the regiment from his earliest childhood, entered into a lengthened detail of its distinguished services since its formation (more particularly adverting to its brilliant achievements in the Peninsula, where on several occasions it received the high approbation of the Duke of Wellington and Lord Hill), and eulogised in warm terms its gallantry and discipline, both in the field and in quarters. Having passed some high encomiums on its present state and appearances, his lordship concluded by expressing his unqualified approval of its conduct during its stay in Scotland, and the great regret he felt at its approaching departure. His best wishes for its welfare and prosperity would accompany it wherever it went, and most welcome would be the contingency which should bring them together again at any future period. His lordship then proceeded to present the colours* to the two senior ensigns, G. H. M. Jones and J. W. Richardson, who received them kneeling.

Lieut.-Colonel Wrottesley then returned thanks to his lordship on behalf of the regiment, and said that while they regretted the absence of Lord Cathcart upon this occasion, it afforded them sincere gratification to receive their new colours from the hands of so distinguished an officer, the immediate descendant of one to whose exertions the 29th was indebted in no small degree for the proud distinction which it had

---

* Writing from the Junior Army and Navy Club, May 25th, 1887, Major Lyle says :— "The colours presented in 1841 were cut up in my presence at Aldershot, I think in 1860, and all the old officers who had seen active service under them got portions. The Colonel of that time, got permission to have colours made up by the schoolmistress, Mrs. Coleman—this was done, and they were attached to the staves. The regimental colour staff is shorter than that of the Queen's, as a bit was knocked off at Sobráon. This was the cause of a new presentation not being desired. I still retain my portion of the Queen's and Regimental colour, and will with pleasure send them to you, if you think them acceptable for your collection."

1841 been its good fortune to earn; he felt confident that the sacred charge now entrusted to them under such favourable auspices would be jealously guarded, and that they would endeavour to preserve untarnished the honour acquired for them by their predecessors, the memory of whose gallant deeds they would ever cherish with feelings of pride and veneration. Colonel Wrottesley concluded by expressing his conviction that they would always entertain a grateful sense of the kindness they had received from Lord Greenock personally, as well as from the Countess, and of the hospitality that had been extended to them during the period of this their first service in Scotland.

After trooping the new colours and marching past in slow and quick time, the regiment returned to barracks, where the men, their wives, and families, were regaled with an excellent and substantial dinner of good old English fare. In the evening, the serjeants of the regiment entertained at dinner those of the 17th Lancers, and of the recruiting staff in Glasgow. Lord Greenock with his staff, the heads of departments, and the commanding officers of corps, dined at seven o'clock with the officers of the 29th, and after the customary toasts, his lordship proposed " Success to the New Colours," which was drunk in a bumper and with the utmost enthusiasm.

The old colours, which were afterwards presented to the Colonel, Lieut.-General John Lord Strafford, are still preserved at Wrotham Park, near Barnet.

A photograph of these colours was taken in 1886, with the help of Mr. Lewis Taylor, and the kind permission of the present Earl, whose father, when serving with the regiment, had often carried them.

Although orders had been received on the 14th of June for the regiment to be in readiness to cross to Ireland, it was not till August the 2nd, 4th, and 6th that it embarked at Glasgow, in three divisions, on board the "Aurora" and "Tartar" steamers for passage to Belfast, where they landed the days following. Whilst stationed here a subaltern's party was detached to Carrickfergus.

By Horse Guards' Letter dated the 6th of January, 1842, twenty **1842** men were allowed to volunteer for service in a corps then being raised to garrison St. Helena. Each individual received a bounty of thirty shillings for so doing, and the number specified were struck off the strength of the regiment on the 1st of February.

COLOURS PRESENTED IN 1841 TO LORD STRAFFORD.

On the 6th of March, with the view of preparing the 29th for service in India, orders were received for its establishment to be raised to 1200 rank and file, and volunteers were received from the 14th, 43rd, 56th, 76th, and 89th Depôts.

1842   On the 29th instant, 3 captains, 5 subalterns, 1 staff, 15 serjeants, 15 corporals, 2 drummers, and 333 privates embarked on board the "Britannia" steamer for Liverpool, *en route* to Weedon. The following day the Carrickfergus detachment marched into Belfast. On the 31st of March and the 2nd of April, the remainder of the regiment embarked in two divisions, on board the "Britannia" and "Duchess of Kent," and on landing at Liverpool also proceeded by train to Weedon.

On the 8th, the establishment of the regiment being fixed at 1 colonel, 2 lieut.-colonels, 2 majors, 9 captains, 20 lieutenants, 7 ensigns, 7 staff; 52 serjeants, 45 corporals, 19 drummers, and 950 privates, Major Hickin was therefore appointed 2nd lieut.-colonel, but as he retired from the service almost immediately, Major R. P. Douglas was promoted in his place. Lieut.-Col. the Honble. C. A. Wrottesley also retired, having exchanged to half-pay with Colonel James Simpson.

Leaving a Depôt of 1 captain, 2 lieutenants, 1 staff; 4 serjeants, 1 drummer, 4 corporals, and 33 privates at Weedon, the regiment proceeded to London by rail, in three divisions, on the 7th, 13th, and 14th, and from thence to Warley Barracks, Tilbury Fort, and Gravesend.

On the 9th of April, the Grenadiers and No. 3 company, commanded respectively by Captains Drake and Kitchener, with Lieuts. Coker and Jones, Ensign the Honble. H. M. Monckton, and Assistant-Surgeon Trousdell, M.D., marched from Warley Barracks to Tilbury Fort, where, having piled arms (the old Brown Bess) the men were put into boats and taken out to the "Beulah." Soon after the Grenadiers had embarked, they were ordered to break up the wicker baskets containing their bearskin caps, and to pack the caps in crates brought on board by some men of the War Department; these were then taken ashore, so, that was the last time bearskin caps were worn by the Grenadiers of the 29th, who received in lieu the chaco with white ball tuft.

About midnight on the 11th of April the "Beulah" ran aground **1842** off Dungeness Light House, and becoming a total wreck the following morning, the detachment was disembarked, one company being sent to Hythe Barracks, the other to Lydd and Dymchurch. Whilst stationed here the establishment of the regiment was completed by 20 volunteers from the 6th Foot. At the end of the month, the two companies marched to Dover castle, where they remained till the 8th of May, when a steamer conveyed them to Gravesend, where they embarked on board the "Buteshire" and sailed once more for Bengal.

The dates of embarkation of the various detachments and of their landing at Chinsará, are as follows:—

Embarked.	Ship.	Officers.	Serjeants.	Corporals.	Drummers	Privates.	Women.	Children.	Landed.
9th April	"Elizabeth"	5	8	7	1	137	18	22	29th July
15th ,,	"Brooke"	6	8	7	4	183	23	15	3rd August
15th ,,	"Thos. Lowry"	5	6	7	2	152	19	14	5th ,,
16th ,,	"Glenelg"	7	17	8	7	145	24	24	9th ,,
May	"Buteshire"	6	6	9	4	160	22	11	21st ,,
15th April	"Chas. Kerr"	4	5	7	1	158	22	23	23rd ,,

On landing at Chinsará, percussion muskets were served out to the regiment.

1842 The following is a list of the officers who were present with the head-quarters on the 1st of September :—

Lieut.-Colonels	Jas. Simpson *(c)*, Robert Percy Douglas.
Majors	Geo. Congreve, Chr. E. Eaton.
Captains	W. W. Drake (Grenadier company), A. T. Hemphill (Light company), H. H. Kitchener, J. O. Lucas, G. Lewis Way, Geo. Brown.
Lieutenants	Edm. Durbin, Geo. Molle, John Power, Lewis Coker, H. Piesley L'Estrange, T. E. Wilbraham, Fred Coventry, Geo. H. M. Jones, Rich Fra. Henry, Alfred A. Simmons, Jas. W. Richardson, Honble. H. Manners Monckton.
Ensigns	Thos. H. Breedon, Wm. H. Macadam, Geo. A. F. Lott, Robert Dobbs, Jas. Johnston.
Paymaster	Jas. Espinasse.
Adjutant	Kenneth Murchison.
Quarter Master	Thos. Kneebone.
Asst. Surgeons	R. Dane, M.D. W. G. Trousdell, M.D. W. Baker Young.

During October, 1 serjeant, 1 drummer, 1 corporal, and 59 privates died of cholera.

On the 8th of November, the regiment left Chinsará; on the 1st of December it camped at Atka, and on the 22nd marched into Gházipúr.

It having been represented to the General Commanding-in-Chief that there existed a want of uniformity in the dress caps, worn by officers of infantry regiments, Lord Hill desired that officers commanding regiments or depôts should cause the following pattern to be strictly conformed to :—

Circular Memo, Horse Guards, 26th of May, 1842.—"The cap to be of black beaver 6¾ inches deep, with lacquered sunk top, 11 inches in diameter, communicating by black leather stitched side straps 3¼ inches wide at the top, with a band of the same which is to encircle the bottom of the cap width ⅞ of an inch—black patent leather peak ; a gilt star plate, 6½ inches in length, with regimental ornaments, surmounted by a crown in front of the cap; lions' heads on both sides, with a gilt chain attached to the left, and to be fastened by a hook on the right side.

A ball tuft and socket."

Colonel Simpson being now in command of the Banáras division, **1843** and Lieut.-Col. Douglas on leave pending retirement on half-pay, the command of the regiment devolved on Major Congreve.

During this year the regiment lost from cholera, remittent fever, &c., two officers and 100 men; amongst the latter was Drummer Geo. Carvell, the last of the black drummers, who died on the 15th of July. Major J. H. Lawrence Archer, who as lieutenant served with the 29th for a short time, and left the regiment on the 1st of November, 1848, says:—"When I was at Gházipúr, about 1850, there was then to be seen the tomb of a 'Private of the 29th,' with the following quaint epitaph, which strange to say I have not forgotten. I forget, however, the man's name and date":—

> "I am billeted here by Death,
> And here I must remain,
> Till the last trumpet sounds,
> When I'll up, and march again."

Circular Memo, Horse Guards, 21st September, 1843.—"A hat of following form and dimensions to be adopted by the officers and men * :—

Depth of crown 7, diameter at top 6¼, breadth of the rim 2 ⅝ inches.

The grenade or ball for Grenadier company to be white throughout; those of the Light company to be green, with a white tuft or fuze; those of the Battalion companies to be red with a white fuze.

Effective field officers to wear a drooping red horse hair plume, 5 inches in height, and which is to droop 2 inches below the top of the hat. The ball or grenade of regimental staff officers to be red throughout.—[*Vide 11th of May, 1846*].

On the 24th of October, Captains Edw. Boyd (M.), Molle; Lieuts. Wilbraham, Jones, Henry, Edw. H. Westropp, Simmons, and Jas. R. Hope; Ensign Henry G. Walker, Assistant-Surgeon Dane, 15 serjeants, 6 drummers, with 300 rank and file, marched for Alláhábád

---

* Although by the Orderly Room Records it appears that the regiment was supplied with this hat, it is very doubtful if it were ever worn by the officers, for Horse Guards' Circular dated the 4th of December, 1843, sanctioned a chaco of an improved form.

1843 to relieve the "Buffs," who had been ordered to join Sir Hugh Gough's army for service against Gwáliár, &c.

This detachment, on the return of the "Buffs," re-joined head-
1844 quarters on the 4th of March, 1844.

On the 27th, Lieut.-Col. Chas. Cyril Taylor, C.B., joined the regiment, and took over the command from Major Congreve.

On the 22nd of September, as the regiment was again suffering from an epidemic of remittent fever, the right wing and No. 6 company marched to camp at Boorkah, returning to Gházipúr on the 30th inst.

On the 13th of October, the regiment marched for Ágrá. On account of its sickly state, a detachment consisting of Captain Stepney, Lieuts. Coker, Chas. E. MacDonnell, and Walker, Assistant-Surgeon Trousdell, 14 serjeants, 26 corporals, 14 drummers, and 352 privates, who were too ill to march, proceeded in boats up the Ganges towards Ghurmuktisur Ghât.

On the 1st of November, the head-quarters encamped at Kusseah, but on reaching Mainpúri cantonment, its destination was changed to Mírath, which was reached on the 10th of December, and where
1845 Captain Stepney's detachment arrived on the 28th of January, 1845.

When on the 31st H.M. 10th Foot marched into Mírath, the great friendship which had for many years existed between the officers and men of that regiment and the 29th, was renewed, and the bond of union was made still firmer by the friendship existing between Colonel Considine § and Colonel Taylor.

Whilst stationed here, the officers of the two regiments joined in giving a ball, and it was after supper on that occasion, that Colonel Taylor made a speech, at the conclusion of which, the wife of an officer of the 10th rose to respond, and said "There ought to be a Colonel Taylor at the head of every regiment!"

---

§ Died 4th September, 1845, previous to the Ball.

Some time previous to this, "Our Cousins," as the 10th were always **1845** called by the 29th, made the latter permanent honorary members of their Mess, and I am indebted to Captain P. R. Newbury, Mess President 1/10th, for the following extract from the Mess Regulations of his battalion :—

"*Honorary Members.*—It is here recorded that the 2nd Battalion of the Regiment, and also the 29th (Worcestershire) Regiment, are permanent honorary members of the Mess, and that the same privilege appertains to the Officers of the 1st Battalion 10th Regiment, with the 2nd Battalion 10th Regiment and 29th Regiment."

It is difficult to ascertain precisely when this honour was conferred on the 29th. General Sir R. P. Douglas, writing on the 5th of March, 1889, says, "I think, if my memory at my advanced age is to be trusted, that the 10th made the 29th perm^t hon. members of their mess about the end of '41 or early in '42."

General Lindsay Farrington writes :—" The arrangement by which the 10th and 29th became permanent honorary members of one another's mess dates back certainly as far as 1838, if not further. When I landed in Calcutta in the beginning of 1844, the 10th Regt. was quartered there, and although at that time I was in the 39th, and not the 29th, I heard of the arrangement ; when we were quartered together at Mírath in 1845, the privilege was largely used."

By Circular Memo, Horse Guards, 30th April, a new shoulder knot was approved of for the non-commissioned officers and men.

By General Order dated the 6th of August, the serjeants' sash of coloured stripes was ordered to be discontinued, and one of crimson colour universally adopted.

During this year, regulations were issued forbidding any regimental record or device being placed on the " Queen's Colour," other than the number of the regiment, in gold Roman characters, surmounted by the Imperial Crown.

1845 General Return of the Country, Size, Age, and Service of the Serjeants, Corporals, Drummers, and Private Men of the Twenty-ninth Regiment of Foot. Inspected by Major-General Woodhouse at Mírath on 28th May, 1845.

Number of Each Country.

	Colonel.	Lt.-Colonels.	Majors.	Captains.	Lieutenants.	Ensigns.	Staff.	
English	1	1	2	4	11	4	3	Paymaster. Qr. Master. Surgeon. Adjutant. 1 Asst. Surgeon.
Scotch		1		1		3	2	
Irish				4	10		2	2 Asst. Surgeons.
Foreign								
Total	1	2	2	9	21	7	7	

Number of Each Country.

	Serjeants.	Corporals.	Drummers.	Privates.
English	22	21	4	516
Scotch	4	3	1	29
Irish	27	21	14	321
Foreign				
Total	53	45	19	866

Number of Each Size.

	Serjeants.	Corporals.	Drummers.	Privates.
6 ft. 0 in. and upwards	2	2		27
5 „ 11 „ „	2			23
5 „ 10 „ „	2	4	1	51
5 „ 9 „ „	9	7	2	132
5 „ 8 „ „	13	12	2	213
5 „ 7 „ „	17	11	1	178
5 „ 6 „ „	8	8	1	218
5 „ 5 „ „		1	5	19
Under			3	
Lads			3	5
Total	53	45	19	866

Men's Service.

	Serjeants.	Corporals.	Drummers.	Privates.
25 Years and Upwards				
20 „ „	2			3
18 „ „	3	2		40
14 „ „	7	1	1	34
12 „ „	9	2		66
10 „ „	1	3		22
9 „ „	3			5
8 „ „	4		1	9
7 „ „	5	4		13
6 „ „	5	5	1	44
5 „ „	7	15	2	123
4 „ „	6	7	2	149
3 „ „	1	6	3	139
2 „ „			4	172
1 „ „			2	42
Under			3	5
Total	53	45	19	866

Age.

	Serjeants.	Corporals.	Drummers.	Privates.
45 years and upwards				
40 „ „	2	1		7
35 „ „	5	4		69
30 „ „	16	3	1	124
25 „ „	21	7	4	163
20 „ „	9	30	7	442
18 „ „			4	56
Under			3	5
Total	53	45	19	866

During the month of August, the 29th were again attacked by **1845** cholera, but the epidemic, though still raging among the other troops in garrison, suddenly left the regiment on the 14th of September.

On the 15th of October, the regiment marched for Kasauli; on reaching Ambálah on the 28th, orders were received for it to halt, and on the 31st Major-General W. R. Gilbert, commanding the division, reviewed it for the inspection of H.R.H. Prince Waldemar of Prussia, who, accompanied by his staff, took breakfast with the officers.

On the 11th of November the march was resumed, and on reaching the foot of the hills, the regiment was drawn up in line, on the road, for inspection by H.E. Sir Hugh Gough, G.C.B., G.C.H., the Commander-in-Chief. Kasauli was reached on the 21st.†

Extract from General Order, Horse Guards, 20th November, 1845 :—

"The Commander-in-Chief having considered it his duty to order a Court of Enquiry to assemble, in order to enquire into the transactions which occurred in the —— Dragoons on the 28th Sept. last, desires that the report of the Court may be published in the General Orders of the army.

He entreats the commanding officers of regiments to draw the attention of officers under their command, respectively to the consequences resulting from the practice of gymnastic exercises, after the Mess dinner. . . . . . The Commander-in-Chief has been informed that the practice of smoking, by the use of pipes, cigars, or cheroots, has become prevalent among the officers of the army, which is not only in itself a species of intoxication occasioned by the fumes of tobacco, but, undoubtedly occasions drinking and tippling by those who acquire the habit; and he entreats the officers commanding regiments to prevent smoking in the Mess Room of their several regiments, and in the adjoining apartments, and to discourage the practice, among the officers of junior rank in their regiment.

By command of Field Marshal
The Duke of Wellington,
Commander-in-Chief.
JOHN MACDONALD,
Adjutant-General."

---

† *Vide* Extracts from letters of General Hawes, Colonel Hook, and Captain Wallack, late of the 9th Foot, pages 384 and 386.

1845 Whilst at Ambálah, orders had been received for the regiment to hold itself in readiness for active service; and on the evening of the 10th of December, whilst the officers were sitting in their mess-room smoking, and sipping their after-dinner wine, an officer of the governor-general's staff arrived with a despatch, desiring Col. Taylor and the 29th to march with the utmost speed and join the army then assembling under Sir Hugh Gough to repel the Sikhs, who, having coerced or induced the Láhor authorities to commence hostilities, had crossed the Satláj, invested Firúzpúr on one side, and taken up an entrenched position at Fírúzshahar, about ten miles in advance of the former place, and nearly the same distance from Múdkí. These orders were received with great enthusiasm, and the remainder of that night was passed in packing and getting ready for the campaign. The men were medically inspected, and each served out with 100 rounds of ball ammunition.

MONTHLY RETURNS, 1ST DECEMBER, 1845.

HEAD QUARTERS, KASAULI.

Officers Present.

Lieut.-Colonel—C. C. Taylor, C.B.   Major—Congreve.

Captains   Lucas, Stepney, E. Boyd (*m.*), J. D. Young, Molle, Power, Coker.

Liuetenants   Jones, Henry, W. Kirby, E. Westropp, C. Handfield, Simmons, J. F. Galiffe, C. E. MacDonnell, W. F. Stehelin, H. G. Walker, St. G. M. Nugent, L. Farrington, O. Carey, J. M. Lyle.

Ensigns   H. Francis, Hans R. White, G. St. J. Henderson, E. T. Scudamore, A. A. Dick.

Paymaster—Clay.   Adjutant—Murchison.   Quarter Master—Kneebone.

Surgeon—Taylor.   Asst. Surgeons—Trousdell, M.D., and Young.

Leaving the women and heavy baggage in charge of Major Boyd, **1845** Ensigns Francis, White, Quarter-Master Kneebone, and Assistant-Surgeon Trousdell, the regiment marched early on the morning of the 11th to Kálka, where arms having been piled, the officers proceeded to the commissariat stores to superintend the issue of tents and the packing of them on the camels.

About 4 p.m., the men being somewhat rested, the regiment started for Munnymajra, and accomplished that day a march of about 23 miles. Being here joined by the 1st (Bengal) European Light Infantry, the two regiments continued their advance towards Múdkí in charge of some heavy artillery.

On the 13th, Lieut.-Col. Taylor being appointed brigadier to the 3rd infantry brigade of the army of the Satláj, Major Congreve assumed the command of the regiment.

On approaching Wadní, a fortified town of some importance, much excitement was caused by the receipt of an order from the commander-in-chief, to the effect that, as the inhabitants of that place had refused provisions to a part of the British force a few days previously, H.M. 29th and the 1st En. Light Infantry were to reduce the fort to submission.

These orders were however countermanded on account of information being received that an immediate action was expected to take place between the rival armies near Múdkí. During the night another dispatch was received from the governor-general, allowing a short halt.

The following morning the march was resumed, and late on the evening of the 19th, the regiments joined the army of the Satláj then encamped at Múdkí, from which position the enemy had been driven the previous day.

1845   The 2nd dispatch, which had caused the regiment to halt, had also prevented it participating in the glorious victory, and occasioned much discontent in the 29th, for the men, on hearing of the action, exclaimed with unfeigned disappointment, "The regiment was late for Waterloo, and now we are late again!"

The 29th was played into camp by the band of the governor-general, who very kindly sent the officers some supper. The men having piled arms, were supplied with rations and bivouacked for the night; but on the arrival of the tents early next morning, camp was immediately pitched. It being decided to attack the enemy on the 21st, the troops were given a day's rest.

On joining the army, H.M's 29th and 80th regiments, together with the 45th Native Infantry were placed in the 3rd (Lieut.-Col. Taylor's) brigade, of Major-General W. R. Gilbert's (the 2nd) division, but the following day, the 80th was removed to another brigade.

The regiment had during the past nine days traversed a distance of about 170 miles by a succession of forced marches; the roads the whole way were deep in dust, the days hot, nights cold, wells were scarce, and the men had consequently suffered greatly from thirst. So rapidly had one march succeeded another that bread could not be made, and in lieu of it, flour and ottah were served out to the men to make chapatties of.

On the 21st, with the exception of 1 lieutenant and 7 men, who were left in charge of the baggage, tents, and servants at Múdkí, the regiment went into action the same strength as it had left Kasauli.

That morning (Sunday) no bugles were allowed to sound or drums to beat, the regimental parade was formed up at 2.30 a.m., and, in anticipation of the action, each man carried 60 rounds of ball ammunition and had two days' rations in his haversack.

No camp followers, excepting one servant for each officer, were **1845** permitted to accompany the troops.

Crossing the field of Múdkí, which was still strewn with dead, the several columns under Sir Hugh Gough marched to effect a junction with Major-General Sir J. Littler's force, which was advancing from Firúzpúr. The junction having been made about 1.30 p.m., the army marched on Fírúzshahar, where the enemy, posted in great force, and with a most formidable artillery, had remained since the action of the 18th, incessantly employed in throwing up entrenchments.*

Nothing was seen of the Sikhs till about 3 p.m., when on approaching their works, the skirmishers exchanged shots. Their main position was soon afterwards discovered to be, to use Lord Gough's words, "a parallelogram about a mile in length, and half-a-mile in breadth, including within its area the strong village of Ferozeshah; the shorter sides looking towards the Sutlej and Moodkee, the longer towards Ferozepore and the open country."

Instead of advancing to the direct attack of these formidable works, the force manœuvred to their right, and the 2nd and 4th divisions of infantry in front, supported by the 1st division and cavalry in second line, continued to defile for some time out of cannon shot between the Sikhs and Firúzpúr. Preparations which were at once commenced for a united attack, were not completed till an hour before sunset. On the right, was Gilbert's division, which was to attack part of the south and as much of the east side of the entrenchments as it could manage.

A heavy cannonade was now opened by the enemy, who had dispersed over their position upwards of 100 guns, more than 40 of which

---

* No trace of the earthworks now remains, but a monument erected on their site perpetuates the memory of the officers and men who fell in their capture.

GG

1845 were of battering calibre; these kept up a well-directed fire, which the practice of our far less numerous artillery of much lighter metal checked in some degree, but could not silence. Having wheeled from column into line, the 2nd division advanced in a direct echelon of regiments from the right, the 29th leading.† By previous concurrence of the commanding officer, the bandsmen now acted as hospital orderlies, and two of them in the performance of this duty were amongst the first wounded. The field hospital was opened on the ground where the first casualties occurred, and Private Wm. Hearn, who previous to enlisting in the English army, had served as adjutant in the Queen of Spain's service, was the first man killed of the Grenadier company. The 29th advanced in quick time, file firing as it approached the entrenched position; nothing could equal its steadiness while exposed to well-directed discharges of shell, grape shot, and musketry. In one case, an entire section was swept away by a single discharge.

Unflinchingly, and pouring in a heavy fire, the regiment with a loud cheer, charged up to the guns, crossing the entrenchments only to find that their work was just commencing, for behind the captured guns, were posted the enemy's unsubdued infantry, who poured forth a continuous galling fire. Undismayed, however, the men pushed on and drove back the foe. It was only on the approach of darkness that they retired, and took up a position about 300 yards from the trenches ready to advance again at daybreak. About an hour after the commencement of the action, Colonel Taylor, whose charger had been killed under him, was brought wounded to the field hospital, having been struck by a round-shot on the side, and suffered a good deal from the effects of the blow and shock together. He was laid on the ground with the rest of the wounded, and later in the evening, having been attended to, and feeling better, went away on a gun carriage.

---

† In the subsequent action, when there was only one white regiment in the brigade, it took the central position.

Major Congreve was twice wounded, the last time so severely as **1845** to be obliged to leave the field; Captain Stepney then succeeded to the command, and was also soon afterwards wounded. Captain J. O. Lucas (brigadier-major) was killed, as were also Captain G. Molle and Lieut. A. A. Simmons. The latter, who was commanding the Grenadier company in Capt. Lucas' absence, had been wounded in the foot, and was limping away leaning on Lieut. Murchison, when a bullet struck him in the head, and he fell dead at Lieut. Kirby's feet; this latter officer had also a narrow escape, for a round shot killed two men alongside of him.

As evening closed great confusion prevailed, the Sikh camp being on fire in several directions; constant explosions of mines and magazines took place, and part of the position was still occupied by the enemy, who kept up a harassing fire during the early part of the night, and obliged the troops constantly to change their positions. At length, near midnight, the wearied soldiers lay down to such rest as they could find on a damp sandy soil, without any covering to protect them from the bitter cold, and suffering from excessive thirst, not having had any water during the whole day, except some little they had carried in tins, and which had all been consumed by an early hour.

Surgeon J. R. Taylor's report of killed and wounded in Her Majesty's 29th Regiment with the army of the Satláj, in 1845-46, contains many interesting extracts, some of which are here inserted:—

"In the midst of our labours at the field hospital, darkness set in. The candles we had brought were now lighted with a view to continue the dressings of the wounded, though all parties were fairly worn out with fatigue and want of refreshment. Orders soon arrived however to put out the lights; these not being at first attended to, were repeated, with the explanation that we should draw upon us the fire of the enemy; we were further ordered to remove the wounded from that place, which we were told was unprotected, and to join the regiment, which was said to be, a short distance to our right. With the few means of conveyance

1845 at hand, it was impossible to move all the wounded. But with the help of the ammunition camels, officers' horses, stray horses, and the doolies still remaining, the greater number who could not walk, were provided for, and it may be said of those that were left on the ground, that they had no chance of living under any circumstances.

In endeavouring to make our way to the regiment, we approached fires, which on nearing were discovered to be tents on fire within the Sikh entrenchments. Here we were assailed with cries from numbers of the wounded of the regiment, who recognised the voices of our party. Urgent were their entreaties for water, and removal. To remove these men was impracticable, but I assured them they should have assistance in the morning. It was very dark, but I think I counted fifteen men in a small space close to the trenches, most of them were very severely wounded in the lower extremities. To finish the history of these men, I shall here add, that when our troops had retaken this ground the next day, I found most of those I had seen there overnight, with their throats cut. One man, Corporal Withey, though he had a dreadful gash in his throat and another across his face, could still articulate faintly. After leaving these men, we skirted along the entrenchments towards another line of fires, running at a right angle to those we had just seen before. There also, we heard much noise of voices and hammering, and made pretty sure of falling in with the regiment. We had not time, however, to approach very near before some musket shots were discharged at our party, and one man on a camel was wounded. In the hurried retreat which immediately ensued, the natives threw down the petarrahs containing instruments, and everything else, and made off as fast as they could. Every particle of hospital equipment was lost in the darkness and confusion, and the wounded were dispersed. As we were retiring we were challenged, and upon advancing, I recognised Sir Henry Hardinge, who hastily interrogated me about the camp. Whilst replying to him, an officer of my own regiment recognising my voice, and hearing my difficulty, came up and said 'Taylor, here is your regiment!' It was in fact bivouacking within musket shot of the trenches, but lying silent and without fires, so we had missed it. Thus our capability of further assisting the wounded was altogether lost."

"The night of the 21st December," wrote Sir Henry Hardinge to Sir Robert Peel, "was the most extraordinary of my life. I bivouacked with the men without food or covering, and our nights are bitter cold. A burning camp in our front, our brave fellows lying down under a heavy cannonade which continued during the whole night, mixed with the wild cries of the Sikhs, our English hurrahs, the tramp of men, and groans of the dying.

In this state, with a handful of men who had carried the batteries the night before, I remained till morning, taking very short intervals of rest by lying down with various regiments in succession, to ascertain their temper and revive their spirits. I found myself again with my old friends, the 29th, 31st, 50th, and 9th, all in good heart. My answer to all and to every man was, that we must fight it out, attack the enemy vigorously at daybreak, beat him, or die honourably on the field."

The following morning at dawn, the troops were formed in line, and benumbed with cold as the men were, they needed no cheering on. The "Advance" sounded, and dashing forward, the occupation of the enemy's camp, and capture of their baggage, and stores of all kinds, was soon completed. In this charge the 29th captured several guns which had continued to fire on them as they advanced. The regiment then formed on the opposite side of the camp, and on Sir Hugh Gough and Sir H. Hardinge riding down the line, they were received with a gratifying cheer. Parties were now sent in search of water, which was found in some chatties in the camp, and as the men had been almost entirely without any since the previous morning, such refreshment was exceedingly welcome. The men were beginning to congratulate themselves on the victory, and looking forward to a short rest, when the

1845 regiment was suddenly called to arms and ordered to advance, for the advance guard of a fresh army, under Sidar-Téj-Singh, who had been watching Firúzpúr, had arrived on the scene, and was making an attempt to re-take the captured guns and camp.

Being menaced by large bodies of cavalry, the 29th formed square, but on the cavalry retiring, and the enemy's artillery finding the range, it deployed and lay down along one of the faces of the camp to guard the captured guns. Being partially sheltered by a small embankment, the men suffered scarcely at all, for the shots passed over them and pitched in the regiments in their rear. In this position the 29th remained for about an hour and a half, when the enemy's flanks being simultaneously threatened by cavalry, the Sikh guns ceased firing, and retired precipitately towards the Satláj.

The men were now able to procure abundance of water, bullocks, grain, etc., in the captured camp, and what proved most acceptable as the cold night set in, plenty of warm covering. During the night the companies lay in quarter-distance column, with arms piled in front of each.

The following day, the 23rd, Lieut. Kirby being sent with some men to spike six or seven guns, numbers of tumbrils, full of grape, canister, and round shot, were discovered. In the afternoon the regiment had the melancholy duty of burying its dead; three of its officers who had been killed on the 21st, were laid in one grave.

By a Return furnished at the time, Surgeon Taylor says:—

"The number of each description of wounded in the 29th Regiment at Firúzshahar was as follows:—

By Artillery	137
„ Musketry	43
„ Explosion	4
„ Sword	1
Total	185

"A great many men suffered from more than one wound. Private Gray had as many as six grape shots through various parts of his body, and, curious to say, without one bone being broken; he did not however recover. Pte. Mulling had six grape shot wounds with only two bones broken; he was invalided, but was afterwards reported to have died. Further, in considering the proportion of mortality amongst the wounded, it must be remembered that they all lay upon the field from the 21st to the 24th, when they were conveyed in hackeries to Firúzpúr. During the three days they thus remained exposed to the powerful heat of the sun by day, and the very disproportionate cold air by night, many of them suffered from most agonising thirst, and little water could be got, and that very putrid.

Their excessive thirst and the impossibility of obtaining water, may be judged by the fact that on the morning of the 22nd, men of this, and other regiments, were reduced to the direst expedients for quenching their thirst. A great number had not their wounds dressed till the 25th, for it was late on the evening of the 24th when they reached Firúzpúr, and nothing more could be done that night, than to get them housed, and give each some bread and tea; some narcotic, and other draughts were also administered."

3RD BRIGADE 2ND DIVISION BRIGADIER TAYLOR, C.B., H.M. 29TH & 45 N.I. REGIMENTS.

Firúzshahar, 21st and 22nd December, 1845.	Lieut.-Col.	Major.	Captains.	Lieutenants.	Ensigns.	Staff.	Serjeants.	Drummers.	Rank and File.	Officers' Chargers.
Strength of the 29th Regt. going into action	1	1	6	12	3	4	42	18	698	3
Killed †			2	1			1		51	2
Wounded †	1	1	1				10	2	180	1

† The above Return is copied from the Orderly Room Records, and corresponds with the Regimental Muster Roll, and Pay List. In the "*Gazette*" the casualties were published as follows:—

29th Foot { Killed— 1 Serjeant, - Drummer, 67 Rank and File.
          { Wounded—6   ,,   4   ,,   106   ,,

1845

OFFICERS KILLED OR WOUNDED.

Killed—
- Captain J. O. Lucas *(Major of Brigade)*.
- „ Geo. Molle.
- Lieut. Alf. Angelo Simmons.

Wounded—
- Lieut.-Colonel C. C. Taylor, c.b. *(Brigadier)*.
- Major Geo. Congreve.
- Capt. A. St. G. H. Stepney.

NON-COMMISSIONED OFFICERS, RANK AND FILE KILLED.

Extracted from the Muster Rolls, Pay Lists, and Monthly Returns of 29th Foot :—

Serjt. Smith, John	Pte. Fuller, Edward	Pte. Sands, George
Corpl. Evans, Thos.	„ Giles, John	„ Sands, James H.
„ Teasdale, James	„ Green, George	„ Sheldon, William
„ Withey, Charles	„ Greenway, Francis	„ Shelton, William
Pte. Beaumont, James	„ Hadkinson, Thomas	„ Smith, Chas., 1458
„ Bentley, Rich^d., No. 2212	„ Hastewell, John	„ Sullivan, Daniel
„ Bentley, Rich^d., No. 1864	„ Halter, William	„ Sutton, George
„ Beresford, Charles	„ Hearne, William	„ Warren, James
„ Blackburn, Michael	„ Heburn, William	„ Watts, John
„ Blazer, William	„ Hodkinson, David	„ Webb, Henry
„ Boardman, William	„ Illingworth, Thomas	„ Whinyates, Robert
„ Bobbin, Isaac	„ Langhan, Thomas	„ White, Charles
„ Bromhead, Benjamin	„ Larner, William	„ White, Thomas
„ Brown, Joseph	„ Laughlin, Mathias	„ Wilson, Henry
„ Challener, Charles	„ McCrackin, John	„ Winn, Winford
„ Courtnay, Edward	„ Neal, John	„ Woodcut, James
„ Donaughey, John	„ O'Connor, Michael	
„ Drew, James	„ Reed, George	

Lieut. Octavius Carey, who had sent in his papers, and was about to retire from the service, hearing of the outbreak of hostilities, had attached himself to the 3rd Light Dragoons, and was blown to pieces by a shell in the action of Múdkí.

For the distinguished part taken by the regiment in the late action, Sir Hugh Gough was pleased to appoint Serjeant-Major G. Mitchell, of the 29th, to a vacant ensigncy in the regiment.

On the death of Captain Lucas, Lieut. and Adjutant G. H. M. Jones took up the duties of brigade-major.

On the morning of the 24th, the regiment advanced to Sultan- **1845**
Khan-wálá, where in the evening it was joined by its baggage. On
Christmas Day the officers of H.M. 80th dined with those of the 29th,
and all things taken into consideration, a pleasant evening was spent.

The battle of Fírúzshahar threatened to prove a fruitless victory,
for on the 26th it was reported that the enemy, with the intention of
renewing the struggle, had re-crossed the Satláj. A further advance
was therefore made on the 28th, and Sir Hugh having taken up a
strong position on the left bank, awaited the arrival of the siege train,
and reserve ammunition from Delhí.

On the 1st of January, the regiment was encamped at Arufka, but **1846**
on the 10th Taylor's brigade was ordered to advance to Chota Sobráon,
which it occupied with two companies, whilst the remainder encamped
a short distance in rear. Being joined by a party of Sappers, the
regiment immediately commenced to entrench the village. From a
tower, the Satláj could be seen about a mile distant, and large bodies of
the enemy throwing up entrenchments and batteries on the left bank.
As soon as it was dark, a covering party of an officer and 40 men,
having been extended, Lieut. Kirby and 80 others were ordered out to
clear the ground of some high jungle within musket shot of the village,
and having accomplished this without molestation, the party returned to
camp about 11 p.m.

The entrenching of this post being completed on the 18th, three
companies were left to hold the work, and the remainder of the brigade
marched back to its former camp. This outpost was subsequently only
occupied during the day time.

The regiment, which since the battle of Fírúzshahar had remained
encamped with the head-quarters of the army, marched on the 26th with
the remainder of the 3rd brigade, a troop of horse artillery, and a
regiment of irregular cavalry, towards Lodiáná for the purpose of
co-operating with Sir H. Smith, who had marched a few days previously

1846 to its relief. On reaching Dharmkót, heavy firing was heard from the direction of Alíwál, and a messenger arriving that evening with a letter announcing Sir H. Smith's victory over Ranjúr Singh, the troops under Brigadier Taylor started the next morning to rejoin Sir H. Gough.

OFFICERS PRESENT.

1st February, 1846.   Camp Akbarwálá.

Captains—Stepney, Young, Coker, and Murchison.

Lieutenants—Henry, J. Æ. Duncan, Kirby, Westropp, Handfield, *acting Adj^t.*, Galiffe, MacDonnell, Stehelin, Walker, H. T. Metge, Nugent, Farrington, Lyle, Henderson, Scudamore, Dick, *sick in camp.*

Ensigns—V. Tonnochy, G. Mitchell.

Pay-Master—Clay.   Surgeon—Taylor.   Asst. Surgeon—Young.

JOINED HEAD-QUARTERS 7TH FEBRUARY.

Lieut.—F. Coventry; Ensign—F. Kneebone; Qr.-Master—T. Kneebone.

Sir Harry Smith and the heavy ordnance having joined the main body, it was decided to attack the enemy's position on the 10th, and between 3 and 4 a.m. that day the troops marched from their camp with that object. The morning being very dark, Taylor's brigade moved cautiously towards its former outpost at Chota Sobráon, which being unoccupied was taken possession of without opposition. A thick haze favoured the British advance, but as day dawned, and the approaching troops were discovered, the Sikhs opened a smart cannonade.

About the centre of the line, and facing the strongest part of the enemy's position, was Gilbert's division, the 3rd brigade of which was composed of the 41st N.I., H.M. 29th Foot, and the 68th N.I.* The

---

* Gazette.

services of these regiments not being at this time required they moved **1846**
to a neighbouring nullah for shelter.

At 7 a.m. a heavy cannonade, which lasted for about two hours, was commenced by both sides, when, as but little impression had been made on the well-constructed batteries, and the ammunition for the heavy guns was reported to be running short, Sir R. Dick's division was ordered to attack the enemy's right. As on entering the entrenchments these troops encountered formidable obstacles and were opposed by far superior numbers, Sir Hugh Gough decided on a general attack. Having up to the present time been under shelter, the 29th had but one man wounded.

It was about ten o'clock when the 1st and 2nd divisions received orders to storm the works in their front. Moving out of the ravine, Taylor's brigade advanced in line for about three-quarters of a mile, exposed to a heavy fire from a battery of 13 guns. A nullah about 70 yards from the entrenchments being reached, the brigade halted for a minute or two previous to delivering the assault.

Wild and long was the shout that rose from the regiment, as amidst showers of grape and musketry it dashed forward towards the large ramparts of clay and wood, upwards of 10 feet high; nothing appeared to view but the muzzles of the guns, behind which the Sikh infantry were lining the entrenchment, four deep.

Notwithstanding its undaunted courage, the 29th, having in the charge far outstripped the Native regiments, and in consequence not receiving proper support, now found itself after a hard struggle constrained to fall back to the shelter of the nullah, whence it again rushed forward, maddened at seeing the Sikh soldiery come from their entrenchments and cut the throats of their brave comrades who were lying wounded. Being a second time repulsed, and obliged to return to the friendly nullah, the regiment waited there for a few moments to re-form and allow the men to get their wind, when, nothing daunted, it charged the enemy for a third time, and entering the entrenchments, captured

1846 the whole of the guns in its front. The defences being now stormed in all directions, the enemy retired towards the bridge of boats and the ford across the Satláj. It was not until the weight of all three divisions of infantry, in addition to several regiments of cavalry and the fire of every available piece of field artillery had been felt, that the foe gave way. Retreating at first, in good order, the incessant volleys soon caused them to seek safety in a rapid flight, and finding their bridge of boats broken, they attempted to ford the river. Then occurred a scene of carnage, for the horse artillery galloping up, threw shrapnel with deadly effect into the dense masses, whilst the infantry poured in a murderous fire.

Brigadier Taylor, who at the head of the regiment, in the third charge, was shot behind the ear close to the enemy's guns, had previous to receiving his mortal wound, been cut across the face. Lieut. G. H. M. Jones, his brigade-major, "who was riding the same charger ridden by Captain Lucas at Fírúzshahar when he was killed," was severely wounded by a cannon ball, which carried away the greater portion of his right forearm, including the elbow joint. The death of this officer was however the effect of dysentry, under which he had laboured ever since the 21st of December; he never rallied in spirits, but died at Fírúzpúr on the 23rd of February. Ensign Mitchell was struck either by a grape or gingall shot, which pounded the shin bone close to the ankle joint, into fragments. Amputation was performed at the calf of the leg, and never was an operation borne with more firmness, nay positive indifference, the patient himself assisting. Irritative fever having set in, he died on the 18th. Captain Stepney being wounded by a grape shot through the thigh, it fell to Captain Coker's lot to bring the regiment out of action.

During this day there were lucky escapes; amongst others was that of Lieut. Kirby, who commanded No. 1. Whilst advancing in line, this company was ordered to ease off to its right, when a round shot, fired considerably within point blank range, struck the left-hand man of the Grenadier company (who was on Kirby's right), killing **1846** both him and his rear rank man on the spot. A few seconds later Kirby fell near the batteries, shot through the right leg, his sword was knocked out of his hand, and his scabbard shot in two. Whilst lying thus helpless, some Sikhs attacked him and inflicted two severe sabre cuts on his neck and shoulders. Fortunately Corporal Hall succeeded in shooting one of the assailants and bayonetting another, when the regiment returning to the charge, Kirby was saved.

3RD BRIGADE 2ND DIVISION H.M. 29TH FOOT, 41ST, AND 68TH N.I.*

Sobráon, 10th February, 1846.	Lieut.-Col.	Major.	Captains.	Lieutenants.	Ensigns.	Staff.	Serjeants.	Drummers.	Rank and File.	Officers' Chargers.
Strength of the 29th Regt. on going into action	1	1	4	16	2	5	30	14	469	
Killed *	1						1		34	1
Wounded *		1	3	8	1	1	6		130	

OFFICERS KILLED, WOUNDED, DIED OF WOUNDS.

KILLED.

Lieut.-Colonel C. C. Taylor, C.B., commanding 3rd Brigade.

WOUNDED.

Major Marcus Barr, *l.c.s., Actg. A.G.* — Severely and dangerously. Died.

Captains:
- A. St. G. H. Stepney. — Severely.
- J. D. Young. — Slightly.
- Kenneth Murchison. — Slightly.

Lieutenants:
- G. H. M. Jones, *major of brigade.* — Very severely. Died.
- Rich. Fra. Henry. — Severely.
- J. Æneas Duncan. — Severely.
- Walter Kirby. — Very severely.
- C. E. MacDonnell. — Severely. comm^{dg}. Grenadier co^y., *vice* Stepney.
- H. G. Walker. — Slightly, by an arrow.
- St. Geo. Mervyn Nugent. — Severely.
- G. St. Julien Henderson. — Contusion.
- E. T. Scudamore. — Severely.

Ensign George Mitchell. — Severely. Died.

---

* *Gazette.*

29 Foot { Killed— 1 Sergeant, 35 Rank and File.
{ Wounded—7 ,, 132 ,,

1846

KILLED.

Extracted from Muster Rolls, Pay Lists, and Monthly Returns 29th Foot:—

Cr.-Serjt. Swaby, John	Pte. Harrison, William	Pte. O'Donnell, James
Corpl. Colquhoun, Andrew	,, Hodder, Robert	,, Roebuck, John
Pte. Box, William	,, Hunt, William	,, Scott, Robert
,, Boyce, George	,, Jackson, John	,, Smith, Michael, 875
,, Clee, Charles	,, Keelan, Patrick	,, Stanton, William
,, Corbett, James	,, Lane, Henry	,, Steward, Hugh
,, Deeran, John	,, Locock, James	,, Taggert, Hugh
,, Duncan, William	,, Lord, William	,, Wason, James
,, Dunphy, Patrick	,, McManus, Thomas	,, Weathers, James
,, Fitton, Edmund	,, Mawhinney, James	,, Wilson, John
,, Flood, William	,, Mulholland, William	,, Wotton, George
,, Goodier, Thomas	,, Murphy, Jeremiah	

A monument in memory of the officers and men of the 29th (Worcestershire) Regiment who fell in the Satláj campaign was afterwards placed by their surviving comrades in Worcester Cathedral. It is said that the figure on this monument represents Colonel Taylor. There is also a tablet in memory of Brigadier-General Taylor in Canterbury Cathedral.

During the 11th and 12th of February the wounded were removed to Firúzpúr, *en route* to Kasauli.

The 29th, with the remainder of the 2nd division, remained encamped in front of Sobráon till the 15th when it marched to Kunda Ghât, crossed the Satláj by a bridge of boats, and proceeded to join the head-quarters of the army encamped at Kasúr.

Extract from General Order by the Right Honble. the Governor-General of India:—

"Camp, Kussoor, 14th Feb., 1846.

. . . . The army has also sustained a heavy loss by the death of Brigadier Taylor, commanding the 3rd Brigade 2nd Division, a most able officer, and very worthy to have been at the head of so distinguished a corps as Her Majesty's 29th Regiment, by which he was beloved and respected.

Her Majesty's 29th, and the 1st European Regiment, and the 16th, 48th, and 61st Native Infantry, and the Simoor Battalion have entitled themselves, by their gallant conduct, to the thanks of the Government."

Amongst the officers in command of regiments, etc., whose services were acknowledged by Sir Hugh Gough were Captain Stepney, and Lieut. Jones, brigade-major.

"We were in this battle," says Sir Hugh, "again honoured with the presence of Prince Waldemar of Prussia, and the two noblemen in his suite, Counts Oriola and Greuben. Here, as at Múdkí and Fírzúshahar, these distinguished visitors did not content themselves with a distant view of the action, but throughout it were to be seen in the front, wherever danger most urgently pressed."

The Prince's medical attendant, Dr. Hoffmeister, being shot through the head, an officer of the 29th ventured to remark how unfortunate it was that a non-combatant should have been killed, to which the Prince replied, "What more could a soldier want!"

On the morning of the 18th the whole army advanced upon Láhor, before which city it encamped on the 20th. Whilst here, the regiment was joined by Captain H. H. Kitchener with a detachment of 87 recruits from England, and 4 corporals, 1 drummer, and 10 privates who had been left sick at Mírath.

On the 9th of March, the Flank companies, under command of Captains Stepney and Wilbraham, formed part of the guard of honour present at the ratifying of the Treaty between the British Government of India, and the Láhor Darbár on the part of Mahárájah Dhulíp Singh, then a minor. The following day the army paraded in review order for

1846 inspection by the Governor-General, the Commander-in-Chief, Major-General Sir Chas. Napier, G.C.B., governor of Sind, and H.H. Dhulíp Singh.

Captain A. T. Hemphill, who had been doing duty with invalids since the 11th of October, 1845, and who had in the meantime succeeded to a majority, joined and took over the command of the regiment on the day of the inspection.

On the 15th of March, the army of the Satláj was broken up, and on the morning of the 23rd, the regiment commenced its return march, and re-crossing the Satláj on the 26th, it arrived at Kasauli on the 11th of April, having been absent from that station exactly four months, during which period it sustained the following losses in killed, died of wounds, or invalided as unfit for further service:—1 lieut.-colonel, 1 major, 2 captains, 2 lieutenants, 1 ensign, 1 staff; 7 serjeants, 2 drummers, 186 rank and file.

Bt.-Lieut.-Col. Barr, who had accompanied the wounded to Kasauli, died there on the 26th of March, without hearing of his having been made a Companion of the Bath.

The new chaco, as prescribed by Circular Memo, Horse Guards, 21st September, 1843, was issued to the regiment on the 11th of May.

In 1846, the waist-belt for regimental field officers was directed to be of buffalo leather, the plate gilt, having the letters "V.R.," with a crown above, and the number of the regiment in silver below. The other officers wore the shoulder-belt.

Shell jacket for the 29th was the same as that worn in 1829, with Prussian collar, but pointed cuffs.

A worsted ball tuft, $\frac{2}{3}$ white and $\frac{1}{3}$ red at bottom, was at this period worn on the chaco of the Field, and battalion company officers; that of the Grenadier company was all white; that of the Light company, green throughout.

Trousers. 15th Oct.—30th April, of Oxford mixture; 1st May—14th Oct., in United Kingdom, grey tweed; in East Indies, white linen.

A new shako plate (5 inches in diameter) was introduced this year, viz., a gilt star, **1846** surmounted by a crown, and bearing within a wreath formed of laurels, a garter inscribed with "*Honi Soit*," &c., &c., in the centre of which was a gilt lion crowned, &c., standing on a wreath.

EXTRACT FROM GENERAL ORDER, HORSE GUARDS, 1ST JUNE, 1847.

" Her Majesty having been graciously pleased to command that a **1847** medal should be struck to record the services of her fleets and armies

OFFICERS' CHACO PLATE—1846-1856.

during the wars commencing in 1793, and ending in 1814, and that one should be conferred upon every officer, non-commissioned officer, and soldier of the army who was present in any battle or siege, to commemorate which, medals have been struck by command of Her Majesty's royal predecessors, and have been distributed to the general

H H

1847 or superior officers of the several armies and corps of troops engaged, in conformity with the regulations of the service at that time in force.

"* * *"

The following is a list of actions, for serving in which officers and men of the 29th Foot became entitled to medals :—

Lord Howe's Action ...	1st June, 1794.
Roleia	17th) August, 1808.
Vimiera	21st)
Talavera	27th and 28th July, 1809.
Busaco...	27th September, 1810.
Albuhera	16th May, 1811.

These medals were not distributed till the end of 1848-49.

On the 30th of June permission was granted the regiment to bear on its regimental colours and appointments the words "Ferozeshah," "Sobraon," in commemoration of its distinguished conduct in those battles.

In the clothing issued this year (21st August) the scales on the coatees were of a different pattern, and the lace on the skirts was discontinued.

By a special order of the Governor-General, the regiment paraded on the 27th October for his lordship's inspection. On this occasion Lord Hardinge addressed the 29th in the most laudatory terms; he spoke of the conduct of the regiment during the Peninsular War and the recent campaign on the Satláj, as having been most conspicuous for gallantry, and at all times deserving of the highest praise. His lordship, after reminding them of the high character the old 29th had borne for upwards of a hundred years, concluded by expressing his highest approbation of the very soldierlike appearance they now presented.

1848 On the 18th of March Major Gregory Way, Lieuts. Honble. H. M. Monckton and G. St. J. Henderson arrived at Kasauli with a draft from England.

On the 15th of May the regiment was inspected by Major-General **1848** Sir W. R. Gilbert, K.C.B., when its effective strength was 1 colonel, 2 lieut.-colonels, 2 majors, 9 captains, 21 lieutenants, 7 ensigns, 1 paymaster, 1 adjutant, 1 quarter-master, 1 surgeon, 3 assistant-surgeons, 51 serjeants, 45 corporals, 20 drummers, 1,034 privates.

NUMBER OF EACH COUNTRY.

	Serjeants.	Corporals.	Drummers.	Privates.
English	18	23	7	551
Scotch	3	2	2	48
Irish	30	20	11	435
Foreign				
TOTAL	51	45	20	1034

NUMBER OF SIZE.

	Serjeants.	Corporals.	Drummers.	Privates.
Of 6 ft. 0 in. and upwards	3	2		16
5 ,, 11 ,, ,,	2	2	2	34
5 ,, 10 ,, ,,	7	2		66
5 ,, 9 ,, ,,	8	7	1	116
5 ,, 8 ,, ,,	9	11	5	187
5 ,, 7 ,, ,,	15	8		251
5 ,, 6 ,, ,,	6	8	4	282
5 ,, 5 ,, ,, Under	1	5	4	70
Lads			4	12
TOTAL	51	45	20	1034

Circular Memo, Horse Guards, 30th June, 1848.

The officers' dress coat,* to be made without either lace or embroidery on the skirts other than the authorised regimental skirt ornament.

The blue frock coat to be entirely discontinued in the infantry, and a plain shell jacket,† made with the facings of the regiment, but without lace, or any ornament, to be worn with forage cap and without the sash, in quarters, on fatigue, or on orderly duties, at drill, and on parade when the non-commissioned officers and men happen to be dressed in the same manner.

Field officers to be distinguished by a small embroidered crown, or star (or both, according to their rank), at each end of the collar of the shell jacket.

---

* The 29th coatees were edged with white.

† The officers of the 29th continued to wear the shell jacket, with hooks and eyes, in lieu of buttons, and plain twisted crimson silk shoulder cords.

1848   In lieu of the blue frock and cloak, officers are to be provided with a grey cloak coat, to be worn over their uniform in wet or cold weather.

A black leather sling waist belt with snake clasp may be worn with the shell jacket.

On the breaking up of the army of the Satláj, Major-General Sir John Littler had been left at Láhor in command of about 10,000 men, pending the reconstruction of the Government of that district, and everything appeared to be progressing in a satisfactory manner, until April 1848, when Mr. Vans Agnew, of the Civil Service, and Lieut. Anderson, of the Bombay army, who had been sent to Multán, were murdered. This murder was followed by a general outbreak at Láhor, and endeavours to expel the British from the Panjáb.

The standard of rebellion being raised in the capital, and numerous bodies of disbanded Sikhs assembling in all directions, the British troops were for a time prevented from marching against Multán, which the enemy had occupied.

The 29th being directed to march to Firúzpúr, and relieve H.M. 32nd Foot, "which had been detailed as part of the force to march against Multán," left Kasauli on the 22nd of August. On the 1st of September it encamped at Bussee Kusba, and arrived at its destination on the 14th.

Early in October, it was announced in General Orders, that a force would be assembled under the personal command of Lord Gough, and designated "The Army of the Punjaub." Major-General Sir W. Gilbert, K.C.B., was to have command of the 2nd infantry division, the 3rd brigade of which was to be commanded by Colonel A. S. H. Mountain, C.B., of H.M. 29th Foot. This brigade was finally designated the 4th. At Chiliánwálá and Gujrát it was composed of H.M. 29th, the 30th and 56th Native Infantry regiments. ‡

---

‡ The 30th and 56th Bengal Native Infantry regiments disappeared from the Army List in 1859.

The present 30th Native Infantry was formerly the 22nd Punjabi Regiment.

Leaving at Firúzpúr a depôt of 8 serjeants, 1 drummer, 6 corporals, **1848** and 106 privates, under command of Lieut. Stehelin, on the 9th of November the regiment marched with the head-quarters of the army, and having crossed the Satláj by two bridges of boats, the first to the tune of "The Royal Windsor March," the second, to that of the "British Grenadiers," it that day reached Gunda-Singh-wálá, and on the morning of the 13th encamped at Mían Mir. On the 16th, the march was continued, and the Rávi crossed.

When Bena Mullian was reached on the 18th, it was ascertained that Chattar Singh had joined Shér Singh, and that the two had crossed the Chínáb; the advance guard was therefore increased from one, to two companies, and placed under the command of a field officer, whilst the baggage for the next day's march was put in charge of a wing of the 45th Native Infantry.

Early next morning the regiment, accompanied by the commander-in-chief, left its camping ground and advanced to Muttah.

About 2 a.m. on the 20th, a body of the enemy's cavalry being observed hovering about, the Flank companies, under command of Captains Murchison and Fraser, were immediately ordered out; everything however passed off quietly, and at daybreak the regiment fell in and continued its march. On reaching Mianwálá on the 21st, it found H.M. 24th encamped on its left, and H.M. 61st about a mile and a half to its right.

At sunrise the following morning, soon after the inlying picquet had been dismissed, the "Assembly" was sounded, orders having been received for the immediate advance of the troops. It then became known that Lord Gough had, at an early hour, placed himself at the head of an advance force and pushed on towards Rámnagar. All speed was made, and on reaching that town the regiment passed through it, and halted under a tope of small trees.

The guns in front were still firing, but the 29th remained as spectators of an action chiefly confined to artillery and occasional

1848 charges of cavalry. It was in one of the latter, that General Cureton and Colonel Havelock lost their lives.

After a short halt, the regiment advanced about half a mile, when it again halted, and was ordered to pitch camp.

A look-out, being erected next day at the quarter-guard, with the aid of glasses, a good view was obtained of the enemy, who appeared to be raising a battery on the left of their position. In the afternoon the regiment marched out of camp to attend the burial of General Cureton, and it had just reached the grave, when intelligence was received that the enemy were advancing in force, on the right; returning therefore to camp, it at once fell in, but no attack being made, the parade was dismissed.

On the 30th, whilst a strong party was sent to occupy a tope, in front of Mountain's brigade, and to erect a battery for the heavy guns, another was employed in throwing up a redoubt on the right. These parties were at first fired on by the enemy's heavy artillery, which however later on ceased to molest them.

A council of war being held, it was decided to strike a decisive blow, and with a view of so doing, on the 1st of December, Major-General Sir Joseph Thackwell was detached with a force to turn the enemy's left, whilst the main body attacked the position in front. In the afternoon, the left wing of the regiment, under Major Way, marched to the battery on the right, and on its being ascertained the following day that Thackwell had crossed the Chínáb at Vazírábád, the batteries opened fire on the enemy, in order to distract their attention from him. On the evening of the 3rd, the other wing of the regiment took up a position about 500 yards in front of the right battery, and commenced to construct two others about 500 yards apart and connected by a ditch and breastwork; being relieved about 2 a.m., by the left wing, the works were finished before dawn, and the ford at Rámnagar secured.

Shér Singh, who had in the meanwhile become aware of **1848** Thackwell's successful passage, broke up his camp and retired. In the afternoon therefore, many of the officers of the regiment rode over to inspect the enemy's late position.

The bodies of several of those who fell in the action of the 22nd of November were now recovered, and on the afternoon of the 5th, 300 of the regiment paraded, under command of Lieut.-Col. Congreve, for the interment of Colonel Havelock's remains.

On the morning of the 18th, the regiment paraded at ten o'clock, with a view of crossing the Chínáb by a pontoon bridge which the engineers had constructed. Having to wade through, at a part where the road had been carried away, the men were halted on the bank to take off their boots and socks, and on reaching the other side, waited to allow the 30th Native Infantry, which was following, to come up. Moving on again and crossing another stream, the regiment encamped that day at Tokailsi, about four miles from its late position, and three from General Thackwell's.

The Monthly Returns dated the 1st of January, 1849, Head- **1849** quarters, Camp, Januki, show the following officers as present with the regiment :—

- Lieut.-Colonel—Congreve, C.B. Majors—M. Smith and Way.
- Captains—Power, Murchison (Grenadier company), Æ. W. Fraser (Light company), *sick in field hospital at Rámnagar*.
- Lieutenants *—Honble. H. M. Monckton, Metge, Farrington, Dick, Tonnochy, Kneebone, E. T. Fitzgerald *(sick in camp)*, W. S. Simmons, C. H. Levinge *(sick in camp)*, R. J. Evans, J. E. Henderson, and E. H. Pery.
- Ensigns—W. L. D. Smith, A. R. Mowbray, G. A. Ferris, G. H. Nevill, W. D. Chapman, and E. H. Paske.
- Paymaster—Clay. Qr. Master—Dowson. Assistant-Surgeons—Trousdell, Macbeth, and Stewart.

Whilst in this camp, the officers amused themselves by hunting jackals, and occasionally foxes; by riding over to view the scene of the late attack on Sir Joseph Thackwell, and by playing cricket.

---

* Lieut. and Adjutant MacDonnell was on the 1st of January appointed brigade major to Mountain's brigade.

1849 On the 2nd of January, Major Way, "who always took a great interest in the welfare and amusements of the officers and men," turned out a regimental team to play "The Officers of the Army." It was a two days' match. In the 1st innings the 29th scored 78 runs, the Army 60; the second day the Regiment scored 60 to their opponents' 24.

Leaving this camp on the 9th, the regiment arrived on its new ground at Loah Tibbah a little before mid-day.

The fall of Atak, and consequent advance of Chattar Singh with reinforcements for the enemy, having been communicated to Lord Gough, the governor-general urged him to strike an effectual blow at Shér Singh without loss of time. On the morning of the 12th therefore, the army advanced towards Dinghí. The route lay through a very jungly country, the march was tedious, and it was nearly 2 p.m. before the regiment reached its new ground.

"It was now ascertained," says the author of the Decisive Battles of India, "that the Sikh army was in position some 14 miles distant, that its left rested on the low hills of Rasúl, its centre on the village of Fathsháh-ki-chak, its right on Múng; that though its front was covered by a thick belt of jungle, yet along the frequented road, which led from Dinghí straight upon Rasúl, the country was more open. A Council of War being held, it was decided to march the following day on Rasúl; that Gilbert's division, forming the extreme right, should force the enemy's left, whilst the heavy and field artillery, massed together, should sweep in enfilade the curvilinear position of their centre and right."

At midnight the officers were warned that an advance would be commenced early next morning.

The regiment having fallen in about 7 a.m., the brigades formed up in masses of quarter distance columns, the heads of which during the advance kept their dressing with a battery of 18-pounders stationed in the centre of the line. Skirmishers having been thrown out, an advance straight across country was commenced. Mountain's brigade was on the right of the heavy guns, whilst Pennycuick's was on their left.

Sketch of the Field of Chiliánwálá, made in January, 1849, by Ensign W. L. D. Smith.

1849 Unlike other corps, the 29th took the precaution to keep their colours cased, for the ground was covered nearly the whole way with a low dog jungle, intersected in many places with long prickly fences which offered no inconsiderable impediment.

Shér Singh perceiving the object of this march, determined if possible to force an action, before the British could reach the open ground on his left; he had therefore, under cover of the dense jungle, thrown forward his centre and part of his right, and occupied a mound near Chiliánwálá with a small detachment.

It having been reported to Lord Gough that the enemy were in possession of this mound, and that parties of their cavalry had been seen in advance of it, he altered the direction of his advance, and marched on Chiliánwálá. About mid-day the regiment halted whilst the enemy's picquets in front of this village were being driven in.

This having been accomplished, Pennycuick's brigade then deployed into line, whilst Mountain's moved off a little to the right and halted. In front of the latter brigade was a mound covered with tents and men, which being evidently an advance post of the enemy, the heavy guns opened fire upon it, and the Light companies (that of the 29th under command of Lieut. Metge) rushing forward to secure it, the Sikhs retired, and only one man who was taking a pot shot at an officer of the *Light Bobs* was taken prisoner. Later on, Major Way, meeting a private of the Light company arrayed in a very fine fur-lined coat with what appeared to be gold buttons, stopped the man and asked him where he got his handsome garment. "Please sir," replied the soldier, "me and a Sikh nobleman had a few words, and I came away with his coat!"

The brigade which had in the meantime been halted, now received orders to advance, and on arriving at the edge of a high jungle deployed, piled arms, and lay down.

The 29th formed the right, the 30th N.I. the left, and the 56th N.I. the centre of the brigade.*

Lord Gough, who did not appear to have any intention of engaging the enemy that day, had given his Q.M.G. orders to take up ground for encamping, and the troops were in the act of falling out, when a loud report was heard, and some shots fell near the commander-in-chief. One bounding over the colours of the 29th, pitched amongst the dhooli bearers behind, and sent them flying across the country.

Lord Gough at once directed his heavy guns to respond. Shér Singh now determined to complete the operation he had so successfully begun, and sent the whole of his field artillery to the front, upon which our infantry were ordered to advance and charge them. This order was given about 3 p.m., and it fell to Mountain's brigade to attack the most formidable part of the position.

Lord Gough, who was near the 29th at this time exclaimed, "We are at the ould work again, boys!" Whilst passing through the thick, thorny, and dense jungle which intervened, the men were much annoyed by the fire of sharpshooters who were posted in the trees, and whose signals enabled the Sikh artillery to make excellent practice against the advancing troops. One gun on the left, placed so as to enfilade the advance of the regiment, was doing much damage. Observing this, Lieut. W. S. Simmons broke off with a few men of the Light company, and charging it, after a most determined hand to hand fight, the gunners were bayonetted and the gun captured. Not having any spikes at hand, and wishing to render the piece useless, a bright idea occurred to this officer, who, seeing a bewildered Sepoy of the 56th near at hand, pulled off his forage cap and rammed it up the gun; this was the means of saving many lives. The amusing part was to follow, for the day after the action the gun being brought in, was examined

---

* Official Regimental Records 29th Foot; and sketch of the battle, drawn by Capt. E. Haythorne, 98th Regiment, A.D.C. to General Campbell, C.B., Camp Chiliánwálá, 29th January, 1849.

1849 and the Sepoy's forage cap being extracted, its innocent owner was sent for, complimented, and promoted on the spot, for his bravery in capturing and rendering useless the gun. The desperation with which the artillerymen stood to, and defended their guns, may be judged, when it is stated that one of these men with the bayonet right through him, clutched hold of his assailant's musket, and with uplifted arm was about to cut him down, when the latter in self-defence pressed the trigger of his musket and shot the brave Sikh.

The regiment which was still advancing, could now no longer preserve its dressing, for the men having to force their way through the dense jungle, had to get through when and where they could, and therefore at times found themselves in large groups. On approaching the more open ground where the Sikh artillery supported by infantry was posted, the former opened fire with grape.

As the right of the line was this day saved by General Colin Campbell with H.M. 61st, so was the centre by Col. Congreve with the 29th Foot,* for riding through the jungle in front of his regiment, this officer at once grasped the situation, viz., the complete isolation of the 29th in consequence of the Native regiments of the brigade failing to support it ; its unfavourable position whilst exposed to frequent discharges of grape, and the critical position of the 5th brigade. A moment's hesitation would have entailed the destruction of the centre of the line of battle.

Wishing, therefore, to get his men out of the jungle with the least possible delay, and to charge the enemy, the colonel, noticing a gun on the left which was causing much annoyance, pointed to it, and shouted, " 300 Rs. to the man who takes that gun !" Then ordering his bugler, whom he had mounted on an enormous horse cut loose from a Sikh limber, to sound the " Double," he gave the word to charge. Followed

---

* *Vide* General Grant's address to the regiment on 17th January, 1857.

by some of his men, Colonel Congreve dashed forward towards the gun, and being the first to reach it, struck the piece with his sword, exclaiming, "My gun!" In the meanwhile, the remainder of the old regiment had broken their way through the jungle, and with a shout such as moments of pride and triumph like these, and these alone, can produce, made bravely to the front, rushing headlong into the thick of the enemy. Then commenced a struggle the like of which is but seldom seen, for casting aside their matchlocks as of no further use, the desperate Sikhs, sword in hand, awaited the onslaught. Numbers of their artillerymen were bayonetted in the act of serving the guns, whilst others continued the contest till they were either shot, or cut down. The guns, 12 in number, were captured, but in so doing upwards of 60 of the regiment were incapacitated by sword cuts alone. As previous to going into action two men per company had been provided with spikes, the guns were immediately disabled.

Ensign Smith, in a letter written home just after this action, gives the following account :—

"At first the regiment lost but an occasional man or two, killed by round shot, but as it neared the enemy a heavy fire of musketry and grape was opened on the men, who in forcing their way through the jungle and bushes, at times got into groups. Then came a grand explosion, a crashing smashing sound, and heaps of men came rolling down, some uttering low cries of pain, others falling without a sound. This was the effect of grape. When the smoke cleared away a little, there began an infernal clatter of musketry. 'There they are by ——!' shouted a fellow near me, and there they were. An immense line of infantry was standing behind the bushes in rear of their guns, their long matchlocks pointing in a very ominous way towards us. Our men with one accord raised their firelocks, and sent a tremendous volley into them, and with a shout went at them with the bayonet. They let us approach to within about 30 yards, when having fired, they threw

1849 away their matchlocks, and drawing their swords, awaited our attack. Some ten or twelve stood close before our colours; they were fine large fellows dressed in red jackets with green facings, black crossbelts and continuations; all had beards reaching down to their waists, and long hair at the back of their heads. They fired, but missed us, we dashed at them round the bush, one of the men on my right shot one dead, and dashed his bayonet at another, who however seized the dreaded point with his left hand, and cut down his assailant. I came next, the Sikh threw the bayonet away and turned towards me, holding his sword straight up in the air ready to put my head between my heels. I hit the very nick of time, and making a plunge at him, he looked at me for a moment, and then dropped off my sword, the point of which had penetrated beneath his right shoulder blade, having previously struck him on the left side somewhere very near the heart. All the others shared his fate. One man threw out his arms, took the point of a bayonet into his body, and held it there with his left hand whilst with his right he severely wounded his antagonist."

Line having been re-formed, the regiment continued to press the enemy's infantry, which retired in the greatest order, loading, halting, and fronting to deliver their fire, as if on parade, thereby giving an excellent illustration of their good drill and discipline.

As Pennycuick's brigade had been repulsed, and its assailants were advancing along the line, to attack the remaining regiments on the right, the 29th received orders to change front to the left on its Light company. This occasioned a gap in the line, of which the enemy were not long in taking advantage, for suddenly there was an alarm that some of them were in rear, endeavouring to withdraw the spiked guns. This proving to be the case, Colonel Congreve turned the regiment about, and charged back to defend them. Shortly after this some Sikh cavalry were observed approaching at a steady canter, who having advanced to within about 200 yards, slackened their pace to a walk; one, however, continued his advance from bush to bush, until **1849** he at last got within 100 yards of the regiment, when one of the men ran out a few yards, and as the Sikh appeared between the last two bushes, dropped him dead from his horse. The remainder thereupon galloped up, but every firelock was brought up to the "present," and many a bullet told, as men dropped from their saddles or horses rolled over. Being thrown into some confusion, another well-directed volley sent the enemy to the right about, and away they went helter-skelter. Two of the Sikhs, however, previous to so doing spread a white cloth over the body of the man who was shot first, and who appeared to have been their leader.

The regiment then fronted, and continuing its advance became again opposed to some infantry and a battery of seven guns, which were firing on the 5th brigade. On their charging these guns, six of them limbered up and galloped away, the seventh however turned round and taking a shot at the colours succeeded in clearing away every man to the right and left of them. The gun was captured, the gunners bayonetted, and H.M. 24th was saved from any further loss.

Having driven the enemy into another open space beyond the jungle, the regiment in order not to expose its small numbers to the enemy's view, was directed to halt in rear of the jungle, and soon afterwards orders were received for the men to pile arms and lie down. Presently Lord Gough rode along the front of the 29th which received him with a hearty cheer, the result being some round shot from the enemy, which wounded two men just in front of the commander-in-chief, upon which he pulled up exclaiming, "Them be hard dumplings, boys!" In this position the regiment remained for some time, till all firing having ceased and the enemy having withdrawn, No. 1 company, under command of Lieut. Kneebone, with Ensign Ferris, was ordered to hand over its arms to No. 2, and to collect the wounded. Whilst this was being done the remainder of the regiment fell back on Chiliánwálá

1849 and bivouacked for the night, a short distance in rear of where it had that morning first deployed; for near this village alone could food and water be obtained. By the time the wounded had been collected, it was so dark that Lieut. Kneebone's company had great difficulty in finding its way back to the regiment.

Unarmed, surrounded by jungle, and with the enemy in the vicinity, it was an anxious moment when advancing footsteps were heard. The approaching party on being challenged, proved fortunately to be an escort with ammunition and grog for the regiment; these had also lost their way. The men now halted, and a tot all round being served out, the parties eventually reached the regiment without further adventure, and to the pleasure of their comrades who were getting anxious at their long absence.

During the change of front, which had enabled the enemy to get in rear of the regiment, five out of the twelve guns which had been spiked, were withdrawn by the Sikhs.

In this action the centre of the Queen's colour, which Ensign Smith ‡ carried, was shot out, and that officer twice hit by spent bullets; Ensign Mowbray, ‖ who had charge of the regimental colour, had the badge shot off his forage cap, but happily escaped without wounds.

Major-General Sir W. Gilbert, in his despatch, mentions the undaunted bravery on this occasion of Her Majesty's 29th Regiment, under Lieut.-Colonel Congreve, and the manner in which Majors Smith and Way seconded their brave commander; as also of the conduct of Lieut. MacDonnell, § major of brigade.

---

‡ Died at Vazírábád on the 29th of November, 1849.

‖ Promoted the following day into H.M. 24th Foot. Died on the 16th of February, 1850.

§ The only officer of the Queen's army under the grade of Captain rewarded with a step of honorary rank for this action.

From Muster Rolls, Pay Lists, and Monthly Returns 29th Foot:—

Chiliánwálá, 13th January, 1849.	Lieut.-Cols.	Majors.	Captains.	Lieutenants.	Ensigns.	Staff.	Serjeants.	Drummers.	Rank and File.
Strength of Regiment going into action	2	2	2	12	6	6	29	12	771
Killed *							2		33
Wounded *		1		2	1		6	4	200
Missing									2

OFFICERS WOUNDED.

Major—Matthew Smith   Slight contusion.

Lieutenants { Honble. H. M. Monckton   Severely.
             { H. T. Metge   Very severely.

Ensign—G. H. Nevill   Slightly.

KILLED.

Serjt. Carey, Patrick
 ,,   Long, Robert
Pte. Beech, Richard
 ,, Buckley, Charles
 ,, Bunting, Thomas
 ,, Campbell, James
 ,, Cooney, Edmund
 ,, Cotter, Pierce
 ,, Dailey, Barnard
 ,, Darmon, Joseph
 ,, Dawkins, Henry
 ,, Dempsey, Patrick

Pte. Donovan, John
 ,, Farnol, John
 ,, Fidler, John
 ,, Giles, William
 ,, Gastiler, John
 ,, Guest, Frederick
 ,, Haggett, George
 ,, Hopkins, Michael
 ,, Hussey, John
 ,, Jenkins, William, 2682
 ,, McDermott, Dominick
 ,, McGlaughlin, Charles

Pte. Marriott, Thomas
 ,, Mayo, James
 ,, Mullin, Thomas
 ,, Naylor, William
 ,, Pratt, William
 ,, Shenton, James
 ,, Taylor, Jonas
 ,, Twambley, John
 ,, Walker, Thomas
 ,, Walsh, Thomas
 ,, Wildbore, James

MISSING.

Privates—T. Taylor and T. Vornem (in Indian battles the missing may generally be counted as killed).

---

* *Gazette.* 29th Foot { Killed— 2 Serjeants, - Drummers, 29 Rank and File.
                      { Wounded—5   ,,   4   ,,   194   ,,

1849 The following anecdotes about the fight are mentioned in Ensign Smith's letter, part of which has already been quoted:—

"The Sikhs always mutilate any wounded they come across, and when they got in our rear they found under a bush two men of the Light company, both badly wounded, and pretending to be dead. They stripped one of his haversack, pouch, etc., he never moving in the slightest; they then went to the other and commenced to rifle him. I suppose he gave a twitch, or something of the sort, for one of the Sikhs gave him a cut right down his back, but the fellow never flinched even for that, and the Sikhs, thinking them certainly dead, went away; both men are recovering fast. One man near me in the charge knocked down a fellow and bayonetted him, then putting his hand to his victim's waistband to feel if he had a stray rupee or so about him, but finding none, looked at him with a mock appearance of pity, and shaking his head said, 'Ah, you poor devil, you hadn't received your daily pay!' This was under as infernal a fire as any man could wish to be in. Another fellow, coming from behind a bush, where he had evidently been slaughtering somebody, being asked what he had been doing there, replied, 'Me, and another gen'elman, has just been settling our little differences round the corner.'

The Sikhs have a way of dropping as if shot, and when the regiments have passed, of taking a steady shot at an officer or anyone at all conspicuous: this has often been done, not only by men who were unhurt, but also by those actually badly wounded, and they, when they get hold of our wounded, treat them barbarously; the consequence is that our men having experienced these annoyances, both in the Sutlej and this campaign, never spare a soul, never pass a Sikh, even though he be in the agonies of death, without helping him off, and therefore many an unpleasant scene takes place. Nothwithstanding this, Monckton received a shot in his back which narrowly missed being fatal."

Lieut. Thackwell, in his " Narrative of the Second Sikh War," **1849** says :—

"After the battle, Padre Whiting (Rev. W. J. Whiting, chaplain to the army), by which name he will be ever known, earnestly entreated Lord Gough to grant him an escort to enable him to recover and bury the bodies of his poor countrymen. The escort consisted of four companies of Englishmen, 200 sappers and miners, and two troops of native cavalry. Whilst they were collecting the dead, the Sikhs in great force approached close, but did not offer any molestation. Their attitude was however so threatening that Mr. Whiting was compelled to leave untouched four men of the 29th Foot, who had fallen far in advance. Such an attempt would have precipitated an action."

When, after the battle,* the troops retired to Chiliánwálá, the Sikhs fell back and re-occupied their position at Rasúl, and there awaited the arrival of reinforcements under Chattar Singh and a contingent from Afghanistan.

On the 14th, Lord Gough took up a position between Chiliánwálá and Mujiánwálá, where he remained pending the fall of Múltán and arrival of troops engaged in its siege under General Whish.

H.M. 24th Foot having had 21 officers killed or wounded in the late action, amongst whom were its three field officers, Major M. Smith, of the 29th, was on the 14th of January appointed lieut.-colonel of the former regiment, in which also Ensign Mowbray was given his lieutenancy ; whilst Captain W. G. Brown, who had commanded the Light company of the 24th the previous day, was promoted major in the 29th Foot.

---

* An obelisk was subsequently erected upon the scene of action, in memory of the British officers and men who had lost their lives upon the field, which is known to the natives as " Katalgarh," or the House of Slaughter. This neighbourhood is also celebrated as the scene of a battle between Alexander the Great and Porous, in 327 B.C.

1849 The posting of field officers, not meeting with the approval of the Home authorities, Colonel Smith, and Major Brown, were in July re-transferred to their former corps.

During the next few days, earthworks were thrown up to protect the camp, and the regiment was at first employed in cutting down bits of jungle in the direction of Múng, and subsequently in constructing on a mound about a mile to its right, a square redoubt, the angles of which were pierced for three guns, and which was capable of holding about 300 men.

On the evening of the 18th, Lieut. Metge died from the effects of his wounds, and was buried the next morning.

Multán having fallen on the 21st, General Whish immediately set out for Rámnagar.

In the meanwhile the enemy made several attempts to induce Lord Gough to leave his position.

Monthly Returns, 1st of February, 1849—Camp at Chiliánwálá.

OFFICERS PRESENT.

Lieut.-Colonel—Congreve, C.B. Majors—Way, and W. G. Brown (*sick in camp*).

Captains—Power, Coker (*m.*), and Murchison.

Lieutenants—Monckton, Farrington, Dick, Tonnochy, Kneebone, Fitzgerald, Simmons, Levinge, Evans, Henderson, Pery, and Smith.

Ensigns—Ferris, Nevill, Chapman, and Paske.

Pay Master—Clay. Qr. Master—Dowson.

Assistant-Surgeons—Trousdell, M.D., Macbeth,‡ and Stewart.

ALTERATIONS DURING THE MONTH.

Lieut. H. P. Onslow joined on the 2nd, and Surgeon Dane, M.D., on the 10th inst.

On the 2nd, it being observed that the greater part of the Sikh camp had been struck, reconnoitering parties were sent to watch the

---

‡ On account of ill-health, obtained leave of absence from the 12th of February to the 11th of May following.

mouth of a gorge in rear of the British army. Nothing, however, being seen of the enemy in that quarter, it was thought they had retreated. Shér Singh, however, finding his endeavours to draw out Lord Gough of no avail, shortly afterwards returned to Rasúl, and on the evening of the 13th, having completed all his preparations for a decisive move, succeeded in turning the British position, and in gaining a march towards the Chínáb, which he was however prevented from crossing, as General Whish, on reaching Rámnagar, had sent detachments to guard the fords. The Sikhs then marched to Gujrat, and there took up a position.

1849

Early in the morning of the 15th, Lord Gough's army marched in pursuit, and reached Shadáwálá, distant but a few miles from Gujrát, on the 20th. The enemy's picquets were now well in sight, and it was discovered that the Sikh camp nearly encircled that town. The strength of their army was about 60,000 of all arms, with 59 pieces of artillery, and a body of 1,500 Afghan horse led by Akram Khan. Sirdar Chattar Singh and his son, Rajah Shér Singh, were their chief commanders. To meet the attack which they expected to be made that day, the enemy's leaders had posted their troops as follows, says Colonel Malleson: " Their centre was formed behind the village of Kálrá; their left, rested on the Kátelah, a rivulet which flows into the Chínáb at a point above Vazírábád; their right, refused, was covered by the Dwárah, a dry, sandy-bedded rivulet of some breadth." This order they maintained on the 21st. About 6.30 a.m. that day, the 29th having formed square, Colonel Mountain told the men they were to attack an outpost of the enemy's, and carry it without firing a shot. The army having formed up in line of quarter-distance columns at deploying intervals, marched at 7.30 a.m. to its pre-arranged position. In the centre of the line were the heavy guns, 10 in number, drawn by elephants, on the right of which were the 56th Native Infantry, H.M. 29th Foot, and the 30th Native Infantry.

1849   Finding the Sikhs had evacuated the outpost, the regiment pushed on until it came within range of the enemy, when the artillery, galloping to the front from between the brigades, opened fire. The infantry in the meantime lay down a short distance in rear of the guns, and regulated their movements in all cases by those of the batteries.

After some time the enemy's infantry attemped to advance, but being received with a fire of shrapnel and grape, were compelled to retire.

During this action, an onslaught was made by a party of Sikh horsemen, who being mistaken for some of our own irregular cavalry, rushed past the skirmishers, and riding down the rear of the 29th, continued their course towards the commander-in-chief's staff. Some of them were shot by the rear rank of the regiment, which had at once faced about; the remainder being charged by Lieut. Stannus, of the 5th Light Cavalry, who commanded Lord Gough's escort, but few escaped.

Orders to advance being now received, the regiment marched through the enemy's camp, and whilst so doing passed many disabled guns. As quickly as the enemy had taken up a fresh position, they had been driven from it by the fire of the artillery, which broke their ranks at all points; in fact, towards the end of the action they retired so fast that the regiment had not a chance of closing with them.

"The British cavalry," says Major L. Archer, "was now launched in pursuit, while the infantry, advancing through the gaily striped tents, which had been abandoned, drew up in line on the left, and a little in advance of the town of Gujrát. It was nearly sunset, arms were piled; and, while here and there mines and combustibles were exploding, the bands of the various regiments struck up at the hour of retreat, their martial music, dominated by the spirit-stirring 'Rule Britannia.'"

The action having been chiefly confined to artillery, the casualties of the 29th were trifling, viz., 2 killed and 6 wounded. The total losses in the brigade being only 2 killed and 10 wounded.

KILLED.
Private—Gibson, John
     „   Sullivan, John

Sketch of the Battle of Goojirat, by Lieut. W. S. Simmons.

1849   In this action Ensign Ferris* carried the Queen's Colour, and George Nevill†, the Regimental. This was destined to be the last occasion on which the regiment ever carried colours on active service.§

Next day General Gilbert started in pursuit of the enemy, and marching by Dinghí, the regiment reached Naurangábád, on the left bank of the Jhelam on the 24th, where it remained encamped till the flight of the Afgháns beyond the Khaibar, which brought the campaign to an end.

On the 1st of March brigadier Mountain was brought into camp badly wounded, having accidentally shot himself through the hand, whilst placing his pistol in his holster.

On the 23rd and 24th, the regiment marched in two divisions for Khowar, and thence to Vazírábád, where, there being a want of barrack accommodation, it encamped first at Tonekí and afterwards at Serokí.

On the 30th, the annexation of the Panjáb was proclaimed, Dhulíp Singh, the titular Sovereign, yielding up his rights in consideration of an annual pension. The royal treasures of Láhor were secured, and out of the spoil, the celebrated Koh-i-Nor was reserved for Queen Victoria.

Col. Congreve and Major Way having obtained leave of absence early in April, the command of the regiment devolved on Major Brown, who on the 15th of June presented the medals for the Satláj campaign to those entitled to receive them.

The Depôt, which had been stationed at Firúzpúr under command of Lieut. Stehelin since November 1848, rejoined head-quarters toward the end of December, 1849.

---

* Capt. Ferris exchanged to 97th Foot, on the 18th of March, 1859, and retired as Major on full pay, with rank of Lieut.-Colonel, 17th of January, 1877.

† Was on the 12th of July, 1850, appointed Lieut. 12th Foot. Retired from 7th Fusiliers as Captain on the 13th of July, 1855.

§ *Vide 1882.* "Regiments ordered on active service, to leave their colours at the base of operations."

1849 During this campaign the officers wore over the plain hooked-up shell jacket which has already been described, a plain double-breasted red serge quilted jacket, with roll collar and buttons covered with the same material. Field officers wore a belt with slings, company officers carried their swords suspended in a sliding frog on a black patent leather waist-belt, with snake clasp. Cap covers were worn by all ranks, the non-commissioned officers, rank and file having their badges, which were of brass, outside the cover. The Battalion companies wore a "29," Flank companies a grenade or bugle, as the case might be, above the numerals; in each case a small piece of red cloth was placed under the badge. The "tuft" on the top of the cap was—white for the Grenadiers, green for Light company. The shoulder belt plate for the non-commissioned officers, rank and file, was perfectly smooth, with a raised "29" in the centre.

1850 Being relieved by the 10th Foot, the regiment left Vazírábád about the middle of February, 1850, and marching by Firúzpúr arrived at Mírath on the 29th of March.

A plain shoulder-belt without a breast-plate, was authorized this year, for the pouch; and a waist-belt with a frog for the bayonet was introduced.

On the 15th of August Lieut.-General Ulysses Lord Downes, K.C.B., was appointed Colonel of the regiment, *vice* General, the Earl of Strafford, transferred to the Coldstream Guards.

Whilst at Vazírábád the officers adopted a red waistcoat to wear with the shell jacket at Mess.

Having unexpectedly received orders to march with as little delay as possible to Kánhpúr, and to proceed thence by water to Dánápúr, to relieve the 80th Foot sent on active service to Burma, the regiment, under command of Lieut.-Colonel Congreve, C.B., left Mírath on the 2nd of March, 1852, and on reaching Kánhpúr, encamped there until **1852** the 5th of April, when it embarked on a fleet of 91 boats and reached its destination on the 28th inst.

The sick and women proceeded direct from the Ghurmuktisur Ghát to Dánápúr by water.

1852 A wing of the regiment, under command of Major Stepney, with Captain Farrington, Lieuts. Lyle, Dick, Kneebone, Henderson, J. T. James, Chapman, Ensigns J. J. H. Gordon, Henry W. S. Carew, J. F. Page, J. C. Langford, Assistant-Surgeon Macqueen, M.D., 20 serjeants, 8 drummers, 21 corporals, and 352 privates, proceeded in two divisions, on the 10th and 23rd of July, by steamer to Fort William, Calcutta there to be stationed.

On the 30th the medals for the Panjáb campaign were issued. They had been received a month previous, but no ribbon having been sent with them, the distribution was delayed.

By Circular Memo, Horse Guards, the 8th of July, 1852, a plain double-breasted blue frock coat, with plain covered buttons, was sanctioned to be worn by officers when riding or walking in the neighbourhood of their quarters; this coat was to be worn with the forage cap, sash, sword, and waist-belt, with a black stock, and buttoned up.

From a pattern taken out of the book of a well-known London military tailor, it appears that the facings on the officers' coatee were about this time altered from the very pale yellow, almost primrose colour, which had been worn certainly for the last hundred years, to a deeper yellow.

Being relieved by the 2nd European Regiment, on the 11th of November, the wing stationed at Fort William (with the exception of No. 1 company) moved to Chinsará. On the 3rd of December, No. 1, under command of Lieut. Lyle, with Ensigns Gordon, Page, and **1853** Langford, rejoined head-quarters. On the 3rd of January, 1853, No. 3, with Lieuts. Kneebone, James, and Chapman, arrived at Dánápúr from Chinsará. The Grenadier company and part of No. 2, under Captain Stehelin, having embarked at Chinsará on the 16th of January, reached head-quarters on the 5th of February. The remaining portion of No. 2, under command of Captain Farrington, arrived at Dánápúr on the 2nd of March.

By General Orders dated Head-quarters, Umballa, the 9th of March, 1853, it was intimated that Her Majesty had been pleased to approve of the words " Panjaub," " Chillianwallah," and " Goojerat " being borne on the Regimental colour* and appointments of the 29th **1853** Regiment, in consideration of its services during the campaign of 1848-49 in that country.

On the 5th of December, Nos. 4, 5, 6, and 7, and the Light company (Captain H. G. Colvill), under command of Major J. Ross Wheeler, embarked for Calcutta, whence on the 28th of January, 1854, **1854** it sailed on board the H.C. steamer "Bernice," with the "Agha Buckha" transport, for Moulmein, where it arrived on the 6th of February.

At 3 p.m. on the 20th, orders having been received for the head-quarters, under command of Major Smith, with the right wing and Grenadier company (Captain Walker) to be in readiness to embark at 4 p.m.; they left Dánápúr that afternoon, and Calcutta on the 9th of March, arriving at Moulmein on the 15th.

From this place, detachments were sent to Bassein, Shwegyeen, and Sitang.

Information being received that a party of convicts which was being conveyed to Singapore on board the "Clarissa," had, after murdering the captain of the ship and the havildar of the native guard, made for shore near Amherst, a detachment consisting of 2 subalterns, 1 staff, 3 serjeants, 1 drummer, with 52 rank and file of the Grenadiers, under command of Captain Walker, embarked on the 19th of May on board the Hon. Company's steamer "Sesostris" in search of the gang. Owing, however, to the dense jungle and want of transport, the search proved fruitless, and on the 28th the troops returned to head-quarters.

By Circular Memo, Horse Guards, the 21st of July, 1854, the General Commanding-in-Chief authorized the practice, in the army generally, of allowing the moustache to grow, subject to the following regulations, which were to be strictly obeyed on home and colonial service. A clear space of two inches to be left between the corner of the mouth and the whisker, when whiskers are grown. The chin, the underlip, and at least two inches of the upper part of the throat must be clean shaved. The wearing of the moustache was optional with all ranks.

---

* The battle scrolls for the Satláj and Panjáb campaigns were not sewn on the colour till 1871-72; this accounts for the unequal interval between these, and those commemorating the Peninsular victories.

1854   By a General Order, Commander-in-Chief in India, dated the 27th of July, the service companies of the regiment were formed into ten instead of nine.

Towards the end of October, the regiment received orders to proceed to Rangoon, and thence to Thayetmyo, where the head-quarters, the Flank companies, with Nos. 1 and 8, arrived on the 15th of November, and relieved the 1st European Bengal Fusiliers.

Nos. 2 and 3 from Moulmein, and No. 5 from Bassein, joined head-quarters on the 30th. No. 4 from Sitang, and Nos. 6 and 7 from Shwegyeen arrived at Thayetmyo on the 19th of December. Early this month, Nos. 2 and 3 embarked for Prome, but on reaching that place were ordered to Shwedoung, a small station on the left bank of **1855** the Irawaddy. At the latter place, on the 10th of February, 1855, several of the phoongee or priests' houses which were occupied by No. 3 company, were burnt down, and a great quantity of the arms, accoutrements, and bedding destroyed. Captain Dick mentioned the cheerful and unceasing exertions displayed by the officers, non-commissioned officers, and men of the detachment, in arresting the progress of the fire, to which he attributed the safety of the other buildings occupied by No. 2 company. This detachment rejoined head-quarters on the 15th of April.

On the 17th of February, Colonel Congreve, C.B., the senior lieut.-colonel of the regiment, was appointed quarter-master-general to the forces in India; and Col. Smith, who succeeded to the command, exchanged in June with Lieut.-Colonel John H. Stewart, of the 81st Foot, who, however, did not join the regiment till the 20th of September following.

On the 13th of March, the Depôt, consisting of 3 serjeants, 2 drummers, 32 rank and file, which had been left at Moulmein under command of Lieut. Langford, when the regiment proceeded to Thayetmyo, joined head-quarters.

Nos. 1 and 8 proceeded on detachment to the frontier post at **1855** Meeaday on the 20th, but returned to head-quarters on the 28th September on being relieved by Nos. 4 and 5, under command of Major Wheeler with Captain Westropp, Lieuts. Ferris, De Vic Valpy, and Assistant-Surgeon Chartres.

On the 8th of August a guard of honour, consisting of the Flank companies and band, under command of Captain Colvill (Light company), received Major Phayre, agent of the governor-general of India, and envoy to the Court of Ava. In obedience to Garrison Orders, on the 10th of August a portion of the band embarked on board the Satláj and accompanied the envoy to the capital.

Great changes in the uniform of officers and men were this year authorised. Coatees were abolished, and on the 16th of January, a scarlet double-breasted tunic, with collar rounded off in front, lappels and cuffs of regimental facing was substituted; the lappels were made to be worn either turned back or buttoned over, the latter if on duty. Cuff, round; on sleeve, a slashed flap of regimental facing with three loops of regimental lace and buttons. Two rows of buttons, at equal distances down the front, nine in each row. Scarlet slashed flap on skirt behind, with three loops of regimental lace and buttons. Coat, collar, cuffs, and slashes to be edged with white. On left shoulder, a crimson silk cord to retain the sash, with a small regimental button. Field officers to be distinguished by lace round top and bottom of collar, down edge of skirts behind, also on edge of skirt and sleeve flaps; two rows of lace round top of cuffs, and badges of rank on collar. Other officers to have lace on top of collar only, and one row round top of cuffs. Badges of rank on collar.

"*Chaco*" of black felt 5¼ inches deep in front, 7⅛ inches behind, 1 inch less in diameter at top than at bottom. Patent leather sunk top, a peak in front and behind, and chin strap. Gilt *plate, star of eight points, surmounted by a crown, having the regimental number in bright gold, on a black ground, within a garter proper. A bronze gorgon's head at the back for ventilation.

"*Worsted ball tuft*," and gilt socket as in 1846.

"*Waist belt*." Enamelled leather with slings. *Plate*, a round clasp, having on the centre piece, the number of the regiment surmounted by a crown, both in silver, and on the outer circle the regimental title in silver letters.

---

* For non-commissioned officers and privates, Brass.

1855 "*Shell jacket.*" Scarlet, with rounded collar and pointed cuffs of the regimental facing. A row of small regimental buttons down the front at equal distances, and two on each sleeve. Field officers alone, distinguished by collar badges.

"*Frock coat.*" Blue, double breasted, stand-up collar rounded off in front, cuff and lappels all blue, slashed flap on sleeve with three small regimental buttons. Slash and flaps on skirts, as in tunic and crimson shoulder cord like in tunic. Field officers only, to wear collar badges.

"*Trowsers.*" 15th October to 30th April, Oxford mixture. 1st May to 14th October, dark blue. In hot climates, white linen.

The buttons of the non-commissioned officers and privates, which had up to the present been of pewter, quite flat, with "29" in centre encircled by a small raised ring, were now changed to brass and made convex. With the introduction of the tunic, the white tape across the breast of the men's coats, and the regimental mode of wearing the buttons, in pairs, disappeared.

1856 By Circular Memo., Horse Guards, 28th March, 1856, a single * instead of a double-breasted tunic was approved of for all ranks; this alteration to take effect from the 1st April, 1857. The rank of an officer was denoted by a badge on the collar, in addition to which officers of the Flank companies wore an embroidered grenade or bugle, according to their company.

On the 5th of September Nos. 4 and 5 having been relieved by Nos. 6 and 7 companies, rejoined head-quarters from Meeaday.

Orders having been received for the regiment to proceed to Calcutta and relieve H.M. 53rd Foot, a wing consisting of Nos. 1, 2, 3, 4, and 5 companies, under command of Major Wheeler, left Thayetmyo on the morning of the 29th November for Rangoon, where it disembarked on the 3rd of December, but on account of the disturbed state of the country, the previous orders were cancelled, and the wing returned to Thayetmyo on the 22nd, when Major Wheeler was ordered to take command of the garrison at Meeaday.

An important change was made this year by the abolition of the Board of General Officers, the duty of supplying the soldiers' clothing being transferred from the Colonels of regiments to the State.

---

*The single breasted tunic was not adopted by the officers of the regiment till October 1858.

By Sealed Pattern, dated Horse Guards, 12th January, 1857, the officers' buttons were assimilated to those of the men; and a big embroidered "29" was directed to be worn on the forage caps of the battalion company officers.

On the 16th a guard of honour, under command of Captain Colvill, composed of 50 rank and file from each of the Flank companies, received H.E. Lieut.-General Grant, C.B., commander-in-chief of the Madras army.

The following day the regiment, under command of Lieut.-Colonel Stewart, was reviewed by His Excellency, who expressed his entire

Officers' Tunic and Coatee Button.

satisfaction with the manner in which the different evolutions were performed, as also with everything that came under his observation, and paid it a high compliment in the following speech made on parade:—

"Twenty-ninth Regiment, I am glad to have met you again, we are old friends, for I have served with you through two campaigns, and I must say I consider you second to none. You upheld the honour of the British arms at Roleia, Vimiera, Talavera, and Albuera, and more recently under that renowned general, Lord Gough, at Ferozeshah, Sobraon, and Chillianwallah, when whatever may have befallen others, you at least carried all before you, and retained undiminished the lustre of your ancient name, and again at the crowning victory of Goojerat, when we finally defeated and overthrew the Sikh power.

1857 "I believe you are about to go home, and wish you all, health and happiness, and am sure that wherever you are, you will always retain undiminished the lustre of your present name, you will carry with you the good wishes of all with whom you may have served; they will regret the departure of a corps so distinguished for its gallantry in the field, and uniform good conduct in quarters."

On the 11th and 12th of March, Nos. 6 and 7 companies rejoined head-quarters from Meeaday, having been relieved by Nos. 2 and 3 under command of Captain Farrington, with Lieuts. Evans and Ledgard.

On the 9th of June, Captain and Brevet Lieut.-Colonel S. Fisher,* 29th Foot, commanding the 15th Irregular Cavalry, was killed at Súltánpúr by the mutineers.

Colonel Malleson, in the "History of the Indian Mutiny," gives the following account of this officer's death:—

"Súltánpúr was the head-quarters of the 15th Regiment of Irregular Cavalry, commanded by Colonel S. Fisher, one of the most gallant and daring officers in the service. Early on the morning of the 8th June, 1857, the 1st Regiment of Military Police, commanded by Captain Bunbury, rose in revolt. Colonel Fisher rode down to their lines, followed by his men, to endeavour to recall them to order. Whilst he was addressing them, a policeman came round and shot him in the back. He fell mortally wounded from his horse. His own men had been passive spectators of the deed. They would not approach him, although they allowed the adjutant, Lieut. Tucker, to tend him in his last agony. Whilst they permitted this, however, they turned upon the second in command, Captain Gubbins, shot him, and then shouted to Lieut. Tucker to be off. By this time Colonel Fisher's last agony was over, and Tucker, having nothing more to do, mounted and rode for his life."

---

* Exchanged from the 3rd Light Dragoons with Capt. Honble. H. M. Monckton, 2nd August, 1850.

On the 24th and 28th of June, a wing of the regiment, consisting **1857** of Nos. 1, 6, 7, and 8 companies, embarked in two detachments, the first under command of Captain Duncan, the second under that of Major Wheeler, for Rangoon, *en route* to Calcutta. The officers with this wing were Major Wheeler, Captains Duncan, Westropp, Fred Middleton; Lieutenants Levinge (from the 31st of October), Evans (disembarking officer), Gordon (acting quarter-master), Smith (acting adjutant to the wing), J. Dane; Ensign G. F. Hart, and Assistant-Surgeon Macqueen, M.D. Having disembarked at Calcutta about the 27th of July, the wing occupied the Town Hall, which had been fitted up as a barrack.

In October, Nos. 1 and 8 companies, under command of Captain Kneebone,† marched to reinforce the garrison at Bárrákpúr, where some native regiments had already been disarmed by H.M. 35th Foot. Later on they were joined by Major Wheeler with the remainder of the wing. On the 9th and 12th of December, three mutineers of the 32nd Bengal N.I. having been convicted by General Court Martial, were on a garrison parade, blown away from guns. On the 21st the wing marched to Calcutta, where it embarked on board the "Belgravia" for Rangoon, which was reached on the 29th.

On the 17th of July, Captain Farrington, with No. 2, rejoined head-quarters, from Meeaday.

On the 19th, the Flank companies and No. 4, under command of Captain Colvill, with Captain F. Sorell, Ensigns W. Winn and K. V. Bacon, embarked for Rangoon, where they were joined on the 7th of August by the head-quarters, consisting of the staff, band, and attached men of companies previously embarked for Calcutta. Captain Farrington, with Lieut. F. S. Eckersall, 3 serjeants, 3 drummers, 73 rank and file, remained at Thayetmyo, and were on the 21st of

---

† This officer was on leave in the Mauritius, when news of the outbreak of the mutiny arrived; sacrificing his leave, he took passage on board the first steamer bound for Calcutta, and on going ashore was surprised to see some of his own company on sentry.

1857 November joined by the Grenadier company, under command of Lieut. H. E. Quinn.

On the 24th of July, the establishment of the regiment was fixed at 1 colonel, 2 lieut.-colonels, 2 majors, 10 captains, 12 lieutenants, 8 ensigns, 7 staff, 51 serjeants, 50 corporals, 20 drummers, and 900 privates.

1858 On the 14th of January, 1858, No. 4 and the Light company, under command of Captain Colvill, with Lieut. E. Gorton and Assistant-Surgeon Farmer, embarked at Rangoon for Thayetmyo, where they arrived on the 24th.

On the 10th of February, No. 3, under command of Captain Walker, joined the right wing at Thayetmyo, from detachment at Meeaday.

Embarking on the 27th of March at Rangoon on board the Hon. Company's steamer "Damoodah" and the flat "Bhagaretty," the head-quarters, consisting of the staff, band, with Nos. 7 and 8, under command of Major Wheeler, arrived at Thayetmyo on the 5th of April, and the following day, the two companies, with Captain Kneebone, Lieut. Hart, Ensign A. G. Black, L. A. Shadwell, and Assistant-Surgeon Farmer, proceeded to Meeaday to relieve Captain Beauchamp Seymour, R.N., and his ship's company, who had lately been doing duty there.

In the Regimental Orders of the 14th of April was published the H.G. Order doing away with Flank companies.* The companies were therefore re-numbered, and the Grenadiers, "Captain Walker's company," became No. 1; the Light company, "Captain Colvill's," No. 10.

On the 21st, Captain Stehelin in command of Nos. 2, 6, and 7 companies, with Captain Levinge, Lieuts. G. W. F. D. Smith, Dane, and Hart, Ensign J. R. Bomford, and Assistant-Surgeon Macqueen, joined head-quarters from Rangoon.

---

* *Vide* page 504.

In the meanwhile Captain Middleton,‡ who in March, had been **1858** appointed extra A.D.C. to Lieut.-General Sir E. Lugard, G.C.B., was distinguishing himself in India, and was recommended by Sir Edward to Lord Clyde for the Victoria Cross for two acts, but no notice was taken of this recommendation.

Colonel Malleson, writing of the forcing of the passage of the Tons on the 15th of April, 1858, says: "Hamilton, of the 3rd Sikhs, a very gallant officer, was wounded and unhorsed when charging the squares. As he lay on the ground, the rebels cutting at him, Middleton, of the 29th Foot, and Farrier Murphy rushed to his assistance, and succeeded in rescuing his body from being cut to pieces. The wounds Hamilton received were, however, mortal. A little later, when a body of rebels, who had re-formed, left their ranks with drawn tulwárs in their hands, to cut down a dismounted wounded trooper of the Military Train, Middleton dashed out at them, drove them back, dismounted, and placed the wounded trooper on his horse."

These two acts of bravery were at the time vouched for by the following eye witnesses, viz., Captain J. H. Wyatt, commanding 2nd Bn. Mil. Train; Lieut. and Adjutant Wm. Thompson, 2nd Bn. Mil. Train; Lieut. and Adjutant John Briggs, Mil. Train; Pte. Jas. Penman, B Troop, Mil. Train; and Lieut. Frederic L. H. Lyon, R.H.A.

Previous to this, Captain Middleton, who had served at the siege and capture of Lakhnao, had been mentioned in dispatches.

On the 19th of July, No. 10 received the Enfield rifle. This completed the re-arming of the regiment with the new weapon.

On the 8th of September, two companies under command of Captain Levinge, with Lieuts. Eckersall and Winn, proceeded to relieve Captain Kneebone's detachment at Meeaday, which rejoined head-quarters the same day.

---

‡ Now Lt.-General Sir F. D. Middleton, K.C.M.G., C.B.

1858   Orders having been received for the regiment to proceed to Bengal, on the 16th of October the head-quarters, consisting of staff, band, Nos. 1, 8, 9, and 10 companies, under command of Major Wheeler, embarked at Thayetmyo for Rangoon, where they landed on the 21st. This division, with the exception of No. 9, re-embarked on the 27th, on board the s.s. "Sidney," and landing at Calcutta on the 1st of November, marched up to the Conductor's Barracks, where orders were received for it to parade in full dress, at 2.30 p.m. that afternoon, and march to Government House, where the proclamation of Her Majesty taking over charge of the H.E.I.C's possessions was read. The Royal standard, which had been escorted by some blue-jackets from H.M. ships of war, was then run up ; a general salute was given, and 21 guns fired as the Imperial flag floated from the masthead.

On the 4th, the head-quarters marched from the barracks to the Armenian Ghât, where, being joined by some 40 recruits from Dum Dum, under Ensign H. Davis, they crossed the river by steam ferry to Howrah, and there took train to Ránígang, which was reached about 4 p.m.

The regiment being ordered to place itself under command of Lieut.-Colonel W. W. Turner, at Sásserám, with a view of being detached in pursuit of some parties of rebels, and also to guard the Grand Trunk Road, on the 9th inst. No. 8, with Lieuts. E. W. Kent and Hart, started by bullock train for Sherghátí. Captain Stehelin's detachment from Rangoon, consisting of Nos. 2, 4, and 5, reached Ránígang that day, and the remaining companies, on arrival, proceeded to be detached on the Grand Trunk Road.

<small>During this duty the men were supplied with Kharkee cap covers, and the officers wore a white shoulder-belt with a small pouch. Kharkee tunics were not issued till the 21st of February, 1859.</small>

On the 11th of November, No. 9 company, under command of Captain Kneebone, marched for Sherghátí ; and No. 10, with Captain Colvill and Ensign Bacon, for Dehri. Here fresh orders were received from Lieut.-Col. Turner, for No. 10 to proceed at once to Thiloulta, **1858** where Lieut.-Colonel J. McN. Walter's field force was then encamped.

As this officer had commenced his military career in the 29th, Captain Colvill's company met with a hearty reception.

Instructions having arrived for the company to push on at once, in pursuit of some rebels, to Tepa, situated at the foot of the Rehul Pass, the men bivouacked for the night, and early next morning continued their march. When, on the 22nd, the pass was reached, it was discovered that the enemy, after having constructed an abbatis and some stone breastworks, had retired. Having made preparations to occupy this post, and stationed there a picquet under command of Ensign Bacon, Captain Colvill, with the remanider of the company, took up a position a little lower down, and as the nights were very cold, the men set to work to hut themselves.

This detachment was visited by Lt.-Col. Turner on the 28th, when orders were given for the company to march the following morning for Sásserám, where it arrived on the 1st of December and joined the head-quarters of the regiment, which with No. 5, had arrived there a few days previously.

In the meanwhile, No. 1, with Captain Walker and Assistant-Surgeon John, had marched from Ránígang in pursuit of a party of rebels, reported as being in the Behter neighbourhood; No. 2, with Captain Stehelin, Lieut. Dickinson, and Assistant-Surgeon Farmer, had been detached to Hazáribagh, whilst Nos. 3, 4, 6, 7, and 8 had marched independently up the Grand Trunk Road to Alláhábád, where, under command of Captain Farrington, they were stationed till about the end of the following February.

The head-quarters of the regiment being ordered to join a Field force, assembling under command of Lieut.-Colonel Turner, with a view of operating against a large body of rebels who, under the leadership of Ummur Singh, were plundering in the Palamau district, on the

1858 afternoon of the 6th of December, Major Wheeler, Captains Colvill and Walker, Lieutenants Kent, Smith (acting adjutant), Black, and Bacon, Qr.-Master W. Smith, Surgeon Moorhead, with about 200 non-commissioned officers, rank and file,§ marched from Sásserám for Barun, where they were joined by a company of H.M. 37th Foot, and some irregular cavalry. These marched early the following day, and during the afternoon of the 9th, when near Mahometgáng, on the right bank of the Koel, were joined by Captain Kneebone's company from Sherghati.

On reaching Chynepúr, information was obtained that the rebel's main position was at Sunnya, a village about 35 miles distant, situated in a valley behind the passes of the mountains; that their strength was about 1400, and that they had fortified the passes with the intention of defending them. These passes were three in number. First, and the strongest by nature, was the Panch Nudia, said to be held by 1200 men; the second, the Buglu Mara, on the direct road from Chynepúr, defended by 800; the third, the Bunjunna Pass, a mile and a half west of that road, was ascertained to be held by a small picquet only.

It having been decided to attack the centre pass, the march was continued without delay, and on the afternoon of the 14th the rebels, who were seen crowning its summit, were summoned to lay down their arms. Having in reply, opened what proved fortunately to be a harmless fire, it was determined to force their position the next day. Shortly after midnight the enemy made an attack on the outposts, but were compelled to retire.

As the Buglu Mara Pass was found to be a strong position, flanked on either side by steep wooded spurs, and defended near the top by an abattis, which in its turn was flanked by three circular loop-holed stone breastworks, a detachment was sent early the following morning with orders to engage the picquet stationed in the Bunjunna,

---

§ The Mutiny medal was presented to the detachments serving under Colonel Turner.

to turn the enemy's flank and to descend into the plain beyond, which was directly in rear of the centre pass.

As soon as it was ascertained that the flank attack had commenced, 40 men of H.M. 37th, supported by Captain Colvill's company, the whole under command of that officer, were ordered to the front to seize the spur commanding the left of the centre pass, whilst a similar detachment under Captain Kneebone, advanced to secure the spur on the opposite side. Having given these flanking parties half-an-hour's start, Lieut.-Colonel Turner, supported by the reserve of the detachment of the 29th, under command of Major Wheeler, advanced into the Buglu Mara. The enemy, however, after firing a few shots at the flanking parties, retired, and skirting the edge of the Koel which flows round the base of the pass, dispersed in all directions through the jungle which lined its banks.

The main body having got safely through the pass, crossed the river, and the flanking parties being reinforced, skirmished through the jungle to Sunnya, which was found deserted. There not being any signs of the enemy in the neighbourhood, the force bivouacked for the night.

When, the following morning, the Ramgarh battalion and 100 of the 29th, under Captain Colvill, attacked the Panch Nudia Pass in rear, the enemy at once dispersed, leaving their cooking vessels hanging on sticks. Here also were found traces of about 40 or 50 horses, and a bivouack for at least 400 men.

Further on, was an abattis of large timber, which had been thrown across the stream for about a hundred yards. The pass was also defended by four different lines of loop-holed breastworks, flanked by small rifle pits.

Having destroyed these obstructions, and handed over the passes and plateau beyond them to the deputy commissioner, the force commenced its return march, and Sásserám was reached on the 26th.

1858   Two days after this, Captain Kneebone's company was ordered to march to Jehanabad to relieve No. 5, which, under command of Ensigns Shadwell and W. M. Cochrane, had been stationed there during the last three weeks.

1859   Orders having been received on the 11th January for the 29th to join another field force under Colonel Turner, C.B., for the pursuit of rebels, the Jehanabad detachment was recalled, and on the 14th, the head-quarters of the regiment, under command of Major Wheeler, with Nos. 1, 5, 9, and 10 companies, left Sásserám.

From this day till the 28th of February, these companies were employed in clearing the Ramghar and Behar districts of the rebels, who, now completely beggared and starving, were reported to be retiring towards Mongarh and the Ganges.

On the 1st of February head-quarters, under command of Lieut.-Colonel Wheeler, with Captains Colvill and Kneebone, Lieuts. Kent, Smith (acting adjutant), Black, Bacon, Ensign Shadwell, Pay-Master Longden, Quarter-Master Smith, Surgeon Moorhead, and Assistant-Surgeon Farmer, were encamped near the village of Hutkona, about eleven miles from Hazáribágh, where a Depôt company, under command of Captain Stehelin and Ensign Cochrane was stationed; No. 1 with Captain Walker was at Sherghátí, and five companies under command of Captain Farrington were on command at Alláhábád.

On the afternoon of the 5th, when head-quarters were encamped near Juree on the right bank of the river Lilajun, No. 5, under Lieut. Kent, was ordered out after rebels; some shots were exchanged and one private was wounded, but none of the enemy were captured.

Considering the nature of the service on which the head-quarters were now employed, not only was the band a useless encumbrance, but the instruments, which had but a short time previously been received from Hanover, were very liable to get damaged. For the last three weeks the companies had been continually on the march through a jungly country, and the big drum had been generally carried on the **1859** head of a native. Being now within 14 miles of Sherghátí, it was thought to be a good opportunity of getting rid of the band, which was therefore sent to join the detachment stationed there.

On the 28th, orders were received for the companies to concentrate at Sherghátí, preparatory to their march down country and embarkation for England.

The regiment was at this time stationed as follows:—

Head-quarters and 3 companies at Dungain, Captain Walker's company at Huntergang, Captain Stehelin's at Hazáribágh, 5 companies under Captain Farrington at Sásserám. Colonel Stewart, Ensign Prittie, 5 serjeants, 2 drummers, 3 corporals, and 71 privates were at Sherghátí, where they were joined on the 1st of March by the head-quarters, and on the 4th by the left wing from Sásserám. On the following morning the right wing paraded to discharge rifles.

A few days later, Major Kent and Surgeon Franklyn of the 77th Foot arrived to superintend the volunteering of the regiment, and on the 20th, the companies commenced to march independently for Ránígang. Proceeding thence by rail to Calcutta, on the 3rd of May the left wing, under command of Captain Colvill, with Captains Chester, S. W. Clarke, Ledgard; Lieutenants Gorton, Black, Fursden, Shadwell; Ensigns Prittie, A. Fawcett, and Assistant-Surgeon John, embarked on board the "Clasmerden." On arriving at Portsmouth on the 18th of September, this wing proceeded by rail to Weedon, there to be stationed.

On the 16th of May the head-quarter division, under command of Major Westropp, with Captains Walker, Kneebone, H. Wilkie; Lieutenants Gordon, Smith, Hart, Winn, Bomford, Bacon, Cochrane; Ensign Davis, Quarter-Master Aylett, Surgeon Moorhead, and Assistant-Surgeon Farmer, embarked at Calcutta on board the "Gipsy Bride."

1859   One night in July, when off the Cape of Good Hope, the "Mary Sheppard" with a wing of the 78th on board, came in collision with the "Gipsy Bride." It being dark and stormy, some time elapsed before the ships got clear of each other, and in consequence of damages received, it was found necessary for the latter ship to put into Simon's Bay, where she was detained two weeks whilst undergoing repairs.

When on the 29th of September the head-quarters disembarked at Portsmouth, they proceeded by rail to Preston, and took up quarters in the Fulwood Barracks, where on the 11th of October H.R.H. the Commander-in-Chief inspected them.

On the 19th of December, the wing stationed at Weedon, with the following officers, Captains Dick, Middleton (M), and Chester, Ensigns Fawcett, E. P. H. Everard, R. Berkeley, J. H. H. Croft, and Assistant-Surgeon John, joined head-quarters.

By Horse Guards' Circular, dated the 31st of October, officers were ordered to provide themselves with leather leggings.

During this tour of foreign service, the regiment received by

Drafts from England	10 Serjeants.	9 Corporals.	1506 Privates.
Volunteers from Regiments in India ...	1 ,,		380 ,,

Between the 1st of August, 1842, and the 1st of November, 1859, the deaths in the regiment were 32 officers, 79 serjeants, 11 drummers, 57 corporals, and 1255 privates.

Between the 9th and 20th of March, 1859, 7 serjeants, 6 drummers, 3 corporals, and 215 privates volunteered to regiments in the Bengal Presidency.

Whilst in India, the 29th was nicknamed the "Europe Regiment," on account of its being the only British corps from which native servants were rigidly excluded, cooks and washermen excepted.

Names of Officers who Died or were Killed: 1859

1843.	January 28th.—Lott, Ensign Geo. Aug.; at Gházipúr.	
,,	December 30th.—Moore, Lieut. James; ,,	
1844.	June 25th.—Durbin, Capt. Edmd.; at Haidarábád Sind, whilst doing duty with the 86th Regt.	
,,	September 24th.—Hope, Lieut. Jas. R.; at Mírath.	
1845.	,, 13th.—Dobbs, Lieut. Robt.; ,,	
,,	December 18th.—Carey, Lieut. Octavius	⎫
,,	,, 21st.—Lucas, Capt. J. O., major of brigade.	⎪
,,	,, 21st.—Molle, Capt. G.	⎬ Killed in Action.
,,	,, 21st —Simmons, Lieut. A. A.	⎪
1846.	February 10th.—Taylor, C.B., Lieut.-Colonel C.	⎭
,,	,, 18th.—Mitchell, Ensign G.	⎱ Died of Wounds at
,,	,, 23rd.—Jones, Lieut. G.H.M., major of brigade.	⎰ Firúzpúr.
,,	March 26th.—Barr, C.B., *l.c.; s.*, Major Marcus, actg. adjt. general.	⎱ Died of Wounds at ⎰ Kasauli.
.,	July 30th.—Coventry, Capt. F.; at Kasauli.	
,,	November 24th.—Henderson, Lieut. G. St. Julien; at Ambálah.	
1847.	August 4th.—Kirby, Captain Walter; at Kasauli.	
,,	September 11th.—Kneebone, Qr. Mr. Thos.; at Calcutta.	
1849.	January 18th.—Metge, Lieut. H. F.; died of Wounds, near Chiliánwálá.	
,,	April 29th.—Fraser, Capt. Æneas W.; on passage home.	
,,	November 29th.—Smith, Lieut. W. L. Davies; at Vazírábád.	
1850.	March 2nd.—Handfield, Capt. Carey; at Mírath.	
1853.	—August 6th.—MacDonnell (M), Capt. C. E.; at the Depôt, Chatham.	
1854.	January 8th.—Young, Capt. J. D.; at Calcutta.	
1855.	June 13th.—Power, Major John.	
,,	,, 21st.—Hart, Lieut. E. Browne; at Amritsar.	
,,	July 20th.—Walsh, Qr.-Master Timothy; at Thayetmyo.	
,,	December 4th.—Simmons, Lieut. W. Septimus; at Langford, Somerset.	
1856.	June 13th.—Jameson, Paymaster H. F.; at Rangoon.	
,,	August 16th.—O'Loghlin, Lieut. Joseph; drowned in Irawadi by upsetting of a boat during a gale.	
,,	November 30th.—Henderson, Lieut. J. Sheridan; at Kyouk-hpyú.	
1857.	June 9th.—Fisher, *l.c.* Capt. Saml.; killed by mutineers at Sultánpúr.	
,,	August 12th.—Duncan, Capt. J. Æneas; at Calcutta.	

Depôt Companies, 1842—1873.

1842 Depôt When in 1842 the regiment was ordered on foreign service, the following were selected to remain at home to form the Depôt:—Captain S. H. Palairet, Lieutenants D. Mackworth, G. P. Stanhope, Surgeon C. T. Ingham, M.D., 4 serjeants, 1 drummer, 4 corporals, and 33 privates.

Battalion Company Drummer,* 1849.

These marched from Weedon on the 13th and 14th of May, for Chatham, to join the Provisional battalion there stationed under command of Lieut.-Colonel Thos. Weare, K.H.

---

* The wings, and lace across breast of coatee, were chevroned with yellow, dark blue, and black, alternately.

1852
Depôt

At the funeral of Field Marshal the Duke of Wellington, which took place on the 18th of November, 1852, a detachment of 1 captain, 1 subaltern, 1 serjeant, 1 corporal, and 5 privates, with side arms, from every regiment of infantry, was ordered to take part in the procession which followed the *cortège* to St. Paul's. In the case of regiments being on foreign service, these parties were drawn from the Depôt companies.

The following officers were on the 1st November on the strength of the Depôt :—

Captain K. Murchison, on leave 20th August to 14th November, 1852.

Lieuts.
- W. S. Simmons „ „ „ 20th „ „
- H. P. Onslow „ 29th September „ 31st December, „ „
- H. E. Quinn „ 29th October „ 28th „ „

1857

The designation of Depôt in place of "Provisional" battalion took place in September, 1857; there were eventually 23 Depôt battalions. The 1st and 2nd, which consisted of depôts of regiments in India, were stationed at Chatham, and at this time Colonel H. Jervis commanded that to which the 29th companies belonged.

1858

In February, 1858, the Depôt companies joined the 2nd Depôt battalion, commanded by Colonel Newton Phillips, to which Captain Lyle was shortly afterwards appointed I. of M.

1859

The other officers on the strength of the Depôt on the 1st of September, 1859, were Lieut. T. P. Wood, Ensigns E. P. H. Everard, R. Berkeley, H. W. Kindersley, F. C. Ruxton, W. G. Arnold, and H. W. S. Carew who had been recruiting at Aberdeen since the 9th of October, 1858.

On the 4th of October the 29th Depôt companies vacated the lines at Fort Amherst, Chatham, in which they had been encamped during the summer, and proceeded to Devonport to join the 11th (British) Depôt battalion, commanded by Colonel G. W. Franklyn. At this time the battalion consisted of the depôts of the 1st and 2nd battalions of

1859 the 10th Foot, of the 32nd, 41st, and 55th regiments, and later on that **Depôt** of the 59th joined it.

1860 On the 15th of January, the 11th Depôt battalion, under command of Colonel H. D. Crofton moved from Devonport to Preston, where the 29th Regiment was stationed.

1865 In February 1865, this Depôt battalion comprised the depôts of the 1st and 2nd battalions 10th Foot, of the 29th, 55th, 90th, and 91st regiments, and was commanded by Lieut.-Colonel William Hardy. At the end of the month the Depôt companies joined the 2nd Depôt battalion at Chatham, which consisted of the depôt companies of the 2nd battalion 2nd Foot, 1st and 2nd battalions 12th, 1st battalion 20th, 40th, and 52nd regiments, and was commanded by Col. E. Newdigate.

1868 On the 8th of November, 1868, the Depôt companies left Chatham for Colchester, where, on arrival, they joined the 8th Depôt battalion, which consisted of the depôts of the 1st battalion 6th, 2nd battalion 18th, 32nd, and 96th regiments, and was commanded by Lieut.-Colonel P. Robertson Ross. The officers then serving with the 29th Depôt companies were Captains Boycott, C. E. Phipps; Lieuts. Berkeley, J. W. Boyfield, W. Evans, C. A. P. Cooper, and Ensign T. C. Yard.

1870 By a General Order issued the 22nd March, 1870, the several Depôt battalions of infantry, "with the exception of one to be temporarily retained," were ordered to be broken up from the 1st of April. The Depôts of battalions of infantry serving abroad, were then severally attached to regiments, and battalions serving at home, and directed to move with them on change of quarters.

In consequence of this order, on the 31st of March the Depôt companies of the 29th proceeded to Portsmouth to await the arrival home from India of the 77th Foot, but as this regiment did not land till the 25th of May, they were, as a temporary measure, attached to the 1st battalion 25th Foot.

From December, 1870, to April, 1873, the Depôt companies were attached to the 77th Regiment at Portland.

1873 Depôt

On the 21st of the latter month, the companies, under command of Captain Davis, with Captain Carrington, Lieuts. Dalgleish and Anstice, Sub-Lieuts. O. H. Oakes and H. Bailey, 6 serjeants, 7 corporals, 2 drummers, and 96 privates joined the head-quarters of the regiment, which had a short time previously returned from the West Indies, and was then stationed at Templemore.

CHAPTER XIII.

HAVING given an account of the Depôt companies up to 1873, let us now resume the history of the regiment from the time we left it stationed at Preston in December, 1859.

1860 During the following February, Nos. 3, 5, 7, and 9 companies proceeded on detachment to Bury, where, on the 6th of March, they were joined by the head-quarters and No. 1, under command of Major Westropp.

On the 20th, Nos. 2 and 4, with Captains Dick, Chester, Lieuts. Hart, Shadwell, Ensigns Fawcett, Everard, and Assistant-Surgeon Farmer, proceeded from Preston to Sunderland for ball practice. Here, on the 7th of April, they were joined by No. 6, also from Preston. On the 26th, Ensign Everard, whilst returning with his company from the range, to barracks, was knocked down by a train whilst passing over a level crossing of the Seaham and Sunderland Railway, and died the following day from injuries received.

Head-quarters, under Major Westropp, proceeded from Bury to Newcastle-on-Tyne on the 27th, where they were joined the same day by Nos. 8 and 10, under Major Farrington, from Preston.

On the 24th of May, a detachment, under Captain Chester, was ordered from Newcastle to North Shields in aid of the civil powers, but affairs having passed off quietly, it returned to head-quarters the same day.

On the 6th of August, Lieut. Bomford, with 30 non-commissioned officers and men, was ordered to Liverpool, but rejoined head-quarters on the 31st.

1860 On the 12th of September, head-quarters, under Lieut.-Colonel Westropp, including one company from Tynemouth and the detachment from Sunderland, under command of Major Farrington, proceeded to Aldershot, where, on arrival the following day, they were quartered in the North Camp huts, and attached to the 3rd brigade commanded by Brigadier-General D. Russell, C.B.

1861 The regiment moved on the 31st of December, 1861, into the east block, Permanent Barracks, South Camp. On this occasion H.R.H. the General Commanding-in-Chief, was pleased to express the great satisfaction he derived from the report of the creditable state in which the hut accommodation occupied by the regiment for the last 15 months had been handed over to the barrack-master.

During this year the officers' chaco was changed to one of ribbed blue cloth, with a patent leather peak and chin strap. Colonels and lieutenant-colonels were distinguished by two rows of regimental lace round the top. Majors by one. Cap-plate, a gilt star of eight points surmounted by a crown, and having the number of the regiment cut out, within a garter.

At this period the band in undress wore white shell jackets, yellow collar and cuffs, with a red piping round them, also round the shoulder straps and up the back of jacket and sleeves.

1862 On the 21st of May, 1862, head-quarters and the 1st division, under command of Lieut.-Colonel Farrington, proceeded by rail to Liverpool, where they embarked on board the "Heron" steamer for Glasgow, and arriving there on the 24th, marched into barracks.

The 2nd division, under Major Walker, consisting of Nos. 2, 7, 10, and part of No. 6, arrived at Glasgow on the 28th, when Nos. 2 and 7, under command of Captain Chester, proceeded by rail to Paisley, where they were stationed till the 5th of June, when they returned to head-quarters in consequence of the Renfrew Militia being ordered to occupy those barracks during their annual training. These companies returned to their former quarters on the 9th of July.

LL

1862 The 3rd division, under Major Lyle, consisting of Nos. 1, 4, 5, and part of No. 6, landed at Glasgow on the 30th of May, and with the exception of the latter company, proceeded the same day to Ayr.

On the 9th of June, Major-General Walker, commanding the North British District, inspected the regiment, and it was shortly after this, that the men composing Nos. 1 and 10, "the late Grenadier and Light companies," were distributed amongst the other companies, and the last vestige of Flank companies disappeared.

On the 15th of September a guard of honour, under command of Captain Dick, with Captain Clarke, Lieut. Davis, Ensign T. C. Lambert, the Queen's colour, band, and No. 1 made up to 80 rank and file, paraded at the Queen's Hotel, George's Square, to receive the Judges, Lords Deas and Ardmillan, and accompany them to the Court House.

1863 On the 21st of April, 1863, the 1st division of the regiment, under Major Wilkie, on the 27th, the head-quarters, under command of Lieut.-Colonel Farrington, on the 4th of May, the 3rd division under Captain Wm. Boycott, and on the 11th of May, the 4th division under Major Clarke, proceeded by the "Lord Clyde" steamer from Glasgow to Dublin, *en route* to the Curragh, where on arrival they were quartered in huts in C. Square.

On arrival in camp, the regiment once more met its "*Cousins*," when each company of the 10th entertained the corresponding one of the 29th with the greatest hospitality. Old soldiers relate that when in '60 the Depôt companies of the two regiments lay at Devonport, the men were constantly seen in each others' barrack-room helping to clean their accoutrements.

General the Right Honble. Ulysses Lord Downes, G.C.B., having died on the 26th of July, General Sir James Simpson, G.C.B., was transferred from the colonelcy of the 87th to that of the 29th Foot.

On the 2nd and 3rd of November, the regiment marched in two **1863** divisions for Dublin, halting *en route* for a night at Naas. On arrival at its destination, head-quarters and 6 companies were quartered in the Ship Street, the remaining four in the Royal Barracks. Whilst stationed here, there being many officers in the regiment of a musical turn, an officers' band was organised.

OFFICER AND CORPORAL IN UNDRESS—1863.

On the 18th of May, 1864, the regiment proceeded by train from **1864** King's Bridge Station, to the Curragh, where on arrival it was quartered in huts in H. Square.

1864   The 36th Foot, which in 1881 became the 2nd battalion Worcestershire Regiment, was also stationed at the Curragh this year.

In consequence of the Belfast Riots, and disturbed state of the north of Ireland, orders were received for the regiment to proceed to Newry and Enniskillen. Having paraded at 4.15 a.m. on the 19th of August, it went by rail to Dublin, and refreshments having been obtained at the Royal Barracks, it marched to the Drogheda Station, whence it proceeded by special train to Dundalk, where four companies were left under command of Major Clarke. The head-quarters and other companies continued their journey to Newry.

On the 25th, Major Clarke's detachment moved to Enniskillen.

1865   On the 13th of March, 1865, two companies, under command of Captain Ledgard proceeded from Newry to Belfast, to aid the civil power during the assizes. On completion of this duty the detachment returned by march route, *via* Banbridge, and rejoined head-quarters on the 26th of April.

On the 30th, the regiment proceeded by rail to Dublin, and pending embarkation for Malta, was stationed in Richmond Barracks.

Before leaving Ireland, the silver head of the drum-major's staff was so worn down and thin with holes, that a new one was obliged to be bought. When shortly after at Malta, Colonel Farrington enquired for the old one, it was found that the drum-major had cooly disposed of it for old silver.

On the 20th of June, the regiment, under command of Lieut.-Colonel Farrington, with Majors Clarke, Wilkie; Captains Kneebone, Ledgard, Boycott, Davis, Berkeley, Ruxton, J. C. Douglas, Lambert; Lieuts. J. Bourke, A. W. Matchatt, R. J. Watson, C. E. P. Simpson, Honble. W. S. H. Jolliffe, D. D. Dick, E. Carrington, J. W. Boyfield, C. H. M. Paget, F. Russell, J. H. Pitfield; Ensigns G. W. F. Claremont, W. M. Prendergast, C. W. H. Helyar, W. Evans, C. A. P. Cooper, F. C. H. Littledale, E. J. H. Spratt, J. O. Dalgleish; Pay-

master W. F. Scott, Adjt. Wm. Winn, Lt.; Surgeon Moorhead, M.D.: **1865**
Asst.-Surgeon J. P. H. Boileau, M.B.; and Quarter-Master R. Erwin, embarked at Kingstown on board H.M.S. "Orontes."

On landing at Malta, head-quarters and seven companies were stationed in Fort Ricasoli, one company at Zabbar Gate, one at Fort St. Salvator, and one at Zeitun Gate.

By the Monthly Return dated the 1st of July, the strength of the regiment, and nationality of the officers, etc., were as follows:—

	Officers.	Serjeants.	Drummers.	Corporals.	Privates.
English	25	25	13	22	394
Scotch	5	3	1		18
Irish	7	18	7	16	203
Foreign					
Unknown	2				
Total	39	46	21	38	615

For musketry instruction, the several companies used to proceed to Pembroke Camp.

During 1866 all, except field officers, adopted steel in place of leather sword **1866** scabbards, and the drummers' regimental lace was abolished, a universal pattern having been sanctioned for infantry regiments.

In June, 1867, the regiment received the Snider breechloading **1867** rifle.

On the 2nd of July, the 29th embarked on board H.M.S. "Tamar" for conveyance to Canada. Having landed at Quebec on the 27th, the companies were transhipped to river steamers for passage to Montreal, where, on disembarking, they marched to Logan's Farm.

On the 10th of September, head-quarters, with 8 companies, embarked on board the steamers "Grecian" and "Kingston" for Hamilton, where they relieved the 1st battn. 16th Foot, and were

1867 stationed in McNab Street and the Crystal Palace Barracks. On the 13th, they were joined by A. and H. companies from Chambly.

A blue patrol jacket, for officers of infantry regiments of the Line, was this year approved of instead of the double-breasted blue frock coat. Field officers were distinguished by badges of rank embroidered in gold on the collar.

1868 General Sir James Simpson, G.C.B., having died on the 18th of April, 1868, Major-General J. Longfield, C.B., was appointed Colonel of the regiment.

On the 13th of May, head-quarters with band and 6 companies, relieved the 2nd battn. 17th Foot at Toronto.

In June, a new pattern chaco of blue cloth, ornamented with gold braid round the bottom, up sides and back, and with two lines round the top, was authorized for officers. Colonels and lieut.-colonels had two lines of regimental lace round the top instead of braid. Majors, one, instead of the upper line of braid. A gilt burnished chain was introduced instead of the chin strap.

Gilt cap plate with "29" in the centre of a garter bearing the Royal motto, a laurel wreath round it, and a crown above.

This chaco was worn by the officers and men up to the embarkation of the regiment for India in '79, and by the Depôt companies till August, 1881.

A General Order was issued in September, abolishing the slash flap and buttons on the cuffs and skirt of the tunics; in place of the round cuff of regimental facing, a similar but pointed one, with regimental lace, and tracing braid, was introduced.

A gold and crimson, dress sash, belt, and stripes for trousers, was at this time authorized to be worn by officers at levees, balls, etc.

On the 10th of November, A, B, D, and E companies left Hamilton for London, Ontario; the last three of these companies **1869** joined head-quarters at Toronto in May, '69.

On the 12th of June, E. and K. companies proceeded by river steamers to Quebec, where on arrival they encamped at Point Levis. Here, on the 17th and 18th they were joined by head-quarters and 7 companies, and on the 29th of July by A. company from London, Ontario. Whilst stationed here, the 29th, 53rd, and 3 companies of the 1st battn. Rifle Brigade were employed in working at the new forts.

Orders having been received for the regiment to proceed to **1869** Jamaica, on the 28th of October it embarked on board H.M.S. "Tamar." On arriving at Halifax, N.S., a Board of Naval Officers pronounced the transport as unfit for service; the regiment was therefore disembarked

OFFICER AND SERJEANT IN CANADIAN DRESS—1869.

on the 10th of November, and distributed as follows:—Head-quarters and 5 companies to the Wellington Barracks, 3 companies to Glacis Barracks, and 2 to the South Artillery Barracks.

1869 On the 17th of December, the regiment, under Lt.-Col. Farrington, embarked on board H.M.S. "Orontes," but in consequence of fogs, it did not sail till the 20th. Having disembarked at Kingston, Jamaica, on the 30th, it bivouacked for the night at the gardens, and relieved the 84th Regiment the following morning at Newcastle.

1870 On the 25th of May 1870, F. company, under command of Captain Davis, with Lieut. A. T. Ross and Ensign Wm. Barlow, proceeded on detachment to Up Park Camp, but rejoined head-quarters on the 9th of July. G. company, with Captain Ruxton, Ensigns Barlow and C. de F. Green, marched to Up Park Camp on the 3rd of September, where it was stationed till the 20th of October, when it returned to Newcastle.

On the 29th of November, head-quarters, under command of Major Wilkie, with 5 companies and the following officers, viz.: Captains Davis, Ruxton, Douglas, Simpson, Boyfield; Lieutenants Paget, Claremont, Cooper, Littledale, Dalgleish, T. C. Yard; Ensigns Clarke, C. P. Cubitt, Green, N. Sadlier, A. G. St. George; Paymaster R. Smyth, Adjutant Spratt, Qr. Master W. H. Martin, and Assistant-Surgeon Boileau, M.B., marched to Kingston and embarked on board H.M.S. "Himalaya" for passage to the Leeward Islands.

Reaching Trinidad on the 5th of December, H. company, with Captain Simpson, Lieut. Paget,* and Ensign Cubitt, was disembarked. On the 8th the head-quarters and 3 companies landed at Barbadoes, and relieved the 53rd Foot at St. Anne's. Captain Ruxton's company, with Lieut. Dalgleish and Ensign Green, remained on board the "Himalaya" till St. Vincent was reached, when it disembarked and relieved a similar detachment of the 53rd.

---

* Fort Adjutant at Trinidad, from the 14th of December, 1870, till promoted, when he took command of H. company. Lieut. Prendergast was then ordered from Jamaica to take up the duties of Fort Major at Trinidad.

On the 20th of July, 1871, a Royal Warrant was promulgated prohibiting all officers **1871** from selling or bargaining for the sale of any commission in the forces, under the penalty of forfeiture of their commissions and of being cashiered.

By Royal Warrant, dated the 30th of October, the rank of cornet, and ensign, was abolished, and all such officers appointed before the 26th of August, 1871, were given the rank of lieutenant. Officers, on first appointment, were gazetted as sub-lieutenants.

Lieutenants of militia, were also for the first time allowed, under certain conditions, to qualify and obtain a commission as lieutenants in the army.

In February, 1872, pantaloons and high boots were ordered to be worn by mounted **1872** officers of infantry on all mounted duties; also a sabretasche. A mess jacket, with stand-up collar, was also approved of.

On the 23rd of August, D. company, under command of Captain Claremont, embarked on board H.M S. "Sphinx" for conveyance to St. Vincent to relieve Captain Ruxton's detachment.

Information being received, whilst the officers were at mess during the evening of the 28th of October, that several lawless attacks had been made during the course of the afternoon, on the police and porters employed in escorting some goods, part of the cargo of the wrecked steamer "Cuban," to the stores of the persons who had purchased them, and that a riot was taking place at Bridgetown, orders were given for the regiment to be got under arms.

G. Company, with Captain Ruxton, Lieuts. J. W. Jameson and St. George, having been served out with ball ammunition, at once repaired to the scene of the disturbance. On reaching the Wharf, where much damage had been done, a very disorderly mob was discovered; these were driven away, and several prisoners made. Leaving here, a detachment under Lieut. St. George, and having posted a party near the goods, the remainder of the company marched to the lower part of Broad Street, by Sir John Arnott's stores. On their way there, some of the soldiers were very severely wounded by stones and glass bottles thrown at them by the mob, and its sympathisers in the adjacent houses, upon which it became necessary to clear the street at the point of the bayonet.

1872   When, about midnight, affairs appeared to have quieted down a little, the prisoners, escorted by detachments of the Royal Artillery and 29th, were marched to the Central Police Station, where Captain Ruxton's detachment remained during the night.

Lieut. Senhouse Clarke, who had arrived on the scene early in the evening in company of Col. Sargent, A.A.G., was now put in command of the Wharf House Guard detachment. During the night a mob assembled in the vicinity of this post and assumed a menacing attitude. Their leader, a powerful negro, endeavoured to force one of the sentries, but a quickly-delivered thrust with the bayonet cooled his ardour, and the mob taking the hint, gave the soldiers a wide berth.

During the next day the remaining exposed goods were removed in safety, but as a number of idlers had again assembled near the wharf, and were parading the streets, Captain Helyar's company was ordered to relieve Captain Ruxton's at the Central Station, and to hold itself in readiness to aid the police.

Here it remained during the ensuing night, though happily its services were not required.

"War Office,

20th November, 1872.

"Sir,

By desire of the Field-Marshal Commanding-in-Chief, I have the honour to acknowledge the receipt of your letter of the 29th ultimo, reporting upon the conduct of the troops, consisting of two companies of the 29th regiment, and 20 gunners under the command of Major De Moleyns, Royal Artillery, sent on the requisition of His Excellency the Governor of Barbadoes, to assist the civil power in quelling a serious riot which occurred in that island on the night of the 28th Idem.

In reply, I am instructed to acquaint you, that the behaviour of **1872** the troops is considered to have been highly creditable, and you will accordingly be so good as to express His Royal Highness' approval of their conduct upon this trying occasion.

I have the honour to be,

Sir,

Your obedient servant,

(S)   J. W. ARMSTRONG,

D.A.G."

In August, a scarlet patrol jacket for officers of infantry was approved of. This jacket was of cloth or serge, according to the climate, of the same shape and size as the blue patrol, with a collar of the regimental facing; sleeves braided as the shell jacket, according to rank. Scarlet shoulder-straps, with a small button, and the number of the regiment in gold embroidered figures. White cloth edging round shoulder-strap and jacket, except the collar. Field officers, gold embroidered collar badges. This jacket was worn without the sash, at drill and on parade when the men were dressed in frocks. The blue patrol was permitted to be worn on regimental boards, and on fatigues, but officers were not required to provide themselves with it.

Orders having been received for the regiment's return to Europe, **1873** on the 28th of February, 1873, head-quarters, under command of Lieut.-Colonel Hales Wilkie, embarked at Barbadoes on board H.M.S. "Orontes," and having picked up the Trinidad, St. Vincent, and Jamaica detachments, reached Queenstown on the 10th of April. Here the men were transhipped on board two river steamers for conveyance to Cork. On landing they proceeded to Templemore by rail, and were joined by the Depôt companies on the 21st inst.

A plan having been approved of, for localizing the forces in the United Kingdom, the military districts of Great Britain and Ireland were, from the 1st of April, 1873, divided into 66 infantry and 12 artillery sub-districts.

1873   Colonel R. White, C.B., h.p., late 17th Light Dragoons, was on that day appointed to command the 22nd sub-district, which included the counties of Herefordshire and Worcestershire. The line battalions, militia battalions, the brigade depôt, rifle volunteer corps, and infantry of the army reserve of these two counties constituted the infantry sub-district brigade.

All first appointments to the line, and all enlistments for line service, were for the future made for the brigade, instead of as heretofore for a particular regiment, and the brigade depôt was ordered to furnish the permanent staff of the militia battalions as the present staff of these battalions was absorbed.

Although the 29th, and 36th (Herefordshire) now became linked, still each regiment was permitted to retain its distinctive number, precedence, traditions, colours, and facings.

In May, orders were received for the band in future to be dressed in clothing of the same colour as worn by the regiment.

Soon after landing in Ireland, the men were supplied with the Glengarry, *in lieu* of the round forage cap; the bandsmen received scarlet caps, which, however, when worn out, were replaced by blue ones. The badge worn with the Glengarry was of brass, viz., "29" encircled by a garter, bearing the title "Worcestershire" in raised letters, the whole surmounted by a crown.

The non-commissioned officers, when not on duty, continued for some years after this to wear their small circular forage cap with "29" in copper in front. These caps, with the exception of their not having a peak, were similar to those worn by the officers. When later on the officer's forage cap badge was altered, that of the non-commissioned officers was changed to a copper star, with garter and the lion in centre, and a small "29" below.

Red kersey frocks, with collars of the regimental facing, a plain braided cuff, and shoulder-strap with brass numerals, were also issued to the regiment *in lieu* of the shell jacket. The Depôt companies had the previous year received a similar frock, but with collar and shoulder-straps of yellow; also the Glengarry cap.

It was an old custom in the regiment to have the shell jackets of the non-commissioned officers piped with white, round the top of the collar, down the front and round the bottom of the jacket.

1873 Whilst stationed at Templemore, Captain Ruxton's company was detached to Nenagh, Captain Claremont's to Tralee, and a wing under Major Boycott was employed as a working party at Carlisle Fort, Cork Harbour.

Permission, dated Horse Guards, War Office, 12th August, 1873, was received from the Commander-in-Chief, authorizing the following alterations of badges, viz. :—

Officers' forage cap.—A gold embroidered star of garter, with Royal motto, solid silver lion device in centre, and a small gold embroidered "29" below the star.

Shoulder-strap officers' scarlet patrol.—A similar device, but on a larger scale, having the garter of blue enamel with Royal motto in gold letters.

Collar badge for tunics of non-commissioned officers, rank and file.—A similar shaped star, etc., but of brass, with "29" in centre; this was instead of the metal crown, which had been recently approved of as a universal collar badge.

The shoulder-straps on tunics of non-commissioned officers, rank and file, were this year changed from yellow piped with white, and with the regimental number embroidered thereon in white, to scarlet edged with white braid and brass numerals.

In September the scarlet patrol jacket was directed to be worn by officers whenever the men wore chacos, on all garrison duties, and whenever they were on brigade parades. The blue patrol was permitted to be worn for regimental duties, except on parade, when the men wore chacos.

1874 In August 1874, the scarlet patrol was ordered to be discontinued, but officers in possession of them were permitted to use them till worn out.

On the 30th of June the regiment proceeded to the Curragh Camp, there to be stationed during the drill season, and on the 16th of September it moved to Dublin and took up quarters in the Richmond Barracks.

1875 The Martini-Henry rifle was taken in use on the 12th of January, 1875.

Whilst stationed here, companies were detached to Pigeon House Fort for their annual course of musketry.

Orders having been received for the regiment to proceed to Jersey, on Sunday, the 12th of June, the old knapsacks and pouches were returned into store, and the valise equipment fitted.

1875   The "*Star*" was now transferred from the pouches to the flap of the valises, and small stars were placed on the black pouches † worn in front, on either side of the locket of the waist belt.

Proceeding by rail to Kingstown on the 14th, the regiment embarked on board H.M.S. "Simoon," and sailing the following day, put into Milford on the 16th, where the Depôt companies of the 36th Regiment, under command of Lieut. F. L. Harford, with Lieut. H. C. Cowell, were taken on board.

Having reached St. Aubin's Bay on the afternoon of the 17th, about 9 p.m. E. company, under command of Captain Watson, with Lieutenants Ross and H. E. E. Everard, was ordered ashore, and marched up to Fort Regent. Landing early next morning, head-quarters, under command of Lieut.-Col. Wilkie, with I. company, and the Depôt of the 36th Regiment, relieved head-quarters of the 2nd battn. 5th Fusiliers at the Fort; D. and G. companies, under Captain Ruxton, marched to Grève-de-Lecq; K. company, with Captain Matchett and Lieut. Oakes, to Rozel, and the remaining 5 companies, under Major Boycott, to St. Peter's, there to be stationed.

On the 18th of July, I. company with Captain Carrington, took up quarters in Mont Orgueil Castle, Gorey.

On the 28th of December, the Depôt companies 36th Foot under command of Captain C. D. James, with Surgeon Boileau, of the 29th, embarked on board H.M.S. "Assistance," for passage to Devonport, to join the head-quarters of their regiment, which had lately returned from India.

1876   In 1876, a universal button, with Royal arms thereon, replaced the regimental button on the clothing of the non-commissioned officers, rank and file.

Orders being issued for the mobilization of the 2nd and 5th Army Corps, the regiment, having been relieved by the 47th Foot, embarked

---

† *Vide* Regimental Order, page 519.

on the 3rd of July, by companies, in barges from the Albert Pier, St. **1876** Helier's, for conveyance to H.M.S. "Assistance," then anchored in St. Aubin's Bay.

An accident having occurred to the machinery of the troopship, whilst in the "Race of Alderney," she was delayed there until the arrival of a Government tug, which towed her into Portsmouth.

Disembarking on the 5th, the regiment proceeded by rail to Petersfield, where, with the 49th, 52nd, a detachment of the 61st Foot, and of the Army Service Corps, they encamped on the heath. These troops formed the 2nd brigade of the 2nd division, 2nd army corps, and were commanded by Major-General H. J. Warre, C.B.

A detachment under command of Captain Matchett and Lieut. Dalgleish, proceeded direct from Portsmouth, with the women and children of the regiment, to Chatham, there to await the arrival of the head-quarters.

At the time of this mobilisation, the 36th Foot and the two battalions of the Worcestershire Militia, formed part of the 5th army corps assembled in the vicinity of Salisbury. The localization scheme had now been in force three years, and it is a pity the authorities did not take advantage of this opportunity to bring together the line and militia battalions of the 22nd sub-district brigade, for never again is it likely they will be so near together.

On the 14th, two parties proceeded from Petersfield, one under command of Captain Claremont, with Lieut. Cooper, to St. John's Wood, London, the other, under Lieut. Littledale, to Dorchester, for the purpose of conducting back to the camp men of the 1st class army reserve, who had been called out for a week's drill, and ordered to be attached to the regiment for instruction in the use of the Martini-Henry rifle.

At 5.30 a.m. on the 19th, the brigade, with attached army reserve men, paraded in marching order, and proceeded to Woolmer Forest,

1876 where they encamped for the night. Tents having been struck at 2 a.m. the following day, the brigade continued its march, and on arriving at Aldershot about 9.45 that morning, encamped near the church in the North Camp.

The army reserve men returned to their homes from Woolmer.

The 2nd army corps being now concentrated at Aldershot, a review of the troops took place on the 22nd, in the presence of the Prince of Wales; and H.R.H. the Field-Marshal Commanding-in-Chief, in a General Order, expressed his entire satisfaction with the result of his inspection of the several divisions of the army corps which had been brought together under the new system of mobilization.

On the morning of the 25th, the regiment marched to Farnborough, whence it proceeded by special train to Chatham. Whilst stationed here, detachments were sent to Gravesend, Upnor Castle, and Chattenden.

1877 From January 1877, officers on joining the army were gazetted as 2nd lieutenants instead of sub-lieutenants.

Musketry having been suspended at Gravesend on account of the insecurity of the Milton Ranges, in April the musketry detachment stationed there proceeded to Littlehampton, and thence, towards the end of May, to Dymchurch Redoubt, near Hythe, where having remained about six weeks, it rejoined head-quarters.

On the 21st of June, the regiment, strength—2 field officers, 9 captains, 8 subalterns, 2 staff, 41 serjeants, 41 corporals, 19 drummers, 918 privates, proceeded to Aldershot by train, and encamped on Rushmoor Bottom.

Orders having been received for the troops stationed at Aldershot to proceed to Windsor, the several camps and lines were left in charge of the recruits, and the infantry of the division marched on the 9th of July to Chobham Common, where it encamped for the night; the artillery and cavalry of the army corps being at Ascot Heath.

The following day the march was continued to Windsor, where **1877** the troops, under command of Lieut.-General Sir T. Steele, K.C.B., were reviewed by Her Majesty the Queen. It was not till after midnight that the regiment returned to camp at Chobham. Rushmoor Bottom was reached the following day in time for the men's dinners.

During the last two months 471 recruits joined the regiment; and when on the 9th of October H.R.H. the Duke of Cambridge inspected the division, he specially commended the 29th for its smart, soldier-like appearance, which he considered highly creditable to a regiment which had lately received so many recruits, and was able to appear with so few casualties.

Extract from Regimental Orders.

"Aldershot, 27th September, 1877.

5. The following extract from a letter, dated Horse Guards, 7th August, 1877, is published for general information:—

"I am directed by H.R.H. the Field-Marshal Commanding-in-Chief to acquaint you that as the Stars which were recently ordered to be removed from the pouches of the 29th Regiment, were granted to that corps as a special distinction for service in the field, His Royal Highness, with a view to the assimilation, as much as possible, of the pouches of the 29th Regiment to those of the Guards, has approved of white ammunition pouches being issued *in lieu* of black ones."

On the 17th of December, Captains Claremont and Cooper, Lieutenants Littledale and Ross, with Serjt.-Major T. Shattock, 4 serjeants, 5 corporals, and 12 privates, under command of Major Berkeley, proceeded by train to Worcester, whence they marched to Norton Barracks, which had recently been completed for the accommodation of the depôt companies of the 29th and 36th Regiments.

To the Depôt of each regiment was assigned a block of buildings, over the doorway of which is painted the name of the officer who raised the particular regiment.

1877	The building assigned to the Depôt companies of the 29th was by mistake named "Albemarle" instead of "Farrington" as it should have been.

The depôt 36th Regiment had arrived at Norton towards the end of November for the purpose of equipping the barracks.

On the 19th of December, Colonel F. F. Hunter, of the latter regiment, was appointed to command the sub-district brigade.*

During this autumn the course which events were taking in the east, subsequent to the outbreak of the Russo-Turkish war, occupied the serious attention of the English nation, and it seemed highly probable that we should once more be brought into contact with our old Crimean foe. Hopes of peace became less as the divergence of opinion which existed in the Cabinet increased.

1878	Early the following year the Mediterranean Squadron, which had been wintering in Besika Bay, received orders to proceed through the Dardanelles and hold itself in readiness to protect the lives and property of British subjects in Constantinople, should disturbances arise there on account of its threatened occupation by the Russians.

The Government having obtained a vote of credit of £6,000,000, preparations were at once made for the threatening war.

On the 28th of February orders were received for the formation of a regimental transport consisting of 1 serjeant, 22 privates as drivers, 27 horses (3 riding and 24 draught), and 12 waggons. These were placed under command of Lieut. Cubitt.

Lieut.-Colonel and Bt.-Colonel Wilkie having on the 2nd of March retired on h.p., the following paragraph was published in Regimental Orders, 3rd March, 1878.

5. "Colonel Hales Wilkie, on resigning the command of the 29th Regiment, desires to express the great regret he feels at leaving

---

* The following officers have since had command of the regimental district :—
19th Dec. 1882—Colonel R. E. Carr, late commanding 2nd Bn. Worcestershire Regiment.
19th Dec. 1887—Colonel F. C. Ruxton,	,,	1st Bn.	,,	,,

after a lengthened service in the corps. Colonel Wilkie begs to thank **1878** all ranks for the hearty support he has invariably received, in the performance of duty, and will always look back with pleasure to the many happy years spent in the regiment, and if hereafter he can be of service to any of his old comrades, it will be to him the greatest satisfaction."

On the 1st of April, the establishment of the regiment was ordered to be increased to 30 officers, 50 serjeants, 40 corporals, 17 drummers, and 960 privates.

The following day a proclamation was issued calling out the reserve for permanent service, which, adding as it did 40,000 men to the strength of the army, showed that the Government considered war as imminent.

On the 16th, a conducting party, under command of Captain Simpson, with Captain Helyar, Lieut. Everard, and 2nd Lieut. E. A. Pym, proceeded to St. George's Barracks, London, for 176 non-commissioned officers and men of the 1st class army reserve, who were ordered to join the regiment.

Affairs were rapidly approaching a crisis; a contingent of Indian troops was embarked for Malta, where also the Channel Squadron was ordered to concentrate.

On the 13th of May, Her Majesty the Queen arrived at Aldershot to review the division, which was drawn up for her inspection on the Queen's Parade.

The climax appeared imminent when Germany stepped in as mediator. A congress to enquire into the lately ratified Russo-Turkish Treaty of San Stephano, assembled at the German capital on the 13th of June, and that day month the plenipotentiaries signed the Treaty of Berlin.

Orders having been received for the regiment to move to Dover, on the 24th of September an advance party, under Lieut. Everard, left

Group of Regiment in 1878.—By R. Simkin.

Aldershot to take over the regimental transport of the 2nd battn. 6th **1878** Foot, and on the 30th the regiment, under command of Lt.-Colonel Davis, arrived to take up quarters in the Citadel and Drop Redoubt.

In December, 36 men volunteered to the 2nd battn. 24th Foot, then stationed in South Africa.

A cork helmet covered with blue cloth, with a gilt spike, etc., was this year authorized for the officers. As its adoption was to be gradual, and it was expected that the regiment would within a year or two be ordered on foreign service, all officers appointed to the 29th were requested to supply themselves with the chaco, so as to be in uniformity with the majority.

The plate for this helmet was, a gilt star, with the number of the regiment in the centre, within a garter bearing the Royal motto; a laurel wreath round the garter, and a crown above.

The tunics issued to the men this year, instead of having a whole collar of yellow, were made with patches of the regimental facing at either end, and only the outside of the cuff was faced with yellow cloth. After the amalgamation of regiments in 1881, the white facing on the collar was made to go all round, also on the cuff, which was changed from the pointed shape to a circular one.

Orders having been telegraphed on the 2nd of January 1879, for **1879** the regiment to be held in readiness to embark for India, on the morning of the 29th, it proceeded by rail to Portsmouth, embarked on board H.M.S. "Serapis," and sailed the following day.

As the troopship remained at Malta for a day, an officer of the 2nd battn. 10th Foot, which formed part of the garrison of that island, came on board to remind those of the 29th that they were permanent honorary members of their mess.

The regiment—strength 22 officers, 2 staff; 38 serjeants, 14 drummers, 821 rank and file—landed at Bombay on the afternoon of the 4th of March, and having been served out with white helmets, and the usual amount of ball ammunition, it proceeded by rail to Máu, which was reached on the morning of the 9th. A. company, with Captain Carrington and 2nd Lieut. Hardisty, having been detached, *en route*, for duty at Asírgarh.

1879 On the 14th, Lieut.-General J. Forbes, C.B., commanding the division, inspected the regiment, and the following day, B. company with Captain Prendergast and 2nd Lieut. Conyngham, marched to Indúr, there to be stationed.

The following is a list of the officers who embarked with head-quarters for India:—

Colonel—Davis; Captains—Douglas (M.), Watson (M.), Simpson, Carrington, Helyar, Prendergast; Lieutenants—Cubitt (Instructor of Musketry), Oakes, Everard, F. J. W. Bennett, D'A. R. Chapman, A. J. Erskine; 2nd Lieutenants—Pym, M. V. Hilton, A. H. K. Ward,* E. A. Williamson,† W. A. L. Conyngham, W. F. J. Hardisty, E. A. D'A. Thomas, H. L. Haughton, C. M. Edwards; Adjutant—W. S. Clarke, *lt.*; Quarter Master—J. Brogden.

Previous to leaving England, the following device was decided upon as the ornament to be worn on the puggaree of the officer's helmet. A gilt oblong star, in centre XXIX., encircled by a garter inscribed "Worcestershire;" above the garter was a small silver lion. In 1883 a frosted silver centre, with castle device, was substituted for the Roman letters.

1880 On the 25th of February, 1880, three companies, under Major Ruxton, proceeded on detachment to Dísá; two of these moved to Baroda on the 6th of August, and rejoined head-quarters at Máu on the 8th of September.

In June, a new pattern forage cap of blue cloth, with patent leather drooping peak ornamented with gold embroidery, was approved of for the officers of infantry regiments; also a blue glengarry for active service and peace manœuvres. On the black cockade of the latter, was placed the star which in '77 had been removed from the small black pouches. This badge was similar to that worn on the glengarry and helmets of non-commissioned officers and men.

Shoulder straps, with badges of rank thereon, were in October ordered to be added to the officers' uniforms.

---

* Died at Máu, of fever, on the 26th of November, 1879.
† Died at Baroda, on the 7th of September, 1880.

On the 29th of January, 1881, the company left at Dísá rejoined **1881** head-quarters.

E. company, under command of Captain Claremont, was detached to Ahmadnagar, from the 21st of May to the 14th of September, when it rejoined at Máu.

On the 11th of April, a General Order was promulgated for general information, changing the organization, titles, and uniforms of regiments of the line.

It was directed, that from the 1st of July, 1881, the infantry of the line, and militia, should be organized in territorial regiments, each of four battalions, for England; the 1st and 2nd being line battalions, the remainder militia. The words "regimental district" were also substituted for "sub-district."

To the 29th "Worcester" regimental district, were allotted the 29th (or the Worcestershire) Regiment, the 36th (Herefordshire),‡ and two battalions of the Worcestershire Militia.* These four battalions now form "*The Worcestershire Regiment*," the uniform of which was ordered to be scarlet, with white facings, and rose pattern lace. The officers, non-commissioned officers, and men of the 3rd and 4th battalions were directed to wear the letter "M"§ on their shoulder straps. Not only did regiments now lose their particular facings,

---

‡ On the 28th of June, 1701, a Royal Warrant was issued authorizing Wm., Viscount Charlemont, to raise a regiment of foot in Ireland. In 1751, this regiment was numbered the 36th; in 1782, it was given the title of "Herefordshire;" and in 1881 was the first of the line regiments to lose its identity.

* The Worcestershire Militia was raised in 1770, by George Wm., 6th Earl of Coventry.

The Herefordshire Militia, which had since 1873 formed part of the 22nd Sub-District Brigade, was in June 1881 transferred to the 25th Sub-District Brigade, and the following month became the 4th Battn. the Shropshire Regiment (late 53rd and 85th.)

§ By Army Order 428, of 1889, the number of the battalion (in lieu of "M") was directed to be worn on the shoulder straps of warrant officers, non-commissioned officers, and men of infantry militia.

1881 regimental lace, and numbers, by which they had for the past 130 years been known, but their well-known, and to the soldier, much-prized regimental devices were ordered to be amalgamated with those of other regiments with which they had nothing in common.

Regiments were even directed to sew on their Colours, which recorded the brave and heroic deeds of their ancestors and which still in many instances bore the traces of active service, the names of engagements in which the colours had never been carried, of battles won by regiments with which they never had any connection, and consequently no sympathy. Up to this date, soldiers looked upon their colours with reverence, and considered them a most sacred trust.*

On the whole, the 29th is one of the lucky regiments, for it continues to be known by its old County Title; its former number is borne by the regimental district, and the four battalions have been ordered to adopt its "*Quick-Step*," the "Royal Windsor March."

The device on the officers' helmet and waist-belt plate of the present Worcestershire Regiment, was supposed to be an amalgamation of the badges of the late 29th and 36th Regiments and of the Worcestershire Militia. The well-known motto "FIRM" of the 36th, and the "Castle" device of the militia, are certainly portrayed, but neither the "*Garter Star*" nor the "*Lion*," both devices worn by the 29th for upwards of 100 years, were represented.

When, a short time afterwards, a collar badge was authorized for the officers' tunics, this defect was in a measure rectified, for a silver star (but not yet of the proper shape), with the gilt lion device in the centre, encircled by a garter, pierced with the Royal motto, and the word "FIRM" on a gilt scroll below the garter, was approved of.

---

* Major Erwin relates that in 1864, an old serjeant who had served his full period of 21 years in the regiment, and had been discharged in 1823, walked a distance of 19 miles to the Curragh Camp, "just to see," said the serjeant, "the old colours of the regiment;" he remarked that he did not see any black drummers, and that in his time they were all blacks

Colours Presented in 1841.

Photographed by Lieut. E. A. Williamson, at May, in 1880.

1881 Beneath the lion and the garter, was some blue enamel, for which in 1883 frosted silver was substituted, and the ornament was then sanctioned for the collar of the mess jacket.

NAMES OF OFFICERS BELONGING TO THE 29TH (OR WORCESTERSHIRE) REGIMENT, 30TH JUNE, 1881.

Colonel—John Longfield, C.B., *General.*

Lieut. Col. H. Davis.

Majors. { F. C. Ruxton. / J. C. Douglas. }

Captains { R. J. Watson, M. / E. Carrington. / H.G. MacGregor,* M., *p.s.c.; s.* / G. W. F. Claremont. / W. M. Prendergast, *d.* / E. J. H. Spratt, M. / W. S. Clarke. / J. Cooke. / S. Watson, M. / A. H. Atkinson. ‖ }

Lieuts. { O. H. Oakes. † / H.E. E. Everard, *d.* / F. J.W. Bennett, *d.* / D'A. R. Chapman. / A. J. Erskine, *I of M.* / E. A. Pym. / M. V. Hilton, *Adjt.* / W. L. A. Conyngham. / W. F. G. Hardisty. / E.A. D'A. Thomas. / H. L. Haughton. }

2nd Lieuts. { C. M. Edwards. / H. L. Begbie. / A. R. Browning. / T. B. French. / A. E. Aitken. / W. A. Watson. / C. H. Dawson. / A. G. Smith. / C. R. Mallaby. }

Paymaster—W. L. Fleury, *Hon. Capt.* A. P. Dept.
Quarter-Master—J. Brogden.

Important alterations were now also made in the establishment of the senior regimental officers, and the strength of the 1st Battn. was fixed at 2 lieut.-colonels, 4 majors, 4 captains, 16 lieutenants, 1 adjutant,

---

† Sub-Lieut. 29th Foot, 10th January, 1872; Captain 1st Battn. Worcestershire Regiment, 17th December, 1881; transferred to the 2nd Battn. in November, 1882; appointed Superintendent of Gymnasia, Dublin District, July, 1883; Adjutant 3rd Lanark R.V.C., 8th November, 1886, to 1891; Major Worcestershire Regiment, 9th October, 1889.

* *Garrison Instructor, Natal.*
‖ *Exchanged from 55th Foot, 29th June, 1881.*

1 quarter-master, 2 warrant officers, 48 serjeants, 40 corporals, 16 drummers, 780 privates. In consequence of this, Major Ruxton was promoted to be lieut.-colonel, and the three senior captains to be majors; the latter officers, however, still continued to perform all regimental duties as captains. For the next seven years, officers who held commissions previous to the 1st of July, 1881, were promoted as vacancies occurred in their own battalions, and not in the regiment.

In August, numerals and regimental badges were ordered to be removed from the shoulder straps of the scarlet patrol jackets worn by officers in India, and badges of rank, in gold, substituted.

In September, the designation of serjeant-drummer was substituted for drum-major.

Being rejoined by the Indúr and Ásírgarh detachments, and relieved by the 2nd battn. Lancashire Regiment (late 20th Foot), the battalion, under command of Lieut.-Col. Davis, commenced its march from Máu for Nasírábád on the 28th of October.

At Sadúlpúr, which was reached on the 30th, the Mahárájáh of Dhár visited the camp, on which occasion the battalion paraded and marched past.

Rutlam was reached on the 4th of November, the Mahárájáh of which State was received in camp by a guard of honour of 50 men.

On the 7th, when at Jowra, the Nawab of that place was also received in camp.

Nímach being reached on the 13th, the battalion halted for two days, and a detachment of the 2nd battn. Leicestershire (late 17th Foot) was relieved by B., G., and H. companies, under command of Lt.-Col. Ruxton. B. and G. companies subsequently formed part of the Viceroy's (Lord Ripon) escort, when His Excellency at Chitorgárh on the 23rd, invested the Mahárájáh of Udaipúr, with the Order of the Star of India.

1881   The head-quarters and the remaining companies continued their march on the 15th, and on the 22nd encamped close to the Bhilwara railway station. Here Lord Ripon alighted, *en route* from Ájmír to Chitorgárh, and was received by a guard of honour of 100 men with the Queen's colour. *Apropos* of this, the following letter was received by the officer commanding at Nasírábád :—

"Sir,

"I am desired to inform you that the Major-General has been commanded, by His Excellency the Viceroy, to express His Excellency's appreciation of the compliment paid him, by the guard of honour from the battalion under your command, on the occasion of its being turned out to him when His Excellency passed your camp during his journey by rail from Ájmír. The Major-General has much pleasure in adding, that His Excellency expressed his special satisfaction at the clean, smart, soldier-like appearance of the men, and of the manner in which they turned out."

On the 28th, the head-quarter division reached its destination at Nasírábád, but the companies did not move into barracks till the 30th, when they relieved the head-quarters of the 2nd battn. Leicestershire Regiment.

Lieut.-General E. A. Somerset, C.B., was on the 19th of December, appointed Colonel of the 1st battn. Worcestershire Regiment, *vice* General John Longfield, C.B., transferred to the colonelcy of the 8th (King's) Foot.

1882   On the 2nd of March, 1882, the following Circular Letter was received :—

"I have the honour, by desire of the Field-Marshal Commanding-in-Chief, to convey to you, Her Majesty's command, that in consequence of the altered formation of attack, and extended range of firing, regimental colours will not necessarily in future, be taken with the battalion on active service. When, however, a battalion proceeds abroad in the ordinary course of relief, colours will accompany the **1882** battalion, but in the event of its being ordered on active service, they will be left at the base of operations, unless the general officer commanding, should be of opinion that the nature of the service in which a force is about to be engaged is such as to render the possession of the colours with the battalion undoubtedly expedient, when he may as a special matter give directions for their accompanying it. Except in this respect, no change will be made, both colours being retained as affording a record of the services of the regiment, and furnishing to the young soldiers a history of its gallant deeds.

At reviews and occasions of ceremony, they will be usually taken with the battalion."

On the 2nd of June, authority was received for the word "Ramillies" to be inscribed on the colours of the Worcestershire Regiment, in commemoration of the part taken by Farrington's regiment in that victory.

Mounted officers of infantry regiments of the line were this year ordered to discontinue the use of the saddle cloth.

On the 18th of July, Lieut. Haughton, who had served as transport officer in the late Afghán campaign, for which he received the medal, died of cholera at Banáras, whilst attached to the 10th Bengal N.I.

Extract from Regimental Orders, Nasírábád, 1st March, 1883:— **1883**
"In taking leave of the battalion he has had the honour to command for the last five years, Colonel Davis wishes to thank all ranks for the invariable good conduct and devotion to duty, which has made it such a pleasure to do so."

On the 8th of May, the following letter from the adjutant-general Bombay army, to Col. Davis, late commanding the 1st battn. Worcestershire Regiment, was received:—

"I am directed by His Excellency the Commander-in-Chief, Bombay Army, to express to you on this occasion of your relinquishing

1881 the command of your battalion, his entire satisfaction at the manner in which you have exercised your command.

Nothing could have been more favourable than the reports of the General Officer commanding the Máu division, both on the state of the 1st battalion of the Worcestershire Regiment, and on your personal qualifications for command; and from what His Excellency saw and heard of that battalion, he entirely concurs, in Sir Robert Phayre's opinion.

I am desired to add, that but for an oversight, through which a long delay has been incurred, the above would have been published in Division Orders."

On the 5th of May, it was officially intimated to the battalion, that the Star, worn on the valises of the late 29th Regiment, had been approved of, for the "*Worcestershire Regiment*,"† with the exception that the letters "W.R." be substituted for the numerals "29."

Under the feudal system which formerly prevailed in Rájputáná, the Thákurs were obliged to furnish a certain number of cavalry for the Mahárájáh's service. This liability had of late years been compounded for, by the payment of an annual sum, which the Rájah having recently tried to increase, led to disturbances in Bikanír. The Politicals tried to settle the matter, but having failed, the Thákurs fortified to the best of their ability, and shut themselves up in Bidassur. To this place the Political agent, escorted by the Irinpúrah battalion and a few Deoli irregular cavalry, repaired; but as the rebels would not listen to his proposals, and the troops with him were too few, he retired to Sujangarh, there to await the arrival of the "Bikanír Field Force," which had been despatched to restore order.

On the 15th of December, three guns of the R.A.; B. and G. companies 1st battn. Worcestershire Regiment (under command of Major Carrington, with Lieuts. Conyngham and Edwards); a wing of the 8th Bombay N.I.; a detachment of Bombay sappers and miners;

---

† The 3rd and 4th battns. do not wear the valise ornament.

and the Irinpúrah battalion, left Nasírábád under command of Brigadier- **1883** General R. R. Gillespie, C.B.

On reaching Ájmír, these were joined by the Mairwarra battalion. It was here ascertained that the rebels, numbering 2,500 under command of Bhadur Singh, chief of the malcontents, still occupied Bidassur, a walled town about 150 miles distant, also that they had sent away their women and cattle, had loopholed the walls, and were prepared to defend the town.

When, however, after a nine days' march, General Gillespie's force reached Sujangarh, the Thákur leader, having been deserted by many of his followers, came out and surrendered himself.

Having halted for a couple of days, a detachment composed of some sappers and miners, a few cavalry, and two companies of the 8th N.I., proceeded to Bidassur to mine the fort, which, with its four bastions and gateway, was effectually demolished in the presence of the General, Colonel Bradford (governor-general's agent for Rájpútáná), the Rájah of Bikanír, his followers, and several of the European officers.

After this, the field force returned to Nasírábád, where it arrived **1884** on the 9th of January, 1884.

Much of the country which this force traversed consisted of loose sand, which lay in long, low, rolling hills, the only vegetation being sand-grass, burrs, and a small thorny scrub. Several dry salt lakes were also crossed, and both men and guns had a hard time of it.

With reference to this march, the following letter was received:—

"His Royal Highness the Field Marshal Commanding-in-Chief has been pleased to remark upon the exemplary conduct and creditable march, with Brigadier-General Gillespie's column to Bikanír."

It having been ascertained that a great number of Gházis, who had opposed our forces in the actions near Kandahár during the late Afghán campaign, were Kakar Pathans from the Zhob district, which

1884 flanked the line of communication with Sind, it was proposed to chastise them when the war was over ; but a change of Ministry having taken place at the termination of the campaign, a policy of non-intervention ensued. When however, in 1883 and '84, these tribes made raids on our outposts, and seemed inclined to threaten the construction of the Sibi-Quetta railway, it was decided to send a punitive expedition into the Zhob, or "Long" Valley, and at the same time to explore that unknown district.

The expedition, which consisted of about 5,200 troops of all arms, was placed under command of Brigadier-General Sir Oriel Tanner, K.C.B., and ordered to rendezvous, about the 27th of September, at Dukki.

Orders having been received for a wing of the regiment to act as part of the reserve to the 1st division of the expeditionary force, on the 5th of September, A, C, D, and H companies, under command of Lieut.-Colonel Douglas, with Majors Watson and Carrington ; Lieuts. Chapman, Hilton (adjutant), Mallaby, B. H. Randolph, R. M. Betham, and A. L. S. Ogilvie, left Nasírábád by rail for the Nari Gorge, eight miles north of Sibi, at that time the terminus of the Sibi-Quetta railway. Travelling all night, and having halted *en route* at Bandikin, Delhí, Ambálah, Mian Mir, Multán, Khánpúr, and Sukkur ; the Nari Gorge was reached on the 13th. The following day, the wing commenced its march to Dukki, where it arrived on the 24th, and was met by the band of the 3rd Bombay L.I., which played it into camp to the tune of "Far Away."

Owing to the great heat, the march was a very trying one, and three men died from sunstroke.

Much to the disappointment of all, the wing was kept in reserve, during the operations, at the termination of which, a thorough survey of the country having been made, the field force was divided into two columns, and returned to India by different routes.

Leaving Dukki on the 28th of November, the wing of the Worcestershire Regiment retraced its steps to Tung. Here it branched off to Maudai, and marching through the Kujjak Pass to Kujjak, Sibi was reached on the 8th of December. The following day A. and H. companies proceeded by train to Haidarábád, whilst C. and D. companies joined head-quarters of the regiment, then stationed at Karáchí.

1884

On the 14th of September, Lieut.-General (hon. General) R. W. Disney Leith, C.B., had been appointed Colonel of the 1st battalion Worcestershire Regiment, in place of Lieut.-General Somerset, C.B., transferred to the King's Royal Rifles.

On the 22nd of October, the head-quarters of the battalion, with E. F. and G. companies, had left Nasírábád by rail for Bombay, where they embarked on board the Indian marine steamer "Clive" for passage to Karáchí. Reaching that post on the 31st, they disembarked and went under canvas till the 2nd of November, when they moved into barracks and relieved the 2nd battn. Gloucestershire Regiment (late 61st Foot).

On the head-quarters leaving Nasírábád, Brigadier-General R. R. Gillespie, C.B., caused the following order to be published:—

"During the three years the 1st Worcestershire Regiment has been at Nasírábád, its conduct has been most excellent, and the Brigadier-General has great pleasure in placing on record his appreciation of it, and of the good discipline of the battalion, and is sure that the strong feeling for the credit of the regiment that influences all ranks, will, so long as it exists, be conducive to these good results, which make it efficient, and a credit to its country and to the British army.

The Brigadier-General will bring his opinion of the very satisfactory condition of the battalion to the notice of His Excellency the Commander-in-Chief."

1885 On the 1st of June, 1885, the first of the annual dinners of the 29th (Worcestershire) Regiment took place at the Freemasons' Tavern. On account of the battalion being on foreign service, the attendance was small; the following officers were however present:—

Lieut.-Colonels—J. J. Bailey, R. J. Watson; Majors—G. W. F. Claremont, C. H. Helyar,† A. W. Matchett; Captains—H. G. Colvill, C. A. P. Cooper, W. S. Clarke, J. O. Dalgleish, H. E. E. Everard,‡ Hon. S. Hylton Jolliffe, F. C. Littledale; Lieutenants—H. L. Begbie, F. J. W. Bennett,§ and Mr. R. A. Oswald.

After dinner, H.R.H. the Duke of Cambridge, who was presiding at the annual regimental dinner of the Grenadier Guards, which was taking place under the same roof, was pleased to send word that the Guards were drinking the health of the 29th Regiment. This honour, coupled as it was with the old regimental number, was greeted with three hearty cheers.

1886 On the 3rd of December, F. company, under Captain A. Moss, proceeded on detachment to Haidarábád, where, on the 8th of January, 1886, head-quarters of the battalion under command of Colonel Ruxton, with C., E., and G. companies, arrived. On the 30th inst, head-quarters, with A., C., E., F., and G. companies, marched to Panwarkojat, and joined a camp of exercise formed there under command of Brigadier-General G. Luck, C.B., commanding the Sind district. Having remained here encamped, till the 2nd of February, the battalion returned to Haidarábád, where three companies under command of Major Carrington were left on detachment. Head-quarters, with A., F., and H. companies, under command of Lieut.-Colonel Douglas, marched thence to Karáchí, where they arrived on the 16th instant.

---

† 3rd Hussars.
‡ 3rd Battn. Worcestershire Regiment.
§ North Somerset Yeomanry.

REGIMENTAL ORDERS. **1887**

"Karáchí, 1 March, 1887.

"In handing over to-day the command of the battalion, Colonel Ruxton desires to express to all ranks, his great appreciation of the support which he has invariably met with, and of the good conduct and soldierlike behaviour of the non-commissioned officers and men during the period that he has had the honour to command them.

After a service of 28 years, Colonel Ruxton bids farewell with his best wishes to the regiment, in whose reputation and welfare he will always take the deepest interest."

The left wing of the battalion under command of Captain J. R. Rainsford left Haidarábád by rail, on the 2nd of March, for Mach in the Bolan Pass, whence it marched to Quetta, and on arriving there on the 8th, encamped. On the 12th it was joined by the head-quarters and right wing, under command of Lieut.-Colonel Carrington.

Having remained under canvas for about two months, the regiment moved into the quarters lately occupied by the 2nd battn. King's Own (Royal Lancaster) Regiment.

Whilst stationed here, two or three companies were employed till about the end of October, 1888, in road-making near Sarakula.

On the 7th of October, Quarter-Master F. Bradley died of cholera.

On the 18th of November, 1888, Major Spratt, Lieut. J. G. R. **1888** Swanson, with Lieut. B. C. Holt, of the 2nd Bn. K.O.L.I. (105th Madras L.I.), a jemidar of the 5th Bombay Cavalry, and 30 native troops, left Quetta on a reconnaissance. Marching by the Sini Bolan, Rod Bahar, Johan, Kelát, across the Sarun plateau to Kotree, Gundava, Shorun, and Dadur, they returned to Quetta on the 10th of February, 1889.

1888   The strength of the battalion on the 31st of December, was 30 officers, 46 serjeants, 35 corporals, 15 drummers, 988 privates.

Size.	Serjeants.	Corporals.	Drummers.	Privates.
6 ft. & upwds.	1	2	1	13
5 ,, 11	2	1		22
5 ,, 10	4	2	1	46
5 ,, 9	3	4	2	69
5 ,, 8	6	5	3	122
5 ,, 7	9	6	2	238
5 ,, 6	11	9	4	212
5 ,, 5	8	5		171
Under	2	1		91
Lads				4
Total	46*	35	15	988

Country.	Serjeants.	Corporals.	Drummers.	Privates.
English	41	35	13	945
Scotch	3		1	6
Irish	2		1	37
Total	46*	35	15	988

(Signed)   D'A. Thomas
Capt. and Adjt. 1st Worc. Regt.

1889   On the 1st of January, 1889, the officers consisted of 13 of the late 29th Foot, 6 of the late 36th, and 11 who had joined the army since the introduction of the territorial scheme.

On the 5th of March, the average height of the battalion was 5 feet 7½ inches.

1890   On the 7th of March, 1890, the battalion—strength, 22 officers, 954 rank and file—left Quetta by rail for Karáchí. Halting that night at Sharigh, and at Sibi on the 8th and 9th, it embarked on the 11th on

---

* Includes 2 Warrant Officers and an Armourer Serjeant.

board the Indian Marine s.s. "Canning" for Bombay, which was reached on the 14th; here it disembarked the same day, and proceeding in two trains to Púna, it was met at the station the following morning by the band of the 1st battn. Royal Fusiliers, which played it up to the Ghorpúri Barracks, recently vacated by the 2nd battn. Durham Light Infantry (106th Foot.)

OFFICER—1887-1890.

By letter dated Horse Guards, War Office, the 17th of October, 1890, it was intimated to the General Officer commanding the N.W. District (Chester) that the Queen had been graciously pleased to approve of the pattern badges submitted to her for the officers and men of the Worcestershire Regiment. The principal alterations were the granting of a proper shaped star (oblong) with the garter, and lion device in place of the castle, and the substitution of the lion device in lieu of "W.R." in the centre of the valise and forage cap ornaments of the non-commissioned officers, rank and file.

1891   On the 3rd of January, the battalion—strength, 17 officers, 649 rank and file—marched out to Camp Yerroda, to take part in extensive manœuvres in the vicinity of the "Three Sisters" Hills.

REGIMENTAL ORDERS.

"Poona, 28 February, 1891.

"Colonel E. Carrington, on giving up command of the battalion in which he has had the honour of serving for 29 years, wishes heartily to thank all ranks for the unfailing support and assistance they have given him in carrying out the duties of the regiment. He also thanks the men for their good behaviour and the way in which, both in cantonments and on parade, they have kept up the character of the regiment. With best wishes for their welfare, he wishes all 'Good-bye.'"

The Napier Memorial Shield, besides several challenge cups, was this year won by the battalion at the Bombay Rifle Association meeting.

1ST BATTN. WORCESTERSHIRE REGIMENT, 30TH MAY, 1891.

Colonel—Leith, Lt.-Gen. *(Hon. Gen.)*, R. W. D., *C.B.*

Lt.-Colonel—Spratt, E. J. H.

Majors—*m.* Clarke, W. S. C.; Rainsford, J. R.; Moss, A.

Captains—Lenox-Conyngham, W. A.; *s.* Thomas, E. A. D'A., *D.A.A.G., Kamptee;* Begbie, H. L., *Adjt. Burma State Ry. Vols.;* Newton-King, A. C., *Comdt. Khandalla Sanitarium; d.* Monro, G. N.; Randolph, B. H., *Adjt.;* Wilkie, E. O. H.; Hovell, H. de B.; Peacock, G. T.; How, C. C.

Lieutenants—Bell, E.; Nunn, M. H.; *d.* Swanson, J. G. R.; Carey, de V., *Comdt. Puna Rest Camp*; Thomas, B. H., *S.S.O., Purundhur;* Westmacott, C. B.; Bennett, C. H.; Gordon, J. L. R.; Taylor, E. F.; Stubbs, A. K.; Brock, E. N. L.; Cassels, G. R.; Hannyngton, J. A.

2nd Lieutenants—Harold, C. F.; Drever, T. I.; Stuart, B. F. B.; Wooldridge, H. C.; Seton, C. H.

Paymaster—Moss, A., *Maj. (acting);* Adjutant—Randolph, B. H.; Qr. Master—Young, I. *Lt.*

APPENDIX.

Succession Roll of Regimental Staff Officers, Chaplains, and Agents.—1694-1890.

Colonels Commanding.

Thomas Farrington
Lord Mark Kerr
Henry Disney
William Anne, Earl of Albemarle
George Read
Francis Fuller
Peregrine Thomas Hopson
Honble. George Boscawen
George, Earl of Granard
William Evelyn
(11) William Tryon
(12) Charles, Earl of Harrington
William, Lord Cathcart, K.T.; K.A.N.; K.A.; K.S.A.; K.T.S.
Gordon Forbes
W John, Earl of Strafford, G.C.B.; G.C.H.; K.M.T.
Ulysses, Lord Downes, G.C.B.; K.T.S.; S.A.
W Sir James Simpson, G.C.B.
John Longfield, C.B.
Edward Arthur Somerset, C.B.
Robert William Disney Leith, C.B.

Lieutenant Colonels.

William Froude
William Watkins
Sir Christopher Wray, Bart.
Charles Cratchrode
Benjamin Columbine
William Kennedy
Peregrine T. Hopson
Caroline Fredk. Scott
Lord Frederick Cavendish
Henry Richardson. *c.*
John Conynghame
(12) Maurice Carr
(13) Patrick Gordon
Thomas Carleton. *c.*
Lord Henry FitzGerald
William, Lord Cathcart
Archibald Campbell. *c.*
Hugh Dickson
John Enys
Lord Frederick Montagu
John Byng
Frederick Maitland, M. GENL.
Daniel White
Sir Gregory H. B. Way, C.B.; K.T.S.

Lieutenant Colonels.—*Continued.*

(25) John Tucker
Peter Hodge
W Honble. James Stanhope
Sir John Buchan, C.B.; K.T.S.
W James Simpson
Henry Christmas Cash
John Viney Evans
Honble. Charles Alexr. Wrottesley
W James Simpson. *c.*
George Congreve, C.B.

(35) John Hamilton Stewart. *c.*
John Ross Wheeler
Edward Henry Westropp
Lindsay Farrington. *c.*
John Flanagan
Hales Wilkie. *c.*
Howell Davis. *c.*
Frederick Charles Ruxton. *c.*
Edmund Carrington. *c.*
Edward J. H. Spratt.

Junior Lieut.-Colonels.

In November, 1793, a new plan was made for recruiting the army, by offering to such regiments as could raise a certain number of men in a given time, an additional lieut.-colonel, and major; the promotion to go in the regiment.

Hugh Dickson.   1 March, 1794.
John Enys
Lord Frederick Montagu
(4) John Byng

(5) George A. F. Lake
John Agmondisham Vesey
Honble. Geo. A. F. Lake
Daniel White.   1805—3 Sept., 1808.

On proceeding to India in 1842, the establishment was again raised to 2 lieut.-colonels, and 2 majors.

Thomas Bennett Hickin
Robert Percy Douglas
Charles Cyril Taylor, C.B.
George Congreve, C.B.
(5) Henry Robartes Wyatt

(6) Andrew T. Hemphill
Arthur Simcoe Mountain, C.B. *c.*
Honble. Thomas Ashburnham, C.B. *c.s.*
Mathew Smith
John Hamilton Stewart. *c.* 1855—30 Sept., 1859.

Under provision of Royal Warrant, 25th of June, 1881, the establishment of field officers was, from the 1st of July, increased to 2 lieut.-colonels and 4 majors.

Frederick Chas. Ruxton.
John Charles Douglas.
Edmund Carrington.

By A.C., 1st of February, 1887, the number of lieut.-colonels was reduced to one per battn., and as each lieut.-colonel who thus became supernumerary was absorbed, a captain was added to the establishment of the territorial regiment.

MAJORS.

Christopher Wray	(28) John Tucker. *l.c.*
Charles Cratchrode	Peter Hodge. *l.c.*
Benjamin Columbine	George Tod. *l.c.*
William Kennedy	William Elliot
Charles Pawlett	John V. Evans
James Kennedy	Honble. Charles A. Wrottesley
Charles Crosbie	Thomas B. Hickin
George, Lord Forbes	Robert P. Douglas
Hugh Scott	George Congreve
Montagu Wilmot	Marcus Barr. C.B. *l.c. ; s.*
James Gisborne	Andrew T. Hemphill
Bartholemew Blake. *l.c.*	Mathew Smith
Maurice Carr	Gregory Lewis Way
Pierce Butler	John Ross Wheeler. *l.c.*
Jeremiah French	Edward H. Westropp. *l.c.*
Christopher Carleton. *l.c.*	Lindsay Farrington
Archibald Campbell	John Mackenzie Lyle
William Monsell. *l.c.*	Somerset Molyneux Clarke
Henry Hervey Aston	Hales Wilkie
Hugh Dickson	Nathaniel Polhill Ledgard
John Mallory (on increase of establishment, 1794)	William Boycott
	Howell Davis
John Enys	Robert Berkeley
James Kirkman	Frederick C. Ruxton
George Johnstone	Edmund Carrington
Daniel White. *l.c.*	H. J. de B. de Berniere
Gregory H. B. Way	John Lewis Rose
(27) Thomas Egerton	William Senhouse Clarke

JUNIOR MAJORS.

John Enys (1st March, 1794)	(8) Gregory H. B. Way
Ralph Ramsay. *l.c.*	Thomas Egerton
James Kirkman	John Tucker
Francis William Farquhar	Peter Hodge
George Johnstone	George Tod
Daniel White. *l.c.*	Thomas Gell
(7) William Edgell Wyatt	William Elliot

Junior Majors.—*Continued.*

(15) Robert Stannus
John V. Evans
John Walter
Honble. Charles A. Wrottesley
Thomas B. Hickin
Alexander Sharrock
Richard Lucas
Robert P. Douglas
George Congreve
Christopher Edward Eaton
Marcus Barr. *l.c. ; s.*
Andrew T. Hemphill
Henry H. Kitchener
Mathew Smith
Gregory L. Way
William Gustavus Brown

(31) Arthur St. George Stepney
John R. Wheeler
John Power
Sir Edward Lugard, K.C.B. *c. ; s.*
Edward H. Westropp
Lindsay Farrington
James McK. Lyle
Henry G. Walker
Somerset M. Clarke
Hales Wilkie
Nathaniel P. Ledgard
William Boycott
Howell Davis
Robert Berkeley
Frederick C. Ruxton
John C. Douglas

Junior Majors. (Under provision of Royal Warrant, 25 June, 1881.)

Robert John Watson
Charles Edward Pinckney Simpson
Edmund Carrington
George Wm. Fredk. Claremont
John Francis Egerton
Edward James Henry Spratt
William Senhouse Clarke
Joseph Ryland Rainsford
Allan Moss

Adjutants.

John Wright
Francis Lewis
Hugh Montgomery
Andrew Charlton
William Groves
Archibald Cunningham
Charles Phillips
William Cockcroft
(9) John Montagu Blomer

(10) William Lindsay
Samuel Barrett
John Hallowes
John Roberts
James Kirkman
George Johnstone
Thomas Comber
Thomas O'Neil
William Wade

Adjutants.—*Continued.*

(19) Benjamin Wild
John Vesie
William Gilbert
John Weir
George Foskey
Morgan Morgan
Andrew T. Hemphill
John Owen Lucas
Kenneth Murchison
George H. Jones
Charles Eustace MacDonnell

(30) Lindsay Farrington
Hugh George Colvill
Valens Tonnochy
Robt. Cathcart Dalrymple Bruce
John James Bailey
William Winn
Edward J. H. Spratt
Wm. Senhouse Clarke
Murray Venables Hilton
Edward Algernon D'A. Thomas
Bernard H. Randolph

Quarter Masters.

James Howard
John Miller
John Lewis
Peter Bonafous
John Miller
Thomas Farrington
Samuel Hurst
John Fuller
Francis William Kinner
James Vibart
Alexander Saunders
Alexander Dalgetty
Richard Nosworthy
(14) Thomas Stott

(15) William Gillespie
James Mitchell
Thomas Kneebone
Charles Sutherland Dowson
Timothy Walsh
John J. Bailey
William Smith
James Aylett
Richard Erwin
William Henry Martin
Henry Hill Bray
James Brogden
Frederick Bradley
Isaac Young

When, previous to 1765, the regiment happened to be on the Irish establishment, a Quarter Master was not allowed on its strength.

Surgeons.

Abraham Silk
Marsh Hollingsworth
Bartholomew Black
Bartholomew Blake
Archibald Dickson
(6) John Robertson

(7) George Hoyer
Robert Scott
John Offral
Joseph Skinner
Thomas Gregg
Samuel Irving

SURGEONS.—*Continued.*

(13) Thomas Carter
Henry Lennon
George Guthrie
Joseph Arthur Stanford
William Milton
Charles Thomas Ingham, M.D.

(19) Arthur Wood, M.D.
Charles Thos. Ingham, M.D.
John Robert Taylor, M.D.
Richard Dane, M.D.
Edward Moorhead, M.D.
Richard William Meade

Regimental surgeons, and assistant surgeons were abolished by Royal Warrant, 1 March, 1873.

MATES, OR ASSISTANT SURGEONS.

* * * * * * * *
George Mackenzie
Mathew Leslie
James Mills
Mathew Leslie
Robert Scott
Henry Duggan
Thomas Smith
John Dickson Reed
Philip Staples
William Marson
Peter Simpson
William Marson
Charles Pugh
Anthony Bishop
George Miller
Thomas Gregg
Alexander Hodge
John Wilson
Edward Walsh
Arthur Dowdell
. . . . . Gibson
(23) George Guthrie

(24) Frederick Dawes
Edward Curby
Lewis Evans
William Parker
James Lawder
James Smith
George Dunlop
John Hawkey, M.D.
Peter Robertson
George Alexander Cowper, M.D.
Richard Dane, M.D.
William Green Trousdell
William Baker Young
Alexander Mackay Macbeth
Charles Ludovic Stewart
Robert McGregor
Daniel Macqueen, M.D.
John Smith Chartres
William Langford Farmer
William Alexander Mackinnon
Walter John
St. John Killery
John Peter Hamilton Boileau, M.D.

PAYMASTERS.

Prior to 1798, an officer, under the rank of a field officer, was appointed by the colonel to act as paymaster. Regimental paymasters were first appointed in that year;

they ranked as captains in their respective regiments, but had no military command. They gave security to the Secry. at War for the time being, themselves of £2,000, and two sureties of £1,000 each. The above sums were forfeited on proof of malversation, criminal neglect of duty, or if it appeared that any valuable consideration had been directly or indirectly given in order to obtain the appointment.

Thomas Fitzgerald
Thomas Stott
Christopher Humphrey
Benjamin Wild
Nathaniel Farewell
(6) James Espinasse

(7) James Herbert Clay
Charles Scarlin Naylor
Tennent Jameson
John Edward Longden
William Fortescue Scott
Robert Smyth

Regimental paymasters were abolished by Royal Warrant, 22nd of October, 1877.

From the 26th of October, 1875, when Major R. Smyth retired, to the 1st of January, 1880, there was a paymaster's committee of which Captain R. J. Watson was president; after this an officer of the Pay Department was attached to the regiment.

Instructors of Musketry.

William Boycott
Robert Berkeley
George Wm. F. D. Smith
Charles E. P. Simpson
(5) Edmund Carrington

(6) George W. F. Claremont
Clement Astley Paston Cooper
Wm. Senhouse Clarke
Charles Percy Cubitt
Archibald J. Erskine

The appointment of instructor of musketry was abolished by G.O., 31st March, 1883.

Chaplains.

John Hancox
Robert Cox
Henry Bland
John Clifton
John Devie
(6) John Spicer

(7) Joseph Cowper
John Rogers
James Stewart
John Forbes
George Turner. 1774, to 24 Dec., 1796.

Regimental chaplains were abolished the latter end of 1796.

Regimental Agents.

1694—1702	Mr. Peter Bernard	Rose Street, Covent Garden.
1719	Colonel Campbell	Blind Key, Dublin.
1745	Captain Alexander Wilson	Queen Street, Westminster.
1749—1752	Captain George Johnston	
1752—1762	Mr. William Chaigneau	Dublin Castle.
1762—1766	Captain Theoph. Desbrisay	Cork Hill.
1760—1776	Mr. Cowden	In the Meuse, Charing Cross.
1776—1780	Mr. Bishopp	Vine Street, Piccadilly.
1780—1785	Mr. Cowden	In the King's Meuse.
1785—1788	Mr. Elwin	Gray's Inn.
1788—1891	Messrs. Cox, Cox, and Greenwood	Craig's Court.

In addition to the above, between 1863 and 1879 the Irish regimental agents were—

Sir E. R. Borough, Bart.
Messrs. Armit & Co.

ALPHABETICAL LIST OF REGIMENTAL STAFF OFFICERS, WITH A SHORT ACCOUNT OF THEIR SERVICES UP TO THE TIME OF THEIR LEAVING THE REGIMENT.

Farrington's Regiment was allowed complete from 20th March, 1694, to 28th Feb., 1698, when its officers were placed on half-pay.

ALBEMARLE, W.A.,

2nd Earl of, born at Whitehall in 1702, was apptd. on 25 Aug. '17 Capt. and Lt.-Col. in the 2nd Foot Guards; on 31 Mar.'27 A.D.C. to King Geo. I. with the rank of Col. in the army; on 22 Nov.'31 Colonel of the late Col. Disney's Regt. (29th Ft.), and on 8 May '33 transfd. to the Colcy. of the 3rd Troop of Horse Gds. In Sep. '37 was made Govr. of Virginia, on 2nd July '39 apptd. Brigadier; Maj. Genl. 18 Feb. '42. The following year served on the Continent, and led his Troop to the charge, at Dettingen. In Oct. '44 was removed to the Colcy. of the C. Gds.; Lt. Genl. 3 Jan. '45. Distinguished himself at Fontenoy, commanded the rt. wing of the army at Culloden, and in '47 a division of infantry at the battle of Val or Laffeld. Was subsequently apptd. Ambassador to the Court of Versailles, and died in Paris 22 Dec. 1754.

ASHBURNHAM, C.B., HONBLE. T.,

Brev. Col. exchgd. 8 Feb. 1850 fm. h.p. 62 Ft. to junr. Lt.-Col. of 29th. Commanded the Kánhpúr brigade from 15 May '50 to July '52; Banáras Brigd. 3 July—7 Aug. '52, when transfd. to the Firúzpúr brigade. Retd. fm. Regt. 19 Aug. '54, on being promtd. Maj. Genl. *Prev. Service*, Ens. C. Gds. 30 Jan. 1823, and commanded a brigade of the army of the Satláj at Firúzshahar and Sobráon. Was on 3 Apl. '46 apptd. A.D.C. to the Queen with rank of Col. in the army.

ASTON, H. H.,

Was on 13 Nov. 1793 promtd. from Capt. of a new Independent Compy. to Maj. of the 29 Ft., and on 4 Feb. '94 to Lt.-Col. 82nd Ft. *First Comsn.*, Ens. in the Buffs, 27 Jan. 1779.

AYLETT, J.,
> Exchgd. on 23 Mar. 1859 from Qr. Mr. 20 Ft., to that of the 29th. Retd. on h.p. with rank of Capt. 30th Jun. '65. *Prev. Service* in the 20th Ft., with which he was present throughout the Crimean Campaign and Indian Mutiny.

BAILEY, J. J.,
> Ens. 3 Aug. 1855, Qr. Mr. 5 Nov. follg., Adj. 29 Feb '56, Lt. Jun. '57. Apptd. P. Mr. 31 Ft. 6 Nov. '63. *Prev. Service*, Entered the army in 1835, served with the 13th Lt. Infantry throughout the Áfghán campaign of '38-'42, and at the assault of Gházni (July '39) had command of six volunteers who carried up the powder bags with which the gates of that fortress were blown down, after which he entered with the storming party under Col. Dennie. Lt.-Col. Bailey, who retired from the army in 1882, after a service of 47 years (10 only of which were passed in the United Kingdom, the remaining 37 having been served in India, Áfghánistán, Scind, Bilúchistán, Burma, and the operations in the Malay Peninsula of '75-'76), served with the 4th Bn. R. B. in the '78-'79 Áfghán war, and was the only individual of the British or Indian armies who had been through the whole of the '38-'42 campaign in that country.

BARR, C.B., M.,
> Exchgd. 15 Dec. 1843 fm. Maj. in the Buffs. Served from 12 Nov. '42 to 10 Feb. '46 (including the battles of Mahárájpúr, Fírúzshahar, and Sobráon) as A.A.G. to H.M. Forces in India. Died at Kasauli 26 Mar. '46 fm. effects of wounds recd. at Sobráon. *First Comsn.*, Ens. in the Buffs 9 Apl. 1825.

BARRETT, S.,
> Ens. 19 Jun. 1751, Lt. 16 Feb., and Adj. 1 Jan. '56. Out of Regt. 1759.

BERKELEY, R.,
> Ens. 24 Sep. 1858, Lt. 11 Sep. '60, I. of M. 21 Jan. '61, Capt. 13 Feb. '63, A.D.C. to Maj.-Genl. Vaughan Maxwell, C.B., '70-73, Maj. 26 July '76. Retd. 29 Jan. 1879.

BISHOP, A.,
> Surg. Mate 25 Dec. 1792. Retd. 8 Mar. '93.

BLACK, B.,
> Was Surg. on 1st Jun. 1715.

BLAND, H.,
> Chapl. 17 Jan. 1709.

BLAKE, B.,
> Was Surg. in 1715.

BLAKE, B.,

 Ens. 27 Dec. 1727, Lt. 19 July '39, Capt. 1st Jun. '50, Maj. 10 Dec. '55, Brev. Lt.-Col. 2 Jan. '62. Out of Regt. the follg. month.

BLOMER, J. M.,

 (late of Ancaster's Regt.) Ens. 27 Nov. 1746, Adj. 10 Mar., and Lt. 20 Jun. '53, was promtd. Capt.-Lt. in 55 Ft. 25 Dec. 1755.

BOILEAU, M.D., J. P. H.,

 Asst. Surg. 9 Jun. 1865, Surg.-Maj. 30 Sep. '76, left the Regt. the follg. month on appmt. to Asst. Professor of Pathology at Netley.

BONAFOUS, P.,

 Ens. 16 Feb. 1694, h.p. 28 Feb. '98 to 10 Mar. 1702, Lt. . . . ., Qr. Mr. . . . . to 12 Jan. '07, when promtd. Capt. Out of Regt. 10 Aug. 1715.

BOSCAWEN, HONBLE. G. E.,

 Born 1 Dec. 1712, Ens. 1st Foot Gds. 24 Nov. '29. Capt. and Lt. Col. 9 Apl. '43 ; distinguished himself in the battles of Dettingen and Fontenoy. Apptd. A.D.C. to King Geo. II. with rank of Col. in the army, 18 Aug. '49. Col. of 29th Ft. 4. Mar. '52. Maj. Genl. 14 Jan. '58, Lt. Genl. 22 Feb. '60. Was on 16 Jan. '61 removed to Colcy. of 23rd R.W. Fuziliers, and died in York Street, St. James, 3 May, 1775.

BOYCOTT, W.,

 Ens. 18 Dec. 1857. I. of. M. 31 Jan., and Lt. 2 Dec. '59. Capt. 2 Dec. '62, Maj. 31 Oct. '71, retd. 26 July '76, and died at Hawkston, Woodside, Natal, 11 Mar. 1884.

BRADLEY, F.,

 Exchgd. in Oct, 1885 fm. Qr. Mr. 2nd Bn. Worc. Regt. to that of the 1st Battn. Died of cholera at Quetta, 7 Oct. 1887.

BRAY, H. H.,

 Promtd. 13 May 1874 to be Qr. Mr. of the Regt., and exchgd. 13 Mar. '78 to the 87th R.I. Fusiliers.

BROGDEN, J.,

 Exchgd. on 13 Mar. 1878 from Qr. Mr. of 87th R.I. Fusiliers, and in Oct. '85 to the 2nd Battn. Worc. Regt. *Prev. Service*, with the 87th, with which he was present on the N.W. frontier during the Mutiny of 1857-'58.

Brown, W. G.,

Of the 24 Ft., was on 15 Jan. 1849 posted to a Majority in the 29 Ft. in place of Brev. Lt.-Col. M. Smith apptd. to command the former Regt. after the battle of Chiliánwálá. Major Brown commanded the Light compy. of the 24th at Chiliánwálá. Served with 29th at Gujrát, and commanded the Regt. fm. Apl. to July, when his promotion in the 29th not being sanctioned by the Home Authorities, he was re-transfd. to his old corps as Major. *First Comsn.*, Ens. 24th Ft., 7 July 1825.

Bruce, R. C. D.,

Was on 18 Aug. 1848 transfd. fm. Lt. 2nd W.I. Regt. ; apptd. Adjt. 29 July '53, and on 21 Sept. '55 was promtd. Capt. in 82nd Ft. *First Comsn.*, Ens. 2nd W.I. Regt. 10 Nov. 1843.

Buchan, c.b., k.t.s., Sir J.,

Was on 28 Feb. 1822 apptd. Lt. Col. fm. Brev. Col. on h.p. Exchgd. to h.p. 10 Jun. '26. *Prev. Service*, Ens. 1st Battn. Scotch Brigade 1 Aug. 1795, was actively employed in the Mysore war, and in Guadaloupe. Served in the Peninsula as Col. of 7th Portuguese Regt. from 1811 to end of war. Was present at the battles of Vittoria, Pyrenees, Nivelle, Nive, Orthes, and Toulouse. Died 2 Jun. 1850.

Butler, P.,

Fm. Capt. Plymouth Division of Marines, 30 July 1762 ; Maj. 22 Apl. '66 ; Retd. 26th July '73. *Prev. Service*, Capt. of 135th compy. of Marines 20 Mar. 1761.

Byng, J.,

Was on 14 Mar. 1800 promtd. fm. Maj. 60 Ft. to junr. Lt. Col. of 29th. In Aug. '04 was apptd. to 3rd Foot Gds.—[*Vide Strafford J., Earl of.*]

Campbell, A.,

The younger son of an old Argyllshire family, was born in 1738, apptd. Ens. 22 Jun. '57, Lt. (Grenadier compy.) 13 Feb. '62, Capt. (Gr. compy.) 2 Aug. '69. On the 5th Mar., '70 afforded his Colonel considerable assistance in the riots which took place at Boston, N.A. In '75 on becoming senior Capt., according to the established custom, he gave up the command of the Grenadier company. Early the following year he sailed with the regiment for the relief of Quebec. Shortly after landing, Lt.-Col. Patk. Gordon being apptd. Brigadier-General, he selected Capt. Campbell to be his Major of brigade, but on the brigade, which consisted of the 21st, 29th, and 62nd regiments, being broken up, in Aug. he rejoined his regiment. On the 8th Oct. embarked with his company on board the "Inflexible," which was engaged with the American fleet on Lake Champlain on the 11th and 13th insts.; was on 26 Jun. '77 apptd. by H.E. Genl. Sir Guy Carleton, Commissary of Musters of the British forces under his command, in which capacity he accompanied Genl. Burgoyne's Expdn. from Canada, but after the action of Hubberton (when Capt. Visct. Petersham of the Grenadier compy. was apptd. A.D.C. to the General), was given a command in the battalion of Grenadiers, with which he served the remainder of the campaign; in Oct., under an Article of the Convention of Saratoga, several officers of Burgoyne's army were permitted to return to Canada on condition they did not serve, till exchanged, but the American Congress failing to fulfil the articles agreed upon, Sir Guy Carleton ordered Captain Campbell, amongst others to do duty. Promtd. Brev. Maj. 17 Nov. '80. In '82 the advance posts of the army at the entrance of Lake Champlain were entrusted to his care. In '85 was apptd. Commandant of all the posts situated on the five great Lakes; Maj. 22 Aug. '87, Brev. Lt. Col. 18 Nov. '90, Lt. Col. 21st Ft. 23 Aug. '92, but on 5th Dec. follg. was re-transferred to the 29th, which he commanded in the Expdn. to Grenada. Brig. Genl. 3 Apl. '95, Brev. Col. 21 Aug. follg. Govr. of Grenada in '96, and died that year on 15 Aug. whilst on a tour of inspection in the island.

CARLETON, C.,

Promoted 13 Sep. 1777 fm. Capt. 31st Ft. to Maj. of 29th; the following year commanded an Expdn. on the American frontier, and in '80 one against Forts Anne and George; Brev. Lt. Col. 19 Feb. '83. Died at Quebec 14 Jun. '87. *First Comsn.*, Ens., the Buffs 12 Dec. 1761.

CARLETON, T.,

On 2nd Aug. 1776 was promtd. fm. Maj. and Brev. Lt. Col. 20th Ft., to Lt.-Col. of 29th, Brev. Col. 20 Nov. '82. In '84 was apptd. Govr. of the newly-formed Province of New Brunswick. Exchgd. on 25 Sep. '88 to 5 Ft. Died 2 Feb. 1817. *Prev. Service*, Ens. 20 Ft. 12 Feb. 1755, and was present at battle of Minden 1 Aug. 1759.

CARR, M.,

On 16 Dec. 1752 was transfd. fm. Capt. of the Battle Axes * in Ireland, to the 29th Ft.; Maj. 13 Feb. '62, Lt. Col. 23 Apl. '66, sold out the same year, and obtained an appnt. in the Barrack Depmt. *Prev. Service*, Born 1730. Lt. in Army 1 Dec. 1745.

---

* A company of Foot Guards armed with battle-axes, whose duty it was to attend the State Captain and Colonel.

CARRINGTON, E.,

Ens. 7 Nov. 1862, Lt. 4 Nov. '64, I. of M. 21 Aug. '66, Capt. 9 Oct. '69, Maj. 1 July '81. In '83 commanded a detchmt. of the Regt. employed with the Bikanir Field Force, and the follg. year served with the Zhob Valley Expdn. Lt. Col. 11 Aug. '86; on 2 Mar. '87 succeeded to the command of the Battn. Col. 11 Aug. '90. Having completed 4 years' service in command, was on 2 Mar. '91 placed on h.p., and apptd. D.Q.M.G. Bombay army from the 8th inst.

CARTER, T.,

Was on 28 July 1795 apptd. Surg., but retd. Dec. 1796.

CASH, H.C.,

Apptd. Lt. Col. from h.p. 31 May 1839. Retd. the next day. *First Comsn.*, Ens. 96 Ft. 16 July 1808.

CATHCART, W. LORD,

Born 17 Sep. 1755. Accompanied his father to St. Petersburg in '68. After his return home he studied the law of Scotland, and in '76 was admitted a Member of the Faculty of Advocates. On his father's death, his lordship took up the army as a profession, and in Jun. '77 was gazetted to a Cornetcy in the 7th Queen's Dragoons; proceeded as extra A.D.C. to Sir Henry Clinton to the seat of war in America, and in Oct. was present at the storming of Forts Clinton and Montgomery. In Nov. was apptd. to a Ltcy., and on 10 Dec. was promtd. to a Troop in the 17th Light Dragoons; present at the engagement of Monmouth Court House. In '78 raised the British Legion, of which he was given command and provincial rank of Col. On 13 Apl. '79 was apptd. Maj. of 38th Ft., with which he served in the affairs of Springfield and Elizabeth Town Point. On 2nd Feb. '81 was apptd. Capt. and Lt. Col. in the Coldstream Gds., and on 6th Oct. '89 exchanged to the Lt. Colcy. of the 29th Ft.; Brev. Col. 18 Nov. '90, and on 5 Dec. '92 was apptd. Colonel of the Regiment; in Nov. '93 was given a brigade in the Expdn. which, under Lord Moira, was intended to help the French Royalists of La Vendee and La Loire. On 3 Oct. '94 was promtd. Maj. Genl.; served in Flanders, and the followg. year in Holland and N. Germany, when he commanded the whole of the Light Cavalry; returned to England in '96; in '97 commanded a brigade of Cavalry at Weymouth, and was on 7 Aug. transfd. to the Colcy. of 2nd Life Gds. Promtd. Lt. Genl. 1 Jan. 1801; in the autumn of '05 was ordered to Russia as Ambassador. His Lordship was next apptd. commander-in-chief of the Forces in Scotland, and in May '07 to command the Mil. Forces in the Expdn. to Copenhagen; in '14 was created Earl Cathcart, and died at Cartside, Glasgow, 16 Jun. 1843.

CAVENDISH, LORD F.,

   Of the Coldstream Gds., was on 18 Jun. 1755 apptd. Lt. Col. of the 29th Ft., but on 1st Jun. '56, was transfd. to Capt. and Lt. Col. 1st Ft. Gds. *Prev. Service*, Ens. 1st Ft. Gds. 20 Apl. 1749.

CHARLTON, A.,

   Appointed Lt. and Adjt. 24 Nov. 1713. Capt. 4 Mar. '23. Out of Regt. Jan. 1738.

CHARTRES, J. S.,

   Asst. Surg. 11 Jun. 1852 ; on 10 Dec. '57 was apptd. to the Staff.

CLAREMONT, G. W. F.,

   Ens. 24 Mar. 1863, Lt. 22 Aug. '65, I. of M. 9 Oct. '69, Capt. 31 Oct. '71, attached to Worc. Militia as Adjt. for the trainings of '75 and '77. Extra A.D.C. to Govr. of Bombay 8 Sep. '80—31 May, '81. Maj. 1st Bn. Worc. Regt. 2 Mar. '83. Adj. to 4th Bn. Scottish Rifles 1 Jan. '84—89, when posted to 2nd Bn. Worc. Regt. Prom. Lt. Col. h.p., and retd. on retd. pay 2 Mar. '90. Died in London 5 Apl., buried at Malvern Wells 11 Apl. '91.

CLARKE, S. M.,

   Exchgd. as Capt. on 2 Feb. 1859 fm. the 93rd Highlanders ; Maj. 16 Jan. '63. promtd. to h.p. Lt. Colcy. 20 May '68. *Prev. Service*, Ens. 93rd Ft. 23 Nov. '49., and was present with that Regt. in the Crimea and Indian Mutiny.

CLARKE, W. S.,

   Ens. 8 Jan. 1868, Lt. 27 Oct. '71. Served in the Ashanti Expdn. of '73-74 in the Transport Service, and was in charge of the port of Sutah. I. of M. 4 Sep. '76 to 11 Oct. '78, when apptd. Adj. Capt. 1st Feb. '79. In '86 served as Commandant of the Colaba Depôt. Maj. 11 Aug. '86. Adj. to 3rd Bn. Worc. Regt. fm. 7 Jun. '86—91.

CLAY, J. H.,

   P. Mr. on 31 May, 1844, fm. Lt. 59 Ft. Served with the 29th in the Satláj and Panjáb campaigns. On 20 Apl. '49 was apptd. P. Mr. to 3rd Light Dragoons. Died 1854. *First Comsn.*, Ens. 59th Ft. 5 May 1837.

CLIFTON, J.,

   Chapl. 28 Feb. 1728. Out of Regt. 1735.

COCKCROFT, W.,

   Ens. 11 July 1741, Lt. 22 Nov. '46, Adj. 19 Jan. '47. Retd. 9 Mar. 1753.

COLUMBINE, B.,

Was Capt. in Farrington's Regt. in 1703. Maj. 23 Nov. '10, Lt. Col. 28 Jan. '17, out of Regt. the follg. Dec. *Prev. Service,* Appears to have been gazetted Lt. in Col. Edwd. Leigh's Dragoons 1 Mar 1697.

COLVILL, H. G.,

Exchgd. as Lt. on 13 Oct. 1843 from 39th Ft., apptd. Adj. 22 Oct. '50, Capt 10 Dec. '52. Served with the wing of the Regt. that went from Burma to Calcutta during the Mutiny and was employed fm. 9 Nov. '58 to 28 Feb. '59 with Brigadier Turner's field force in clearing the Palámao, Ramgarh, and Bihár districts of the rebels. Was the last Capt. of the Light company, which he commanded fm. Dec. '53. Sold out 31 July '60. *Prev. Service,* Ens. 39 Ft. 10 Jan. '40, and was on 29 Dec. '43, when serving with that Regt., severely wounded in the action of Mahárájpúr.

COMBER, T.,

Was on 16 Feb. 1795 apptd. Adj. of the newly-formed 2nd Bn. 29 Ft., but died 14 May follg, whilst serving in Grenada with the 1st Bn. As Serjt. served with a detachmt. of the Regt. on board H.M.S. "Glory," in Lord Howe's victory of 1st June, 1794.

CONGREVE, C.B., G.,

Ens. 8 Apl. 1825, Lt. 12 Jan. '26, Capt. 12 Jun. '28, Brev. Maj. 23 Nov. '41, Maj. 8 Apl. '42. Commanded the Regt. at Fírúzshahar (severely wounded). Lt. Col. 11 Feb. '46. Present at battles of Chiliánwálá, Gujrát, and pursuit of the Sikhs to the Jhelam. Brev. Col. 20 Jun. '54. On 17 Feb. '55 was apptd. Q.M.G. to H.M. Forces, and in '57 officiated as Adj. Genl. of Forces in India. Present with the Force which proceeded under the commander-in-chief against the mutineers at Delhí, at the battle of Budli-ki-Serai, and the heights of Delhí on 6 Jun. ; also the subsequent siege operations until the end of July '57. Placed on h.p. 29 Sep. 1859.

CONYNGHAM,* J.,

Promtd. on 13 Feb. 1762 fm. Maj. and Brev. Lt. Col. 1st Bn. 1st Ft. to Lt. Col. of 29th. Out of Regt. 22 Apl. 1766. *Prev. Service,* Capt. 1st Bn. 1st Ft. 1 Apl. 1744.

COOPER, C. A. P.,

Ens. 19 Apl. 1864, Lt. 28 Dec. '66, I. of M. 31 Oct. '71, Capt. 26 July '76. Retd. on a gratuity 2 Feb. 1878.

---

* Sometimes spelt Cuninghame.

COWPER, M.D., G.A.,
> Apptd. Asst. Surg. from the Staff 20 Sep. 1839. Exchgd. to 90th Ft. 18th Dec. 1840.

COWPER, J.,
> Chapl. 16 Dec. 1752. Out of Regt. 31 Jan. 1762.

COX, R.,
> Chapl. 10 Mar. 1702. Out of Regt. 16 Jan. 1709.

CRATCHRODE, C.,
> Was apptd. to Farrington's Regt. as Capt. 16 Feb. 1694; h.p. 28 Feb. '98 to 10 Mar. 1702. Maj. 1 July '07, Lt. Col. 23 Nov. '10. Out of Regt. Dec. '17. *Prev. Service*, Capt. in Army 1 Nov. 1689.

CROSBIE, C.,
> Apptd. Maj. 14 July, 1737, promtd. Lt. Col. of T. Fowke's (43rd) Regt. 17 Feb. '41. *Prev. Service*, Ens. in Army 1703.

CUBITT, C. P.,
> Ens. 20 May 1868, Lt. 27 Oct. 71, I. of M. 13 Nov. '78 to 1 Dec. '81, when promtd. Capt. in 105 Ft.

CUNNINGHAME, A.,
> Ens. 6 May 1723, Lt. 8 May '30, Adj. 14 Jun. '34, Capt.-Lt. 26 July '45, Capt. 22 Nov. '46. Out of Regt. 1756.

CURBY, E.,
> Asst. Surg. 20 Mar. 1806; present at Roliça, Vimiero, passage of Douro, Talavera; was taken prisoner at Plasencia 7 Aug. '09 whilst in charge of the sick; rejoined the Regt. in Oct. '10; present at Albuera. Apptd. to the Staff Nov. 1812.

DALGETY, A.,
> Promtd. Qr. Mr. 7 Mar. 1792, Ens. 1st Bn. 29 Ft. 16 Apl., and Lt. 1st Sep. '95. Retd. 24 Apl. 1799.

DANE, M.D., R.,
> Exchgd. 18 Dec. 1840 from Asst. Surg. 90th Ft. In '42 sailed with Regt. for Bengal; did duty with, and was subsequently in medical charge of the Landúr Depôt fm. 18 Mar. '44 to 21 July '46, when promtd. Surg. in 11 Ft. On 7 July '48 was apptd. fm. the 63 Ft. to the 29th; joined Hd. Qrs. 10 Feb. '49. Was present at the battle of Gujrát, and subsequent pursuit of the Sikh army to the Jhelam. In May '55 was apptd. to the Staff. *Prev. Service*, Asst. Surg. 90 Ft. 18 Sep. 1835.

DAVIS, H.,
>Ens. 19 Dec. 1857, Lt. 12 Jun. '60, Capt. 16 Jan. '63, Maj. 23 Jan. '75, Lt. Col. 2 Mar. '78, Col. 2 Mar. '82. Having completed 5 years as a Regtl. Col., was placed on h.p. 2 Mar. 1883.

DAWES, F.,
>Asst. Surg. 9 Jun. 1803, but never having joined, was on 7 Nov. '05 superseded for absence without leave.

DE BERNIERE, H. J. DE B.,
>Was in May 1887 transferred fm. Maj. 2nd Battn. Worcestershire Regt. to the 1st Battn., and joined Hd. Qrs. at Quetta in the autumn. On 22 Oct. '89 was promtd. to command the 2nd Battn. then stationed at Limerick. *Prev. Service*, As H. J. de B. Smart was apptd. Ens. 58th Ft. 24 Nov. 1863.

DEVIE, J.,
>Chapl. 19 Dec. 1735. Out of Regt. 1747.

DICKSON, A.,
>Surgeon 21 Dec. 1748. Out of Regt. Dec. 1755.

DICKSON, H.,
>Exchgd. on 7 Dec. 1764 from Lt., late 108 Ft.; promtd. Capt.-Lieut. and Capt. 26 Dec. '75, and the following year sailed with Regt. for relief of Quebec; in Sep. served on board the "Inflexible" in actions on Lake Champlain. Capt. 1 Aug. '79, and on 1 Oct. '81 was appointed to the Grenadier coy. Brev. Maj. 18 Nov. '90. Commanded a detachmt. of Regt. doing duty as Marines on board H.M.S. "Egmont" 23 July—15 Nov. '93. Maj. 5 Feb. and junior Lt.-Col. 1 Mar. '94. Sailed with Regt. for Grenada, where he was actively employed in '95-'96; apptd. Lt. Col. 2nd Battn. 29th Ft. 25 Feb. '95. Sold out 16 July '97. *First Comsn.*, Ens. 31st Ft. 29 Sep. 1757.

DISNEY, H.,
>Ens. 1st Ft. Gds. 1 May 1694, was wounded the followg. year at the capture of Namur, Capt. and Lt. Col. 11 Mar. 1708. Apptd. to command Archibald, Earl of Isla's late Regt. (36 Ft.) 23 Oct. '10, to 10 July '15. Colonel of Lord Mark Kerr's late Regt. (29th Foot) 25 Dec. '25. Died 19 Nov. 1731.

DOUGLAS, J. C.,
>Ens. 3 July 1860, Lt. 7 Nov. '62, Capt. 25 Apl. '65, Brev. Maj. 1 Oct. '77, Maj. 29 Jan. '79, junr. Lt. Col. 2 Mar. '83. Commanded a wing of the Regt. in the Zhob Valley Expdn. of '84. Retd. fm. Service 11 Aug. 1886.

DOUGLAS, R. P.,

Ens. 16 Mar. 1820, Lt. 19 Feb. '24, Capt. of Grenadier compy. 11 Jun. '28, A.D.C. to Govr. of Mauritius 10 Dec. '32—31 Jan. '33, A.D.C. to Sir Howard Douglas, Bt., Lord High Comr. Ionian Islands 30 Apl. '35—12 Jan. '37; Asst. Mil. Sec. Ionian Islands 13 Jan. '37—16 Jun. '41. Promtd. Maj. 26 Oct. '41, junr. Lt. Col. 15 Apl. '42, sailed with the Regt. for Bengal, but soon after landing there obtained the commander-in-chief's leave to return to England, and retd. on h.p. unatt. 30 Jun. 1843.

DOWDELL, A.,

Asst. Surg. 7 Sep. 1797. Retd. 24 Dec. following.

DOWNES, U., LORD,

Born 15 Aug. 1788, was, as Ulysses Burgh, apptd. Ens. 54th Ft. 31st Mar. and Lt. 21 Nov. 1804. Capt. 9 Oct. '06; was transfd. to 92nd Ft. on 25 Nov. '08, and proceeded to Portugal as A.D.C. to Sir J. Cradock. In '09 was made A.D.C. and Asst. Mil. Sec. to Sir Arthur Wellesley; present at Talavera (slightly wounded), and at Busaco the year followg.; promtd. Maj. 31 Mar. '11; was present at Fuentes d'Onor, El Boden, the siege of Cuidad Rodrigo, of Badajos, and battle of Salamanca; promtd. Lt. Col. 92nd Ft. 5 Sept. '12, present at battles of Vittoria, the Pyrenees, Siege of San Sebastian, battle of Nivelle (horse killed), Nive, and Toulouse (slightly wounded). On 25 July '14 was apptd. Capt. and Lt. Col. Grenadier Gds.; Surveyor General of Ordnance Mar. '20, and A.D.C. to the King with rank of Col. in the army on 27th May, '25. Succeeded as 2nd Baron Downes 2nd Mar. '26. Retd. on h.p. 5 July '27. Maj. Genl. 10 Jan. '37. Col. of 54th Ft. 4 Apl. '45, Lt. Genl. 9 Nov. '46. Was on 15 Aug. '50 transferred to the Colonelcy of 29 Ft. General 20 Jun. '54. Died at Bert House, Athy, co. Kildare, 26 July 1863.

DOWSON, C. S.,

Promtd. 27 Mar. 1846 fm. 25th Ft. to a Ltcy. in the 29th. Qr. Mr. 10 Dec. '47. Served with Regt. at Chiliánwálá, Gujrát, and subsequent pursuit of Sikh army to the Jhelam. On 11 Oct. '53 was apptd. Lt. 8th Ft. *First Comsn.*, Ens. 90th Ft. 3 Jun. 1842.

DUGGAN, H.,

Surg. Mate 16 July 1765. Out of Regt. Mar. 1773.

DUNLOP, G.,

Asst. Surg. fm. h.p. 90 Ft. 22 Jun. 1820. Died at Buttevant 20 Aug. '27. *Prev. Service*, Asst. Surg. 66 Ft. 19 Oct., 1815.

EATON, C. E.,

Ens. 28 Apl. 1825, Lt. 20 May '26, Capt. 30 Dec. '31; Maj. 15 Apl., and exchgd. to the Buffs 15 Dec. 1843.

EGERTON, J. F.,

On 27 Aug. 1884 was promtd. fm. 2nd Bn. Worcestershire Regt. to a Majty. in the 1st Battn., which four years later on, he joined at Quetta. In Mar. '90 was transfd. to "second in command" of the 2nd Battn. *Prev. Service*, Ens. 36th Ft. 21 Aug. '66. Adj. 4th Bn. Worc. Regt. 10 July '83—'88.

EGERTON, T.,

Exchgd. on 20 Oct. 1796 fm. Capt. 56th Ft. In '99 was present with the Regt. in the Expdn. to Holland. Brev. Maj. 25 Apl. '08, and on 17 Aug. follg. was severely wounded at Roliça. Maj. 2 Sep. '08. Retd. from service 29 Aug. '11. *First Comsn.*, Cornet 23 Light Dragoons 29 Nov. 1794.

ELLIOT, W.,

Exchgd. on 14 Apl. 1808, fm. Lt. in the 4th Garrn. Battn., and was present with the 29th Regt. at Vimiero, passage of the Douro, battles of Talavera and Busaco, 1st siege of Badajos, and battle of Albuera. Capt. 9 Oct. '11. From '15 to '18 served as Maj. of Brigade with the Army of Occupation in France. Maj. 2 May '22; was on 13 July '32 promtd. on h.p. unatt., and apptd. D.Q.M.G. in Jamaica. *First Comsn.*, Ens. 96 Ft. 28 Nov. 1807.

ENYS, J.,

Ens. 22 Apl. 1775, sailed the follg. year with the Regt. for relief of Quebec, and in Sep. served on board the "Thunderer" in actions on Lake Champlain; Lt. 16 Feb. '78, served that year and in '80 with the 29th Rangers under Maj. Carleton. On 25 Jan. '83 was promtd. Capt. of an additional compy, which being reduced that year, Capt. Enys was placed on h.p. till 14 Apl. '84. Maj. 1 Mar. '94, and on 25 Feb. '95 was posted to the newly-raised 2nd Bn. 29th Ft. Lt. Col. 6 Sep. '96. Commanded the Regt. throughout the Expdn. to Holland in '99, and retd. fm. service 14 Mar. 1800. Died at Bath 30 July '18 in his 61st year.

ERSKINE, A. J.,

Sub-Lt. 11 Sep. 1876. Lt. 11 Sep. '77. I. of M. 15 Jan., '81. Capt. 1 Jan., and on 24 Mar. '84 was seconded for service as Dep.-Asst. Com.-Genl. on probn. with the Commissariat and Transport Staff; was finally transfd. to the A.S. Corps 1 Apl. 1889.

ERWIN, R.,
Served with Regt. through the latter part of the Satláj, and throughout the Panjáb campaigns, also with wing stationed at Calcutta and Bárrákpúr during the Mutiny; was present with Brigdr. Turner's Field Force when clearing the Palámao, Ramgarh, and Bihár districts of rebels 9 Nov. '58 to 28 Feb. '59. Apptd. Qr. Mr. on 30 Jun. '65, and was transfd. to 2nd Battn. 21st Ft. on 16 Jan. 1866.

ESPINASSE, J.,
P. Mr. of Regt. on 8 Feb. 1839 (fm. Capt. 97th Ft.); on 31st May '44 was transfd. to 1st Ft. *First Comsn.*, Ens. 4th Ft. 8 Feb., 1821.

EVANS, J. V.,
Born 12 Apl. 1792; served in 1808 as a volunteer with 40th Ft. at Roliça and Vimiero. Apptd. Ens. 29th Ft. 2nd Sep. '08, was present the followg. year at passage of Douro, and battle of Talavera (when he took a French Standard), promtd. Lt. 14 Dec. '09. Present at Busaco in '10, and the next year at 1st siege of Badajos and battle of Albuera. In '14 served in the Expdn. up the Penobscot (N. America) and was present at the affair of Hampden. Capt. 20 May '19, Maj. 22 Nov. '27; Lt. Col. 1 Jun., and died in London 1 July 1839.

EVANS, L.,
Asst. Surg. 22 Nov. 1807, was present with Regt. throughout the Peninsular campaign, and apptd. Asst. Surg. to the Forces at the Army Depôt on 19 Dec. 1811.

EVELYN, W.,
Ens. 2nd Regt. of Foot Guards 17 July 1739, Lt. 16 Apl. '44, Capt.-Lt., with rank of Lt.-Col. of Foot, 27 Aug. '54, Capt. 24 Mar. '55, 2nd Maj. 20 Aug. '62, 1st Maj. 23 Dec. '63. Was on 3 Nov. '69 apptd. Colonel of the 29th Ft. Maj.-Genl. 3 Apl. '70, Lt. Genl. 29 Aug. '77. Died 13 Aug. '83. In the churchyard of Send, Surrey, is a handsome sarcophagus with the follg. inscription: " Sacred to the memory of Lieut.-General William Evelyn, Col. of the 29th Regiment of Foot, fourth son of Sir John Evelyn, Bart., of Wotton, in this county. He sat two Sessions in Parliament for Helston, in the county of Cornwall, by the friendship of Lord Godolphin, and departed this life looking forward to, and trusting in a better, the 13th day of August, 1783. Aged 60."

FAREWELL, N.,
Transfd. 25 May 1826 from P. Mr. of 19 Ft. to that of 29th. Died at Plymouth 16 Nov. '38. *Prev. Service*, As Capt. of 1st Somersetshire Militia was on 25 Dec. '13 gazetted Capt., with temp. rank, in 40 Ft.; the followg. year was placed on British h.p. and on 6 Mar. '23 apptd. P. Mr. 19 Ft.

FARMER, W. L.,

Asst. Surg. 6 Nov. 1857. Served with Brigdr. Turner's Field Force whilst clearing the Palámao, Ramgarh, and Bihár districts of rebels from 9 Nov. '58 to 28 Feb. '59; was transfd. to 16th Lancers 9 Jun. 1865.

FARRINGTON, L.,

Exchgd. 22 Feb. 1845 fm. Lt. 39 Ft. Served with the 29th at Fírúzshahar, Sobráon, Chiliánwálá, and Gujrát; was apptd. Adj. 1 Mar., and Capt. 9 July '50; Maj. 2nd Dec. '59, Lt. Col. 25 Mar. '62, Brev. Col. 25 Mar. '67. Retd. on h.p. 31 Oct. '71. *First Comsn.*, Ens. 86th Ft. 23 Jun, 1843.

FARRINGTON, T.,

Born 1664 (son of Thos. Farrington, of St. Andrew Undershaft, merchant, who was a younger son of Wm. ffarington of Worden, and in Nov. 1663 married Miss Mary Smyth, dau. of the Speaker of the House of Commons), was on 31 Dec. '88 given a Commission * in the 2nd Regt. of Foot Guards; Capt. and to take rank as Lieut.-Colonel of Foot 1 Jun. '93. On the subsequent augmentation of the army, he was on 16 Feb. '94 apptd. Colonel of a newly-raised Regt., which was reduced in '98, when its Officers were placed on h.p. till early in 1702. On the 12 Feb. that year, Col. Farrington was placed on full pay, and on 16 Aug. '03 was promtd. Brigadier; on 1 Jun. '06 Maj. Genl., and on 1 Jan. '09 Lt. Genl. General Farrington, who was M.P. for Malmesbury from 12 May '05 to 9 Oct. '10, died at Chislehurst 6 Oct. '12, and was buried in the chancel of St. Nicholas church. By his marriage with Miss Betenson he had issue one son † and two daus. and from the followg. letter ‡ to the Duke of Marlboro' it appears that the son joined his father's Regt. :—

"My Lord,

"There is a Company vacant in my Regiment, by the death of Captain Young. I humbly begg your Grace will be pleased to give it to my son, he is now learning his exercises, and fortification to qualifie him for the Service this will be a favour ever acknowledged by him who is wth. all due respect.

Your Graces
Most dutifull
& Obedient Servant
THOS. FARRINGTON."

London 6 August 1706.

---

* Lieuts. of Guards, to take rank as Captains of Foot $\frac{9}{15}$ Jul. 1691.—*Mil. Entry Bks.*

† Thomas, was M.P. for Ludgershall, Wilts, 29 Jun. 1747—'54; dying without issue the 29th Jan. 1758, he left Chislehurst to his nephew, Lord Robt. Bertie.

‡ Blenheim Palace. Letters A.I., 1706.

FARRINGTON, T. D.,

>Ens. 9 Dec. 1695 ; h.p. 28 Feb. '98 to 10 Mar. 1702, Lt. 28 Aug. '07 ; was Capt. previous to 21 Dec. '08. Apptd. Qr. Mr. 23 Nov. '09, and placed on h.p. when the Regt. was reduced in 1713.

FARQUHAR, F. W.,

>Transfd. fm. Ens. 69 Ft. 25 Dec. 1775 ; embarked the follg. year for relief of Quebec, and that autumn served on board the "Inflexible" in the actions on Lake Champlain. In '77 served with the Flank compys. in Genl. Burgoyne's Expdn. fm. Canada. Lt. 17 Feb. '78, and that year, as well as in '80, served with Maj. Carleton's Expdns. against the American frontier. Capt. 28 July '90, Brev. Maj. 20 Jun. '94, Capt. 2nd Bn. 29th Ft. 16 Apl. '95. Served on the Staff. at Chatham fm. Jan. '95 to '97. Maj. 6 Sep. '96, and was promtd. Lt. Col. 2nd Bn. 17 Ft. on 5 Aug. '99. *First Comsn.*, Ens. 69 Ft. 9 Oct. 1775.

FITZGERALD, LORD H.,

>Exchgd. on 26 Sep. 1788 fm. Lt. Col. 5 Ft., and on 6 Oct. '89 to Capt. and Lt. Col. Coldstream Gds. *First Comsn.*, Cornet 3rd Regt. of Horse (or Carabineers), 4th Oct., 1777.

FITZGERALD, T.,

>Brev. Maj. was on 17 Nov. 1796 transfd. fm. Capt.-Lt. and Capt., h.p. 90th Ft. to the 29th. Brev. Lt. Col. 1 Jan. '98, and on 19 Apl. follg. was apptd. P. Mr. to the Regt. fm. h.p. Lt. Col. In '99 served with Regt. in Expdn. to Holland. Retd. in May 1805. *First Comsn.*, Ens. the Buffs, 5 Oct. 1777.

FLANAGAN, J. B.,

>Who was apptd. Lt. Col. fm. h.p. 81st Ft., on 31 Oct. 1871, was retd. in the same *Gazette*. *First Comsn.*, Ens. 76th Ft. 3 May 1831.

FORBES, LORD G.,

>Born in 1710, was on 6 Oct. '26 apptd. Ens. in R. Handasyd's Regt. (22nd Ft.). Capt. in H. Disney's (29th) 25 Apl. '29, Maj. 17 Feb. '41. On 11 Oct. '46 was promtd. Lt. Col. of Thos. Fowke's Regt. (2nd Ft.), Bt. Col. 31 Dec. '55 ; served as Q.M.G. to the army in Ireland, and on 22 Nov. '56 was apptd. Col. of 61st Ft., which subsequently was numbered the 76th Ft. Maj. Genl. 25 Jun. '59, and on 16 Jan. '61 was transfd. to the Colonelcy of 29 Ft., Lt. Genl. 19th inst. Succeeded to the Earldom of Granard in '65, and died in Ireland 24 Oct. '69.

FORBES, G.,
> Of the Forbes of Skellator, in Aberdeenshire, was born in 1738, apptd. Ens. 33rd Ft. 27 Aug. '56; Lt. in the 2nd Battn. (afterwards numbered 72nd and disbanded in 1763) 2nd Oct. '57. Capt. 7 Oct. '62; served with this Regt. at Havannah; exchgd. to 34th Ft. 12 Apl. '64, and served with it in Louisiana. Promtd. Maj. 9th Ft. 11 Nov. '76, and the followg. year served with Burgoyne's Expdn. fm. Canada (twice wounded). On 24 Sep. '81 was promtd. Lt. Col. of 102 Ft., a newly-raised Regt., with which he sailed for the E. Indies. On 13th Jun. '82 was given the local rank of Col. On 12 Oct. '87 was made Lt. Col. of 74th Ft., which appointmt. he appears to have vacated in Nov. '88; Bt. Col. 18 Nov. '90, and on 18 Apl. '94 was apptd. Colonel of 105 Ft., Maj. Genl. 3 Oct. followg.; Governor of Cape Nicola Mole, in St. Domingo, 25 Mar. '95; Colonel of 81st Ft. 24 Jan. '97, and on 8 Aug. followg. was transfd. to the Colonelcy of the 29th Ft., Lt. Genl. 1 Jan. 1801, General 1 Jan. '12. Died at Ham, Surrey, 17 Jan. 1828, and was buried at Petersham.

FORBES, J.,
> Chapl. 26 Aug. 1767. Died Mar. 1774.

FOSKEY, G.,
> On 29 Jan. 1824 was transfd. fm. Lt. 54 Ft., and apptd. Adj. Retd. on British h.p. 31 Dec. '33. *First Comsn.*, Ens. 7th W.I. Regt. 4th Apl. 1811.

FRENCH, J.,
> Was on 7 Dec. 1764 promtd. fm. the 59 Ft. to Capt. in 29th; Maj. 26 July '73. Sailed with the Regt. for relief of Quebec in '76 and accompanied it to Crown Point. On 14 Sep. '77 was promtd. Lt. Col. 31st Ft. Died at Parsonstown, King's Co., Sept. 1819. *First Comsn.*, Ens. 59th Ft. 4 Mar. 1760.

FROUDE, W.,
> Apptd. Lt. Col. of Farrington's Regt (29 Ft.) 1 Apl. 1694. On the reducing of the Regt. in '98 was placed on h.p. till 12 Feb. 1702; exchgd. to Capt. and Lt. Col. 1st Ft. Gds. 10 Mar. followg. *Prev. Service*, 2nd Lieut. Royal Fuziliers 21 Jun. 1685.

FULLER, F.,
> Elder son of Edward Fuller, a direct descendant of the Fullers of Uckfield, Sussex, was on 19 July 1711 apptd. Lt. and Capt. 1st Ft. Gds., Capt. and Lt. Col. 11 Jun. '15, 2nd Maj. 5 Jun. '33, 1st Maj. 5 July '35, Lt. Col. 15 Dec. '38. Colonel of G. Reade's late Regt. (29 Ft.) 28 Aug. '39. Brigdr. Genl. 18 Feb. '42, Maj. Genl. 12 July '43, and died whilst serving with the Regt. at Cape Breton 10 Jun. 1748.

FULLER, J.,
> Qr. Mr. 18 Aug. 1744. Out of Regt. Apl. 1748.

GELL, T.,
> Ens. 5 Oct. 1804, Lt. 12 Dec. '05, Capt. 17 Nov. '08, served with the Regt. throughout the Peninsular war, and subsequently received the Silver Medal with the Roleia, Vimiera, Talavera, and Busaco clasps. At Albuera brought the 29th out of action, for which he was awarded the Gold Medal. In '14 served with the Expdn. up the Penobscot, N. America, and on 3 Sep. was severely wounded at the affair of Hampden. Brev. Maj. 22 Jun. '15, Maj. 28 Dec. '20. Retd. 2 May '22, and died at Spondon, nr. Derby, 14 Nov. 1865, aged 77.

GIBSON, * * * *
> Asst. Surg. 28 Aug. 1800, but failing to join the Regt., was struck off its strength in March, 1801.

GILBERT, W.,
> Was on 22 July 1819 apptd. Lt., and Adj., fm. h.p. 66th Ft. Died in May '22
> *First Comsn.*, Ens. 66 Ft. 22 Dec. 1813.

GILLESPIE, W.,
> Qr. Mr. 13 Jun. 1805. In 1799 served with Regt. in Expdn. to Holland; throughout the Peninsular campaign 1808 to '11, and Expdn. up the Penobscot in '14. Retd. on full pay 23 May 1822.

GISBORNE, J.,
> Transfd. 22 Apl. 1755 fm. Maj. 30 Ft.; promtd. 18 Nov. follg. to Lt. Col. 10 Ft.
> *Prev. Service*, Capt. in Col. C. Frampton's Regt. (30 Ft.) 26 Feb. 1746.

GORDON, P.,
> Was on 7 Feb. 1776 apptd. fm. Lt. Col. h.p. late 108 Ft., and sailed in command of the Regt. for relief of Quebec. Soon after landing, was given command of a brigade consisting of the 21st, 29th, and 62nd Regts. On 25 July was shot at, and severely wounded, by Lt. Whitcombe, an American. Died of his wounds 1 Aug. '76, and was buried at Montreal. *Prev. Service*, in 1754 was one of the senior Lts. of 2nd Bn. 1st Ft.

GREGG, T.,
> Surg. Mate, 25 Dec. 1793, Surg. 1st Bn. 29th Ft. 31 Dec. '94. Died whilst on service in Grenada 23 July 1795.

GRANARD, G., EARL OF,
> *Vide* Forbes Lord G.

GROVES, W.,

As Ens. was placed on h.p. when the Regt. was reduced in 1713; placed on full pay 28 Aug. '16. Adj. 29 Aug. 1719.

GUTHRIE, G.,

Born 1785, was on 5 Mar. 1801 apptd. Asst. Surg.; promtd. Surg. 20 Mar. '06. In '08 was present with Regt. at Roliça and Vimiero; in '09 at passage of the Douro, and battle of Talavera. In Jan. '10 was apptd. Surg. to the Forces, on Hosp. Staff. After the campaign Mr. Guthrie returned to London, and in '23 was elected Asst. Surg. to the Westminster Hospital, Surg. in '27. President R. Coll. of Surgeons in '33, '42, and '55. Died 1st May 1856.

HALLOWES, J.,

Ens. 10 Mar. 1753, Lt. 16 Feb. '56, Adj. 19 May '59; out of Regt. 1762.

HANCOX, J.,

Was on 16 Feb. 1694, apptd. Chaplain; on 28 Feb., 1698, was placed on h.p.

HARRINGTON, C., EARL OF,

Born 1753, was, as Visct. Petersham, apptd. Ens. Coldstream Gds. 3 Nov. '69; on 26 July '73 was promtd. to Capt. 29th Ft. (Light compy.); early in '76 exchgd. to the Grenadier coy., with which he served at relief of Quebec. In '77 accompanied General Burgoyne's Expedition fm. Canada, and commanded the 29th Grenadiers in the affair of Hubberton; on 12 July was apptd. Supernumerary A.D.C. to Genl. Burgoyne, with whom he served the remainder of the campaign; on 16 Jan. '78, was apptd. Capt. and Lt. Col. 3rd Ft. Gds.; in Apl. '79 succeeded to the Earldom of Harrington. Raised, and was apptd. Lt. Col. Commandant of 85th Ft. 30th Aug. '80, and embarked with the Regt. for Jamaica; Col. 20 Nov. '82 (this Regt was lost in '83 whilst on passage home). On 12 Mar. '83 was apptd. Col. of 65 Ft., fm. which, on 29 Jan. '88, he was transfd. to the 29th Regt. On 5 Dec. '92 was transfd. to the Colcy. of 1st Life Guards, Maj. Gen. 12 Oct. '93, Lt. Genl. 1 Jan. '98, Genl. 1803. Was in '06 apptd. commander-in-chief of the Forces in Ireland; and at the Coronation of King Geo. IV. was bearer of the Great Standard; was subsequently apptd. Capt. Govr. and Constable of Windsor Castle. Died 5 Sep. 1829.

HAWKEY, M.D., J.,

Was transfd. 27 Apl. 1826 fm. Asst. Surg. 4 Ft.; promtd. on the Staff 20 Sep. 1839. *Prev. Service*, Asst. Surg. 4th Ft. 16 Jun. 1825.

HEMPHILL, A. T.,
   Ens. 7 Apl. 1825, Lt. 16 Apl. '29, Adj. 1 May '34, Capt. 3 July '39 (Light compy.), Maj. 11 Feb., and junr. Lt. Col. 8 Dec. '46. Mil. Sec. to Govr.-Genl. of India 12 Jan. '48, and exchgd. to 26 Ft. 8 Mar. follg. Genl. Hemphill died in Dublin 3 Mar. 1863.

HICKIN, T. B.,
   Exchgd. 28 Jan. 1819 fm. Capt. h.p. 66th Ft.; Brev. Maj. 10 Jan. '37, Maj. 31 May '39, junr. Lt. Col. the 8th, and retd. 15 Apl. '42. *Prev. Service*, Ens. 38 Ft. 4 May 1805, Lt. 2nd W. I. Regt. 31 Oct. '05, Lt. 66 Ft. 28 Jan. '08, served with the latter Regt. in the Peninsular campaign, including capture of Oporto, and battles of Talavera, Busaco, Albuera (wounded), Vittoria, Roncesvalles, Pyrenees, Pampeluna (severely wounded), Nivelle, Nive, Bayonne, Aire, Heights of Garris, Orthes, and Toulouse.

HILTON, M. V.,
   2nd Lt. 30 Jan., and Lt. 31 Aug. 1878. Adj. 24 Apl. '79. In '84 served with the wing of Regt. in Zhob Valley Expdn.; Capt. 20 Nov. '85, transfd. to 2nd Bn. Worcestershire Regt. Jun. 1886.

HODGE, A.,
   Surg. Mate, 2nd Bn. 29 Ft. 2 Apl. 1795. On 25 Feb. '96 was transfd. to the 5 compys. serving in Grenada. Retd. 24 May, 1797.

HODGE, P.,
   Ens. 3 Mar., and Lt. 31 May 1798; the followg. year served with the Regt. in Expdn. to Holland. Capt. 2 May 1800; was present at Roliça (wounded), Busaco, 1st siege of Badajos, and Albuera (slightly wounded). Brev. Maj. 20 Jun. '11. In '14 served with the Regt. in Expdn. up the Penobscot, N. America (mentioned in dispatches.) Brev. Lt. Col. 21 Jun. '17, Lt. Col. 28 Dec. '20, exchgd. to Capt. and Lt. Col. Grenadier Gds. 14th, and retd. fm. service, 28 Feb. 1822.

HOLLINGSWORTH, M.,
   Surg.; left the Regt. in 1714.

HOPSON, P. T.,
   Ens. 3rd Ft. Gds. 25 Apl. 1712, Capt. in J. Clayton's Regt. (14th Ft.) 3 Apl. '18; was on 1st Apl. '43 transfd. fm. Lt. Col. of Lord H. Beauclerk's Regt. (48 Ft.), to that of F. Fuller's (29th.) In Mar. '48 was made Govr. of Cape Breton, and the 6 Jun. followg. succeeded to the Colonelcy of the Regiment. Apptd. Govr. and Commander of the Forces in Nova Scotia, 4 Mar. '52, and on 4 Mar. '54 was transfd. to the 40th Ft. Maj. Gen. 15 Feb. '57. On 10 Nov. '58 sailed in command of an Expdn. against Martinico and Guadaloupe. Died at the latter island 27 Feb. 1759.

HOWARD, J.,
> Was on 16 Feb. 1694, apptd. to Farrington's Regt. (29 Ft.) as Capt.-Lt., also Qr. Mr.; Capt. 12 Sep. followg.; placed on h.p. 28 Feb. '98. On 10 Mar. 1702 was apptd. Lt. in 1st Ft. Gds., which he appears to have originally joined as Ens. 22 July, 1693.

HOYER, G.,
> Surg. 4 Dec. 1767. Resigned 21 Dec. 1769.

HUMPHREY, C.,
> Apptd. P. Mr. 25 Apl. 1811. Retired on h.p. 5 Jun. '17. Died 1830.

HURST, S.,
> Qr. Mr. of H. Disney's Regt. (29 Ft.) 25 Dec. 1726.

INGHAM, M.D., C. T.,
> Was promtd. 25 Jun. 1826 fm. 3 D. Gds. to Surg. 29 Ft. On 21 Aug. '40 was apptd. to 9th Light Dragoons, but on 23 July '41 exchgd. back to the 29th. Apptd. Surg. 54 Ft. 14 Jun. '42. *Prev. Service*, Asst. Surg. 8th Ft. 16 Aug. '10; Served in American war of '13, and was present at the affairs of Fort George, Chippewa, and Falls of Niagara.

IRVING, S.,
> Surg. 2nd Bn. 29 Ft. 6 May 1795; exchgd. to h.p. 107 Ft. 20 July followg.

JAMESON, H. T.,
> P. Mr. 28 Dec. 1855 fm. Lt. 3rd W.I. Regt. Died at Rangoon 13 Jun. '56. *First Comsn.*, Ens. 15th Ft. 26 Dec. 1851.

JOHN, W.,
> Asst. Surg. 14 May 1858, and the following Novr. was employed with Brigdr. Turner's Field Force in clearing the Behter district of rebels. Was apptd. to Staff 24 May 1861.

JOHNSTONE, G.,
> Joined as a volunteer and was gazetted Ens. 1 Nov. 1780, Lt. 24 Sep. '87. Capt.-Lt. and Capt., 24 Aug. '92. Adj. 9 Jan. '93, Capt. 5 Feb. '94. Served with Regt. in Grenada '95-'96. Maj. 9 Aug. '99, and was promtd. Lt. Col. of the New Brunswick Fencibles 9 July 1803.

JONES, G. H. M.,
> Ens. 13 July 1839, Lt. 16 Nov. '41. Served with the Regt. at Fírúzshahar; apptd. on 22 Dec. '45 Brig. Maj. 3rd Inf. Brigade army of Satláj. Died 22 Feb. '46, of wounds recd. at Sobráon. On 20 Mar. followg. his name appeared in the *Gazette* as being apptd. Adj. to the Regt.

KENNEDY, J.,

Apptd. to Lord Mark Kerr's Regt. (29th Ft.) as Capt., on 29 Jun. 1715. Maj. 15 Apl. '20; promtd. to Lt. Col. Earl of Rothes' Regt. (25 Ft.) 30 Jun. 1737.

KENNEDY, W.,

Was on 28 Jan. 1717 apptd. Maj. of Lord Mark Kerr's Regt. (29th Ft.) and on 9th Dec. followg. promtd. Lt. Col. Died 1 Apl. '43. *Prev. Service*, With Ld. M. Kerr's *late* Regt. which was reduced in 1712. Capt.-Lt. 28 Jan. '09. Capt. 10 Jan. '10, placed on h.p. 23 Feb. '13 to 22 July '15, when apptd. to Brigadier Grant's Regt.

KERR, LORD M.,

4th son of Robert, 4th Earl and 1st Marquis of Lothian, was on 1 Jan. 1694 apptd. Capt. of a company of infantry, and served under William III. in Flanders; on 15 Apl. '97 was apptd. Capt. in Lord Jedburgh's Dragoons. On the breaking out of the war in Queen Anne's reign obtained the Lt. Colcy. of Macartney's, a newly-raised regiment (subsequently disbanded), with which he embarked from Scotland in the spring of 1704, and served the campaign of that year on the Dutch frontier. On 1 Jan. '06 was given the command of a newly-raised Regt. of Foot, which sailed with the Expdn. under Lord Rivers to Portugal, and thence to Spain; was wounded at the battle of Almanza 25 Apl. '07; promtd. Brigdr. Genl. 12 Feb. '11. It having been decided to reduce a certain number of Regts., his lordship's was disbanded early in '12, and on the 7th Oct. he was apptd. to the Colonelcy of the late Thos. Farrington's Regt. (29th Ft.) In '16, at the time of a threatened Jacobite rising in Ireland, was appointed Govr. of Carrickfergus, Belfast, and of all H.M's Forces in the counties of Down and Antrim. In '19 commanded a Brigade of Infantry in the Expdn. to Spain under Lord Shannon; was present at the capture of Vigo, Rodendella, and Port-a-Vedra. On 25 Dec. '25 was transfd. to the Colcy. of the late Stanhope Cotton's Regt. (13 Ft.) Maj. Genl. 10 Mar. '27, and on 19 May '32 was removed to the Colcy. of Philip Honeywood's Dragoons (11th Hussars); Lt. Genl. 1 Nov. '35, Govr. of Guernsey '40, Genl. '43, Govr. Edinburgh Castle '45; placed on the Staff in Ireland '51. Died in London 2 Feb. 1752, and was buried in Kensington church.

KILLERY, ST. J.,

Asst. Surg. 25 Mar. 1859, but was transfd. to the Staff 1 Dec. followg.

KINNER, F. W.,

Ens. 8 May 1730, Lt. 23 Jan. '41, Qr. Mr. 23 Apl. '48. Retd. Jun. 1751. This officer's name was sometimes spelt Kinnier, also Skinner.

KIRKMAN, J.,

Ens. 14 Mar. 1775. Adj. 31 Jan., and Lt. 28 Mar. '76. Embarked that year with the Regt. for relief of Quebec; in '80 accompanied Major Carleton's Expdn. against Forts Anne and George; Capt.-Lt. and Capt., 24 Sep. '87; Capt. 24 Aug. '92; on 13 Feb. '93 embarked with his compy. to do duty as Marines on board H.M.S. "Duke" during the Expdn. to Martinico, and on his return to England in the autumn, was apptd. Maj. of Brigde. to Lord Cathcart, in which capacity he served on the Continent till '96; Brev. Maj. 6 May '95, Maj. 10 Feb. '96. In '99 served with the Regt. in Expdn. to Holland, and on 3 Dec. was promtd. Lt. Col. 2nd Bn. 52nd Ft.

KITCHENER, H. H.,

On 26 Jan. 1841 exchgd. from Capt. 13 Light Dragoons. Maj. 27 March '46 and exchgd. 27 Sep. followg. to 9 Ft. *First Comsn.*, Cornet 13 Lt. Dns. 29 Jun. 1830.

KNEEBONE, T.,

Joined the Regt. 4 May 1812 as a volunteer fm. Royal Cornwall Militia. Apptd. Qr. Mr. 15 July '24. Was present at battle of Sobráon. Died at Calcutta 11 Sep. 1847.

LAKE, HONBLE. G. A. F.,

Promtd. 12 Nov. 1803 fm. 40 Ft. to junr. Lt. Col. 29th; retired on h.p. of the Regt. the followg. year, and on 20 Dec. was apptd. D.Q.M.G. to the King's troops in the East Indies; returned to England in '07, and on 5 Nov. exchgd. back to full pay. Was killed at Roliça 17 Aug. '08. *Prev. Service*, In 1798, whilst serving as A.D.C. to his father (afterwards Lord Lake) was present at the affairs of Castlebar, Vinegar Hill, and Ballynamuck. In 1801 was apptd. A.A.G. to the King's Forces and Mil. Sec. to the Commander-in-Chief in India. His conduct during the Marátha War was particularly distinguished; on 1 Nov. '03 was severely wounded at Laswárí. *First Comsn.*, Cornet 8th Light Dragoons 20 Aug. 1796.

LAWDER, J.,

Was on 12 Nov. 1812 apptd. Asst. Surg.; exchgd. to h.p. 66th Ft. 22 Jun. 1820. *Prev. Service*, Surg. Mate, Meath Militia 23 Mar. 1812.

LEDGARD, N. P.,

Ens. 1 May, and Lt. 27 July 1855; Capt. 29 Apl. '59; Maj. 20 May '68. Retd. 23 Jan. '75, and died in Kensington 13 Apl. 1889.

LEITH, C.B., R. W. D.,

Ens. 1st Bo. Eur. Fusrs. 4 Sep. 1837; served at Karack on the Persian Gulf fm. '38 to '41, Lt. 10 Jan. '39, Capt. 10 Jun. '45. In '49 was present at siege, and led the storming party at the capture of Multán; was dangerously wounded, losing his left arm, which was twice severed by sabre cuts from two of the enemy, both of whom he cut down; ball in the right shoulder, unextracted, besides other sabre cuts on the right arm. Brev. Maj. 7 Jun. '49. Brev. Lt. Col. 28 Nov. '54. A.A.G. Bombay 9 Nov. '55 to Dec. '59. Col. 106 Ft. 1 Jan. '62; placed on h.p. 29 May, '66. Maj. Gen. 6 Mar. '68, Lt. Genl. 1 Oct. '77. Genl. 1 July '81. Col. 1st Battn. Worcestershire Regt. 14 Sep. 1884.

LENNON, H.,

Exchgd. 20 July 1795 fm. Surg. h.p. 107th Ft. to that of 2nd Bn. 29th. Was dismissed the service by sentence of Court Martial, Mar. 1806. *Prev. Service*, Surg. 107 Ft. 9 May 1794.

LESLIE, M.,

Surg. Mate, 19 Aug. 1749. Out of Regt. 1757.

LEWIS, F.,

2nd Lt. of Grenadier compy. in Farrington's Regt. (29 Ft.) 16 Feb. 1694; placed on h.p. 28 Feb. '98 to 10 Mar. 1702, when apptd. Adj. of the Regt.

LEWIS, J.,

Apptd. Qr. Mr. of Farrington's Regt. (29th Ft.) in 1702.

LINDSAY, W.,

Apptd. Lt., and Adj., on 12 March 1754, fm. Lt., Horse Grenadier Gds.; on 25 Dec. '55 was promtd. to Capt. 11 Dragoons. *Prev. Service*, Adj. of 2nd Troop H. Gr. Gds. 20 May 1751.

LONGDEN, J. E.,

Apptd. P. Mr. 26 Dec. 1856, from late P. Mr. of Turkish Contingent. Was present with the Hd. Qrs. of the Regt., when employed under Brigdr. Turner fm. 9 Nov. '58 to 28 Feb. '59 in clearing the Palámao, Ramgarh, and Bihár districts of rebels. Exchgd. on 19 Aug. '62 to 77th Ft. *Prev. Service*, 1 year 246 days with the Turkish Contgt.

LONGFIELD, C.B., J.,

Son of John Longfield of Longueville, nr. Mallow, was apptd. Ens. 8th (King's), 28 Jun. 1825, Lt. 26 Sep. '28, Capt. 30 Jan. '35, Maj. 19 Nov. '44, Lt. Col. 3 Apl. '46; Brev. Col. 20 Jun. '54; Brig. Genl. Bengal, May—Nov. '55, Apl. to Dec. '56, and Jun. '57 to Apl. '59; commanded the 2nd Brigade at

LONGFIELD, C.B., J.,—*Continued*.

siege of Delhí in '57, the Reserve during the assault, and served in the city during the six days' fighting that ensued. Maj. Genl. 3 Aug. '60, Col. 29 Ft. 19 Apl. '68, Lt. Genl. 5 Sep. '69, Gen. 19 July '76. Was on 19 Dec. '81 transfd. to Colcy. of his old Regt. the 8th (King's), and died at Kilcoleman, nr. Bandon. 27 Feb. 1889.

LUCAS, J. O.,

Ens. 15 Jun. 1830, Lt. 27 Jun. '34, Adj. 3 July '39, Capt. 19 Mar. '41. Commanded the Grenadier comy. fm. '43, to 13 Dec. '45, when apptd. Brig. Maj. to 3rd Inf. Brigde. army of Satláj; was killed at Fírúzshahar 21st Inst.

LUCAS, R.,

Ens. 5 Apl. 1810; present at Busaco the followg. Sep. Lt. 24 Oct. '11, Capt. 22 Apl. '26. Commanded the Light compy fm. '33, to 3 July '39, when promtd. Maj. Retd. 6 Sep. followg.

LUGARD, K.C.B., SIR E.,

Exchgd. 18 Sep. 1846 fm. Capt. and Brev. Maj. 31st Ft.; Brev. Lt. Col. 7 Jun. '49; A.D.C. to the Queen and Brev. Col. 20 Jun. '54. Maj. 13 Jun. '55. Became non-effective by promotion 22 Oct. '58. Sir Edward never joined the Regt., for he held Staff appointments continuously fm. 10 Feb. '46—1 Nov. '71. *Prev. Service*, Ens. 31st Ft. 31 July '28, served throughout the Afghán campaign of '42, the Satláj and Panjáb campaigns, and Persian Expdn. of '57. Commanded a Division at capture of Lakhnao, and subsequently the Azamgarh Field Force.

LYLE, J. M.,

Ens. 19 May 1843, Lt. 2 Sep. '45, served with Regt. at Fírúzshahar and Sobráon, Capt. 6 Aug. '53. I. of M., 2nd Depôt Battn. 1 Mar. '58, Maj. 12 Jun. '60. Retd. 20 Feb. '63.

MCGREGOR, R.,

Asst. Surg. fm. the Staff 8 Nov. 1850, and on 2 Oct. '57 was promtd. on the Staff.

MACBETH, A. M.,

Asst. Surg. 21st July 1846. Served with the Regt. at Chiliánwálá, and on 8 Nov. '50 was apptd. to the Staff.

MacDonnell, C. E.,
Ens. 21 Apl. 1842, Lt. 23 Jan. '43. Served with Regt. at Firúzshahar, and at Sobráon was wounded by a musket ball in the jaw, and lost left eye. Adj. 20 Mar. '46. On 1st Jan. '49 was apptd. Brig. Maj. to 4th Inf. Brigade army of the Panjáb; was present at Chiliánwálá (mentioned in dispatches), Gujrát, and subsequently served with the force sent in pursuit of the enemy, till the final occupation of Paswhár, part of the time as D.A.A.G. of Division. Capt. the 1st, and Brev. Maj. 2nd Mar. '50. Died at Chatham 6 Aug. 1853.

Mackenzie, G.,
Was Surg. Mate, in 1727.

Mackinnon, W. A.,
Apptd. on 18 Dec. 1857 Asst. Surg. fm. the Staff. Never joined the Hd. Qrs. of the Regt., for soon after landing in India was apptd. to the Staff of H.E. the Commander-in-Chief, and on 11 Apl. '59 was transfd. to 42nd Highlanders. *Prev. Service*, Asst. Surg. 42nd Hdrs. 24 Mar. '54, present at battles of the Alma, Balaklava, Expdn. to Kertch, siege and fall of Sevastopol.

Macqueen, M.D., D.,
Asst. Surg. 15 Nov. 1850, promtd. on Staff 26 Jan. 1858.

Maitland, F.,
Who on 3 Dec. 1800 had been apptd. Brigadier in the Leeward Islands, was on 4 Aug. '04 transfd. fm. Lt. Col., and Brev. Col. 27th Ft., to the 29th. In Mar. '05 was apptd. Govr. of Grenada, and on 30 Oct. followg. promtd. Maj. Gen. Was given the Colcy. of 1st Ceylon Regt. on 24 Feb. '10. *Prev. Service*, In '81 served at relief of Gibraltar; attack on Tobago, and siege of Nieuport in '93; attack on Martinico, St. Lucia, and Guadaloupe in '94, and commanded a brigade at attack on Surinam in Apl. 1804. *First Comsn.*, Ens. 14 Ft. 1 Sep. 1779.

Mallory, J.,
Ens. 23 Jun. 1774, Lt. 27 Dec. '75, Capt.-Lt. and Capt. 7 Oct. '82. In '90 did duty with his compy. on board H.M.S. "Courageux." Capt. 24 Sep. '87, Maj. 1 Mar. '94; the followg. year proceeded with the Regt. to Grenada, where he died 22 Apl. '95 from effects of wounds recd. on service.

Marson, R.,
Surg. Mate, 12 May 1789, retd. 16 Nov. '90, re-apptd. 1 Jun. '91. Retd. 11 July 1792.

Martin, W. H.,
Qr. Mr. 26 Jan. 1866, fm. Staff Serjt.-Maj. at Chatham. Died 3 Apl. 1874.

MEADE, R. W.,
>Fm. Staff Surg. 14 Sep. 1867. Retd. on h.p. 7 Mar. '77. *Prev. Service*, Asst. Surg. 88 Ft., 1 Sep. '54, with which Regt. he served in the Crimea from 1 Dec. follg., also in the Indian Mutiny, including the affair of Bhognapúr, siege of Lakhnao (Mar. '58), and Kálpi.

MILLER, G.,
>Surg. Mate, 9 Mar., and retd. 24 Nov. 1793.

MILLER, J.,
>Ens. Farrington's Regt. (29 Ft.) 18 Oct. 1694, placed on h.p. 28 Feb. '98 to 10 Mar. 1702, when apptd. Qr. Mr.; re-apptd. Qr. Mr. 12 Sep. '07, promtd. Capt.-Lt. 21 July, and Capt. 23 Nov. '09 (Grenadier compy.) Out of Regt. Oct. 1717.

MILLS, J.,
>Was Surg. Mate, in 1755. Out of Regt. 1758.

MILTON, W.,
>Exchgd. 14 Oct. 1824 from Surg. h.p. of the Cape Regt. Retired on h.p. 25 Jun. '26. *Prev. Service*, Asst. Surg. 21st Light Dragoons 15 May, 1806.

MITCHELL, J.,
>Qr. Mr. 23 May 1822 from Serjt.-Maj. late of the Regt. Died at Tralee 23 Jun. 1824.

MONSELL, W.,
>Promtd. fm. the 26th, to Lt. 29 Ft. 13 Feb. 1762; Capt. 13 Sep. '69, Brev. Maj. 17 Nov. '80. In '90 did duty with his compy. on board H.M.S. "Gibraltar." Brev. Lt. Col. 18 Nov. '90, Maj. 24 Aug. 92, retd. 12 Nov. '93. *First Comsn.*, Ens. 26 Ft. 3rd Mar. 1760.

MONTAGU, LORD F.,
>Was promtd. 19 July 1797 fm. 98 Ft. to Lt. Col. of 29th. In '99 served with Regt. in Expdn. to Holland. Retd. 11 Nov. 1803. *First Comsn.*, Ens. 1st Foot Gds. 15 Jun. 1791.

MONTGOMERY, H.,
>Lt. 8 Nov. 1708, Adj. 16 Dec. '10, Capt. 21 Nov. '13, out of Regt. Nov. '17. *First Comsn.*, Ens. in C. Churchill's Regt. (3rd Ft.) 7 July 1702.

MOORHEAD, M.D., E.,
>Promtd. fm. 32 Ft., to Surg. 29th on 25 May, 1855. Served with Brigdr. Turner's Field Force whilst clearing the Palámao, Ramgarh, and Bihár districts of rebels, 9 Nov. '58—28 Feb. '59. On 13 Sep. '67 was apptd. to the Staff. *Prev. Service*, Asst. Surg. 32nd Ft. 2 Aug. '42, with which he served during the 1st and 2nd siege operations before and capture of Multán.

MORGAN, M.,
On 27 Apl. 1826 was promtd. to Adj. with rank of Ens.; Lt. 11 Jun. '30. Retd. 9 Oct. 1835.

MOSS, A.,
Promtd. from Lt. 2nd Battn. Worcestershire Regt. to Capt. 1st Bn. on 1 Jan. 1884. S.S.O. Haidarábád '85, Major 2 Mar. '91. *First Comsn.*, Sub.-Lt. 36th Ft. 19 Apl. 1876.

MOUNTAIN, C.B., A. S. H.,
Brev. Col., Exchd. on 8 Feb. 1850 fm. the 26th Ft. to junior Lt. Col. of 29th. Commanded the 4th Brigade during the Panjáb campaign, including the battles of Chiliánwálá and Gujrát. Served as Brigdr. Genl. in Bengal Inf. Division of Sir W. Gilbert's Force at the passage of the Jhelam. Retd. on h.p. 1 Nov. '49. *Prev. Service*, As D.A.G. was present throughout the war in China of '41-'42; and at the capture of Chapoo 18 May, '42, received 3 severe wounds. Ens. 97 Ft. 20 July, 1815.

MURCHISON, K.,
Joined the 29th Depôt comps. 1 Mar. 1831 fm. 1st Bn. 3rd Ft. Gds. and on 1 Feb. '39 was promtd. Ens.; was apptd. Adj. 20 Mar. '40, Lt. 20 May, '41. Served throughout the Satláj campaign, including the battles of Fírúzshahar (promtd. Capt. 22 Dec. '45) and Sobráon (wounded.) Commanded the Grenadier compy. from '47 to '49, and served with it at battles of Chiliánwálá, Gujrát, and subsequent pursuit of enemy to the Jhelam. Retd. on full pay 10 Dec. '52, and died at St. Heliers, Jersey, 24 Dec. 1883.

NAYLOR, C. S.,
Was on 20 Apl. 1849 transfd. from P. Mr. of 40 Ft. to 29th, and on 13 Aug. '55 was apptd. to the Staff for Army Service. *Prev. Service*, in '18 in S. Marátha country, and the follg. year in the Serwent Waree State; was severely wounded in both legs at the assault of Roree 13 Feb. '19. Served in the Burmese war of '25-'26, and capture of Karáchí in 1839. Ens. 87th Ft. 3 Jun. 1815.

NOSWORTHY, R.,
Ens. 26 Jan. 1789; Qr. Mr. 2nd Bn. 29th Ft. 3 Jun. '95; but on 16 Feb. '97 was removed to 50 Ft.

OFFRAL, J.,
Surg. 28 Feb. 1776; embarked that year with Regt. for relief of Quebec, and in '78 served with Maj. Carleton's Expdn. against the American frontier; was apptd. Apothecary to the Forces on the Continent 24 Apl. 1793.

O'Neil, T.,

Apptd. fm. Serjt. Maj. to Adj. 20 Oct. 1796; Ens. 9 Feb. '97; served with the Regt. throughout the Expdn. to Holland in '99; Lt. 20 Feb. 1800. Retd. 6 Aug. 1801.

Parker, W.,

Asst. Surg. 19 Mar. 1812. Retd. on h.p. of 4th Ft. Dec. 1815.

Pawlett, C.,

Apptd. Maj. in Lord Mark Kerr's Regt. (29 Ft.) 12 Dec. 1717. Out of Regt. Apl. 1720.

Phillips, C.,

Ens. 28 Apl. 1741; Adj. 24 Feb. '44; died 1746.

Power, J.,

Ens. 5 May 1837; Lt. 12 July '39; Capt. 29 Dec. '43; served with Regt. at Firúzshahar, Chiliánwálá, Gujrát, and subsequent pursuit of the enemy to the Jhelam; commanded the Grenadier compy. fm. '51, to 20 Jun. '54, when promoted Maj. Died 13 Jun. 1855.

Pugh, C.,

Surg. Mate, 12 July 1792; retd. 24 Dec. followg.

Rainsford, J. R.,

Was in Oct. 1884 transfd. fm. Capt. 2nd Bn. Worcestershire Regt. to the 1st Battn., which he joined at Nasírábád; Maj. 26 Mar. '90. *Prev. Service*, Sub. Lt. 36 Ft. 10 Sep. 1875; I. of M. 13 Sep. '80; Capt. 2nd Bn. Worcestershire Regt. 29 May 1883.

Randolph, B. H.,

Lt. 10 Mar. 1883; served the followg. year with the Zhob Valley Expdn., and on 9th Oct. '89 was promtd. Capt. in the 2nd Bn. Worc. Regt. On 26 Nov. '90 sailed to rejoin his former Battn., of which he was apptd. Adj. on 28 Dec. followg.

Ramsay, R.,

Maj. 1st Bn. 29th Ft. 2 May 1795, fm. Capt. and Brev. Maj. 61st Ft.; Brev. Lt. Col. 21 Aug.; died in Grenada the followg. Nov. *First Comsn.*, Ens. 61st Ft 27 Jun. 1758.

READ, G.,
> Capt. in the army 16 Aug. 1703; Capt.-Lt. 1st Ft. Gds. 13 Mar. '08; 2nd Maj. with rank of Lt. Col. of Foot 24 Nov. '29. On 3 Jun. '33 was apptd. Colonel of Lord Albemarle's late Regt. (29th Ft.); Brig. Genl. 2 July '39; and on 28 Aug. followg. was transfd. to the Colcy. of W. Hargrave's late Regt. (9th Ft.); Maj. Genl. 1 Jan. '43; Lt. Genl. 3 Aug. '47. On 1 Nov. '49 was removed to the Colcy. of 9th Dragoons; and died 28 Mar. 1756.

REED, J. D.,
> Surg. Mate, fm. 25 Jun. 1776 to 9 May 1788.

RICHARDSON, H.,
> Brev. Lt.-Col., was on 23 Jun. 1756 promtd. fm. Maj. 13 Dragoons to Lt. Col. 29th Ft.; Bt. Col. 19 Feb. '62; out of Regt. Feb. '62. *Prev. Service*, Maj. 13th Dragoons 4 Feb. 1749.

ROBERTS, J.,
> Joined Fuller's Regt. (29 Ft.) in 1742; apptd. Adj. 13 Feb. '62. Retd. Jan. 1776.

ROBERTSON, J.,
> Surg. 10 Dec. 1755; died Dec. 1767.

ROBERTSON, P.,
> Asst. Surg. 1 Nov. 1827 fm. Asst. Surg. 70 Ft.; was apptd. to the Staff 22 Jun. 1838. *Prev. Service*, Asst. Surg. 70th Ft. 12 Jan. 1826.

ROGERS, J.,
> Chapl. 1 Feb. 1762; retd. 1765.

ROSE, J. L.,
> Transfd. 9 Oct. 1889 as Major fm. 2nd Battn. Worcestershire Regt. to 1st Battn.; promtd. Lt. Col. on h.p. 18th, and died in London 22 Feb. 1891. *First Comsn.*, Ens. 36 Ft. 2 Jun. 1865.

RUXTON, F. C.,
> Ens. 3 Jun. 1859; Lt. 3 Dec. '61; Capt. 20 Feb. '63; Brev. Maj. 6 July '77; Maj. 2 Mar. '78; junr. Lt. Col. 1 July '81; to command the Battn. 2 Mar. '83; Col. 1 July '85; placed on h.p. 2 Mar. '87, on completion of four years service in command of a Battn. Apptd. to command 29th Regtl. Dist. 19 Dec. 1887.

SAUNDERS, A.,
> Apptd. Qr. Mr. 22 Sep. 1775; Ens. 27 Feb. '76; embarked that year with the Regt. for relief of Quebec, and was taken prisoner the followg. Sep.; Lt. 10 Mar. '81; Capt. 25 Aug. '90. Was killed on board H.M.S. "Brunswick" 1 Jun. 1794.

SCOTT, C. F.,
: Promtd. 5 Jan. 1749 fm. Maj. of J. Guise's Regt. (6 Ft.) to Lt. Col. of Hopson's (29th Ft.) Died 18 Jun. '55. *First Comsn.*, Cornet R.N.B. Dragoons 20 Jun. 1727. When in Guise's Regt. distinguished himself in the rebellion in Scotland by his gallant defence in Mar. '46 of Fort William.

SCOTT, H.,
: From Lt. and Capt. 3 Foot Gds. to Capt. Disney's Regt. (29th Ft.) 16 Sep. 1731; Maj. 22 Nov. '46. Died '48. *First Comsn.*, Ens. 3rd Foot Guards 24 Dec. 1720.

SCOTT, R.,
: Promtd. fm. Surg. Mate to Surg. 22 Dec. 1769. On 28 Feb. 1776 was removed to 3rd (or Prince of Wales) Dragoon Gds.

SCOTT, W. F.,
: As P. Mr. exchd. fm. 77th Ft. on 19 Aug. 1862. Hon. Maj. 13 Jan. '64, and exchgd. 17 Apl. '66, to 69th Ft. *Prev. Service*, Ens. 1st Ft. 15 July '43, in January '54 was apptd. P. Mr. 77 Ft., with which he served the Crimean campaign.

SHARROCK, A.,
: Exchgd. as Capt. fm. 35 Ft. on 29 Nov. 1827. Maj. 27 Sep. '39. Retd. on full pay with rank of Lt. Col. 26 Oct. '41. *First Comsn.*, Ens. 35 Ft. 12 Aug., 1806.

SILK, A.,
: Apptd. Surgeon to Farrington's Regt. (29th) 28 Feb. 1694, placed on h.p. 28 Feb. '98 to 2nd May, 1702, when re-appointed.

SIMPSON, C. E. P.,
: Ens. 19 Mar. 1861, Lt. 20 Feb. '63, I. of M. 14 Jan. '65, Capt. 21 Aug. '66, Brev. Maj. 17 Nov. '79, Maj. 1 July '81. Ret. on retired pay with rank of Lt. Col. 19 Mar. 1886.

🞠 SIMPSON, G.C.B., SIR J.,
: Son of David Simpson, Esqre. of Teviot Bank, was born in 1792, and after having served two years in the Company's service at Madras, was apptd. Ens. 1st Foot Gds. 3 Apl. 1811; served in the Peninsula fm. May '12 to '13 including the latter part of siege of Cadiz and the defence of Seville. Lt. and Capt. 25 Dec. '13; served the campaign of '15 and was severely wounded at Quatre Bras. Adj. 1st Bn. Grendr. Gds. 8 Feb. '21, and on 25 Apl. '25 was promtd. to an unatt. Lt. Colcy., fm. which on 10 Jun. '28 he exchd. to the 29 Ft.; Brev. Col. 28 Jun. '38, exchgd. to h.p. unatt. 31 May '39. On 8 Apl '42,

exchd. back to full pay, and proceeded to Bengal in command of the Regt. Commanded the Banáras Division fm. 15 Jan.—May '43; was fm. July '43 employed on the Staff in Sind, and was subsequently apptd. second in command to Sir Charles Napier during the campaign against the mountain and desert tribes on the right bank of the Indus. On 8 Dec. '46 exchgd. to h.p. unatt., and was soon afterwards apptd. Commandant of Chatham. Maj. Genl. 11 Nov. '51, Lt. Genl. 29 Jun., and Genl. 8 Sep. '55. Served in the Crimean campaign, first as Chief of the Staff and afterwards as Commander-in-Chief. On 27 July '63 was apptd. Colonel of the 29th Ft., and died at Horringer, nr. Bury St. Edmunds, 18 Apl., 1868.

SIMPSON, P.,

Surg. Mate, 17 Nov. 1790. Retd. 31 May 1791.

SKINNER,

See Kinner, F. W.

SKINNER, J. W.,

Apptd. fm. Hosp. Mate at Grenada, to Surg. of 29th Ft. 24 May 1793. Died at Plymouth 31 Dec. 1794. *For Prev. Service see page 138.*

SMITH, G. W. F. D.,

Ens. 13 May 1853, Lt. 13 June '54, I. of M. 2 Mar.'63, Capt. 4 Nov.'64. Exchgd. to 5th Fusiliers 17 Jan. 1865.

SMITH, J.,

On 25 Dec. 1815 was apptd. Asst. Surg. from 4th Ft. Retd. on British h.p. 25 Dec. '18. *Prev. Service*, Asst. Surg. 4 Ft. 25 Sep. 1812.

SMITH, M.,

Exchgd. as Maj. fm. 9 Ft. 21 Sep. 1846. Served with the Regt. at Chiliánwálá on 13 Jan. '49, and the followg. day was apptd. to command H.M. 24th Ft.; present at Gujrát; Brev. Lt. Col. 7 Jun. '49. This officer's appmt. to the 24 Ft. not having been sanctioned by the Home Authorities, he was on 2 July followg. re-transfd. to the 29th Ft. Lt. Col. 20 Jun. '54, and exchgd. to the 81st Ft. 5 Jun. '55. *Prev. Service*, As Maj. of Brigade was present with General Pollock's army during the Afghán campaign of '42. Ens. 16 Ft. 5 Aug. 1819.

SMITH, T.,

Surg. Mate, 3 Mar. 1773. Out of Regt. 1776.

SMITH, W.,

Who served at Fírúzshahar (severely wounded), also at Chiliánwálá and Gujrát, was on 18 Jan. 1856 apptd. Qr. Mr. fm. Hosp. Serjt. ; was present with Brigdr. Turner's Field Force whilst employed fm. 9 Nov. '58—28 Feb. '59 in clearing Palámao, Ramgarh, and Bihár districts of rebels. Exchgd. to 1st. Bn. 20 Ft. on 23 Mar. 1859.

SMYTH, R.,

Exchgd. on 17 Apl. 1866 fm. P. Mr. 69 Ft. Retd. with rank of Lt. Col. 26 Oct. '75. *Prev. Service*, With 69th Ft., in which he became P. Mr. 10 Nov. '54.

SOMERSET, C.B., E. A.,

Born 1817, was apptd. Ens. R. Brig. 29 Jan. '36, Lt. 9 July '40, Capt. 31 Jan. '45. Served in the Kaffir war of '52-'53, Maj. 12 Nov '54, was present at battles of the Alma, Balaklava, Inkerman, also siege and fall of Sevastopol, Lt. Col. 23 Mar. '55, Brev. Col. 29 May '58. Maj. Genl. 6 Mar. '68, Lt. Genl. 1 Oct. '77. Apptd. Col. 1st. Bn. Worcestershire Regt. 19 Dec. '81, but was on 14 Sep. '84 transfd. to Col. Commandant 1st Bn. King's Royal Rifles. Died at his residence, Troy House, Monmouth, 12 Mar. 1886.

SPICER, J.,

Chapl. 17 Jan. 1747 to Dec. 1757, when he resigned.

SPRATT, E. J. H.,

Ens. 3 Mar. 1865, Lt. 12 Dec. '68, Adj. 22 Jun. '70, Capt. 31 Aug. '78. Served in S. Africa fm. 1 Nov. '78 to 20 Feb. '80, was present at Ulundi ; served in the operations against Sekukuni, and as Orderly Officer to Col. Russell, comdg. the troops, was present at the storming of the Chief's stronghold (mentioned in dispatches.) Brev. Maj. 24 July '80. Served in the Boer war of '81 as D.A.A.Q.M.G. Maj. 19 May 1886. Lt. Col., and to Command the Battn. 2 Mar. '91.

STANFORD, J. A.,

Was promtd. 4 Jan. 1810 fm. 3rd Ft. to Surg. 29th Ft. Served with the Regt in '10 at Busaco, and the following year at Albuera. Exchgd. 14 Oct. '24 to h.p. of The Cape Regt. *Prev. Service*, Asst. Surg. the " Buffs " 25 Oct. 1803.

STANHOPE, HONBLE. J.,

Exchgd. 14 Feb. 1822 fm. Capt. and Lt. Col. Grenadier Gds., to Lt. Col. 29th Ft., and to h.p. on 28th inst. *Prev. Service*, in Spain, Portugal, and was present at Waterloo. Ens. 1st Ft. Gds. 26 Dec., 1803.

STANNUS, R.,
Ens. 24 Jan. 1805, Lt. 5 Feb. '08. Served with Regt. at Roliça (wounded and taken prisoner), in '09 was present at Talavera (severely wounded), and the followg. year at Busaco; in '11, at 1st siege of Badajos, and battle of Albuera (severely wounded). Capt. 1 July '13, commanded the Light compy. fm. '19, till promtd. Maj. 22 Apl. '24. Retd. Nov. '27, and died at Sandy Brook Beaumont, Jersey, 23 Oct. 1862.

STAPLES, P.,
Surg. Mate, 10 May 1788. Retd. 11 May, 1789.

STEPNEY, A. ST. G.,
Ens. 16 May 1834, Lt. 10 Nov. '37, Capt. 15 Apl. '42. Commanded the Grenadier compy. fm. '45—Aug. '47; brought the Regt. out of action at Fírúzshahar and commanded it at Sobráon (severely wounded.) Brev. Maj. 3 Apl. '46, Maj. 9 July '50. Exchgd. to 54th Ft. 5 Nov. 1852.

STEWART, C. L.,
Exchd. 20 July 1847 fm. Asst. Surg. 50 Ft.; present in '49 at battles of Chiliánwálá and Gujrát. On 11 Jun. '52 was promtd. in 94th Ft. Died at Highbury 5 Dec., 1888. *First Comsn.*, Asst. Surg. 39 Ft. 8 Jun., 1841.

STEWART, J.,
Chapl. 17 July, 1765. Died the followg. year.

STEWART, J. H.,
Exchgd. 5 Jun. 1855 fm. 81st Ft. to junr. Lt. Col. of 29th. Brev. Col. 8 Mar., '57, and retd. on full pay with rank of Maj. Genl. 2 Dec., '59. Died at Southsea 14 Jun. '75. *First Comsn.*, Ens. Royal African Colonial Corps 23 July 1827. This officer's widow, who died about 1879, left by bequest a sum of £400, the interest on which was to be paid annually to H.R.H. the Duke of Cambridge, or to the Comr.-in-Chief for the time being, for the benefit of daughters of married private soldiers of the 29th and 81st Regts.

STOTT, T.,
As Serjt., served with a detachmt. of the Regt. on board H.M.S. "Thunderer" 1 Jun. 1794; apptd. Qr. Mr. 25 Apl. '99, and served that year with the Expdn. to Holland. On 4 May 1805 was apptd. P. Mr. and served with the Regt. in the Peninsular campaign until 25 May '10, when he returned to England, and on 25 Apl. '11 was apptd. P. Mr. to the 10th Royal Veteran Battn.

STRAFFORD, J. LORD,

3rd son of G. Byng, Esqre., of Wrotham Park, Barnet, was born 1772; as John Byng, was apptd. Ens. 33rd Ft. on 30 Sep., and Lt. 1 Dec. '93; Capt. 24 May '94. Served in Flanders and Holland, and was wounded on 8 Jan. '95 at Guildermalsen. Maj. 60 Ft. 28 Dec. '99; was promtd. to Lt. Col. 29 Ft. 14 Mar. 1800. On 4 Aug. '04 was removed to 3rd Ft. Gds., and the following year served in the Expdn. to Hanover. In '07 took part in the Expdn. to Copenhagen. Succeeded to Earldom of Strafford 14 Aug. '09, and that year served with the Expdn. to Walcheren. Was apptd. Col. on the Staff in the Peninsula in '11; commanded a Brigade in the 2nd Division of army under Lord Hill, and was present with it in all the movements and affairs with the enemy in S. Spain. Maj. Genl. 4 Jun. '13; was engaged at Vittoria, the Pyrenees, Pampeluna (wounded), Nivelle (wounded and had 2 horses shot under him), passage of the Nive, and affair before Bayonne on 13 Dec. '13, when he had another horse shot under him. In '14 was engaged with the enemy at Espellette, Heights of Garris, Orthes, Aire, and Toulouse. Commanded the Brigade of Guards at Waterloo, and the first Corps of the Army which marched on Paris, and by occupying the Heights of Belleville and Montmartre, subsequently gained possession of that city. Was apptd. Colonel of 2nd W. I. Regt. on 26 July '22, Lt. Genl. 27 May '25. On 23 Jan. '28 was transfrd. to the Colonelcy of the 29 Ft. In '35 was created a Baron, and in '47 advanced to 1st Earl of Strafford. Transfd. to Colcy. of Coldstream Guards on 15 Aug. '50. Field Marshal 2 Oct. '55, and died in Lower Grosvenor St. 3 Jun. 1860.

TAYLOR, C.B., C.C.,

Apptd. junr. Lt. Col. 30 Jun. 1843 fm. Lt. Col. on Particular Service in Canada; on 13 Dec. '45 was given the command of 3rd Infantry Brigde. army of Satláj; was wounded at Fírúzshahar, and killed at Sobráon 10 Feb. 46. The *Gazette* of 3rd Apl. 1846 contained this Officer's appmt. of A.D.C. to the Queen with rank of Col. in the army. *Prev. Service*, In '27-'28 served in the Expdn. to Kolapúr; and during the Canadian rebellion of '38 was actively employed on the frontier. Ens. 46th Ft. 26 Mar. 1823.

TAYLOR, M.D., J.R.,

Was promtd. from the Staff, 14 Jun. 1842, to Surg. 29 Ft., with which he served at Fírúzshahar and Sobráon. On 7 July '48 was apptd. to 80 Ft. *Prev. Service*, Asst. Surg. 58 Ft. 2 Aug. 1833.

THOMAS, E. A. D'A.,

    2nd Lt. 11 May 1878, Lt. 8 Sep. '80, Adj. 14 Apl., and Capt. 1 Sep. '86. Resgd. Adjcy. 15 Dec. '90, when apptd. S.S.O. Puna. Apptd. D.A.A.G. Puna disct. 11 Feb. 1891.

TOD, G.,

    On 17 Apl. 1795 was apptd. Ens. 2nd Battn. 29 Ft., from Ens. 6th Fencibles, and the 2nd Sep. followg. was promtd. Lt. Served in the Expdn. to Holland in '99; Capt. 23 July 1803; commanded the Grenadier compy. at Roliça (made prisoner). In '09 was present at passage of the Douro and battle of Talavera; in '10 at Busaco; was slightly wounded the followg. year at Albuera. Brev. Maj. 31 Oct.'11, Maj. 2 Dec. '13, Brev. Lt. Col. 12 Aug. '19. Retd. Apl. 1824.

TONNOCHY, V.,

    Ens. 2 Sep. 1845, was present at Sobráon, and promtd. Lt. 20 Mar. '46. Served in Panjáb campaign, including battles of Chiliánwálá, Gujrát, and pursuit of enemy to the Jhelam. Adj. 29 July '53 (which he resigned same day), Capt. 20 Jun. '54. Exchgd. to 81st Ft. 7 Aug. 1855.

TROUSDELL, W. G.,

    Asst. Surg. 8 Apl. 1842, present at Chiliánwálá, Gujrát, and pursuit of enemy to the Jhelam. Was transfd. to 3rd Light Dragoons 15 Nov. 1850.

TRYON, W.,

    Was on 12 Oct. 1751 apptd. Lt. and Capt. 1st Ft. Gds., Capt.-Lt. 30 Sep., and Capt. and Lt. Col. 9 Dec. '58. As Governor of N. Carolina (28 Mar. '65 to July '71) evinced great zeal and ability in suppressing the rising seeds of insurrection, and conciliating the loyal British subjects. Was apptd. Govr. of New York (9 July '71—'78), and Commander-in-Chief of the Forces there; Col. in the army 25 May '72, 3rd Maj. 1st Ft. Gds. 8 Jun. '75. On 1st Jan. '76 was apptd. Maj. Genl. with local rank in America, and 2nd Maj. 1st Ft. Gds. 19 Feb. followg. Maj. Genl. 29 Aug. '77. Colonel of 70 Ft. 14 May '78. On 16 Aug. '83 was transfd. to the Colonelcy of 29th Ft., and died 27th Jan. 1788.

TUCKER, J.,

    Ens. 13 Mar. 1793, Lt. 16 Apl. '94, and whilst serving on board H.M.S. "Alfred" was present at Lord Howe's Victory of 1st Jun. '94. Served on board the Fleet fm. July '93 to Mar. '97; in the Expedition to Holland in '99, and was promtd. Capt.-Lt. and Capt. 21 Nov., Capt. 5 Dec., '99. In 1808 was apptd. Brig. Maj. in Nova Scotia, but rejoined the Regt. shortly before the battle of Talavera, at which he was present. On 25 Sep. '10 was apptd.

TUCKER, J.—*Continued*.

Commandant at Belem. After Albuera, was ordered to rejoin the Regt.; Brev. Maj. 4 Jun. and Maj. 4 July '11. Brev. Lt. Col. and Inspecting F.O. of Militia in Canada, 30 Sep. '13, Lt. Col. 22 Ft. 10 Feb. '14, but exchgd. to 29 Ft. on 29 Sep. followg. Retd. 27 Dec. 1820.

TURNER, G.,

Chpl. 17 Mar. 1774. Proceeded on King's leave from 21 Jun. '76 to 24 Jun. '94. Retd. on abolition of appmt. in Dec. 1796.

VIBART, J.,

Apptd. to Regt. as Lt., 13 Feb. 1762. Qr. Mr. 17 July '65. Died 1775.

VESEY, J. A.,

On 31 Jan. 1805 was apptd. fm. Lt. Col. of the Nova Scotia Fencibles to the junr. Lt. Colcy. of 29th Ft., but on 7 Feb '07 exchgd. to h.p. of the Regt. *First Comsn.*, Ens. 11 Ft., 5 Jun. 1778.

VESIE, J.,

Ens. 13 Apl. 1809, and the followg. year was present with the Regt. at Busaco. Lt. 19 Jun. '11. Adj., 21 Dec. '18; Died at Limerick 23 Sep. 1823.

WADE, W.,

Served with the Regt. in Expdn. to Holland 1799. On 7 Aug. 1801 was promtd. Adj. and Ens., Lt. 18 Sep. '04; in '08 was present at Roliça and Vimiero, in '09 at the passage of the Douro and Talavera. Capt. 17 Aug. '09; in '10 was present at Busaco, and the followg. year at Albuera. Retd. 25 July, 1821.

WALKER, H. G.,

Ens. 29 Apl. 1842, Lt. 31 Dec. '43, whilst acting A.D.C. to the Govr. General, at battle of Fírúzshahar had his horse shot under him, and at Sobráon was slightly wounded. Capt. 15 Mar., '53. Commanded the Grenadier compy. fm. '54 to '58 (last Capt. of Grenadiers.) Served fm. 9 Nov. '58 to 28 Feb. '59 with Brigdr. Turner's Field Force in clearing the Palámao, Ramgarh, and Bihár districts of rebels. Maj. 25 Mar. '62. Retd. 16 Jan. 1863.

WALSH, T.,

Apptd. on 11 Oct. 1853 from Lt. 8th (King's) to Qr. Mr. of 29th. Died at Thayetmyo 20 July '55. *Prev. Service*, With 48th Ft. in the Coorg campaign of '34, and with the 55th Ft. in Chinese war of 1840-42. Ens. 78th Highlanders 28 Nov. 1845.

WALTER, J.,
> Was transfd. on 13 July '32 fm. Maj. 62nd Ft. Exchgd. 7 Sep. '38 to 95 Ft. *Prev. Service*, Ens. 62nd Ft. 15 July '06. Served in the Peninsular war, and in France from Oct. '13 to the end of the campaign in '14, including the passage of the Bidassoa, battles of Nivelle, Nive, passage of the Adour, and investment of Bayonne; was present at the surrender of Paris in 1815.

WATKINS, W.,
> Exchgd. 10 Mar. 1702 from Capt. and Lt. Col. 1st Ft. Gds. to Lt. Col. of Farrington's Regt. (29th.) Was out of Regt. July '07. *Prev. Service*, Lt. 2nd Regt. of Ft. Gds. 7 Apl. 1691.

WATSON, R. J.,
> Ens. 21 Dec. 1860, Lt. 13 Feb. '63, Capt. 1 Dec. '65, Brev. Maj. 20 Aug. '78, Maj. 1 July '81; served with wing of Regt. in Zhob Valley Expdn. of '84, promtd. Lt. Col. in 2nd Bn. Worcestershire Regt. 28 Oct. followg, and on 19 Dec. '86 to its command. Retd. on retired pay 12 Dec. 1888.

WAY, C.B., K.T.S., SIR G. H. B.,
> Was on 25 Feb. 1808 promtd. from 5 Ft. to Maj. of 29th. Was present at battles of Roliça (wounded, and taken prisoner). In '09 commanded the Light Infantry of Lt. Genl. Stewart's brigade, which led the advance of the British army in the actions of 10th, 11th, and 12th May, and terminated in the passage of the Douro and capture of Oporto. Was present at Talavera; commanded the Regt. at Busaco '10; the following year served with it at 1st siege of Badajos, and succeeded to its command at Albuera (wounded slightly) for which he was awarded the Gold Medal. Brev. Lt. Col. 30 May, and Lt. Col. 4 July '11. Exchgd. on 29 Sep. '14 to the 22nd Ft. Died 19 Feb. 1864. *Prev. Service*, Ens. 26 Ft. 24 Aug. 1797, but on his passage to America to join, was taken prisoner. Having been exchanged, he was on 3 Nov. '99 apptd. Lt. 35 Ft. In 1800 was engaged at the siege of Valetta, and capture of Malta. Capt. 5 Ft. in '03; embarked with Expdn. to Hanover '05, but was shipwrecked off the Texel, and made prisoner by the Dutch. In '06 served as A.Q.M.G. to the Forces under Lt. Col. Whitelocke, and led the right wing of the Infantry brigde. at the storming of Buenos Ayres.

WAY, G. L. (NEPHEW OF SIR G. WAY, C.B.),
> Was apptd. Ens. 17 Feb. 1832, Lt. 30 July '36, Capt. 21 May '41, Maj. 8 Dec. '46. Served in '49 with the Regt. at battles of Chiliánwálá, Gujrát, and pursuit of the enemy to the Jhelam; on 30 Apl. proceeded on leave of absence to England, and retd. 9 July '50. A short time previous to his death, which occurred at Wick Hall, Brighton, on 14 Jan. 1889, he presented a very handsome centrepiece to his old Regt.

WEIR, J.,

On 16 May, 1822 was apptd. Lt. and Adj. fm. h.p. 69 Ft., Cap. 1 Sep, '25. Drowned off the Cape of Good Hope, whilst on passage home fm. the Mauritius 17 July, '36. *First Comsn.*, Ens. 69 Ft. 1 Dec. 1814.

WESTROPP, E. H.,

On 8 Apl. 1842 was promtd. Lt. in 29th Ft. from Ens. 67th Ft.; served with Regt. at Fírúzshahar and Sobráon. Capt. 5 Aug. '47. Maj. 20 July '58, Lt. Col. 12 Jun. '60. Retd. 24 Mar. '62. *First Comsn.*, Ens. 67 Ft., 2 Nov. 1838.

WHEELER, J. R.,

As Maj. exchgd. fm. 54th Ft. 5 Nov. '52. Commanded a wing of the Regt. which formed part of Brigdr. Turner's Field Force, and was engaged in clearing the Palámao, Ramgarh, and Bihár districts of rebels (9 Nov. '58—28 Feb. '59.) Brev. Lt. Col. 26 Oct., and Lt. Col. 13 Dec. '59. Retd. 11 Jun. '60. Died at Northam, N. Devon, 4 Aug. 1890. *First Comsn.*, Ens. 54th Ft. 30 July 1828.

WHITE, D.,

Ens. 27 Sep. 1787. In '90 served on board H.M.S. "Egmont," and on 25 Aug. was promtd. Lt.; served on board H.M.S. "Duke" in '93, and accompanied the Expdn. to Martinico; promtd. Capt.-Lt. and Capt. 5 Feb., and Capt. 1 Mar. '94. Served with the Regt. in Grenada '95-96, Expdn. to Holland in '99, and was wounded, 2nd Oct., at Bergen. Maj. 5 Dec. followg. Brev· Lt. Col. 1 Jan. 1805. Succeeded to the command of the Regt. at Roliça, for which he received the Gold Medal; present at Vimiero, and was promtd. Lt. Col. 2 Sep. '08; the followg. year served at the passage of the Douro and capture of Oporto, also at Talavera; in '11 at 1st siege of Badajos and Albuera (severely wounded). Died of wounds, at Eylas 3 Jun. '1811.

WILD, B.,

Was apptd. Ens. 28 Sep. 1807, frm. Lt. 1st Lancashire Militia, and the followg. year served at Roliça and Vimiero; in '09 was present at passage of the Douro, and capture of Oporto. Lt. 8 Jun. '09, Adj. 18 Jan. '10, was present at Busaco 27 Sep. followg. and on 16 May '11 at Albuera was severely wounded. Capt. 21 Dec. '15. Early in '17 retd. on h.p. of the Regt., but on the 15 Jun. was brought in as P. Mr. Retd. on h.p. 25 May '26. Died 1839.

WILKIE, H.,

As Capt. exchgd. 18 Mar. 1859 fm. 97 Ft., Maj. 20 Feb. '63, Lt. Col. 31 Oct. '71, Brev. Col. 31 Oct. '76. Retd. on h.p. 2 Mar. '78. *Prev. Service*, Ens. 97 Ft. 18 Aug. '54. Served in the Crimea fm. 16 Jun. '55, including the siege and fall of Sevastopol; also in the Indian Mutiny, and was present with the Jánpúr Field Force in the actions of Chánda, Hamirpúr, and Súltánpúr, besides the siege and capture of Lakhnao.

WILMOT, M.,

Was transfd. on 23 July 1748 fm. Maj. late Halifax's Regt. Promtd. Lt.-Col. 45 Ft. 8 Apl. 1755.

WILSON, J.,

Surg. Mate 25 Jun. 1795. Retd. 24 May 1797.

WINN, W.,

Apptd. fm. Ens. 76 Ft. 14 Dec. 1855. Lt. 13 Aug. '57. Adj. 6 Nov. '63 and on 27th May '70 was promtd. to a h.p. company. *First Comsn.*, Ens. 76 Ft. (fm. Lt. 1st Durham Militia) 30 Nov. 1855.

WOOD, M.D., A.,

Promtd. Surg. fm. 3 Light Dragoons 21 Aug. 1840, but exchgd. 23 July '41 to 9th Lt. Dragoons. *Prev. Service*, Asst. Surg. 78 Highlanders 19 Nov. 1826.

WRAY, SIR C., BART.,

Born before 1672, entered the army at an early age, and fought on the side of King William at the battle of the Boyne 1 July '90, on which occasion his father, Sir Drury Wray, Bt., a Capt. in Col. H. Sutherland's Horse, fought for King James. Was on 16 Feb. '94 apptd. Maj. in Col. Farrington's Regt. (29th Ft.), placed h.p. 28 Feb. '98 to 10 Mar. 1702. Lt. Col. 1 July '07. On the death of his father 30 Oct. '10 became 10th Bart. of Glentworth. Died at Portsmouth 21st Nov. followg, when his brother Cecil, a Capt. in Farrington's Regt. succeeded to the title. Sir Cecil served as High Sheriff of Lincolnshire in '16 and died 9 May 1736.

WRIGHT, J.,

Apptd. Lt. and Adj. of Farrington's Regt. 16 Feb. 1694. Capt.-Lt. 12 Sep. followg.; placed on h.p. from '98 to 10 Mar. 1702, when promtd. Capt. in the Regt., from which he retd. shortly after.

WROTTESLEY, HONBLE. C. A.,
>Exchgd. as Maj. fm. 95th Ft. on 7 Sep. 1838. Lt. Col. 3 July '39, and exchgd. to h.p. 8 Apl. '42. Died 24 Feb. 61. *Prev. Service*—Present at siege of Bhártpúr in 1826, and battle of Fírúzshahar '45. Cornet 16 Light Dragoons 21 Dec. 1815. Col. Wrottesley was 2nd son of Sir J. Wrottesley, Bt. (afterwards 1st Baron Wrottesley) who on 25 Jun. 1790 was apptd. Lt. in the 29th fm. the 35th Ft.

WYATT, H. R.,
>Exchgd. 8 Dec. 1846 fm. Brev. Col. h.p. unatt., to junr. Lt. Col. of 29th, and retd. same day. *First Comsn.*, Cornet 1st Life Gds. 22 Sep. 1812.

WYATT, W. E.,
>Ens. 22 Feb. 1793. Served on board the Fleet on the Newfoundland and Channel Stations fm. 31 May '93 to May '95 ; Lt. 5 Feb. '94, Capt.-Lt. and Capt. 1st Battn. 29th Ft. 25 Apl. '95 ; on 23 Feb. '96 was transfd. to the 5 compys. actively engaged in Grenada. Capt. 6 Sep. '96. Served as Capt. of Grenadier compy. in Expdn. to Holland, and was shot through the thigh at the landing at the Helder 27 Aug '99. Maj. 24 July 1803, promtd. Lt. Col. 23rd Fusiliers 18 Feb. 1808.

YOUNG, I.,
>Apptd. Qr. Mr. fm. Lt. King's (Liverpool) Regt. on 25 Jan. 1888. *Prev. Service*, with 42nd Highlanders in Ashanti Expdn. of '73-'74 ; Egypt '82, Soudan, '84, Nile Expdn. '84-'85. Promtd. Lt. in King's (Liverpool) Regt. 19 Sep. 1885.

YOUNG, W. B.,
>Asst. Surg. 8 Apl. 1842, was present at Fírúzshahar and Sobráon. Exchgd. to 50 Ft. 18 Mar. 1847.

The Services of the above Officers are taken from the Military Entry Books, etc. The Official, and Hart's Army Lists.

Extract from the History of the Coldstream Guards :—

"It was the practice, up to the Reign of Queen Anne, to grant fresh Commissions to Officers who exchanged, or were removed from one Company to another. When a Regiment was on foreign service, the Commander of the Forces filled up all vacancies without the knowledge or control of the Government at home : this privilege continued till the Peace in 1748 ; and it is in many instances become extremely difficult, and frequently impossible to ascertain the names of the Officers appointed abroad, or the date of their Commissions on promotion.

War Office, Janry., 1833."

29th Regimental Call.

Slow March.

Small caps: Composed by H.R.H. THE DUCHESS OF KENT.

"The Royal Windsor" Quick March.

COMPOSED AND PRESENTED TO THE 29TH FOOT BY PRINCESS AUGUSTA IN 1791.

Regimental Double March.

INDEX.

	PAGE.
Accoutrements	... 60, 101, 367, 373
Adams, Mr. John	 69
Age of Men,	42, 73, 123, 262, 330, 434, 457, 507, 538
Albuhera, Authority for	 354
Allegiance, Attempts to seduce Soldiers from	 217
American Stamp Act	 56
Ammunition, how to be carried	... 100
Amusement, A morning's	 317
Appointments in *Gazette*	 56
Arms, Bells of	 45
„ Rifles, etc.	70, 351, 429, 489, 507, 515
Army, Localization of	 513
„ Re-organization of	 525
„ Reserve	... ... 517, 521
Arnold, Benedict	... ... 82, 88
Ascent of the Peter Botte	 371
Augusta, Princess	... ... 124, 590
Band	... 118, 361, 370, 503, 514
Barbadoes, Riots at	 511
Barrákpúr, A wing sent to	 487
Battalion, Depôt, and Provisional	498, 499, 500
„ 2nd 29th	 158
Battle Axes, The	 553

	PAGE.
BATTLES, SIEGES, AND ENGAGEMENTS :	
Albergaria Nova	 295
Albuera	 320
Badajos	... ... 320, 325
Bemis Heights	 90
Bennington	 87
Bergen	 239
Boston, Massacre at	 62
Buglu Mara Pass	 492
Champlain, Lake	 81
Chiliánwálá	 462
Douro	 297
Firúzshahar	 438
Gibraltar	 40
Grenada, Actions in	191, 193, 198, 206
Grijo	 296
Gujrát	 475
Hamden	 345
Helder, Landing at the	 233
Hubberton	 86
Neer Hespern	 21
Ostend	 26
Quebec	 77
Ramillies	 24
Roliça	... ... 277, 291
Sobráon	 448
St. Jago, *Registership*	 141
Stillwater	 88
Talavera-de-la-Reyna	 301
Toulon	 44
Ushant	... ... 140, 148, 150
Vimiero	 283

	PAGE.
Bayonet Belt, 310, 365, 367, 373, 377, 415	
Black Jack 280, 289, 323	
Board of General Officers ...	... 484
Boileau, Chas. de C.	8, 12, 20
Boston, N.A., Disturbances at	58, 62
Braid, &c., Regimental, 44, 52, 57, 59, 106, 339	
Buttons, Regimental, 6, 52, 57, 59, 91, 340, 361, 372, 484, 485	
„ Universal	... 516
Calkers, or Caucus Meetings	... 62
Calpe Hunt, The	... 342
Caps, Chaco, &c., and Plates, 3, 37, 45, 52, 58, 59, 60, 70, 71, 101, 102, 106, 118, 119, 122, 128, 137, 181, 183, 222, 246, 249, 261, 265, 334, 337, 347, 352, 353, 361, 365, 369, 374, 376, 416, 428, 430, 431, 454, 455, 483, 503, 508, 522, 524	
„ Cockade on, 60, 125, 246, 261, 273, 290, 352, 365	
„ Feather, 106, 119, 128, 352, 369, 370, 374, 381	
„ Forage, or Undress, 365, 367, 374, 479, 490, 514, 524	
„ Lace, 37, 60, 339, 352, 365, 503, 508	
„ Lines and Tassels, 261, 352, 364, 365, 369	
„ Tufts, 122, 246, 261, 352, 370, 381, 431, 454	
Captain-Lieutenants	4, 71, 258
Cathcart, Correspondence of Lord W., 109—212	
Chaplains, Regimental ...	84, 211
Chartist disturbances ...	... 417

	PAGE.
Charlotte, Letter from Queen	... 126
Chevrons	... 252
Chelsea Hospital	... 4
Chilliánwálláh, Authority for...	... 480
Chudleigh's Regt., Col. Thos.	33, 34
Clothing, Dress, etc., 3, 6, 23, 37, 44, 52, 58, 59, 60, 70, 71, 102, 122, 125, 218, 221, 334, 337, 338, 339, 353, 355, 357, 364, 366, 367, 368, 370, 373, 374, 375, 456, 484, 490, 514, 515, 522	
Coatee abolished	... 483
Coats, Issue of great ...	... 251
Colonels of Foot, List of Reformed	10
Colours, 29, 41, 44, 52, 55, 107, 220, 250, 265, 327, 338, 340, 341, 342, 358, 424, 427, 433, 470, 478, 481, 526, 527, 530	
„ Capture of French	305, 309
„ Lions on the Poles ...	... 377
„ Third, discontinued	... 388
Commissions, Price of ...	38, 71
„ Purchase abolished	... 511
Company to be formed from Officers on h.p.	... 8
Corporals' Epaulettes ...	... 59
Courts Martial Punishments	15, 16, 19
Cymbals	... 339
Depôt Companies 340, 347, 351, 353, 390, 498	
„ 22nd Brigade (sub-district)	514
Deserter, Fate of a	... 95
Desertion, punishment for ...	... 101
Discipline, Treatise on ...	... 41
Drummers, Black, 55, 74, 122, 222, 355, 358, 367, 373, 375, 526	
„ Hangers	... 370
Drum Major	... 529

	PAGE.
Drum Major's Staff	121
Drums, Brass	137
Ensign, Rank of, abolished	511
Enys, Lt. Col. John,	IX., 78, 81, 92, 93, 95, 100, 102, 120, 135, 136, 158, 165, 167, 173, 178, 179, 214, 218, 220, 231, 239, 241, 244, 246, 248, 560
Esprit de Corps	361, 526
Everard, Ensign E. P. H.	499, 502
Expeditions:	27, 30, 31, 39
" in America,	81, 85, 93, 94, 96
" Bikanír	532
" Penobscot	344
" Zhob Valley	533
Farrington, Lt.-Gen. Thos.,	x., xi., 1, 8, 9, 10, 32, 562
" Ensign Thos. D.	8, 12, 563
" Lt.-Col. Lindsay	433, 562
Ferozeshah, Authority for	456
Field Exercise approved of	126
Fifes, Adoption of	48
Fisher, Lt.-Col. S.	486
FitzHugh, Capture of Ensign	49
Flank Companies,	3, 70, 84, 96, 234, 453, 488, 504
Frills	128, 337, 377
Furnace, Ensign Edwd.	323
Fusiliers, Offer to be made	411
Gates, General Horatio	88
Gaiters,	59, 74, 101, 102, 130, 261, 337, 357
Gauntlope, The	16
Germain, Carelessness of Lord G.	84
Ghost at Sable Island	253
Gipsy Bride in collision	496
Goojerat, Authority for	480

	PAGE.
Gordon, Col. Patk.	80, 565
Grenadier, Swords, Matches, etc.,	3, 101, 365, 376
Guns, Battalion	45, 215, 249
" Curricle	225
Hair, mode of dressing	26, 42, 46, 100, 102, 127, 135, 221, 233, 260, 275, 278, 283
Halberts	3, 59, 125
Halifax, N.S., Founding of	50
" Presentation from Inhabitants of	263
Half Mounting	168
Harrington, Lady; and the children	116
Hatchets	3, 71, 101
Horse, The Wooden	15
" Officers'	131, 132
Inspection Reports,	72, 105, 106, 119, 122, 260, 262, 330, 337, 340, 342, 355, 357, 358, 365, 367
Johnson, Sir John	79
Joke, A practical	335
Kelát, Reconnaissance in	537
Kinsale, Address from the Sovereign of	358
Knapsacks	261, 283, 515
Lake, Lt.-Col.	268, 269, 277, 318, 570
Lieutenant of Guards, Army rank of,	562
Light Company raised	70
Lillingston's Regt., Col. Luke	5
List of Officers:	x., 8, 11, 36, 51, 72, 166, 172, 173, 196, 197, 219, 286, 311, 316, 326, 349, 430, 436, 448, 461, 474, 495, 506, 510, 524, 528, 540

	PAGE.
List of Officers: dead or killed (1843 to 1859)	497
„ „ on board the Fleet, 43, 120, 152	
„ with Burgoyne's Expdn.	85
„ „ Turner's Field Force	492
„ „ the Bikanír Field Force	532
„ „ with Zhob Valley Expdn.	533
List of N.C. Officers, Rank and File, killed or wounded, 41, 82, 87, 90, 155, 191, 194, 199, 209, 236, 241, 283, 285, 295, 296, 307, 324, 325, 332, 333, 346, 445, 446, 451, 452, 471, 476	
List of Casualties (1843 to 1859)	496
London, City of x., xi., 109, 244, 420, 421	
Looping, Regimental mode of	57, 106
Louisburg, Winter at	47
Machias, Taking of Fort	346
Madras, Exchange of	48
Manual Exercise	125
Marines, Service as 42, 120, 134, 139, 262	
Martinico, Detacht. land in	143
Masonic Lodge	55
Medals, Issue and sale of, 139, 318, 331, 456, 478, 480, 492	
Mess Bills	115, 221
„ —Hour of	118
„ —Officers eat together	74
„ —Permanent Hon. Members	382, 433
„ —Regulations revised	378
Middleton, Captain F., recommended for V.C.	489
Militia—Antrim 223; Bucks 229; Devon 231, 252; Herefordshire 525; Renfrew 503; Staffordshire 335; Suffolk 134; Warwick 229; Worcestershire 105, 182, 517, 525	

	PAGE.
Militia, Lieuts. of, permitted to enter Army	511
Miquelets, Officers posted to the	28
Montgomery, Genl.	76
Moustaches, Introduction of	481
Musketeers	3
Mutiny, Indian	487, 490
Necessaries, Camp	76
„ Men's	338
Neckcloths discontinued	125
Norwich	4, 5, 28, 29, 33
Numbers, Regimental, 6, 43, 44, 54, 57, 529	
Officers—Band	505
„ —Boots and Shoes, 102, 130, 221, 261, 511	
„ —Breeches, 52, 60, 129, 130, 221, 261, 334, 337, 357	
„ —Corporal Punishment	8
„ —Country, Age, &c., 72, 122, 262, 330, 434, 457, 507	
„ —Dress of, 3, 52, 58, 59, 60, 73, 91, 106, 119, 127, 129, 130, 221, 222, 233, 337, 339, 387, 454, 457, 479, 480, 483, 484, 508, 513, 515, 529	
„ —Mess Dress, 221, 261, 511, 528	
„ —Epaulettes, Wings, etc., 58, 91, 125, 129, 314, 318, 334, 338, 339, 361, 366, 368, 374, 375, 524	
„ —Feathers in Hats	106, 119
„ —Companies of Field	4, 258
„ —Fusils	44, 59, 125
„ —Gaiters, &c., 59, 74, 102, 130, 337, 357, 496	
„ —Gorget 59, 130, 182, 337, 370, 377	
„ —Lace, Gold	369, 525

	PAGE.
Officers—Lace, Silver	339, 368
„ —Oath	2, 4
„ —Partizans, Pikes, &c.	3, 41, 44
„ —Sabretasche	511
„ —Saddle Cloth discontinued	531
„ —Salute	41
„ —Sash, 4, 45, 52, 59, 107, 130, 259, 337, 364, 368, 508	
„ —Shell Jacket	367
„ —Shoulder Belt, and Plate, 59, 91, 184, 339, 353, 361, 364, 368, 371, 372, 490	
„ —Spontoon	44, 59, 102
„ —Spurs	130
„ —Swords, Belts, and Scabbards, 4, 59, 102, 107, 125, 130, 182, 221, 318, 334, 338, 365, 368, 371, 374, 454, 507	
„ —take possession of Chudleigh's Regiment	33
„ —Trowser Lace	357, 508
Offreckonings	37
Ostend	26, 30, 145, 349
Owling	106
Parisian Bully	350
Pay, Rate of	4, 14, 217, 259
Pershore, Stationed at	105
Peninsula, Authority for	348
Picket, The	19
Pikemen	3, 13
Pioneers	60
Pouch Ornaments, 101, 365, 376, 408, 516, 519, 532, 539	
Preston, Capt. Thos.	63, 71
Prize Money	141, 165, 173, 252
Punjaub, Authority for	480

	PAGE.
Quebec, Relief of	76
Quota Men	213
Rangers, The 29th	93, 94
Ramillies, Authority for	531
Rammers, Steel	38
Recruiting, at Birmingham, 136; Middlesex, 45; Surrey, 30; Worcester, 98, 104, 213	
Regiment, Description of the	265, 283, 313
„ Last to wear Frills	377
„ „ „ Matches	365
„ „ „ Queues	275
Regimental—Badges, 91, 101, 184, 526, 539	
„ —Customs	221, 379, 413
„ —Designations 6, 32, 39, 42, 43, 53, 54, 97, 525	
„ —Dinner	536
„ —District 29th	525
„ —Marches	124, 589
„ —Mess Regulations	378
„ —Monument	452
„ —Nicknames, 65, 131, 221, 415, 496	
„ —School	251, 339
„ —Standing Orders	127, 337
Rifle Corps, Formation of the	245
Roleia, Authority for	335
St. Jago, Capture of the	141
St. John's Island, Surprise at	46
Saunders, Captn. Alexr.	80, 157
Scotland threatened	29, 36, 37
Scott, Captn. Hugh	46
Scott, Monument to Sir W.	423
Serjeants—Cane	376
„ —Chevrons	252

	PAGE.
Serjeants—Coats	59, 370
„ —Braid	59, 387
„ —Epaulette, Wings, &c.	252, 387, 433
„ —Fusil	59, 70, 125, 370
„ —Girdle	45, 59, 339, 433
„ —Halbert, Pike	3, 59, 125, 370
„ —Skirt Ornaments	373
„ —Shoulder Belt Plate	479
„ —Swords	38, 59, 97, 101, 105
Serjeant, Colour	340
„ Major	39, 252
Serjeant-Major Richards	282
Singular occurrence, A	355
Smoking, Orders relative to	380, 435
Sobraon, Authority for	456
Soldier, Position of the	41
Southampton, Disturbances near	181
Stocks	102, 125, 128
Sub-Lieutenant, Rank of, abolished	518
Sunday, Dark	102
Sunk	76
Sword Exercise	183
Swords, Rank and File	3, 38, 46, 101, 105, 370
Talavera, Authority for	354
Tambourines	339, 375
Teetotum Expdn.	93
Tewkesbury, Stationed at	105

	PAGE.
Thirty-fourth Foot	33
Thirty-sixth Foot	39, 74, 75, 506, 514, 517, 520
Tithe collecting at Gurthroe	396
„ process-serving at Midleton	393
Treeing	93
Trowsers	135, 357, 373, 374, 377, 455
Tunics, Introduction of	484
Turner, Rev. Geo.	84, 211
Union of England and Scotland	29
„ Great Britain and Ireland	250
Valise Equipment, Issue of	515
Vance, Ensign Richd.	325
Vimiero, Authority for	354
Wallace, Wm. Vincent	347
Washington, George	54
Waterdeck	76
Way, Lt.-Colonel Sir G. H. B.,	280, 286, 296, 331, 340, 347, 585
Way, Major Gregory	292, 456, 585
Wellington, Funeral of the Duke of	499
Wexford, Outrages at	225
William Henry, Prince	103
Winkfield Plain, Review on	248
Windsor, Stationed at	122, 335
„ Review at	519
Worcester	13, 104, 519
Yarmouth, Landing at	243

www.ingramcontent.com/pod-product-compliance
Lightning Source LLC
Chambersburg PA
CBHW080325020526
44117CB00036B/2806